## DATE DUE

| JAN 4 1988 | | |
|---|---|---|
| OCT 5 1994 | | |
| OCT 04 1998 | | |
| | | |
| | | |
| | | |
| | | |
| | | |
| | | |
| | | |
| | | |
| | | |
| | | |
| | | |
| | | |
| | | |
| | | |
| | | |

DEMCO 38-297

GARY ORFIELD

# MUST WE BUS?

*Segregated Schools and National Policy*

THE BROOKINGS INSTITUTION
*Washington, D.C.*

*Library of Congress Cataloging in Publication Data:*
Orfield, Gary.
  Must we bus?
  Includes bibliographical references and index.
    1. School integration—United States.   2. School
children—United States—Transportation.   I. Title.
LC214.5.O73      370.19'342      77-91803
ISBN 0-8157-6638-6
ISBN 0-8157-6637-8 pbk.

9 8 7 6 5 4 3 2 1

THE BROOKINGS INSTITUTION is an independent organization devoted to nonpartisan research, education, and publication in economics, government, foreign policy, and the social sciences generally. Its principal purposes are to aid in the development of sound public policies and to promote public understanding of issues of national importance.

The Institution was founded on December 8, 1927, to merge the activities of the Institute for Government Research, founded in 1916, the Institute of Economics, founded in 1922, and the Robert Brookings Graduate School of Economics and Government, founded in 1924.

The Board of Trustees is responsible for the general administration of the Institution, while the immediate direction of the policies, program, and staff is vested in the President, assisted by an advisory committee of the officers and staff. The by-laws of the Institution state: "It is the function of the Trustees to make possible the conduct of scientific research, and publication, under the most favorable conditions, and to safeguard the independence of the research staff in the pursuit of their studies and in the publication of the results of such studies. It is not a part of their function to determine, control, or influence the conduct of particular investigations or the conclusions reached."

The President bears final responsibility for the decision to publish a manuscript as a Brookings book. In reaching his judgment on the competence, accuracy, and objectivity of each study, the President is advised by the director of the appropriate research program and weighs the views of a panel of expert outside readers who report to him in confidence on the quality of the work. Publication of a work signifies that it is deemed a competent treatment worthy of public consideration but does not imply endorsement of conclusions or recommendations.

The Institution maintains its position of neutrality on issues of public policy in order to safeguard the intellectual freedom of the staff. Hence interpretations or conclusions in Brookings publications should be understood to be solely those of the authors and should not be attributed to the Institution, to its trustees, officers, or other staff members, or to the organizations that support its research.

*To Amy, Sonia, and Rosanna*
*with love*

# Foreword

SOMETIMES it seems that the more that is said about an issue the less is known about it. Certainly no one could claim that the issue of busing students for purposes of school desegregation has received insufficient attention from political leaders or the mass media. On some occasions, more attention has been given to this one question than to all the other national policy issues presented in major education and appropriations bills before Congress. When Chicago began busing 496 children in September 1977, an almost equal number of reporters from around the world arrived to cover the story. Yet little effort has been made to explore the issue in breadth and depth as a question of national policy and to analyze objectively the choices before the nation in dealing with urban segregation.

In this book, Gary Orfield subjects this hotly controverted issue to systematic investigation and analysis. He draws together materials from many disciplines, from a wide range of school systems, and from courts, the Congress, and federal and state administrative agencies. He recounts the evolution of the law on school desegregation, reviews the political turmoil surrounding the busing issue, traces the administration—or nonadministration—of the law by the federal executive agencies, analyzes the practical problems that must be confronted in school desegregation, and dispels the myths that have grown up around the busing issue. In the end, he outlines a constructive program of action to make desegregation work.

Orfield's research on this issue, over a period of more than a decade, took him to many communities involved in desegregation struggles. He attended numerous conferences and drew on his experience as scholar-in-residence at the U.S. Commission on Civil Rights and as a staff member of the Senate Committee on Labor and Public Welfare. The book would have been impossible without the generous assistance of school officials, lawyers, government officials, and civil rights groups across the country. Its completion was greatly facilitated by a grant from Carnegie Corporation of New York.

For numerous editorial suggestions and for help in simplifying a long and complex manuscript, the author particularly thanks William Taylor, Noel Epstein, Gilbert Y. Steiner, James L. Sundquist, and the editor, Elizabeth H. Cross. Other readers who made valuable suggestions include Meyer Weinberg, David Kirp, Vilma Martinez, Robert Crain, Richard Hiller, and Michael Ross. The preparation of the manuscript depended on the skills of Radmila Nikolić, Donna Verdier, and Gloria Jimenez. The index was prepared by Diana Regenthal.

As with all Brookings publications, the conclusions are those of the author and should not be ascribed to Carnegie Corporation or to the trustees, officers, or other staff members of the Brookings Institution.

BRUCE K. MACLAURY
*President*

*January 1978*
*Washington, D.C.*

# Contents

   Text Tables

# MUST WE BUS?

# Important Decisions Affecting School Desegregation

## SUPREME COURT DECISIONS

### Brown v. Board of Education, 347 U.S. 483 (1954)
A unanimous decision that schools segregated by state laws are "inherently unequal" and violate the Fourteenth Amendment's guarantee of equal protection under the law.

### Brown v. Board of Education, 349 U.S. 294 (1955)
School desegregation should take place "with all deliberate speed" and under primary control of a federal district court.

### Green v. Board of Education of New Kent County [Virginia], 391 U.S. 430 (1968)
This decision settled the long dispute about whether the Constitution requires that southern students be offered an opportunity to desegregate voluntarily or whether it requires that the dual school system be abolished. The Court ruled that school districts must adopt a plan that promptly produces schools not identifiable by race.

### Swann v. Charlotte-Mecklenburg Board of Education, 402 U.S. 1 (1971)
The Court sustained a countywide desegregation plan requiring extensive busing, ruling that cities whose schools have historically been segregated by law cannot defend continuing school segregation after they have adopted a neighborhood school plan. The schools must be actually integrated no matter how much inconvenience and extra transportation are entailed.

### Keyes v. School District No. 1, Denver, Colorado, 413 U.S. 189 (1973)
The Court outlined the kind of proof necessary to show that a northern school system has violated the Constitution and is therefore subject to the same sort of desegregation requirement as a similar southern city. The Court held that when there is proof that a substantial portion of a city has been purposely segregated by official action the entire city should be presumed to be afflicted with de jure segregation unless local officials can prove it was accidental. The case also established the right of Mexican-American children to the same desegregation remedies as those available to blacks.

### Lau v. Nichols, 414 U.S. 563 (1974)
The Court established the obligation of school districts, under the Civil Rights Act of 1964, to provide appropriate education for non-English-speaking children.

### Milliken v. Bradley, 418 U.S. 717 (1974)
In this 5–4 decision denying Detroit and its suburbs metropolitan desegregation, the majority ruled that plans must be limited to a single school district, regardless of its racial composition, unless violations affecting the distribution of students among the districts could be proved.

## LOWER COURT DECISIONS

### Adams v. Richardson, 356 F. Supp. 92 (D.D.C. 1973)
The first of a series of decisions by federal district courts and courts of appeals finding the Department of Health, Education, and Welfare guilty of intentional nonenforcement of the Civil Rights Act of 1964 in the seventeen southern and border states.

### Brown v. Weinberger, 417 F. Supp. 1215 (D.D.C. 1976)
Federal District Judge John J. Sirica found the Department of Health, Education, and Welfare guilty of intentional nonenforcement of the Civil Rights Act of 1964 by continuing to subsidize unconstitutionally segregated schools in the North.

# School Desegregation and the Cities

BUSING was the last important issue to emerge from the civil rights movement of the 1960s and the only one to directly affect the lives of large numbers of whites outside the South. The legal principles and social ideals
originating with the landmark case *Brown* v. *Board of Education*[1] started
the drive for urban school desegregation but it never enjoyed broad public
support. Civil rights groups turned to the courts in the early sixties when
they realized there was no other route open. When they finally prevailed,
their achievement was incomplete and in many ways ironic.

Victory came not from the Warren Court, which refused to hear urban
cases, but from the more conservative Burger Court. In a surprising, unanimous decision in 1971,[2] the Court sustained busing as a remedy for unconstitutional segregation. As plans were adopted first in the South and then
in some northern cities, opinion polarized against the desegregation orders.
Within a year many political leaders, much of the mass media, and some
members of the academic community had joined the opposition for the
first time since 1954. Rarely have the courts been so isolated.

In the years that followed, an intense but confusing debate raged across
the country. Integrationists supporting the Court saw state-imposed (de
jure) school segregation as an evil and desegregation as an important end
in itself. Antibusing leaders claimed that segregation was the accidental
result of private decisions (de facto segregation) and that desegregation
should be carried out only if educational gains could be conclusively
proved. Critics said that hopes for elimination of the achievement gap between white and minority children were futile, but supporters argued that

1. 347 U.S. 483 (1954).
2. *Swann* v. *Charlotte-Mecklenburg Board of Education*, 402 U.S. 1.

1

the results were positive. Opponents claimed that busing sped white flight from the cities and concluded that the cure was worse than the disease of segregation. Supporters found this untrue or irrelevant and saw busing as a first step away from urban apartheid.

Much of the debate was not pertinent to the work of the courts. The task of judges was not to design the optimal social policy but to rule on evidence of illegal segregationist practices and devise plans to correct their effects. The courts found that segregation existed in such large parts of the cities that there were no simple answers—the choice was segregation or busing. For the judges, once a constitutional violation was proved, there was no choice.

The busing issue has become explosive for three reasons. First, the schools are the largest and most visible of public institutions, directly affecting millions of families. Second, school assignment patterns, unlike housing or job patterns, are wholly determined by public officials and can thus be rapidly changed by a court order to those public officials. Third, because of the strong base of constitutional law and the massive evidence of illegal local actions, school desegregation is still proceeding at a time when action against housing and job discrimination has been hampered by weak enforcement and controversial Supreme Court decisions. In a sense the school desegregation movement looks powerful because it is moving slowly forward at a time when most of the other major initiatives are failing. Actually, however, only a few cities desegregate each fall.

The courts could not ignore the issue, nor could they effectively explain the changes. After years of proceedings, they found constitutional violations and prescribed remedies. Their complex and technical rulings, dealing with a single school district at a time, have failed to explain and justify the radical changes in the local schools. The courts have engaged in elaborate consideration of a community's racial history, the way school district boundary lines had been drawn years before, the segregation of teachers, and other evidence of de jure segregation, and then have tried to devise remedies to repair the damage. The judges do not consider it their job to discuss parental worries about education, violence, and racial change, and they seldom do. The local plans have often seemed arbitrary. The issues have increasingly been defined by political opponents, including presidents, and by the mass media, which naturally concentrated on the most dramatic stories with the strongest visual content—angry local conflicts in the early phase of the desegregation process.

Most elected leaders have ignored the issue of spreading urban segregation though they assail the solutions devised by the courts. As the presidential commissions of the 1960s predicted, our metropolitan areas are splitting into separate and unequal societies and a number of our big city school systems have few whites left. The 1968 fair housing law was the last positive step toward integration, but its impact has been slight. Since then, Congress has spent part of each session working on legislation intended to restrain or even reverse school integration in the cities. During the same years, as the economy of the central cities has deteriorated and the loss of middle class residents has accelerated, Congress has enacted legislation cutting the cities' share of funds for education and housing.

After a tumultuous decade of social and cultural change, a nation that had been torn by war, stunned by urban riots, and shaken by assassinations was not prepared to recognize or cope with metropolitan apartheid. People denied that the problem existed, claimed that it was being solved, argued that blacks and Hispanics liked segregation anyway, or, most often, attacked the proposed solutions.

## Implementation

This study is based on two assumptions: first, that the courts will continue to require urban desegregation, and second, that successful and stable integration is an important goal for American society. Most social science research has been concerned only with measuring the short-term effects of new policies. Although this study draws on those data, it concentrates on the practical and political problems of carrying out policies designed to eliminate urban school segregation.

The book is built around two political and social questions that have received little systematic study. First, has the Court defined a policy that *can* be implemented? Given the structure of urban society and the nature of school systems, can urban schools feasibly be integrated without excessive cost, educational damage, or resegregation? Second, *will* the constitutional requirements proclaimed by the courts be implemented? With almost no voluntary compliance, can a judiciary with limited administrative capacity and power transform urban public schools? Have the judges overlooked easier or better ways to achieve integration? Has the federal executive branch enforced the law? To what extent can private civil rights groups enforce the law themselves through case-by-case litigation? What policy options remain?

The National Context

Although the urban desegregation issue affects hundreds of cities, most people tend to think of the experiences of only one or two. This is not uncommon—a concrete image is usually more powerful than a set of statistics. Certainly many more people were moved to action in the 1960s by the spectacle of police beating civil rights marchers than by the decades of reports on segregated public accommodations. The problem is that the dominant public image of busing, the picture of hatred and violence outside some Boston schools, is misleading; it does not portray the normal pattern but rather the worst failure of local leadership. Yet this image not only energizes the antibusing movement but also leads many citizens to conclude that "busing has failed."

School systems and communities across the United States differ in their segregation problems, in the history of their race relations, in the stance of local political leaders, in the skills and attitudes of school administrators, in the role of the mass media, and in many other ways. One goal of this book is to explore this diversity, examining the distinctive problems and possibilities that arise in different urban contexts. The legal framework is constant, but the practical meaning of the policies varies greatly as one moves from a small city in South Carolina to the huge Hispanic and black ghettos of Los Angeles, to the inner suburbs of Cleveland, or to the ghetto school system of Newark. Some have already had years of experience with peaceful citywide integration. Others have done nothing and become more segregated each year.

Three broadly different settings for desegregation are examined in part 1 —the rural South, the largest metropolitan centers, and the nation's other cities and suburbs. Although this is an analysis of urban desegregation, the rural South must be briefly considered because the long battle there has shaped many of the legal, administrative, and social issues that are now germane to the urban setting. Because substantial long-term desegregation has so far been largely limited to the rural South, it also provides a model for examining the prerequisites for change.

Urban school districts are basically divided by size and racial composition. The five largest districts, which enroll about one-fifth of the nation's minority students, are so much bigger than all others that they must be considered special cases. Conclusions about the feasibility of desegregation in New York or Chicago imply little about the best policies for Omaha or

Duluth. Techniques that successfully end segregation in a suburb or a small city may well be irrelevant in integrating a city with huge ghettos and barrios.

Even among communities of similar size the feasibility of desegregation is affected by the racial and social composition of the city, the way the metropolitan area is divided into school districts, and the strength of local private schools, all of which influence the desegregation process. The old, decaying industrial cities of the East and Midwest, which were cut off by independent suburbs generations ago, present far more serious barriers to desegregation than younger, more prosperous cities elsewhere. The schools in many of the old cities are often dominated by minority children and have been losing middle class families for decades. There is little chance of true integration, which is not the case in newer cities or cities with few minority children. Similarly, the prospects for aging suburbs close to expanding ghettos are far different from those for new subdivisions on the suburban fringe.

Although desegregation is usually described as a black-white issue, in many cities it is not. The nation's second largest minority group—the Hispanics—are crucially important in the Southwest, in California, and in New York, Chicago, Miami, and other cities. Many school districts have at least two significant minority groups and must find ways to reconcile integration with the special educational needs and desires of non-English-speaking children. Careful planning and mutual accommodation are essential for success in such a complex setting.

Consideration of the diversity of American communities leads logically to the question of the practicality of judicial requirements in each kind of community. Thus the costs, the educational effects, and the technical problems of transporting children are studied.

Even if desegregation is feasible, implementation may be impossible, and the second part of the book explores this problem. Students of the Supreme Court and the federal judiciary are skeptical about the capacity of the courts to impose changes that go against a consensus of public opinion. The courts by themselves, for example, accomplished little in a decade of trying to desegregate southern schools.

The enforcement breakthrough that desegregated the rural South was the result of the commitment of Congress and the executive branch. Only after Congress passed the 1964 Civil Rights Act, forbidding the payment of federal aid to school districts that continued to discriminate and authorizing the Justice Department to bring civil rights cases, did change come rapidly. Vigorous enforcement by the Departments of Justice and Health,

Education, and Welfare under President Johnson created a momentum for desegregation and took the pressure off the courts.

When the issue shifted to the North, the Civil Rights Act remained in force and the executive branch remained responsible for enforcement of constitutional requirements. This meant that, if the executive branch decided to enforce the law, the power available to enforce desegregation requirements would be far greater than is normally at the disposal of the courts.

Shortly before the courts began to require citywide desegregation, a new administration took office and brought the most sudden shift on civil rights policy in the century. President Nixon had in his campaign promised to restrain HEW's efforts in the South and to produce a more conservative Justice Department and Supreme Court. The conflict between the judicial requirements for busing and the President's active leadership of antibusing forces produced a severe institutional crisis in HEW and Justice. Bureaucracies created to enforce civil rights laws found themselves with controversial responsibilities in a political climate that had suddenly changed.

The executive branch led the movement against busing, but there was soon active competition from antibusing leaders in Congress. Even as the President ordered the civil rights agencies to resist urban desegregation requirements, Congress moved toward a direct attack on the courts. The story of the early 1960s seemed to be unfolding in reverse. Opposition grew, the elected branches withdrew their support and turned against the courts, whites' opposition to urban desegregation crystallized, and the mass movement taking to the streets marched not under the banner of "INTEGRATION NOW" but with signs reading "PRESERVE OUR NEIGHBORHOOD SCHOOLS." The political and administrative decisions left the courts isolated and threatened, as they had been in the South in the 1950s.

The final portion of this book discusses the future. If there is to be integrated education, there must be a sober recognition of both the responsibilities and the limitations of the courts and a national debate about positive policies supporting integration. The most basic question is, can some kind of metropolitan approach to integration in the older cities be found? Large southern districts have had wide experience with metropolitan plans, and the national applicability of this experience is assessed. In addition, a wide range of policy options must be considered if there is to be a successful transition from segregation to lasting and effective integration. These options range from relatively simple ways to improve planning to complex relationships between school and housing policies designed to stabilize and expand integrated neighborhoods.

Desegregating big city schools through busing is not an ideal or even a natural solution to segregation, but it is quite simply the only solution available if there is to be substantial integration in this generation. (Housing policies could play a useful supporting role.) There is no neat package of policies and programs that would solve all local problems, but there are many constructive policies that could ease the transition in the schools. Each year it will be harder to reverse the momentum of segregation in the big cities. The real choice now is not between busing and doing nothing, but between busing in an intelligent way that will begin to consolidate integration and busing in an ill-planned way that will reinforce the existing separation and deepen racial polarization. The choice should be self-evident.

# PART ONE

# The Law and Urban Segregation

# 1

# The Courts and the Law

THE SUPREME COURT did not set out to transform urban schools in the busing cases. It has plainly been uncomfortable in consistently confronting a hostile public and angry political leaders. The issue before the Court was not even, strictly speaking, an educational one. Faced with evidence of local official actions producing racial segregation in public schools, the justices had to decide whether these actions violated the Constitution. If they did, the Court had to set standards for repairing the damage.

The Court's solutions, of course, were legal ones. Given the unwillingness of elected officials at any level of government to devise their own policies to end segregation in American cities, the Court's solutions were usually the only solutions there were. Analysis of school desegregation policy must therefore begin with an understanding of the Court's basic doctrines and what they mean in practice.

The dispute came before the federal courts when civil rights lawyers offered evidence that black children had been denied their right to public education provided without racial discrimination. Local school systems fought judicial intervention, insisting that their schools operated on a racially neutral basis and that segregation was the unfortunate by-product of housing patterns they were powerless to change.

The Supreme Court passed judgment not on the way the schools taught children but on the segregationist practices of school boards and school administrators. In the cases it heard the Court found local officials guilty of fostering a castelike segregation in urban public schools and supported the use of a remedy, extensive busing, that was anathema to most white Americans and political leaders. The national mood had turned against the rapid social change of the 1960s, and many denounced this judicially imposed racial change. When the Court held that most urban school segregation was unconstitutional, it made a judgment few white Americans understood or accepted. When it supported citywide busing, it stirred sustained opposition across much of the political spectrum.

Announcing a new application of constitutional requirements was only the beginning of a long process of law enforcement. Not one major school system complied voluntarily. Each case required years of litigation, almost always against determined local resistance. Enforcing the law presented the courts with an unprecedented challenge—could they, acting by themselves, successfully restructure the largest and most important public institutions of the nation's cities? In view of the importance to American city dwellers of both their schools and their homogeneous middle class communities, could a nonelected branch of government alter these entrenched social patterns?

In the 1950s, though they had asked only for small, slow changes in the segregationist practices of one region, the courts had been unable to desegregate more than a tiny fraction of southern blacks. In the 1970s, the task was much more formidable: they were attempting to change racial practices that were the general rule in urban America. In the fifties and sixties, most Americans saw the South as a place apart from the rest of the country and supported sweeping congressional action in 1964 and 1965 against southern discrimination. But in the seventies the courts were attempting to change the practices of the majority. The urban desegregation cases polarized public opinion and generated sustained criticism of the courts.


## Toward Urban Desegregation

The Supreme Court's decisions on city school desegregation required no great innovation in legal theory. They did, however, represent a momentous change in federal urban policy.

During the half-century 1918–68, when ghettos formed and grew in northern and western cities, segregation was usually supported by local officials and federal housing administrators, who saw it as a desirable goal. The courts treated it as an accident, a kind of natural phenomenon, calling it de facto. As southern cities began their late but rapid growth, few were surprised to see racial patterns develop like those of the North.[1] Even at

1. Karl E. Taeuber and Alma F. Taeuber, *Negroes in Cities* (Atheneum, 1969), pp. 43–64.

the height of concern about urban policy and civil rights during the Johnson administration, the only significant action against northern segregation was the 1968 passage of a fair housing law that lacked workable enforcement machinery.[2]

Although the Warren Court carried judicial activism on behalf of equal rights to a new high, it carefully sidestepped the issue of urban segregation throughout the fifties and sixties. As the seventies began, the legal issues had developed to a point where the cases could no longer be delayed. Lower courts were making contradictory decisions. The Supreme Court had to resolve the conflict and confusion.

For almost two decades after 1954 the Court's understanding of the basic legal requirements resulting from the landmark *Brown* decision had grown.[3] Change came slowly at first, then much more rapidly after Congress and the President committed the power of the other branches to desegregation in the mid-1960s.

In 1954 the Supreme Court held that segregated schools are "inherently unequal" and that when racial segregation results from state laws those laws are unconstitutional and must be struck down.[4] Some interpreted this decision as ordering rapid integration of schools in the South. A year passed, however, before the Supreme Court in a unanimous decision spelled out the requirements: districts need do only what the local federal judge thought was adequate locally, and (subject to broad, vague guidelines) change would come "with all deliberate speed."[5] Three years later the Court responded to defiance in Little Rock with another unanimous decision establishing the principle that initial desegregation could not be delayed because of intense local community resistance, even if local officials said there was danger of violence.[6]

Throughout the first ten years of desegregation the Supreme Court continued to insist that some change take place but avoided defining what the final goal of the desegregation process was. Then, in an extremely important 1968 case, the Court held that southern school districts were obligated not merely to get rid of the old school segregation laws but also to adopt desegregation plans that produced the most rapid movement toward a

2. Public Law 90-284, Title VIII.
3. *Brown* v. *Board of Education,* 347 U.S. 483 (1954). This is the principal title of four cases in Kansas, Delaware, Virginia, and South Carolina.
4. Ibid.
5. *Brown* v. *Board of Education,* 349 U.S. 294 at 301 (1955).
6. *Cooper* v. *Aaron,* 358 U.S. 1 (1958).

system in which individual schools were no longer racially identifiable.[7] The next year the Court, under its new chief justice, Warren Burger, announced that the time for gradualism was over and that southern school districts must correct continuing constitutional violations immediately.[8]

From the 1954 *Brown* case to the 1968 *Green* case, it was not clear whether rural southern school systems were required merely to offer a formal opportunity for integration or actually to abolish segregation. Even after the *Green* decision it was not clear how the requirement for positive desegregation action applied in the urban setting. In rural areas, where there was relatively little residential segregation, actual desegregation could usually be accomplished by assigning all students to the nearest school. In southern cities, however, residential segregation had become intense and many schools were in the segregated areas. Much more drastic remedies would be necessary to create genuinely biracial schools.

Finally, in 1971, the Supreme Court decided its first major case about the goal of desegregation in the urban South.[9] The problem in Charlotte, North Carolina, was that merely applying a "neutral" neighborhood school procedure for assigning students would mean continued segregation, but actual desegregation would require transporting students to new schools. Either the courts must choose a seemingly equitable procedure guaranteed to segregate most black urban children or they must support integration through a procedure moving black and white children from their neighborhoods.

The federal district court in Charlotte decided that breaking down segregation was the goal. The Supreme Court agreed, ruling that the lower courts had wide discretion in ordering whatever changes were necessary to overcome the continuing impact of the South's long history of segregation imposed by law.

School desegregation law had developed more dramatically in the three years from 1968 to 1971 than in the preceding fourteen years. Until the late 1960s the courts demanded only gradual achievement of token integration through "freedom of choice" at some distant future time. By 1971 the courts required that desegregation be thorough and as rapid as possible and that it actually integrate city schools rather than merely exchang-

7. *Green* v. *County School Board of New Kent County*, 391 U.S. 430 (1968), dealt with a small rural Virginia county.

8. *Alexander* v. *Holmes*, 396 U.S. 19 (1969). This decision concerned some thirty districts in rural Mississippi.

9. *Swann* v. *Charlotte-Mecklenburg Board of Education*, 402 U.S. 1 (1971), dealt with the largest metropolitan area in the Carolinas.

ing a segregated dual school system for a segregated neighborhood school system.

## Unconstitutional Segregation in the North

Northerners had watched the legal developments with considerable detachment. None affected northern racial patterns, which were almost always characterized as de facto segregation caused by private not public action. As the 1970s began, however, the federal courts were scrutinizing a number of northern and western districts. The lower federal courts were finding that much northern urban school segregation was de jure, the result of official action. The Supreme Court said nothing.

The Court's 1971 decision upholding busing in Charlotte quickly influenced pending northern cases. Once the Supreme Court gave southern judges discretion to do whatever was necessary and reasonable to end de jure segregation, northern judges who concluded that the segregation they were examining was also de jure obtained the same powers. In several cases, they ordered prompt citywide busing. Television newscasters began to report antibusing protests in California, Michigan, and Colorado. National controversy mushroomed when the lower federal courts began to explore the possibility of ordering desegregation across school district boundary lines.

It was time for Supreme Court guidance. Finally, in its 1973 decision on the Denver school system, the Court began to spell out constitutional requirements for northern and western cities.[10]

The Court's principal task was to develop some workable definition of de jure segregation or dispense with the de jure–de facto distinction altogether. The Court had three broad choices. First, it could insist on a rigid definition of de jure segregation requiring, before the courts acted, unambiguous proof that local officials had *intended* to segregate the schools. Second, it could accept the claim of some civil rights groups that all segregation, however caused, was inherently unequal and violated the "equal protection" guarantee of the Constitution. Third, it could spell out some less demanding standards of proof for de jure segregation, relying more on the *results* of patterns of official action and less on proving the motives of the officials.

The Supreme Court examined these issues in the context of litigation

10. *Keyes* v. *School District No. 1, Denver, Colorado,* 413 U.S. 189 (1973).

about the Denver school system. Denver was a city with relatively few blacks. The local lawsuit had been filed because a new school board decided to abandon an earlier voluntary plan to end segregation in part of the city containing 7 of the system's 119 schools. Civil rights lawyers presented the kind of evidence that would later be uncovered in city after city. The school officials had, for instance, built a new, segregated school in the middle of a small pocket of black population, the Park Hill neighborhood. The school board had also employed optional zones, which allow white students to leave schools in integrated neighborhoods, thus accelerating resegregation. It had dealt with school crowding by placing mobile classrooms where they intensified rather than diminished segregation.

The federal district court had ruled that segregation in the Park Hill community was the result of unconstitutional school board actions, and it later ordered changes in the rest of the city on the ground that the other segregated schools were also unequal and violated the Fourteenth Amendment.[11] The court of appeals overturned this second decision, limiting desegregation to the single neighborhood.[12] The conflicting decisions offered the Supreme Court an opportunity to define its view of de jure segregation in the northern context.

The Court took none of the options. It neither limited desegregation orders to schools where there was strong evidence of intentional segregation nor dispensed with the de facto theory. It held that the mere fact of segregation was not necessarily a constitutional violation but that there should be a presumption that an entire school system had been segregated by official action if civil rights groups proved violations in a substantial part of the city. Once guilt was established in part of a district, the courts could desegregate the entire system unless local officials could prove that the remaining segregation was not related to school system policies.

The Court did not define unconstitutional urban segregation. Instead it indicated that the courts should follow a new procedure with a new set of assumptions. The decision pushed the lower federal courts toward less demanding standards of proof of intent to segregate without ever saying just what those standards should be.

The logic of the *Keyes* case suggested that, when school authorities made a series of decisions that had the easily foreseeable effect of intensifying segregation and rejected alternatives that would foster integration, this was sufficient proof of a violation. The majority of the Court agreed that

11. *Keyes* v. *School District No. 1,* 303 F. Supp. 279 (D. Colo. 1969); 313 F. Supp. 61 (D. Colo. 1970).

12. *Keyes* v. *School District No. 1,* 445 F.2d 990 (10th Cir. 1971).

Denver's discriminatory site selection and assignment methods in the small Park Hill neighborhood did constitute a violation of the Constitution. The Court pointed out that the Park Hill area contained more than an "insubstantial or trivial fragment of the school system."[13] The neighborhood held more than a third of the city's black students (though not many Mexican-Americans, the city's largest minority group).

The decision incorporated a legal theory one scholar has described as the "spread theory," which asserts that increasing segregation in one area usually has spillover "reciprocal" effects on other city neighborhoods and their schools.[14] The Court held that "where plaintiffs prove that the school authorities have carried out a systematic program of segregation affecting a substantial portion of the students, schools, teachers and facilities within the school system, it is only common sense to conclude that there exists a predicate for a finding of the existence of a dual school system."[15] The Court concluded that decisions by government agencies segregating some areas inevitably affect other sections of a city.

First, it is obvious that a practice of concentrating Negroes in certain schools by structuring attendance zones or designating "feeder" schools on the basis of race has the reciprocal effect of keeping other nearby schools predominantly white. Similarly, the practice of building a school . . . to a certain size and in a certain location, "with conscious knowledge that it would be a segregated school" . . . has a substantial reciprocal effect on the racial composition of other nearby schools. So also, the use of mobile classrooms, the drafting of student transfer policies, the transportation of students, and the assignment of faculty and staff, on racially identifiable bases, have the clear effect of earmarking schools according to their racial composition, and this, in turn, together with the elements of student assignment and school construction, may have a profound reciprocal effect on the racial composition of residential neighborhoods within a metropolitan area, thereby causing further racial concentration within the schools.[16]

The Court stated that it was simply "common sense" that racially inspired school board actions have an impact beyond the particular schools directly involved except in "rare" cases where a court concludes that there are natural boundaries within a district so important that they create "separate, identifiable and unrelated units."[17] (In Denver, though, the Court held that a six-lane freeway probably was not a sufficient physical barrier

13. *Keyes* v. *School District No. 1*, 413 U.S. at 199.
14. Owen M. Fiss, "School Desegregation: The Uncertain Path of the Law," *Philosophy and Public Affairs*, vol. 4 (Fall 1974), pp. 22–23.
15. *Keyes* v. *School District No. 1*, 413 U.S. at 201.
16. Ibid. at 201–02.
17. Ibid. at 203.

to justify separate treatment of schools on different sides of the road.[18])
Except in such rare cases, "proof of state-imposed segregation in a substantial portion of the district will suffice to support a finding by the trial
court of the existence of a dual system."[19] Once this finding was made,
school authorities would be under the same obligation as their southern
counterparts to abolish illegal segregation. There could be citywide busing
in the North.

*Keyes* was the first major school decision after 1954 that was not unanimous—Justice William Rehnquist dissented. He said that it "certainly
would not reflect normal English usage to describe the entire district as
'segregated' on such a state of facts, and it would be a quite unprecedented
application of principles of equitable relief to determine that if the gerrymandering of one attendance zone were proven, particular racial mixtures
could be required by a federal district court for every school in the
district."[20]

For civil rights advocates, the chief question in the case was whether the
Court had shaped legal standards that could permit substantial desegregation without impossible litigation costs. If the Court had adopted an approach suggested by the Justice Department—to require school-by-school
proof—the practical difficulties of gathering sufficient evidence would
mean that there would be virtually no desegregation.

The net outcome of the Denver case was that the courts no longer required comprehensive citywide proof of local constitutional violations. The
situation, however, was still confused. The old standard had been replaced
not by a new definition but by a new procedure. Litigants did not have to
show local intent to segregate each part of the entire system, though they
did have to make a convincing showing in a "meaningful" section, whatever
that meant. Once this showing was made they could follow two courses of
argument. They could either cite the Supreme Court's practical finding that
localized segregation had a reciprocal racial impact on other sections of
the system or rely on the new legal presumption shifting the burden of
proof to local school authorities. Unless the school board could come up
with strong evidence that the segregation was isolated in its effect and that
it had never been influenced by racial considerations, the federal district
judge could do whatever was necessary to eliminate segregation throughout
the city.

18. This judgment may have been reached in part because of evidence that children
had been assigned across the highway in other circumstances.
19. *Keyes* v. *School District No. 1*, 413 U.S. at 203.
20. Ibid. at 256.

The Supreme Court decision was seen by some legal scholars as the end of the de facto defense in desegregation litigation, but it was viewed more cautiously by others. Some who were hesitant to celebrate victory were civil rights lawyers. In almost two decades of southern enforcement litigation, they had often seen promising legal principles diffused and refracted into strange new shapes in the prisms of the lower courts.

The Denver plan was the first test of what the Supreme Court meant, and it was a clear victory for the NAACP Legal Defense Fund. After the Supreme Court laid down the ground rules, the district court had to decide whether the city's segregation was unconstitutional. Judge William Doyle promptly held that it was and ordered half-day integration of all but a few Denver schools.[21] Later the court of appeals ordered full-day integration of all schools in the city, finding Doyle's remedy inadequate under the Supreme Court's standard.[22] The lower courts believed that the Court's rulings left them no alternative to citywide desegregation in Denver.

Though most judges elsewhere eventually ordered desegregation too, some did not. Supreme Court decisions deflect or deepen the channels of case law, but they rarely set firm boundaries to its flow. To minimize division within the Court and to permit flexible adaptation to diverse local needs, the Court normally limits itself to broad formulas, leaving much discretion to district courts. This has been particularly clear in school desegregation law.

### Constitutional Violations

Before there can be any thought of a desegregation plan, the courts must first find state-imposed segregation. Although critics of the busing orders claim that the courts have been trying to break up de facto segregation, the fact is that they must decide the local authorities are guilty before they can do anything. Evidence of violations is uncovered in the great majority of cases in the North and West. The violations range from openly segregationist policies, recorded in school board minutes, to more subtle patterns of site selection and drawing of attendance zones in ways that consistently maximize segregation, not integration. In many cases the violations have continued for years and they include a wide variety of practices. Table 1-1 shows the violations found in a sampling of cases.

21. *Keyes* v. *School District No. 1*, 380 F. Supp. 673 (D. Colo. 1974).
22. *Keyes* v. *School District No. 1*, 521 F.2d 465 (10th Cir. 1975).

Table 1-1. *Discrimination Found by Federal Courts in Northern School Desegregation Cases, 1956–76*[a]

| Type of discrimination found by courts | Benton Harbor | Boston | Buffalo | Cincinnati[b] | Cleveland | Dayton | Denver | Detroit | Gary | Grand Rapids | Hillsboro | Indianapolis | Kalamazoo | Kansas City | Las Vegas | Manhasset | Minneapolis | New Rochelle | Omaha | Oxnard | Pasadena | Pittsburg | Pontiac | San Francisco | South Holland–Phoenix | Phoenix | Springfield |
|---|---|---|---|---|---|---|---|---|---|---|---|---|---|---|---|---|---|---|---|---|---|---|---|---|---|---|---|
| Discriminatory drawing or alteration of attendance zones | | × | × | | × | | × | × | | | × | × | × | | | × | × | × | × | × | × | | | × | × | × | |
| Discriminatory location of new schools | | × | × | | × | | × | × | | | | × | × | | × | | × | | × | × | × | | × | × | × | × | |
| Discriminatory expansion of existing schools (such as enlarging minority schools rather than transferring minority students to nearby white schools with available space) | | × | | × | × | | × | | | | | × | × | | × | × | × | | × | | × | | | × | | × | |
| School board's failure to relieve overcrowding at white schools by transferring white students to nearby minority schools with available space | | | | | | | | | | | | | | | | | | | | | | | | | | | |
| Discriminatory hiring of teachers and administrators | | × | × | | × | | | × | | | × | × | | | × | | | | | | × | | × | × | | | |
| Discriminatory assignment of teachers and administrators | | × | × | | | | | | | × | | | | | | | × | | | × | × | | × | | | | |
| Discriminatory promotion of teachers and administrators | × | × | | | × | | × | | | | | | | | | | | | × | | × | | | | × | | |
| School board's perpetuation or exacerbation of school segregation by its strict adherence to neighborhood school policy *after* segregated school system had developed | | × | × | × | | × | | × | | × | | × | × | | | × | × | | | × | × | | × | × | × | | × |
| School board's failure to adopt a proposed integration plan or to implement previously adopted plans | | × | × | | × | | | | | | × | × | | | | × | × | | × | × | × | | | | | | |

School board's adoption of "open enrollment" or "free transfer" policies, with the effect of allowing whites to transfer out of black schools without producing a significant movement of blacks to white schools or whites to black schools ... X X ... ... X ... X ... X X X X ... ... ... ... ... ... ...

School segregation de facto rather than the result of state action ... X X ... ... X ... X ... ... ... ... ... ... ...

Source: Center for National Policy Review, Catholic University Law School, "Why Must Northern School Systems Desegregate? A Summary of Federal Court Findings in Recent Cases" (Washington, D.C., January 1977; processed).

a. Below are listed the decisions in the cases in the twenty-six school districts.

Benton Harbor, Michigan
Berry v. School District of City of Benton Harbor, 505 F.2d 238 (6th Cir. 1974).

Boston, Massachusetts
Morgan v. Hennigan, 379 F. Supp. 410 (D. Mass. 1974). 509 F.2d 580 (1st Cir. 1974). Cert. denied, 95 S.Ct. 1950 (1975).

Buffalo, New York
Offerman v. Nitkowski, 248 F. Supp. 129 (W.D.N.Y. 1965). 378 F.2d 22 (2d Cir. 1967).

Cincinnati, Ohio
Deal v. Cincinnati Board of Education, 244 F. Supp. 572 (S.C. Ohio 1965). Aff'd 369 F.2d 55 (6th Cir. 1966). Cert. denied, 389 U.S. 847 (1967). On remand, 419 F.2d 1387 (6th Cir. 1969). Cert. denied, 402 U.S. 92 (1971). Bronson v. Board of Education of Cincinnati, C.A. No. C-174-205 (S.D. Ohio, filed September 29, 1976).

Dayton, Ohio
Brinkman v. Gilligan, 503 F.2d 684 (6th Cir. 1974).

Denver, Colorado
Keyes v. School District No. 1, 303 F. Supp. 279 (D. Colo. 1969). 303 F. Supp. 289 (D. Colo. 1969). 313 F. Supp. 61 (D. Colo. 1970). 313 F. Supp. 90 (D. Colo. 1970). 445 F.2d 990 (10th Cir. 1971). 413 U.S. 189 (1973). 368 F. Supp. 207 (D. Colo. 1973). 380 F. Supp. 673 (D. Colo. 1974). 521 F.2d 465 (10th Cir. 1975). Cert. denied, 96 S.Ct. 806 (1976).

Detroit, Michigan
Bradley v. Milliken, 433 F.2d 897 (6th Cir. 1971). 438 F.2d 945 (6th Cir. 1971). 338 F. Supp. 582 (E.D. Mich. 1971). 468 F.2d 902 (6th Cir. 1972). Cert. denied, 409 U.S. 844 (1972). 345 F. Supp. 914 (E.D. Mich. 1972). 484 F.2d 215 (6th Cir. 1973). 418 U.S. 717 (1974). 402 F. Supp. 1096 (E.D. Mich. 1975).

Gary, Indiana
Bell v. School City of Gary, 213 F. Supp. 819 (N.D. Ind. 1963). 324 F.2d 209 (7th Cir. 1963). Cert. denied, 377 U.S. 924 (1964).

Grand Rapids, Michigan
Higgins v. Board of Education of Grand Rapids, 395 F. Supp. 444 (W.D. Mich. 1973). 508 F.2d 779 (6th Cir. 1974).

Hillsboro, Ohio
Clemons v. Board of Education of Hillsboro, 228 F.2d 853 (6th Cir. 1956). Cert. denied, 350 U.S. 1006 (1956).

Indianapolis, Indiana
United States v. Board of School Commissioners of Indianapolis, 332 F. Supp. 655 (S.D. Ind. 1971). 466 F.2d 573 (7th Cir. 1972). 474 F.2d 81 (7th Cir. 1973). Cert. denied, 413 U.S. 920 (1973).

Kalamazoo, Michigan
Oliver v. School District of City of Kalamazoo, 346 F. Supp. 766 (W.D. Mich. 1972). 448 F.2d 635 (6th Cir. 1972). 368 F. Supp. 143 (W.D. Mich. 1973). 508 F.2d 178 (6th Cir. 1974). Cert. denied, 421 U.S. 963 (1975).

Kansas City, Kansas
Downs v. Board of Education of Kansas City, 336 F.2d 988 (10th Cir. 1964). Cert. denied, 380 U.S. 914 (1965).

Las Vegas, Nevada
Kelly v. Guinn, 456 F.2d 100 (9th Cir. 1972). Cert. denied, 413 U.S. 919 (1973).

Manhasset, New York
Blocker v. Board of Education of Manhasset, 226 F. Supp. 208 (E.D.N.Y. 1964). 229 F. Supp. 709 (E.D.N.Y. 1964). 229 F. Supp. 714 (E.D.N.Y. 1964).

Minneapolis, Minnesota
Booker v. Special School District No. 1, 351 F. Supp. 799 (D. Minn. 1972).

New Rochelle, New York
Taylor v. Board of Education, 191 F. Supp. 181 (S.D.N.Y. 1961); appeal dismissed as premature, 195 F. Supp. 231 (S.D.N.Y. 1961); remedy considered, 288 F.2d 600 (6th Cir. 1961). 294 F.2d 36 (2d Cir. 1961); aff'd on rehearing. Cert. denied, 368 U.S. 940 (1961). 221 F. Supp. 275 (S.D.N.Y. 1963); decree modified.

Omaha, Nebraska
United States v. School District of Omaha, 389 F. Supp. 293 (D. Neb. 1974).

Table 1-1 footnotes continued

521 F.2d 530 (8th Cir. 1975). *Cert. denied*, 44 U.S.L.W. 3280 (1975).

Oxnard, California

*Soria v. Oxnard School District Board of Trustees*, 328 F. Supp. 155 (C.D. Calif. 1971). 467 F.2d 59 (9th Cir. 1972). 409 U.S. 945 (1972); *application for stay denied*. 488 F.2d 579 (9th Cir. 1973). *Cert. denied*, 416 U.S. 951 (1974). 386 F. Supp. 539 (C.D. Calif. 1974).

Pasadena, California

*Spangler v. Pasadena Board of Education*, 311 F. Supp. 501 (C.D. Calif. 1970). 415 F.2d 1242 (9th Cir. 1970). 427 F.2d 1352 (9th Cir. 1970). *Cert. denied*, 402 U.S. 943 (1971). 375 F. Supp. 1304 (C.D. Calif. 1974).

Pittsburg, California

*Brice v. Landis*, 314 F. Supp. 974 (N.D. Calif. 1969).

Pontiac, Michigan

*Davis v. School Board of Pontiac*, 309 F. Supp. 734 (E.D. Mich. 1970). 443 F.2d 573 (6th Cir. 1971). *Cert. denied*, 404 U.S. 913 (1971). 374 F. Supp. 141 (E.D. Mich. 1974). 474 F.2d 46 (6th Cir. 1973).

San Francisco, California

*Johnson v. San Francisco Unified School District*, 339 F. Supp. 1315 (N.D. Calif. 1971). *Stay denied*, 404 U.S. 1215 (1971). 500 F.2d 349 (9th Cir. 1974).

South Holland-Phoenix, Illinois

*United States v. School District 151 of Cook County, Illinois*, 286 F. Supp. 786 (N.D. Ill. 1968). 404 F.2d 1125 (7th Cir. 1968). 301 F. Supp. 201 (N.D. Ill. 1969). 432 F.2d 1147 (7th Cir. 1970). *Cert. denied*, 402 U.S. 943 (1971).

Springfield, Massachusetts

*Barksdale v. Springfield School Committee*, 237 F. Supp. 543 (D. Mass. 1965). 348 F.2d 261 (1st Cir. 1965).

b. The original Cincinnati case (*Deal*) was prosecuted on a de facto theory and was unsuccessful. A more recent suit (*Bronson*), now in litigation, alleges several of the types of discrimination listed above.

The evidence is striking in Boston, for instance, where Judge W. Arthur Garrity, Jr., handed down page after page of findings of unconstitutional action by local authorities. The Boston school authorities were found guilty of building facilities "to increase racial segregation"; attendance zone lines rarely followed natural boundaries and were drawn to increase segregation by school authorities "at all times displaying an awareness of the potential racial impact of their actions." Patterns of assigning elementary school students to high schools were "manipulated with segregative effect." What natural integration grew out of residential desegregation was dissipated by a system that permitted white students to transfer from integrated to white schools. Busing had sometimes been used to increase segregation. Black teachers and administrators were commonly assigned to black schools.[23]

Lower court decisions do not, of course, prove that all segregation in a city's schools is produced by illegal school board actions. No one doubts that private action plays a role, and neither law nor social science has devised techniques that would permit any precise estimate of the long-run impact of segregationist decisions taken many years earlier. Nor is it possible to know how many of the actual violations have been detected by the judges. What is important is that significant violations are almost always found and that they contribute to increasing segregation. The legal rights of minority children have been abused, often with ingenious thoroughness.

The courts do not always find violations, of course. Since the Supreme Court granted wide discretion to the district courts and the appellate courts were to intervene only when the district court findings were "clearly erroneous," district courts may refuse to take any action if they consider the evidence of local violations unconvincing.

When the *Keyes* decision was handed down, two cases were pending in the Federal Court of the Western District of Michigan, Southern Division. The first concerned the schools of Grand Rapids and contained many of the elements that other judges had cited as proof of unconstitutional segregation. The local school board, for instance, had added capacity to overcrowded segregated ghetto schools rather than reassigning black children to nearby white schools. It had built new schools it knew would be segregated, rejecting integrated alternatives. It had established "optional" attendance zones, a device allowing white students in changing neighborhoods to transfer to all-white schools elsewhere. The civil rights lawyers also presented substantial evidence that there was a history of assigning black teachers only to black schools. Judge Albert Engel ruled that such assign-

23. *Morgan v. Hennigan,* 379 F. Supp. 410 (D. Mass. 1974).

ments had "seemed entirely logical at the time." Since some whites were hostile, it "made the practice seem acceptable and even desirable."[24]

Though the discriminatory assignment of teachers was wrong, the court held, it only created a rebuttable presumption that the segregation of the school system was not accidental. Judge Engel concluded that other evidence presented by the school board was sufficient to rebut the presumption. No busing was required.[25]

A similar case in the nearby city of Kalamazoo, however, produced an order for comprehensive desegregation. Judge Noel Fox decided that the failure of the board to accept "rational alternative" policies that would lessen segregation constituted de jure segregation.[26]

These two cases showed that federal judges still had differing concepts of de jure segregation. The Sixth Circuit Court of Appeals' decision to sustain both judgments suggested that the confusion reached up into the appellate tribunals as well.[27]

Although the courts almost always found school districts guilty of unconstitutional segregation when litigation was seriously pursued, there were enough contrary decisions to trouble civil rights lawyers. A case in San Jose, California, for instance, was dismissed for lack of proof. Sometimes even the appellate courts raised obstacles. The Ninth Circuit Court of Appeals, for example, read the requirements for proof very strictly, overturning pre-*Keyes* desegregation decisions in San Francisco and Oxnard and sending the cases back for further proof.[28]


## —And Remedies

Usually when appeals were finished the guilt of local authorities was established. Even then, however, the implications for a local school system were uncertain. Although judges normally ordered plans to end segregation throughout a school system by distributing students proportionately at each school, some signed orders leaving a great deal of segregation untouched.

24. *Higgins* v. *Board of Education of the City of Grand Rapids, Michigan,* unpublished decision, July 18, 1973, at 71. See also Margaret Marshall, "The Standard of Intent: Two Recent Michigan Cases," *Journal of Law and Education,* vol. 4 (1975), pp. 227–41.

25. *Higgins* v. *Board of Education.*

26. *Oliver* v. *Michigan State Board of Education and School Board of Kalamazoo,* 368 F. Supp. 143 (W.D. Mich. 1973); Marshall, "Standard of Intent," pp. 235, 236.

27. Marshall, "Standard of Intent," p. 241.

28. *Soria* v. *Oxnard School District Board of Trustees,* 488 F.2d 579 (9th Cir. 1973); *Johnson* v. *San Francisco Unified School District,* 500 F.2d 349 (9th Cir. 1974).

These differences resulted from the ambiguities of the Supreme Court's 1971 *Swann* decision, a ruling that upheld a plan of approximate racial-balance desegregation in Charlotte while explicitly stating that this was not a required approach. The Court said there was a "presumption" against schools that diverged substantially from districtwide racial proportions but still insisted that federal district judges had wide discretion. In a number of cases, the courts failed to follow the *Swann* model.

Within months of the 1971 decision, there were more than forty court decisions embodying its principles. Federal courts in the South rapidly updated old desegregation plans to conform to their interpretation of the new requirements. Most decisions imposed a plan requiring approximately proportional enrollment at all schools; others left substantial segregation intact. A few even decided that doing anything further would only be self-defeating. In major districts in Florida and North Carolina, in Nashville, Mobile, Pontiac, San Francisco, and other communities, the courts ordered approximately balanced enrollments throughout the school systems. Chief Justice Warren Burger, however, confused things by criticizing a Winston-Salem, North Carolina, desegregation decision because of the judge's assumption that racial balance was required.

Judges in some cities approved less extensive and more gradual approaches. In Chattanooga and Dallas, orders required only partial desegregation.

When districts had a black majority, decisions were perplexingly diverse. Several systems were desegregated by placing a minority of white students in each school. In one 65 percent black Virginia county system, on the other hand, the district court concluded that nothing more should be done because "there are just not enough whites to go around."[29] A similar decision in Atlanta simply pronounced the city desegregated and said that further busing would lead to rapid flight from the city by the remaining whites. (This Atlanta "compromise," which provided for hiring more black administrators instead of desegregating, was actively supported by Governor Jimmy Carter and Judge Griffin Bell. When the decision was sustained by the court of appeals, all the major Atlanta-based civil rights groups condemned the action and concluded that "constitutionally mandated desegregation is the most important issue to be resolved.")[30]

Many of these decisions were appealed, and in several cases the appeals

29. Robert F. Campbell, "Busing Decisions Provide Leeway," *Race Relations Reporter* (September 7, 1971), pp. 4–6.

30. *Calhoun* v. *Cook,* 332 F. Supp. 804 (N.D. Ga. 1971); press release, Southern Regional Council, November 5, 1975.

courts insisted on greater desegregation. In other important cases, however, partial desegregation or no real desegregation at all was accepted as an adequate approach, particularly in school systems with minorities of whites.

The federal district court in Memphis devised a plan that left about one-third of the city's black children in all-black schools. Civil rights groups attacked the decision, claiming that it was "a gross distortion" of the Supreme Court's position. The court of appeals, however, upheld it because of "practical considerations."[31] The Supreme Court refused to review the case, permitting the plan to stand.[32]

The skeptical federal district judge handling desegregation in Detroit after the Supreme Court had rejected a metropolitan plan in its 1974 *Milliken* decision[33] ordered "the minimum law will allow." Under the plan about one-eleventh of Detroit students were bused, integrating the white schools but leaving most schools all-black.[34] In an unusual decision, the court of appeals ordered further integration but conceded that it did not know how to accomplish it.

The court of appeals noted that Ronald Bradley, the black student whose parents had sued the school system when he was assigned to a 97 percent black kindergarten, would now be attending a 100 percent black sixth grade after six years of litigation and full implementation of the "desegregation" plan. There were, in fact, about 83,000 black children in intensely segregated inner city schools that would be "virtually untouched" by the plan. The plan, the appellate court said, had "glaring defects that could never pass constitutional muster and would not be countenanced by this court in a different factual situation." Spreading the small number of white children among all city schools, however, would only "accelerate the trend toward rendering all or nearly all of Detroit's schools so identifiably black as to represent universal school segregation within the city limits." In an unusual show of open disagreement with the Supreme Court, the judges of the Sixth Circuit repeated their conviction "that genuine constitutional desegregation can not be accomplished within the school district boundaries."[35]

During the same period the Fifth Circuit Court of Appeals upheld lower court decisions permitting the retention of extensive segregation in Atlanta and Montgomery, Alabama. In the Atlanta case, the courts simply declared

31. *Washington Post*, December 6, 1973.
32. Ibid., April 23, 1974.
33. *Milliken* v. *Bradley*, 418 U.S. 717 (1974).
34. *Christian Science Monitor*, January 26, 1976.
35. *Bradley* v. *Milliken*, 540 F.2d 229 (6th Cir. 1976).

desegregation to be complete in a community that had never carried out a citywide plan.[36] A district court in St. Louis approved a plan requiring only gradual desegregation of teachers and minimal student integration, suggesting that this was a way out of the busing controversy.[37] (The case was appealed.) Plainly, many judges were troubled about the value of desegregation plans that ended up with all children in predominantly minority-group schools.

The real possibility that the lower federal courts would interpret Supreme Court precedents narrowly meant that civil rights lawyers had to prepare far stronger cases than a reasonable interpretation of the *Keyes* decision would suggest. Though *Keyes* had shifted the burden of proving there had been no unconstitutional action to the local school system, some federal judges were shifting the burden of proof back to the civil rights lawyers. Even when de jure segregation was proved, a major effort was often required to obtain a workable remedy. In important respects, then, it was still necessary to prepare a case as if *Keyes* had not been decided.

Theoretically the *Keyes* decision eased the task of winning urban cases. But while the Court had greatly improved the chances for ultimate victory in nonsouthern cases, its new standards lacked the precision and clarity necessary to produce consistent, strong responses from all the lower federal courts. Desegregation litigation remained an expensive and time-consuming task with uncertain results. Even within the Supreme Court serious disagreement about the meaning of *Keyes* persisted.

## The Rights of Hispanic Children

The *Keyes* decision not only opened the way for more extensive litigation in the North and West but also extended the reach of the 1954 *Brown* decision to the nation's second-largest minority, Mexican-Americans, the dominant group in the Hispanic population. In many cities west of the Mississippi, Chicano students are the largest minority group in the schools, a group often growing far more rapidly than blacks. Their educational levels are frequently below those of their black counterparts. Sometimes they face severe prejudice and discrimination. Until recently Chicanos in Texas and some other states were subjected to open de jure segregation.[38]

36. *Calhoun* v. *Cook*, 332 F. Supp. 804.
37. *Christian Science Monitor,* January 16, 1976.
38. Jorge Rangel and Carlos Alcala, "Project Report: De Jure Segregation of Chicanos in Texas Schools," *Harvard Civil Rights–Civil Liberties Law Review,* vol. 7 (1972), p. 307.

In many western cities the treatment of Mexican-American children in a desegregation plan was an even more important and difficult issue than the treatment of black children.

Until the Supreme Court spoke, there had been considerable confusion on this score. In some districts, including Houston, the courts had treated Chicanos as part of the white majority, allowing the school board to desegregate blacks with Mexican-Americans while leaving many Anglos (Caucasians of non-Latin extraction) in all-Anglo schools.[39] In other cases, including that of Denver, the courts had ruled that Mexican-Americans were also victims of segregation and must be integrated with Anglos.[40]

The Supreme Court decision on *Keyes* resolved this important question in an aside as if it were merely a matter of common sense. The Court reasoned that the situation of Chicano students was similar to that of blacks, that they had faced the same kind of discrimination, and that they were entitled to the same remedy. It decided that "Hispanos and Negroes have a great many things in common," citing a Civil Rights Commission study that had actually made no recommendations about school desegregation. The Court ruled that Denver blacks and Mexican-Americans "suffer identical discrimination in treatment when compared with the treatment afforded Anglo students."[41]

The decision about Mexican-Americans greatly increased the burden on the courts and the school system in cities like Denver, but it should have also led to the development of remedies that made more educational sense. Since Denver had a Chicano population about twice as large as its black population, desegregating all the minority-group children was about three times as big a job as simply desegregating black children. Fully desegregating schools in this situation often meant moving two major ethnic groups rather than one into a previously homogeneous school, creating a complex tri-ethnic situation. Schools would simultaneously face desegregation and the special problems of children with little or no working knowledge of English.

The Supreme Court's approach had the advantage of forbidding desegregation plans like Houston's, but it also introduced new problems. The decision said nothing about the special linguistic and cultural situation of many Chicano children, an issue not present in simple black-white desegregation. The difficulty and sensitivity of the issue would soon become evident in the battle over the Denver remedy. The decision had major implications for other large systems with many Hispanic children (see table 1-2).

39. *Ross* v. *Eckels*, 434 F.2d 1140 (1970).
40. *Keyes* v. *School District No. 1*, 313 F. Supp. 61.
41. *Keyes* v. *School District No. 1*, 413 U.S. at 198.

Table 1-2. *Enrollment of Hispanic Children in Selected Large School Districts, 1974–75*

| School district | Number | As percent of total enrollment |
| --- | --- | --- |
| Albuquerque | 32,729 | 39.0 |
| Austin | 12,808 | 21.9 |
| Chicago | 67,508 | 12.7 |
| Corpus Christi | 23,808 | 54.9 |
| Dade County (metropolitan Miami) | 72,872 | 29.6 |
| Dallas | 18,426 | 12.3 |
| Denver | 20,541 | 25.8 |
| El Paso | 39,856 | 62.9 |
| Fresno | 12,439 | 22.5 |
| Houston | 40,190 | 19.0 |
| Los Angeles | 167,606 | 27.8 |
| Newark | 12,520 | 16.6 |
| San Antonio | 45,682 | 66.7 |
| San Diego | 14,384 | 11.9 |
| San Francisco | 10,604 | 14.0 |
| Tucson | 11,787 | 27.9 |

Source: U.S. Department of Health, Education, and Welfare, Office for Civil Rights, "Distribution of Minority Students by School Composition, 1970–1974" (May 27, 1976; processed).

After the Supreme Court had ruled on *Keyes*, the district court permitted the Mexican-American Legal Defense and Education Fund (MALDEF) to enter the case to represent the interests of the city's largest minority. MALDEF worked with local Chicano leaders, concentrating on devising educational policies to protect and expand existing bilingual-bicultural programs as part of the desegregation program. MALDEF lawyers explained to a largely hostile Chicano community that desegregation was inevitable and that it could be a vehicle for improving educational programs for Mexican-American children.[42]

At first, the approach seemed to work. The district court ordered the Denver school system to adopt an educational program designed to correct the many "incompatibilities" between existing local practices and the special needs of Hispanic students, as described by MALDEF consultant José Cardenas.[43] Judge Doyle's decision left segregation untouched at a few Hispano schools that were conducting experiments in bilingual-bicultural education. The ruling supported a program for the "transition of

42. Remarks of Carlos Alcala at Conference on the Courts, Social Science, and School Desegregation, Hilton Head, South Carolina, August 20, 1974.

43. *Keyes* v. *School District No. 1*, "Memorandum Opinion and Order," 380 F. Supp. 673.

Spanish-speaking children to the English language" as "clearly . . . a necessary adjunct to this court's desegregation plan."[44]

School officials strongly objected to judicial intervention in educational
issues and moved very slowly. The Community Education Council, appointed to monitor compliance, charged that the school authorities were
sabotaging the bilingual plan.[45] School district lawyers appealed, attacking
the bilingual directives. In an August 1975 ruling the Tenth Circuit Court of
Appeals sustained their challenge and reversed both the requirement for
bilingual-bicultural education and the retention of a few segregated
experimental schools. Such programs, the court ruled, were "not a substitute
for desegregation." Broad educational changes were not the proper concern
of the judiciary: "Instead of merely removing obstacles to effective desegregation, the court's order would impose upon school authorities a pervasive
and detailed system for the education of minority children."[46]

The appellate court rejected what it described as the assumption that
"minority students are entitled under the fourteenth amendment to an
educational experience tailored to their unique cultural and developmental
needs." "Although enlightened educational theory may well demand as
much," the court observed tartly, "the Constitution does not."[47]

Although the Supreme Court had expanded the reach of desegregation
requirements to include the largest minority group in the Southwest, experience in working out an actual remedy in Denver suggested both that the
Court had oversimplified the situation in equating Hispanics with blacks
and that desegregation plans affecting Spanish-speaking children would
raise substantive educational issues difficult for the courts to ignore but also
difficult to decide.


The City Line

Once the Supreme Court had supported citywide desegregation plans in
the *Swann* and *Keyes* cases, the courts soon had to grapple with the problem of desegregation across school district boundary lines. The issue arose
immediately in a number of the large central cities where minority children

44. Ibid.

45. Report from Community Education Council, appointed by the federal district
court, to Judge William E. Doyle, February 10, 1975. The Council observed: "No
effort has been made to adopt the Cardenas Plan. . . . There is a widespread belief in
the Hispano community that a vigorous and effective bilingual/bicultural program is
unlikely to emerge from present operations."

46. *Keyes* v. *School District No. 1, Denver,* 521 F.2d at 482.

47. Ibid.

already outnumbered whites. Civil rights lawyers argued that effective orders must encompass the "real city"—the entire metropolitan community.

During 1973 the Supreme Court deadlocked 4–4 on the metropolitan issue in the Richmond, Virginia, case. The following year the issue came before the Court again, when it reviewed a lower court decision ordering desegregation of metropolitan Detroit, the nation's fifth largest urban complex. In its decision, the Court held, 5–4, that desegregation must stop at the city line in Detroit.

The lower courts had found Detroit guilty of unconstitutional segregation but concluded that there could be no sensible remedy within a city where the enrollment was already two-thirds black and whites were rapidly leaving. The courts then decided to order preparation of a desegregation plan to include the city and fifty-three of the surrounding suburban school districts.[48]

The Supreme Court heard the arguments in an atmosphere of extreme political tension. The district court's decision had ignited a drive in the House of Representatives to prohibit court-ordered desegregation. President Nixon had strongly backed this approach during the 1972 presidential campaign. There had even been congressional hearings on a constitutional amendment.[49]

In its eagerly awaited Detroit decision, *Milliken* v. *Bradley*, the Court reaffirmed the rule of the *Keyes* decision on within-school-district discrimination, but refused to carry its assumptions about segregation across school district boundary lines in metropolitan areas. Whereas the Court was still prepared to liberally interpret the reciprocal effects of the intentional segregation of a neighborhood's schools on the rest of the schools within a city and to presume violation throughout a school district once some local problem was demonstrated, the standards of proof required were far higher when a school district boundary line was involved—the litigants had to *prove* that the violations had effects that crossed the district lines. Reciprocal effects of racially identifiable schools, the Court considered, stopped at the city-suburban line. Such effects presumably were metropolitan in Charlotte, which happened to have a metropolitan school district, but were limited to individual jurisdictions in metropolitan Detroit.

Civil rights lawyers, who believed that desegregation would not require

48. *Bradley* v. *Milliken*, 345 F. Supp. 914 (E.D. Mich. 1972). The ruling on the inadequacy of Detroit-only plans was published as part of the court of appeals decision, 484 F.2d 215 at 242 (6th Cir. 1973).

49. The controversy is reflected in the statements and materials printed in the House Judiciary Committee's hearings on constitutional amendments. See *School Busing*, Hearings before Subcommittee No. 5 of the House Committee on the Judiciary, 92:2 (Government Printing Office, 1972).

excessive busing, requested the Court to delay consideration of the case until a definite desegregation plan had been drawn up.[50] The Court, however, denied the request and decided to rule on the constitutional issues rather than the equity of the Detroit remedy.

When the Court heard the case in February 1974 the courtroom was jammed. A number of state attorneys general had signed briefs urging the Court to reject the thesis that a state government was responsible for designing a metropolitan remedy for segregation in school districts that were legally the state's local instrumentalities. On the other side, civil rights organizations, the Mexican-American Legal Defense Fund, and the cities of Hartford and Boston joined in arguing that failure to implement a metropolitan remedy would make a mockery of the whole concept of the right to a desegregated education in central cities with heavily nonwhite enrollment.[51]

The civil rights groups thought they had a strong legal argument in stating that school district boundary lines must give way if their maintenance violated constitutional rights. The Supreme Court, in its reapportionment decisions of the 1960s, had concluded that local political boundaries must yield when they made it impossible to protect the constitutional right of each citizen to exercise equal power in the selection of his representatives in Congress and in the state legislatures. Protecting the right justified forcing the states to abandon traditional legislative and congressional districts.[52]

The reapportionment decisions, which eventually resulted in the redistricting of virtually the entire country, were attacked in Congress and state legislatures, but they represented judicial overturning of the local political structure on behalf of a principle that had wide public support, the principle of "one man, one vote." The Detroit case asked the courts to restructure a basic part of local government, public school districts, on behalf of a goal that was strongly opposed by the public.

Although school districts have no legal right to autonomy in most states, the Supreme Court's decision recognized the underlying social and political reality. In theory suburban governments were mere creatures of state governments and could be altered at will, but in practice they were centers of great and rapidly growing political power, power committed to a determined defense of suburban autonomy. State governments recognized this. They had given the suburbs wide powers to determine their residential character by means of zoning, land use, and building code requirements

---

50. Brief of NAACP Legal Defense Fund, *Milliken* v. *Bradley*.
51. Briefs on file at Supreme Court Law Library, no. 71-507.
52. *Baker* v. *Carr*, 369 U.S. 186 (1962); *Wesberry* v. *Sanders*, 376 U.S. 1 (1964).

that could be used to exclude lower class residents and virtually all families relying on multiple unit rental housing. When these regulations were super-imposed on a pattern of almost complete segregation in subdivision devel-opment and marketing, it meant that the suburbs could largely control both the economic class and the race of their residents.[53] These patterns were, of course, reinforced by the existence of separate suburban school systems.

Chief Justice Burger's majority opinion firmly rejected "the notion that school district lines may be casually ignored or treated as a mere admin-istrative convenience" as "contrary to the history of public education in our country." "No single tradition in public education," he said, "is more deeply rooted than local control over the operation of schools; local auton-omy has long been thought essential both to the maintenance of community concern and support for public schools and to the quality of the educational process."[54] If forced to choose between desegregating schools and recogniz-ing the tradition of local autonomy, the Supreme Court was willing to move back toward more limited definitions of constitutional violations and de-segregation.

The Court ruled that breaching the boundary lines was permissible only where there was clear evidence of intentional violation of the rights of black students which demonstrably increased segregation in the suburbs. The task of the courts was to shape the best remedy available within the boundaries of the guilty school district. Overriding the existing structure of local government was an extreme remedy which would make the district court "first, a *de facto* 'legislative authority'" and "then the 'school super-intendent'" of a vast new super school district.[55]

Burger's opinion said that the civil rights litigants had to prove either that the district lines had been drawn for racial purposes or that uncon-stitutional segregation within one district had definitely caused substantial segregation in each of the other districts involved. "Without an inter-district violation and inter-district effect," he said, "there is no constitutional wrong calling for an inter-district remedy."[56]

The Court dismissed the conclusion of the lower courts that a city-only plan was not really desegregation and would not work. Chief Justice Burger said the lower courts were trying to produce "the racial balance

53. Anthony Downs, *Opening Up the Suburbs: An Urban Strategy for America* (Yale University Press, 1973), pp. 49–52; Michael Danielson, *The Politics of Exclusion* (Columbia University Press, 1976).

54. *Milliken* v. *Bradley*, 418 U.S. 717 at 741–42 (1974).

55. Ibid. at 743–44.

56. Ibid. at 745.

which they perceived as desirable." The Constitution, he said, "does not require any particular racial balance."[57] There could be full desegregation in school systems with a majority of blacks.

The four dissenting justices argued that the practical effect of the decision was to elevate the prerogatives of the suburbs above the constitutional rights of the black children. They insisted that integration would be both meaningless and temporary without suburban involvement. The decision meant, they said, "that deliberate acts of segregation and their consequences will go unremedied, not because a remedy would be infeasible . . . but because an effective remedy would cause what the Court considers to be undue administrative inconvenience to that State."[58]

Justice Thurgood Marshall, who had been the NAACP attorney in the 1954 *Brown* case, dissented more bitterly. He asserted that "the Court's answer is to provide no remedy at all for the violation proved in this case, thereby guaranteeing that Negro children in Detroit will receive the same separate and inherently unequal education in the future as they have been unconstitutionally afforded in the past."[59]

Marshall insisted that the Court's responsibility was to draw up a plan that actually worked. "One cannot ignore the white-flight problem," he said, "for where legally imposed segregation has been established, the District Court has the responsibility to see to it not only that the dual system is terminated at once but also that future events do not serve to perpetuate or reestablish segregation."[60]

Under a Detroit-only decree, Detroit's schools will clearly remain racially identifiable. . . . Schools with 65 percent and more Negro students will stand in sharp and obvious contrast to schools in neighboring districts with less than 2 percent Negro enrollment. Negro students will continue to perceive their schools as segregated educational facilities and this perception will only be increased when whites react to a Detroit-only decree by fleeing to the suburbs to avoid integration.[61]

The ultimate meaning of the case was muddled by the concurring opinion of the fifth member of the majority, Justice Potter Stewart. Stewart joined in the Chief Justice's analysis, but said that a metropolitan approach might be necessary if civil rights litigants proved "purposeful, racially discriminatory use of private housing or zoning laws." In an important footnote, Stewart expressed his belief that much of the segregation in Detroit was caused by "unknown and perhaps unknowable factors such as in-

57. Ibid. at 740–41.
58. Ibid. at 763.
59. Ibid. at 782.
60. Ibid. at 802.
61. Ibid. at 804.

migration, birth rates, economic changes, or cumulative acts of private, racial fears." These, he said, had somehow produced a black "core," which "has grown to include virtually the entire city." A metropolitan desegregation plan would be possible, Stewart concluded, only if "it is shown that the State, or its political subdivisions, have contributed to cause the situation to exist. No record has been made . . . showing that the racial composition of the Detroit school population or that residential patterns within Detroit and in the surrounding areas were in any significant measure caused by governmental activity."[62]

The import of Justice Stewart's comments and his footnote generated intense debate among civil rights lawyers. In a hearing before the U.S. Civil Rights Commission in October 1974 and in Washington strategy sessions the next month, some lawyers dismissed the comment as a largely meaningless effort to tone down the harsh impact of the Detroit decision. Others either saw it as an invitation to litigants to return to the Court with another case based on proof of discriminatory housing practices or confessed their uncertainty about what it might mean.[63] NAACP leaders shared Justice Marshall's perception that the decision reflected the political judgment of the Court majority and that the Court would not risk its prestige on the issue until the political climate changed.[64] The lawyers most involved in the Detroit case felt that they had presented substantial evidence of intentional housing desegregation in the Detroit suburbs but that the Court had ignored it.[65] The Court's majority opinion had specifically excluded consideration of the housing issue.

While most civil rights lawyers believed that the *Milliken* decision precluded any frontal attack on metropolitan segregation for the foreseeable future, actions by the Supreme Court during 1975 showed that crossing city-suburban boundary lines would sometimes be possible, at least in special local situations. The first cross-district plan was carried out in the fall of 1975 in Louisville. After the court of appeals had ordered metropolitan desegregation,[66] the Louisville school board had voted to dissolve. Under Kentucky law this forced the surrounding county system to take responsi-

62. Ibid. at 755–56.

63. Civil Rights Commission, *Milliken v. Bradley: The Implications for Metropolitan Desegregation* (GPO, 1974). See also William Taylor, "The Supreme Court and Urban Reality: A Tactical Analysis of *Milliken v. Bradley*," *Wayne Law Review*, vol. 21 (1975), p. 751.

64. Nathaniel R. Jones, "An Anti-Black Strategy and the Supreme Court," *Journal of Law and Education*, vol. 4 (1975), p. 203.

65. Panel discussion, Washington, D.C., by Paul Dimond (a principal attorney in the Detroit litigation), November 15, 1974.

66. *Newburg Area Council v. Board of Education of Jefferson County*, 510 F.2d 1358 (6th Cir. 1974).

bility. When the case reached the Supreme Court the cross-district issue was moot and the high court left the appellate court judgment in force. A more important case reached the Court in late 1975. In a brief decision the Court sustained a finding of de jure segregation by the state of Delaware in the metropolitan Wilmington area.[67] But on the whole the *Milliken* decision will surely prevent rapid and widespread cross-district integration.

## The Principles of Law

The Supreme Court's school decisions between 1968 and 1975 built a rough framework of constitutional law on urban school segregation. While the policies often contained disturbing ambiguities and enforcement varied from court to court, the basic principles seemed reasonably clear.

1. Urban school districts have a positive duty to do whatever is necessary to end unconstitutional segregation within their boundaries.

2. Segregation will be presumed to be unconstitutional throughout an entire school district whenever litigants can prove that the school officials intentionally foster segregation in any significant area of the city.

3. Intent to segregate can be inferred from an examination of the clear and readily foreseeable racial consequences of a school board's selection of certain school sites, boundary lines, and so forth.

4. Mexican-American students in the Southwest (and perhaps other groups with a clear history of discrimination) must be desegregated with Anglo children.

5. Remedies must be confined to a single school district in the absence of proof that children are distributed on different sides of the city-suburban line as a result of government action, not private discrimination.

## The Law and the Split in the Court

Seldom in its history had the Supreme Court staked out a position on so controversial an issue with so little support from either elected officials or the public. Attacks on the decisions were incessant. Appeals came from all sides as virtually every major school board affected vowed to "fight it to the Supreme Court." The appeals were supported by state officials of major states and even the Department of Justice. Across the street from the Court,

---

67. *Evans* v. *Buchanan,* 423 U.S. 963 (1975). In October 1977 the Court refused to delay implementation of the Delaware order for desegregation.

in the Capitol, legislative attempts to nullify the judicial rulings passed annually in the House and stirred bitter fights in the Senate. Presidents of both parties—Nixon, Ford, and Carter—proclaimed their opposition to desegregation through busing.

This angry criticism fell on a Court ideologically divided on many other issues, as the conservatives appointed by President Nixon fought the shrinking number of liberal and moderate justices over the constitutional heritage of the Warren Court. The *Harvard Law Review*'s annual tabulations of votes showed a striking pattern of polarization.[68]

Chief Justice Warren had worked very hard to unite the Court behind unanimous rulings on the controversial school issue.[69] This tradition of unanimity persisted through the 1971 *Swann* decision.[70] The *Keyes* decision in 1973, however, brought the open dissent of one justice, Rehnquist, and a concurring opinion by Justice Powell criticizing busing as a remedy.[71] The metropolitan issue deadlocked the Court in 1973 and brought a narrow one-vote decision in the 1974 *Milliken* case, the first clear defeat for civil rights groups since 1954.[72]

There were some signs of erosion of the principles of the *Keyes* decision and return to a narrower view of de jure segregation in a series of Supreme Court actions in 1976 and early 1977.

The change in tone was first apparent in a case on employment discrimination, *Washington* v. *Davis*. In its decision the Supreme Court pointed out that some lower courts had erred in ordering desegregation where there had been no explicit proof of "discriminatory racial purpose." The Court, in passing, summarized the law on school desegregation as follows:

> The essential element of *de jure* segregation is "a current condition of segregation resulting from intentional state action . . . the differentiating factor between *de jure* segregation and so-called *de facto* segregation . . . is *purpose* or intent to segregate."[73]

School cases reflected the more cautious attitude. In its decision on the

---

68. "The Supreme Court, 1971 Term," *Harvard Law Review*, vol. 86 (November 1972), p. 297. The shift on the Court was unusually clear: "With one exception, each of the four Nixon Justices agreed with each of the other four Nixon Justices a higher percentage of the time than he agreed with any of the five non-Nixon Justices."

69. The story of the background of the 1954 Supreme Court decision is skillfully told by Richard Kluger, *Simple Justice* (Knopf, 1976).

70. *Swann* v. *Charlotte-Mecklenburg Board of Education*, 402 U.S. 1.

71. *Keyes* v. *School District No. 1*, 413 U.S. 189.

72. *Milliken* v. *Bradley*, 418 U.S. 717.

73. *Washington* v. *Davis*, 426 U.S. 229 (1976).

*Pasadena* case, the Court limited the power of judges to deal with resegregation developing after a school integration plan had been implemented.[74]

The Court's desire to restrict remedies seemed apparent when it vacated lower court desegregation orders in important cases in Austin and Indianapolis in late 1976 and early 1977. The justices directed the lower federal courts to reconsider their decisions in light of its pronouncements in *Washington* v. *Davis* and similar language in a decision upholding exclusionary zoning in the suburbs.[75] Civil rights groups were also deeply disturbed by a January 1977 Court decision to review a court order that had already been implemented in Dayton, Ohio.[76]

The Supreme Court offered little new guidance in its June 1977 decision in *Dayton Board of Education* v. *Brinkman.* Although there had been much speculation that the Court had chosen this case as a means of abandoning the principles of *Swann* and *Keyes,* the decision was disconcertingly vague. The Court sent the case back for further argument, holding that the district court had not found sufficient de jure segregation to justify a citywide desegregation plan (something that even the civil rights groups had conceded). The Court emphasized the necessity of such proof and held that the court of appeals had exceeded its legitimate role in the case by insisting on more desegregation than the trial court had found to be justified. At the same time, however, the case reaffirmed the *Swann* and *Keyes* decisions, prompting Justice Brennan to note that the broad powers of the federal courts to remedy school discrimination "continue unimpaired."[77]

Perhaps there was greater significance in two brief orders from a divided Court sending both the Omaha and Milwaukee cases back for further evidence. In both cases, three justices held that this action was unnecessary but the majority insisted that further proof be produced in two more cities that were implementing desegregation plans.[78]

Although the decisions did not renounce the principles of *Swann* and *Keyes,* they made it more difficult for civil rights lawyers both to prove de jure segregation and to obtain a comprehensive remedy when they did. Judges were put on notice that they must require more evidence of viola-

74. *Pasadena City Board of Education* v. *Spangler,* 44 U.S.L.W. 5114 (1976).

75. *Austin Independent School District* v. *United States, judgment vacated,* 45 U.S.L.W. 3409 (1976); *Board of School Commissioners* v. *Buckley, judgment vacated,* 45 U.S.L.W. 3508 (1977). The suburban housing case is *Arlington Heights* v. *Metropolitan Housing Corporation,* 50 L.Ed. 2d 450 (1977).

76. *Dayton Board of Education* v. *Brinkman, cert. granted,* 45 U.S.L.W. 3485 (1977).

77. *Dayton Board of Education* v. *Brinkman,* 45 U.S.L.W. 4910 (1977).

78. *School District of Omaha* v. *United States,* 97 S. Ct. 2905 (1977); *Brennan* v. *Armstrong,* 97 S. Ct. 2907 (1977).

tions and that they must limit remedies to repairing the damage done by the violations.

Although the Court had not yet abandoned the principles of *Keyes*, the indications of a change in emphasis convinced some observers that a new policy was emerging. Attorney General Griffin Bell told a national television audience that he believed the Court had implicitly accepted the policy of limiting busing to an absolute minimum.[79] While legal scholars and civil rights leaders hotly disputed this conclusion, school boards across the country filed new appeals, delayed action, and awaited future decisions clarifying the law.[80]

The tension and stress so evident in the Court arose from its unique role in the urban school cases. The angry resistance to court orders to restructure massive urban educational systems tested the limits of judicial power. In its decisions, the Court had concluded that it must attempt to impose a policy supported by no powerful political movement and never voluntarily adopted by any major American city.

In an atmosphere of confusion and pressure, cases dragged on for years with appeals and remands up and down the judicial hierarchy. (The Indianapolis case, for instance, was nine years old when the Supreme Court remanded it for new hearings in 1977.) Even though few cities outside the South had actually desegregated by 1977, resistance remained intense. As the Court appeared to waver on its own decisions, confusion multiplied.

Frequently, as the national debate grew, emotions became so intense, rhetoric so heated, and public confrontations so acrid that it was all but impossible to focus on what had been learned and what lay ahead if there were to be integrated schools in our cities. Little effort was made to evaluate and draw lessons from the many southern busing orders that have been in effect since 1971.

Ending illegal segregation in the cities of the North and West remained a massive task in the late 1970s. It was by no means certain that the courts had provided all the necessary tools. Without powerful assistance from elected officials and administrative agencies, lasting effective urban integration was unlikely. If the Supreme Court's effort failed or were abandoned, the country would face a future of vast separate and unequal systems of training its children in the metropolitan areas where most people live.

79. Bell's statements on "Face the Nation" were reported in *New York Times*, February 14, 1977.

80. Local efforts to use the new Court rulings to minimize desegregation rapidly appeared in cases pending in Milwaukee, St. Louis, El Paso, Detroit, and elsewhere.

# 2

# Segregated Cities, Segregated Schools

A FIRST STEP in understanding what the legal principles would mean if applied nationally is understanding the dimensions of the segregation problem in our urban centers and their school systems. One often hears critics of the court decisions claim either that the problem is so immense that it is beyond the reach of federal policy or that the problem is being solved by residential integration and that judicial intervention is unnecessary. Current statistics on urban racial patterns, however, support neither conclusion.

## Minority Children

One child in four born in the United States is a member of a minority group. Most are black, but a large and growing number are Hispanic. Most live in urban areas, but they are distributed quite unevenly both among the metropolitan centers and within them. Most live in cities of the southern or border states or in the older urban industrial centers of the East, the Midwest, and California. Many cities and states have very few. Most of the children are segregated.

The schools in a growing list of big cities are predominantly black and Hispanic (though the cities themselves have English-speaking white majorities) because the minority population is young and unusually reliant on the public schools. The concentration of blacks and Latinos in certain areas of some large and middle-sized cities is the result of rapid migration from rural areas to a few metropolitan areas, high birthrates, and extreme residential segregation.

## Migration

The migration of blacks from the rural South to the nation's large urban centers is perhaps the most important movement of American citizens since the settlement of the western frontier. This and the more recent influx of Latinos have greatly changed the social structure of the metropolitan centers where a large majority of Americans reside. The movements not only carried patterns of deep racial division from the South across much of the country, creating physical segregation more extreme than ever before in American history, but also raised doubts about the long national effort to forge a shared culture in American society.

The black migration did not begin in earnest until World War I. In 1910 nine-tenths of blacks were still living in the South, but the 1970 Census showed that this number had shrunk to 53 percent. There were fewer than a million blacks in the North and West in 1900 but about eleven million in 1970.[1] The black migration to the West came even later, having become substantial only in World War II.

Only a third of blacks were urban dwellers in 1920, but by 1970 almost three-fourths were. (Northern blacks had always been highly urbanized.)[2] Black migration from the South peaked after World War II. During the 1950s it equaled about one-sixth of the black population base of the South and during the 1960s about one-twelfth.[3] From 1950 to 1970 the total U.S. black population increased about a third of a million a year, with all of the increase in the cities.

The 1970s apparently brought a demographic reversal. Census Bureau analyses disclosed an end to the historic pattern of northward migration which had brought 4.5 million blacks north between 1940 and 1970. There was no net migration at all through the mid-1970s. In fact, there may be slightly more blacks moving south than coming north.[4] This can be attrib-

1. Reynolds Farley, "The Urbanization of Negroes in the United States," in Raymond A. Mohl and Neil Betten, eds., *Urban America in Historical Perspective* (Weybright and Talley, 1970), pp. 322–23; U.S. Bureau of the Census, *Current Population Reports,* Series P-23, no. 48, "The Social and Economic Status of the Black Population in the United States, 1973" (GPO, 1974), p. 10.

2. Farley, "Urbanization of Negroes," p. 323.

3. George W. Groh, *The Black Migration: The Journey to Urban America* (Weybright and Talley, 1972), p. 48.

4. *New York Times,* September 1, 1977, quoting Census Bureau migration expert Larry H. Long.

uted to the robust condition of the economy of the southern states when
that of the urban Northeast was weakening.

Although the great black migration is now history in most cities, many
are still receiving large numbers of Latinos from international as well as
internal sources. The migrants bring with them not only ethnic identification but a distinctive linguistic background.

Until recently little public attention was paid to this immigration, which
has quietly transformed large areas of a number of the nation's cities. Many
Spanish-speaking Mexican-Americans have lived in Texas, California, and
the states of the Southwest since the time the area was taken from Mexico;
many more are entering the United States from Mexico legally and illegally
and settling in city barrios. The movement of Puerto Ricans to the mainland has changed New York City and a growing list of other communities.
Migration from Cuba resulted in there being 733,000 native Cubans in
the United States in 1973, a population that has transformed much of
Miami, one of the South's largest cities.[5]

The immigrant stream has been swollen in recent years by many hundreds of thousands of illegal newcomers from not only Mexico but nations
of the Caribbean and Central and South America. If this migration continues and the Hispanic residents already here continue to reproduce at
their present rate, Latinos may replace blacks as the largest minority group
in many areas.

The interaction of three forces—the immigration law reforms of 1965
ending national quotas that discriminated against Asians, the decline in the
U.S. birthrate, and the skyrocketing level of illegal immigration—has made
immigration a major source of annual population growth, producing an
increase of Spanish-speaking and Asian minority groups in a number of
big cities. In the school systems of these cities the cumulative effect is
striking.

### Growth of the Spanish-Origin Population

The Census Bureau reported in 1974 that the Spanish-origin population
had reached 10.8 million, more than one-twentieth of the national total.
The percentage is certain to increase substantially because the Latino population is much younger than the average for the United States, with a
median age below twenty-one. Future trends are evident in the national

5. Bureau of the Census, *Current Population Reports*, Series P-20, no. 259, "Persons of Spanish Origin in the United States, March 1973" (GPO, 1974), p. 3.

figures for children under five years of age—one-twelfth of these children are Latinos. Levels are especially high in some regions, particularly the states of the Southwest; overall population figures show:[6]

| | Number (thousands) | As percentage of state population |
|---|---|---|
| California | 3,153 | 15.4 |
| Texas | 2,099 | 17.8 |
| New York | 1,485 | 8.3 |
| Arizona, Colorado, and New Mexico | 1,067 | 18.9 |
| All other states | 2,991 | 1.9 |

## Mexican-Americans

The largest single group of newcomers is Mexican-American. Mexican immigration grew rapidly after the policy changes of the 1960s, which restricted migrant agricultural work and imposed a ceiling on western hemisphere immigration and resulted in a boom in illegal immigration. Arrests of illegal entrants climbed from 55,000 to about 800,000 a year between fiscal years 1965 and 1974, and many were never apprehended.[7] In late 1974 the Immigration and Naturalization Service estimated that there were at least 6 million illegal residents in the country and perhaps as many as 12 million.[8]

Mexican-American families live in a wide variety of settings but generally are far less ready than earlier immigrant groups to adopt English as their dominant language. Their settlements extend from the rural Texas counties along the Rio Grande to the great metropolitan centers of Los Angeles and Chicago.

Levels of Mexican-American segregation vary from rigid patterns in Texas to considerably more openness in parts of California. Mexican-Americans in much of the Southwest once faced segregation analogous to

6. Bureau of the Census, "Persons of Spanish Origin in the United States, March 1974," pp. 1–2, 23.

7. Leo Grebler, Joan W. Moore, and Ralph Guzman, *The Mexican American People: The Nation's Second Largest Minority* (Free Press, 1970), p. 81; "How Millions of Illegal Aliens Sneak into U.S.: Interview with Leonard F. Chapman, Jr., Commissioner, Immigration and Naturalization Service," *U.S. News and World Report* (July 22, 1974), pp. 27–30. Eighty-nine percent of the illegal immigrants arrested in fiscal year 1975 were Mexicans; U.S. Comptroller General, "Immigration—Need to Reassess U.S. Policy" (October 19, 1976; processed), app. I, p. 3.

8. M. A. Farber, "Battle Expected on Tighter Laws to Curb Illegal Aliens," *New York Times,* December 31, 1974.

that of blacks in the Deep South.[9] School segregation in some districts was so severe and persistent that federal courts had to strike it down in 1947 and 1948 decisions in California and Texas, the two states that have educated the most Chicano children—in 1970 they accounted for 80 percent of total Chicano school enrollment.[10]

Both school and residential segregation of Chicanos was most severe in Texas. Some school districts there had historically been reluctant to provide any education at all for Mexican-American children; others had operated segregated "Mexican" schools.

Analysis of 1960 census data showed that the residential segregation of blacks was usually greater than that of Chicanos even though the income and education of blacks were usually higher. A study of thirty-five cities in the Southwest found, however, that Mexican-Americans were almost always segregated from both whites and blacks to some extent. The most thoroughgoing patterns of three-way, black-Chicano-Anglo segregation were found in large cities such as Dallas, Fort Worth, Denver, Houston, Los Angeles, Phoenix, and San Antonio.[11]

The wall between Anglos and Mexican-Americans is more porous than that between blacks and whites. Nothing illustrates this so clearly as the question of intermarriage. While Anglo-black intermarriages are still quite rare, intermarriages of Mexican-Americans and Anglos have increased. More and more Chicanos are forming new families with Anglo spouses and Anglo relatives.

A 1963 Los Angeles study found that even among immigrants from Mexico an eighth of the men and a fifth of the women married outside the Chicano community in spite of the language problem. In the third generation, almost a third of both sexes marry non-Latinos. By the early 1960s Los Angeles Chicanos in general were no more likely to marry within their own ethnic group than were Americans of Italian or Polish ancestry three decades earlier.[12]

9. U.S. Commission on Civil Rights, *Ethnic Isolation of Mexican Americans in the Public Schools of the Southwest,* Mexican American Education Study, Report 1 (GPO, 1971), p. 13.

10. Jorge Rangel and Carlos Alcala, "Project Report: De Jure Segregation of Chicanos in Texas Schools," *Harvard Civil Rights–Civil Liberties Law Review,* vol. 7 (1972), pp. 311–38; Commission on Civil Rights, *Ethnic Isolation of Mexican Americans,* p. 17.

11. Grebler and others, *The Mexican American People,* pp. 273–75.

12. Frank G. Mittelbach, Joan W. Moore, and Ronald McDaniel, "Inter-Marriage of Mexican-Americans" (Los Angeles: Mexican-American Study Project, 1966; processed), p. 10. In contrast, in the 1970s, more than 98 percent of black marriages were

Though the Supreme Court has tended to equate the situation of Mexican-Americans with that of blacks, there are actually striking differences. It is clear that there is less social distance between Anglos and Mexican-Americans, particularly as the social and economic status of the latter rises. This suggests that, at least in some areas, Chicano school integration will be seen by Anglos more as a social class threat than as a racial one.

### Puerto Ricans

Puerto Ricans, the nation's second largest Spanish-speaking group, are concentrated in a small number of school systems. They are more segregated than Chicanos and their socioeconomic status is lower.

Migration of Puerto Ricans to the mainland in large numbers came relatively late and most of its impact has been limited to the New York City metropolitan area and surrounding smaller cities. The World War II labor shortage brought a sudden boom in Puerto Rican migration. The prosperity of the 1950s doubled the number of migrants.

The 1970 census showed that the mainland Puerto Rican population was still growing rapidly and still highly concentrated. The total figure was 1.39 million, a 56 percent increase during the 1960s. Seven states contained 91 percent:[13]

|              | Number (thousands) | As percentage of total Puerto Rican population in mainland U.S. |
|--------------|--------------------|----------------------------------------------------------------|
| New York     | 879                | 63.2                                                           |
| New Jersey   | 137                | 9.8                                                            |
| Illinois     | 88                 | 6.3                                                            |
| California   | 47                 | 3.4                                                            |
| Pennsylvania | 45                 | 3.2                                                            |
| Connecticut  | 38                 | 2.8                                                            |
| Florida      | 30                 | 2.1                                                            |

To an extent that was impossible at the time of other immigrant waves, the Puerto Ricans maintained close communication with their native area. Many, in fact, were more sojourners than immigrants, and decisions to leave the cities and return to the island were commonplace. In a typical year more

---

to other blacks. Bureau of the Census, "Social and Economic Status of the Black Population in the United States, 1973," p. 78.

13. Bureau of the Census, *Census of Population, 1970: Puerto Ricans in the United States,* Final Report PC(2)-1E, pp. xi, 1. There had been a 196 percent increase in the 1950s.

Puerto Ricans traveled to and from New York than the total resident
Puerto Rican population of the city. In one year, for instance, there were
3.4 million arrivals or departures on low-cost flights between New York and
San Juan.[14]

Puerto Rican communities were spared the continuing wave of immigrants that inundated Chicano communities in the early 1970s. In fact,
officials in San Juan reported net reverse migration to the island in 1972–
74.[15] The increase in the mainland Puerto Rican population was due to the
high fertility of young families. (The median age of all Puerto Ricans was
only nineteen in 1970.)[16] At the same time, mainland Puerto Ricans were
slowly dispersing to secondary centers within the United States. In some
cities in Connecticut, New Jersey, Pennsylvania, and Massachusetts large
Puerto Rican settlements were developing.

In Chicago, as in many other big systems, the huge number of black
students has been declining for several years as the number of Hispanic
students (one-seventh of the enrollment in 1976–77) has been rising. In
the 1973–74 school year there were about 29,000 Puerto Rican children, an
increase of 6 percent in only two years. The city had become the second
most popular destination of Puerto Rican newcomers.[17]

The problem of Puerto Rican students is more localized than that of
Chicanos, but their situation is even more dismal. Most Puerto Ricans are
in cities that are highly segregated and in a severe economic decline,
whereas Chicanos are more widely dispersed, with many in healthier, less
segregated communities with better economic bases. In the early 1970s
Puerto Ricans were concentrated in the Northeast, the only region where
the segregation of both blacks and Latinos had increased. Lower rates of
intermarriage and more severe housing segregation suggest more prejudice
against Puerto Ricans than against other Hispanics and less likelihood of
assimilation.

Puerto Rican residential segregation is usually less extreme than that
of blacks. The huge Puerto Rican population of New York City is considerably more concentrated in the three central city boroughs (Manhattan, the Bronx, and Brooklyn) than blacks are, but their neighborhoods are

14. Commission on Civil Rights, *Education, Housing, Employment, Administration
of Justice,* Hearing Held in New York before the United States Commission on Civil
Rights, February 14–15, 1972 (GPO, 1972), p. 255.

15. *New York Times,* March 22, 1975.

16. Commission on Civil Rights, *Education,* Hearing, p. 229.

17. Illinois State Advisory Committee to the U.S. Commission on Civil Rights,
"Bilingual/Bicultural Education—a Privilege or a Right?" (May 1974; processed);
p. 7.

less likely to go through the inexorable process of transition to almost complete segregation that is usual for neighborhoods with large black populations. Most New York neighborhoods with substantial Puerto Rican populations did not become all-Latino during the 1960s, particularly where the Puerto Ricans had relatively high socioeconomic status. There was little evidence in New York of whites fleeing Puerto Rican neighbors.[18] At the same time, analysis of Puerto Rican segregation in three other cities—Boston, Cleveland, and Seattle—showed segregation there to be severe, close to the level of segregation of blacks in Boston and Cleveland, even higher in Seattle. This segregation did not diminish between 1960 and 1970.[19] Few Puerto Ricans, however, were confined to the monolithic ghetto that formed the life experience of many blacks.

### Cubans

The third major group of Hispanic immigrants is the most recent, the most localized, and the most successful—the refugees from the Cuban revolution. Cubans began to arrive in the United States in significant numbers only in the early 1960s, and most settled in Miami. Within a decade they had strongly affected the city, its economy and culture, and the metropolitan Dade County school system, the country's sixth largest.

There were 446,000 American residents of Cuban origin in 1970, more than three-fourths of whom were still aliens. Forty-two percent lived in the Miami metropolitan area. The secondary center of settlement was New York City.[20]

The distinctive feature of the Cuban immigration was the class structure and educational background of the group. Most other Hispanic newcomers were refugees from poverty and joblessness. The Cubans, on the other hand, had often been relatively prosperous and had fled from a political and social revolution. The migration included many of Cuba's most successful families, with a level of education, business experience, and skills equaled by few immigrant groups. The difference between their relative success and the tribulations of the other groups strengthens the hypothesis that some

18. Terry J. Rosenberg and Robert W. Lake, "Toward a Revised Model of Residential Segregation and Succession: Puerto Ricans in New York, 1960–1970," *American Journal of Sociology*, vol. 81 (March 1976), pp. 1142–50.

19. Avery M. Guest and James A. Weed, "Ethnic Residential Segregation: Patterns of Change," *American Journal of Sociology*, vol. 81 (March 1976), p. 1097.

20. Bureau of the Census, *Census of Population, 1970: National Origin and Language*, Final Report PC(2)-1A (GPO, 1973), pp. 462, 226, 247.

Spanish-speaking citizens may confront more serious barriers of class and education than of racial and ethnic prejudice.

The rapid and impressive economic achievements of the Cubans were striking. Although relatively few obtained citizenship quickly and fewer spoke English than in other Latino groups, their income rose rapidly. The 1970 census showed the average income of a foreign-born Cuban was $8,684, more than $2,000 above the average for immigrants born in Mexico, although the latter had typically been in the United States longer and almost 40 percent had become citizens.[21] By 1974 there were more than 6,000 Cuban-owned businesses in Miami.[22]

A survey of metropolitan Miami in the fall of 1975 reported that Latin families had slightly higher incomes than other white families. Although this was partly because more members of the bigger families worked, the Cubans, who had been impoverished on arrival, had achieved financial power equal to that of Anglo families in an extraordinarily short period of time.[23]

## Other Minority Groups

The only other significant minority groups in American schools are Orientals and Indians, each of which accounted for about 0.5 percent of national enrollment in 1972. Both groups are growing rapidly. Indians have an extremely high birthrate, and Oriental immigration, which has been rapid since the 1965 immigration reform, jumped at the end of the Vietnam War. Except for Orientals in San Francisco, neither group is highly segregated in urban areas, and both present only local problems for desegregation policy.

In most communities, neither group has shown much support for deseg-regation. Like the Cuban population, they will be primarily considered in this study only when particular local problems are described.

## Demographics and the Urban Future

Projecting population trends is risky, but statistics strongly suggest a continued rise in the proportion of the minority population in the central

21. Ibid., pp. 171–72, 461.
22. Susan Jacoby, "Miami Si, Cuba No," *New York Times Magazine*, September 29, 1974.
23. *Miami Herald*, February 21, 1976.

cities and their school systems. The average minority-group woman is younger and has more childbearing years ahead, and both Latino and black families are larger than white families. The Latin population will also grow through immigration.[24]

The national trend toward smaller families was set in the late 1950s and the birthrate reached its low point in 1976, declining to almost half its post–World War II peak.[25] In 1970–73 the number of Anglo children below five fell slightly while the number of children of minority groups rose. By 1973 more than one-seventh of all children under five and one-seventh of those born in 1972 were black. Other non-Anglo groups were growing even faster, as were immigrants, who accounted for 30 percent of the nation's net population growth.[26] In 1970 one study showed that the black fertility level was dropping toward the Anglo level, but the Mexican-American rate remained 42 percent higher.[27] Even if the annual levels were the same, the younger minority families would have more childbearing years. Since minority children rely on public schools more than Anglos, the growth in minority-group enrollment will be even larger.

Each year, therefore, the proportion of minority children to desegregate will grow, with the great majority of them concentrated in central city school systems. National Institute of Education Director Harold Hodgkinson estimated in 1976 that, by 1985, 30 percent of all eighteen-year-olds in the United States would be members of a minority group.[28]

### Black Majorities in the Cities

Perhaps the greatest obstacle to school desegregation policy is the concentration of black families in segregated areas of central cities.[29] A far higher proportion of blacks than of whites continue to live in central cities, particularly in the few large cities that were magnets for migration from the South.

24. Bureau of the Census, *Current Population Reports,* Series P-25, no. 519, "Estimates of the Population of the United States by Age, Sex, and Race: April 1, 1960 to July 1, 1973" (GPO, 1974), p. 12; *Washington Post,* June 23, 1974.

25. Bureau of the Census, *Current Population Reports,* Series P-25, no. 614, "Estimates of the Population of the United States by Age, Sex, and Race: 1970 to 1975" (GPO, 1975), pp. 5, 76. The birthrate increased slightly in early 1977; *New York Times,* July 24, 1977.

26. Bureau of the Census, "Estimates of the Population . . . April 1, 1960 to July 1, 1973," pp. 5, 76.

27. Data reported in *Washington Post,* June 23, 1974.

28. Council for American Private Education, *Outlook* (February 1976), p. 1.

29. A central city is the core city (or cities in some cases) of a recognized standard metropolitan statistical area.

Although the black proportion of central city population rose sharply, reaching more than one-fifth in 1970, the percentage of blacks living in suburbs was lower in 1970 than in 1900. And in the suburbs, they were apt to live in old black communities or extensions of city ghettos across the city-suburb boundary line. Chicago's black suburban population, for example, was concentrated in black suburbs and older, decaying industrial suburbs. In the more typical Chicago suburban areas, with more than 3 million white residents in 1970, about one-third of one percent of the population was black.[30]

There were black majorities in the central cities of only three (Washington, Newark, and Atlanta) of the fifty largest metropolitan areas in 1970, and the trends suggested that most cities would retain white majorities for some time but the proportion of minority groups would continue to rise.[31]

In the first half of the 1970s, 13 million people left the central cities, almost 10 million of them moving to suburbs. Six million moved into the central cities during this period, about one-eighth of them black. Metropolitan areas as a whole experienced a net national out-migration of 1.6 million people between 1970 and 1975. More than half the loss was due to movement to fringe settlements in counties next to urbanized areas, just beyond the suburbs.[32]

Census reports in the early 1970s showed net out-migration not only from central cities but also from large parts of some suburban rings. In Maryland, for example, the formerly booming suburban areas of Baltimore County and Prince Georges County had net out-migrations between 1970 and 1974.[33]

A study of eleven of the twelve largest central cities (Houston is excluded because its boundaries changed) found that during the 1960s eight still had a net in-migration of minority residents, but ten lost a substantial number of their white residents (table 2-1). The effects on public schools are dramatic. Many big cities still have "net *in*migration of whites at ages

---

30. Karl E. Taeuber, "Race and the Metropolis: A Demographic Perspective on the 1970's," Institute for Research on Poverty, Discussion Paper (March 1974; processed), pp. 4–5.

31. Ibid., p. 17; also table 1.

32. Bureau of the Census, *Current Population Reports*, Series P-20, no. 285, "Mobility of the Population of the United States: March 1970 to March 1975" (GPO, 1975), pp. 1–2.

33. Bureau of the Census, *Current Population Reports*, Series P-25, no. 596, "Estimates of the Population of Maryland Counties and Metropolitan Areas: July 1, 1973 and 1974" (GPO, 1975), pp. 3–4.

Table 2-1. *Changes in White Population in Cities and Suburbs during the 1960s, Selected Metropolitan Areas*
Percent

| City | Decrease in whites in city | Increase in whites in suburbs |
|---|---|---|
| Atlanta | 27 | 51 |
| Baltimore | 25 | 23 |
| Chicago | 24 | 20 |
| Cleveland | 33 | 12 |
| Detroit | 32 | 12 |
| Los Angeles | 2 | 2 |
| New Orleans | 23 | 27 |
| New York | 13 | 14 |
| Philadelphia | 16 | 26 |
| St. Louis | 34 | 23 |
| Washington | 39 | 61 |

Source: Adapted from Larry H. Long, "How the Racial Composition of Cities Changes," *Land Economics* (August 1975), pp. 263–64.

20–24,"[34] but there is a high level of out-migration among young white families of child-raising age.

Although the number of blacks in the suburbs has increased fairly rapidly, the base from which they began was so small that they still constitute an insignificant fraction of suburban residents. In three of the eleven large metropolitan areas studied—Atlanta, Baltimore, and New Orleans—the black portion of the suburban population fell during both the 1950s and the 1960s; only in New York, Los Angeles, Chicago, Cleveland, and Washington were there small net increases. The most striking changes during the 1960s came in Los Angeles and Cleveland, where ghettos rapidly spilled over from the city into the inner suburbs—a "suburbanization" with little resemblance to that of whites. In most big metropolitan areas the proportion of black suburban residents was no higher in 1970 than in 1950. The first seven years of the 1970s showed little change.[35]

### The Impact on City Institutions

The erosion of the white middle-class tax and employment base of the older cities produced not only spreading ghettos but also severe financial strain threatening the maintenance of basic public services, including the

34. Larry H. Long, "How the Racial Composition of Cities Changes," *Land Economics* (August 1975), p. 266.
35. Ibid., pp. 264–65; Bureau of the Census, *Current Population Reports,* Series

schools. During the mid-1970s, when these cities' school systems had to cope with unprecedented concentrations of low-income minority-group children, tight money led to larger class sizes and shorter school years.

Detroit and Chicago, long two of the nation's healthiest industrial and commercial centers, showed symptoms of decay. New York City's fiscal collapse and major retrenchments were a national spectacle. Detroit's racial transition and fiscal crisis were less noticed but even more severe. During the 1960s Detroit's white population dropped 29 percent while its black population grew 37 percent.[36] By 1970 the city's population had dropped from its peak of 1.9 million to 1.3 million and was 44 percent black. By 1975 the city had lost 200,000 more people and was predominantly black. Between 1970 and 1974 school enrollment went from just above half to more than 70 percent black. Detroit faced a large and chronic fiscal deficit and had already begun to lay off large numbers of city workers.[37] In September 1976 some first graders went to school for only half a day.

Chicago showed signs of a similar decline. During the 1960s it lost about a fifth of its white population and about 211,000 jobs while its suburbs' white population climbed 800,000 and the suburban job base grew by half a million jobs. Chicago added 90,000 welfare recipients to its rolls. Pierre de Vise, an expert in Chicago demographics, concluded that "its population, jobs and fiscal base are on a downhill course that cannot easily be reversed."[38]

People in the older central cities could not keep up with the nation's rising average income. A study of nineteen major cities showed that income growth was lowest in St. Louis, New York, Cleveland, Los Angeles, and Baltimore, all cities with minority-dominated school systems.[39] Not only were cities less and less able to finance good schools, but they also offered fewer job opportunities for the graduates.

### The Largest Cities

Minority population concentration is most acute in the five largest central cities in the United States—New York, Chicago, Los Angeles, Phila-

---

P-20, no. 305, "Geographical Mobility: March 1975 to March 1976" (GPO, 1977), pp. 1, 5, 8.

36. Bureau of the Census, *Statistical Abstract of the United States: 1973* (GPO, 1973), pp. 850–51.

37. Ibid., pp. 850–53; *New York Times*, May 15, 1975.

38. Pierre de Vise, "Social Change in Chicago," quoted in *New York Times*, April 1, 1975.

39. Council on Municipal Performance statistics quoted in *New York Times*, July 8, 1974.

delphia, and Detroit. In 1972, when the last national summary statistics were issued, these five cities served more than one-fifth of all the black and Latino public school students in the United States.[40] (This amounts to about two black children in five who live outside the South.) These cities, whose wealth and rich job opportunities had been powerful magnets to both Latinos and southern blacks, now show, in the most acute form, the immense difficulty of adapting old, fragmented institutions of local government to the demographic and economic effects of this migration and to the movement of middle-class white families and jobs to the suburbs and beyond.

With the exception of Los Angeles, the five largest cities have been in a severe demographic decline since World War II. All five of the metropolitan areas are experiencing a net outflow of people for the first time in American history. And all cities will suffer a serious loss of political power to the suburbs when state legislatures and Congress are redistricted after the 1980 census.

Among the largest cities the decline was most precipitous in Detroit and least so in Los Angeles, where the central city includes large areas that would be suburbs in older urban centers. Detroit's white population fell so rapidly that the overall city population shrank about 1 percent a year from 1970 to 1975. This was faster than Chicago's and Philadelphia's decline in the early 1970s.[41] In the first three years of the 1970s, New York City lost 0.75 percent of its population each year.[42] The number of middle-class taxpayers was shrinking most rapidly.

The long-term implications of these figures can hardly be exaggerated. A study by the Regional Plan Association in New York, for example, points out that by 1980 the inner core of the New York metropolitan area could lose a million people. This change and a huge growth in the outlying suburbs would have distressing effects not only for the city but for the fabric of the whole metropolitan area:

The labor market of Manhattan would be greatly weakened, and economic opportunity in New York City severely undermined. Segregation would increase further. Taking a million people from the highest density parts would increase

40. Department of Health, Education, and Welfare, Office for Civil Rights, *Directory of Public Elementary and Secondary Schools in Selected Districts, Fall 1972* (GPO, 1973), pp. viii, 115, 311, 627, 936, 1212. Hereafter *Directory, 1972.*

41. The Conference Board, *The Philadelphia Market, 1972–1973, The Chicago Market, 1972–1973,* and *The Detroit Market, 1972–1973* (New York: Conference Board Major Market Data Series, 1975), p. 7 in all; and Bureau of the Census statistics in *Chicago Tribune,* April 14, 1977.

42. Regional Plan Association, "The State of the Region: A Digest of Selected Trends Through 1974," *Regional Plan News,* no. 97 (March 1975), p. 27.

Table 2-2. *Central City and Suburban Residents in Metropolitan Areas of at Least One Million Population, by Race and Income Class, 1970*

Percent

| Race and income class (dollars) | Central cities | Suburban rings |
|---|---|---|
| White | 35.3 | 64.7 |
| Under 4,000 | 46.4 | 53.6 |
| 4,000–10,000 | 41.6 | 58.4 |
| Over 10,000 | 30.9 | 69.1 |
| Black | 81.1 | 18.9 |
| Under 4,000 | 85.5 | 14.5 |
| 4,000–10,000 | 82.5 | 17.5 |
| Over 10,000 | 76.8 | 23.2 |

Source: Census Bureau calculations for U.S. Commission on Civil Rights, 1971.

the energy consumption of that million people perhaps on the order of 50 percent. The Region's public transit system would be weakened and auto dependency reinforced.[43]

These projections were made before the city's 1975 financial collapse forced cutbacks in public employment, which had been the only actively expanding source of jobs in the city.

### Demographics and Desegregation

Central city demographic change was most rapid in the old industrial centers. In the Middle Atlantic and New England states the decade brought a 10 percent decline in whites and a 45 percent increase in blacks in the central cities.[44]

Trends showed steady growth in the economic and social gap between city and suburbs, with increasing class segregation even among blacks (see table 2-2). As ghettos spread into the suburbs or integrated suburban housing became available in some areas, the black middle class began to leave the city—its departure is well advanced in cities such as Washington and Newark.[45]

Noting the suburbanization of blacks in a few metropolitan areas, some policymakers suggested that the school issue might solve itself. Sizable increases in blacks living in suburbs of St. Louis, Washington, Los Angeles,

43. Ibid., p. 8.
44. Bureau of the Census, *Census of Population and Housing, 1970: General Demographic Trends for Metropolitan Areas, 1960 to 1970,* Final Report PHC(2)-1 (GPO, 1971), pp. 5, 23.
45. Ibid., pp. 4–5, 34, 62.

and a few other cities seem grounds for optimism. Figures showing that in a few metropolitan areas black newcomers now tend to move directly to the suburbs are similarly encouraging.

On closer inspection, however, the new black settlement pattern in the suburbs is depressingly like that in the central cities. It is usually a process of ghetto formation, only the ghettos are finally spilling across the city boundaries or new ones are forming in suburban communities.

A generation ago it would have been considered remarkable that the mass migration from the South to urban ghettos was ending, that the rate of population growth was falling rapidly, and that substantial black migration across the once sancrosanct suburban line had begun, at least in some metropolitan areas. These changes would have been expected to signify the amelioration of urban segregation or even the beginning of a genuine solution to the problem.

The changes, however, came in unexpected ways, with consequences that offer little, if any, reason for optimism. The rapid departure of young white middle class families from the central cities, together with the plummeting birthrate, means that an increasing number of cities and some inner suburbs are left with few whites to integrate. Few foresaw that a second large urban minority group—the Latinos—with severe problems of their own would descend upon the central cities before the problems of the blacks had been addressed. Most assumed that black migration to the suburbs would breach the wall of racial separation to include new families in successful and integrated communities. Few projected that urban ghettos would engulf parts of the suburbs.

Population statistics clearly show that there is no equilibrium in urban racial patterns, only rapid change, which is not favorable to integration. A policy of governmental nonintervention will neither protect the existing residential status quo nor produce any significant increase in school integration; it will merely permit ghetto and barrio expansion, rapid white suburbanization, and the further spread of segregated education.

## Enrollment Trends

Many large American cities now have predominantly black school systems. Others are moving steadily in this direction. Many of the white students who remain are members of quickly growing Hispanic communities. Eventually some major cities will have predominantly Spanish systems, with black and Anglo minorities.

Central city school systems are rapidly becoming less and less significant for English-speaking white families but remain critical to the future of vast numbers of black and Hispanic children. The large urban school systems that were the model for American public education a generation ago are often isolated and trouble-plagued institutions serving mostly poor minority-group children who have no other choice. This pattern is characteristic of the large cities of the East and Midwest but there is much diversity elsewhere. When one considers the patterns of minority concentration, the arrangement of school districts in various metropolitan areas, and the levels of school segregation, it is immediately apparent that no simple national generalization describes the problem of achieving desegregated schools. In spite of the bitter political debate that portrays busing as a national issue, the fact is that desegregation is essentially complete in many areas, is a negligible problem in others, is manageable within single school districts in a third category, and presents unusual challenges only in some large metropolitan areas.

## Distribution of Minority Students

Of the 44.6 million students enrolled in the U.S. public schools in the 1972–73 school year, almost 22 percent were members of a minority group.[46] Almost three-fourths of the minority children, and 15 percent of total national enrollment, were black. Latino children accounted for most of the remainder, and for 5.4 percent of the national total. The remaining 1 percent was composed of almost equal numbers of Oriental and off-reservation Indian children,[47] most of whom now attend schools with a majority of white English-speaking students. In 1974 national estimates showed that about 67 percent of blacks and 67 percent of Latinos were in schools more than half of whose enrollment was from minority groups. Black students were by far the most likely to be in the most segregated schools. Forty-one percent of the blacks, 30 percent of the Latino children, and a few from the other groups were in schools with more than 90 percent minority children.[48]

While only one-fifth of the black children in the large districts attended

46. Meyer Weinberg, "Desegregation and Achievement," paper presented at Conference on the Courts, Social Science, and School Desegregation, Hilton Head, South Carolina, August 20, 1974, p. 5B.

47. Ibid.

48. HEW enrollment statistics contained in press release of Senators Edward Brooke and Jacob Javits, June 20, 1976. The statistics were released in this way because HEW had failed to publish them.

predominantly white schools, more than half of the blacks in the smaller systems did. The smaller districts (enrollment of less than 38,000) accounted for almost three-fourths of all black students in well-integrated schools.[49]

Most of the smaller districts in the South are under desegregation plans; most have had at least five years' experience with substantial integration. In the North the smaller districts often have few minority students. While there are only 0.7 million black students in intensely segregated (80 percent or more minority) schools in the smaller districts, there were more than three times as many in the larger systems.[50] Of the hundred largest school districts, forty-nine are in the North and West—twelve in California, six in Ohio, three in New York, and the rest scattered widely.[51] The greatest segregation problems are in a few states.

Systematic study of statistics from large cities outside the southern and border states shows astonishingly high levels of school segregation, particularly in the older cities. In most there has been little, if any, improvement— no desegregation plan has been prepared and no litigation is pending.[52] Even in the few cases where a court order has produced a decline in racial isolation within the central city, there is usually increasing segregation and racial separation on a metropolitan scale. By 1970 the northern schools had become more segregated than those of the South—and the difference was growing. The following table shows the percentage of black students in predominantly white schools:[53]

|  | 1968 | 1970 | 1972 |
|---|---|---|---|
| Southern states | 18.4 | 39.1 | 44.4 |
| Northern and western states | 27.6 | 27.5 | 29.1 |

Statistics on changes in urban school districts between the 1970–71 and the 1974–75 school years show that segregation is actually becoming worse in the northeastern states while it is stagnant in the Midwest and continues to fall in the South.[54]

49. Weinberg, "Desegregation and Achievement"; author's calculations.

50. Ibid.; Marian Wright Edelman, "Winson and Dovie Hudson's Dream," *Harvard Educational Review,* vol. 45 (November 1975), pp. 417–50.

51. Jeffrey W. Williams and Sally L. Warf, *Education Directory, 1973–74: Public School Systems,* HEW, National Center for Educational Statistics (GPO, 1974), pt. 2, p. 251.

52. Gordon Foster, "Desegregating Urban Schools: A Review of the Techniques," *Harvard Educational Review,* vol. 43 (February 1973), p. 10.

53. HEW, Office for Civil Rights, April 12, 1973.

54. HEW statistics in Brooke-Javits press release, June 20, 1976.

The political passions about school busing arise more from the fear than from the reality of desegregation. A study of ninety cities outside the South between 1964 and 1971 showed that more than one-third did not transfer a single student, black or white. Fewer than one-tenth of the cities bused as many as one-third of their black students—the median level was 2 percent. Only three cities among the ninety studied had "reverse bused" as many as one-seventh of their white enrollment by 1971. Twenty-three other districts had bused or reassigned some white students, but in fourteen of them it was only a fraction of 1 percent. In most of the rest it was under 2 percent. All of the battles in New York City had produced the transfer of only seven in every ten thousand white students.[55]

There have, of course, been more court orders since 1971, but surprisingly few outside the South. Schools in Denver, San Francisco, Pontiac, Dayton, Boston, and part of Indianapolis have desegregated, as have a number of smaller systems. But in the great majority of northern and western school districts with significant enrollment of minority students, nothing has been done about segregation. In the fall of 1975, as Congress was engaged in another stormy antibusing debate, the Justice Department reported only two new federal court orders outside the southern and border states. One integrated a single junior high school in New York City. The fall of 1976 brought desegregation in Omaha, Dayton, and the first phase of a three-year plan in Milwaukee, but most cities were untouched. New busing for integration in the fall of 1976 affected only 0.1 percent of U.S. students.[56]

Substantial progress was made during 1968–72 in lowering the national level of school segregation, but it was largely limited to the South. The regional differences were striking. In 1972 the typical southern white child in a class of thirty had more than six black classmates. Nowhere else was the average more than two. In New England, the north central states, and the Pacific states it was one or less.

Even though the northern states had far fewer black students to integrate proportionally, blacks there usually had fewer white classmates than in the South (see table 2-3). While the typical southern black child was in

55. Christine H. Rossell, "Measuring School Desegregation," in David J. Kirby, T. Robert Harris, and Robert L. Crain, *Political Strategies in Northern School Desegregation* (D.C. Heath, 1973), pp. 185–87.

56. List prepared by the Justice Department, Civil Rights Division, September 1975; Justice Department analysis of 1976 desegregation cases, in *Congressional Record* (daily edition), May 18, 1976, p. S7398; the 1976 busing figure is my calculation from statistics reported by United Press International in *New York Times*, September 8, 1976.

Table 2-3. *Regional Variations in Black Enrollment and in White Classmates of Average Black Child, 1972*

| Region | Blacks as a percentage of total enrollment | Percentage of white classmates[a] for average black child |
|---|---|---|
| Southeast | 30 | 44 |
| Middle Atlantic | 6 | 28 |
| Border | 21 | 28 |
| New England | 6 | 47 |
| West south central | 17 | 28 |
| East north central | 13 | 28 |
| West north central | 9 | 30 |
| Mountain | 3 | 52 |
| Pacific | 8 | 29 |
| United States | 16 | 34 |

Source: Adapted from James S. Coleman, Sara D. Kelley, and John A. Moore, *Trends in School Segregation, 1968–73* (Urban Institute, 1975), p. 24.

a. Includes Latinos (since Hispanic enrollment is higher outside the South, the table understates the differences between the regions).

a class that was 44 percent white, the typical black child in the Pacific states was in a class only 29 percent white.[57]

### Private School Enrollment

One of the factors that makes school desegregation particularly complex in some parts of the country is the existence of a large network of private schools, which may impede school integration. The problem appeared first in the South, but some northern cities are now affected.

The Southern Regional Council (a private development and civil rights agency) has been especially active in pointing out the threat to the desegregation process posed by the emergence of "segregation academies" in the South, which were opened in many communities beginning in the mid-1960s. Experts estimated that they drew as many as half a million white students out of the public schools from 1964 to 1975. Urban desegregation was most affected in Memphis, where a newly organized system of private religious academies attracted thousands of children. Southern private school enrollment appears to have stabilized at about 10 percent of the

57. James S. Coleman, Sara D. Kelley, and John H. Moore, *Trends in School Segregation, 1968–73* (Urban Institute, 1975), p. 24.

region's white pupils.[58] In some districts children are now returning to public schools.

Although private schools have been expanding in the South, nationally they have been shrinking until recently, with most of the losses in the Catholic system, long the dominant sector of American private education. In the 1973–74 school year, one in nine whites and one in twenty-five blacks attended private schools. The declining birthrate had brought a 6 percent drop in public elementary school enrollment between 1970 and 1973, but private school enrollment had fallen 17 percent during the same period. Private elementary enrollment reached its low point in 1974 and rose modestly in 1975–76; private high school enrollment began to grow in 1972–73. Overall, however, private schools still serve a substantially smaller percentage of children than they did a decade ago.[59]

Both black and Hispanic enrollments in Catholic schools grew, reaching 13 percent in 1974–75. Schools serving low-income central city areas held onto their enrollment better than other parochial schools.[60] Though blacks made up only 1.8 percent of the Catholic population in 1970, they constituted 5.1 percent of the parochial system's elementary students at that time.[61]

During the 1970–71 school year Catholic schools enrolled 88 percent of the private school students in forty-three of the nation's largest cities. In Cleveland and Philadelphia private schools, including Catholic schools, enrolled about a third of all school age children. Approximately a fourth of schoolchildren went to private schools in Chicago, Boston, Milwaukee, New Orleans, New York City, and San Francisco, all cities with severe segregation problems. Cleveland had more whites in Catholic than in public schools by 1970. Detroit had three-fourths as many.[62] Although trends indicated that parochial schools would enroll large fractions of the white chil-

58. John Egerton, *Promise of Progress: Memphis School Desegregation, 1972–73* (Atlanta: Southern Regional Council, 1973), pp. 16–19, 32; *New York Times,* September 22, 1975.

59. Bureau of the Census, *Current Population Reports,* Series P-20, no. 294, "School Enrollment—Social and Economic Characteristics of Students, October 1975" (GPO, 1976), p. 7.

60. *Integrated Education* (March–April 1975), p. 25; Chris Ganley, ed., *Catholic Schools in America* (Denver: Curriculum Information Center with National Catholic Educational Association, 1975), p. iv.

61. Andrew M. Greeley, "Catholic Schools Are Committing Suicide," *New York Times Magazine* (October 21, 1973), p. 65.

62. Diane B. Gertler, *Nonpublic Schools in Large Cities, 1970–71 Edition,* HEW, National Center for Educational Statistics (GPO, 1974), pp. 2, 5.

dren remaining in many older central cities, in a number of southern and western cities fewer than one-tenth of the children were involved.

Most of the private schools in big cities were predominantly white. In Boston, Cleveland, Buffalo, Cincinnati, and Rochester minority group children accounted for less than one-tenth of private school enrollment in 1970; in most other cities the fraction was substantially below one-fourth. In the inner city sections of these communities, however, the minority-group portion of private school enrollment was much higher, often reaching almost 50 percent, though it never (except in Fort Worth) assumed the monolithic segregated character of the public schools in most of these communities.[63] Almost half the Catholic schools are in central cities and one in seven is in a poverty area. Between 1970 and 1974 inner city enrollment rose from one-ninth to one-sixth of the Catholic total.[64] In some cities Catholic schools were providing the only integrated, middle class education available to minority children.

The top two Catholic systems were among the ten largest school systems in the United States (see table 2-4). Each of the twenty-one largest systems would have been among the hundred largest in the United States had it been a public system.[65]

In most cases, when a desegregation order is handed down, the Catholic schools attempt to support it by endorsing the plan and refusing to accept transfer students from public schools. Nonetheless, the very fact that a substantial portion of the city's white children are not in the public system impedes effective desegregation. In a city with a rapidly declining white population even a stable private enrollment rapidly diminishes the proportion of whites enrolled in public schools. Ironically, a school system originally built to aid a religious minority group encountering severe discrimination now has the unintended side effect of making the repair of public school discrimination against racial minorities far more difficult in some big cities. The great concentration of parochial schools in the older industrial central cities has increased the urgency of a metropolitan approach to desegregation in these areas.

63. Ibid., pp. 13–16.

64. National Catholic Educational Association, *Catholic Schools in the United States, 1973–74* (Washington: NCEA, 1974), pp. 8–11; Ganley, *Catholic Schools in America,* p. vii; Edward B. Fiske, "Inner City Catholic Schools Find Stability," *New York Times,* October 9, 1977.

65. Ganley, *Catholic Schools in America,* p. vi; Williams and Warf, *Education Directory, 1973–74,* pt. 2, p. 251.

Table 2-4. *Largest Catholic School Systems, 1974–75 School Year*

| Rank | Diocese | Enrollment |
|------|---------|------------|
| 1 | Chicago | 224,100 |
| 2 | Philadelphia | 205,800 |
| 3 | New York | 156,400 |
| 4 | Brooklyn | 146,000 |
| 5 | Los Angeles | 131,700 |
| 6 | Newark | 101,700 |
| 7 | Detroit | 93,000 |
| 8 | Cleveland | 87,000 |
| 9 | Boston | 81,500 |
| 10 | St. Louis | 72,500 |
| 11 | New Orleans | 68,500 |
| 12 | Milwaukee | 63,400 |
| 13 | Trenton | 62,200 |
| 14 | Cincinnati | 61,300 |
| 15 | Rockville Center, N.Y. | 59,600 |
| 16 | Pittsburgh | 59,100 |
| 17 | Buffalo | 57,400 |
| 18 | Baltimore | 48,200 |
| 19 | San Francisco | 47,300 |
| 20 | St. Paul | 45,700 |
| 21 | Washington, D.C. | 42,800 |

Source: Chris Ganley, ed., *Catholic Schools in America* (Denver: Curriculum Information Center with National Catholic Educational Association, 1975), p. xiii. Diocesan boundaries often do not coincide with city boundaries.

## Regional Differences in School District Composition

Minority children in the South and some parts of the West are much more likely to live in urban school districts where desegregation in predominantly white schools is feasible because the central cities usually encompass a larger segment of the metropolitan area than do the older industrial cities. In southern, border, and some western states school district organization is often less fragmented; in several the county is the basic unit of educational organization.

These differences in organizational structure affect policy. In an old eastern city, where the city limits were fixed before the advent of streetcars or automobiles, the central city is likely to contain only a narrow segment of the white population, which often includes a high proportion of elderly people and of working-class ethnic groups. The situation of such a city (for instance, Boston) in a desegregation crisis is very different from that of a city like Phoenix, which has many middle-class whites.

The differences are even greater between countywide school districts and central-city-only districts. In 1970 the metropolitan area of Charlotte, North Carolina, had 571,000 residents, with all the children in a single school district; and Richmond, Virginia, had 553,000 residents, but most lived in suburbs with their own school systems.[66] The schools in metropolitan Charlotte could be and were desegregated, with a large white majority in each school. Since the school district includes most housing within reach of local jobs, there was no practical alternative for most white families. In Richmond, on the other hand, 70 percent of the students in the city were black.[67] There white families could choose between a central city system dominated by schools with an increasing number of black children and two large nearby suburban systems with few black children. Whereas the percentage of white enrollment stabilized after metropolitan desegregation in Charlotte, it continued to decline after central city desegregation in Richmond.[68]

A minority student's right to a desegregated education may well depend on whether he or she happened to be born in an area that, for wholly unrelated reasons, suburbanized late. A black student in Richmond is, in effect, denied the right to a desegregated education, though the bus ride would be no longer than that already provided for children living in the inner city of Charlotte. Students in Richmond were bused to so-called desegregated schools with a small number of white students. Under the Supreme Court's holding in the *Milliken* case in Detroit such schools could fulfill all constitutional requirements. Surveys show, however, that few whites or blacks think of this as genuine desegregation.[69]

Because Florida adopted countywide school districts while New Jersey has fragmented districts, black students in the former attend integrated schools while those in the latter must attend segregated schools. North-South differences in suburbanization are striking. Whereas in the eleven southern states suburban enrollment averaged only about one-fourth, in the most populous states of the North and West it usually averaged more than

66. Bureau of the Census, *Statistical Abstract of the United States: 1973*, pp. 850, 890.

67. HEW, Office for Civil Rights, *Directory, 1972*, p. 1430.

68. HEW, Office for Civil Rights, Form OS/CR 101 submitted by school districts for the 1974–75 school year.

69. Year after year, Gallup polls have found sharp resistance to predominantly minority schools among whites who support integration. Surveys of the parents of bused black children have found the least support when the child was bused to a school with a predominantly black enrollment. School systems in Detroit and Wilmington led by blacks have supported metropolitan plans, sacrificing their own authority in the quest for genuinely integrated schools.

Table 2-5. *Central City and Suburban School Enrollment as a Percentage of Total State Enrollment, Selected Northern and Western States with Large Minority Populations, 1973–74 School Year*

| State | Central city | Suburb |
|-------|:------------:|:------:|
| California | 34.1 | 57.9 |
| Colorado | 26.7 | 44.6 |
| Connecticut | 30.1 | 50.3 |
| Illinois | 30.0 | 47.9 |
| Indiana | 28.8 | 31.4 |
| Massachusetts | 24.7 | 56.1 |
| Michigan | 22.8 | 51.6 |
| New Jersey | 14.4 | 59.1 |
| Ohio | 26.6 | 48.2 |
| Pennsylvania | 23.7 | 52.6 |
| New York | 38.1 | 44.7 |

Source: Unpublished tabulations by the National Center for Educational Statistics, HEW, 1974.

half. Substantial desegregation will not be easy in states such as New Jersey, only one-seventh of whose students were enrolled in the declining central city systems in the 1973–74 school year, or Michigan, where the figure was little more than one-fifth (see table 2-5).

## Problems of Desegregation

Although the large numbers of minority children in central city school systems sometimes make the obstacles to desegregation seem almost insurmountable, there is much variation in the country. Most minority children still live in districts where desegregation is feasible. Many live in states where there is no significant problem.

### The Smallest Problems

Although busing has been pictured in congressional debates as a grave national problem, most senators and congressmen represent constituencies where the minority population is so low that even total desegregation would be a minor operation. This is true of the states reaching from the Pacific Northwest to the Mississippi River, in which 1972 statistics from the Department of Health, Education, and Welfare show there is little segregation.

Oregon, for example, had 8,518 black students in its public schools, 85 percent of whom were in Portland, the state's largest city. Black students made up 10.6 percent of Portland's 68,000 pupils. Only ten schools had predominantly minority enrollment; in four of them just over half were minority students who could easily be desegregated. Subsequently the city desegregated under state guidelines.[70] Clearly, in Portland reassigning and transporting a few hundred children wiped out significant segregation of black students in a large school system and thus in an entire state.

In the neighboring state of Washington, the largest school district, Seattle, had a much higher proportion of minority children, but its problem was manageable. In 1974, 26 percent of Seattle's 69,000 schoolchildren were from minority groups. Many were Orientals; only 15 percent were black. Only 22 of the 128 schools in the system were close to half white.[71] The city adopted a voluntary desegregation plan in 1977.

Even Oregon and Washington, however, had far more minority students than such states as Idaho, Montana, Wyoming, North Dakota, South Dakota, and Utah. It was possible for the whole northwestern quarter of the United States to achieve general desegregation without extensive changes.

Further east, in Minnesota, the largest system, Minneapolis, has desegregated, and the second largest system, St. Paul, had only 11.6 percent minority enrollment in 1972 and five predominantly minority schools, which enrolled 1,076 blacks.[72] The state could be desegregated with minimal effort. Iowa had only 10,000 black students and a few segregated schools. State education officials required local development of desegregation plans in 1976. Des Moines desegregated in 1977. Still further east, in Wisconsin, the numbers were more substantial. Milwaukee's public schools contained 37,000 black children in 1975, or 33 percent of the system's total enrollment. Thirty-seven schools, containing more than two-thirds of the black students, had more than 90 percent minority enrollment by 1974; in twenty-five of them, minority enrollment was more than 99 percent.[73]

Milwaukee faced difficult problems. Substantial busing was needed to achieve integration. A federal district court found the city guilty of uncon-

70. HEW, Office for Civil Rights, *Directory, 1972,* pp. 1151–52; *Portland Oregonian,* July 3, 1977.

71. HEW, Office for Civil Rights, Form OS/CR 101 submitted by Seattle school system, 1974.

72. HEW, Office for Civil Rights, *Directory, 1972,* pp. 717–18.

73. Ibid., pp. 1505–07; *Des Moines Register,* August 29, 1977; *Milwaukee Journal,* January 19, 1976; HEW, Office for Civil Rights, "Distribution of Minority Students by School Composition, 1970–1974," report to the U.S. Senate (May 27, 1976; processed), pp. 61–63, published in Center for National Policy Review, *Trends in Black School Segregation: 1970–1974,* vol. 1 (Washington: CNPR, 1977).

stitutional segregation in early 1976, which set the desegregation process in motion.[74] The second phase of a three-year plan, which used educational innovations to attract many voluntary transfers, began in September 1977.[75] Wisconsin's second largest city, Madison, has no segregated schools. The other Wisconsin city with a significant minority population, Racine, implemented metropolitan desegregation in September 1975.[76]

There are other states where desegregation is essentially a one-city problem, where one piece of litigation or one federal enforcement action can desegregate most of the minority children in the state. In Colorado, Denver contains more than two-thirds of the black students in the state and about one-third of the Chicanos. It is desegregated. In Nevada, Las Vegas contains more than 90 percent of the state's black students and they have been desegregated under a federal court order. Statistics for 1972 show that no schools except those serving American Indians are segregated.[77] In Nebraska, more than 90 percent of the black students and more than two-thirds of all minority students were in the Omaha schools, where white enrollment was 78 percent and there were only thirteen segregated schools.[78] Omaha desegregated in September 1976.

New England, excluding Boston, is another region with easily manageable desegregation problems. In Massachusetts almost three-fifths of the black students are located in Boston.[79] All Massachusetts districts are now desegregated. In 1972 total minority enrollment in Maine was 0.5 percent.[80] In Vermont the percentage was even lower, and in New Hampshire only slightly higher. About one-twentieth of the schoolchildren in Rhode Island were from minority groups, but state policy has now desegregated all systems. Only Connecticut, with one-eighth of its children from minority groups, faces severe problems with its central city systems, which are predominantly black and segregated. In 1977 the state board of education announced a desegregation policy, threatening to withhold state aid from Bridgeport.[81]

Thus most of the thirty-three states outside the southern and border state

74. *Armstrong v. O'Connell*, 408 F. Supp. 825 (D. Wis. 1976); *aff'd*, 539 F.2d 625 (1976).

75. *Milwaukee Journal*, September 7, 1977. More than 14,000 students transferred.

76. *New York Times*, October 22, 1975. Racine is a consolidated metropolitan district.

77. HEW, Office for Civil Rights, *Directory*, 1972, pp. 808–11.

78. Ibid., pp. 802–03.

79. Ibid., pp. 569–609.

80. Ibid., p. 537.

81. Ibid., p. ix; *New York Times*, September 22, 1977.

regions have either negligible segregation problems or ones that are manageable without basic change.

### The Biggest Problems

The desegregation process was proceeding unevenly and irregularly in the large urban areas in 1976. Indiana had partial desegregation in Indianapolis and Fort Wayne, full desegregation in Evansville, and one major metropolitan case pending, which called for the completion of countywide desegregation in Indianapolis.[82] In Ohio, Dayton desegregated in the fall of 1976, and desegregation litigation was in process in four large cities—Cleveland, Columbus, Cincinnati, and Youngstown. The pending Ohio litigation will affect almost one-fifth of the state's children and most of its minority students.[83] In California, San Francisco, Sacramento, Pasadena, Berkeley, and a number of smaller systems had been desegregated and litigation was pending in the state courts against other districts. The state supreme court had ordered desegregation in Los Angeles. The largest system in Texas, Houston, had begun a partial desegregation plan; Dallas had desegregated. In Missouri, St. Louis had been ordered to begin desegregating and Kansas City school officials had accepted a plan.[84] The Philadelphia school system was under court order to prepare a desegregation plan to comply with state agency requirements which had produced desegregation in many smaller Pennsylvania districts, but enforcement was unlikely. Michigan shares with California and Ohio the distinction of having faced the most active program of litigation outside the southern and border states. Detroit, Pontiac, Kalamazoo, and some other districts desegregated under federal court orders. Action was pending elsewhere. Progress came most slowly in New Jersey, Illinois, and New York, where desegregation plans were limited largely to small suburban communities with relatively few minority students and litigation made little progress. State

82. *United States v. Board of School Commissioners of City of Indianapolis,* 503 F.2d 68 (7th Cir. 1974), *cert. denied,* 95 S. Ct. 1655 (1975). The Supreme Court remanded this case for further evidence early in 1977.

83. Citizens' Council for Ohio Schools, "Desegregation in Ohio, Background for Current Litigation" (January 1976; processed), p. 1.

84. The St. Louis case was settled out of court without any provision for substantial desegregation of students. Judith Frutig, "St. Louis Plan—Without Busing," *Christian Science Monitor,* January 16, 1976. The NAACP later intervened and, with the support of the Justice Department, appealed for an order including substantial busing. *St. Louis Globe-Democrat,* May 25, 1977. HEW refused to accept the Kansas City plan.

Table 2-6. *Selected Major School Districts with Predominantly Minority Enrollment, 1974–75*

| School district | Percent |
|---|---|
| Atlanta | 85 |
| Baltimore | 72 |
| Chicago | 71 |
| Cleveland | 60 |
| Dade County (Miami) | 56 |
| Dallas | 55 |
| Denver | 53 |
| Detroit | 74 |
| District of Columbia | 96 |
| Gary, Indiana | 81 |
| Houston | 61 |
| Kansas City, Missouri | 62 |
| Los Angeles[a] | 58 |
| Memphis | 71 |
| Newark | 89 |
| New Orleans | 81 |
| New York City[b] | 64 |
| Philadelphia | 66 |
| St. Louis | 70 |

Source: HEW, Office for Civil Rights, Elementary and Secondary School Civil Rights Survey report forms.

a. Includes 5 percent Oriental students.

b. Figures for 1973–74.

officials brought about desegregation in ten of the smaller cities in September 1977.

Two different kinds of obstacles to national school desegregation remain. The first is that of bringing cases in hundreds of smaller school districts where desegregation requires little change but local officials will not take action voluntarily. The second is the need for complex litigation in larger cities and metropolitan areas where both prosecuting the case and carrying out desegregation plans are substantial undertakings. The greatest obstacles are the older central cities where few whites remain. The difficulties encountered have constrained effective relief where such cases have been prosecuted (Detroit, St. Louis, Atlanta, Baltimore, Cleveland, Los Angeles, and others) and prevented the filing of litigation in other major systems (New York, Chicago, Newark, Pittsburgh, San Antonio, Oakland, and New Orleans).

Table 2-6 lists the major districts where some metropolitan desegregation would be required to place all minority children in predominantly white schools. Demographic trends indicate that imbalances will become more extreme and that the list will lengthen in years to come.

## Social Class and Educational Effects of Central-City-Only Desegregation

The demographic trends underlying changes in central city enrollment not only make it difficult to achieve desegregation but also reduce the likelihood that desegregation will produce any educational benefits.

Educational research suggests that the basic damage inflicted by segregated education comes not from racial concentration but from the concentration of children from poor families. The studies show that the economic and social background of the majority of the children affects the educational achievement of a school more than any other single school factor, so there is no reason to be optimistic about the integration of two lower-class groups. Although the responsibility of the federal courts reaches neither to educational programs nor to consideration of social class as a relevant legal category, social scientists normally see social class integration as a prerequisite to successful school integration.[85]

The distribution of students in schools with substantial numbers of very poor children is almost as skewed as that in schools with substantial numbers of minority children. Three-fourths of American children attending public school are in schools where fewer than one-fifth of the children are from families receiving food stamps, welfare, or other special assistance. On the other hand, one-tenth attend schools where most of the children come from such a background. Another one-tenth go to school with at least one-fourth very poor children.[86]

The central educational problem is that not only are many children in racially—and linguistically—identifiable segregated schools but their classmates are from poor families. With their limited resources, these schools must cope with large numbers of children from families that are disorganized, in grave financial difficulty, and constantly moving.

Often a partial desegregation plan, which brings together white and black students from both sides of the ghetto boundary line, merely pools students with special needs from two hostile neighborhoods. In older

85. Frederick Mosteller and Daniel P. Moynihan, eds., *On Equality of Educational Opportunity* (Random House, 1972), pp. 22–24.

86. *Equal Educational Opportunities Act of 1972*, Hearings before the Subcommittee on Education of the Senate Committee on Labor and Public Welfare, 92:2 (GPO, 1972), p. 288.

central cities, the entire school system may serve children from a narrow social and economic range, thus minimizing the possibility of any academic benefits from desegregation.

## Falling Enrollment and Desegregation Possibilities

Enrollment statistics, of course, are not static, either nationally or within individual communities. Planners for school systems, however, can make reliable predictions by looking at life expectancy statistics and making some allowance for immigration. For instance, the children who will be first graders six years from now have already been born. Projections for metropolitan areas also require estimating urban migration. These projections are far less definite but are still invaluable in planning.

The most important single consideration is the sharp fall in the American birthrate. The number of children born each year per 1,000 population peaked in 1947, continued high until 1957, then began to drop, reaching a new low in 1976.[87] Total elementary enrollment peaked in 1970 and had declined 9 percent by 1975, a drop of 2.9 million students. School systems that had struggled to alleviate a chronic shortage of classrooms in the 1950s and early 1960s had trouble filling them in the early 1970s. Birth statistics through 1975 show that the decline will continue for at least the next few years and that public schools will probably have lost a million more students by 1980. And the Office of Education projected in 1977 that enrollment in the nation's schools will have dropped another 10 percent by 1983.[88]

Although the overall national enrollment is dropping, it is up in some districts. Areas of the South and West that are experiencing rapid in-migration and outer suburbs where young families in major metropolitan areas live still have some problems of overcrowding and inadequate facilities. By the same token, the decline is most precipitous in the areas with out-migration and an aging population—the central cities and the inner suburbs. Between 1971 and 1973 total enrollment in the forty-nine largest

87. HEW, National Center for Health Statistics, in *Monthly Vital Statistics Report* (August 27, 1976), p. 1, reported that the birthrate continued to decline through the first half of 1976.

88. W. Vance Grant and C. George Lind, *Digest of Education Statistics, 1975 Edition*, HEW, National Center for Educational Statistics (GPO, 1976), pp. 95, 7; *Washington Post*, July 30, 1977.

cities declined from 7.3 million to 6.8 million while their minority enrollment rose from 44 to 53 percent.[89]

For desegregation policy this means, first, that the overall task is no longer expanding. In many areas, there are fewer students to bus each year, at least at the elementary level. Second, desegregation plans are less likely to involve competition for overcrowded classrooms. There are now excess classrooms, even schools, in both cities and suburbs, which lend flexibility to desegregation planning and may require reassigning children whether or not desegregation takes place. Finally, the minority population has begun to decline in a number of the older central cities, the most segregated school districts. A greater number of minority-group children are moving from these metropolitan areas to suburban districts, where desegregation may be easier; this reduces the scale of city-suburban busing necessary for metropolitan desegregation. All these trends tend to make metropolitan desegregation somewhat more feasible.

## Decline of Whites in the Cities

The principal negative trend is the continued rapid decline of Anglo enrollment in many central cities (see table 2-7). Calculations suggest that the rate of loss accelerates as the black proportion of the enrollment rises, even if the school system remains segregated. From 1968 to 1973 the average big city whose enrollment was half black lost one-sixteenth of its remaining Anglos *each year*, and the average smaller city with similar enrollment proportions lost about one in every twenty-three white students each year. These were the average changes in cities where there was no increase in desegregation.[90]

Important statistical studies during 1976 and 1977 found strong, close relationships between the percentage of black population in a city and the speed of the white population's decline. Fitzgerald and Morgan concluded that for northern cities "two factors stand out in the prediction of percent white change ... between 1968 and 1974—the relative presence of blacks ... within the community and the 1960–70 growth of the black population."[91]

89. "Fewer Pupils, Greater Concentration of Minorities Seen in Big City Schools," *The School Administrator* (May 1975), p. 13.

90. Coleman, Kelly, and Moore, *Trends in School Segregation*, p. 51.

91. Michael R. Fitzgerald and David R. Morgan, "Assessing the Consequences of Public Policy: School Desegregation and White Flight in Urban America," paper pre-

Table 2-7. *Changes in Enrollment of Anglos, Selected Cities, 1968–74*[a]
Percent

| City | 1968 | 1974 | Change |
|------|------|------|--------|
| Atlanta | 38 | 15 | −23 |
| Baltimore | 35 | 28 | − 7 |
| Boston | 68 | 55 | −13 |
| Chicago | 38 | 29 | − 9 |
| Cleveland | 42 | 40 | − 2 |
| Columbus | 74 | 69 | − 5 |
| Dallas | 61 | 45 | −16 |
| Detroit | 39 | 26 | −13 |
| Houston | 53 | 39 | −14 |
| Indianapolis | 66 | 57 | − 9 |
| Los Angeles | 54 | 42 | −12 |
| Memphis | 46 | 29 | −17 |
| Milwaukee | 73 | 63 | −10 |
| New Orleans | 31 | 19 | −12 |
| New York | 44 | 36 | − 8 |
| Philadelphia | 39 | 34 | − 5 |
| St. Louis | 36 | 30 | − 6 |
| San Diego | 76 | 74 | − 2 |
| Tampa[b] | 74 | 75 | 1 |
| Washington | 6 | 4 | − 2 |

Sources: HEW, Office for Civil Rights; Coleman, Kelly, and Moore, *Trends in School Segregation*, p. 24.
a. Excludes Latin population.
b. Metropolitan district.

Plummeting enrollment means that central city school systems often have half-empty schools. Since many of the costs of a school are fixed (salaries for administrators, janitor, librarian, office and other staff, maintenance, electricity, and heating), continuing to use these half-empty schools constitutes a major financial burden, substantially increasing costs per student and narrowing the curriculum that can be offered in any one school. Half the U.S. school districts had begun to close schools by 1974.[92]

---

sented to the annual meeting of the Midwest Political Science Association, April 22, 1977 (processed), p. 16. This research reinforced earlier findings by James Coleman, Luther Mumford, Reynolds Farley, and others on the importance of the community's racial composition. Fitzgerald and Morgan found no significant additional white flight following implementation of a desegregation plan in the typical city.

92. Cyril G. Sargent, "Fewer Pupils, Surplus Space: The Problem of School Shrinkage," *Phi Delta Kappan*, vol. 56 (January 1975), pp. 352–54. When New York City's financial crisis intensified in 1976, one response was a decision to close approximately fifty schools. Board of Education officials estimated that this plan would save the city $13.5 million a year. Most of the buildings were more than fifty years old and a number were more than half empty. *New York Times*, January 29, 1976. Miami projected that

The constraint on closing schools is the reluctance both to deny certain neighborhoods a school and to transport their students. If a desegregation plan ends the neighborhood school assignment pattern and transports students anyway, it offers an opportunity to save money and improve curriculum by closing obsolescent schools.

## Decline of Blacks in the Cities

As national school enrollment has dropped, minority enrollment in many of the largest central city systems has also fallen. The Washington, D.C., public schools, for example, reached their peak in the enrollment of blacks in the 1969–70 school year. It fell more than 2,000 in the fall of 1970, the first such decline since 1942. Between 1969 and 1977 black enrollment in the city fell from more than 140,000 children to approximately 115,000, with particularly sharp annual drops at the elementary school level.[93] This did not reflect a drop in the number of black children in the whole metropolitan area—for instance, the suburban system of Prince Georges County, Maryland, gained black students more than twice as fast in 1970 as the Washington schools lost them.[94]

The same pattern of black enrollment growing in the suburbs and shrinking in the central cities occurred in several other major metropolitan areas, though it was not yet a national pattern. Statistics show an emerging pattern of "black flight" from Newark, St. Louis, San Francisco, and elsewhere. The black proportion of total enrollment in these systems continued to increase only because whites moved to the suburbs even more rapidly and their birthrate declined even more steeply. The five years 1970–74 brought declines in the black enrollment in a number of cities and stabilization in others. Cleveland lost 14 percent of its black students, St. Louis 11 percent, San Francisco 10 percent, Los Angeles 4 percent, and New Orleans and Philadelphia 3 percent.[95] San Francisco also experienced a "brown flight" of Mexican-American students, with Hispanic enrollment dropping 14 percent

---

twenty-six of its schools would be substantially below capacity by 1977. *Miami Herald,* February 26, 1976.

93. District of Columbia Public Schools, Division of Research and Evaluation, *Data Resource Book, 1974–75,* pp. 6–7. Black enrollment for the 1975–76 school year declined while white enrollment rose slightly. The decline accelerated in 1977, with elementary schools losing 6.5 percent of their students in one year. *Washington Post,* November 23, 1975, November 13, 1977.

94. *Washington Post,* December 15, 1970.

95. Center for National Policy Review, *Trends in Black School Segregation,* pp. 16, 18, 26, 34, 36, 50.

during the period.[96] This flight, like much of the white exodus, was probably due more to the desire for suburban housing and escape from urban decay than to the racial composition of city schools. As housing becomes available to blacks in inner suburbs in other areas, similar patterns may develop.

The flight of middle-class black children and their families from the central city schools may bring some suburban desegregation but it also robs the schools of one of their most important assets. Remembering the remarkable achievements of students from black elite institutions like Washington's Dunbar High School, scholars wonder why the same results have not been achieved in today's inner city schools.[97] Although Sowell notes that Dunbar was not primarily middle class, the school was the focal point for ambitious families that would experience great upward mobility and provide Washington with black leaders. Most of these families have now abandoned the public school system in Washington and a growing number of central cities for private schools or schools in the inner suburbs. This not only removes a great many of the best prepared children from the classrooms, but also denies the public schools the informed support and assistance of some of the most talented and politically effective parents. The remaining minority children attend schools stigmatized as inferior not only by whites but also by the successful members of the minority communities.

### Decline in the Suburbs

While central city enrollments have been falling for years, the impact of the "baby bust" on suburban districts has often been much more sudden and traumatic. Systems that had strained to educate the students pouring into classrooms suddenly began to shrink in the 1970s. Now administrators, who had until recently fought hard to build schools, had to select those to be closed. By the mid-seventies the decline was endemic, for instance, in the once-booming suburban counties surrounding New York City. The *New York Times* reported:

Bergen and Essex, New Jersey's most populous counties, recorded an enrollment drop last year of more than 9,000 pupils, a combined decline of some 3 percent.

Enrollments in Nassau and Westchester are going down steadily. Nassau has lost some 25,000 pupils in the last three years.[98]

96. Center for National Policy Review, *Trends in Hispanic Segregation: 1970–1974,* vol. 2 (CNPR, 1977), p. 50.
97. Thomas Sowell, "Black Excellence—The Case of Dunbar High School," *Public Interest,* vol. 9 (Spring 1974), pp. 3–21.
98. *New York Times,* January 15, 1975.

In Chicago from 1966 to 1974 elementary enrollment dropped in 54 percent of the 115 suburban districts. Just between 1973 and 1974, enrollment dropped in five of every six elementary systems and in the high schools in half the districts.[99]

The aging population in the inner suburbs, the falling birthrate, building restrictions, money market problems that held new construction well below predictions, and skyrocketing housing prices that were keeping many young families with children out of the housing market were all curtailing suburban enrollments. City-suburban desegregation in the 1960s would have had to cope with overcrowded schools. By the mid-1970s many classrooms on both sides of the city-suburban boundaries were empty. The high cost of operating half-empty schools meant that many neighborhoods would lose their schools unless more students could be found.

### Black Suburbanization

Rapid black suburbanization in some metropolitan areas has had a disappointingly small effect on school desegregation statistics. At least two kinds of suburbanization have taken place. The first is ghetto expansion into communities across the city line. This was the dominant pattern and could be seen, for example, in the suburban communities adjoining Watts in the Los Angeles area and in a number of the inner suburbs around Washington, D.C. The second, which occurred particularly in high-cost suburbs, is modest, stable housing integration.

Ghetto expansion into suburbia can influence school desegregation very differently, depending on the way the school districts in the metropolitan area are organized and whether the courts have ordered desegregation. If the suburban schools are part of large countywide systems, desegregation remains a real option, although student transportation is required. This was the prevailing pattern in the Washington suburbs. Most had well-integrated schools in 1975, though the massive black in-migration and white out-migration in Prince Georges County suggested that stable integration might be impossible there. Baltimore County, on the other hand, failed to desegregate when it received a rapid influx from the city. Baltimore County's black enrollment climbed 54 percent between 1970 and 1975, and a pattern of segregated schools developed.[100]

99. Cook County Educational Service Region, "Enrollment Comparisons, 1966–67 to 1974–75" (February 1975; processed), pp. 2–5.

100. *Baltimore Sun*, November 4, 1974, and November 20, 1975; Center for National Policy Review, *Trends in Black School Segregation*, p. 28.

But most metropolitan areas have small fragmented school districts, often scores of them. Fragmented suburban areas in the path of expanding ghettos need cross-district desegregation more urgently than most central cities. A small suburb is like a single city neighborhood in that traditional methods of ghetto growth can rapidly change the racial composition of the entire system. Already the highest levels of segregation in some metropolitan areas are found in the inner suburbs.

Advocates of fair housing often fallaciously equate black access to suburban housing with integration, perhaps because they assume that economics will restrict the option to relatively few blacks. Actually, if access to housing became relatively free, a great many black families could afford to purchase housing, particularly in the older, less exclusive suburbs. If large numbers of blacks began to move, the result might well be the familiar urban one of spreading ghetto schools rather than integration.

### The Meaning of the Enrollment Trends

School segregation is bad and getting worse in the largest cities in the North. In the South, on the other hand, and in the many northern states with few black and Latino students, major progress has been made.

The data show that, because of the unusual concentration of black and Hispanic children in the biggest cities and because of the fragmented governmental structure in the older metropolitan areas of the East and Midwest, the North faces special institutional barriers to integration. Neither the shrinking of minority enrollment in some cities nor black suburbanization offer real solutions though they could lessen the difficulty of metropolitan integration. Similarly, the concentration of private education in the very cities most important to minority children creates an added obstacle.

Our largest central cities are wasting away; the cancers of spreading segregation and urban decay are making lasting integration impossible within these cities' boundaries. Only drastic policy changes can contain their effects and begin to reverse the trends. If the Supreme Court holds to the doctrines of its Detroit decision, integration in the largest cities promises to be partial and transitory.

# 3

# Integration of Housing

ACCORDING TO public opinion polls, many people hope or believe that there is a better, more "natural" way to achieve integrated schools. The most frequently mentioned is to wait until housing integration automatically produces integrated neighborhood schools.[1] The passage of state and federal fair housing laws persuaded many that open housing was a reality and that the busing issue was only a bitterly divisive diversion. This is an extremely serious criticism, implying that the country is passing through needless turmoil over something that can be accomplished simply by the passage of time.

Given the demographic patterns of American metropolitan areas, there are only two alternatives to the steady expansion of ghettos and barrios and the continued decline of white middle class population in the metropolitan cores. Either a major effort must be made to open up housing choices for blacks and integrate suburban housing or policies must be designed that will attract jobs and white middle class residents back to the urban core in substantial numbers. Existing national policy does neither.

In urban America, ghettos continue to grow and subdivisions for young white families cut deeper and deeper into the countryside, producing a race and class separation so far-reaching that a child can grow up with virtually no contact outside his racial or social group. The implications of this became apparent in the late 1960s in riots in cities across the country and the final flash of upheaval after the killing of Martin Luther King, Jr. The strobe light of the riots, the killing, and the grim report of President John-

1. Gallup Polls in 1973 and 1975 showed considerable support for housing solutions. The 1973 survey appears in *Gallup Opinion Index* (December 1973), p. 25.

son's Riot Commission soon faded, however.[2] In the early 1970s the issue disappeared from political discussion as quickly as it had emerged.


## The Record

Those who suggest housing integration as an alternative to school desegregation rarely acknowledge that busing plans are often necessary because of the past role of government policy in creating cities and suburbs with rigidly segregated neighborhoods. Before one can assess the possibility that government agencies will desegregate housing, one must understand how segregation came about. Federal housing programs and local officials have usually reflected the racial views of the realtors, homebuilders, lending institutions, and other powerful components of the housing and home finance industries.[3]

Government agencies openly supported housing segregation throughout the period of development of the modern ghetto system and through the early years of white-only suburbanization after World War II. All levels of government were implicated.

After the Supreme Court acted in 1917 to strike down local ordinances setting up separate zones in which whites and blacks were permitted to reside, the chief device for enforcing segregation was the restrictive covenant.[4] The covenant was an agreement by the initial owners of property, irrevocably written into the deed of the property, which forbade the sale of the property to blacks and other minorities and was enforced by municipal and state courts. This policy of public enforcement of private discrimination was reinforced by denying adequate police protection to black families who bought houses in white neighborhoods. Mob violence and other forms of intimidation were commonplace in such circumstances. Several cities experienced major race riots. Terror and threats of various forms of reprisals, which had been central to the maintenance of white

2. National Advisory Commission on Civil Disorders, *Report of the National Advisory Commission on Civil Disorders* (GPO, 1968).

3. Charles Abrams, *The City Is the Frontier* (Harper, 1965), provides an excellent overview of federal policy. For a description of the NAACP legal campaign against restrictive covenants, see Clement E. Vose, *Caucasians Only* (University of California Press, 1959); and Loren Miller, *The Petitioners* (Pantheon, 1966).

4. Much of this section originally appeared in Gary Orfield, "Federal Policy, Local Power, and Metropolitan Segregation," *Political Science Quarterly*, vol. 89 (Winter 1974–75), pp. 777–802. See especially pp. 784 ff.

supremacy in the South, played an important role in the establishment of white residential separation in the North.[5]

Government support of private segregation helped impose a pattern of extreme segregation on urban blacks. Chicago is a good example. As late as 1910 blacks there were still living in small scattered pockets though they were less segregated than the city's Italian population.[6] During the next decade the city's black population tripled, a terrible wartime housing shortage increased racial hostility, and the city was torn apart by its 1919 race riot, in which more than thirty-eight people died and hundreds of others were injured. Blacks outside the ghetto that was forming were subjected to threats and bombings; whites remaining inside were driven out by escalating racial tension and the high cost of ghetto housing.[7] By 1920 Chicago and other major cities had large, rigidly defined, and almost completely segregated ghettos. A major study concludes:

The development of the physical ghetto . . . was not the result chiefly of poverty; nor did Negroes cluster out of choice. The ghetto was primarily the product of white hostility. . . . As the Chicago Negro population grew, Negroes had no alternative but to settle in well-delineated Negro areas. And with increasing pressure for Negro housing, property owners in the black belt found it profitable to force out white tenants and convert previously mixed blocks into all-Negro blocks.[8]

The collapse of the private housing market during the depression brought heavy government participation in the housing business. The new federal agencies adopted and reinforced prevailing racial practices. The industry was a wreckage. Funds for mortgage financing evaporated as banks collapsed and were forced to call in many of the short-term renewable mortgages then widely used. Mounting unemployment brought widespread foreclosures. There was no money for new construction.

The federal government intervened decisively. Federal insurance for bank deposits and federal regulation of insured banks restored bank assets

5. NAACP pioneer Mary White Ovington writes of the World War I period: "The attempted destruction of homes bought by Negroes in white neighborhoods was becoming frequent, and cities were passing segregation ordinances to prevent such transfer of property. Homes of Negroes who had bought houses in white blocks or nearly white blocks were bombed, dynamited, and occupants were intimidated in many cities." *The Walls Came Tumbling Down* (Harcourt Brace, 1947), p. 115.

6. Allan H. Spear, *Black Chicago: The Making of a Negro Ghetto, 1890–1920* (University of Chicago Press, 1967), pp. 14–19.

7. William M. Tuttle, Jr., *Race Riot: Chicago in the Red Summer of 1919* (Atheneum, 1970), pp. 161–67.

8. Spear, *Black Chicago*, p. 26.

by eliminating the risk of loss for depositors. Federal Housing Administration mortgage insurance eliminated the lending institution's risk. The assets of savings and loan associations, the dominant source of mortgage money, multiplied more than 200 times in the sixteen years after the federal deposit insurance system began. By 1960 they had invested $67 billion, mostly in home mortgages.[9]

FHA mortgage insurance revolutionized home financing by guaranteeing payment of mortgages on properties that met the agency's standards. With risk eliminated, lenders were willing to accept lower interest rates and much longer periods of repayment. Conventional lenders adopted similar approaches. These changes substantially cut the size of monthly payments, helping millions of Americans become homeowners. Since approval for FHA financing greatly expanded the potential market for new developments, builders complied with the agency's intricate quality standards. At the same time, the FHA became the leading force in systematizing national home appraisal practices. Within a year of its creation, the FHA was insuring 40 percent of new home mortgages. Home building had doubled and mortgage costs were at an all-time low.[10]

The FHA adopted a segregationist policy and refused to insure projects that did not comply. The common wisdom of white appraisers was that integration damaged property values. Although there was no evidence for this assumption, it became official FHA policy for appraisals.

The FHA helped shape the housing market through policies spelled out in its *Underwriting Manual,* a decisive though little known bureaucratic document. It stipulated that FHA officials were to prevent fiscal risk by requiring effective guarantees against "inharmonious racial groups." Appraisers were told to look for physical barriers between racial groups or for restrictive covenants. "Incompatible racial elements" was officially listed as a valid reason for rejecting a mortgage.[11]

While the FHA provided an important service for young white families, blacks were viewed as a liability on an appraisal balance sheet. Other FHA policies deepened the discriminatory effect. Since it was easier to accurately appraise the value and life expectancy of housing in new developments of similar units, the FHA refused insurance for mortgage commitments in large areas of central cities it judged to have uncertain future value, thus

9. U.S. Commission on Civil Rights, *1961 Report,* vol. 4: *Housing* (GPO, 1961), p. 61.
10. Federal Housing Administration, *Annual Report* (GPO, 1935), p. vi.
11. Rose Helper, *Racial Policies and Practices of Real Estate Brokers* (University of Minnesota Press, 1969), p. 202.

channeling funds and buyers outward and denying federal assistance for the only housing on the black housing market. This redlining[12] policy discouraged investment in inner city ghettos and barrios and in the integrated neighborhoods adjoining them.

The New Deal also saw the first tentative efforts to construct public housing for a small fraction of the millions of families still priced out of the private housing market. The Public Works Administration accepted the policy of segregation. Congress set up a public housing agency in 1937 largely limited to financing projects in which local authorities made most of the decisions. Federal officials were considered bold when they enforced a separate but equal policy requiring that black projects get a share of the units built "in the same proportion as they are at present represented in the neighborhood."[13] Tax money paid for the construction of racially defined projects that tended to intensify ghetto segregation. Sometimes the projects even included their own segregated schools.

When Congress finally committed the country to a permanent public housing program in 1949, it set off local political battles over the location of the new housing. Blacks urgently needed housing, especially after the large-scale destruction of ghetto housing authorized by the slum-clearance sections of the 1949 law. It would have been logical to build housing on vacant sites available at reasonable cost in the outlying areas of cities. These areas, however, were white. The issue came to a head in a period of tense, sometimes violent race relations that were intensified by the rapid black urbanization of World War II when there were acute housing shortages in the industrial cities. Blacks came seeking jobs at a time when there was virtually no new housing construction.[14]

Federal officials permitted pervasive segregation of residents in buildings constructed on segregated sites and employing discriminatory tenant assignment policies. Instead of increasing the black housing supply, the net effect of the new urban programs was to diminish it, since more black housing units were eliminated for "slum clearance" than were constructed under the public housing program. The urban renewal record was particularly dismal. By 1967 about 400,000 units of housing had been destroyed in urban renewal areas, displacing a great many poor black families, but

12. Redlining is the practice of outlining in red on a city map an area where no financing will be considered.
13. Richard Resh, *Black America* (D. C. Heath, 1969), pp. 104–05; Martin Meyerson and Edward C. Banfield, *Politics, Planning, and the Public Interest: The Case of Public Housing in Chicago* (Free Press, 1955), p. 121.
14. Charles Abrams, *Forbidden Neighbors* (Harper, 1955), pp. 86–87.

less than 3 percent of these units had been replaced by new public housing in the renewal areas.[15] The failure to build replacement housing tended to accelerate the ghettoization of neighborhoods adjoining the renewal area. Ironically, much of the land that had been bulldozed was never developed. No one would invest in the deteriorating cities.

The public housing that was constructed for blacks often offered a concentrated version of ghetto life. To maintain segregation the local public housing authorities usually purchased and cleared expensive, intensively used ghetto land. Since the site cost was so high, the planners could stay within federal per-unit cost ceilings only by constructing high-rise buildings. Many housing experts knew from the start that high-rise buildings containing hundreds of apartments built on ghetto sites were unsuitable for families with small children.[16] As the policy of constructing "vertical ghettos" unfolded, thousands of black and Hispanic families desperate for decent housing found themselves trying to survive in the midst of social chaos and even physical terror.[17] The environment, of course, was one of almost absolute racial separation.

Federal housing and renewal policies respected the fragmentation of local power in metropolitan areas. Few suburban communities built any public housing and some even used the urban renewal program to wipe out small pockets of long-time poor black residents.[18] Most of all, however, the FHA and Veterans Administration mortgage insurance programs shaped and reinforced the racial and economic segregation of suburbia. FHA appraisers required assurances that insured properties "shall continue to be occupied by the same social and racial group." The agency even drafted a model restrictive covenant and urged its adoption.[19]

FHA policy was so entrenched that the agency initially tried to evade the Supreme Court's 1948 ruling against restrictive covenants. FHA admin-

15. U.S. National Commission on Urban Problems, *Building the American City: Report of the National Commission on Urban Problems to the Congress and to the President of the United States*, II.Doc. 91-34 (GPO, 1968), p. 163.

16. An excellent history of the choices in Chicago can be found in Meyerson and Banfield, *Politics, Planning, and the Public Interest*.

17. See Lee Rainwater, *Behind Ghetto Walls: Black Families in a Federal Slum* (Aldine, 1970), pp. 8–16, for a description of the social conditions affecting the 10,000 people who lived in the massive Pruitt-Igoe project in St. Louis. See also William Moore, Jr., *The Vertical Ghetto* (Random House, 1969), pp. 9–16.

18. Baltimore County, Maryland, for instance, sent displaced poor families into the city for public housing.

19. George and Eunice Grier, *Equality and Beyond: Housing Segregation and the Goals of the Great Society* (Quadrangle Books, 1966), pp. 54–55.

istrators claimed that administrative agencies still had the right to insist on segregation. After the agency officially reversed its policy on covenants in 1950, realtors soon learned that the agency had no objection to "gentlemen's agreements." The FHA also accepted new covenants requiring approval of sales by a group of neighbors, screening by the board of a community club, options to repurchase property, and other devices.[20]

The Veterans Administration had a similar record, with nonwhites holding only 2 percent of its guaranteed mortgages in 1950. The generous VA program allowed families to become homeowners with virtually no down payment, but minority veterans were rarely offered the opportunity to obtain inexpensive new housing and begin building an equity. Since homeownership is the only form of personal wealth most American families have, the long-term social consequences of cutting off this opportunity were great. Most families purchasing new homes today must have large equities to meet high, inflation-produced down payments. Whites are far more likely to have such an equity.

Although there were rhetorical changes in the programs during the 1950s, a 1958 study concluded:

Indirectly, Federal policies have stimulated segregation in two important ways. The changes in the housing industry which have so largely increased the power of private builders to determine community patterns . . . have been made possible by the Federal mortgage insurance systems. The FHA and VA policies of giving commitments to insure the mortgages on entire housing tracts in advance of construction provide the necessary basis for corresponding advance commitments of financing by lending institutions; thus enabling builders to construct hundreds and even thousands of houses. . . .

The other indirect Federal support of segregation has been the moral sanction given to the racial discrimination practices of private business. . . . Federal agencies . . . aside from verbal pronouncements for equality, continue to tolerate the discriminatory practices of those who distribute Federal benefits.[21]

The first positive action against discrimination in federal housing programs did not come until 1962, when President Kennedy signed an executive order on the subject. The order, however, covered only a small portion of housing. A tiny staff was provided to oversee the policy's implementa-

20. National Committee Against Discrimination in Housing, *Trends in Housing* (New York: NCDH, 1956); Richard O. Davies, *Housing Reform During the Truman Administration* (University of Missouri Press, 1966), pp. 124–25; Abrams, *Forbidden Neighbors*, pp. 224–25.

21. Commission on Race and Housing, "Where Shall We Live?" in William L. C. Wheaton, Grace Milgram, and Margy Ellin Meyerson, eds., *Urban Housing* (Free Press, 1966), p. 281.

tion, and sanctions were almost never invoked. In 1967 a study by a fair housing group testing how much actual access potential black buyers had to FHA-insured housing concluded that virtually nothing had changed. When the FHA finally conducted its own national survey on the race of those benefiting from its programs, its findings were similar. The agency's deputy commissioner, Philip Maloney, reported in late 1967 that in "a number of large urban centers . . . virtually no minority family housing has been provided through FHA."[22] Only in the late 1960s did the Department of Housing and Urban Development begin to act against segregation in public housing.

A number of federal court decisions have now held both local and federal housing and other urban agencies guilty of unconstitutional residential segregation. In Philadelphia the federal court of appeals ordered HUD to approve no further programs without considering their impact on segregation.[23] The court of appeals in Chicago found both the Chicago Housing Authority and HUD guilty of a long history of intentional segregation of public housing. Eventually the court ordered not only the dispersal of future public housing in Chicago, but also the construction of public housing in the suburbs to remedy the past violations of suburban communities.[24] This decision was upheld by the Supreme Court in 1976.[25] An analysis by the Commission on Civil Rights indicates that major federal subsidy programs were continuing to intensify segregation into the 1970s, and another study shows segregation continuing in new projects in Chicago even after the court orders.[26]

A number of the courts hearing school cases have made explicit findings about the role of federal and local officials in creating segregated neighborhoods where the schools were automatically segregated. Federal courts have found that housing policies increased school segregation in Charlotte, Wilmington, Cleveland, New York City, and a number of other cities. In the 1976 Cleveland case *Reed* v. *Rhodes*, for example, the federal district

22. National Committee Against Discrimination in Housing, *How the Federal Government Builds Ghettos* (NCDH, 1967); speech by Maloney, reprinted in *Congressional Record* (December 5, 1967), p. 35023.

23. *Shannon* v. *HUD*, 436 F.2d 809 (3d Cir. 1970).

24. *Gautreaux* v. *Chicago Housing Authority*, 503 F.2d 930 (7th Cir. 1974).

25. *Hills* v. *Gautreaux*, 425 U.S. 284 (1976).

26. Commission on Civil Rights, *Home Ownership for Lower Income Families: A Report on the Racial and Ethnic Impact of the Section 235 Program* (GPO, 1971); Frederick Aaron Lazin, "Public Housing in Chicago, 1963–1971: *Gautreaux* v. *Chicago Housing Authority*: A Case Study of the Cooptation of a Federal Agency by Its Local Constituency" (Ph.D. dissertation, University of Chicago, 1973).

court found both the federal government and the Cuyahoga Metropolitan Housing Authority partially responsible for the city's segregated schools:

It is clear that the presence of racially segregated public housing in conjunction with school board policies operated to spawn racially segregated schools. There can be little doubt that this result was the natural, probable, foreseeable, and actual effect of the school board's "neighborhood school policy."[27]

## The Nature and Limits of Fair Housing

The first significant federal actions against segregated housing came in 1968—the enactment of the federal fair housing law and the Supreme Court's decision in *Jones* v. *Mayer,* which held that all housing discrimination was illegal under a Reconstruction Era law.[28] When Congress completed action on the open housing bill, the press hailed the action as a start in dismantling the racial barriers around American ghettos.

In some ways, it seemed a reasonable hope. Public opinion surveys of blacks consistently show a preference for living in integrated neighborhoods, and most whites say they would accept a black family living next door.[29] As the black middle class expanded rapidly in the 1960s, more and more families had the means to buy suburban homes.

Public officials, too, showed signs of changed attitudes. Many of the most populous states had been under state fair housing laws for the better part of a decade by 1970. Secretary of Defense Robert S. McNamara had attempted to use Pentagon influence to break up segregation in off-base military housing. Martin Luther King's last major civil rights drive, the Chicago Freedom Movement, produced some local promises to open up the suburbs. The federal open housing law was enacted though it had been badly defeated only two years earlier. More units of subsidized housing were being produced than ever before. Legal strategies were being shaped to challenge the exclusionary zoning practices of the suburbs. Never before had there been so much reason to hope for a reversal in the momentum of segregation.

27. *Reed* v. *Rhodes,* 422 F. Supp. 708 (N.D. Ohio E.D. 1976).
28. *Jones* v. *Mayer,* 392 U.S. 409 (1968).
29. Surveys conducted by the Institute for Social Research at the University of Michigan show that the percentage of whites believing that blacks should have the right to move wherever they could afford housing rose from 65 to 87 from 1964 to 1974. *New York Times,* August 18, 1975.

Early data from the 1970 Census on the effect of various fair housing laws punctured dreams of rapid change. White suburbanization continued on a massive scale, the percentage of black and Hispanic central city residents rose sharply in many metropolitan areas, and black suburbanization remained at a very low level.

The most common measure of residential integration at any one point is the Taeuber index, a statistical measure that shows the percentage of local residents who would have to move to achieve a random nonracial residential distribution. When this index was calculated in 1970 for 109 cities, the data showed that in 80 of the cities at least four of every five black families would have to move to achieve full integration. The index of segregation had declined at least five points in two-fifths of the cities during the 1960s but had risen in only one city in eleven.[30] The increased neighborhood desegregation was largely confined either to cities with few blacks or to those with an unusually large number, and the statistics probably reflected two quite different kinds of change.

Historically, where black populations have been small, they have been somewhat less segregated, even in the largest cities at the early stages of ghetto formation. Cities with black majorities seemed more integrated, but it was often integration only in a technical sense. In cities like East St. Louis, Illinois, Wilmington, Delaware, East Orange, New Jersey, and Oakland, California, very rapid neighborhood transition took place in various parts of the city. This meant that, at any one time, many blacks and whites appeared to be living in biracial neighborhoods on the periphery of expanding ghettos. The result of this kind of trend was apparent in Newark, the only major city where segregation was worse in 1970 than 1960. What had statistically appeared to be integration in Newark was really the rapid emergence of a ghetto city.[31] Because the Taeuber index identifies such transitional areas as integrated, it offers an optimistic estimate of the level of housing desegregation.

Two other measures of trends in housing segregation are used in a recent study by scholars at the Urban Institute, who note that the Taeuber index is limited to central cities, while housing markets cover entire metropolitan areas. Calculating the index on a metropolitan level, they found increased segregation during the 1960s. Their new statistical measure of

30. Annemette Sorensen, Karl Taeuber, and Leslie J. Hollingsworth, "Indexes of Racial Residential Segregation for 109 Cities in the United States, 1940 to 1970," Institute for Research on Poverty Discussion Papers (University of Wisconsin, 1974; processed), pp. 7–9.

31. "City Housing," *Municipal Performance Report* (November 1973), pp. 16–18.

"exposure" to the other race, based on a calculation of the percentage of black and white neighbors in twenty-four metropolitan areas in four widely scattered states, yielded similar results. The average family had fewer neighbors of the other race in 1970 than ten years earlier. These negative trends were particularly evident in large metropolitan areas with large minority populations.[32]

## Impact on the Black Middle Class

Not only do blacks prefer to live in integrated areas, but those forced to accept segregation are also forced to accept a variety of burdens not imposed on white families at similar income levels. In many cities, black families must pay a significantly higher fraction of their income for housing, are much less likely to own their homes, have less freedom to move to new job sites, and are less likely to enjoy the benefits of either homeowners' tax privileges or suburbanites' equity growth. It is impossible for the growing black middle class to achieve any approximation of the homogeneous neighborhoods with high social and economic status so eagerly sought by the white middle class.

A national study of mobility in the late 1960s found that whites moved frequently, with 43 percent changing homes in a three-year period, and that blacks moved even more often, but that all this moving left segregation virtually intact. While many of the whites moved because of changes in jobs, more than 90 percent of the blacks moved within the same community.[33] Blacks moved more often largely because they relied on rental housing, housing they could not control. The most common reason for blacks moving was the one that affected whites *least*—they moved because they had to, because the landlord or some other external force took the housing from them.

An important consequence of residential segregation is that black families find it far more difficult than whites to live in a neighborhood where their children are not constantly exposed to poverty and to people with little education. Typical white professionals and managers, for instance, live in neighborhoods where fewer than a fourth of the workers are un-

32. Frank deLeeuw, Anne B. Schnare, and Raymond J. Struyk, "Housing," in William Gorham and Nathan Glazer, eds., *The Urban Predicament* (Washington: Urban Institute, 1976), pp. 145–55.

33. Ronald J. McAllister, Edward J. Kaiser, and Edgar W. Butler, "Residential Mobility of Blacks and Whites: A National Longitudinal Survey," *American Journal of Sociology*, vol. 77 (November 1971), pp. 447–48.

skilled or semiskilled while black professionals and managers live in areas where most of the workers hold lower status jobs. "The educational composition of the neighborhood of the most highly educated black person," according to a 1975 study, "is approximately comparable to that of a white high school drop-out." The average white family with an income below the official poverty line lives in a neighborhood with a higher average income than the neighborhood where the average black family with $25,000 a year lives.[34]

Since neighborhood composition basically shapes the character of elementary schools, even an unusually successful black family normally finds its children enrolled in a public school where most of the students come from families with relatively low educational levels, careers, and standards of living. Because of the adults they encounter, the experience and aspirations of their classmates, and the expectations of their teachers, children from successful black families often find themselves in a discouraging, unchallenging educational setting.

These disturbing data directly contradict the optimistic conclusions of the "neo-conservative" intellectuals who oppose further civil rights enforcement initiatives. Wattenberg, for example, argued in his widely read 1974 book, *The Real America,* that the black middle class had full access to the housing market:

Blacks with decent jobs, middle-class blacks, don't need . . . the artificial integration of scatter-sitism—they can buy their way into decent neighborhoods, black or white. Middle-class blacks, living in good neighborhoods black or white, neither need nor want busing—they want good schools and they have the wherewithal to get them.[35]

Wattenberg cites no evidence that there is either an open market in housing or homogeneous middle class black neighborhoods and schools. He simply assumes it. (National polls show that both whites and blacks also assume it.) But studies conducted for HUD in 1976 show the persistence of high levels of overt discrimination in the housing market.[36] A 1976 psychiatric study of the personal and family consequences of blacks'

34. Brigitte Mach Erbe, "Race and Socioeconomic Segregation," *American Sociological Review,* vol. 40 (December 1975), pp. 804, 809.

35. Ben J. Wattenberg, *The Real America: A Surprising Examination of the State of the Union* (Doubleday, 1974), p. 256.

36. Judith A. Haig, "A Study to Determine the Extent of Compliance Among Developers/Sponsors with Equal Housing Advertising Guidelines and Affirmative Marketing Regulations," submitted to HUD by Jaclyn, Inc., April 1976 (processed); Mark Battle Associates, Inc., and the National Committee Against Discrimination in Housing, "Affirmative Fair Housing Marketing Techniques: Final Project Report," submitted to HUD, January 23, 1976 (processed).

encounters with segregationist practices in searching for a home showed they are deep and many-sided.[37]

Being trapped in the ghetto, Brigitte Erbe notes, may explain one of the most disturbing problems of the black middle class. Studies of black economic mobility have observed "the low degree of occupational inheritance between high-status black fathers and their sons and the high degree of intergenerational downward mobility among blacks compared to whites."[38] Even after it has achieved middle class status, a black family finds it extraordinarily difficult to escape the downward pull of ghetto conditions. Often such middle class families provide the core of black support for school desegregation.

## Prognosis and Proposals for Change

Any major gain in residential desegregation in the near future is unlikely. After a number of years of significant growth in the relative family income of blacks, the ratio stopped rising in the early 1970s. During the 1960s and 1970s enormous inflation in the cost of housing gave a large unearned equity to those who already owned homes but screened out more and more people who could not come up with the down payment and closing costs of a first home. This hurt minority families, which were usually renters. (More than two-thirds of white families owned their own homes.) Blacks who had achieved solid middle class status found that housing prices were rising beyond their reach. Unlike 1950, when two-thirds of American families could afford a new home,[39] less than one-third could afford the median-priced new home in 1975. Between 1967 and 1977 the cost of home-ownership rose 107 percent.[40] The long segregation had denied many minority families the price of admission to the contemporary housing market.

As housing costs skyrocketed, the government shut down the federal housing subsidy programs for families unable to afford private housing. Spurred by the 1968 housing legislation, these programs had been an extremely important part of the housing market in the early 1970s, sometimes accounting for one-fourth of all new housing units.[41] Virtually all new commitments were terminated in January 1973, when President Nixon froze

37. William H. Grier, "The Psychic Effects of Housing Discrimination," report to HUD, 1976 (processed).

38. Erbe, "Race and Socioeconomic Segregation," p. 803.

39. Congressional Record (daily edition), March 15, 1977, p. S4129.

40. Housing Affairs Letter (September 23, 1977), p. 6.

41. Commission on Civil Rights, Home Ownership for Lower Income Families, p. viii.

the basic housing programs of the 1968 act.[42] Little subsidized moderate-income housing was begun in the following years. New programs begun in 1975 operated on a small scale and were aimed at higher-income groups.

None of the numerous proposals for accelerating the rate of residential desegregation seem likely to have much impact in the near future. An active campaign of litigation against exclusionary zoning in the suburbs has produced few substantive gains except in the courts of New Jersey.[43] The Supreme Court has placed massive procedural and legal obstacles in the way of successfully raising these issues in the federal courts.[44] Presidents Nixon and Ford, as well as all the major candidates in the 1976 presidential campaign, rejected proposals that federal urban programs require dispersion of subsidized housing units in middle class communities.[45] HUD and the Department of Justice have been given very small staffs to meet their investigative and litigation responsibilities under the 1968 law.[46] The law gave HUD no enforcement sanctions even when it proved violations. The Justice Department settles an average of twenty-three cases a year in the entire country. A number of states have never had a case.

The most comprehensive reviews of the issue—by Anthony Downs of the Real Estate Research Corporation and by the Commission on Civil Rights—conclude that only fundamental reshaping of housing market practices in major metropolitan areas will produce change.[47] Both propose stringent limitations on the housing and land-use authority of local governments and greatly expanded government intervention in the housing market, including the formation of metropolitan housing agencies to carry out national dispersion policies. Both express the judgment that not only sanctions but also positive incentives are necessary to break up the en-

42. Testimony of James T. Lynn, secretary of HUD, in *Oversight on Housing and Urban Development Programs, Washington, D.C.,* Hearings before the Senate Committee on Banking, Housing, and Urban Affairs, 93:1 (GPO, 1973), pt. 1, pp. 243–94.

43. *Southern Burlington County NAACP* v. *Township of Mount Laurel,* 67 N.J. 151, 336 A.2d 713 (1975).

44. *Warth* v. *Seldin,* 422 U.S. 490 (1975); *Jefferson* v. *Hackney,* 406 U.S. 535 (1971); *James* v. *Valtierra,* 402 U.S. 137 (1972); *Village of Belle Terre* v. *Boraas,* 416 U.S. 1 (1974).

45. Christopher Lydon, "Carter Defends All-White Areas," *New York Times,* April 7, 1976; James M. Naughton, "Ford Says Nation Should Preserve 'Ethnic Treasure,' " *New York Times,* April 14, 1976.

46. Commission on Civil Rights, *The Federal Civil Rights Enforcement Effort—A Reassessment* (GPO, 1973), pp. 38, 103. Investigatory staffing continued to decline through 1976.

47. Anthony Downs, *Opening Up the Suburbs: An Urban Strategy for America* (Yale University Press, 1973); Commission on Civil Rights, *Equal Opportunity in Suburbia* (GPO, 1974).

trenched patterns of the housing market. But barring a sudden change in national policy there is no likelihood of any significant change in residential patterns in the foreseeable future.

## Residential Change and School Segregation Levels

The small decline in residential segregation in some cities and some suburban areas during the 1960s might lead one to expect at least temporary local declines in the level of school segregation. Even this modest hope, however, may be unjustified. The findings of an analysis of residential trends over three decades in the central cities and inner suburbs of twenty-nine large metropolitan areas were disappointing. As the 1970s began the central cities studied had an average of 42 percent black students and their inner suburban rings had 94 percent white enrollment.[48] Reynolds Farley, a leading racial demographer, concluded that "the nation's neighborhoods are almost as segregated now as they were thirty years ago. If present trends persist, schools organized on a neighborhood basis will remain racially segregated indefinitely."[49]

Black suburbanization continued to be uncommon, and researchers found that black suburbanites through the late 1960s were highly segregated from whites in the suburbs just as in the central cities. Nowhere did the number of black suburbanites come close to the number of blacks who could afford suburban homes during the 1960s. Farley concluded that if actual income or housing costs were the governing factor "levels of residential segregation would be low."

In most urbanized areas, the racial composition of the suburbs would be greatly altered if blacks occupied housing according to their ability to pay. In 1970, 73 per cent of the Detroit area's white families, but only 12 per cent of the area's black families actually lived in the suburban ring. If blacks were as well represented in the suburbs at each income level as whites, 67 per cent of the black families—rather than 12 per cent—would be suburban residents.[50]

The results were similar in city after city. In Chicago only one-sixth of blacks with the necessary income were suburbanites; in Philadelphia, one-third; in Boston, about one-fifth; in Baltimore, about one-tenth.

---

48. Albert I. Hermalin and Reynolds Farley, "The Potential for Residential Integration in Cities and Suburbs: Implications for the Busing Controversy," *American Sociological Review*, vol. 38 (October 1973), pp. 597–601.

49. Reynolds Farley, "Residential Segregation and Its Implications for School Integration," *Law and Contemporary Problems*, vol. 39 (Winter 1975), p. 167.

50. Ibid., pp. 169, 175, 177.

The discrepancies among individual suburbs and school districts within a metropolitan area—the major question for school integration—were even more extreme. In 1970 in each of more than half the Detroit suburbs there were fewer than *five* black families, although a random distribution of people at appropriate income levels would have produced many hundreds of black residents. In the industrial suburb of Warren, for example, economic factors alone would lead one to expect 6,600 black families, but there were only 31.[51]

The suburbs as a whole were never so totally white as the image of the "white noose" suggested. For decades about 3 percent of suburban residents in the North and West were black, but most lived in segregated developments, often originally constructed for blacks. When larger black settlements began to develop in some suburbs they tended to grow around the old nuclei, to be in decaying older towns and cities incorporated into the sprawling suburbs, or simply to result from a central city ghetto's expansion across the suburban boundary line.

Racial change in the New York metropolitan area, for example, is under way in parts of the inner ring of suburban counties in northern New Jersey, Westchester, and Long Island. These aging suburbs experienced a net average yearly loss of about 3,000 whites and gained an average of more than 9,000 blacks and almost 2,000 Puerto Ricans in the 1960s, and the minority proportion of their population increased 57 percent.[52]

Metropolitan St. Louis also saw the beginning of significant black suburbanization as the city lost an astonishing 17 percent of its population during the 1960s. The suburban black population more than doubled, reaching more than 45,000.[53]

Although the proportion of blacks in the St. Louis suburbs was still relatively small (5 percent), there was evidence both of the channeling of black home buyers into areas already integrated (thus defining integration as a transitional phenomenon) and of the replacement of white homeowners in such areas by newcomers more likely to be renters and transients.[54] By 1974 the school system of the principal center of suburban integrated housing, University City, was 65 percent black, even higher at the elementary school level.[55]

51. Ibid., pp. 175–76.
52. Regional Plan Association, "The State of the Region: A Digest of Selected Trends Through 1974," *Regional Plan News*, no. 97 (March 1975), pp. 26–27.
53. Solomon Sutker and Sara Smith Sutker, eds., *Racial Transition in the Inner Suburb: Studies of the St. Louis Area* (Praeger, 1974), pp. 6, 9.
54. Ibid., pp. 32–40.
55. HEW, Office for Civil Rights, "Pratt Report," data submitted to Federal District Court (D.C.), undated (1974).

The same sequence of development was taking shape around Los Angeles and Newark. Small inner suburbs sometimes change very rapidly. Near Los Angeles, the suburban community of Compton, adjoining the Watts ghetto, has a predominantly black school system, far more segregated than the central city's. About 40 percent of the students in the central city but only 2 percent in Compton are Anglo. In Newark not only is the school system segregated, but some nearby communities like East Orange, once a site of black middle class escape from the city, also have ghetto school systems. By 1972 East Orange schools were more than 90 percent black.[56]

A small suburban system in the path of ghetto expansion may be much like a transitional "neighborhood" in the cities. Suburban districts are often more vulnerable to a small influx of black students than central city systems. While adding a thousand black students to a neighborhood in New York City hardly changes a decimal point in the citywide enrollment statistics and has no effect at all on children attending school in the isolated white areas of the city, the same group of students entering a small suburban district would make a visible change in the whole district and give the affected system a different identity in the surrounding suburbs.

An example of this is the Los Angeles suburb of Inglewood, a community of 97,000 also adjoining Watts, which began substantial housing integration only in the 1960s. The town was a gradually declining area of housing for whites with moderate income. It was a natural target for black families, many of whom came from Compton. While the blacks were trying to flee the ghetto, whites feared a repeat of Compton, which had changed from a segregated white community to part of the central city ghetto in just a few years.[57]

Implementation of a 1970 desegregation plan in Inglewood was followed by a rapid fall in white enrollment. Researchers examining the plan concluded that when "demographic forces are very strong" from an expanding ghetto it is extremely difficult to do anything significant about school segregation without speeding the transition process.[58] The fragmentation of the suburbs into small isolated districts, the report stated, greatly increases the difficulty of desegregation. Opponents, who are free to leave if they are not satisfied, are offered the alternative of nearby segregated school systems.

56. HEW, Office for Civil Rights, *Directory of Public Elementary and Secondary Schools in Selected Districts, Fall 1972* (GPO, 1973), p. 832.

57. Edna Bonachich and Robert F. Goodman, *Deadlock in School Desegregation* (Praeger, 1972), pp. 3–4, 17–18, 26.

58. Ibid., pp. 96, 11–12.

People are able to take hard-line positions, saying in effect: "If you don't satisfy me, I will move out." They can take nonnegotiable stands because they are not ultimately dependent on a negotiated settlement. . . . The process is exacerbated by the fact that each individual decision to move out increases the pressures on the remaining residents to move.

When looked at in this way, the problem . . . takes on a metropolitan significance. People may relocate from community to community within the same metropolitan area without affecting their job and other important social relations. . . . In short, they have a stake in the metropolitan area that they do not have in a particular suburban community.[59]

In the fall of 1972 the Inglewood school system had become 59 percent minority.[60] Two years later, few white students remained.

There has been much speculation and scholarly argument about whether central city desegregation plans accelerate white flight from the cities. This debate is inconclusive. The ironic reality may be that suburban whites are fleeing to more distant, "whiter" suburbs. This problem appears to be particularly acute in areas with many small suburban school systems.

Black suburbanization, where it has occurred at substantial levels, has usually been subject to the same inevitable racial transition as the cities. "Suburbanization to date," Karl Taeuber concludes, "has occurred with the same racially discriminatory channeling of black residents into selected localities that characterizes central cities."[61] Unless this vicious circle can be broken, minority suburbanization seems likely to push the boundary line of racial separation ever farther into the countryside.

### Effect of School Segregation on Young Families

When the decisions of whites to migrate to the suburbs are studied, families usually say that the school issue plays a fairly small role. There are many reasons for leaving the city, including better housing, access to suburban jobs, larger yards, and shopping. Few cities offer new, reasonably priced, relatively low-down-payment housing competitive with that in the suburbs. Many cities have deteriorated in so many different ways that it is difficult to untangle the overlapping negative influences. Because jobs have shifted rapidly to the suburbs, in only a few areas do a large number of successful white families want or need to live in old central cities of declining importance.[62]

Washington, D.C., provides clear evidence of the influence of schools.

59. Ibid., p. 86.
60. HEW, Office for Civil Rights, Directory, 1972, p. 105.
61. Karl E. Taeuber, "Racial Segregation: The Persisting Dilemma," Annals of the American Academy of Political and Social Science (November 1975), p. 95.
62. Orfield, "White Flight Research," Educational Forum (May 1976), pp. 527–29.

Most federal agencies are in the heart of the city, and the press, trade associations, embassies, a wide variety of national organizations, and many of the city's other major employers need access to the federal agencies. Washington's national cultural institutions and historic neighborhoods have stimulated the desire to live in the city, and there is a substantial migration into the city of young white adults.

But the population ratios of various age groups in the city differ so much that they can only be explained by the school situation. Black children five to fourteen years old, for example, outnumber white children more than ten to one. The ratio is more than eight to one among those aged fifteen to nineteen. After children finish school, the ratio shifts. Almost one-third of the residents aged twenty to twenty-four are white. As people move into the child-raising years, however, the ratio changes again: in the thirty-five- to thirty-nine-year-old group, there are about four blacks for every white. For families over fifty the ratio shifts again in the other direction: with no school problems, more whites remain in the city.[63]

Statistics from other big cities are similar, showing falling white populations in spite of a net in-migration of young white adults.[64] Clearly families with school age children, including large numbers of middle class black families, feel they must live outside the city. (The Washington black population declined 27,000 from 1970 to 1974 as the suburban black population rose 110,000. In addition, 10,000 black children in the city attended private schools.[65]) Thus the existence of a ghetto school system undermines an otherwise excellent potential for residential integration and economic revitalization in major parts of the city. The interaction of school and housing segregation spurs not only the separation of whites and blacks but also the loss of the middle class black families so important to the schools and the cities.

## Housing Integration and School Integration

If one were to select a national sample of Census tracts that had substantial black and white housing integration in 1960 and examine their

63. District of Columbia Municipal Planning Office, Demographic Unit, "Estimated Population of the District of Columbia by Age, Color and Sex: July 1, 1973" (processed).

64. Larry H. Long, "How the Racial Composition of Cities Changes," Land Economics (August 1975), pp. 261, 266.

65. School year 1974–75 statistics from District of Columbia Public Schools, Division of Research and Evaluation, Data Resource Book, 1974–75 (Division of Research and Evaluation, December 1974), pp. 6–7; District of Columbia Public Schools, "Pupil Membership in Regular Day Schools on October 17, 1974, Compared with October 18, 1973" (November 8, 1974; processed), p. 1.

schools a decade later, one would normally find not integrated but ghetto schools. This is because residential integration has often begun at or near the periphery of an expanding ghetto, where the integration has been evanescent. Only a few neighborhoods in the United States have had stable integration for a generation.[66]

This belief that the beginning of integration produces a segregated ghetto neighborhood is the cause of much of the white resistance to residential change and school desegregation. Lower income whites living in traditionally ethnic areas are often particularly hostile. They occupy housing that many blacks and Latinos can afford, and they often lack the means to purchase similar housing in the suburbs.

One student of Boston segregation, Michael Ross, noted that antibusing voting in local elections was more intense in some middle class city neighborhoods than in the lower income neighborhoods right across the line from the ghetto. He found a consistent correlation during the 1960s between the percentage of owner-occupied homes and support for antibusing leader Louise Day Hicks.

The residents of these neighborhoods have typically moved from less affluent ethnic enclaves into these all-white middle class sections of Boston. While upwardly mobile, they did not have the financial resources or the desire to leave the city and reside in the suburbs. . . .

In leaving the deteriorating central city, these individuals sought a desirable neighborhood, better schools, and more privacy. With their middle-class status, they now had the financial resources to purchase a home, and this decision reinforces their commitment to their neighborhood. However, their aspirations for a better future become less certain when the addition of "culturally disadvantaged" blacks becomes even a remote possibility. Besides the multitude of negative racial stereotypes, this type of racial change also symbolizes the encroachment of urban problems.[67]

Similar fears have been observed in aging suburban communities experiencing integration. A growing number of them have adopted various local ordinances to try to prevent resegregation. One of these was a Willingboro (formerly Levittown), New Jersey, ordinance banning "for sale" signs in front yards, which the Supreme Court struck down in 1977 as a violation of the right to free speech.[68]

66. Nina Jaffe Gruen and Claude Gruen, *Low and Moderate Income Housing in the Suburbs* (Praeger, 1972), pp. 119–38.

67. J. Michael Ross, "Resistance to Racial Change in the Urban North" (Ph.D. dissertation, Harvard University, 1973), pp. 821, 823, 824.

68. David F. White, "Sign Ruling Presents Problem in Suburbs," *New York Times*, May 4, 1977.

The damaging results of the normal process of residential "integration" suggest not only the need for policies that permit the black population to move farther away from ghetto locations, but also the possibility that school integration of a certain kind may be a *prerequisite* for stable housing integration. If all neighborhoods in a city had integrated schools and the movement of black families into a neighborhood made no difference to the local school, the cycle might be broken.

According to the 1970 census data, two of the cities that had successfully carried out school desegregation in the mid-1960s had among the lowest levels of housing segregation in the United States in 1970. Berkeley, California, where voters had defeated a fair housing referendum in the early 1960s, now ranked fifth in housing integration among 109 U.S. cities. Sacramento, which carried out a systemwide desegregation plan in 1966, ranked third. Also, Evanston, Illinois, another early pioneer in desegregation, has reduced its high level of housing segregation in spite of the high cost of much of the housing in the community's white area.[69] These results suggest that under some circumstances districtwide school desegregation plans may contribute to residential integration.

The chief problem in sustaining residential integration, according to recent sociological studies, usually does not stem from "white flight" but from the difficulty of maintaining the desirability of the neighborhood to new families. Studies of racial change in neighborhoods in Chicago and Cleveland showed that the so-called flight of residents differed little from the normal patterns of residential mobility before racial factors were introduced. In a highly mobile society (more than one-sixth of the people in the country move each year) change is substantial and continuous. For a neighborhood to remain well integrated, it must continually be able to attract new home buyers of both races. White home buyers, however, are reluctant to make such a long-term commitment in the face of uncertainty, and realtors commonly steer them to "safer" neighborhoods.[70]

If this description of the underlying dynamics of neighborhood change is accurate, equalizing the school racial balance throughout a housing market might change the incentives. It would mean, in effect, that a white family

69. Sorensen, Taeuber, and Hollingsworth, "Indexes of Racial Residential Segregation," pp. 7–9.

70. Harvey Molotch, "Racial Change in a Stable Community," *American Journal of Sociology*, vol. 75 (September 1969), pp. 226–38. In Cleveland "white flight" did not exceed normal levels of mobility, except in a small minority of neighborhoods. Avery M. Guest and James J. Zuiches, "Another Look at Residential Turnover in Urban Neighborhoods: A Note on 'Racial Change in a Stable Community' by Harvey Molotch," *American Journal of Sociology*, vol. 77 (November 1971), pp. 457–67.

purchasing a home in an integrated or largely black area would run no risk of their children ending up in segregated ghetto schools. Nor would a black family moving into a white neighborhood be seen as a threat to the local school's racial balance.

A study of Riverside, California, detected what may be another effect of prolonged desegregation. After some years, students and their parents had become acquainted with the new neighborhoods and the people around the new school and some of them decided to move within walking distance of the school to which the children were being bused.[71] Similar moves have been observed in Louisville, where the court order exempted integrated neighborhoods from busing. The Kentucky Commission on Human Relations reported that there had been a significant increase in residential integration.[72]

Some researchers conclude that attending integrated schools encourages people to live in integrated neighborhoods. One barrier to residential integration is that though most blacks want to live in integrated neighborhoods few want to be the only black in an area.[73] Obviously, substantial suburban integration requires many black pioneers willing to move into predominantly white areas. Research shows that black adults who attended integrated schools are more likely to take the first step in integrating new neighborhoods. A study of Los Angeles black adults in the 1960s found, for example, that experience with school integration was a major factor in the decision to live outside the ghetto. Willingness to undergo the tension of living in a white neighborhood was directly related to childhood contacts with whites.[74]

A study of black adults by the National Opinion Research Center reported similar findings:

Respondents who attended integrated schools have had more contact with whites, have less anti-white feeling, and thus make a conscious effort to live in integrated situations. The persistence of patterns of association with whites from elementary

71. Christine Rossell, "The Social Impact of School Desegregation," Research Proposal to National Institute of Education (1974; processed), p. 11.

72. Kentucky Commission on Human Rights, "Fair Housing—A Better Answer than Busing" (September 22, 1975; processed). The number of blacks living in the suburbs increased 63 percent between 1973 and 1977; residential segregation diminished in exempt neighborhoods. Integrated Education (September–October 1977), p. 33.

73. A. Campbell and H. Schuman, "Black Views of Racial Issues," in Marcel L. Goldschmid, ed., Black Americans and White Racism (Holt, Rinehart, and Winston, 1970), p. 347. However, if blacks move mostly to areas already well integrated, they may be unwitting participants in the resegregation process.

74. Bonnie Bullogh, "Social-Psychological Barriers to Housing Desegregation" (UCLA Graduate School of Business Administration, Special Report 2, 1969; processed).

school and high school to adulthood is not surprising when one remembers the large number of hours which every person spends in schools and the importance of school as a socializing agency. The most plausible explanation is that school integration develops a set of attitudes about whites that makes contact with whites less uncomfortable. Certainly it is clear from our data that many Negroes find association with whites distressing.[75]

School integration does not always foster housing desegregation nor did it bring about rapid change even in the cases cited. Research is still sparse. Obviously, some kinds of desegregation plans may merely speed up traditional patterns of racial transition, particularly small-scale "pairing" programs, which extend integration only a few blocks beyond current ghetto boundaries in a big city by merging schools on opposite sides of the ghetto line. Though these plans involve no busing, they may speed ghetto expansion and "white flight" by accelerating the normal process of neighborhood transition.

It is important to remember that school and housing policies have reciprocal effects. School segregation is often caused by housing policies, and in the long term stable housing integration may greatly ease school integration. Without school integration, on the other hand, it is extremely difficult to stabilize housing integration unless the minority population is relatively small or the white population can afford private schools.

### Does School Desegregation Cause Residential Resegregation?

During 1975 debate among both scholars and policymakers was stimulated by a brief paper by James Coleman in which he stated that increases in school desegregation under some circumstances produced an accelerated departure of white families from the cities.[76] Antibusing leaders used this research to argue that busing students was not only unpopular but senseless, producing a result exactly opposite from its intent.

But Coleman's actual assertions were far more limited than the antibusing argument implied. Declines in white enrollment, Coleman reported, were rapid in central cities with sizable black populations *whether or not* schools were integrated. Desegregation, he suggested, may intensify the problem temporarily in the largest cities. (Very few big cities had carried out any kind of citywide desegregation plan by this time.) This does not

---

75. Robert L. Crain, "School Integration and the Academic Achievement of Negroes," *Sociology of Education*, vol. 44 (Winter, 1971), p. 19.

76. James S. Coleman, Sara D. Kelley, and John A. Moore, *Trends in School Segregation, 1968–1973* (Urban Institute, 1975).

mean, of course, that people were fleeing solely because of the race issue. A city with a high proportion of minority residents usually has a number of other problems—housing decay, outward migration of jobs, rising crime rates, increases in the costs of public services and tax levels. All of these may influence the decision of a family looking for housing or of a realtor recommending locations to a newcomer to the area. In larger urban areas the problems are often compounded when the number of private homes in the central city steadily declines and virtually all new construction is in the outer suburbs.

The waning attractiveness of central cities is mirrored in the attitudes of the people still living in them. Surveys by leading polling organizations— Gallup, Harris, Roper, and Opinion Research Corporation—have shown that the percentage of city residents who would stay if they had a choice has shrunk—from 22 percent in 1966 to 13 percent in 1972—in part, perhaps, because of the riots of the late 1960s.[77]

After two years of heated dispute over Coleman's argument it was still not clear whether desegregation plans increased the rate of white departure. One 1977 study, for example, argued that public reaction to underlying demographic changes in the city and to deteriorating city conditions would explain the statistical trends of white enrollment without any reference to desegregation plans at all.[78] Most scholars believed, however, that there was a significant one-year acceleration of white flight in big cities where a plan limited to the city only was implemented. Perhaps the enrollment decline in a single year would be that normally expected in two years.

Desegregation, in any case, neither creates flight where there was none nor has a long-term impact on the rate of declining white enrollment. Large central cities are losing their remaining white students rapidly even in neighborhoods with all-white schools. Often the decline is sharpest in aging, well-to-do white communities some distance from minority areas. To understand, one needs only to look at the age level of the female population remaining in the city. In 1970 the median age for white females still in Washington, D.C., was forty-six, in Chicago thirty-seven, in St. Louis forty-four, in Detroit forty, in San Francisco forty-one. On the average, black women in these cities were seventeen years younger. Black families

77. See summary of poll data in James L. Sundquist, *Dispersing Population: What America Can Learn from Europe* (Brookings Institution, 1975), pp. 24–29.

78. Michael R. Fitzgerald and David R. Morgan, "Assessing the Consequences of Public Policy: School Desegregation and White Flight in America," paper presented at the annual meeting of the Midwest Political Science Association, April 22, 1977 (processed).

were often in the middle of their child-bearing years. Young white families were in the suburbs. The imbalance in school enrollments could only increase.[79]

Coleman's study, as well as an intensive study of Florida school districts based on interviews with thousands of parents, suggests that where the desegregation plans include the suburbs residential stability is greater. Coleman and Farley report that the problem becomes most difficult when the central cities have large minority populations and the suburbs are virtually all white. There is considerable stability, on the other hand, in metropolitan school districts where there is no place to flee to.[80]

Desegregation of entire metropolitan areas maximizes stability. In other words, the smallest desegregation plans may have the worst effects on housing integration and the largest may create the most favorable conditions. The smallest create easily accessible havens of segregation; the largest equalize the burden, raise the cost of flight, and diminish the differences between city and suburban schools. Policymakers and judges who attempt to minimize flight by limiting the area of desegregation may be following exactly the wrong strategy.

79. David Sly and Louis Pol, "White Flight, School Segregation and Demographic Change," in Meyer Weinberg and others, *Three Myths: An Exposure of Popular Misconceptions about School Desegregation* (Atlanta: Southern Regional Council, 1976), pp. 62–63.

80. Coleman found that flight was greatest "where there was a high degree of between-district segregation in the metropolitan area (thus providing a supply of predominantly white suburban schools to which families could move)," and "in districts with higher proportions of Black children." He explains the stable enrollment of a district like Hillsborough, Florida (metropolitan Tampa), by pointing out the absence of white suburban sanctuaries and the relatively small proportion of black students in the district as a whole. James S. Coleman, "Liberty and Equality in School Desegregation," *Social Policy*, vol. 6 (January–February 1976), pp. 10–12. Reynolds Farley, "Can Governmental Policies Integrate Public Schools?" (University of Michigan, Population Studies Center, 1976; processed).

# 4

# A New American Dilemma

IT IS HARD to find a political leader who opposes integrated education and equally hard to find one who supports busing. Polls of white people across the country show strong support for educating black and white children in the same schools but strong opposition to the technique used to bring them together. Though the courts have found no other way to end unconstitutional segregation in the big cities, the public is not convinced and does not want to make a choice between segregation and busing.

Most political leaders respond by denying that a choice has to be made. Busing, they say, is unnecessary, the unhappy result of arbitrary court decisions. Something else—usually something unspecified—should be done about urban school problems; busing is not only unnecessary but extremely costly and damaging to the educational process.

If the federal courts are right and the choice between busing and segregated education is often unavoidable, one can interpret the political rhetoric and the public opinion polls in only two ways. Either the consistently expressed preference for integration is meaningless and cynical or it represents genuine misunderstanding of what the courts have chosen and what the consequences of their decisions have been.

There is no way to measure people's underlying motives accurately, but it seems most reasonable to begin with the assumption that the public and its elected leaders are usually sincere when they affirm the values both of integration and of neighborhood schools. Public rhetoric and poll data provide important background information, but they say less about policy than has often been assumed. If the values are mutually exclusive, the real policy issue is which value should have priority if a choice is inevitable.

Are neighborhood schools the most important thing, even if they guarantee perpetuation of unconstitutional segregation? Or is integration primary, even if it requires busing?

## The Attack on Busing

The policy of urban desegregation through busing, as portrayed by its critics from the White House to the school board meeting room, is both arbitrary and self-defeating. It is described as a costly and rigidly formalistic approach to integration likely to worsen race relations and accelerate the exodus of the remaining white residents from central cities. Polls show most people believe these claims. Public perception has doubtless been reinforced by the way the national media, particularly television, have covered the story. For example, during October 1975 the national evening news programs carried twenty-six reports on urban school desegregation. Nine of the reports concerned conflicts in Boston and Louisville. The only two cities in the country experiencing active and tumultuous protests, in other words, accounted for more than a third of the news on desegregation. In Boston the coverage focused on two high schools where most of the city's problems had arisen. Much of the remaining news concerned statements of antibusing leaders and the antibusing legislation being considered by Congress. There were two brief stories on the courts. Five of the reports were devoted to the experience of desegregated communities in other parts of the country, and the emphasis was on white flight from desegregation.[1] Few viewers could realize that in most affected communities desegregation had been accepted peacefully.

Political leaders have also done much to shape public perception. The central themes of busing opponents were contained in President Nixon's 1972 message to Congress. In the future, he said, the drive for equality in the schools must "focus much more specifically on education." Busing, as contrasted to education, he said, had "been a classic case of the remedy for one evil creating another evil." Not only was desegregation distinct from education, but they were in direct conflict. "Schools," said Mr. Nixon, "exist to serve the children, not to bear the burden of social change." The school bus, once a "symbol of hope," was becoming a "symbol of social engineering on the basis of abstractions."

1. *Television News Index and Abstracts* (Nashville, Tenn.: Vanderbilt Television News Archive, October 1975), pp. 1956–2198.

In too many communities today, it has become a symbol of helplessness, frustration and outrage—of a wrenching of children away from their families, and from the schools their families may have moved to be near, and sending them arbitrarily to others far distant.[2]

Black parents too, said Mr. Nixon, had moved toward "far greater balance" on the issue. They now wanted "emphasis on improving schools, on convenience, on the chance for parental involvement—in short, on the same concerns that motivate white parents."[3]

According to the President, some federal courts had adopted such "extreme remedies" that they were creating problems "severe enough to threaten" everything that had been achieved since 1954. The answer, he said, was to end the hardship caused by busing for some poor children and recognize that the largest urban ghettos could never be desegregated. "Rather than require the spending of scarce resources on ever-longer bus rides . . . we should encourage the putting of those resources directly into education."[4]

The President's position was endorsed by Gerald Ford, then House Republican leader, who supported not only legislation to prohibit court-ordered busing for racial integration but also a constitutional amendment forbidding even voluntary local busing.[5] "The best way in this emergency to obtain that best education," he had earlier said, "is to provide Federal financial assistance rather than to force busing. Forced busing to attain racial balance is not the best way to get good education."[6]

The Nixon and Ford assertions were backed by Secretary of Health, Education, and Welfare Elliot Richardson, who said that the "fabric of the body politic" was being torn by the almost unbearable strain of the busing issue on the educational process. "If one thing is clear," he testified, "it is that we cannot continue the current degree of pressure on our school systems." Richardson spoke of the "widespread belief that remedies have been imposed that harm more than they help."[7]

The alternative approach outlined by Richardson simply called for concentrating larger amounts of the existing compensatory aid on fewer

2. "Special Message to the Congress on Equal Educational Opportunities and School Busing, March 17, 1972," *Public Papers of the Presidents: Richard Nixon, 1972* (GPO, 1974), p. 432.

3. Ibid., p. 433.

4. Ibid., pp. 435, 437–38.

5. *Congressional Record*, August 17, 1972, p. 28909.

6. Ibid., November 4, 1971, p. 39304.

7. *Equal Educational Opportunities Act of 1972*, Hearings, pp. 25–26.

children. A reordering of priorities was evident in the proposal. The administration wished to divert much of the money being used to help school districts make desegregation work into compensatory education in the ghetto.[8] The assumptions underlying the position were simple. First, children were being hurt in some way by desegregation. Second, busing was very expensive. Third, the money being used for desegregation could be spent instead to achieve substantial educational gains.

Richardson testified for the change though he conceded that the findings of HEW's latest research on desegregation, which dealt with 225 desegregating southern school systems, were encouraging. The study showed that "it can be said clearly that the educational results are affirmative." The results for compensatory education, he conceded, were less clear.[9]

## Congressional Critics

Many legislators simply assumed that education had been harmed. Opponents of desegregation hammered on the themes of excessive cost and educational harm. Nebraska conservative Senator Roman Hruska insisted that busing "will hamper rather than help progress."[10] Representative Richardson Preyer of North Carolina asserted that most people supported integrated education but were "heartsick to see the deterioration in discipline and in the quality of education in our schools and what that means for the future of their children." He said parents were bitterly opposed to "leveling down" in the school system and saw "the educational life chances of their children being jeopardized in the interest of improving others."[11]

Senators from states where busing was beginning were particularly vocal. Senator Howard Baker reported that the Tennessee plans had caused "enormous hardships." "For local communities," he said, "busing orders have often meant that funds which could be used to make needed improvements in educational facilities or to provide better pay for teachers are instead spent to buy, fuel, and maintain buses."[12] Senator Dewey Bartlett said that desegregation plans had "created a state of social and educational chaos in Oklahoma's two largest cities."[13] Senator William Roth, Jr.,

8. Ibid., pp. 28–29.
9. Ibid., p. 289.
10. *Busing of Schoolchildren,* Hearings before the Subcommittee on Constitutional Rights of the Senate Committee on the Judiciary, 93:2 (GPO, 1974), p. 27.
11. Ibid., pp. 72–73.
12. Ibid., p. 234.
13. Ibid.

of Delaware announced: "As an alternative to busing, I favor the development of first-rate, high-quality, neighborhood schools for all students,
regardless of race."[14]

The issue arose whenever an education bill began to move through
Congress or an election campaign got under way. Usually the main lines of
attack were familiar. Desegregation was defined as impractical, expensive,
and a poor alternative to "educational" programs. In early September 1975,
in the first tense weeks of desegregation in Louisville and of Boston's Phase
II plan, President Ford assailed the federal courts for the many instances
where, he said, they had required unnecessary busing. Although the
Justice Department later conceded that it could find no instance of such
judicial failure, the President's comments reflected, and doubtless deepened, the belief that there were alternatives, which had been willfully
ignored.[15]

When Senator Joseph Biden, a young Delaware Democrat, led his
Senate battle to restrict HEW's power to enforce urban desegregation,
his arguments sounded much like those of the Republican presidents. He
drew national attention, attacking busing as a "bankrupt concept" that
violates the "cardinal rule of common sense."[16] Senator Thomas Eagleton
questioned whether this remedy was "creating greater problems than those
it is intended to remedy."

Looking at the experience of the last decade, I find no compelling reason to
maintain busing as a congressionally authorized procedure in school desegregation cases when . . . in a great many cases, the social problems created by busing
now outweigh the social advantages to be derived from bringing black and white
students together.[17]

Throughout the 1975 debates, member after member cited James Coleman's controversial argument that school desegregation accelerated white
flight as if it were a proven conclusion. Coleman was the principal witness
at Senate hearings organized by busing opponents, and his articles and
speeches were quoted continually by sponsors of major amendments, who
argued that his earlier research had been the basis for the busing policy in
the first place and that no defense remained for the policy now that he had

14. Ibid., p. 237.
15. Statement of President Ford in an interview on Providence station WJAR-TV,
Newport, Rhode Island, August 30, 1975, *Weekly Compilation of Presidential Documents*, vol. 11 (September 8, 1975), p. 921.
16. *Congressional Record* (daily edition), September 24, 1975, p. S16643.
17. Ibid., pp. S16643, S16644.

changed. Senator Biden, sponsor of the first major antibusing amendment ever passed by the Senate, reflected this view:

The architect of the concept now opposes it. Professor Coleman, an educator, first suggested the possible benefits of busing in a 1966 report. Now in 1975 Coleman says, "Guess what? I was wrong. Busing doesn't accomplish its goal."[18]

## The 1976 Presidential Campaign

The 1976 Democratic primaries brought forth another flood of rhetoric about busing. None of the candidates saw it as a good solution to segregation. Of the six candidates still active after the first few primaries, the most liberal, Morris Udall, spoke of an "emerging consensus" against busing and favored voluntary plans. Jimmy Carter praised the approach adopted in Atlanta, where the local branch of the NAACP had accepted a bargain putting more black administrators in the school system instead of introducing a desegregation plan. Both Governor Edmund (Jerry) Brown and Senator Frank Church criticized busing, Senator Henry Jackson proposed legislation to restrict busing, and former Governor George Wallace favored a constitutional amendment banning it.[19] Although most Democratic candidates pledged to uphold court orders, Carter's comments were typical of the campaign discussion: "This well-intentioned idea has contributed little to the equalization of educational opportunity, has often resulted in a decreased level of integration over the long term, and has divided and sidetracked our efforts toward improving education of all children."[20]

The arguments in the campaigns and on the floor of Congress were not unique. Newspaper articles and editorials frequently made similar assertions.[21] Some prestigious academics supported the claims. Local educators and school board members echoed them. Perhaps most important, the claims reflected widespread public beliefs on an issue that was receiving a great deal of attention.

It was no conspiracy. It was much more like a consensus. Parents were deeply concerned about sending their children to schools in strange neigh-

18. Interview in *TV News*, September 20–26, 1975; inserted in *Congressional Record* (daily edition), October 2, 1975, p. S17372.

19. John Matthews, "How Democratic Candidates Stand on the Busing Issue," *Washington Star*, January 19, 1976.

20. Ibid.

21. See editorials reprinted in Judith F. Buncher, ed., *The School Busing Controversy: 1970–75* (New York: Facts on File, 1975).

borhoods. Everyone knew that there was severe racial tension in the country and feared that it would spill over into desegregated schools. Few understood the reasons for the courts' orders, and national leaders had made no effort at all to reassure parents about the consequences of desegregation for their children's education. Critics constantly stated that there were alternative ways to solve the problem. Almost no one in a position to be heard would defend the policy.

## Public Beliefs

In his classic 1944 study, *An American Dilemma,* Gunnar Myrdal probed the contradictions between American ideals of racial equality and American practices of segregation.[22] Each step toward desegregation since then has required recognition of these contradictions. Eventually, for example, it became clear that the only way to achieve desegregation in the South was to alter the tradition of local control in major ways. Contradictory beliefs about local control and equal rights were held for as long as possible. Only at a time of crisis—blatant actions by Alabama and Mississippi officials in 1963–65—was the contradiction resolved in favor of decisive national action. But there has been neither a major social movement nor political leadership to effectively point out that a dilemma still exists. People continue to support school desegregation and to oppose busing, refusing to recognize the incompatibility of their values and believing that there is some other way to achieve integration.

### Growing Support for Integration

Increasing support for integrated schools has been a clear pattern in successive studies of public opinion over the decades. Three decades of surveys by the National Opinion Research Center showed remarkable growth of a consensus supporting integrated schools between 1942 and 1970. In 1942 only two northern whites in five supported integrated schools. Support had risen to three in five by 1956 and to more than four in five by 1970. The changes were notable in the South. In 1942 supporters of integrated education were a tiny minority, only 2 percent, of white southerners. Two years after the 1954 Supreme Court decision in *Brown,* the level had risen to 14 percent. By 1970 almost half of southern whites favored inte-

22. Gunnar Myrdal with Richard Sterner and Arnold Rose, *An American Dilemma: The Negro Problem and Modern Democracy* ( Harper and Row, 1944 ).

Table 4-1. *Percentage of White Parents Objecting to Integrated Education, by Proportion of Black Students, Selected Years, 1959–75*

| School level of black enrollment | 1959 | 1963 | 1965 | 1966 | 1969 | 1970 | 1973 | 1975 |
|---|---|---|---|---|---|---|---|---|
| *South* | | | | | | | | |
| Few | 72 | 61 | 37 | 24 | 21 | 16 | 16 | 15 |
| Half | 83 | 78 | 68 | 49 | 46 | 43 | 36 | 38 |
| Majority | 86 | 86 | 78 | 62 | 64 | 69 | 69 | 61 |
| *North* | | | | | | | | |
| Few | 7 | 10 | 7 | 6 | 7 | 6 | 6 | 3 |
| Half | 34 | 33 | 28 | 32 | 28 | 24 | 23 | 24 |
| Majority | 58 | 53 | 52 | 60 | 54 | 51 | 63 | 47 |

Sources: *Gallup Opinion Index* (February 1976), p. 9; George H. Gallup, *The Gallup Poll: Public Opinion 1935–1971* (Random House, 1972), vol. 3: *1959–1971*, pp. 1598, 1940–41, 2010, 2211.

grated schools.[23] A social movement—civil rights—had brought congressional action and administrative enforcement. After desegregation was imposed, the inconceivable became the new status quo.

Answers to a related series of questions asked by successive Gallup polls in eight different years from 1959 to 1975 showed dwindling public opposition to integrated schools during the period, especially in the South during the 1960s, the region and the period in which massive desegregation was concentrated (see table 4-1). Southern attitudes steadily moderated as integration proceeded. Between 1959 and 1975 the percentage of southern whites willing to send their children to school with a few black children grew from 28 to 85, while the number expressing "no objection" to their children's enrollment in half-black classrooms grew from 17 to 62 percent. At least nine-tenths of northerners were willing to accept some blacks in their schools throughout this period, and the number claiming that they had "no objection" to half-black schools grew from 66 percent to 76 percent.

## Declining Support for Civil Rights Enforcement

Even as acceptance of integration was growing, public support for further action against racial discrimination virtually disappeared. The issue had dominated American politics at the time of the Birmingham crisis in 1963, during the subsequent congressional battle over President Kennedy's civil rights bill, and during the Selma march and voting rights struggle of

23. Andrew M. Greeley and Paul B. Sheatsley, "Attitudes Toward Racial Integration," *Scientific American* (December 1971), pp. 13–14.

1965. Polls at that time showed that people saw action against discrimination as the most important question before the country. This public concern supported congressional passage of the two most important civil rights laws since Reconstruction, but it soon waned. Between March 1965 and May 1966, the percentage of people convinced that civil rights was the nation's most important problem plummeted from 52 to 9.[24] Though these levels later fluctuated considerably, there was little support for accelerating integration. The social issues of crime and violence became dominant, urban riots across the country increased racial tension, and the polls showed growing resistance to further racial change. One scholar concludes that the opposition of national leaders (including the President after 1968) to desegregation enforcement may well have accelerated the trend. By the end of the 1960s, public opinion approximated "a state of moderate consensus *against* these civil rights initiatives."[25]

During the early 1970s, the public seemed less and less concerned. A national study of the hopes and fears of Americans in 1971 found that only one person in ten rated "settlement of racial problems" as a hope for the nation, down substantially from earlier measures in 1959 and 1964.[26]

The "problems of black Americans" again received low priority in a 1972 public ranking of national matters of concern. On a list of twenty-seven issues, they ranked twenty-fourth.[27]

A similar careful study of public attitudes, two years later in April 1974, found that the "problems of black Americans" ranked lowest among thirty issues studied. The most important issues were inflation, violence, and crime.[28]

Perhaps people paid little attention to civil rights because they believed that progress was occurring spontaneously. Almost one-fifth thought there had been substantial recent progress and another half believed there had been some. Only one in nine thought that blacks were losing ground. In fact, the American public expressed more optimism about progress on race relations than on any other domestic problem studied.[29]

24. George H. Gallup, *The Gallup Poll: Public Opinion 1935–1971* (Random House, 1972), vol. 3: *1959–1971*, pp. 1934, 2009.

25. J. Michael Ross, "Resistance to Racial Change in the Urban North" (Ph.D. dissertation, Harvard University, 1973), p. 123, chap. 3, and p. 253.

26. Albert H. Cantril and Charles W. Roll, Jr., *Hopes and Fears of the American People* (Universe Books, 1971), p. 23.

27. William Watts and Lloyd A. Free, eds., *State of the Nation* (Universe Books, 1973), p. 35.

28. William Watts and Lloyd A. Free, *State of the Nation 1974* (Potomac Associates, 1974), pp. 20–21.

29. Ibid., pp. 278, 305. Earlier research showed that most white Americans believed the problems of blacks were the result not of discrimination but of some failing of the

These feelings were evident in public responses to Harris Survey questions asked in 1976 and 1977. During 1976 pollsters found that a 75–7 percent majority of whites believed that blacks were not discriminated against in public education. After more than two-thirds of the American public watched the 1977 eight-day television series *Roots*, which portrayed the history of slavery and discrimination, the Harris Survey asked white viewers the same question. White attitudes were held so strongly that this unprecedented experience had had little effect: 73 percent of the white viewers said there was no school discrimination and only 18 percent took the opposite position.[30]

Even at the height of the civil rights movement, when there were large majorities for action against segregation in public accommodations and other distinctively southern problems, the public was lukewarm on the issue of federal action to assure integrated schools. Polls conducted between 1964 and 1970, as well as a follow-up survey in 1974, showed that white support for such action never came close to 50 percent, and the unpublished 1974 data reportedly showed less white support than any of the previous polls.[31] Equally interesting in the survey was the strong and consistent black support for federal enforcement of school desegregation, even after the rise of the black power and community control movements:[32]

|       | Percent favoring federal action | |
|-------|-------|-------|
|       | *Black* | *White* |
| 1964  | 68 | 38 |
| 1968  | 84 | 33 |
| 1970  | 84 | 41 |

The confidence of blacks in the federal government, however, had sharply declined. A 1972 Harris Survey found that most of them believed the Justice Department had become antiblack. While 72 percent said they had "depended on the Federal government a great deal for black progress" under Presidents Kennedy and Johnson, only 3 percent expressed similar faith about the commitment of the Nixon administration.[33]

---

blacks themselves. The reason most commonly cited was lack of motivation. Howard Schuman, "Free Will and Determinism in Public Beliefs about Race," in Norman R. Yetman and C. Hoy Steele, eds., *Majority and Minority: The Dynamics of Racial and Ethnic Relations* (Allyn and Bacon, 1971), p. 390.

30. Harris Survey, published in *Chicago Tribune*, April 11, 1977.

31. Institute for Social Research Survey reported in *New York Times*, August 18, 1975.

32. Angus Campbell, *White Attitudes Toward Black People* (Institute for Social Research, 1971), pp. 130–31.

33. Louis Harris, *The Anguish of Change* (Norton, 1973), pp. 231, 232, 240.

*Skepticism*

When the busing issue arose in the 1970s, then, the public was not only uninterested in further desegregation but also skeptical about the national government and the nation's schools. Most respondents to a question in a 1974 survey, for example, said that the "people in power" no longer cared about ordinary people, a severe erosion of confidence since 1966, when the same question was asked. More than two-thirds of the public believed that the government had "consistently lied to the American people over the last ten years."[34]

Nor was there much public confidence in the school system. A Gallup poll conducted in late 1973 showed, for instance, that the general level of dissatisfaction with schools had risen from a low of 18 percent to 29 percent in just seven years. It was highest in the largest cities, reaching 40 percent in cities of over a million people and 34 percent in those of half a million to a million.[35] Although a 1966 Harris Survey found that 61 percent of the people had "a great deal of confidence" in education, in 1972 only 31 percent held similarly positive views. Much of the southern desegregation had taken place in an atmosphere of public support for education and rapidly growing national aid. Both were diminishing when the issue came up in the big cities of the North and the West.

Things were even worse by the mid-1970s. Only one-eighth of the respondents rated the schools as excellent in 1975 and 1976 surveys. The young and the college-educated were even more critical. People were most concerned, as they had been for seven of the eight previous years, about the lack of discipline in public schools.[36] Conditions could hardly have been less favorable for launching a governmentally imposed racial change in the public schools.


*A Consensus Forms*

Busing became a national issue distinct from school integration in the late 1960s and early 1970s. The major developments took place between 1970 and 1972, a period that brought the first major urban court orders, the first decisions in the North, the threat of suburban desegregation, and a presidential campaign emphasizing the issue.

34. Patrick Cadell survey, reported in *New York Times,* April 15, 1974.
35. *Gallup Opinion Index* (December 1973), p. 25.
36. Gallup polls, as reported in *New York Times,* December 17, 1975, and September 21, 1976.

At first public opinion about busing was confused. Basically the same question, if worded differently, produced different answers. By the early seventies opposition had become intense on virtually any question touching on busing.

The shift from indecision to polarized opposition is shown in two Harris Surveys. One, in 1971, found that Americans were willing to have their children bused for court-ordered desegregation by a slim 47–41 percent majority. The next year, during the presidential primary campaigns, opponents outnumbered supporters almost 3–1.[37]

The early Gallup polls asked the question differently and got a more negative response. In 1970 and 1971 Gallup asked whether people supported "busing of Negro and white school children from one school district to another." The question not only neglected to say why they were bused but also could be read as referring to city-suburban cross-district busing. Because it ignored the goal, integration, respondents did not have to make the difficult choice. In both years less than one-fifth of the public supported busing.[38] Thus interpretation of many of the early polls is complicated because the questions contained misleading, inaccurate, or emotionally laden words like "racial balance" and "enforced busing" but rarely stated the reason for busing.[39]

These subtleties, however, mattered less after the antibusing consensus formed. By the time of the 1972 election, responses were overwhelmingly negative even when the question was carefully phrased:[40]

In areas where the courts have found unlawful segregation of white and black school children the courts have ordered desegregation, including busing where necessary, so that whites and blacks will not be kept from attending school together. Do you favor or oppose such busing?

| Favor | Oppose | No opinion |
|-------|--------|------------|
| 21%   | 70%    | 9%         |

Numerous surveys since that time have shown similar polarization. A February 1976 national poll, for example, found that 71 percent, when asked if they favored "racial integration of the schools . . . even if it requires busing," were opposed.[41]

37. Peter Gall, *Desegregation: How Schools Are Meeting the Historic Challenge* (Arlington, Va.: National School Public Relations Association, 1973), p. 7.

38. *Gallup Opinion Index* (September 1971), p. 20.

39. "Racial balance" was described as the goal of busing in a Harris Survey cited in *School Busing*, Hearings before Subcommittee No. 5 of the House Committee on the Judiciary, 92:2 (GPO, 1972), p. 1751; "enforced busing" was used in Watts and Free, eds., *State of the Nation*, p. 100.

40. U.S. Commission on Civil Rights, "Public Knowledge and Busing Opposition" (1973; processed), p. A-1.

41. New York Times–CBS Survey, *New York Times*, February 13, 1976. Similar

### Causes of the Opposition

Obviously the question of busing raises a distinctive set of fears and beliefs. Available data permit analysis of some of these fears and speculation about others.

People are deeply divided, for instance, about the consequences of desegregation for education and for improving race relations. A 1971 Gallup poll showed that people believed that integration improved education for blacks, but only by a relatively narrow majority of four to three. Most respondents thought it had not helped white children: fewer than one in four thought integrated schools were better for whites,[42] and a large number were convinced that education was downgraded for whites. A 1971 poll found that only 15 percent of whites thought court-ordered integration had a good effect on children in general and 60 percent believed it had a bad effect. Two out of three blacks believed the opposite.[43] When asked in 1972 whether the Supreme Court had "ordered busing in spite of evidence that it would harm a child's ability to learn," 41 percent of the respondents thought the Court had done this, and only 31 percent disagreed. When asked whether "white students' test scores have fallen sharply in desegregated schools," more than one-fourth of the respondents, both white and black, thought this had happened. Public confusion was evident also in the large numbers of people unable to express an opinion on these issues. Those who believed that white students' scores had dropped sharply after desegregation were more than twice as likely to oppose integration as those who did not.[44]

Many people had accepted as true the claims of busing critics. The majority of both whites and blacks, for instance, thought that busing expenses were more than ten times the actual average local cost. Although the cost was usually about 2 percent or less of a school system's budget, six people in seven polled in 1972 thought it was at least 25 percent. Only one

---

results were reported in a May 1976 *Washington Post* poll, which found 76 percent opposition; *Washington Post*, May 16, 1976.

42. Stanley Elam, ed., *The Gallup Polls of Attitudes Toward Education, 1969–1973* (Bloomington, Ind.: Phi Delta Kappa, 1973), pp. 112–13.

43. Opinion Research Corporation poll data reported in Sandra Kenyon Schwartz and David C. Schwartz, "Convergence and Divergence in Political Orientations between Blacks and Whites: 1960–1973," *Journal of Social Issues*, vol. 32 (Spring 1976), p. 66.

44. Opinion Research Corporation, "Public Knowledge and Attitudes Regarding School Busing," report to Commission on Civil Rights, November 1972 (processed), p. 27.

person in six could correctly answer more than half of a short list of true-false factual questions about busing; two out of five either got every question wrong or answered only one correctly. The skewed results, the Civil Rights Commission concluded, showed that people had been actively and successfully "misinformed" about the issue by public leadership. The more accurate a citizen's information, the more likely he or she was to oppose antibusing legislation.[45]

In view of public concern about discipline in all schools and antibusing speeches about endangering children, one would expect whites to fear disorder or danger to children in ghetto schools. A 1977 survey in Los Angeles found that 65 percent of white respondents believed that "deseg-regation will risk the safety of students."[46]


## The Persisting Dilemma

Poll data that consistently show three out of four people against a policy suggest firm, polarized opinion on an issue. The important thing to remember in this case, however, is that these strongly held attitudes coexist with continued affirmation of integrated education as a national goal. The condition for achieving closed minds about busing is success in insisting that it and integration are separate issues.

Virtually all of the court decisions and voluntary local plans, however, are based on exactly the opposite conclusion—that busing is the *only* available way to end urban segregation. In the cities, the courts have found, the issues cannot be separated.

When the Opinion Research Corporation in 1972 asked questions forcing respondents to choose between busing and segregation, its field staff encountered stiff resistance to answering them. Administering the questions took twice as long as normal and many respondents asked the interviewers to stop the interview and note that they were not prejudiced.[47] The answers to the questions were far more complex than those produced by most polls. Although only 21 percent of the respondents favored busing when asked about the question in a general way, a follow-up question showed that another 15 percent would support using existing school buses on new routes

45. Ibid.
46. Los Angeles Unified School District, "Results of L.A.U.S.D. Survey," submitted to the Superior Court for the County of Los Angeles, June 6, 1977 (processed).
47. Comments made to author by Frederick Mason, vice-president, Opinion Research Corporation, November 1972.

Table 4-2. *Public Attitudes toward Integration and Busing, 1974*
Percent

| Policy favored | All respondents | Black respondents |
|---|---|---|
| Integration, even with long-distance busing | 6 | 18 |
| Maximum integration with short-distance busing | 16 | 14 |
| Voluntary open enrollment and busing | 20 | 25 |
| Neighborhood schools | 50 | 33 |
| Don't know | 8 | 10 |

Source: Potomac Associates poll conducted by Gallup, reported in Watts and Free, *State of the Nation 1974*, pp. 109–10.

to increase integration. (This would accomplish substantial desegregation in many districts.) Among those still opposed, another 7 percent said that they would support busing as a "last resort" if they were convinced that there was no other way to overcome unlawful segregation.[48] In the end, more people supported some kind of busing, under some conditions, than opposed it. Among blacks, 71 percent favored some busing if essential for desegregation and 16 percent opposed (some had no opinion).

Related questions were asked in a 1974 survey examining preferred policies on education and race (table 4-2). Forty-two percent of the respondents supported some kind of busing and 50 percent supported a strict neighborhood school policy. A 1972 Harris Survey showed that a major factor in the strong opposition of whites to busing was the fear of reverse busing of white children into central city ghetto and barrio schools. The pollsters found that although three-fourths of the public opposed busing in general only 46 percent opposed one-way busing.[49]

There is little evidence to support the assertion that either busing per se or attachment to neighborhood schools was the cause of white opposition. A 1975 Harris Survey reported that 74 percent of the respondents were opposed to "busing school children to achieve racial balance." The survey also discovered, however, that the children of many of the parents who responded critically were already being bused for other reasons (52 percent of public school students in the United States ride the bus to school). By a 9–1 majority, these parents reported that busing was convenient; seven in

48. Commission on Civil Rights, "Public Knowledge and Busing Opposition," p. 9.
49. Schwartz and Schwartz, "Convergence and Divergence," pp. 157, 158.

Table 4-3. *Preferred Means of Achieving Integration in Schools, 1973 and 1975*

Percent

| Policy favored | 1973 | 1975 |
|---|---|---|
| Low-income housing in middle-income neighborhoods | 22 | 18 |
| Alter school boundaries | 27 | 31 |
| Busing | 5 | 4 |
| Do something else | 22 | 19 |
| No opinion | 17 | 11 |
| Oppose integration | 18 | 17 |

Sources: *Gallup Opinion Index*, October 1973, p. 14, and February 1976, p. 10.

eight expressed general satisfaction with their children's busing.[50] In other words, when people were asked about desegregation, they said they were really only opposed to busing, but when they were asked about busing, they said that it was fine unless it was required for integration.

A very different set of questions asked by the Gallup poll in 1973 and 1975 showed that though busing had little intrinsic appeal most people still wanted to do something to achieve integration in urban schools. When asked "Which, if any, of these ways do you think would be best to achieve integration in public school?" only about one-sixth of the respondents opposed integration (table 4-3). Given the choice of doing something other than busing—and the question clearly implied that there was a feasible choice—most preferred not to rely on buses. (This survey has frequently been cited on the floor of Congress as proof that 95 percent of the public opposes busing. However, the questions were not actually about busing but about *preferred* means to achieve integrated education.) Almost one-fifth of the respondents said they were prepared to support a change in housing policy calling for building low-income housing in middle class communities and almost one-third would support altering school boundaries to increase integration.

Boundary changes are nearly always part of a desegregation plan and are often sufficient for small communities. In large cities, however, such changes tend both to leave most schools segregated and to accelerate racial transition in the neighborhoods immediately adjoining the ghetto, intensifying the very process that undermines stable integration. Constructing

50. Harris Survey, news release, October 2, 1975.

low-income housing in any neighborhood has been extremely difficult since the Nixon administration shut down the major low-income programs in 1973. If these factors had been included in the Gallup questions, the pattern of opinion on busing would almost certainly have been more ambiguous.

Taken together, these surveys show that a great many people wish to do something but that most are reluctant to accept the idea that busing is necessary. For most Americans, the busing issue remains separate from the question of integration.

Some of the basic assumptions, propounded by officials and widely accepted by the public, can be summarized quickly. Busing is very costly. It consumes dollars that could otherwise be spent on educational improvements. It damages the education of white middle class students and does not help minority students. Often it produces increased racial hostility. It tends to speed white flight and urban resegregation. Many of the busing plans are arbitrary and irrational schemes imposed by federal judges with no interest in education. Busing, in short, is described as an extremely expensive, irrational, disruptive, and counterproductive policy. Little wonder that millions of Americans have said they support integration but reject this apparently infeasible approach.

But the dilemma remains. Housing segregation is so severe and demographic trends so unfavorable that busing is the only way to achieve integration for the foreseeable future in many communities. Often the only choice is the one people most wish to avoid—busing or segregation.

# 5

# Is Busing Practical?

IF BUSING is not a feasible policy, the courts have made a gigantic mistake. In an area where there are so many sweeping statements and so few summaries of experience, it is essential to sort out the elements of the antibusing critique and examine the available evidence, one issue at a time. If one sets preconceptions aside, it should soon become evident that the public debate has only a passing connection with the findings of social scientists and the technical information from cities where busing plans are in operation.

## Busing and the Educational Process

Perhaps the most devastating criticism of urban busing plans is that they do not help minority children but do harm middle class students. This assertion is often backed by the claim that *Brown*, the 1954 Supreme Court decision, was based on "social science proof" that racial segregation was educationally harmful and that that premise has now been disproved by better research.

Before examining this criticism, one issue deserves brief attention. Many people who support school integration but oppose busing assume that simply transporting a student to a new school has an adverse educational impact, an impact that is separate from the normal educational effects of integration.

A federally sponsored 1973 study of desegregation in 555 recently desegregated southern school districts, however, found "no evidence that busing per se has any negative consequences." In fact, it reported, there was evidence that race relations were somewhat better in schools where white

students were bused in, and "no evidence that attending *one's own* neighborhood school has any effects, positive or negative, on a school's achievement levels or social climate."[1]

A 1975 review by Weinberg of other studies concludes that the research
is "quite limited" but that "there seems to be little or no reason to believe
that busing children to a newly-desegregated school would have a different
impact on students' academic performance than creating a desegregated
school by re-drawing attendance boundaries or by pairing of schools."[2]

The existing evidence, in other words, strongly suggests that "busing"
is not the issue. Rather it is desegregation, and the research problem is one
of assessing how well desegregation works in diverse urban settings.

The criticism of urban school integration was reinforced by two nationally publicized articles. A 1972 article by David Armor has frequently been
cited as proof that "busing has failed."[3] In a 1975 article, James Coleman,
principal author of the famous 1966 "Coleman report,"[4] announced that his
new research convinced him that urban desegregation was counterproductive.[5]

The actual assertions made by Armor and Coleman are quite different
from those often ascribed to them.[6] Armor concludes that school desegregation does not eliminate the gap between rates of academic achievement
in the first year of the integration process and may increase race consciousness among students. Since he believes that his findings differ from those
presumably underlying the *Brown* decision, he opposes urban desegregation plans.[7] But the *Brown* decision included no findings about academic
achievement and no promise of better test scores.

1. James A. Davis, "Busing," in *Southern Schools: An Evaluation of the Effects of
the Emergency School Assistance Program and of School Desegregation* (Chicago:
National Opinion Research Center, 1973), vol. 2, p. 118.

2. Meyer Weinberg, "The Relationship between School Desegregation and Academic Achievement: A Review of the Research," *Law and Contemporary Problems,*
vol. 39 (Spring 1975), p. 268.

3. David Armor, "The Evidence on Busing," *Public Interest* (Summer 1972), pp.
90–126.

4. James S. Coleman and associates, *Equality of Educational Opportunity* (GPO,
1966).

5. James S. Coleman, Sara D. Kelley, and John A. Moore, *Trends in School Segregation, 1968–1973* (Urban Institute, 1975). This paper was initially publicized in several
draft versions which were far more critical of desegregation policy than the final study
was.

6. For instance, in editorials in *Dallas Morning News,* June 6, 1975; *Richmond
News Leader,* May 1, 1975; and *Boston Herald-American,* May 25, 1975. These are
reprinted in Judith F. Buncher, ed., *The School Busing Controversy: 1970–75* (New
York: Facts on File, 1975), pp. 260–61.

7. Armor, "Evidence on Busing," p. 95.

Sorting out the confusion about Coleman's research is more complex since Coleman directed two totally different kinds of research projects. In his 1966 study, survey and test data from students and teachers across the country were used to try to measure inequalities between black and white schools and to evaluate the educational impact of integration. Coleman's findings then were surprising: in most easily measurable dimensions, black schools outside the South were not notably different from white schools in resources, teacher training, funds spent, and other tangible measures. He also reported that racial integration had little effect on education.

The study suggested that the only way to significantly increase the performance of poor children was to put them in a class with middle class children from families with higher educational levels. This indirectly supported integration since a disproportionate number of minority children were poor and whites were largely middle class. The study concluded, however, that in the best of circumstances the educational results were limited.[8] Coleman subsequently testified in behalf of integration in some areas, but the courts relied on his study in only one major case, that of Washington, D.C.[9]

Coleman's second piece of desegregation research, in 1975, had nothing to do with educational effects and was a lesser undertaking. He attempted to demonstrate a statistical relation between desegregation and increased white flight from the cities. In the resulting study,[10] Coleman claimed that desegregation accelerated white flight from the city schools, but only in the twenty-two largest cities and only in the first year of desegregation. Coleman's articles set off a fierce academic debate on white flight, but they had nothing to do with education and did not disprove the findings of his 1966 study.

### The Education of White Children

If the claim that the quality of education deteriorates for white children in desegregated schools were accurate, civil rights advocates would be asking for something extraordinary: that white parents accept lower-quality education for their children in order to correct the effects of discrimination in earlier generations.

There are many confusing and hotly contested issues in the educational research on desegregation, but this is not one of them. There is clear evi-

---

8. Coleman and associates, *Equality of Educational Opportunity*.

9. *Hobson* v. *Hansen*, 269 F. Supp. 401 (D.D.C. 1967).

10. James S. Coleman, "Liberty and Equality in School Desegregation," *Social Policy*, vol. 6 (January–February 1976), pp. 9–13.

dence that school desegregation has no significant effect on the academic achievement of middle class children. If there were contrary evidence the courts would doubtless give it serious consideration. The Supreme Court recognized the issue in its first decision on big city desegregation: "an objection to transportation of students may have validity when the time or distance of travel is so great as to risk either the health of the children or significantly impinge on the educational process."[11]

The 1966 Coleman report found that whites were substantially less affected by the particular school they attended than most minority children; southern blacks were most affected. There was a different sensitivity to school variations, "with the lowest achieving minority groups showing highest sensitivity." The proportion of white students in a school had no significant effect on white students' achievement.[12]

Thus, if a white pupil from a home that is strongly and effectively supportive of education is put in a school where most pupils do not come from such homes, his achievement will be little different than if he were in a school composed of others like himself. But if a minority pupil from a home without much educational strength is put with schoolmates with strong educational backgrounds, his achievement is likely to increase.[13]

The Coleman report, in general, found that schools are less important to all students, particularly middle class children, than many had hoped. The middle class family is, by all odds, the most effective educational institution in our society. Schools are relatively more important for lower class students. Enrollment in poor ghetto schools can depress achievement levels; enrollment in predominantly middle class schools may narrow the gap between the average achievement levels of minority children and those of white children.

A major reanalysis of the strength of home influences on academic achievement by Harvard Professor Marshall S. Smith concluded that the Coleman report had actually underestimated the influence of the family on achievement levels, particularly for white children. Smith concluded that, for white high school students, two-thirds of the variation in achievement levels between schools was related to the different home environments of the individual students tested, and the figure was only half as high for blacks.[14]

---

11. *Swann* v. *Charlotte-Mecklenburg Board of Education,* 402 U.S. 1 at 30 (1971).
12. Coleman and associates, *Equality of Educational Opportunity,* pp. 22, 297, 325.
13. Ibid., p. 22.
14. Marshall S. Smith, "Equality of Educational Opportunity: The Basic Findings Reconsidered," in Frederick Mosteller and Daniel P. Moynihan, eds., *On Equality of Educational Opportunity* (Random House, 1972), pp. 230–342, 312.

Christopher Jencks's book, *Inequality*, infuriated educators by amassing evidence to argue that changes in the schools have little effect either on achievement levels or on the career patterns of students. Although Jencks is philosophically opposed to large-scale busing plans, he found that desegregation did have a limited positive effect on the education of blacks and that whites were virtually unaffected by it.[15] Jencks wrote later: "Educational researchers have almost never found that white students' test scores actually fell as a result of being in desegregated schools. Nonetheless, both blacks and many whites have been proclaiming the inferiority of schools in black neighborhoods for a generation, so it is not surprising that many white parents believe the difference important."[16]

Since the publication of his 1972 article, David Armor has appeared as an expert witness on behalf of school boards in a number of communities fighting desegregation. In his 1972 testimony at the Senate hearings on anti-busing legislation, however, he conceded that the evidence showed "no worsening of achievement for white students" as a result of busing.[17]

Scholarly surveys of the desegregation literature reinforce these conclusions. A 1970 study by Meyer Weinberg examined scores of studies and reported, "The evidence is even stronger that white children fail to suffer any learning disadvantage from desegregation."[18]

In her comprehensive 1975 survey of the literature, Nancy St. John concluded that desegregation had little if any effect on white achievement.

The longitudinal data from desegregating school systems . . . indicate in every case that racial mixture in the schools had no negative consequences for majority group pupils. In busing experiments in which selected central city children are transported to outlying communities the universal report also is no significant difference in achievement between children in classrooms that do or do not receive bused pupils. . . . It should be noted, however, that in almost all these experiments, white children remained in the majority in their schools and classrooms.[19]

It remained an "open question," she said, whether white children would have lower scores in classes with more than half black enrollment.[20] (A

15. Christopher Jencks and associates, *Inequality: A Reassessment of the Effect of Family and Schooling in America* (Basic Books, 1972), pp. 105–06.

16. Christopher Jencks, "Busing—The Supreme Court Goes North," in Nicolaus Mills, ed., *The Great School Bus Controversy* (Teachers College Press, 1973), p. 18.

17. *Equal Educational Opportunities Act of 1972*, Hearings before the Subcommittee on Education of the Senate Committee on Labor and Public Welfare (GPO, 1972), p. 1196.

18. *Desegregation Research: An Appraisal*, 2d ed. (Bloomington, Ind.: Phi Delta Kappa, 1970), p. 88.

19. Nancy H. St. John, *School Desegregation: Outcomes for Children* (Wiley, 1975), p. 35.

20. Ibid., pp. 35–36.

1975 analysis by researchers at the Federal Reserve Board in Philadelphia did report some crude evidence of low white performance in majority black schools.[21]) Researchers at the National Opinion Research Center noted the possibility of some negative effects on the morale and achievement of white students attending ghetto schools.[22]

Various scholars have also noted cases where there have been positive effects for white students, probably resulting from general educational improvements adopted at the same time as desegregation. St. John reported several studies showing clear white gains.[23] A study by Pettigrew and others noted simultaneous increases in both white and black achievement levels in some districts and offered the following explanation:

the achievement of white and especially of black children in desegregated schools is generally higher when some of the following critical conditions are met: equal racial access to the school's resources; *classroom*—not just school—desegregation; the initiation of desegregation in the early grades; interracial staffs; substantial rather than token student desegregation; the maintenance of or increase in school services and remedial training; and the avoidance of strict ability grouping.[24]

All the evidence is not yet in on whether desegregation affects the educational achievement of white students. Further research may well strengthen existing evidence that the way the desegregation process is handled and the school's *educational* response to its reconstituted student body make a significant difference.

What is remarkable, however, is the consistency of the finding that the desegregation process itself has little if any effect on the educational success of white students, as measured by achievement test scores. (Only when whites are sent to heavily minority ghetto schools is there any ambiguity in this result.) Researchers operating from very different scholarly and ideological starting points support this general finding. Unlike research on other vexing social policy questions, these data present almost a model of consensus.

The commonsense question remains. If the findings are so clear, why are

21. Anita A. Summers and Barbara L. Wolfe, "Equality of Educational Opportunity Quantified: A Production Function Approach," Philadelphia Fed Research Papers (1975; processed), p. 20. This study suffered from a variety of severe methodological weaknesses and its findings should be regarded as highly tentative. In any case, few desegregation plans assign whites to predominantly minority schools.

22. Davis, "Busing," p. 118.

23. *School Desegregation*, pp. 157–62.

24. Thomas F. Pettigrew, Elizabeth L. Useem, Clarence Normand, and Marshall S. Smith, "Busing: A Review of 'The Evidence,'" in Mills, ed., *Great School Bus Controversy*, p. 148.

so many white parents and political leaders convinced that the opposite is true? First, as Jencks points out, most are probably convinced that ghetto schools are inferior places to be. Sometimes they identify the quality of the school with its physical structure. People tend to think of schools as places, not as social institutions made up of children, teachers, and administrators. Rarely do they reflect that their children will actually be going to a new school. Although the school will have the same name and location, it will be restructured in the two things that most influence classroom learning —the composition of the student body and the background of the teachers.

The best recent research shows that the integration process is a long-term one, with changes cumulating over the years. The major national studies published recently strongly suggest that the results depend on how well the individual school handles the changes associated with desegregation.

An important multiyear study was summarized by the Educational Testing Service in a July 1976 report. The study concluded that techniques such as teaching about the contribution of each racial group and assigning children to integrated groups for study and play in school improved racial attitudes. The process worked best where there was strong leadership by the principal, teachers supported the goal of integration, and techniques to minimize racial conflicts were used. Another important 1976 report, by the System Development Corporation, found similar relationships in a different set of schools studied over several years. The report concluded, for instance, that improvement in attitude was closely related to the number of years a student had attended an integrated school.[25] In other words, evidence was accumulating that the *way* the process was handled in the schools made an important difference.

Though it is possible to state with some confidence that desegregation does not hurt students and though we are beginning to understand the complexity of the process, it is not possible to describe the positive educational effects accurately. This is true for several reasons.

1. Evaluation research is still in a primitive phase and seldom reports significant results from any educational program.

2. Though desegregation studies show positive results, most are so poorly designed that one can have no confidence in their findings.

25. Garlie A. Forehand, Marjorie Ragosta, and Donald A. Rock, "Final Report: Conditions and Processes of Effective School Desegregation" (Princeton, N.J.: Educational Testing Service, 1976; processed). John E. Coulson, "National Evaluation of the Emergency School Aid Act (ESAA)" (Santa Monica: System Development Corp., 1976; processed).

3. Desegregation usually is carried out with little educational planning and is assessed only during the transitional year—before any major educational changes have taken place and during the time of maximum tension.

4. Most studies have taken districts as a whole, but evidence now suggests that research must be focused on schools and classrooms.

5. Most of the research has been limited to traditional issues—test scores, self-concept, and so forth—leaving virtually untouched such questions as the impact of integrated schools on higher education, careers, adult racial attitudes, and residential integration.

The National Assessment of Educational Progress, the only organization to measure educational trends nationwide, has recently produced some studies that may reflect the long-term impact of desegregation. Its 1976 reports on achievement in reading and science both single out young southern blacks as making stronger relative progress than either whites or blacks in other regions. Between 1969 and 1973 they showed a 2.8 percent gain in science achievement while northern blacks declined 3.5 percent; whites also declined. Blacks performed best in schools with large white majorities. The report on reading showed that almost all the national gains in primary school reading levels during the 1971–75 period took place in the South, where the scores of young black students rose four times as fast as those of whites, substantially shrinking the black-white achievement gap.[26] These changes cannot now be directly linked to desegregation, but eventually they may be.

A 1977 report on research conducted in school districts across the nation found consistent and substantial educational gains when desegregation had existed since the first grade.[27] Confirmation of this analysis could have major policy implications.


### Violence

A critic might well concede that a child would have the same test score in a desegregated school and yet oppose the policy, fearing the new school might be dangerous.

Although the fear of violence often plays a large role in local debates

26. National Assessment of Educational Progress, *Science Achievement: Racial and Regional Trends, 1969–73* (GPO, 1976), pp. 19–26; *Reading in America: A Perspective on Two Assessments* (GPO, 1976), pp. 10, 25–26.

27. Robert L. Crain and Rita E. Mahard, "Desegregation and Black Achievement," paper prepared for the National Review Panel on School Desegregation Research, October 1977 (to be published in a forthcoming issue of *Law and Contemporary Problems*).

over desegregation plans, a recent Justice Department report indicates that desegregation seldom produces increases in school violence and even lowers the level when a local plan specifically addresses the problem. (The alternative to desegregation plans—"natural" desegregation in interracial neighborhoods—is often tense because the neighborhoods are not yet integrated but merely in transition.) The Community Relations Service of the Justice Department has had experience with this issue in hundreds of communities. Its director in 1976, Assistant Attorney General Ben Holman, reported that most schools and many entire school districts had experienced no injuries related to desegregation. The Detroit school system had fewer racial incidents after desegregation than before. Even in Boston, where resistance was high, only two high schools had a significant in-school problem and only one person was hospitalized overnight.[28] Holman found that students usually adjusted rapidly to desegregated schools, particularly at the elementary level. Most of the violence was among adults outside the school and it diminished after the transition.[29]

A survey of almost a thousand school superintendents by the Commission on Civil Rights turned up little evidence of serious violence accompanying desegregation. Only one district in fifteen had required additional police help, and most of them were back to normal within two months. Very few educators reported that educational activities had been disrupted for more than two weeks.[30] Problems are apt to be greatest during the first year when older, formerly segregated children are first brought together in a school. Attention from the media and the public usually focuses on such schools.

Although school violence is a serious national problem, there is little evidence to show either that desegregation causes it or that reverse busing puts white students in physical danger. Perhaps the national concern about violence, reinforced by 1975 Senate hearings and white parents' fears of ghetto conditions after the riots of the 1960s, help explain an apprehension that does not appear to be related to desegregation experience.[31] There is

28. Letter from Assistant Attorney General Ben Holman to Senators Edward Brooke and Jacob Javits, June 10, 1976, with attachments; reprinted in *Congressional Record* (daily edition), June 26, 1976, pp. S10708–11.

29. Ibid.

30. U.S. Commission on Civil Rights, *Fulfilling the Letter and Spirit of the Law: Desegregation of the Nation's Public Schools* (GPO, 1976), pp. 145–46.

31. Wide publicity was given to the hearings and the report of the Subcommittee on Juvenile Delinquency of the Senate Committee on the Judiciary, issued in April 1975. The report included discussion of the possible connection between desegregation and increased school violence in the South as well as of gang activities in some large

no evidence to show that busing plans are impractical because of physical danger to students in their new schools.

## National Student Transportation

Despite the belief of most Americans that busing for desegregation is massive, expensive, and abnormal, it is a small part of the national student transportation enterprise, which is itself a minor segment of the vast undertaking of public education. Quite apart from desegregation, the majority of American children do not walk to school; they ride, usually on a school bus.

School busing has been increasing steadily for decades, much of it caused by the movement of white families into thinly populated areas. By the 1973–74 school year 52 percent of all public school students rode buses. The annual cost was $1.9 billion, about $87 a student. Buses were driven more than 2 billion miles a year. In addition, more than 600,000 children were bused to private schools at public expense.[32]

More than half of all public school children were bused by 1971 in twenty-five states. In only two states, North Dakota and Louisiana, did busing cost as much as one-sixteenth of school expenditures. In the large industrial states busing usually cost a much lower fraction. According to estimates prepared by federal officials, the effect of desegregation plans on the growth of school busing nationally was minor. No one had precise figures. One guess by the National Institute of Education in 1976 was that integration might account for one bus in eight.[33] This estimate is probably high.

Schools within walking distance were the exception rather than the rule in the United States by the late 1960s. By 1969–70 about two-fifths of students were bused, one-sixth were driven in cars, others rode public transportation, and one in fifty drove his or her own car. Younger children were

---

urban districts. *Our Nation's Schools—A Report Card: 'A' in School Violence and Vandalism*, 95:1 (GPO, 1975). Since the late 1960s fear of crime has figured significantly in surveys of urban attitudes.

32. Department of Health, Education, and Welfare, National Center for Educational Statistics, "Statistics of State School Systems," in table accompanying letters to Senators Edward Brooke and Jacob Javits from W. Vance Grant, April 14, 1976, and to Senator Brooke from Secretary of Transportation William Coleman, Jr., May 4, 1976.

33. U.S. Department of Transportation, "Report on School Busing," submitted to U.S. Commission on Civil Rights, March 10, 1972; National Institute of Education, "Statistics on Selected Desegregation Issues" (1976; processed).

somewhat more likely to live within a mile of school, but the majority did not. Seven in ten elementary students and four-fifths of older children were more than ten minutes from school by 1969.[34]

Children in private schools had to travel farther—much farther at the high school level where 81 percent lived over two miles from school.[35]

Busing for the segregated private schools of the South was particularly striking. These schools, dubbed "segregation academies" by the Southern Regional Council, usually not only had narrower curricula, fewer certified teachers, and inferior facilities, but required more busing as well. While fewer than half the public school students in eight southern states were bused in 1970, the average segregated private school bused 62 percent. Moreover, the bus rides to maintain segregation were more than 70 percent longer on the average. An intensive study of Florida in the 1970s found a similar pattern in private schools that bused children of opponents of busing.[36]

Contrary to public belief, fewer than half of all children in elementary school and only about one-fourth of the older students attend the kind of school so often described in the busing debates—the neighborhood school within a mile of home where a mother can "run over" if her child is hurt. (Since two-fifths of the mothers are away from home working, this picture is not especially apt in any case.)

Before any big city desegregated, schools operated about a quarter of a million buses. Such an enormous national enterprise demonstrates the importance school boards and state legislators have attached to getting isolated students to schools that can offer better programs than the old one-room schoolhouse. Much of this effort is for the benefit of children from upper income suburban families who have chosen to live in areas of such low density that neighborhood schools are impossible and who frequently demand additional buses for safety and convenience. During the five years after court-ordered busing began, the annual increase in the nation's school bus fleet was exactly the same as during the previous five years,[37] but the public reaction was completely different.

Statistics on the huge increases in busing before desegregation show that

34. Department of Transportation, Federal Highway Administration, *Transportation Characteristics of School Children*, National Personal Transportation Study, Report 4 (GPO, 1972), pp. 7, 10–15.

35. Ibid., p. 23.

36. Everett Cataldo, Douglas Gatlin, and Micheal Giles, "Determinants of Resegregation: Compliance/Rejection Behavior and Policy Alternatives," report to National Science Foundation (November 9, 1973; processed), pp. 22–23.

37. Statistics submitted to Senator Brooke by Secretary Coleman, May 4, 1976.

busing in itself was not objectionable. Busing doubled during the 1930s, grew 70 percent in the 1940s, and increased between 1950 and 1960 by more than a third. In the 1960s, however, the rate of increase was much lower, and the proportion of school funds spent on busing declined slightly between 1965 and 1971.[38]

The attack on the expense of busing was full of ironies. Although busing was expanding most rapidly in regions where there were few desegregation plans, there was no attack there. More than fifteen states, including some of the largest, provided free busing to private religious schools, often crossing city-suburban boundary lines. Such service was eagerly sought and energetically defended in legislatures and the courts.[39]

### Costs

Although busing costs a relatively small fraction of school budgets, some believe that any money spent on additional buses damages a school's program and detracts from educational quality. But desegregation costs should be considered in a comparative framework. The data show, for example, that about 7 percent of all the school busing, or 152 million miles a year, is for extracurricular activities—field trips, athletic events, and other nonacademic activities. This is more than twice what the Department of Health, Education, and Welfare had estimated school desegregation would require in 1972.[40] Many states also finance much more free busing for private and parochial schools than for integration.[41]

A largely unnoticed change cost many times more than busing for desegregation. Between 1962 and 1972 the United States substantially raised school expenses by lowering the student–teacher ratio 14 percent. Since teachers' salaries accounted for some 68 percent of total school expenditures, this change alone increased school costs by more than 9 percent. Research has consistently shown that changes in this ratio, even much greater changes, have no clear effect on student achievement. Yet as student populations fell in the early 1970s, the typical local response was to protect teachers' jobs by continuing to lower the ratio.

38. MARC (Metropolitan Applied Research Center) Busing Task Force, *Fact Book* (MARC, 1972), pp. 22–24; HEW, National Center for Educational Statistics, unpublished table, 1975.

39. MARC Busing Task Force, *Fact Book*, p. 24.

40. Testimony of Secretary Elliot Richardson in *School Busing*, Hearings before Subcommittee No. 5 of the House Committee on the Judiciary, 92:2 (GPO, 1972).

41. The number of parochial and private students bused with public funds mushroomed from 146,000 in 1955 to 623,000 in the 1973–74 school year.

Another change that costs much more (about twenty times) than busing for desegregation is bilingual education. Although it has no proven educational value, it has expanded rapidly.[42]

After more than two years of study, the Senate Select Committee on Equal Educational Opportunity reported at the end of 1972 that "there is little evidence, as a general proposition, of the 'excessive busing' which has been discussed in such emotional terms."

Increases of over 20 percent in the proportion of students transported are extremely rare; and the cost of transportation even after desegregation rarely exceeds 3 percent of school district operating budgets. . . .

Transportation under court order has caused serious hardship in a number of communities, not because of the time or distance of travel, but because an insufficient supply of school buses has required schools to be placed on double or even overlapping triple sessions in order to permit existing buses to make several runs.

. . . Although increased transportation expenses are small in terms of total school operating budgets, typically no more than 1 or 2 percent, already overstrained education budgets cannot absorb these increased costs without sacrificing existing education programs.[43]

The committee published data showing that in the great majority of desegregated systems studied the total busing required was well below the average percentage of students bused in a typical district of the state for traditional reasons. In the seventeen systems studied, the average increase in transportation was 16.5 percent. Six of the systems showed increases of 10 percent or less.[44]

### Urban Busing Costs

Enough sizable cities have now carried out desegregation plans to permit some factual discussion of the costs. The Jackson, Mississippi, desegregation plan increased the operating costs of busing from 0.6 percent to 1.8 percent of the total school costs. The Nashville metropolitan plan increased costs from 2.3 to 3.8 percent. In Raleigh, the city with the South's largest 1971 increase in the percentage of students bused, the desegregation plan brought the total expenditure for busing to 1.7 percent. In Richmond the rise was from 0.4 to 1.1 percent; in Winston-Salem, from 1.8 to 4.0 percent;

42. Bilingual classrooms cost 37 percent more than normal classrooms for the average student.

43. Senate Select Committee on Equal Educational Opportunity, *Toward Equal Educational Opportunity,* Final Report, 92:2 (GPO, 1972), pp. 208–09.

44. Ibid., p. 211.

and in Roanoke the new total was 1.1 percent. Integration of the huge 400-square-mile Charlotte metropolitan system raised costs from 0.8 to 1.6 percent. In metropolitan Jacksonville the rise was from 1.3 to 2.2 percent, and in metropolitan Tampa, from 1.35 to 1.7 percent.[45] (Costs for temporary police protection and for new school programs are not included.)

A 1972 study of eleven cities showed that the average time traveled remained the same in the majority of them as for children earlier bused for traditional reasons.[46] More students were bused, but they were not bused distances considered unreasonable before desegregation.

Although the national increase in busing for desegregation has been slight, the increase has been much more visible in certain cities. At the height of southern urban desegregation in 1971, HEW pointed out that in the twenty-three largest districts carrying out desegregation plans busing levels increased 7.5 percent. Cities without desegregation plans showed an average increase of 0.7 percent during the year.[47]

The most heavily populated district now carrying out a desegregation plan that requires substantial busing is Dade County (metropolitan Miami), where a partial plan costs less than 1 percent of local school expenditures. The largest system to have a plan distributing students proportionately in all schools is Prince Georges County, Maryland, the nation's ninth largest system, where the added cost of the 1973 plan was 0.6 percent of the local school budget.[48]

Perhaps the largest school district, in physical size, to undergo desegregation is the huge Clark County, Nevada, system, which includes the city of Las Vegas. The district covers some 8,000 square miles. With more than 72,000 students spread out over an area as big as Connecticut, Rhode Island, and Delaware, it was a formidable challenge in busing logistics. Six thousand additional children were bused, but "the average distance and time of ride for most students was and remains 11 miles and 30 minutes." The additional cost to the district for the first year, including the one-time expense of buying thirty new buses, came to about 2.3 percent of the local school budget.[49]

45. Commission on Civil Rights, *School Desegregation in Ten Communities* (GPO, 1973), pp. 8, 26, 32; Senate Select Committee, *Toward Equal Educational Opportunity*, Final Report, pp. 211–12.

46. Commission on Civil Rights, *Your Child and Busing* (GPO, 1972), p. 14.

47. *School Busing*, Hearings, p. 1205.

48. Commission on Civil Rights, "Public Knowledge and Busing Opposition" (1973; processed), p. 10.

49. Commission on Civil Rights, *School Desegregation in Ten Communities*, pp. 198, 207–09.

Experience with the early desegregation orders in the North and West shows costs similar to those reported in southern cities. For example, a three-way (black-Anglo-Chicano) desegregation plan was required in Denver after the Supreme Court's 1973 decision in *Keyes*. The local plan was able to accomplish a great deal of elementary school desegregation within walking distance of pupils' homes. Only about 6,000 of the 41,000 elementary schoolchildren had to ride the bus to their new schools.[50] In early 1975 the school system's business office estimated that the additional transportation costs resulting from the court order came to about 1.6 percent of the system's budget.[51]

### Small Districts

Discussion of busing is often one-dimensional, but the technical problems of desegregation range all the way from a simple local decision in a small town to have children walk a few blocks in different directions to integrate one or two segregated schools to the prospect of great lines of buses jamming the bridges from Manhattan on the way to outer Queens or the Long Island suburbs. Little attention has been paid to the small districts that serve about two-fifths of the nation's minority students. In many, the process of desegregation can be handled with little cost and few difficulties.

One of the first northern school systems to integrate was the Chicago suburb of Evanston, where the system rezoned its schools to maximize integration, successfully turned one segregated elementary school into a magnet school,[52] and bused the remaining segregated black children to predominantly white schools. It cost 0.4 percent of the school budget. At the Martin Luther King, Jr., Laboratory School, parents throughout the city were willing to pay for their children's busing ($50 a child a semester) to take advantage of special educational programs.[53] The Evanston plan did a great deal to stabilize integration in a major community adjoining Chicago.

In the Dayton suburban school district of Jefferson Township, the cost of busing for integration was less than the saving the district was able to achieve through more efficient use of previously empty classrooms. Although the plan to desegregate the schools required the transportation of

50. *New York Times*, October 26, 1974.

51. Telephone interview with Joseph E. Brzeinski, Division of Business Services, Denver Public Schools, March 14, 1975.

52. A school with a special educational program designed to attract voluntary transfers from outside the area, thus producing integration without compulsion.

53. Commission on Civil Rights, *The Diminishing Barrier: A Report on School Desegregation in Nine Communities* (GPO, 1972), pp. 16–18.

an additional 500 of the system's 2,711 students, the district's assistant superintendent said that the cost was "more than offset by savings accomplished through released classrooms and fewer equipment and furniture outlays."[54]

Union Township, New Jersey, a community of 55,000 and a suburb of Newark, began a plan in 1969 that required busing only a few hundred additional students. Students rode an average of twenty minutes to school. From 1970 to 1972 the district's total busing costs ran 0.7 percent of the local school budget, and a substantial share of that money went to transport private and parochial children to their schools, as required by state law.[55] As in Evanston, the central feature was a plan desegregating one elementary school.

Many small city and suburban districts have only a modest desegregation problem, but the description of the issue as large and explosive affects them when they are considering integration. For these systems, however, there are no real questions of feasibility, only of political will.

### Safety

Busing is an extraordinarily safe operation. The National Highway Traffic Safety Administration reports that in 1971 the total number of passengers killed in the year-long operation of more than a quarter of a million school buses was seventeen. Estimates for 1972 were similar. During these two years deaths caused by automobiles were 54,700 and 57,000 respectively, and included a substantial number of schoolchildren walking to or from school.[56]

The safety of all buses in big cities is shown by mass transit records. Buses accounted for 15 billion passenger miles a year. In intercity travel between 1969 and 1971, for each million miles, people traveling on the airlines and the railroads were twice as likely to be killed; for those in automobiles the fatality rate was forty times greater.[57]

Riding the bus was clearly safer than walking to school, too, though exactly how much safer is difficult to determine. A study by the Pennsyl-

54. Ibid., pp. 37, 39.

55. Commission on Civil Rights, *School Desegregation in Ten Communities*, pp. 126, 128, 133–36.

56. National Highway Traffic Safety Administration, *Traffic Safety '72* (GPO, 1973), pp. 6, 32.

57. "Buses: Backbone of Urban Transit," *The American City* (December 1974), p. 23; National Association of Motor Bus Owners, *Bus Facts*, 39th ed. (NAMBO, 1972), p. 17.

vania Department of Education found that children who walked were in three times as much danger as those who rode the bus. The National Safety Council's *Accident Facts* reported in 1971 that boys and girls walking to class were two to three times as likely to have an accident.[58]

Buses could be made even safer. One sidelight of the busing controversy in Congress is the contrast between statements deploring the dangers of busing and the prolonged failure to take action on legislation to strengthen bus construction standards or on the bus safety measures strongly advocated by Senator Charles Percy of Illinois and other members of Congress. Most states had failed to respond by early 1975 to recommendations for greater safety made in 1972 and 1973 by the National Highway Traffic Safety Administration which called for higher structural standards, better brake systems, changes in injury-causing bus seats, and safety testing of buses.[59]

It is ironic that a great many parents pay to send their children to private schools in buses that are far less safe. Private and parochial schools are primary purchasers of the nearly worn-out buses disposed of by public systems after eight or nine years of use.[60]

## How Much More Busing Is Needed?

No one knows how much transportation will actually be necessary to finish the desegregation process. No one has, for that matter, even given a specific definition to "desegregation." Federal courts sometimes order desegregation of most segregated minority schools and recommend that schools adopt plans approximately reflecting the racial ratio of the district. All plans, however, allow some variance, and the Supreme Court has insisted that racial balance plans are not required. Federal and state courts have at times left a good deal of segregation in school systems.[61] In other words, the most that can possibly be required of school systems is that they approximate districtwide racial patterns in each school, but something

58. Commission on Civil Rights, "Public Knowledge and Busing Opposition," p. 11.

59. *Washington Post*, March 4, 1975; *Congressional Record*, March 28, 1974, p. 8750.

60. School Bus Task Force, in *Congressional Record*, March 28, 1974, p. 8757.

61. *Northcross* v. *Board of Education of Memphis City Schools*, 466 F.2d 890 (6th Cir. 1972), *cert. denied*, 416 U.S. 962 (1974). In this Memphis case the court of appeals approved a plan leaving 21,000 black children in segregated schools. The Supreme Court declined to review the case, permitting this segregation to continue.

less is almost always accepted and major pockets of segregation are some-times left intact.

The burden of desegregation would be considerable if all systems were completely segregated and had no buses. When most systems begin the desegregation process, however, there are not only some integration and a fleet of school buses, but also the possibility that some schools can be inte-grated by reassigning children within walking distance. Most systems also begin with some students who have been bused because they live too far away from any school or from a school that offers some special service they need. In semirural suburban counties, where virtually all the students ride to school, the solution is simply to redirect existing buses. Desegregation in a number of southern districts resulted in a net decline in busing mileage since students had previously been transported long distances to preserve the overlapping assignment areas necessary to maintain segregation.[62] The civil rights organizations litigating the case for metropolitanwide desegre-gation in Richmond concluded that city-suburban desegregation would require very little more busing than the three separate desegregation plans then in existence, in part because a number of children would be able to walk across the city-suburban boundary lines to attend desegregated schools.[63]

### Computerized Bus Routing

One difficulty is that, although some districts operate enough buses to transport the students in a small city, most run on a seat-of-the-pants basis, with little concern for maximum efficiency. Desegregation busing is often simply added to existing busing without any attempt to minimize either busing or its costs. Although HEW has financed research showing that large amounts can be saved through computerized bus routing, few districts make a serious effort to minimize the expenditure of money and time.

It is difficult, of course, to quantify all the issues that eventually enter into transportation decisions. Many decisions are political—for instance, a response to parents who organize to demand additional bus service across "dangerous" streets or highways even though children live close to school.

---

62. Figures prepared by the Atlanta regional office of HEW, reported in *Equal Educational Opportunity*, Hearings before the Senate Select Committee on Equal Edu-cational Opportunity, 91:2 (GPO, 1970), pp. 1777–78.

63. *Bradley* v. *State Board of Education*, Brief for Petitioners, no. 72-550 (1973), p. 69.

The definition of "dangerous" is more often determined by the effectiveness of community demands than by some objective standard. The whole design of desegregation plans is often political. All else being equal, school officials are likely to place most of the burden of busing on the least influential segments of the community.

Despite this, several attempts have been made with computers to find the most efficient way to achieve urban desegregation. They suggest that far less *additional* busing would be required to produce integrated schools than is commonly claimed.

THE LAMBDA REPORT. The first such study was done by a Washington-area research organization in 1971. After the Supreme Court's first busing decision, HEW officials contracted with the Lambda Corporation, a group of former Pentagon systems analysts, for estimates of how much desegregation could be accomplished with a minimum of additional busing. The resulting report, the group's preliminary analysis of forty-four major urban areas of the country, suggested that busing was often a false issue. In most communities busing was already substantial, and rerouting the existing buses could achieve almost total desegregation.[64]

Some HEW officials hoped to use the research to show that the whole busing debate had been misdirected. Others, including the department's top leaders, used it in an attempt to justify the President's proposed restrictions on additional busing by suggesting that desegregation really could be accomplished even if busing were restrained. Eventually, however, the President and the House of Representatives carried this beyond concern about the amount of busing to absolute restrictions on where the buses could go, tacitly conceding that it was the level of desegregation not of busing they were concerned with.

The Lambda report, according to the project director, showed that "the existing school assignments are exaggerating the racial isolation rather than contributing toward desegregation." Another finding was that "with very little additional busing it is possible to greatly increase the amount of desegregation in the schools."[65]

Even in the largest cities analyzed, almost complete elimination of segregation in the schools seems possible without exceeding practical limits for student travel time or economically reasonable limits on the number of students bused. The

64. Testimony of George Pugh (Lambda Corporation), *Equal Educational Opportunities Act*, Hearings before the House Committee on Education and Labor, 92:2 (GPO, 1972), pp. 643, 645.

65. Ibid., p. 645.

analysis also shows that in most school districts very substantial decreases in racial isolation can be accomplished without transporting any students who could otherwise walk to school.[66]

The report pointed out that even more efficient plans might be possible if the planners made good use of existing public transit facilities.[67]

Lambda researchers found that in metropolitan areas efficient planning would require the busing of few additional white children, many of whom lived in thinly settled suburbs where busing was necessary in any case, but substantial numbers of minority children, who were heavily concentrated in old neighborhoods with high population densities and schools within walking distance. The least costly solution would often be to reroute some of the white children already riding buses and to begin busing ghetto children.[68]

THE PRINCE GEORGES COUNTY STUDY. The success of the initial study by Lambda led to another analysis of a large suburban system. After a federal hearing examiner took the extraordinary step of ordering HEW to prepare a desegregation plan for Prince Georges County, Maryland, HEW passed the buck to the computer through another research contract with the Lambda Corporation, which in 1972 produced a sixty-six-page report that outlined a pattern of efficient student assignments, holding maximum travel time to thirty-five minutes after the bus was loaded (to avoid criticism that excessive busing was damaging the educational process).[69]

The study found that slightly more than one-fourth of the children already rode buses because they lived more than a mile away from the nearest grade school. Almost complete racial balance in the county system could be achieved by increasing the level of elementary school busing from 25 to 33 percent, a relatively modest increase involving only one-twelfth of the students in the system. (Fewer students could be bused if the system wished to require students to walk more than a mile to school.) Almost no new busing would be necessary at the junior high and high school levels. Three-fifths of the junior high and four-fifths of the high school students lived beyond walking distance from their schools. Merely rerouting buses would accomplish virtually complete desegregation of these schools.

Optimal desegregation at the elementary school level would require that

66. Lambda Corporation, "School Desegregation with Minimum Busing," report submitted to the Department of Health, Education, and Welfare, December 10, 1971; reprinted in Equal Educational Opportunities Act, Hearings before the House, p. 653.

67. Ibid., pp. 655, 673–74.

68. Ibid., p. 687.

69. George E. Pugh, "School Desegregation Alternatives in Prince George's County" (Lambda Corporation, April 28, 1972; processed).

bused students ride about eight minutes longer each way than they were currently doing. For high school students, the average increase in time would be only two minutes, for a total average ride of twelve minutes.[70]

Few additional white students would be required to ride buses. Since the county had a large white majority and a perfectly balanced school would have less than one-fourth black children, it was obviously more efficient to transport a small group of black children to integrate a school than to transport enough white students to make a black school three-quarters white. Since white children were more likely to be bused because they lived farther out in the less urbanized parts of the county, integrating grade schools would require more than doubling the percentage of black students bused—to approximately 40 percent—while making no significant change in the number of white students transported. The average ride of both groups would be seventeen minutes.[71]

This study, like the first Lambda report, found that existing busing arrangements intensified segregation. In other words, Prince Georges County had been paying significantly more money for busing to make school segregation even more intense than that resulting from the county's housing segregation.[72] No one had complained about this busing.

THE RAND STUDY. In another effort to determine how to handle desegregation in large cities as "cheaply and efficiently" as possible, HEW contracted with the Rand Corporation for the development of a computerized method for examining alternative desegregation plans.

The Rand study of Los Angeles found that this huge school district, where most whites were separated from most blacks and Chicanos by a mountain range, could be desegregated by busing one-fifth of the students. The longest rides would take forty-five minutes, but the average pupil would ride only twenty minutes.[73] (The maximum ride, of course, was likely to be the figure dominating public discussion of such a plan.) Costs suggested by local officials could be cut 60 percent by using the buses more efficiently.[74]

The major costs of busing do not vary much with the distance buses travel but are affected by the number of buses required. This is because "most of the cost is fixed capital, and drivers' salaries do not depend heavily

70. Ibid., p. 33.
71. Ibid., pp. 35–36.
72. Ibid., p. 53.
73. Emmett Keeler, "Planning School Desegregation" (Santa Monica: Rand Corp., 1972; processed), pp. vii–viii. This study is further described in chapter 6.
74. Ibid., pp. xiii–xix.

on distance traveled." The Rand study of ten-year cost data showed that it cost only 5 percent more to double the daily mileage of a bus.[75]

If cost and distance bused were the major reasons for the opposition of whites, there were ways to systematically minimize the change. Busing would involve more minority than white children and no child would have to ride a bus longer than millions of American children already travel routinely every day. In technical terms, at least, desegregation was found to be feasible, even in very large school systems.

### Is Busing Really the Problem?

While carrying out desegregation plans can cost millions of dollars, some districts have cut down on total busing and saved money. Although many southern opponents of busing said they were against busing, not desegregation, they offered no praise for such savings in the South. Busing was assailed even when desegregation actually decreased it. During the late 1960s, when Congressman Fletcher Thompson of Georgia was building a political career on the busing issue by calling for the impeachment of the secretary of HEW and Georgia's Governor Lester Maddox was suggesting that parents resist by letting the air out of school bus tires, busing in Georgia was declining. A study of forty-two desegregating Georgia districts between the start of integration in 1965 and its completion in many of the rural areas in 1969 showed that, although enrollment had risen 92,000, total busing miles had decreased 473,000. The results were similar in Mississippi. In twenty-seven desegregated districts there, annual miles of busing fell 2,500.[76] The amount of busing decreased because school systems were no longer operating two bus systems to carry students from the same area to separate white and black schools.

A study of nine Florida countywide school systems examined busing in great detail. Desegregation brought a total increase of 9,200 in the number of students bused as a "direct effect of desegregation." The affected counties had to purchase an average of seven more school buses each. Daily transportation mileage increased by an estimated 7.5 percent, but local school bus operations tended to be more efficient. The real per-student cost of busing declined in most of the counties, after allowing for inflation. The average percentage of the school budget required for transportation fell

75. Ibid., pp. 6, 70.
76. Commission on Civil Rights, *Your Child and Busing*, p. 14.

significantly in eight of the nine counties in spite of desegregation and population growth.[77]

During a period when desegregation plans had produced as much as a 20 percent decline in the level of busing in some Florida counties (though busing rose in urbanized districts), the state was worked up to a fever pitch over the busing issue. George Wallace swept the state's 1972 Democratic presidential primary. By three to one, state voters supported an anti-busing referendum. Support was strongest in the rural counties where the amount of busing had diminished. If people opposed busing per se, they should have favored many of the state's rural desegregation plans. Their opposition lent empirical support to the proposition that it is integrated schools rather than busing that people oppose.

## Conditions of Difficulty

In view of the minimal rise in busing costs described in this chapter, how can one explain the bitter complaints following the onset of desegregation about the need to cut back local school programs to finance busing? These complaints are not mere rhetoric. In some cases they reflect real difficulties produced by a sudden transition to a new way of operation.[78]

Maximum stress normally comes when a court orders that a far-reaching plan be immediately put into effect in a city with no established bus system. This can cause serious short-term local fiscal problems and may perhaps account for the general perception of the cost and scale of busing required by desegregation.

An urban school system with few or no buses may find it almost impossible even to obtain the necessary vehicles. First, although the buses have a life of nine or ten years, the total cost of a purchase must be paid in a single budget year. Buses are not sold on credit and districts cannot issue bonds to finance them. This is not a serious problem for districts that have a bus fleet, where some vehicles are replaced each year, often with state reimbursement to the local district. But when a district must pay for an entire large new fleet in a single year, it cuts deeply into the budget.

77. Eldridge J. Gendron, "Busing in Florida: Before and After," *Integrated Education* (March–April 1972), pp. 3–5.

78. Costs increase enormously, of course, if there is severe community upheaval. Boston had heavy costs for additional police. But this has seldom happened. Sometimes school systems choose to increase costs by upgrading school programs at the time they integrate or by seeking voluntary integration with expensive magnet programs. These should be considered costs of better education, not of desegregation.

Second, because there are very few suppliers of buses, there is normally a substantial waiting period for delivery of new orders. When desegregation begins, buses must often be used several times a day, usually by staggering school opening and closing hours. Without a careful plan, this can mean that children in the same family go to school from early in the morning to late in the afternoon, superimposing on the racial transition a difficult change in the rhythm of family life. Although staggering the hours of operation tends to minimize costs by using each bus intensively, this is a case where the social costs can outweigh the modest financial savings. Without reserve buses to replace buses that break down, all kinds of problems may arise.

Critics usually cite the expenses of the initial period. The budget figures are presented with all the capital costs of establishing a bus fleet included as part of the costs of the *first year* of desegregation. In other words, added to the operating costs are the costs of purchasing buses, of buying sites and building buildings for parking and maintaining buses, of training new drivers. Few note that costs fall sharply after the first year.

There is no short-run solution to the first-year pinch at the local or state level. Budgets are fixed in advance but these new expenses must be met. Since they are the direct result of federal court action, there are frequent requests for federal assistance. When President Nixon proposed a special desegregation assistance program, school officials eagerly looked to Washington for money to get them out of the financial bind of the transition period.

Predictably, however, the aid program was mired in controversy. The President demanded an amendment to prevent spending the money for busing. Even before Congress acted on the final legislation, HEW administratively determined that local requests for busing money would not be met. Eventually, in 1974, Congress prohibited spending the desegregation program money for busing and also denied local officials discretion to use money from most other federal programs for this purpose.[79]

White House and congressional actions did not prevent busing or desegregation; they only increased the stress of local transition. In its final report, the Senate Select Committee on Equal Educational Opportunity strongly recommended a change:

Great hardship has been caused by administration refusal to permit use of funds for transportation under the special desegregation appropriation. . . . If funds for additional transportation are not supplied by Federal sources, they

79. Public Law 93-380.

must come either from an increase in funds from State or local sources or, far more likely, a cutback in existing services. And the lack of an adequate number of buses, caused by inadequate resources, has forced districts to adopt double or even overlapping triple sessions. . . . These hardships can and should be ended with financial assistance under the Emergency School Aid Act.[80]

The state of Kentucky and several local school systems sued the federal government in 1975, asking for payment of the costs of federal court-ordered plans.[81]

## Minimum Busing and Maximum Trouble

The focus of public attention on the issue of "massive busing" has obscured evidence that desegregation sometimes works better when busing is done on a larger scale. While a number of cities have carried out system-wide and metropolitanwide desegregation on a racial balance model, many cities have had localized busing plans. During recent years civil rights leaders, lawyers, and researchers have argued that metropolitanwide desegregation would be more stable and more beneficial than city-only approaches. Some of the large urban areas whose plans hold down the amount or distance of busing have had far more serious problems than those using metropolitan racial balance approaches.

If people oppose "massive forced long-distance crosstown busing," presumably they will have less objection to plans of smaller-scale, short-distance busing not intended to establish a racial balance but merely to desegregate adjacent neighborhoods. Perhaps plans with less emphasis on spreading minority children around a district would be less "artificial" and better received; the President, the Justice Department, and HEW operated on this premise from 1972 to 1976 in supporting legislative efforts to restrict desegregation to the "next closest school." A similar assumption underlies some court orders and HEW policies that place maximum emphasis on holding down busing. Sociologist James Coleman and Attorney General Edward Levi proposed desegregating only schools where a history of unconstitutional segregation was proved.[82]

80. Senate Select Committee, *Toward Equal Educational Opportunity*, Final Report, p. 268.

81. *Christian Science Monitor*, September 19, 1975.

82. Coleman stated this in frequent articles and statements in 1975–76, and Levi supported 1976 Justice Department briefs following this general approach.

Short-distance busing was tested in the first year of Boston's desegregation when a federal court ordered the implementation of a state plan affecting only parts of Boston. Similar HEW requirements led to the development of a modest desegregation plan for Baltimore. These plans, however, aroused intense local resistance.

The initial experience with each plan was among the worst in the United States. The bitterness of the conflicts may well be related to the social class and neighborhood consequences of concentrating desegregation in areas that happen to be close to the ghetto. At a time of public opposition to "busing," often the courts, federal enforcement officials, or local education leaders faced with the inevitability of desegregation do their best to prevent any child from unnecessarily setting foot on a bus.

The resulting plan may be a masterpiece of efficient transportation planning, but it may make no sense at all educationally and socially. When desegregation planning is dominated by a search for the least amount of transportation, the planning may overlook the reality of the desegregation process. If the process means anything, it is a social and educational reconstitution of a community. If the educational research on the subject shows anything, it is that it works best when minority children are integrated into a middle class white school. There are no apparent educational gains when poor white and black or Latino children are placed together.

### Boston

The assumption that the amount of busing is itself the principal reason for resistance to desegregation can lead to grave errors. For instance, the 1974 Boston desegregation plan, perhaps the least successful in recent years, was supposed to minimize busing distances.

Boston is one of the smallest and most compact of major American cities and has unusually good mass transit, which many students already rode to special schools. A properly prepared plan might have made better use of facilities, since the city had both underenrolled and overcrowded schools. When the desegregation order was handed down, Boston had a white student majority, outnumbering blacks almost two to one, a favorable situation for designing a plan. Finally, unlike most communities, Boston had had considerable experience with integration. For some time children had been voluntarily riding buses to middle class white schools in the city and in the suburbs. These programs had operated virtually without incident.

For years the school committee had refused to honor repeated requests from state and federal agencies and courts to design a desegregation plan that made sense for Boston. The city's schools were segregated so severely by local policies and there was such consistent unwillingness to repair the damage that finally the Nixon administration had initiated fund-cutoff proceedings against the district. Between 1965 and 1971 the number of racially imbalanced schools had increased by more than a third and the number of all-white schools had grown.[83] But the committee believed that preparing a plan would imply support for busing. Thus there was no participation in the initial process by the elected officials and school administrators who knew the city best.

After Judge Arthur Garrity in 1974 found Boston guilty of unconstitutional segregation of the city's schools, he ordered prompt desegregation.[84] When local officials still refused to submit a plan, the judge turned to the state department of education. A staff member was given the assignment of developing a plan. He tried to apply state policy[85] by bringing together black and white children living near each other and integrating as few white schools as possible. His plan affected only 40 percent of the schools; most white schools remained untouched. He found that the shortest bus trips were required to desegregate neighborhoods threatened by ghetto expansion. The city's worst ghetto, Roxbury, was conveniently close to the South Boston bastion of working class whites. Although there was a history of tension and resentment between the two areas, the plan sent large numbers of black students into South Boston. It worked well in the elementary schools, but it proved so explosive in the South Boston high school that it generated a crisis for the entire city.

The desegregation plan cannot be blamed for all the troubles in Boston's schools, but it helped. Ultimately, any money saved on school buses was lost many times over in the form of state aid withdrawn because of the departure of students from the affected schools. Even more striking was the

83. *Washington Post,* December 1, 1971; *New York Times,* December 15, 1971.

84. *Morgan v. Hennigan,* 379 F. Supp. 410 (D. Mass. 1974). The decision contained 148 pages of legal and factual analysis of the de jure nature of Boston's segregation, but only 4 pages of discussion of remedies. This was an example of the frequent disproportion of effort in school litigation—the intense work on proving the violation and the minimal attention accorded the plan. Civil rights lawyers, forced to devote their resources to proving that the segregation is intentional, usually treat the question of what should happen next almost as an afterthought. Too often there is no time to do an educational analysis of the schools or to consult groups and organizations representing the people affected by the changes. The lawyers' basic concern, after all, is breaking down illegal segregation.

85. The Massachusetts Racial Imbalance Act of 1965 required desegregating schools with a bare majority of whites.

financial burden on the city of extra police protection to cope with racial clashes. Police overtime alone cost millions.[86]

Despite the disastrous first phase of a desegregation plan prepared by outsiders, the school committee defied a federal court order to submit a plan designed by its own staff. The court eventually appointed four eminent special masters to design an educationally sound approach to suit local conditions. The four were Charles V. Willie, a black professor at Harvard's School of Education; Francis Keppel, a former U.S. commissioner of education; Jacob Spiegel, a retired state supreme court judge; and Edward McCormack, Jr., a former state attorney general and member of a powerful South Boston Irish political family. After holding hearings on eighteen different plans, they came up with a carefully designed citywide desegregation plan actually requiring the busing of fewer children than the first plan had. The masters proposed to set up nine smaller "community school districts" and a tenth to operate special centralized schools.

The plan combined educational innovations and moves for greater economy and efficiency in the system. Closing about one-eighth of the city's schools eliminated excess school capacity and simplified transportation requirements.[87] The educational innovations included a commitment from the Massachusetts Institute of Technology to work with East Boston High School to develop it into a citywide technical school and from Harvard to work with Roxbury High School in the black ghetto. Local colleges were to play major roles in curriculum development.[88]

The new approach was far from perfect, but the process illustrated the importance of working from an educational concept of the goals of desegregated education rather than a city street map. Too often, because local school officials focus solely on a battle against busing, they lose control over the design of an educationally effective plan. A good plan does not end tension, particularly in a situation like Boston's where a community has been polarized for years, but it does offer some tangible benefits to children at the end of the bus ride. Boston's second year of desegregation was far less explosive than the first. Acceptance of the improved plan may have been indicated by the defeat of Boston's antibusing leaders Louise Day Hicks and Pixie Palladino in November 1977, when Boston voters elected to the school committee its first black member in seventy-six years.[89]

86. *Boston Globe,* May 4, 1976. Mayor Kevin White estimated the city's annual cost at $20 million, primarily for police.

87. *Washington Post,* March 22, 1975.

88. *New York Times,* March 22, 1975.

89. *Boston Globe,* November 9, 1977.

## Baltimore

The nation's eighth largest school system, Baltimore (City), implemented a partial desegregation plan in September 1974. HEW, much against its will, was ordered by a federal court to enforce the 1964 Civil Rights Act in the district, which had a long history of illegal segregation. There was much uncertainty about the value of pursuing substantial desegregation in a system whose enrollment was 70 percent black.[90]

After months of confusing and desultory negotiations, HEW settled for an interim desegregation plan with minimal busing, pairing some nearby elementary schools and integrating the seventh grade of some junior high schools. The high school issue was left for the next year. The school system, however, began to openly violate this small plan early in the school year. Though the distances were short, many whites left school.

The school board soon allowed white students assigned to seven previously black junior high schools to transfer back to schools in or near their own neighborhoods, thus undoing much of the desegregation. The board also reversed one of the limited number of elementary school pairings it had earlier approved.[91] Though there was little busing, there were bitter protests and mass defiance, and the plan was largely nullified.[92]

The federal guidelines themselves showed the peculiar nature of "desegregation" in the large city with few white students. Desegregated schools, under the HEW standards for Baltimore, were supposed to be between 50 and 90 percent black. Even if the city had fulfilled its promises to HEW, most of the city's schools would have retained their black identity.[93]

Defining a 90 percent black school as "desegregated" means little busing is needed, but it does not meet a primary judicial goal of desegregation—removing the stigma of inferiority whites attach to minority schools. A school with 90 percent black enrollment is perceived as a black school, not an integrated one. If Baltimore had been permitted to use more busing to integrate its students with those from the huge adjoining Baltimore County system, real desegregation could have been achieved at a modest cost. Under a minimum busing plan restricted to part of the city, either con-

90. Antero Pietila, "Baltimore Desegregation: Tug of War," *Integrated Education* (November–December 1974), pp. 17–19.
91. *Baltimore Sun*, January 1, 1975.
92. Ibid., December 18, 1974.
93. Ibid., March 14, 1975.

tinued defiance of the law or an accelerated loss of white students seemed likely. Less busing was no solution.

### Other Cities

Similar problems appeared elsewhere. In Detroit the school board strongly supported desegregation through "massive busing" on a metropolitan basis. After the Supreme Court rejected metropolitan approaches, many Detroit black leaders, including Mayor Coleman Young, urged the NAACP to do nothing. They believed that limited busing would bring upheaval and increased white flight from the city.[94] The school board decided to leave many schools segregated.

A small 1970 plan in Trenton, New Jersey, involved transferring only a few dozen black children to nearby white schools serving predominantly working class Italian neighborhoods. Resistance was so strong that state education officials withdrew the desegregation directive and sent the black children back to ghetto schools. It was one of the few cases where local threats prevailed.[95] Similar community uproar over a short-distance busing plan occurred in the Canarsie section of New York City.

Minimizing busing has social class implications. It means that the burden of racial change in old cities will be borne largely by working class white families, those most threatened by racial change and least able to handle it successfully. At the same time, the white middle class on the edge of the city and in the suburbs will retain their schools, segregated along both racial and class lines. Such class differences increase the tension of desegregation.

## Experience with Metropolitanism

If busing is at the core of public resistance to urban integration, one might well assume that carrying desegregation to the metropolitan level would cross the threshold of public tolerance. In fact, however, such plans are already in operation in a number of the nation's largest school systems. A metropolitan plan often requires little more busing than one confined to the city. One reason this is so is that operation of separate city and suburban systems often prevents easy desegregation of adjacent schools

94. *New York Times*, November 9, 1975.
95. *Trentonian*, October 27, 28, 29, 30, 1970.

of different racial composition that happen to be on opposite sides of the city-suburban boundary line. The possibility of combining a number of different transportation systems (already busing many children) into a consolidated operation also offers opportunities for greater efficiency in transportation.

More busing, ironically enough, may produce plans that make more sense educationally (by creating predominantly middle class schools everywhere), may actually end the racial identity of schools, and may minimize the incentive for white flight by assuring equal treatment in all parts of an urbanized area. Experience in the countywide systems of the South (which serve entire metropolitan areas) shows that such desegregation is, in fact, unusually stable.

## Is Busing Practical?

Successful desegregation of an urban school system is unquestionably a complex and difficult process. Achieving real integration in the schools of a society with deep and pervasive racial divisions requires major changes. Southern public schools that passed through physical desegregation years ago are still struggling against "second generation" discrimination.

On the other hand, there is nothing inherently infeasible or impractical about achieving integration by using buses to bring together previously segregated children. The problems, once the political crisis has passed, are simply those of operating integrated schools in a segregated society.

The existing evidence does not sustain any of the claims made by opponents of busing. Busing does not damage the educational process. It is not dangerous. It usually costs a very small fraction of the local school budget, and the cost could be reduced further by more systematic transportation planning and by closing expensive half-empty schools. The bus rides for most students are not long.

Minimizing busing by merely integrating lower class children from adjacent hostile neighborhoods is far less likely to produce lasting success than plans incorporating middle class neighborhoods and schools. The judicial decision to prevent busing across city-suburban boundaries may forestall the development of plans that are much preferable, educationally and socially, and require relatively little additional busing. Minimizing busing may sometimes maximize instability by feeding the syndrome of ghetto expansion into nearby neighborhoods and white flight into sanctuaries of segregation.

The practical problems of busing are not severe enough either to justify people's fears or to dominate the desegregation planning process. Desegregation is usually so feasible technically that policymakers can afford to consider the social and educational desirability of various plans that may require marginally more transportation. They must, in fact, concentrate on just these issues if there is to be a real hope for the schools to move beyond desegregation toward successful integration.

# 6

# The Largest Cities

AMONG the hundreds of American cities, a few are so heavily populated and their metropolitan areas are so large that their problems simply are not comparable with those of typical urban centers. At a certain point, a difference in the scale of urban settlement becomes a difference in kind. The problems of New York or Chicago may be as different from those of Toledo or Omaha as the problems of the smaller cities are from those of small farming towns.

The five largest cities—New York, Los Angeles, Chicago, Philadelphia, and Detroit—are the great centers of communication, commerce, industry, and government, and are the most important loci of the nation's internal migration of minority people. More important, they lie at the heart of urban settlement on a scale unknown anywhere in the world until the recent past. (The five largest U.S. metropolitan areas were among the twenty-two largest in the world in 1960.)[1] They also show, in acute form, the great difficulties of adapting old, fragmented institutions of local government to the complex demands of social and economic change.

When considering the nation's largest school systems, many observers comment that desegregation simply is not practical. In fact, since these systems, particularly the New York City system, tend to get disproportionate attention from both scholars and the mass media, the observers often conclude that desegregation is impossible throughout urban America. This book has reversed that pattern of analysis, first considering general problems and reserving the biggest cities for more intensive analysis. Even if integration is a feasible policy in Indianapolis or Seattle, there could well

1. Robert J. Havighurst, *Education in Metropolitan Areas* (Allyn and Bacon, 1966), pp. 26–30.

be special circumstances that would make it prohibitively difficult in Philadelphia.

This chapter examines the nation's five largest school systems—the only ones with more than a quarter-million enrollment in the 1974–75 school year, each serving the central city of one of the five metropolitan areas in the United States with more than 4 million population.[2]

Even among the five districts there were substantial differences of scale. In 1974 New York City, with over a million students, had a far larger enrollment than Los Angeles (604,000) or Chicago (530,000). Enrollment in these cities in turn was twice as large as that of Philadelphia (267,000) or Detroit (256,000.)[3] Particular attention is given here to New York, Los Angeles, and Detroit. New York's controversies have generated study after study. In Los Angeles and Detroit, active trial of school desegregation lawsuits has produced detailed examination of existing patterns of contemporary segregation and possible remedies.

The metropolitan areas of these five cities contain about one-sixth of the national population. In the 1972–73 school year the five central cities enrolled 18 percent of the black students in the United States (more than one-third of the black children outside the South), 22 percent of the Hispanic students, and 20 percent of the Oriental students.[4] None of them had been significantly desegregated before 1975, when Detroit began a partial plan.

Historically, the desegregation struggles in the five cities were much alike, as were the results during the first two decades after the 1954 *Brown* decision. There had been sporadic protests for a long time, but in the middle 1960s school protests and demands reached their peak. In none of the cities was there early or effective desegregation litigation, but by the early 1970s both Detroit and Los Angeles had generated major legal battles. All

2. Department of Health, Education, and Welfare, Office for Civil Rights, "Distribution of Minority Students by School Composition, 1970–1974," report to the U.S. Senate (May 27, 1976; processed), pp. 1, 5, 9, 13, 17.

The school systems closest in size to the smallest of these five districts, Detroit, were those of Dade County, Florida, and Houston, both of which enrolled far higher proportions of the local metropolitan population and were already partially desegregated. The next largest district was Cleveland, with about half Detroit's enrollment. U.S. Bureau of the Census, *Census of Population and Housing, 1970: General Demographic Trends for Metropolitan Areas, 1960 to 1970*, Final Report PHC(2)-1 (GPO, 1971), p. 47.

3. HEW, Office for Civil Rights, "Distribution of Minority Students," pp. 21, 25, 45.

4. HEW, Office for Civil Rights, *Directory of Public Elementary and Secondary Schools in Selected Districts, Enrollment and Staff by Racial/Ethnic Group* (GPO, 1974), pp. viii, 115, 311, 627, 936, 1212. The current proportion cannot be estimated because HEW has not yet released 1974 totals and did not collect racial statistics in 1975.

faced continuing large increases in minority students and declines in white students, making desegregation more difficult each year. With the exception of a brief and futile effort in Chicago in 1965, none of the cities has faced serious desegregation action by the Departments of Justice and Health, Education, and Welfare under the 1964 Civil Rights Act. HEW urged the desegregation of teachers but ignored the segregation of pupils.

## The Civil Rights Movement and School Integration

The first protests over urban school segregation came long before the *Brown* decision. When W. E. B. DuBois published his classic study, *The Philadelphia Negro*, in 1889, for example, he probed segregation by public school officials violating their own policy of nondiscrimination. There were already a number of segregated schools. He quoted a city councilman justifying faculty segregation: "No matter how well qualified they [blacks] may be to teach . . . it is taken for granted that only white teachers shall be placed in charge of white children."[5]

Black communities in northern cities fought to end open legal segregation of the schools, only to encounter more subtle tactics. In Chicago, for example, black parents fought the attempt to impose "black schools" on children who had previously been allowed to attend nearby public schools. The school board once ruled that no child with more than one-eighth Negro blood could attend a white school. Parents refused to comply, however, and their children "sat in" the regular schools. Finally the school board abandoned this policy.[6] In New York, state law allowed legally segregated schools until 1900. Brooklyn retained some black schools until 1894 and Queens schools were openly segregated until 1900.[7] In California blacks organized in the 1870s to fight total denial of schooling or segregation. Mexican-Americans fought for decades, first to obtain schools and then, particularly after World War II, to end the old system of segregated Mexican schools.[8]

Even after the biggest cities officially abandoned segregation as a policy, it remained as a practice. Minority students, however, were almost invisible

5. W. E. B. DuBois, *The Philadelphia Negro* (Schocken Books, 1967), pp. 89, 94.

6. St. Clair Drake and Horace R. Cayton, *Black Metropolis* (Harper Torchbooks, 1962), vol. 1, p. 44.

7. Seth M. Scheiner, *Negro Mecca: A History of the Negro in New York City, 1865–1920* (New York University Press, 1965), pp. 178–79.

8. Charles M. Wollenberg, *All Deliberate Speed: Segregation and Exclusion in California Schools, 1855–1975* (University of California Press, 1976).

until the great migration of World War I, when large ghettos began to form in Chicago, New York, Philadelphia, and Detroit. But as late as 1930 blacks constituted only 3 percent of the Los Angeles schools' enrollment; not until the region experienced an economic boom during World War II did their number become substantial. Hispanics first became an important minority group in Los Angeles, which has the largest concentration of Chicanos in the United States; they did not become important in New York until the 1950s or in Chicago until the late 1960s. (Detroit and Philadelphia still have not become centers of Hispanic settlement.)

Year by year, school segregation spread in the big cities. Before World War I only two or three of Chicago's schools had black majorities, but by 1931 twenty-six were predominantly black. By 1974, 309 of the city's 643 schools were more than 95 percent black, and 173 contained no students of other races. Less than one-sixth of the schools complied with the state board of education's desegregation requirements.[9] Similar processes took place in the other cities. Although the isolation of black children from whites was more extreme, the segregation of Hispanics also reached high levels.

The *Brown* decision encouraged those who wished to challenge the segregation in the northern ghetto schools. The decision directly affected only the southern and border states, but it legitimated a new set of demands for racial change. Northern blacks poured into local NAACP chapters, increasing the pressure to use against northern segregation the tactics that had achieved the southern breakthrough.

The drive for school desegregation began almost immediately in New York but was not organized as a serious campaign until the early 1960s in the other cities. Puerto Ricans played an important role in the 1960s battle, but their leaders later became less interested in integration.[10] The movement encountered severe obstacles. The cities, for example, usually maintained no public statistics on race, so it was difficult to describe the level of segregation accurately until the federal government in the mid-1960s required that records be kept. Many of the early protests centered on particularly notorious cases of gerrymandering or on the common practice of forcing black students to attend badly overcrowded schools while there were empty seats in nearby white schools.

9. Allan H. Spear, *Black Chicago: The Making of a Negro Ghetto, 1890–1920* (University of Chicago Press, 1967), pp. 203–04; Center for National Policy Review, *Trends in Black School Segregation: 1970–1974*, vol. 1 (Washington: CNPR, 1977), p. 17.

10. Nathan Glazer, "Is 'Integration' Possible in the New York Schools?" in Hubert Humphrey, ed., *School Desegregation: Documents and Commentaries* (Crowell, 1964), p. 186.

*The Movement in New York*

The desegregation issue probably generated more passionate rhetoric and scholarly analysis in New York City than in all the rest of the North through the 1950s and early 1960s. Little happened, however. Sweeping statements were followed by endless bureaucratic delay. The frustration and bitterness engendered by the failure of the city and state authorities to act were signs of things to come in other communities.

A New York City black scholar, Kenneth Clark, had been a leading figure in preparing the famous social scientists' brief submitted to the Supreme Court before the *Brown* decision. Within a month of the Court's decree Clark announced his belief that the decision applied to the North.[11]

The city's school board encouraged supporters of integration with a 1954 policy statement calling segregation "educationally undesirable." It promised to adopt a plan to prevent further segregation and end that already existing "as quickly as practicable."[12] The board set up the Commission on Integration. In response to protests against policies that denied black students access to empty seats in nearby white schools, a small busing program was initiated.[13]

Further progress came much harder. Direct action protests began in 1960. The school board decided that year to allow limited open enrollment.[14] Pressure from blacks and Puerto Ricans for much more substantial change was met by rapidly growing opposition from a coalition of "powerful professional interests inside the school system . . . local parent associations, homeowners, civic groups, and many public and private real estate interests."

They want to keep their new neighborhood "respectable" by preserving uncrowded, "good" schools and safe living conditions. . . . Many of these whites are homeowners anxious about declining property values if Negroes move into their area. As parents, they are concerned about the upward mobility and occupational achievement of their children which they see as threatened by forced desegregation.[15]

11. Diane Ravitch, *The Great School Wars: New York City, 1805–1972* (Basic Books, 1974), p. 251.

12. Will Maslow, "De Facto Public School Segregation," in ibid., p. 157.

13. Meyer Weinberg, "Struggle for Public Policy: Black Children after 1950" (unpublished manuscript, 1973), pp. 41–42.

14. Ibid., p. 42.

15. David Rogers, "Obstacles to School Desegregation in New York City: A Benchmark Case," in Marilyn Gittell and Alan G. Havesi, eds., *The Politics of Urban Education* (Praeger, 1969), p. 127.

Many intellectuals opposed drastic change. Sociologist Nathan Glazer, for example, claimed that there was obviously "no formal segregation in the New York City schools." Therefore, he said, integration should be pursued only if it had demonstrated educational benefits. Glazer saw integration primarily as a symbolic political demand by minority leaders, which was simply infeasible because of the "huge residential concentrations of Negroes and Puerto Ricans." Desegregating Manhattan, where the black and Puerto Rican enrollment was already 75 percent of the total, would require bringing large numbers of children to the island from other boroughs. Even if there were a massive effort to make all schools in the city 40 percent minority, Glazer argued, it might very well be self-defeating:

there are generally not enough "other" children to go around. . . . And in the end, any victories are likely to be Pyrrhic ones. The assignment of a few blocks containing fifty "other" children to a school that is largely Negro and Puerto Rican does not necessarily mean an increase. . . . Maybe only ten or twenty will show up when school opens, and the battle will have been in vain.[16]

The movement for integration, however, intensified. In 1964, at the height of the national civil rights movement, there were huge demonstrations and a boycott of the city schools by more than half a million black and Puerto Rican children. State Commissioner of Education James Allen, Jr., prepared a comprehensive plan for desegregation. Allen's recommendations included the creation of intermediate schools designed to foster integrated education before high school.[17]

Two years after the Allen proposals, the school board opened the first new intermediate school. But the school was in Harlem, and in spite of its earlier commitments, the school board refused to assign white students. Its campaign for voluntary white transfers was a total failure. This retreat helped stimulate a neighborhood demand for "community control of the segregated school."[18] Black integrationists in New York faced the age-old problem of reformers: ideological mobilization over a long time for an improbable end is extraordinarily difficult. Unable to demonstrate any real progress on integration, they found it hard to oppose drives for local community control. Civil rights lawyers were deeply discouraged by their inability to win the major northern desegregation cases of the period.[19] Neither the state nor the federal government acted. Segregation continued to expand.

16. Glazer, "Is 'Integration' Possible?" pp. 186–91.
17. Annie Stein, "Strategies for Failure," *Harvard Educational Review*, vol. 41 (May 1971), pp. 166–67.
18. Rogers, "Obstacles to School Desegregation," p. 133.
19. Robert L. Herbst, "The Legal Struggle to Integrate Schools in the North," *Annals*, vol. 407 (May 1973), p. 52.

## The Movement in Los Angeles

As in many other major cities outside the South, the school issue became important in Los Angeles in the early 1960s and reached its peak from 1963 to 1965. Study of local segregation grew out of an investigation by the American Civil Liberties Union of a black school. The magnitude of the city's segregation soon became evident.

Los Angeles entered the 1960s insisting that it had no segregation. It would not publish racial statistics. In mid-1962 the ACLU, together with the NAACP and the Congress of Racial Equality (CORE), called for school board leadership in overcoming segregation. The state board of education's June 1962 policy urging positive local action for school integration changed nothing.[20]

The initial demands were modest but unsuccessful. The civil rights groups asked for a racial census, reexamination of attendance zone lines, the development of magnet schools (whose special educational programs would presumably attract white students) for voluntary integration, and the future selection of school building sites to foster integration. Finally, in May 1963, with the country in an uproar over events in Birmingham, Alabama, the school board took a modest step. It stepped up compensatory education and pledged to consider the racial consequences of future school zoning decisions.[21]

The local movement reached its zenith in mid-1963. An alliance of seventy-six local groups demanded prompt school board consideration of issues including segregated faculties and the transfer of students from crowded ghetto schools to empty rooms in white schools. The California Supreme Court increased the pressure when it ruled that school boards in the state could not merely be neutral. "The harmful consequences of segregation," the court held, "require that school boards take steps, insofar as reasonably feasible to alleviate racial imbalance in schools regardless of its cause."[22]

Any optimism, however, was soon deflated. The board voted 6–1 against busing students. Following a series of protests, the board permitted voluntary "free choice" enrollment in thirteen schools. A defective transfer plan, however, helped white students leave integrated schools by allowing them to transfer to all-white schools. At the maximum, a few hundred students

20. John W. Caughey and Laree Caughey, *School Segregation on Our Doorstep: The Los Angeles Story* (Quail Books, 1966), pp. 4–5, 14.
21. Ibid., pp. 15–16.
22. Ibid., pp. 17–19.

were desegregated.[23] This was where things stood at the time of the Watts riots.

The fires burning across Watts in August 1965 brought sudden realization that there was a vast, angry black population but it brought no progress on school segregation.[24] The rest of the city reacted at least as much from fear as from concern.

At the first school board meeting after the riots, a program for rapid integration was urged. But only two small programs of voluntary, privately financed integration of three schools began in 1965.[25]

Frustrated with continued local inaction, Los Angeles integrationists began to look outside the city for leverage. Local civil rights leaders urged HEW to withhold federal aid from the schools in 1966, but there was no response. Next, they took the case to the state board of education. The state director of compensatory education, Wilson Riles, announced: "On the question of integration, I plan no compromise."[26] State officials, however, accomplished no more in the City of the Angels than had their counterparts in New York. Finally, the integrationists took the case to court.


## The Movement in Chicago

Chicago has the most segregated school system of any of the five cities. Mass mobilization against segregation came relatively late, but at its peak the struggle had a cast of characters and a sense of confrontation that were probably unsurpassed. The issues were unambiguous, the civil rights movement coalesced for a time with rare unity and sense of purpose, and the school superintendent did not even take the trouble to make a rhetorical promise to try to integrate.

Although there had been scattered protests against school segregation in the city for decades and some active NAACP efforts during the 1950s, the confrontation came the following decade. Successful southern protests and a federal court victory in a widely publicized case in New Rochelle, New York, led many to hope that the courts would eventually force desegregation.[27] Chicago activists documented a growing list of abuses. Super-

23. Ibid., pp. 20–30.
24. National Advisory Commission on Civil Disorders, *Report of the National Advisory Commission on Civil Disorders* (GPO, 1968), pp. 37–38.
25. John Walton Caughey, *To Kill a Child's Spirit: The Tragedy of School Segregation in Los Angeles* (Ithaca, Ill.: Peacock Publishers, 1973), pp. 29–30; Caughey and Caughey, *School Segregation on Our Doorstep,* p. 35.
26. Caughey and Caughey, *School Segregation on Our Doorstep,* p. 44.
27. *Taylor* v. *Board of Education,* 191 F. Supp. 181 (S.D.N.Y. 1961), aff'd, 294 F.2d 36 (2d Cir. 1961).

intendent Benjamin Willis's adamant rejection of modest black requests made him a focal point in the struggle. In contrast to other cities' small efforts, the Chicago school authorities refused to allow blacks to transfer to empty white classrooms and purchased expensive mobile classrooms— "Willis wagons"—to keep children in crowded, segregated surroundings.[28]

Like many other communities, Chicago, under threat of litigation, finally studied local segregation in the mid-sixties. The 1964 report of the Chicago Advisory Panel on Integration documented the system's racial separation. The schools already had 40 percent black enrollment, and 84 percent of the black children attended segregated schools. New schools were even more segregated. Most black schools were overcrowded; white schools were six times as likely to have unused space. Mobile classrooms had indeed been placed where they intensified segregation.[29]

The school board study documented segregation, which led to two school boycotts. Controversy surrounded Superintendent Willis, who refused to enforce the board's limited transfer program. When he threatened to resign, the school board rescinded the policy. In 1965, when Willis was scheduled to retire, the board rehired him, provoking a summer of protests.[30] Martin Luther King, Jr., led thousands of angry demonstrators.

Totally frustrated, Chicago civil rights leaders appealed to Washington to enforce the 1964 Civil Rights Act's fund-withholding provisions. Although the complaint reached HEW in 1965 before the matter of applying the act to northern segregation had been considered, HEW officials, worried about the seriousness of the Chicago allegations and disturbed by the possibility that the first money from the largest federal aid-to-education bill in U.S. history (the Elementary and Secondary Education Act of 1965) would be used to reinforce segregation, decided to hold up $32 million in new funds pending an investigation. The decision, taken without full consideration of the distinctive legal issues in the North and without the approval of either the President or the Justice Department, produced a political uproar in Chicago. Within five days it was reversed.[31] What had started as federal intervention on behalf of desegregation ended with a humiliating retreat that helped keep HEW officials out of northern enforcement efforts for years.

28. See Gary Orfield, *The Reconstruction of Southern Education: The Schools and the 1964 Civil Rights Act* (Wiley, 1969), "Chicago: Failure in the North," pp. 152–57; Weinberg, "Struggle for Public Policy," pp. 43–44.

29. Chicago Board of Education, Advisory Panel on Integration of the Public Schools, "Integration of the Public Schools—Chicago," Report to the Board of Education, City of Chicago (1964; processed), pp. 6, 14–15, 62–63.

30. Orfield, *Reconstruction of Southern Education*, pp. 162–63.

31. Ibid., pp. 167–205.

### Philadelphia and Detroit

The other two cities also had protests but on a lesser scale. In Philadelphia the issue was not seriously confronted until in 1961 a group of black parents, supported by the NAACP and other organizations, sued the board over its plan to install mobile classrooms at a ghetto school rather than using space at a nearby white school.[32] The lawsuit and subsequent community protests in 1962 led to the appointment of a large special committee on nondiscrimination. While the committee was working, the school board succeeded in winning a postponement from the federal court in the litigation. The case was not resumed.[33]

In 1964 the special committee reported that there were a black majority and severe segregation in the school system and that black students were attending the older, inferior, overcrowded schools. The committee recommended that attempts be made to reduce segregation by pairing schools, creating a new organizational structure, and desegregating the faculties. It also proposed accelerated compensatory and early education programs in the ghettos.[34]

A new school board headed by a powerful liberal former mayor, Richardson Dilworth, named a new superintendent, Mark Shedd, an aggressive reformer known for his success in desegregating a New Jersey suburb. The board made many changes and brought talented outsiders into important administrative positions. It did little, however, about desegregation. "Like most American cities," one participant commented, "Philadelphia had begun its reforms too late."[35]

Even though the board avoided action against segregation, black student demonstrations provoked a white reaction that eventually led to the departure of Superintendent Shedd. A violent confrontation with blacks demanding courses in black studies helped make Police Commissioner Frank Rizzo a political force in the city and its next mayor. Rizzo made the school board and the superintendent central targets of his campaign and firmly opposed school desegregation.[36]

32. Conrad Weiler, *Philadelphia: Neighborhood, Authority, and the Urban Crisis* (Praeger, 1974), pp. 79–80; Henry S. Resnik, *Turning On the System: War in the Philadelphia Public Schools* (Pantheon, 1970), pp. 47–53.

33. Marilyn Gittell and T. Edward Hollander, "The Process of Change: Case Study of Philadelphia," in Gittell and Havesi, eds., *The Politics of Urban Education*, pp. 221, 226–27; Weiler, *Philadelphia*, pp. 80–81.

34. Weiler, *Philadelphia*, pp. 85–86.

35. Resnik, *Turning On the System*, pp. 4–6, 42.

36. Fred Hamilton, *Rizzo* (Viking, 1973), pp. 14, 106–10.

Segregation spread and intensified. The only continuing action was a long-drawn-out investigation by the Pennsylvania Human Relations Commission, one of the few state agencies with enforcement powers. Once again, the impulse had to come from outside the city.

Detroit's experience was in some ways comparable to that of Philadelphia. A progressive board came to power, but in Detroit it brought stronger integrationist leadership. A political upheaval ultimately brought about the demise of the Detroit progressives, who were defeated directly on the integration issue. Blacks became a large majority of the school enrollment, and civil rights leaders eventually became convinced that change could only come from outside the political structure.

At first, there were victories. There were meetings and protests and demands and frustrations. Unlike many big cities the political structure of Detroit was not overpoweringly opposed to integration in the 1960s. In fact, one of the dominant local political forces, the United Auto Workers, was strongly integrationist. In 1964 the UAW and other liberal forces in city politics joined to elect three liberal integrationists, headed by activist labor lawyer A. L. Zwerdling, who became president of the board.

Nonetheless, progress toward integration was slow. Although the school system made rapid progress in increasing the number of black teachers and administrators in the late 1960s, its efforts had little impact on segregation. An open enrollment plan and small-scale busing left the great majority of black children in schools with more than 90 percent black enrollment in 1970.

When the state legislature passed a law decentralizing the city's school system, the board responded by selecting districts drawn to preserve the possibility of integration. The board also designed a plan to integrate the city's white schools rapidly. The legislature's response was to pass a law requiring assignment of all students to the school closest to their homes, nullifying the desegregation plan, and to cut the term of office of the school board.

A local recall campaign finally defeated the board's integrationists. For the first time in the history of the school system, the electorate had thrown out elected board members.[37]

Racial polarization had defeated the drive for integration in Detroit, as it had in each of the other largest cities. Like their counterparts in the other cities, Detroit integrationists now looked for leverage from outside to compel local change. The NAACP filed a suit in federal court.

37. William R. Grant, "Community Control vs. School Integration—The Case of Detroit," *Public Interest*, no. 24 (Summer 1971), pp. 62–79.

Table 6-1. *Elementary School Segregation of Blacks in the Five Largest Cities, Fall 1965*

| | Percentage of black children | |
| City | In schools 90 percent or more black | In schools with a majority of blacks |
| --- | --- | --- |
| New York | 20.7 | 55.5 |
| Los Angeles[a] | 39.5 | 87.5 |
| Chicago | 89.2 | 96.9 |
| Philadelphia | 72.0 | 90.2 |
| Detroit | 72.3 | 91.5 |

Source: Commission on Civil Rights, *Racial Isolation in the Public Schools* (GPO, 1967), p. 4.
a. Los Angeles data are for the fall of 1963. Segregation is greatly understated in both Los Angeles and New York because in this table Hispanics are not considered segregated minorities. Thus schools with almost completely black and Hispanic enrollment appear to be integrated.

### The Record of Protest

Each of the nation's largest cities saw a major struggle for school integration. While the history varied from city to city, it was everywhere a major goal of the civil rights movement and one that commanded support from virtually the whole range of black leadership and many Hispanic spokesmen at the height of the movement. Martin Luther King, Jr., led protests in Chicago, SNCC (Student Nonviolent Coordinating Committee) and CORE assailed federal officials for not pursuing integration fast enough, and even Malcolm X joined the picket lines at the second school boycott in New York. It was a call for basic change that united very diverse activists. In some cases the goal was pressed with rare force and insistence, year after year. The result was almost total frustration.

Even token desegregation was won at great cost. As the ghettos expanded, the numbers of minority children in segregated schools remained high. (Table 6-1 shows the segregation of blacks in the five largest cities.) The continued suburbanization of the white population made central city desegregation more and more difficult. Each of the cities experienced a riot between 1964 and 1968, with the upheavals in Detroit and Los Angeles playing a particularly important role in increasing national racial polarization.[38]

Faced with defeat and growing segregation, a large number of black and

38. The history of the struggle in the largest cities parallels that in many smaller cities, which cannot be considered here in detail. In the entire nation, only a few small cities voluntarily desegregated.

Hispanic leaders began to search for another solution in the late 1960s. Many thought that community control might be the answer.

### Community Control

After the integration movement had been stalemated in the nation's largest cities, the community control strategy emerged in minority communities, most fully in New York but also in a few other cities. The goal was to transfer authority over schools in each part of the city from the central school bureaucracy to elected local leaders of the dominant racial or ethnic group, who would then presumably choose sensitive and responsive educators for the top administrative positions.

The assumption was that the problem with urban schools was that they were rigidly bureaucratic and white. Students would learn more in schools accountable to elected minority group leaders where they were respected and where their distinctive values, rather than those of the white culture, were basic to the curriculum.

The idea emerged in New York with the strong support of the nation's largest private philanthropy, the Ford Foundation. Under state legislation the city was eventually divided into community districts.

The scale of the hope for changes was suggested by a Ford Foundation official, Mario Fantini:

The demands call for a new concept of education, one that is fundamentally linked to the concerns and aspirations of the people who depend on it. . . . Attempting to change the community to fit the existing institution has seriously sidetracked us. It is the enlightened refusal of the community to accept this solution . . . which has resulted in the citizens' insistence on taking matters into their own hands.[39]

Political controversy over community control stirred up the powers in the New York educational establishment, including the United Federation of Teachers, against the "good government" and civil rights groups. The battle assumed epic proportions, drawing in the major newspapers and precipitating a severe breach in the black-Jewish coalition that had been so important in the city's politics and the national civil rights movement.

Critics attacked what they saw as a campaign to displace the professionals running the schools with unqualified new minority leaders. Some feared the return of the ward-level patronage-ridden system of school operation

39. Mario Fantini, "Afterward," in Naomi Levine, *Ocean Hill-Brownsville: Schools in Crisis* (Popular Library, 1969), pp. 138–39.

that educators had crusaded against at the beginning of the twentieth century. Some claimed that the separate school systems would be used to teach racial hostility and intensify polarization in the city.

On one side was a vision of releasing a flood of repressed social energy, reviving an unresponsive set of institutions. On the other side was a fear that the changes would create petty localism, reward incompetence, and add to the city's social difficulties.

Community control in the fullest sense was never tried. The three small local demonstration districts produced bitter racial division and an ugly strike in the city. The state legislature refused to authorize full transfer of power to the new community districts. It limited their authority to the selection of local superintendents, a few other specified powers, and any other authority the city school board might choose to turn over to them.[40]

New York has now had community school districts since 1969. While neither the hopes nor the fears have been fully realized, the experience has been informative.

Participation in the elections for the community school boards has been consistently poor and has declined as the years have passed. The limited interest probably resembles a pattern frequently found—research on voting shows that the level of information and of voting is lowest in the most localized elections. Not only is it impossible for the mass media to cover neighborhood campaigns in any detail, but voters usually lack the guidance of party labels, which are extremely important cues for votes, particularly for offices of little public visibility.[41] Across the nation, public information about citywide school board activities is scarce in spite of wide press coverage.[42] In New York it was extraordinarily difficult for an actively concerned voter to follow the candidates for even one of the thirty-two different community boards. Without information about or party identification of candidates, the political vacuum was usually filled by organized groups influenced by school policy, particularly the teachers' union and the

40. Mario Fantini, Marilyn Gittell, and Richard Magat, *Community Control and the Urban School* (Praeger, 1970), pp. 158–70.

41. Lester W. Milbrath cites many studies in the United States and in five other nations to support the proposition that "national elections are nearly always perceived as more important than local elections." *Political Participation: How and Why Do People Get Involved in Politics?* (Rand McNally, 1965), p. 104. See also V. O. Key, Jr., *Politics, Parties, and Pressure Groups,* 5th ed. (Crowell, 1964), pp. 579–80; and Malcolm E. Jewell, *The State Legislature: Politics and Practice* (Random House, 1962), pp. 33–47.

42. *New York Times,* March 24, 1975, reporting a Gallup poll commissioned by the National School Boards Association.

churches. The first elections produced boards dominated by white professionals in a predominantly minority school system.[43]

Less than one-tenth of the electorate voted in the 1975 election. The highest turnouts were in white areas where antibusing candidates promised to use the community board's power to resist desegregation. In part of Brooklyn organizations of both major parties joined to produce an antibusing slate.[44] Decentralization seemingly reinforced segregation.

The dominant force in the elections has been the United Federation of Teachers, which mobilized its 55,000 members to defend their prerogatives. The union candidates won control of twenty-seven of the thirty-two community boards in the 1975 elections. The low turnout was not the fault of the city government, which spent $750,000 in a drive to increase registration but found such lack of interest that it cost an average of more than $100 a voter. The election results quashed the hopes of the early reformers that the boards would counterbalance the power of the union. Decentralization only increased union power, giving the UFT a veto over management in most of the city.[45] The UFT won another major victory in 1977 when only 8 percent of the eligible voters participated.[46]

There was substantial evidence that some of the local boards were engaging in the very kind of patronage politics and small-time corruption that their opponents had originally feared. By 1975 prosecutions of several community board officials were under way and others were being investigated. In some cases the central board had been forced to resume control of local functions.[47]

Some of the strong early supporters of the community control movement were having second thoughts about the system. Kenneth Clark, who had supported the movement, reversed his position and attacked its effects.[48] One of the leading academic proponents, Marilyn Gittell, said that she now favored metropolitan desegregation, which she felt was compatible with some form of administrative decentralization.[49]

43. Reginald Stuart, "Community Boards Have Few Powers," *Race Relations Reporter* (no month or day; 1969), pp. 10–11.

44. *New York Times*, March 27, 1975.

45. *New York Times*, April 23, April 28, and May 14, 1975.

46. *New York Times*, May 18, 1977.

47. Leonard Buder, "City to Take Over 3 School Regions in Fiscal Trouble," *New York Times*, October 29, 1974.

48. Kenneth Clark, "New York's Biracial Public Schools," *Integrated Education* (May–June 1975), pp. 153–55.

49. Marilyn Gittell, "The Political Implications of *Milliken* v. *Bradley*," in U.S.

The New York experience, at a minimum, dispelled the notion that decentralization would lead to major educational breakthroughs. The community boards may well be more conservative than a single central board— they seem to be a device to facilitate UFT control of management. The experience of New York with community authority limited decentralization in other cities. In many cities, the idea was viewed more skeptically.

Detroit's early experience with community control contributed directly to the filing of the federal court case (*Milliken*) for metropolitan desegregation. The city was divided into ten districts, and white candidates won control of six of the eight local school boards in the mostly black school district. Faced first with the adamant resistance to desegregation of twelve high schools and then with a self-defeating community control program, the NAACP decided in 1970 to pursue metropolitan integration as a solution. Three-fourths of Detroit's black children were in schools that had more than 90 percent minority students, but the black public remained strongly integrationist, with 81 percent preferring biracial schools. Half said they supported busing their children into the suburbs for desegregation, and another third were ready to accept this arrangement. Three-fourths believed equal education was more likely in an integrated setting.[50] Decentralization, in other words, generated a distinctly ambivalent reaction and did not displace the belief that integration was the route to educational improvement.

The ideal of decentralization as a way to resist desegregation surfaced again in Illinois when the Chicago school board came under pressure to desegregate in 1977. One Chicago legislator introduced a bill to break up the city into twenty-five separate districts. "This," said Representative Douglas Huff, "would give the blacks a chance to establish themselves."[51]

## The Law and Urban Segregation

When hope for voluntary local action against segregation is gone, civil rights groups often turn to the courts. They had little success in the courts during the 1960s because the constitutional principles of urban school desegregation remained unsettled. Unfavorable decisions in the lower

---

Commission on Civil Rights, *Milliken* v. *Bradley: The Implications for Metropolitan Desegregation* (GPO, 1974), pp. 43–44.

50. Phyllis Myers, "From Auto City to School Bus City," *City* (Summer 1972), pp. 35–37.

51. *Chicago Daily News,* April 7, 1977.

courts, as well as the difficulty and expense of challenging a huge school system, discouraged litigation.

Things began to change in the early 1970s. Federal court orders were won against the Detroit system and parts of New York City, and state courts found against Los Angeles and Philadelphia school authorities. Chicago was pressured by the state board of education.

## The Detroit Precedent

The Supreme Court's first northern urban school decision in 1973 (the *Keyes* decision for Denver) began to clarify the legal status of urban segregation. In 1974 the Court examined the practices of the Detroit school system and held unanimously that Detroit was guilty of unconstitutional segregation.[52]

Compared with most other urban school districts the Detroit school system had been a model for much of the 1960s. Its segregation was less extreme than that in Chicago and Philadelphia. The kinds of violations found in Detroit, like gerrymandering school attendance zones and taking actions with the foreseeable effect of intensifying or perpetuating segregation,[53] have been documented by civil rights groups and scholars in each of the other largest cities. Once the Supreme Court found segregation in Detroit unconstitutional, it seemed unlikely that the practices of any other large district could stand up to careful judicial scrutiny. Any time a civil rights group could get the money toegther to mount a costly legal challenge, Assistant Attorney General J. Stanley Pottinger concluded, federal courts would probably have little choice but to order desegregation.[54]

Each of the five largest districts has already faced some kind of enforcement activity. In Los Angeles, a state court first ordered desegregation of the school system in 1970. A 1976 decision by the California Supreme Court found the city guilty of intentional segregation and concluded that California law required desegregation.[55] The Pennsylvania State Human Relations Commission found Philadelphia's segregation a violation of state law in 1971 and ordered the city to develop a desegregation plan. Chicago briefly lost its federal funds in 1965 and was threatened with litigation by

52. *Milliken* v. *Bradley,* 418 U.S. 717 (1974).

53. *Bradley* v. *Milliken,* 383 F. Supp. at 592–94 (1972).

54. Interview with J. Stanley Pottinger, Assistant Attorney General for Civil Rights, April 22, 1975.

55. The original decision was *Crawford* v. *Board of Education* (Calif. Super. Ct., Los Angeles County, No. 822, 854, 1970); the 1976 decision is *Crawford* v. *Board of Education of the City of Los Angeles,* 130 Cal. Rptr. 724 (1976).

the Justice Department under Attorney General John Mitchell. In 1977 the Illinois State Board of Education gave Chicago a deadline for preparing a desegregation plan.

### New York

After the *Keyes* decision, civil rights lawyers generally agreed that New York City's segregation was unconstitutional. This belief was tested, and confirmed, in a January 1974 decision ordering desegregation of Mark Twain Junior High School in the Coney Island area of Brooklyn. District Judge Jack B. Weinstein concluded that "decisions have been made knowing they would encourage segregation and failures to take available steps to reverse segregative tendencies have made a bad situation worse."[56] A series of actions beginning in the mid-1960s had steadily channeled white students away from Mark Twain though it had more empty space than any school in the district. Between 1962 and 1973 white enrollment declined from more than four-fifths to less than one-fifth.[57]

The segregation of the school was in sharp contrast to the community pattern: there was only one-sixth nonwhite resident enrollment in the district. Even if children bused in from outside were included, the district had only 30 percent black and Puerto Rican students. But the Mark Twain school had 82 percent.[58]

Even though the racial implications of local decisions were apparent, the community board refused to desegregate. The city school chancellor ordered desegregation, then backed down, claiming it would be "self-defeating in that those white students, over a very short period of time, will evaporate."[59]

Judge Weinstein held that much of the increasing racial segregation was caused by the city's housing authority. Decisions about the construction of subsidized housing in the area, together with the authority's policy of giving first preference to families displaced by urban renewal, resulted in a sudden increase in minority pupils in the neighborhood. The projects had large majorities of black and Puerto Rican residents.[60] It was a cycle in which the segregation of the school and the increasing minority population of the

---

56. *Hart* v. *Community School Board of Brooklyn District* #2, 383 F. Supp. 699 at 707 (E.D.N.Y. 1974).

57. Ibid. at 711.

58. Ibid. at 713.

59. Ibid. at 720.

60. Ibid. at 723.

neighborhood, both heavily influenced by public decisions, reinforced each other and made any reversal of the pattern unlikely.

The fact that Central Coney Island . . . has a predominantly nonwhite population, and the fact that Mark Twain Junior High School, which services this area, is severely racially imbalanced, have discouraged, and presumably will continue to discourage, white persons, especially white families with school-age children, from renting or purchasing housing in the area now serviced by Mark Twain.[61]

The court ordered desegregation of the school.

There had been other small desegregation efforts in parts of New York City. Sometimes they produced angry neighborhood protests, as in Canarsie in 1972. The school system made fewer and fewer adjustments.

Since the mid-1960s there has also been intermittent and usually ineffectual pressure for desegregation from the New York State commissioner of education. The most recent was his December 1975 order directing desegregation of two high schools in Queens and Brooklyn. In response, the New York City School Board argued that any such attempts would be futile since demographic changes in the city's population would tend to eliminate more and more majority white schools. Any movement toward racial balance, the board claimed, would merely increase the number of schools that were predominantly minority by 1980.[62] The state commissioner retreated and the NAACP took one of the cases into federal court in 1977.

### Los Angeles

The Los Angeles case, which has been in the courts since 1963, has produced three decisions, and there will be much more litigation before a remedy is devised. After a sixty-eight-day trial in 1968, a desegregation order was handed down by a California superior court in May 1970.[63] The decision was written by Judge Alfred Gitelson. At first highly skeptical, Gitelson conducted extensive research on the issue during the long trial and in preparing his decision. When he found the city schools guilty of illegal segregation, his decision made his court the target of local and national criticism. In the next election, Gitelson lost the seat on the bench he had held for twelve years.[64]

Gitelson ruled that Los Angeles' segregation was de jure rather than

61. Ibid. at 724.
62. *New York Times*, February 19, 1976.
63. *Crawford* v. *Board of Education* (1970).
64. Interview with Alfred Gitelson, June 11, 1974.

de facto. Many of the board's decisions, he said, had "perpetuated and created segregated schools."[65] He also ruled that the board had consistently ignored its responsibility to foster integration. "It lent its power and authority and finances and processes to create, maintain and perpetuate segregated schools and segregated education, and its action 'discourages integration or instigates or encourages segregation.' "[66]

Los Angeles School Superintendent Robert Kelly responded by claiming that the court had departed from existing legal principles and that desegregation would require "enormous sums." "Our studies show that the only feasible way to accomplish racial balance in the schools of Los Angeles is through a program of mass mandatory busing." This, he said, would cost $180 million over the coming eight years.[67] The decision was attacked by President Nixon and the secretary of HEW. The school system won a stay of the order, pending appeal. Seven years later the dispute was still in court, unresolved.

The school board's appeal brief argued that the board had done nothing wrong, that segregation did not harm minority children, and that integration was simply not feasible in the city. It stated that partial desegregation would be self-defeating but that districtwide desegregation was completely impractical. The board's lawyers, however, conceded that any effective plan would have to be mandatory, involve racial quotas, and encompass the entire district or even the metropolitan area.[68]

Fifty percent of Los Angeles' enrollment was minority in 1970. Unfavorable enrollment trends, the board stated, only increased the difficulties caused by the physical separation. A substantial majority of the white students lived in the San Fernando Valley, where the schools were 85 percent white. In the rest of the city, nearly two-thirds of the students were from minority groups. The valley was separated from the rest of the city by the Santa Monica Mountains, with connections limited to three large freeways and a number of winding mountain roads.[69]

The school board urged the courts to do nothing because desegregation did not really help minority children and claimed it would "opt for integration if and when there exists rather convincing evidence that the academic

65. *Crawford* v. *Board of Education* (1970).

66. Ibid.

67. Los Angeles Unified School District, *Spotlight* (February 16, 1970), p. 1.

68. *Crawford* v. *Board of Education*, Appellant's Opening Brief (1972), vol. 1, pp. 17, 135.

69. Ibid., p. 17.

and other benefits of integration exceed the academic and other losses resulting from cutbacks ... required to raise funds for integration." The board argued that the money required for desegregation would produce more educational results if applied to the district's normal program. The courts should therefore permit the schools to operate as they wished.[70]

The civil rights attorneys characterized the school board's view of the law as follows:

Appellants' ultimate contention comes down to the view that the District may lawfully operate an essentially dual school system, that provides admittedly inferior education to minority students, until such time as it has excess funds for integration or until it can be demonstrated with mathematical certainty that funds expended for integration will produce more achievement in the narrow sense than do traditional school inputs.[71]

Attorneys for the ACLU argued that "the District has ... knowingly, affirmatively and in bad faith, segregated its minority pupils *de jure*." The board had built and zoned schools "within racially imbalanced, segregated ghetto areas knowing and intending that the students who live in such areas would be required to attend these schools." Finally, the system's transfer and busing policies, have "compelled its disadvantaged minority pupils to attend segregated neighborhood schools, while permitting white students to escape to predominantly white schools."[72]

The California Supreme Court acted on the case in June 1976. The court held that Los Angeles did have de jure segregation and that, under state law, it had to "take reasonably feasible steps to alleviate school segregation" even if it were de facto. It pointed out that racial balance was not required but that the school board must implement "a program which promises to achieve meaningful progress toward eliminating the segregation in the district."[73] If the school board failed to carry out such a plan, the California courts would order one. The courts could reject a particular school system proposal if they concluded that it would produce excessive white flight and ultimate resegregation of the school system. The courts would also consider "alternative" solutions to the problems of segregation where desegregation was not feasible. The state supreme court found that Los Angeles' long defiance of its responsibility to prepare a working deseg-

70. Ibid., p. 27.
71. *Crawford v. Board of Education*, Respondent's Reply Brief (1972), p. 8.
72. Ibid., pp. 74–75.
73. *Crawford v. Board of Education of the City of Los Angeles*, 130 Cal. Rptr. 724 at 726–27.

regation plan fully justified judicial intervention in demanding school board action.[74]

The ultimate result of this decision is still unclear. The school district prepared its first desegregation plan in 1977, opening a complex legal battle over a remedy. When the court rejected the city's plan for all-voluntary segregation, the district proposed that grades four through eight be partially integrated in the fall of 1978. Further proceedings will be necessary before a final plan is prepared. It is clear, however, that the nation's second largest school system will have to begin desegregation in the coming years.

### Philadelphia and Chicago

Philadelphia and Chicago were the only large cities in which a non-judicial agency took the lead in pressing for desegregation. The Pennsylvania Human Relations Commission was the first state administrative agency in the United States to assert its power to force the integration of a big city school system without a specific directive from its state legislature.

At the beginning of the 1970s, the Philadelphia school system had a predominantly black enrollment (over 60 percent in 1970). Ninety-three percent of the 169,000 black pupils attended schools with black majorities and one-twentieth attended all-black schools.[75]

When the state agency acted, it was very late not only for achieving full desegregation within the central city boundaries, but also because of the political climate of the city. The desegregation directive came in mid-1971, just months before Frank Rizzo became mayor of the city on a strong anti–civil rights platform. Both the progressive superintendent, Mark Shedd, and the Dilworth school board were soon replaced by conservative leaders.

Philadelphia challenged the Human Relations Commission and the case went into state courts. Commission officials brought in the nation's leading desegregation planners, Gordon Foster and Michael Stolee of the University of Miami, to draft a plan for the city.[76] The governor successfully vetoed three state legislative bills to end the commission's enforcement power in 1974, 1975, and 1976. The commission submitted a plan, after many delays, to the commonwealth court in July 1975. It proposed busing some 50,000 students, about one-fifth of the total enrollment, to produce some integration at five-sixths of the city's schools. The cost of the plan was

74. Ibid. at 727.
75. HEW, Office for Civil Rights, May 1976.
76. *Integrated Education* (July–August 1975), pp. 29–30.

in dispute, with commission officials estimating it at $10 million a year and the school board at $35 million.[77] The goal of the plan was not to put black children in predominantly white schools, since that was impossible on a large scale in a school system with almost two-thirds black children, but to substantially reduce the number of schools where the enrollment was 95 percent black or more.[78] This was a very modest definition of desegregation.

The city school board was bitterly opposed. School board attorney Martin Horowitz said that after great effort the plan would leave over a hundred city schools more than 75 percent black. "You're going to disrupt too many lives, spend too much money and accomplish little," he maintained.[79]

The board said it would support a plan merging the city schools with the surrounding suburbs, creating a metropolitan school district, hardly a serious possibility in the wake of the Supreme Court's *Milliken* decision. "Only about six percent of the students in the districts adjoining Philadelphia are black," the board told the court, "and five of the thirteen adjoining districts have fewer than one percent black enrollment."[80] A board spokesman claimed that white children would be "seriously threatened" by black gangs if they were sent into ghetto schools.[81]

The Pennsylvania Supreme Court ruled in 1977 that Philadelphia must desegregate, but the lower court held that the city need only develop magnet schools that might integrate 10 to 15 percent of the students. Superintendent Michael Marcase said that the district probably would not have the money to follow the court order in any case. Substantial desegregation was still a long way off.

The city of Chicago was not only the most severely segregated, both in schools and in housing, but it had a record of harsh race relations and political subordination of black demands unequaled in the other large cities. While significant black suburbanization had begun in New York and Los Angeles by 1970, Chicago's suburbs remained segregated. The city was found guilty of unconstitutional segregation of its public housing in a series of precedent-setting federal court cases culminating in a 1976 Supreme Court decision.[82] It was also the first city to lose revenue sharing funds because of job discrimination.

77. *New York Times,* July 24, 1975.
78. *Philadelphia Inquirer,* August 16, 1975.
79. Ibid.
80. School District of Philadelphia, "Desegregation Plan" (July 1975; processed), p. 20.
81. *Philadelphia Inquirer,* August 16, 1975.
82. *Gautreaux* v. *Chicago Housing Authority,* 265 F. Supp. 582 (N.D. Ill. 1967),

Few observers doubted that sufficient evidence of state action fostering
school segregation could be found in the city, far stronger evidence than
that which satisfied the Supreme Court in the Detroit and Denver cases. Although there had been no trial, there had been repeated investigations of
the schools by a variety of public and private groups and individual scholars. Civil rights organizations had documented individual cases and policies
of discrimination for years.[83]

The first serious school segregation enforcement activity came on the
peripheral issues of faculty segregation and the city's failure to provide
special school programs for the Spanish-speaking student body. In mid-
1973 HEW found the city ineligible for special funds under the Emergency
School Aid Act. Not trusting the Nixon administration, Congress had
written strict civil rights requirements into this legislation intended primarily to assist integration. In 1975 Chicago schools lost almost $8 million
of this money.[84]

The school board's only initiative was a very small desegregation program in one area. Fewer than 500 children were bused to a few schools on
a voluntary plan. It received little support from school officials, and the
number of participating children declined. In 1974, 43 percent of the city's
white students attended virtually all-white schools and 86 percent of the
more than 300,000 minority students attended schools that were at least
nine-tenths minority.[85]

Pressure from two directions brought the Chicago case to life again in
1976. HEW had been ordered by a federal court to resume enforcement of
the 1964 Civil Rights Act. Segregation of faculty in Chicago was one of
the issues the federal agency had illegally postponed. HEW held fund-
cutoff hearings in the fall of 1976, and a federal administrative law judge
found Chicago guilty in February 1977.[86] This decision, which could mean
the loss of more than $80 million a year in federal aid, brought rapid devel-
opment of a plan to desegregate teachers. On the more important issue of

296 F. Supp. 907 (1969), 304 F. Supp. 736 (1969 order), aff'd, 436 F.2d 306 (7th
Cir. 1970), cert. denied, 402 U.S. 922 (1971), 342 F. Supp. 827 (1972 order), aff'd,
480 F.2d 210 (7th Cir. 1973), cert. denied, 414 U.S. 1144 (1974); Hills v. Gautreaux,
425 U.S. 284 (1976).

83. Chicago Board of Education, Advisory Panel, "Integration of the Public
Schools"; Complaint of the Coordinating Council of Community Organizations, July 4,
1965, reprinted in Integrated Education (December 1965–January 1966), pp. 10–35.

84. Washington Post, September 4, 1975.

85. Nathaniel Levin, "Fading Away: Integration in Chicago," Integrated Education (March–April 1976), pp. 8–10; HEW, Office for Civil Rights, May 1976.

86. Chicago Sun-Times, February 18, 1977.

student segregation, the Illinois State Board of Education notified the city in late 1976 that it must develop a plan to comply with state desegregation guidelines or risk losing state aid, which was essential for continued operation.[87] The city began voluntary one-way busing of 496 students in the fall of 1977 and drew up a ten-year plan for more voluntary actions.[88]

Although state authorities in Pennsylvania and Illinois had shown leadership, they were not prepared for a final showdown with the school boards in their largest cities. The Pennsylvania agency postponed its actions year after year. While the state board of education waited for a new proposal from Chicago, the local NAACP began to raise money to sue for desegregation.

## Practicality

Each of the nation's largest cities is almost surely guilty of de jure segregation, as now defined by the Supreme Court. Legally, the cities' school systems have violated the rights of minority children. While considerable effort would be required to prove the violations, there is little doubt that it could be done. A real question remains, however—is there any remedy that would work?

When legal principles clash with realities, the courts may well conclude that a remedy for one legal deficiency would only create new inequities. Even if the children of the largest cities are unconstitutionally segregated, there simply may be no reasonable way to produce integrated schools. Nowhere are the questions of feasibility more urgent than in the largest cities.

While one could wish there were a remedy for every wrong, critics argue that a misguided effort to remedy segregation may accelerate the city's decay. This point of view is by no means confined to conservatives. Even leading civil rights advocates have had misgivings about the staggering job of changing the racial practices of the largest cities.

The NAACP led a nationwide campaign for urban school integration in the early 1960s, working through scores of its local chapters and hoping that the courts would act. The NAACP education director, however, conceded at one point that there were practical limitations that would probably prevent desegregating the largest cities. In 1963 June Shagaloff said:

For the schools in central Harlem, of New York City, or of Detroit, or Chicago—any large city—obviously schools cannot be re-zoned. . . . Here we say open enrollment, to permit children to transfer from Negro schools, segregated schools,

87. Ibid., December 10, 1976.
88. *Chicago Tribune*, October 28, 1977.

to white schools; the assignment of children from over-crowded Negro schools to under-utilized white schools; but for the vast numbers of children who are going to remain, we also urge that the schools be brought up to standard.[89]

Similarly, Kenneth Clark criticized proposals for reverse busing of white students into the schools of Harlem. Such an effort, he said, would generate bitter resistance, producing "disruption of the educational process" without any educational gains. Clark then saw the idea as "unrealistic, irrelevant, emotional and diversionary."[90] He wrote in his classic 1965 study, *Dark Ghetto:*

This plan seems to offer immediate desegregation, but in many cases it would lead to bad education, and, in the end, therefore, to even more segregation. Whites would pull out of the public school system even more rapidly than they are presently doing. In Brooklyn, for example, if real integration were the goal, about 70,000 Negro and Puerto Rican children, under eleven, would have to be transported twice a day, some of them ten miles away. In Manhattan, where schools have an even higher proportion of Negro and Puerto Rican children, even longer travel time would fail to bring about meaningful integration.[91]

Any acceptable plan, he said, must "hold white pupils, even bring more back into the public school system."[92]

As the civil rights movement evolved, these attitudes began to change. Within months, the NAACP was urging integration on the edges of the New York City ghettos. Clark, after a period of enthusiasm for community control, became a militant integrationist. In the mid-1970s, he was calling for complete integration of the school system, which now had two-thirds minority children.[93]

The educational leaders in three of the five largest school systems insist there is no feasible desegregation plan that can successfully accomplish general integration of the city schools. The school boards in the other two, Detroit and Philadelphia, argue that desegregation of the entire huge metropolitan area is much preferable to mere integration of the city's schools. The Supreme Court, however, rejected this view in its Detroit decision.

### The New York View

After two decades of futile battles to desegregate the New York schools, Chancellor Irving Anker announced that even small integration efforts

89. Charles E. Silberman, *Crisis in Black and White* (Random House, 1964), p. 294.

90. Ibid., pp. 300–01.

91. Kenneth Clark, *Dark Ghetto* (Harper Torchbooks, 1965), p. 115.

92. Ibid.

93. Clark, "New York's Biracial Public Schools," pp. 153–55.

should end. New demands for integration, coming at a time of financial trouble, unsuccessful decentralization efforts, and the pressures of the city's rapid social and economic decline seemed too much. The chancellor said there was "a steady shift in population within the metropolitan area," and "so-called minority groups are now heavily in the majority." Racial balance would only create 65 percent minority schools.[94] Outlining various integration steps, like rezoning schools, pairing nearby schools, and permitting open transfers, Anker said that all were undermined by the demographic changes and by the enrollment of 47 percent of the school-age Anglos in the city in private schools during the 1972–73 school year.

New York City had only 15 percent of the state's Anglo enrollment but 72 percent of the state's black children and 90 percent of its Latinos. Outside the city, eight New York school systems in nine had only 10 percent, or fewer, minority children. Governmental fragmentation, superimposed on residential segregation, greatly intensified the problem.[95]

Michael Rosen, the legal adviser to the chancellor, argued that with full desegregation "the whites will disappear."[96] Racial balance by borough, said Chancellor Anker, would mean schools with 32 percent Anglo children in Brooklyn, 19 percent in the Bronx, and 20 percent in Manhattan. The school system had been losing about 1.4 percent of the remaining Anglo students yearly, and the figures would steadily become more lopsided. "Integration does not mean," Anker insisted, "a school that is sixty, seventy, eighty percent minority group youngsters.[97] On this issue, Eleanor Holmes Norton, chairperson of the city's Human Rights Commission, agreed: "To simply distribute a diminishing number of whites thinner and thinner is obviously to get embarked on a process that will not result in integration. A school with twenty percent white students and eighty percent minority children is not integrated. . . . That's why the metropolitan approach has to be looked at very closely."[98]

Anker maintained that moves to increase school integration in the city would be counterproductive unless housing officials acted to stabilize the local proportion of white residents; otherwise whites would merely move faster. Housing policies, he said, often intensified transition.[99]

94. Irving Anker, *Chancellor's Report on Programs and Problems Affecting Integration of the New York City Public Schools* (February 1974), pp. 1–2, 4–15.

95. Ibid., pp. 21–25.

96. Interview with Michael Rosen, March 5, 1974.

97. Irving Anker, "Integration in New York City Schools," *Integrated Education* (May–June 1975), pp. 138–39, 142.

98. Ibid., p. 142.

99. "Report of the Chancellor Pursuant to the Opinion of the Court in Hart, *et al.* v. Community School District 21, *et al.*" (March 1, 1974; processed), pp. 2–5.

*Demographic Trends*

During the time in which the legal issues of northern school segregation were defined and some tentative principles worked out, the entire populations of the largest school districts were transformed almost beyond recognition. In 1960 all of the systems still had large Anglo majorities and little attention had been devoted to the growth of the Hispanic minority.

By the mid-1970s a new situation existed (see table 6-2). New York and Los Angeles, where in 1960 only one-fifth of the children had been minority students, now had rapidly disappearing Anglo minorities. In Los Angeles, where the 1965 Watts riots had focused national attention on black anger, the city faced the unexpected prospect of a Hispanic majority in its schools. Segregation had spread further and whites had left more rapidly and for more distant suburbs than could have been foreseen. The difficult desegregation task of the early 1960s had become the seemingly insurmountable problem of the mid-1970s and promised to produce still greater segregation in the following decades. One could already reasonably assume that a random student in any of the largest school systems was a member of a minority group; soon it would be virtually a certainty.

When the board of education of New York City was sued by the NAACP over the desegregation of a single high school in Queens in 1977, the city argued that it was powerless to accomplish anything. It submitted enrollment projections based on the racial transition experienced in a number of the city's high schools, which, the board claimed, showed that there would not be a single predominantly Anglo high school in Queens by 1985. Racially balancing all Queens schools, the city statisticians argued, would

Table 6-2. *Minority Enrollment of the Five Largest School Systems,* *1974–75 School Year*

| City | Total enrollment | Black | | Hispanic | |
|------|------------------|-------|-------|----------|-------|
| | | Number | Percent | Number | Percent |
| New York[a] | 1,102,905 | 405,311 | 37 | 299,294 | 27 |
| Chicago | 530,188 | 309,473 | 58 | 67,508 | 13 |
| Los Angeles | 603,656 | 149,358 | 25 | 167,868 | 28 |
| Philadelphia | 266,500 | 164,558 | 62 | 12,557 | 5 |
| Detroit | 256,300 | 183,980 | 72 | 4,425 | 2 |
| Total | 2,759,549 | 1,212,680 | 44 | 551,652 | 20 |

Source: HEW, Office for Civil Rights, and school district research departments.
a. Statistics for the 1973–74 school year.

simply speed up the transition by several years.[100] Whatever happened, unless the demographic trends in New York City changed, there was no real hope of avoiding a fast transition to ghetto and barrio schools in the part of the city that had long been the stronghold of the white middle class. With the exception of the small, isolated school population of Staten Island, the entire city would retain few predominantly Anglo schools.

Administrators in other large cities presented similar statistics. During the 1976–77 school year, the Chicago schools enrolled slightly more than three-fourths minority children. Philadelphia schools had only one-third Anglo children and Detroit fewer than one-fifth. The defense of the Los Angeles school board in 1977 litigation was based on projections that the schools would soon have only a small minority of whites and that they would leave much faster if desegregation took place.

After delaying for so long, school boards now argued that unfortunately it was simply too late.

### Defining Feasibility

The question whether there is a feasible desegregation plan for the biggest cities combines several issues. First, one must define "desegregation." If desegregation means racial balance, it is feasible in all the cities. If it means putting all children in predominantly Anglo schools, it is possible in none. Second, one must specify who should be desegregated. Desegregating blacks only, for example, would be relatively easy in both New York and Los Angeles. Third, the answers are obviously different if one thinks on a metropolitan as opposed to a city-only level. Fourth, it is necessary to investigate different components of feasibility—cost, time on the bus, health and safety of children, short-term white flight, and long-term demographic stability.

The legal meaning of desegregation continues to evolve. In 1971 the Supreme Court decided that southern cities with their history of overt segregation must take any necessary positive action to produce actual integration. This would require a major effort to eliminate "racially identifiable" schools.[101] In 1973 the Court extended this obligation to northern and western communities with de jure segregation.[102]

The Court, however, did not spell out clear standards. The tendency of

100. New York Board of Education, Office of Educational Statistics, "Methodology for 1976–1980 Pupil Projections" (1977; processed).
101. *Swann* v. *Charlotte-Mecklenburg Board of Education,* 402 U.S. 1 (1971).
102. *Keyes* v. *School District No. 1, Denver, Colorado,* 413 U.S. 189 (1973).

the lower court decisions has been to distribute students roughly proportionately among the various schools in the district. The Supreme Court has
imposed no such standard.

Proportional plans seem generally workable in districts with a large
white majority, like Charlotte, North Carolina, the first urban case the
Supreme Court considered.[103] The real problem comes in school districts
with black and Hispanic majorities. Here proportionate distribution would
mean all schools were dominated by minority students.

A plan that produced predominantly minority schools would conflict
with another vital aspect of the legal definition of desegregation—the concept that the evil of the segregated school is largely related to the racial
identifiability of the school. Minority schools in a predominantly white
metropolitan area, the argument goes, are seen as inferior and are treated as
inferior, and their students are evaluated as inferior when they go out into
the white-controlled economic and higher education systems. This raises
obvious doubts about the value of desegregation plans that would leave all
students in the central city system in schools dominated by minority
students.

If elimination of the racial identifiability of the school is to remain an
important criterion for desegregation plans, it is obviously impossible to
desegregate all the schools of any of the largest cities. Four choices remain:
do nothing; desegregate on a metropolitan basis; desegregate part of the
city, leaving the rest of the minority children in largely segregated schools;
or simply decide to call predominantly black schools "desegregated," judg-
ing their identifiability by the standard of citywide enrollment, not that
of the white majority in the metropolitan area. In the Detroit decision, the
Supreme Court chose the last alternative, and HEW and the Justice Department have suggested it in some cases.

The question of whom to desegregate is relatively new. In the early years
of desegregation, since virtually all black children in the South were
illegally segregated, the answer was clear.

Urban desegregation cases in the 1970s suddenly began to affect very
large nonblack minority groups, and the courts were confronted with the
problem of defining their status. Basically, there were three choices—
count these groups as part of the majority group and use them to help
desegregate blacks; count them as victimized minorities like blacks and
devise plans to integrate each group with Anglos; or leave them in segregated schools of their own, perhaps providing bilingual-bicultural educa-

103. Swann v. Charlotte-Mecklenburg (1971).

tion. The general assumption has been that both blacks and Puerto Ricans or Mexican-Americans must be desegregated. The status of other groups, including Asian-Americans, is unclear.

### Feasibility in Los Angeles

The Los Angeles litigation has largely revolved around the question of feasibility. The initial 1970 Los Angeles decision was denounced as a classic example of a court's ignoring reality. President Nixon called it "the most extreme judicial decree so far." HEW Secretary Robert Finch, another Californian, said it was "totally unrealistic." The local superintendent said it would lead to "virtual destruction of the district."[104]

One troublesome aspect of the Los Angeles case was that the city has changed in the many years since the case began. Each year there have been fewer white students. In the fall of 1971 minority enrollment was 52 percent but it was approaching 58 percent by the beginning of the 1974–75 school year and reached 63 percent in the fall of 1976.[105] Obviously, desegregation of the school system could not put all minority children in schools with Anglo majorities.

Unlike the other largest cities, blacks constituted only one-fourth of Los Angeles enrollment and the percentage was falling very slowly. In absolute numbers, too, black pupils were declining, though not as fast as white pupils. More than 14,000 fewer black children attended Los Angeles schools in 1976–77 than have five years earlier.[106]

The number of Anglo students fell as the white population aged, fertility dropped, and suburbanization continued. Anglo enrollment plummeted from 352,000 in 1966 to 219,000 in 1976, a decline of 133,000 students.[107] There was every likelihood that this trend would continue.

Feasibility in Los Angeles depends on the definition of who is entitled to desegregation. Certainly it should include black children, 95 percent of whom were in segregated schools in 1976–77.

The situation is complex for Chicanos and other Hispanics, who are

---

104. Caughey, *To Kill a Child's Spirit*, pp. 141, 151–62.

105. Los Angeles Unified School District: press release, January 25, 1974; Fall 1974 Elementary and Secondary School Civil Rights Survey; and "Plan for the Integration of Pupils" (1977; processed), p. 22.

106. HEW, Office for Civil Rights, "Distribution of Minority Students by School Composition, 1970–1974," p. 7; Los Angeles Unified School District, "Plan for the Integration of Pupils," p. 25.

107. Los Angeles Unified School District, "Plan for the Integration of Pupils," p. 27.

Table 6-3. *Levels of Black and Hispanic Segregation in Los Angeles,*
*1974–75*

Percent

| Minority students | Minority enrollment in school attended | | | | | |
|---|---|---|---|---|---|---|
| | 0–50 | 50–70 | 70–80 | 80–90 | 90–99 | 99–100 |
| Hispanic | 20.6 | 15.6 | 8.3 | 9.6 | 36.9 | 9.1 |
| Black | 9.2 | 4.0 | 2.8 | 4.8 | 17.6 | 61.5 |

Source: HEW Office for Civil Rights, "Distribution of Minority Students by School Composition, 1970–1974," report to the U.S. Senate (May 27, 1976; processed). Figures are rounded.

more likely than blacks to live in an integrated neighborhood (table 6-3). Although there is a long history of discrimination against Chicanos in California, the present situation of this group is more ambiguous than that of blacks. Mexican-Americans are less severely segregated; large numbers live outside the traditional barrios. There are increasing signs of assimilation and of intermarriage. A child with a Spanish surname may have a partially Spanish background, may come from a South American or Caribbean rather than a Mexican background, is usually English-speaking, and may be living in a nonsegregated typical middle class neighborhood. If desegregation remedies—and treatment as a victimized minority—were limited to children living in poor segregated barrios and the relatively assimilated families with Spanish surnames were treated simply as part of the majority, desegregation would become more feasible.

The status of the 6 percent of Asian students as a minority group needing desegregation is uncertain. Although the historical anti-Chinese movement in California and the removal of Japanese-Americans to detention camps during World War II showed racial hostility, Judge Gitelson saw no serious problem in contemporary Los Angeles.[108] The ACLU lawyers conceded in 1972 that a desegregation plan might well exclude Asian students, noting that they were highly successful in school and might be considered members of the majority for desegregation purposes.[109]

Financial feasibility depends on desegregation standards. The city's cost estimates were based on the most demanding possible standard—placing about half minority and half Anglo children in each school. The Supreme Court, however, explicitly rejected exact racial balance as a constitutional requirement, though it indicated that seriously disproportionate schools may be suspect. Nor did the Court require that desegregation plans elimi-

108. Interview with Alfred Gitelson, June 11, 1974.
109. *Crawford* v. *Board of Education,* Respondent's Reply Brief, p. 21.

nate every segregated ghetto school. In a city with an enrollment as large as that of Los Angeles, the courts would surely grant substantial discretion to the local judge and the school administration to design a plan likely to work in the local circumstances. The California Supreme Court emphasized this principle in its 1976 ruling.

At first both the school system and the ACLU lawyers assumed that no desegregation plan would work unless it included the entire city. In other words, singling out one part of the city for desegregation and forgetting others would merely give families a powerful incentive to move. Second, the school district officials initially assumed that any plan would have to desegregate all the city's minority groups and maintain equal ratios of Anglo children across the city. The state supreme court rejected these simple assumptions, as did the school district when required to submit a plan in 1977.

The cost figures presented to the courts in Los Angeles in 1970 maximized the possible expenses of the most extensive desegregation. One of the two estimates was prepared in 1967 by Henry Boas, an expert in data analysis, and was a rapid estimate intended, in his own words, "to indicate the economic infeasibility of forcing local school districts to resort to two-way busing to achieve racial balance."[110] The estimate incorrectly assumed that no children could walk to integrated schools and that very few buses could take more than one load of children to school each day.[111] The study was designed to help district officials make their case against state desegregation policies.

The only other source of information was an estimate prepared by the system's director of transportation, which also made several questionable assumptions that increased costs. This quick "pencil and paper" estimate of the cost of busing to approach exact racial balance throughout the school system concluded that putting approximately 49 percent minority children in every school building would take 1,655 buses. With operating and repair costs added to the purchase price of buses, his rough estimate was that the costs could reach $40 million the first year and $20 million each subsequent year. The city would receive about $11.3 million in state reimbursements each year.[112]

Desegregation, according to the school system's high estimates, would have amounted to approximately 3 percent of local school costs for 1969–70.

110. Memorandum from Henry Boas to Superintendent Crowther, November 8, 1967, quoted in ibid., p. 164.
111. *Crawford* v. *Board of Education*, Respondent's Reply Brief, p. 162.
112. Ibid., pp. 209–15, 163–68, 206–17.

More realistic figures, the ACLU suggested, would probably amount to 1 or 2 percent.[113]

But there was a more accurate estimate of the maximum burden of reasonably efficient transportation of children for complete desegregation. Although this analysis, contained in an HEW-commissioned report prepared by the Rand Corporation in 1972, was in the hands of the school administration, it was not released, even to members of the school board.[114]

The Rand study used computer techniques to estimate the minimum costs for both in-district and metropolitan desegregation. It systematically considered many types of desegregation plans, transportation patterns, methods of efficiently using buses, and so forth, calculating the consequences of the many possible different combinations of factors. It also took into account the fact that some students could walk to integrated schools.[115] Rand reported that it would be much less expensive to stop slightly short of perfect racial balance. Fewer students would have to be bused than the school system had estimated—about one-fifth, plus the 5 percent already bused for other reasons. The average bus ride would be only twenty minutes, and the total annual cost of achieving 85 percent desegregation would be "about $25 per public school student." To achieve 91 percent desegregation would cost about $31 per student, amounting to less than 2 percent of the system's annual per-pupil expenditures.[116]

The study found that many of the commonly suggested alternatives to busing did little or nothing to lower costs. The crucial factor for minimizing expense was using each bus for more than one trip to and from school each day.[117]

More surprising, the study reported that a metropolitan plan, serving both the city and several adjacent districts, was feasible even in the sprawling area. Although civil rights groups had not even begun to work on such a plan, the estimates suggested that the costs were modest. While the number of students bused would increase, the proportion of students in the desegregated area who would need busing would decline by about a third. The percentage of white students in the typical desegregated school would be substantially higher. The metropolitan approach took advantage

113. Ibid., pp. 217–18; Los Angeles Unified Public Schools, *Fact Book, 1972.*

114. Interview with Robert Docter (member of the Los Angeles school board), June 11, 1974.

115. Emmett Keeler, "Planning School Desegregation" (Santa Monica: Rand Corp., 1972; processed).

116. Ibid., pp. vii–viii.

117. Ibid., p. ix.

of the several large white systems "located close to the areas of heaviest minority concentration in the central district."[118]

All the cost estimates in Los Angeles were made before the recent rapid inflation of all school costs, but all showed that the cost would be a small fraction of the budget. And each of them was based on more desegregation that will actually be required and far higher enrollments than current levels.

### Feasibility in Detroit

The battle over the Detroit metropolitan plan turned on legal issues. Both sides accepted similar data on the technical feasibility of busing the students. Desegregating dozens of school systems in the nation's fifth largest metropolitan area would require surprisingly low annual costs and surprisingly short bus rides.

The opposing sides, of course, described the facts differently. The state of Michigan argued that "the financial burden of multi-district transportation for the sole purpose of racial balance over a tri-county area is clearly excessive," and estimated that the plan would have an annual operating cost of $17 million. The area to be integrated, the Michigan attorney general claimed, was simply too large for any feasible plan.[119]

The district court observed that the additional percentage of students to be bused would be approximately the same as the average percentage of Michigan students already bused statewide. Judge Stephen Roth concluded that a plan would cost from $40 to $60 per child per year.[120]

The South already had desegregation plans covering more square miles. No student, NAACP lawyers pointed out, would be bused more than forty minutes. The fifty-two suburban districts were within eight miles of the city. In contrast, the average bus ride to school in the whole state was eight and a half miles, and there were existing situations in the Detroit suburbs where some students had to ride an hour and fifteen minutes to school. For a number of suburban children the new bus rides would actually be shorter.[121]

118. Ibid., pp. vii, 22.
119. *Milliken* v. *Bradley*, No. 73-434, Brief for Petitioners (1974), pp. 86, 53, 85–86.
120. *Milliken* v. *Bradley*, No. 73-434, *petition for cert. filed*, Frank J. Kelley, Attorney General, September 6, 1973, pp. 72a–73a.
121. *Milliken* v. *Bradley*, Brief for Respondents (1974), p. 37; Brief for Respondents, Board of Education for the School District of the City of Detroit (1974), pp. 110–11.

The feasibility of a metropolitan plan had to be compared to the feasibility of a Detroit-only plan, which was the only alternative after de jure segregation was proved in the city. The state took the position, ultimately adopted by the Supreme Court, that stable desegregation was possible within Detroit, and overlooked questions about whether 80 percent black schools were really "desegregated."

Detroit's population had peaked in 1950, when it contained 61 percent of the metropolitan area residents. Two decades later it had declined to 36 percent of the area residents, primarily the poor and the aged. The district court pointed out that statistical projections of trends which were well established *before desegregation* showed that the city schools would be 81 percent black in 1980, and almost 100 percent in 1991.[122]

Although Detroit school officials and civil rights lawyers appealed to the Supreme Court to allow them to develop a specific plan proving the feasibility of metropolitan desegregation before passing judgment on the question of areawide integration, a majority of the Court decided that the metropolitan approach must be rejected on legal grounds. Though the majority asserted that there would be complex administrative and financial problems, it did not examine feasibility in any detail. The Chief Justice dismissed concern about the demographic trends in the central city. Courts could not rearrange metropolitan schools, he wrote, to produce "the racial balance which they perceived as desirable."[123]

The dissenters believed that a metropolitan plan was both legally required and eminently feasible. They noted that the majority did not deny that it was feasible. In view of Detroit's existing two-thirds black enrollment and the established patterns of white migration, the dissenters concluded, a city-only plan was completely infeasible unless one twisted the concept of desegregation into a meaningless shape.

Actually, metropolitan desegregation in Detroit could probably have been considerably less costly than the estimates before the Court suggested if efficiency had been made a central criterion in planning busing. Members of a panel appointed by Judge Roth who outlined a metropolitan plan say that minimizing costs and distances was not the chief concern. Rather the panel tried to design a plan that had a good chance of working out both educationally and in community relations.

The outline for the metropolitan plan was drafted primarily by Merle Henrickson of the Detroit schools and Gordon Foster, University of Miami desegregation expert, working with the other members of the panel. The

122. *Milliken v. Bradley, petition for cert. filed*, p. 20a.
123. *Milliken v. Bradley*, 418 U.S. 717 at 740 (1974).

concept was to join a section of the city and a section of suburbia in a single district, where all children would spend some years in the city neighborhood and some years in the suburb. This system, the planners thought, would make each child "a participant in two neighborhoods— one in which he would be a host and one in which he would be a guest."[124]

The panel rebuffed computer firms that offered to design a plan minimizing busing. Henrickson dismissed computerized assignment as a "numbers game." Unless the plan fostered continuous association of children, the planners felt, the whole point of desegregation would be undermined. The transportation distances were moderate in any case.[125]

The plan's estimate of buses was based on rough approximations by the Michigan State Department of Education's supervisor of pupil transportation, Harold Wagner. Busing plans were drawn up, Wagner says, much like the early Los Angeles estimates, which assumed all busing would be additional, not rerouted, and that buses would be used inefficiently. More efficient use of buses might, he said, reduce the number of new buses required by about one-third, but he based his estimates on the number of buses that would be needed if there were no effective coordination between districts. The estimates were prepared by a "paper and pencil procedure," and Wagner conceded that a computerized study was essential for accurate estimates.[126]

The maximum estimated cost of getting the system started would include an initial investment of $65 million for buses and facilities. Operation would cost about $70 per student per year in 1974 prices. The actual cost to the local school districts, however, would be much lower as the state government reimburses about two-thirds of bus operating costs. Since fewer than half the children in the area were to be bused, the annual operating cost of the busing plan to the local district per pupil in the total enrollment would be less than $12 a year.[127] If cost were a primary concern, a more careful study might arrive at a significantly lower cost.

The Detroit area presented no great obstacles to integration in costs and distances. Once the large initial capital investments were made, there would be little effect on local budgets. The distances were not great and the bus rides would not take long. The elements of a plan had been worked out. The problems were, as usual, social and political.

124. Interview with Merle Henrickson, April 18, 1974.
125. Ibid.
126. Interview with Harold Wagner, April 18, 1974.
127. Ibid.; Harold Wagner, "Maximum Bus Requirement for Transportation of Pupils in the Desegregation Area" (undated).

## The Most Difficult Case

New York, a district with far more children than any other, poses the most complex desegregation problem of any American city, but also one of the most urgent because of the huge concentration of minority children. Cases against portions of the system are pending.

The legal situation was analyzed by NAACP general counsel Nathaniel Jones after the NAACP victory in the Coney Island case:

the Fourteenth Amendment applies to New York City as well as it does to Mississippi. . . . That means there can be no racial lines drawn; that school boards cannot allow segregation to come into the schools by means of imposing their attendance patterns on racially segregated housing patterns.

It is not enough for these boards to say that the reason schools are segregated is because housing is segregated, because the courts are clearly stating . . . that, where the school board has options as to the way that it assigns pupils and it accepts a plan which either creates or maintains or perpetuates segregation . . . it is guilty of a de jure act of segregation.[128]

Whatever the legal situation was, many assumed that there was simply no practical remedy in a huge system with less than one-third Anglo students. Judge Weinstein, the author of the Coney Island decision, commented in passing on the question, though it was not directly relevant to his case:

For an area as large as New York City or Metropolitan New York, the problems of practicability become critical. Desegregation may cause such a loss of time and such confusion as to outweigh any possible advantage to the students or society. To require equalization of racial and ethnic percentages in smaller areas such as Brooklyn might also prove abortive because the central portions have such high proportions of Black students. Desegregation that results in every school having an overwhelming Black and Hispanic student body accomplishes little. This suggests that the rule may include an element of reasonableness.[129]

Nathaniel Jones wondered whether a citywide plan would be sufficient. While he strongly supported the need for a plan that dealt with the entire city, he thought suburban involvement also might be needed. Once many jurisdictions were affected, state education officials would "come in and do the type of planning that will have to be done to create some exciting schools so there will not be a temptation to run."[130]

128. Nathaniel Jones, "Implications of the Weinstein Decision," *Integrated Education* (May–June 1975), p. 144.
129. *Hart* v. *Community School Board of Brooklyn District #2*, 383 F. Supp. 699 (E.D.N.Y. 1974).
130. Jones, "Implications of the Weinstein Decision," p. 146.

Two academics who had been involved in the battle since the mid-1950s —Kenneth Clark and Dan Dodson, a veteran New York desegregation researcher and planner—were the most certain about what should be done. Clark now spoke bitterly of litigation as the only thing that would ever make a difference.[131]

During 1974 Clark's research organization, the Metropolitan Applied Research Center (MARC), worked with an ad hoc coalition of major civil rights organizations hoping to initiate litigation against the city. Clark reported:

Representatives from such organizations as the NAACP, the Legal Defense Fund, the Puerto Rican Legal Defense Fund and the New York Civil Liberties Union have [had] a series of meetings. . . . And those lawyers have concluded, after rather serious discussion, that litigation is necessary; that the special machinery for New York City type problems of segregated schools is required in view of the limited resources which have already been over-committed in each of these agencies.[132]

The resources to initiate this litigation had not been found two years later. (MARC itself ran out of money and closed in mid-1976.)[133]

Dodson asserted that resistance to desegregation in New York was "political," not a question of feasibility. He accused school officials of misleading use of the "white flight" issue, arguing that much of the white enrollment decline they attributed to flight was actually caused by general demographic trends, which often occurred most rapidly in parts of the city with no integration at all. An aging population, falling birthrates, and long-established suburbanization were responsible for the decline.[134]

Dodson maintained that desegregation was both feasible and desirable. Principal reliance could be placed on empty seats in good white schools and white integration of the better schools in the inner city, and buildings no longer needed could be closed. It would be particularly easy, said Dodson, to desegregate the black population. Almost no black student would have to be bused beyond the school district adjoining his own.[135]

Clark argued that desegregation was feasible once one stopped thinking of schools as desegregated only if they contained a majority of English-speaking white students. Without much difficulty, he suggested, the city's students could be rearranged to reflect an approximate division of the

131. Clark, "New York City's Biracial Public Schools," pp. 153–55.
132. Ibid., p. 155.
133. New York Times, April 26, 1976.
134. Dan Dodson, "Is Desegregation Possible for New York City?" Integrated Education (May–June 1975), pp. 156, 157.
135. Ibid., p. 157.

total enrollment into equal groups of blacks, Anglos, and Latinos.[136] A metropolitan solution was not necessary:

The Board of Education of the City of New York at present alone has the power, the authority and *the legal responsibility to desegregate the schools of New York City.* It need not look elsewhere in order to effectively desegregate the schools of this city.[137]

The only significant study of desegregating the entire city was a 68-page paper prepared by Dodson for a state commission in late 1971. Dodson demonstrated that it would not be expensive to achieve a substantially better balancing of the city's three major groups. In fact, he stated, the entire effort might cost nothing at all if it were combined with a plan shutting down expensive and inefficient schools that were no longer needed.[138]

Dodson proposed a plan for the entire city, except Staten Island, where the distances and the difficulty of transporting large numbers of children were excessive. He concluded that the city's previous small desegregation efforts had been counterproductive:

Most such patchwork efforts . . . only exacerbate what is a delicate balance in these school enrollments. Usually such piecemeal efforts have accelerated the change from mixed to all-minority schools. This, in part, is the limitation of the neighborhood school. It cannot deal with population changes.[139]

More extensive integration, abandoning the neighborhood school pattern, on the other hand, not only might be more stable but would also permit school authorities to take all children out of "old, outmoded, hazardous buildings." By using the more than 34,000 empty spaces already available in outlying white neighborhoods, the system could save the cost of continuing to operate fifty aging elementary schools in the inner city.[140]

To make all elementary schools approximately representative of the citywide racial distribution, according to Dodson's very rough figures, would have required busing about 78,000 minority elementary school pupils out of the city and sending in 44,000 of the white children attending school outside. Since far more children would be moving outward, most of the

---

136. Kenneth B. Clark and MARC Educational Staff, "Response to Chancellor's Report on Programs and Problems Affecting Integration of the New York City Public Schools" (March 1974; processed), p. 43.

137. Ibid., p. 44.

138. Dan Dodson, "Desegregation of New York City Public Schools: A Feasibility Study," submitted to New York State Commission on the Quality, Cost, and Financing of Elementary and Secondary Education, September 15, 1971.

139. Ibid., p. 24.

140. Ibid., pp. 26–27, 28.

buses would use the uncrowded lanes moving against the flow of rush hour traffic.[141]

In all, Dodson estimated that about one-third of the elementary school children would have to be bused. The figure could be lowered by rerouting some of the 70,000 children already riding buses. When the junior high school reassignments were added in, the total busing through the ninth grade, if no students used the city's mass transit facilities, would amount to about 27 percent of the total enrollment. The total cost, he thought, assuming no saving, could come to about $33 million a year in 1971 prices.[142] The net cost might be much less.

Dodson's analysis was rudimentary and assumed that desegregation in schools that could be as much as three-fourths black and Puerto Rican was meaningful. In the long run, he commented, it might be well to divide up the New York system into several pieces and combine them with nearby suburban counties.[143]

### Feasibility in Chicago and Philadelphia

A 1972 report on metropolitan Chicago concluded that the schools of Chicago and suburban Cook County could be desegregated with school enrollments averaging about one-third black. Both city and county had highly segregated white and black schools, often in easy proximity to one another. The metropolitan area had an unusually effective transportation network of completed freeways and mass transit. Nearly 600 of the 711 suburban schools were more than 90 percent white and half the city schools were more than 90 percent minority.[144] The suburban schools were losing enrollment by the early 1970s and would be increasingly able to accommodate students from outside the district.[145] Illinois State Superintendent Joseph Cronin says that only a metropolitan plan can fully desegregate Chicago.[146]

In 1975 the Philadelphia school board proposed a metropolitan approach, reporting that, if only the immediately adjacent school districts

141. Ibid., pp. 30, 37.

142. Ibid., p. 54.

143. For example, school statistics for 1976–77 showed the Long Island districts adjoining Queens to be mostly white.

144. Meyer Weinberg, "How the Federal Court's Detroit School Decision Might Affect Chicago," *Chicago Reporter* (September 1972), pp. 1–6.

145. Cook County Educational Service Region, "Enrollment Comparisons, 1966–67 to 1974–75" (February 1975; processed), p. 2.

146. Interview with Joseph Cronin, May 6, 1977.

were included, the desegregation area would have equal numbers of blacks and whites.[147] This area would be far smaller and consist of many fewer districts than under the projected Detroit metropolitan plan.

Although geographically these metropolitan complexes seemed enormous, busing times and distances were not unusual. Larger areas with longer bus trips had already been desegregated. The distinctive issues were the political, administrative, and legal questions involved in shaping a new structure to govern local education.


## Can the Central Cities Afford Public Schools?

If hundreds of thousands of minority group children must continue to attend unconstitutionally segregated schools in districts where no remedy is possible, the least one can hope for is that the schools are well provided for. When the busing question arises one of the most common responses is that the money be spent instead on upgrading schools—if they must be separate they could at least be equal. School systems, however, all face severe cutbacks.

In spite of their segregation and concentration of children with learning difficulties, the big city schools were relatively prosperous until the early 1970s. With large industrial, commercial, and real estate tax bases and strong teachers' unions successfully demanding higher salaries, the cities made substantial investments in their schools. While their per-pupil spending was less than that of the affluent suburbs, it was usually higher than the statewide average, and federal aid was growing. Classes were not large and a good many special programs were in operation. Although resources always seemed inadequate to meet the problems, the schools were not poor.

When the decline of the central cities accelerated in the 1970s, there was less possibility of central-city-only integration and an urgent need for metropolitan resources simply to finance a minimal school program. New York City, for example, faced not only firing tens of thousands of teachers it could no longer pay but also the first absolute decline of assessed property values in a third of a century. The prospect was for a continued annual shrinkage of the tax base and mushrooming costs of services.[148]

After the city's brush with bankruptcy in 1975, the school system was forced to cut its teaching staff 23 percent by the fall of 1976. Most high school electives were eliminated, and many of the special accelerated pro-

147. School District of Philadelphia, "Desegregation Plan."
148. *New York Times*, February 3, 1976.

grams intended to keep the schools attractive to talented children and to middle class families were abolished. No major agency in the city had faced a cutback of this speed and scale in the twentieth century, even during the depression years.[149]

The damage to the public school system and the simultaneous ending of the city university's tradition of free higher education threatened to speed the departure of the remaining middle class from the public schools and the city. In one year, for example, one area received 4,000 new students, mostly minority children moving from areas of the Bronx where landlords and vandals were burning block after block of deteriorating apartment buildings, and at the same time it lost about 2,000 children, primarily middle class whites.

The children hurt by the decline were mostly black and Puerto Rican. Since 1960 the minority proportion of the enrollment had doubled and the number of children from families poor enough to qualify for a free lunch had climbed from one-tenth to more than half.[150] The city was caught in a cycle of continuing service reductions and high taxes, which promised to accelerate the process of suburbanization and ghettoization. All this, of course, affected the school system.

New York's problems were the most spectacular, but each of the other cities had serious difficulties. The Chicago schools shut early in the spring of 1976 because they ran out of money. In spite of a salary freeze and elimination of more than 400 jobs, the schools opened in 1976 with a projected $115 million budget deficit.[151] The school system stood to lose some state aid for cutting almost one-tenth of the previous school year. The city's tax base declined $1 billion between 1971 and 1977.[152]

The problems of the schools grew steadily. One-fifth of Chicago's residents were on welfare and 42 percent of the children in public school came from families at the poverty level. The black population of the city continued to increase. A study by the Urban League estimated that black joblessness had reached 36 percent and that the average income of a black family in Chicago, allowing for inflation, had actually declined $178 between 1969 and 1975. The average child in the eighth grade was two years behind the national average in reading. Young blacks were not being equipped with the skills necessary to find work in a shrinking job market;

149. Bernard R. Gifford, "New York City's Schools Are Being Bludgeoned," *New York Times,* September 20, 1976.
150. *New York Times,* June 21, 1976.
151. *Chicago Tribune,* September 15, October 14, 1976.
152. *Chicago Tribune,* June 18, 1977.

the Urban League study found that 53 percent of black male teenagers could not find work.[153] The city was losing approximately 56,000 of its middle class residents each year, and white school enrollment fell 7 percent between school openings in 1975 and 1976.[154]

In Detroit a fiscal crisis forced the dismissal of more than one-sixth of the city employees. The school system had suffered a budget cut as prices continued to inflate. Five hundred teachers and many aides were eliminated in the most drastic cutback in the district's history. In 1976 the system offered only half-day instruction for many first grade children and dropped most high school electives from the curriculum.[155]

Partly as a result of a change in state tax law, Detroit lost almost a sixth of its tax base between 1975 and 1977.[156] With inflation increasing the cost of providing education about 10 percent a year, the city had thus lost about a third of its real capacity to finance good schools from local sources in just two years.

This reflected the dramatic changes in the economic and social structure of the city, changes that only increased the need for strong public schools. The city had become so unattractive to middle class families that a house in a well-preserved neighborhood often sold for half the cost of a similar house in the suburbs. Buyers in the city, however, could have little expectation of the swiftly growing equity that had become usual for the suburban homeowner. Lending institutions had so little confidence in the city that mortgages were virtually unobtainable unless a federal agency guaranteed them. There were no buyers for thousands of houses.[157] School officials, in other words, could only expect continued shrinkage of the tax base and continued loss of middle class students.

Under a state requirement to balance its books, the school system had to reduce its programs. Small classes were banned, so that if not enough students in a ghetto school chose to take college preparatory courses, they were not available to those who needed them. Although the average high school graduate in the city read below the level of almost three-fourths of the nation's graduates, the school system had to increase the size of its classes. More than $20 million worth of needed upkeep in the schools was postponed indefinitely, art and music were eliminated in the early grades, and

153. *Chicago Daily News*, March 21, April 7, 1977; *Congressional Record* (daily edition), May 20, 1977, pp. S8250–51.

154. *Chicago Tribune*, January 26, 1977; *Chicago Daily News*, March 21, 1977.

155. Reginald Stuart, "Detroit's Public Schools Open a Lean Year," *New York Times*, September 9, 1976.

156. *Wall Street Journal*, May 31, 1977.

157. *Detroit Free Press*, June 29, June 21, 1977.

much of the interscholastic athletic program was ended. Even with these cuts, the city faced the prospect of laying off hundreds more teachers before the 1977–78 school year.[158]

The record was similar in Philadelphia. In 1971 School Superintendent Mark Shedd had predicted, "The urban schools of this country are dying. The public schools in the big cities of this nation, including Philadelphia, don't have the money or the staff to provide even a basic education for all of their pupils."[159] By the mid-1970s the deterioration was painfully apparent, with the school system facing a major fiscal crisis each year. During the 1976–77 school year the district operated with a $67 million deficit despite its limited educational program. To finish the school year the school board had to arrange for an emergency $31.5 million loan from local banks. In return, the board had to adopt a balanced budget for the next school year. The budget adopted in June 1977 called for firing almost 10,000 of the 26,000 employees, eliminating kindergartens, libraries, extracurricular activities, counselors, cafeterias, and other services. Superintendent Michael Marcase called the budget "unconscionable, unthinkable, and a travesty."[160] Urgent appeals to the state government and the city council finally narrowed the gap, but the scale of the difficulties was apparent and it would grow in future years.

As the population and wealth of the cities declined, they lost visibility and power. In 1974 Congress changed the Elementary and Secondary Education Act to reduce funds for the big cities of the North and redistribute money to the South and the suburbs (see chapter 8). The low-income voters who stayed in the central cities were far less likely to vote than middle class suburbanites, and this hastened the political transformation. When Congress and the state legislatures are reapportioned after the 1980 Census, the remaining leverage of the older cities will be badly damaged. There is little to suggest a reversal in either the economic or the political decline of the big cities. Unless national policy is changed, they will be unable to finance schools that have any hope of coping with the many problems.

## The Metropolitan Issue

Each of the nation's largest cities faces its problems of segregation and poverty surrounded by some of the wealthiest metropolitan areas in the world, areas where there are many hundreds of empty classrooms, far

158. *Wall Street Journal*, May 31, 1977.
159. *Washington Post*, September 22, 1971.
160. *Philadelphia Inquirer*, June 1, 1977.

more ample tax resources, large existing school bus systems, and lopsided majorities of white children. Except for small plans in parts of the central cities, the future of the desegregation issue will probably be dominated by the metropolitan issue. If lasting large-scale desegregation is to be possible for children in New York, Chicago, Los Angeles, Philadelphia, Detroit, and other large cities, the suburban boundary line must be crossed.

A single metropolitan plan could affect far more people than all the years of struggle to desegregate an entire southern state. Obviously such plans should be developed with the greatest care to suit the unique circumstances of each metropolitan area. If the existing processes continue, however, such planning is extremely unlikely. There will be either metropolitan remedies reluctantly fashioned by courts or piecemeal litigation and small plans as likely to reinforce as to diminish the forces of spreading segregation.

The longer one looks at the demographic and economic trends of the largest cities, the more dangerous the barrier against metropolitan desegregation erected by the Supreme Court in the *Milliken* case appears. With the possible exception of Los Angeles, only local and often transitory integration seems possible in the largest cities. When the Sixth Circuit Court of Appeals reviewed Detroit's central city plan in August 1976, it reflected the frustration of the situation. It was not constitutional, the court said, to leave more than 83,000 black children in segregated schools after the implementation of a "desegregation" plan. Yet the court confessed it could not suggest a way to solve the problem. In spite of the Supreme Court's decision, the judges remained convinced that "genuine constitutional desegregation cannot be accomplished within the school district boundaries of the Detroit School District."[161]

Should the *Milliken* barrier eventually fall, evidence from Detroit and Los Angeles suggests that there are technically feasible ways of desegregating all metropolitan area students in largely white schools except perhaps in New York. Busing costs and distances would not be excessive. Though these cities have the nation's largest concentrations of isolated minority children, they also have mass transit and freeway systems capable of rapidly bringing the children together.

The obstacles to a metropolitan approach would be political. More than elsewhere, the great cities have already built large, segregated, unequal societies. There are not only two separate societies, but also deep class and area divisions within both the majority and the minority. It has come to be

161. *Bradley* v. *Milliken,* 540 F.2d 229 (1976).

accepted by the courts, political leaders, and the public that the white suburban middle class has the right to existence isolated from the problems of the inner city. This class has become pivotal, both economically and politically, and will not surrender its prerogatives easily.

The largest cities can be desegregated, although accomplishing the change through court orders would require a degree of judicial intervention and assertiveness that seems unlikely without a significant change in the Supreme Court. Unless it is done—indeed unless there are powerful supporting policies in other areas such as housing—the racial prospects of these school systems appear to be grim.

If nothing is done it will not be because minority families like segregation. It will not be because nothing can be done, because there are no legal grounds, or because education would deteriorate from the change. It will be because most Americans strongly prefer things the way they are, and the courts will not bear the burden of flying in the face of these deep convictions.

# 7

# The Rights of
# Hispanic Children

ONE CHILD in twelve born in the United States in 1975 was Hispanic. The large majority were Mexican-American. Most lived in cities where their numbers were growing rapidly. Educators, courts, and federal policy-makers, who had shown little success in meeting the needs of blacks, had to consider how to deal with another large minority group whose problems were even more perplexing. Often large groups of both were in the same school systems. Policies designed to respond to one group almost inevitably had consequences for the other.

The swelling Hispanic enrollment of many of the nation's largest urban school systems attracted little national attention until the 1970s. By mid-decade, however, the vacuum had been filled with a series of often conflicting national policies expressing diverse goals for the education of Hispanics.

All three branches of government were involved. Congress acted first, in 1968, attempting to stimulate more appropriate instruction of the children with a small bilingual education program. The Department of Health, Education, and Welfare next decided, in 1970, to prohibit certain kinds of linguistic and cultural discrimination and press for the development of bilingual-bicultural education. The Supreme Court spoke later, in 1973, holding that intentional segregation of Hispanic children was unconstitutional. The next year it sustained HEW's power to prohibit linguistic discrimination. These policies contributed to powerful opposing impulses—one toward integration, the other toward cultural and linguistic particularism.

## The Struggle for Equal Opportunity

The long Hispanic struggle for better education began in the Southwest. Before significant numbers of Puerto Ricans and other Hispanic groups had arrived in the cities, Mexican-Americans had encountered segregation and discrimination. Some of their leaders, like those of the blacks, had turned to the courts, particularly after World War II. Although these struggles were usually ignored outside the region, they helped shape an agenda of issues for Hispanics when they finally became nationally visible and politically important in the late 1960s and the 1970s.

The early segregation of Mexican-Americans was rigid and thorough in many parts of the Southwest. W. Henry Cooke described the California situation in 1948:

Schools for "Mexicans" and schools for "Americans" have been the custom in many a Southern California city. . . . It has been the custom that they be segregated at least until they could use English well enough to keep up with English-speaking children. . . . Since the spring of 1947 . . . it is not now legal. . . . And yet the practice still continues in many cities.[1]

The severest abuses were found in Texas. While there was no state law authorizing the segregation of Mexican-Americans, some districts simply failed to educate Chicanos while many others "established 'Mexican' schools."[2] In 1930 a state court held that open segregation of Mexican-Americans was legal. This remained official Texas policy until it was overturned by a federal court in 1948. Mexican-American children were often sent to a Mexican school though they lived near an Anglo school.[3] In some localities, children were pressured to drop out after the end of the elementary school years.[4] The drive for segregation overrode both the neighborhood school tradition and the obligation to provide equal access to secondary education.

Even after the courts had outlawed segregation, Texas school authorities frequently continued it, building segregated schools in Chicano areas and using a variety of segregationist strategies—gerrymandering, transfer policies permitting white students to escape from integrated schools, and busing for segregation. Other schools used tracking (separate curricula throughout the school career, with initial assignment often based on a

1. W. Henry Cooke, "Segregation of Mexican-American School Children," in Wayne Moquin with Charles Van Doren, eds., *A Documentary History of the Mexican Americans* (Praeger, 1971), p. 326.

2. Jorge C. Rangel and Carlos M. Alcala, "Project Report: De Jure Segregation of Chicanos in Texas Schools," *Harvard Civil Rights–Civil Liberties Law Review*, vol. 7 (1972), pp. 311–14.

3. Until World War II the consensus of professional opinion was that Hispanic children should be segregated for their own good. Some experts held that they were an uncivilized "child race," genetically inferior. Thomas P. Carter, *Mexican Americans in School: A History of Educational Neglect* (Princeton, N.J.: College Entrance Examination Board, 1970).

4. Rangel and Alcala, "Project Report," p. 315.

standardized test given in English) or placed Chicano children in mentally retarded classes to intensify classroom segregation.[5] When the Texas superintendent of public instruction tried to enforce the 1948 court desegregation order by canceling the accreditation of a small school district that segregated students and teachers, the state legislature abolished his office and transferred his powers to a new commissioner of education, who did nothing.[6]

Mexican-Americans, lacking political power, continued the battle in the courts. The campaign was first led by the American GI Forum, a Chicano organization set up after World War II that was particularly influential in Texas.

Hector Garcia, the GI Forum's founder, had traveled the state, studying conditions. He was convinced that separate "Mexican" schools were the cause of poor performance and dropouts. Neglect was symbolized, he said, by an incredible lack even of basic sanitation in the schools in "Little Mexico." Garcia prepared report after report, but little changed.[7]

Lawsuits were filed year after year. Decisions against segregation in Texas and California were followed by a parallel decision in Arizona in 1950. A 1957 decision in Texas went further, declaring separate Anglo and Chicano classrooms illegal.

Although the early cases had documented a history of discrimination and established some legal principles against it, substantive change came slowly. The movement gained important new legal resources in 1968 when the Ford Foundation provided a $2.2 million grant to finance the Mexican-American Legal Defense and Education Fund, modeled on the NAACP Legal Defense Fund. There were now resources for high-quality professional litigation, skillful presentation of issues in the courts of appeals and the Supreme Court, and advocacy in the administrative policymaking processes in Washington.

MALDEF lawyers too found school conditions dismal. Serious segregation was common and little effort was invested in special programs for Spanish-speaking students. In 1970 in the Southwest only about one Chicano student in forty was enrolled in a bilingual program. The schools that had programs often used untrained teachers. Many schools continued to

5. Ibid., pp. 316–19, 331–32, 326. Similar patterns of discriminatory testing and placement were uncovered in California, leading to successful litigation against the practice.
6. Ibid., p. 339.
7. *Equal Educational Opportunity*, Hearings before the Senate Select Committee on Equal Educational Opportunity, 91:2 (GPO, 1970), pp. 2568–72.

discourage any use of Spanish, even on the playground; a few actually punished children for speaking in their native tongue.[8] Most schools simply did nothing.

In many schools Chicanos were concentrated in the lowest levels on the basis of English-language tests. Texts ignored the Mexican heritage. (Student protest in Los Angeles, San Antonio, and elsewhere dramatized this issue.) Parental involvement was minimal; notices were sent home in English though two-thirds of Chicano families speak Spanish at home.

In the beginning, MALDEF was involved in both desegregation and linguistic cases. During its first year, it sued a small Texas district asking the court to end de jure segregation. The next year it sued the Santa Ana, California, system to stop the use of English-language tests on the basis of which Spanish-speaking children were put in classes for the mentally retarded. MALDEF sued for both desegregation and better school programs in Uvalde, Texas. It also tried to intervene in the important Houston and Dallas cases.[9]

In the early 1970s MALDEF's cases showed growing emphasis on bilingualism and a diminishing concern for desegregation. When black litigants in Waco, Texas, appealed a court decision that equalized resources rather than integrating schools, MALDEF stood aside. During 1971 it filed both kinds of action, asking for bilingual-bicultural education and integration in Austin and concentrating on linguistic and curriculum issues in Portales, New Mexico.[10] When *Keyes*, the important Denver desegregation case, was argued, MALDEF was not directly involved even though Mexican-Americans were the largest minority group. Only after the Supreme Court decided that integration was required did the organization step in and help shape the remedy.

One reason for MALDEF's failure to act was the opposition of Denver Chicanos to busing. A public opinion survey of Denver in 1972 showed that, though two-thirds of the blacks thought busing was "a good idea," only about one-fourth of the Mexican-Americans agreed. While Texas Chicanos with a vivid memory of "Mexican rooms" were often preoccupied with ending overt segregation, many big city Latinos showed considerable suspicion of busing plans. A 1974 survey of Los Angeles students found that Chicano

8. U.S. Commission on Civil Rights, *The Excluded Student,* Mexican American Education Study, Report 3 (GPO, 1972), pp. 14–20, 22–24.

9. *Ross v. Eckels,* 434 F.2d 1140 (5th Cir. 1970); *Tasby v. Estes,* 444 F.2d 124 (5th Cir. 1971).

10. *Arvizu v. Waco,* 373 F. Supp. 1264 (W.D. Texas 1973); *Concerned Parents for Equal Education v. Austin* (unpublished opinion); *Serna v. Portales Municipal Schools,* 499 F.2d 1147 (10th Cir. 1974).

attitudes were midway between those of blacks and Anglos on busing.[11] A 1977 survey of parents' attitudes in Los Angeles found that 44 percent of Mexican-Americans, 69 percent of blacks, and 12 percent of whites favored busing.[12]

## The Supreme Court's Actions

As Mexican-American litigation developed momentum and other Hispanic groups began to work through the courts and administrative agencies to change local conditions, the major Supreme Court decision in the *Keyes* case in 1973 altered the entire legal framework.

The *Keyes* case forced the Supreme Court to decide how to treat Mexican-American children in Denver, which had a history of de jure segregation of blacks. In a city with about one-sixth black and one-fourth Hispanic children, the Court had to decide whether to desegregate only the blacks or to recognize Mexican-Americans as an illegally segregated group and desegregate both minorities with the remaining Anglo students. The decision would do much to determine both the scale of the desegregation problem in western cities and whether the result would be putting children from ghetto and barrio schools together and calling it integration.

From 1954 to 1973 the Supreme Court, most lower courts, and HEW had desegregated only blacks, usually ignoring the segregation of Hispanics, even where it was clearly present, as in Texas. Decisions generally were based on the proposition that Mexican-Americans should simply be counted as whites and their distinctive needs ignored. *Keyes* required a Supreme Court definition of the status of Chicanos.[13]

The justices had two choices. They could either define Hispanic students as an undifferentiated part of the majority group in American society and approve a plan that would "desegregate" black students by putting them in Chicano schools or they could accord Chicanos a separate legal status. To give Mexican-Americans special treatment in a desegregation plan, the Court had to conclude that they, as a group, had been subjected to a system of pervasive official discrimination. It decided that, in devising

11. G. Thomas Taylor, Jr., "Citizen Survey Evaluation: Link Between Opinion and Policy," *National Civic Review* (December 1974), p. 580; *Integrated Education* (March–April 1976), p. 40.

12. "Results of the L.A.U.S.D. Survey," submitted to Superior Court of the State of California for the County of Los Angeles (June 6, 1977; processed).

13. *Keyes* v. *School District No. 1, Denver, Colorado,* 413 U.S. 189 (1973).

plans, Hispanics were constitutionally entitled to recognition as a distinct class. The Court held that

there is also much evidence that in the Southwest Hispanos and Negroes have a great many things in common. . . . Though of different origins, Negroes and Hispanos in Denver suffer identical discrimination in treatment when compared with the treatment afforded Anglo students. In that circumstance, we think petitioners are entitled to have schools with a combined predominance of Negroes and Hispanos included in the category of "segregated" schools.[14]

In support of this finding, the Court cited the Civil Rights Commission's conclusion that Mexican-Americans "do not obtain the benefits of public education at a rate equal to that of their Anglo classmates." The commission, however, had never concluded that the educational needs of Chicanos were the same as those of blacks.[15]

Until the Supreme Court acted, the issue had produced serious division and confusion in the lower federal courts. In two of the nation's largest systems, Houston and Miami, the courts had permitted local officials to count Chicanos and Cubans as whites for desegregation purposes. On the other hand, in a case in a small Texas district, the courts had ordered a special form of education (bilingual-bicultural instruction). Another Texas case had defined Mexican-Americans as a separate group for desegregation purposes.[16]

The *Keyes* decision settled the issue of desegregation at least for Chicanos in the Southwest, but in an unsatisfactory way. It simply stated that Chicanos were like blacks and should be accorded the same rights. The conclusion that a group facing linguistic barriers and less interested in desegregation was the same as the local black population was simplistic.

## Unsettled Questions

Even with the legal principle established, many questions remained. The decision mentions conditions prevailing in the Southwest. It is unclear whether the same rights extend to Mexican-Americans in cities outside the Southwest. Would evidence that social conditions had changed in a part of the Southwest remove this special constitutional protection for Mexican-

14. Ibid.
15. See summary, policy recommendations, and list of previous publications in the final volume of Commission on Civil Rights, *Toward Quality Education for Mexican Americans* (GPO, 1974).
16. *Cisneros* v. *Corpus Christi*, 467 F.2d 142 (5th Cir. 1972).

American children? Conditions in the region vary greatly on matters ranging from residential segregation to intermarriage, socioeconomic mobility
to educational achievement. It is not clear what factors would determine
how a particular Hispanic group in a given part of the country should be
treated for desegregation purposes. In subsequent cases, federal judges
in New York and Boston assumed that desegregation could be extended to
Hispanic groups that were primarily Puerto Rican.[17] In Wilmington, Delaware, on the other hand, a federal court held that Latinos would not be
defined as an unconstitutionally segregated minority group unless clear
evidence proving de jure segregation by school officials was presented.[18]

More questions arise when one attempts to extrapolate from the *Keyes*
decision the constitutional status of Oriental and Indian children. The
Chinese and Japanese, for example, were subjected to discrimination in
California, but most are now educationally successful and integrated.
(There are some exceptions, of course, notably in San Francisco's Chinatown.) Should there be four-way distribution of children in towns with
Anglo, Hispanic, black, and Asian students or should the Asian-Americans
be considered majority group children? Should such a decision be based on
a group's history or its present situation?

About one-third of the minority group children in Minneapolis are
Indians. Their desegregation ran counter both to the demand of national
Indian groups for more Indian control of Indian education and to the direction of congressional legislation on Indian education.[19] There is no firm
Supreme Court guidance on the right of Indian children to desegregation,
though in *Keyes* the Court did note that Indian children suffer educational
harm similar to that experienced by Hispanics and blacks.

While the proper treatment of Oriental and Indian children is an acute
issue in a few cities, the constitutional status of Puerto Ricans, Cubans,
and other Spanish-speaking groups is a larger problem. At present, Cubans
are concentrated in metropolitan Miami where the desegregation plan
treats them as part of the white majority group. Whether this decision is in
accord with the later Supreme Court action on the Denver case is unclear.
The legal status of Puerto Ricans is equally fuzzy, with contradictory decisions in different states. It is far from self-evident that Cubans and Puerto
Ricans, to say nothing of the newer South American and Caribbean groups,

17. *Hart* v. *Community School Board of Brooklyn District #2*, 383 F. Supp. 699
at 733 (E.D.N.Y. 1974), *aff'd* 512 F.2d 37 (2d Cir. 1975); *Morgan* v. *Hennigan*, 379 F.
Supp. 410 at 415 (D. Mass. 1974).

18. *Evans* v. *Buchanan*, 393 F. Supp. 428 (D. Del. 1975). A similar conclusion was
reached in the Milwaukee case, *Armstrong* v. *O'Connell*.

19. Indian Elementary and Secondary School Assistance Act, Title II, Public Law
92-318.

have been subjected to official discrimination comparable to that against blacks in the South or Chicanos in the Southwest.[20]

The *Keyes* decision, then, settles only the situation of Chicanos in the Southwest, where school systems found guilty of unconstitutional segregation must desegregate not only blacks but also the usually larger Chicano groups. Ironically, this means that a lawyer representing a black community that makes up 3 percent of a school system can also obtain an order desegregating the 30 percent of the students who are Mexican-American, even though this group may oppose it. Constitutional rights, of course, are not determined by public opinion polls, and most Hispanic people doubtless prefer citywide desegregation to plans that would "integrate" black children by sending them to nearby barrio schools. Nonetheless, something is strange about a legal victory whose benefits are opposed by many of its beneficiaries.

## Segregation

Segregation of Hispanic children across the country was high and still rising in the mid-1970s. Enrollment statistics for the 1974–75 school year showed that there was a slightly higher proportion of Hispanic than of black children in predominantly minority schools. Though the former were still much less likely than the latter to attend schools with almost completely minority enrollments, the trend was toward greater segregation (see table 7-1).

An example is Chicago, the principal midwestern magnet for Chicano

20. According to a recent study a substantial majority of the Caribbean migration in the past generation came from places other than Puerto Rico. Aaron Lee Segal, ed., *Population Policies in the Caribbean* (Heath, 1975), p. 219.

Table 7-1. *Hispanic Children in Predominantly Minority Schools,*
*1970 and 1974*

Percent

| Section | 1970 | 1974 |
|---------|------|------|
| Northeast | 84.2 | 84.2 |
| South | 72.6 | 72.8 |
| Midwest | 52.6 | 57.1 |
| West | 48.5 | 56.3 |
| National | 64.2 | 67.4 |

Source: HEW, Office for Civil Rights, May 1976. These figures are based on data available from school districts that regularly filed reports with HEW. These districts were estimated to include 74 percent of the nation's Hispanic students.

and Puerto Rican migration, where Hispanic enrollment grew from 56,000 to almost 68,000 between 1970 and 1974, although the school system as a whole was rapidly losing students. By the 1974–75 school year 56 percent of the Hispanic children were in schools where the minority enrollment was above 90 percent; most were in schools that had less than 1 percent Anglo students.[21]

### The Language Issue

The striking difference between the black and Hispanic minorities is that, whereas black separation is defined by race, for Hispanics the greatest barrier often seems to be language. Although many Hispanics have Indian ancestry and there has been much black-white intermarriage in Puerto Rico, the racial barriers are usually ambiguous.

Many Hispanic intellectuals and their supporters ascribe the social problems of their people to the linguistic and cultural biases of the English-speaking majority. This has led to a drive for bilingual-bicultural education while the drive for integration is viewed with considerable uncertainty. Sometimes the goals have been in direct conflict. In other cases, working out a solution has required delicate intergroup negotiations.

When Congress and HEW finally recognized the discrimination against Hispanics, they chose to act on the linguistic and cultural issues and ignore the issue of segregation. They used both the carrot and the stick in stimulating the bilingual-bicultural education movement. Funds were provided by the Bilingual Education Act of 1968, creating many jobs for newly trained Hispanic professionals. The pressure for local action was intensified by the decision of HEW's Office for Civil Rights to require the development of special educational programs in all school districts with significant numbers of non-English-speaking children. There has been active litigation on the issue and Hispanic groups have succeeded in winning passage of a number of state bilingual education laws.

Although the linguistic issue is not directly related to school desegregation, it should be examined in considerable detail because it is often presented as a plausible or even preferable alternative to desegregation and because it may split a city's two most important minority groups in the development of a desegregation plan. It has also been used to justify a

21. Department of Health, Education, and Welfare, Office for Civil Rights, "Distribution of Minority Students by School Composition, 1970–1974," report to the U.S. Senate (May 27, 1976; processed), p. 12.

federal program of civil rights enforcement that accepted continued segregation of children of Spanish origin.

HEW's shift in goals began in 1970 with the issuance of the "May 25th Memorandum" declaring that a school system's failure to provide education that met the needs of non-English-speaking children violated the little-noticed section of the 1964 Civil Rights Act forbidding discrimination because of national origin. Language was defined as a basic part of "national origin."

Enforcement of the new policy triggered a number of investigations, the first concentrating on discrimination against Texas Chicanos. In developing remedies the federal agency usually sidestepped the issue of segregation, urging local officials to adopt bilingual-bicultural educational approaches and to hire more Chicano teachers. The idea of beginning instruction in Spanish and preserving Spanish language ability and Mexican cultural traditions strongly appealed to many Chicano intellectuals. A federal court decision requiring such a program for children in the San Felipe–Del Rio school system[22] gave Mexican-American lawyers hope that the courts would define such educational programs as a constitutional right of Chicano children.

The language issue, however, reached the Supreme Court from a different quarter. In March 1970 the Chinatown office of the San Francisco neighborhood legal services program filed suit in federal court, alleging that the city's school system was failing to educate almost 3,000 pupils of Chinese background who could not speak English. It asked the court to require bilingual instruction for the children, ending the tradition of English-only instruction.

The Chinese families lost their case in both the district court and the court of appeals. Both sides agreed that more than 2,800 Chinese students needed special help. District Judge Lloyd Burke concluded that such programs would be "desirable and commendable" but that there was no legal basis to impose such changes. "These Chinese speaking students—by receiving the same education made available on the same terms and conditions to the other tens of thousands of students . . . are legally receiving all their rights to an education and to equal educational opportunities."[23]

The court of appeals reached the same conclusion, finding that "every student brings to the starting line of his educational career different ad-

22. *United States* v. *Texas*, 321 F. Supp. 1043 (S.D. Tex. 1971), *aff'd and modified*, 447 F.2d 441 (5th Cir. 1971).

23. *Lau* v. *Nichols* (unpublished opinion), reprinted in *Equal Educational Opportunity*, Hearings, pp. 4716–17.

vantages and disadvantages caused in part by social, economic, and cultural background, created and continued completely apart from any contribution by the school system."[24] The court held that it would be neither legal nor wise for the courts to prescribe specific educational programs.

The Justice Department intervened when the case reached the Supreme Court, rejecting the contention of the Chinatown legal services group that bilingual education was a constitutional right, but claiming that San Francisco was violating the 1970 HEW policy on national-origin discrimination. Setting such policy, Justice argued, was a legitimate exercise of HEW's authority under the 1964 Civil Rights Act.[25] This approach reduced the issue from defining a new constitutional right to the much simpler problem of construing the 1964 law. It shifted the burden of defining educational standards from the courts to the executive branch.

The Supreme Court adopted the Justice Department's suggestion. In an unusually rapid and decisive action, it unanimously sustained HEW's requirements that the San Francisco schools provide special training for Chinese-speaking children. Its *Lau* v. *Nichols* decision[26] squarely rejected the traditional American assumption that it was the responsibility of immigrant children to somehow learn English on their own.

The Court reasoned that, since the state governments prescribe English as the language of instruction and since mastery of English is a principal objective of the curriculum, "there is no equality of treatment merely by providing students with the same facilities, textbooks, teachers, and curriculum." "We know," the Court held, "that those who do not understand English are certain to find their classroom experiences wholly incomprehensible and in no way meaningful."[27] HEW's 1970 guidelines, which the Court sustained, stated that the district "must take affirmative steps to rectify the language deficiency in order to open its instructional program to these students."[28]

The consequences of the decision were substantial for systems across the country. Although only in San Francisco, where Oriental students accounted for 23 percent of the enrollment in 1972, would the problem of teaching Oriental students assume central importance, Hispanic students accounted for huge portions of a number of the country's largest systems.

24. *Lau* v. *Nichols,* 483 F.2d 791 at 797 (9th Cir. 1973).
25. Memorandum for the United States as Amicus Curiae, *Lau* v. *Nichols* (1973).
26. *Lau* v. *Nichols,* 414 U.S. 563 at 566 (1974).
27. Ibid.
28. Memorandum from J. Stanley Pottinger to School Districts with More Than Five Percent National Origin Children, May 25, 1970.

Leading Hispanic organizations had submitted briefs urging Supreme Court action. In New York and Los Angeles 27 percent of the students were Hispanic; in Chicago and San Diego, 11 percent; in Houston, 19 percent; in Miami, 28 percent; in Denver, 26 percent; in Newark, 15 percent; in Austin, 22 percent; in Dallas, 12 percent. Many Texas cities had a substantial majority of Chicanos.[29] In most cities Hispanic enrollment was growing as white enrollment fell and black enrollment stabilized.

Many suburban and rural districts were also potentially affected. While most blacks outside the South are confined to central city school systems, Spanish-speaking children are less concentrated. In the giant Los Angeles–Long Beach metropolitan area, for example, half of the 296,000 Spanish-speaking children live outside the central city and forty-five of the suburban school districts have at least 10 percent Chicano enrollment each.[30] As they grew, Western cities often incorporated rural Chicano settlements.

*Lau* was important for Hispanics because they are far more likely than other immigrants to rely on their native tongue, even after many years of residence in the United States. The 1970 Census showed that at least 65 percent of the Spanish-surnamed population speak Spanish at home. Even though there was earlier settlement and less segregation of Mexicans in California than in most states, 69.3 percent of all Californians with Spanish surnames considered Spanish their mother language.[31] The proximity to Mexico, the large size of Hispanic communities, and the extensive Spanish-language media have contributed to this.

Many Puerto Rican and Chicano children come to school without having learned any English at home. California school authorities conceded, for example, that there are some 80,000 students who cannot "speak or understand English." More than half of these students were provided "English as a second language" (ESL) training when *Lau* was decided. (ESL programs are often criticized by Hispanic educators for their failure to reinforce a students' native language and culture and their frequent use of brief classes taught by teachers with only marginal knowledge of Spanish.) Far fewer children were in bilingual programs. As for the rest, the California Rural Legal Assistance office described their situation succinctly: "Although they sit for six hours a day in a school room, they are receiving no education."[32]

29. HEW, Office for Civil Rights, 1974 reports and data from *Directory of Public Elementary and Secondary Schools in Selected Districts, Fall 1972* (GPO, 1973).

30. HEW, Data Management Center, "SMSA's Student/Teacher Data" (October 9, 1973; processed).

31. Brief of Amicus Curiae for California Rural Assistance, *Lau* v. *Nichols* (1973).

32. Ibid.

In New York City, a special census conducted by the board of education during the 1971–72 school year found that more than 100,000 students were basically Spanish speaking; of these, more than a third had severe problems. The Puerto Rican Legal Defense and Education Fund showed that, of the sixty-six elementary schools in a city where 85 percent or more of the children were below grade level in reading scores, almost two-thirds were predominantly Puerto Rican. In some cases, the situation was absurd. The true magnitude of New York children's reading problems could not be measured, for example, because the school officials found 28,000 students who knew so little English they could not even be given the test.[33] Something obviously had to be done. Just what was less clear.

The national dimensions of the issue were evident in a 1976 Census Bureau report on language usage, which showed that Spanish was the nation's dominant foreign language, spoken by more than half of all non-English-speaking persons. More than 4 million Americans over the age of four were primarily Spanish-speaking. The next most common foreign language was Chinese, with only one-fourteenth as many people relying on it. All in all, 4.8 million Americans lived in homes where Spanish was the primary means of communication and another 2.3 million in households where it was a regular second language. More than half the people whose usual language was Spanish said that they had difficulty with English.[34]

### Is There a Conflict between Keyes and Lau?

The *Lau* decision was hailed by Spanish-speaking groups, other linguistic minorities, and HEW civil rights officials as the beginning of a new age of linguistic and cultural pluralism in American education. Although the decision only required that the local school board "apply its expertise to the problem and rectify the situation," it was seen as a victory for the bilingual-bicultural education movement. This, some Hispanic leaders claimed, was the central educational and social need of their children.

The bilingual impulse sometimes seemingly ran in exactly the opposite direction from the *Keyes* decision. That case concluded that Chicano children were a victimized minority whose deprivation could be remedied by inclusion through integration. The *Lau* case, on the other hand, was interpreted by some minority activists as support for the theory that the

33. Brief of Amicus Curiae, Puerto Rican Legal Defense Fund, Inc., *Lau* v. *Nichols* (1973).
34. U.S. Census Bureau, *Current Population Reports*, Series P-23, no. 60, "Language Usage in the United States, July 1975" (GPO, 1976), pp. 1–6.

primary problem for non-English-speaking children was the linguistic and social "imperialism" of the public schools. The remedy, they argued, was not inclusion but group solidarity. They advocated using the public schools to develop and preserve competence in the native language, to perpetuate the native culture, and only gradually to introduce English-language instruction. This, some maintained, could often best be accomplished by separating children by language background and concentrating the necessarily limited number of bilingual teachers in the schools where the children were concentrated. Minority leaders accepting these ideas rarely mentioned integration and sometimes actively fought it.

### The Changing Mexican-American Legal Strategy

The private organization most directly affected by the legal imperatives of *Lau* and *Keyes* was the Mexican-American Legal Defense and Education Fund. Although neighborhood legal services lawyers had been victorious in *Lau* and the fledgling Puerto Rican Legal Defense and Education Fund would achieve a major out-of-court settlement on bilingualism with the New York City School Board, MALDEF had the oldest tradition of litigation for Hispanics and represented the largest group.

MALDEF, influenced by the Chicano struggle against segregation, had defended busing. The first MALDEF general counsel, Mario Obledo, had issued a statement denouncing President Nixon's antibusing legislation. It was, he said, "simply an attempt to maintain America as a segregated society."

The purpose of bringing whites, blacks and Chicanos into the same school is to provide a quality education for all and to insure that racial mistrust is not engendered by the simple fact that these groups of children do not know each other. . . .

Chicanos in this country do not want to be isolated in inferior obsolete schools. They want to be integrated into a bilingual-bicultural school system that recognizes the cultural differences they bring to the schools.[35]

The two cities immediately affected by the *Keyes* and *Lau* decisions, Denver and San Francisco, provided an important test for MALDEF. In Denver after the *Keyes* decision MALDEF devoted its resources to the effort to make bilingual programs an integral part of desegregation, leaving the integration issue entirely to the NAACP Legal Defense Fund.

Vilma Martinez, MALDEF's second general counsel, spoke of regional

35. MALDEF press release, March 17, 1972.

differences in 1974. In Texas and New Mexico, she said, Chicano children were often "very very severely deprived," and there was "lots of old-fashioned type segregation." "People there are at a different stage and really want integration." On the other hand, she said, many urban Chicanos do not.[36]

This ambivalence was described by one MALDEF attorney:

While there is a tendency to think that Chicanos, wherever located, share the same educational goals, this is not the case. In rural areas and small urban centers, integration is sought because segregated education invariably means inferior facilities for Chicano schools, as well as psychological feelings of second-class citizenship. In large urban areas . . . however, there is little desire for integration. The leaders of these "barrios" resist education policies which undermine community control of schools and retard the enactment of bilingual/bicultural education.[37]

MALDEF, of course, hoped to attain both goals, using desegregation cases brought by blacks as a vehicle for winning bilingual-bicultural curricula. It hoped that judges, usually leery of curriculum issues, when faced with the immediate practical necessity of designing a desegregation plan would be more open to incorporating educational components. MALDEF claimed that bilingualism would make desegregation work better and ease some group tension. Its strategy was to let black-oriented groups prove the school system had illegally segregated children and then try to piggyback educational change onto the desegregation plan.[38]

While basically supporting desegregation law, MALDEF's staff warned against a "mechanical application" of principles from the South. Proportional distribution of black and white teachers, for instance, was sensible in the South, where there were large numbers of black teachers, but it made no sense to disperse the small numbers of bilingual Chicano teachers in the same way. One MALDEF memorandum commented:

Chicano parents often do not wish to desegregate the *barrio* and they hate busing. For example, in Tucson, Arizona, Chicano parents, who constitute 30% of the city, oppose the integration efforts of the local N.A.A.C.P. . . . .
Theoretically, bilingual-bicultural education and integration are not incompatible. In the Southwest . . . bilingual programs are not integrated and more often than not they are merely . . . historical parallels of the . . . Mexican Schools

36. Interview with Vilma Martinez, June 13, 1974.
37. Alan Exelrod, "Chicano Education: In Swann's Way?" *Inequality in Education* (August 1971), p. 28.
38. Interview with Sanford Rosen, June 13, 1974; interview with Martinez, June 13, 1974.

and Mexican Rooms which have an infamous place in Chicano history. Segregation to remedy English language differences has not been successful in the past.[39]

MALDEF experts expressed the hope that more realistic solutions might come out of negotiations: "Hopefully, the differences between Black and Chicano educational needs will not be competing but complementary. . . . The nub of the dilemma is that bilingual-bicultural education may be played off against integration. At this juncture, it is impossible to tell what is best for Chicano children."[40]

Efforts to meet both goals simultaneously proved to be difficult. After the Supreme Court ordered desegregation in Denver, the NAACP Legal Defense Fund cooperated with MALDEF and local Hispanic educators. MALDEF brought its leading educational consultant, Dr. Jose Cardenas, into court. The district court responded, ordering implementation of bilingualism and review of the system's entire educational program. Some experimental schools for Mexican-American children were left segregated to permit continuation of their programs.[41] But in August 1975 the court of appeals, whose decision was final since the Supreme Court refused to hear the case again, rejected the bilingual program and ordered integration of the experimental schools. Bilingual education, the court held, "is not a substitute for desegregation. Although bilingual instruction may be required to prevent the isolation of minority students in a predominantly Anglo school system . . . such instruction must be subordinate to a plan of school desegregation."[42] The court of appeals held that the district court had exceeded "the limits of its remedial powers":

The court's adoption of the Cardenas Plan, in our view, goes well beyond helping Hispano school children to reach the proficiency in English necessary to learn other basic subjects. Instead of merely removing obstacles to effective desegregation, the court's order would impose upon school authorities a pervasive and detailed system for the education of minority children. We believe this goes too far. . . . The clear implication of arguments in support of the court's adoption of the Cardenas plan is that minority students are entitled under the fourteenth amendment to an educational experience tailored to their unique cultural and developmental needs. Although enlightened educational theory may well demand as much, the Constitution does not.[43]

39. Sanford Rosen and Carlos Alcala, "Principal Legal Issues in School Desegregation Litigation as It Relates to the Mexican American" (memorandum, May 10, 1974), pp. 8–9.
40. Ibid., pp. 11–12.
41. Keyes v. School District No. 1, 380 F. Supp. 673 (D. Colo. 1974).
42. Keyes v. School District No. 1, 521 F.2d 465 at 480 (10th Cir. 1975).
43. Ibid.

The court felt obligated to fully desegregate both blacks and Hispanics, but it pronounced itself powerless to impose a whole new approach to schooling. MALDEF appealed. The Supreme Court refused to review the decision.

Hispanic lawyers, however, could still claim significant victories in 1974 in other appellate court decisions. In *Serna* v. *Portales Municipal Schools,* the Tenth Circuit held in 1974 that the small New Mexico school system was failing to properly educate Mexican-American children, whom the court found far below grade level on achievement tests and much more likely to drop out of school. The judges cited the testimony of expert witnesses that the children's problems were related to the schools' failure to reflect their language and culture in the curriculum and to hire Chicano teachers.

The court of appeals concluded that the district had "a long standing educational policy . . . that failed to take into consideration the specific needs of Spanish surnamed children." Under these "unique circumstances," the courts had broad powers, including the authority to "fashion a bilingual-bicultural program which will assure that Spanish surnamed children receive a meaningful education."[44]

The *Serna* case differed from the Denver litigation in two major respects. First, it was not a desegregation case, so the court was not obliged to meet primary constitutional requirements for integrated schools. Second, there was a specific judicial finding of a school district's failure to provide equal education to Hispanic children, something that had not been part of the Denver case.

In 1977 MALDEF was still actively involved in two important desegregation cases—El Paso and Austin—and in other cases where its role was to press for bilingualism. It remained, said General Counsel Martinez, "committed to desegregation with bilingual education." The two issues could not be separated: "If you have a bilingual education program, this will help desegregate the school district."[45]

### The Puerto Rican Legal Defense Fund

The Mexican-American litigation was concerned with both integration and language, but the litigation filed by the Puerto Rican Legal Defense and Education Fund grew directly from linguistic and cultural concern

44. *Serna* v. *Portales Municipal Schools,* 499 F.2d 1147 at 1154.
45. Interview with Martinez, October 15, 1977; interview with Peter Roos, October 21, 1977.

for the Puerto Ricans, who were concentrated in big city systems with relatively few whites. Integration was never a real possibility for most.

When Puerto Rican lawyers and community leaders organized a public
interest litigation staff, with the support of leading national foundations,
education was a top priority. During its first year the PRLDEF sued the
New York City schools, demanding bilingualism: "The suit demands that
Spanish-speaking children learn their substantive subjects in Spanish while
being taught English. Such a bilingual program would also expose children
to the history and culture of the Hispanic people." The group was also
working for the establishment of bilingual programs in New Jersey. There
was not a word about integrated education in its first annual report and no
litigation was filed on the subject.[46]

When desegregation litigation was brought by other groups in cities
with large Puerto Rican populations, the PRLDEF intervened not for integration but to try to influence the solution. The PRLDEF claimed credit for
having expanded bilingualism substantially in Boston and for bringing
legal actions on the bilingual issue potentially affecting "more than half of
the Puerto Rican school children in the United States." It had also intervened in Wilmington, Buffalo, and Waterbury (Connecticut) desegregation cases. It had a major bilingualism case pending against the Philadelphia school system. Integration cases were seen as a tactic for getting the
bilingual issue into court under favorable circumstances.[47]

## Hispanic Support of Integration

Desegregation litigation is usually triggered by the decision of a substantial element in a minority community which believes that minority
children will never be offered equal education in stigmatized, relatively
powerless minority schools. Surveys of blacks consistently show large
majorities—about eight to one—in favor of the goal of integrated education and consolidated support of busing after a court order has been handed
down. Some Latino communities, in contrast, view integration with misgivings, and busing receives little support. Others are strongly integrationist.

Some Hispanic families, particularly Puerto Ricans, hope to take their

46. Puerto Rican Legal Defense and Education Fund, *First Annual Report, 1972–73*,
p. 9.

47. Ibid., *Annual Report, 1974–75*, pp. 4–6; "Docket of Cases as of May 21, 1976,"
pp. 2–7.

children back to a Spanish-speaking society someday. Although they want their children to have the tools for economic success, they also want them to remain capable of functioning in Spanish. A survey of Puerto Rican parents in two large Connecticut cities found that almost all the parents were born on the island and that almost three-fourths hoped to return even though most of their children had been born on the mainland. Few actually return permanently, but they favored school programs that helped their children gain and hold proficiency in both Spanish and English. At the same time, they expressed hope that their children would be successful in college and find good jobs, both of which depended on mastering English.[48] These opposing desires for cultural continuity and for success in an English-speaking society show up in Puerto Rican attitudes toward busing.

Within the nation's Mexican-American population there were wide divergences. Most Denver Chicanos, for example, were opposed to busing, but a majority of those in Dallas said busing had been good for the school district.[49] A *Los Angeles Times* survey showed that Latino high school students in the city were evenly divided on the value of racially balanced schools and the need for busing.[50] A twelve-year study of the attitudes of Mexican-Americans in one small midwestern city—Racine, Wisconsin— found the search for better jobs an overriding factor in Chicano migration. The families studied were deeply committed to education; they viewed the schools as more important to the mobility of their children than either whites or blacks in the city did. They were the most integrationist of the city's three major groups, with two-thirds favoring more intergroup social contacts.[51] In San Jose, California, and El Paso, Texas, Mexican-American parents unsuccessfully sued the local school district for desegregation in districts where they were the dominant minority. In most urban districts, however, Hispanics avoided desegregation cases, at least until they reached the stage of formulating the remedy.

The cross-currents of opinion were evident in New York City after the

48. Perry A. Zirkel, "Puerto Rican Parents: An Educational Survey," *Integrated Education* (November–December 1973), pp. 20–26. Although most Puerto Rican families return only for visits, a net migration of over 55,000 from the mainland in the 1970s created serious problems for the San Juan schools. *San Juan Star*, June 2, 1975; *New York Times*, October 3, 1975.

49. Taylor, "Citizen Survey Evaluation"; *Dallas Times-Herald*, June 29, 1977.

50. *Integrated Education* (March–April 1976), p. 40.

51. Lyle W. Shannon and Judith L. McKim, "Attitudes Toward Education and the Absorption of Immigrant Mexican-Americans and Negroes in Racine," *Education and Urban Society*, vol. 6 (May 1974), pp. 350–52.

Puerto Rican Legal Defense and Education Fund won approval of the largest bilingual program in the country. In an out-of-court settlement of a lawsuit, the city agreed to test all children with Spanish surnames for language skills and to provide Spanish-language instruction for those who needed it. There was some argument about the procedure adopted in the plan, which automatically placed a student with low scores in a bilingual program unless his parents took the positive step of filling out a form switching their child back to the regular English curriculum. Even small pilot bilingual programs encountered difficulties in attracting and retaining students.[52]

Some of the fears that the program would have the effect of increasing segregation were summarized by Gene Maeroff of the *New York Times:*

A main fear . . . is the possibility that, once a student is assigned to a bilingual program, it may become a permanent feature of his education, rather than it being phased out once he is proficient in English. . . . supporters of the court suit acknowledged their sympathy for a "maintenance approach" that would allow a student to continue to receive a portion of his instruction in Spanish.[53]

Early experience with the New York plan produced evidence of some resistance to bilingualism on the part of Puerto Rican and other Hispanic families. After the consent agreement, the school officials tested most of the Spanish-surnamed students (some refused to take the tests on various grounds—for instance, that their families had been English-speaking for generations). By November 1975 some 80,000 children had been identified as eligible for the program. This was a much smaller number than the PRLDEF had expected. The number declined significantly with later testing, indicating that many children were learning English. As of May 1976 the reports to the court indicated that there were 58,448 eligible children in the city schools. Of these, 8,532 were withdrawn by their parents. Withdrawals were highest at the high school level because about one-sixth of the families refused to participate.[54]

Since parents, particularly those with low income and little knowledge of English, are often reluctant to question the wisdom of school administrators, these high withdrawal rates show considerable uneasiness about the bilin-

52. Gene Maeroff, "Billingual Education Plan for City's Schools," *New York Times,* March 12, 1974. For the text of the New York agreement, see *Aspira of New York, Inc. et al. v. Board of Education,* Consent Decree (S.D.N.Y. August 29, 1974).
53. Maeroff, "Bilingual Education Plan."
54. Irving Anker, "Progress Report on the Implementation of Consent Decree of August 29, 1974 in *Aspira of New York, Inc. et al. v. Board of Education.*"

gual approach. If parents had to choose whether to put their children *into* the program, fewer might be enrolled. (Colorado state law, for example, requires advance written consent from parents.)

The New York experience also demonstrated another important fact—language is not the overriding problem of Hispanic children. Even among Puerto Ricans, the least successful of the Hispanic groups, a large majority of the children can speak English, and the number who cannot may be falling rapidly. This means that the long-term practicality of bilingual-bicultural education as a strategy for Latino education may be questionable.

National survey data collected in 1965 showed that, even then, the average Mexican-American first grader had slightly higher verbal achievement scores than the average black student. Puerto Rican scores were only slightly lower.[55] One New York bilingual education coordinator said in 1976 that Puerto Rican children were learning English fast enough to end the need for bilingualism in "a couple of years" unless the justification was changed to one of maintaining Spanish culture.[56] And a 1977 report showed that two-thirds of Hispanic children in bilingual programs could speak English and that more than four-fifths of the programs held on to children after they were ready to function in a regular classroom.[57]

If there are to be bilingual programs, they can be operated in quite different ways. Most existing programs are segregated. The National Task Force de la Raza, reporting on the fifth year of federal bilingual programs in 1974, found that the enrollment in programs for Chicano children was 88 percent Spanish-speaking and only 12 percent English-speaking students. Almost nine-tenths of the programs were aimed at permanent maintenance of Spanish competence rather than at a more effective transition to English. National figures three years later were similar.[58]

Although Hispanic educators tended to agree that bilingual programs should be provided for as many Hispanic children as possible, they disagreed about whether they should be integrated. Gloria Zamora, former director of the HEW bilingual program, told a Senate committee that children should not be segregated for bilingual training: "I believe that

55. W. Vance Grant and C. George Lind, *Digest of Education Statistics, 1975 Edition,* HEW, National Center for Educational Statistics (GPO, 1976), p. 187.

56. *New York Times,* June 21, 1976.

57. American Institutes for Research, "Evaluation of the Impact of ESEA Title VII Spanish/English Bilingual Education Program," AIR 48300 (February 1977; processed), pp. xxxi–ii.

58. Report printed in *Congressional Record,* March 4, 1974, pp. 5060–61; American Institutes for Research, "Evaluation," pp. V-1, V-20–21.

segregation of children of diverse language groups is a pedagogically un-sound practice and it may also be a violation of their civil rights. . . . A skill-ful teacher will integrate children of the two language groups so that language learning can be stimulated."[59] On the other hand, the Puerto Rican Association for National Affairs denounced proposals that at least 30 percent of English speakers be included in bilingual programs as an un-necessary waste of scarce funds.[60]

Such contradictory statements show a conflict between two apparently desirable objectives. Closer examination of the court decisions and their application to local circumstances, however, suggests that there need not be a conflict.

The *Lau* decision is far less specific than its enthusiasts often claim. It affirms HEW's power to insist that school systems do something to help children unable to understand English-language instruction. While the Supreme Court recognizes that it offends common sense simply to put these children in an English-language classroom and expect everything to work out, it does not prescribe any remedy. The Court merely said to the local school officials "Do something."

"Teaching English to the students of Chinese ancestry who do not speak the language is one choice," the Court held. "Giving instructions to this group in Chinese is another. There may be others. Petitioner asks only that the Board of Education be directed to apply its expertise to the problem and rectify the situation."[61] Making the choice is apparently the responsibil-ity of local school officials. The basis for the *Lau* right vanishes once the child can function in the normal curriculum.


## The Trend toward Segregation

The sparse language of the *Lau* decision produced an explosion of bi-lingual education, often directly in response to a federal requirement. HEW attempted to use and broaden its newly recognized regulatory au-thority by spelling out detailed requirements for testing non-English-speaking children and automatically placing them in programs of bilingual-

59. *Education Legislation, 1973*, Hearings before the Subcommittee on Education of the Senate Committee on Labor and Public Welfare, 93:1 (GPO, 1973), p. 2932. For a summary of research showing the educational benefits of integrated classrooms, see American Institutes for Research, "Evaluation," pp. A-25, A-29–30.

60. *Education Legislation, 1973*, Hearings, pp. 3060–62.

61. *Lau* v. *Nichols*, 414 U.S. 563 at 565.

bicultural education. This policy, backed with the threat of fund cutoffs, hastened the change begun by the Bilingual Education Act of 1968. The Supreme Court's goal was to foster the effective participation of excluded groups in the normal English curriculum, but the result has been the development of multiyear parallel curricula, defined by children's linguistic and ethnic background.

Federal programs in bilingual education aid and in civil rights enforcement, though nominally affirming integration, have actually strengthened separation. The regulations of the Bilingual Education Act include language prohibiting recipients to "subject an individual to segregation," and HEW's policy memorandum of May 25, 1970, calls for transitional programs that "must not operate as an educational dead-end or permanent track." HEW brought in a group of experts to formulate national standards for school district compliance with the Supreme Court's *Lau* decision; the standards incorporated a statement that remedying language problems could "not justify the existence of racially/ethnically identifiable classes, *per se.*"[62] This is commonly ignored.

The resulting programs are highly segregated for several reasons. First, Hispanic students normally attend schools with considerable segregation. Second, though HEW has brought heavy enforcement pressure on school systems to provide bilingualism, it has done virtually nothing about desegregation. Finally, the regulations in the various programs are full of loopholes so large that they make a mockery of the policy statements about segregation. The regulations permit segregation of groups defined by linguistic ability where local school officials say it is educationally necessary. In practice there have been almost routine segregation at the local level and no federal enforcement of integration policies.

The San Francisco school system illustrates both the problems of desegregating a school system dominated by nonblack minority groups and the high-voltage politics of designing bilingual plans. The court in the San Francisco case found proof of illegal segregation for only the 29 percent of students who were black, but the court order encouraged the city to also desegregate Hispanics and each of the various large Asian-American groups with Anglos, who accounted for little more than one-fourth of the total enrollment. Supreme Court Justice William O. Douglas rejected an appeal for a stay from lawyers representing Chinatown parents who did not want their children desegregated. Complex reassignments of nine racial and ethnic categories of students temporarily produced approximate balance

62. These provisions are summarized in Herbert Teitelbaum and Richard J. Hiller, "Bilingual Education: The Legal Mandate," *Harvard Educational Review* (May 1977), p. 160.

in the schools and substantially reduced the segregation of black children.[63]

When desegregation had been only partially carried out, the school district lost the *Lau* case and San Francisco became the first major city under court order to solve the problems of non-English-speaking students. Advocates of bilingual-bicultural education wanted special programs not only for an estimated 7,200 children who spoke no English but for all children of different linguistic heritage. They demanded special classes for the city's largest ethnic groups and also for many others ranging from Arabic to Hindi.

The activists appointed to the school district's Citizens' Task Force on Bilingual Education concluded that the "burden should be on the school to adapt its educational approach" to the needs of the linguistic minorities. The task force called for instructing each of the groups primarily in its native language and culture throughout their entire school careers, teaching English as a secondary language.[64]

Needless to say, this attempt to use the schools for new goals produced strong resistance. In San Francisco a grand jury issued a report claiming that the approach would only "keep the young pupil from becoming assimilated into our existing society, which is English-speaking." The school system's associate superintendent, Lane De Lara, believed that the best answer was "pure and simple" training in English.[65] The school officials maintained that simple English training would fulfill the command of the Supreme Court's decision, but HEW lawyers said the agency would not approve it. Activists assailed the whole idea of assimilation. Some claimed that the Court had ordered full bilingual-bicultural education, no matter how high the cost or how small the group; some argued angrily that "there is something inherently racist about assimilation." The city's Human Rights Commission attacked the segregationist implications of the recommendations, urging concentration on teaching English and "return to regular school classes."[66]

The Citizens' Task Force supported its policy recommendations with a major report prepared by the Center for Applied Linguistics.[67] The re-

63. David L. Kirp, "Multitudes in the Valley of Indecision: The Desegregation of San Francisco's Public Schools" (unpublished paper, 1975), pp. 87–101.

64. Dexter Waugh and Bruce Koon, "Breakthrough for Bilingual Education: *Lau* v. *Nichols* and the San Francisco School System," *Civil Rights Digest* (Summer 1974), pp. 20–21; Kirp, "Multitudes in the Valley of Indecision," p. 129.

65. Waugh and Koon, "Breakthrough for Bilingual Education," p. 24.

66. San Francisco Human Rights Commission, Position Paper, March 24, 1975.

67. Center for Applied Linguistics and Citizens' Task Force on Bilingual Education, "A Master Plan for Bilingual-Bicultural Education in the San Francisco Unified School District" (February 25, 1975; processed).

search summary, however, was produced under peculiar conditions: the researchers were told by the task force to report only "positive instances." One recalled: "We told them that in terms of reading, there wasn't much evidence to show that bilingual education helped. But they didn't want us to say anything like that. They had a political job to do."[68] The recommendations for far-reaching changes in the San Francisco schools, changes working toward ethnic separation, were the basis for official policy adopted by the school board.

San Francisco provides a good example of carrying the principles of both *Keyes* and *Lau* to their illogical conclusions. In both cases, as they were applied to the city, there were largely unexamined assumptions that produced more rigid ethnic divisions. It was simply assumed, for instance, that the Asian-American children were a minority victimized by segregation that must be desegregated. But by any reasonable standard, most of them were successful. A comparative study in the spring of 1973 in the San Francisco district found that they viewed themselves more positively than any other group, including Anglos. Sixth grade reading achievement scores showed Asian-American children to be at the 64th percentile, whereas blacks were at the 26th percentile and Latinos at the 32d.[69] One must ignore the normal meaning of the words to define most Asians in San Francisco as a deprived minority. The bitter discrimination once practiced against Chinese, Japanese, and other Asians appears to have little present effect.

Carrying the idea of bilingualism to its ultimate conclusion, some enthusiasts would use public education to keep alive distinctive group identities and languages that might not otherwise survive as new groups became successful. For a society that has traditionally viewed its schools as a necessary institution for the building of a common culture and a civic consciousness, this would be a striking departure.

## Does Segregation Help Hispanic Children?

There is no conflict between bilingual education and school integration if the bilingual program is integrated and if it is primarily aimed at moving children as rapidly as possible into the normal school program. But most

68. Noel Epstein, *Language, Ethnicity, and the Schools* (Institute for Educational Leadership, 1977), p. 50.

69. Jane R. Mercer and Lulamae Clemons, "Summary Report, Evaluation of Integrated Education in Forty-Eight San Francisco Elementary Schools," report to San Francisco Unified School District (May 1973; processed).

programs are segregated and their primary goal is the maintenance of the children's separate linguistic and cultural identity. They have a sequence of separate courses that continue through much of a student's school career. Officials in New York City claimed in 1977 that they should be exempt from HEW's desegregation requirements because of their bilingual programs.

If it could be proved that children's education was damaged by desegregation, this would raise a serious legal issue. The Supreme Court, in its initial 1971 decision (*Swann*) sustaining busing, clearly recognized that educational harm would be a valid ground for limiting the extent of busing plans.

A review of the research uncovers no evidence that segregated bilingual programs work better; in fact, there is no convincing evidence that bilingualism works at all. Some of the research from other countries frequently cited in defense of the American programs suggests that learning a second language is easiest in classes where most of the children speak the language the minority children must acquire. It may well be, in other words, that integration would increase the possibility that Latino children will rapidly and successfully become bilingual.

There is little reliable information on the impact of the hundreds of functioning bilingual programs. The scattered research results now available do not sustain the argument that these programs are crucial to minority children, much less the assertion that they should be offered on a segregated basis.

Martin Gerry, formerly director of the Office for Civil Rights, described the research situation succinctly in 1974: "There aren't any federal studies worth a damn." Gerry, a lawyer who had been a leader in developing federal requirements, was skeptical about educational research anyway. He relied strongly on his own conviction that all-English school programs tell children that there is "something wrong with their language and their culture."[70]

Gilbert Sanchez, then director of the bilingual-bicultural program at the Center for Applied Linguistics, told a Senate committee in 1973 that "one of the major shortcomings of bilingual education in the past has been the total lack of basic research."[71] After reviewing the available research, Development Associates, a leading Hispanic consulting firm, concluded in 1974 both that the Hispanic population was deeply divided over educational strategies and that the evidence so far was inconclusive. It urged

70. Interview with Martin Gerry, September 10, 1974.
71. *Education Legislation,* Hearings, p. 3141.

experimentation not only with bilingualism but also with other methods, including better preparation of teachers, that might "produce results better than or equal to those produced by bilingual/bicultural programs."[72]

When the Commission on Civil Rights issued a 1975 report highly supportive of bilingual-bicultural education, it too conceded that there was virtually no evidence on the probable effect. The introduction included this unusual disclaimer: "In undertaking this study, the Commission . . . did not analyze findings from existing bilingual-bicultural programs, since few reliable evaluation data are available."[73]

The commission noted that the following problems were among those for which no reliable solutions were currently available: (1) how to measure achievement in bilingual children; (2) whether learning two languages tended to limit facility in each; (3) whether particular kinds of teaching methods worked better with bilingual children; (4) whether mathematics should ever be taught in a non-English setting; and (5) whether bilingualism lowered measured intelligence.[74]

A 1973 review of research on Mexican-American education by Norma G. Hernandez summarizes some of the arguments. On the important issue of intelligence, she says, though many researchers found either negative or neutral effects on intelligence from bilingual programs, they did not have adequate statistical controls. The best support she could find for bilingualism was a relatively sophisticated 1962 Canadian study of a group of ten-year-old bilinguals, which suggested that bilingual children scored higher than expected on intelligence tests.[75]

This Canadian research (the St. Lambert study) has frequently been called the most important scholarly evidence supporting American bilingualism, although it involved a different language, a social setting unlike any in the United States, and a group of middle class, not lower class, bilingual children. The bilingual training of middle class English-speaking Canadian children was accomplished by immersion in a French-speaking educational environment (in a predominantly French-speaking city and province). Though this study is often cited in defense of separate linguistic

72. Development Associates, Inc., report in Robert L. Crain and associates, *Design for a National Longitudinal Study of School Desegregation* (Santa Monica: Rand Corp., 1974), pp. 71–75, 76–95.

73. Commission on Civil Rights, *A Better Chance to Learn: Bilingual-Bicultural Education* (GPO, 1975), p. 3.

74. Ibid., pp. 127–36.

75. Norma G. Hernandez, "Variables Affecting Achievement of Middle School Mexican-American Students," *Review of Educational Research*, vol. 43 (Winter 1973), p. 21.

and cultural programs, it more logically supports an integrationist policy—immersion of Spanish-speaking children in English language curricula—rather than one of segregated bilingualism.

Pursuit of bilingual competence may have costs in some cases. An early study, for example, concluded that students remember least from courses they study in their first language and then are asked to recall in their second language.[76] If this is true, beginning basic courses in Spanish may be a poor way to convey skills that must later be used in English-speaking surroundings. And the results of the first national evaluation of the impact of the federally funded programs (a study of 11,500 students in 150 schools), which appeared nine years after the enactment of the Bilingual Education Act, were discouraging. The study showed that the children in the average bilingual program, which was costly, did less well on English reading and vocabulary tests than Hispanic children who had remained in English-speaking classes. Bilingual-bicultural programs made no difference either in attitudes toward school or in absenteeism.[77]

These negative findings do not mean that bilingual education is an unworkable idea. Evaluation of educational policies is complex and rarely shows strong positive effects. Research throughout the world contains ambivalent findings and contradictory policy recommendations.[78] The programs may become more effective, and better ways of measuring their impact may be developed. But according to the best existing evidence, the highly segregated programs have produced no educational gains that justify modifying desegregation orders.

It seems clear that bilingualism can be achieved in an integrated setting, perhaps far more effectively.[79] More troublesome is the associated idea of biculturalism, which has come to mean using the public school curriculum to strengthen the ethnic identity of a linguistic minority group. Even if one believes that this is a proper function of public education, it raises perplexing questions.

What cultural traditions, for instance, should the schools try to convey to a Mexican-American child? Mexican-Americans cannot even agree on

76. Cited in ibid., p. 18.

77. American Institutes for Research, "Evaluation," pp. xxx, xxxi, V-26, V-27, VI-75, VI-76. This study's methodology has been seriously criticized, and its findings should not be regarded as conclusive.

78. Frederick Shaw, "Bilingual Education: An Idea Whose Time Has Come," New York Affairs (Fall 1975), p. 108.

79. In an important early program in Miami, the most successful classes were those that were half Anglo. Interview with Rosa Inclan, director, Miami bilingual program, December 6, 1972.

a name for their group. One study in New Mexico shows a strong identification as "Spanish."[80] Others see themselves as Mexicans, Chicanos, Mexican-
Americans. Different names symbolize different cultural identities. The
following themes are among the many that might occur to a curriculum
developer:

> The history of Spanish-Americans in the Southwest
> The Hispanic literary tradition
> The political tradition of the Mexican revolution
> The Indian ancestry of most Chicano students
> The cultural impact of Mexican Catholicism
> Contemporary Mexican or Latin culture and values
> Controversies over the U.S. war with Mexico, Mexican land claims, and
>     Mexican attitudes toward American society

Who should choose among these and other possible themes? The materials used are bound to conflict either with basic values of American political
culture or with the views of many Hispanic parents. Which should it be?
Which children should be exposed to biculturalism? Is there, for instance,
any reason for an assimilated English-speaking child of Mexican ancestry to
be specially treated by the public schools? Should Puerto Ricans, Cubans,
South Americans, and others with Spanish names be channeled into the
same programs?

Two purposes of American education have been to teach at least minimal
competence in reading and writing English and to impart the basic principles of a political culture. Whether or not the policy was right, the
evidence suggests that it was stunningly successful in its own terms. In spite
of frequent rural and urban concentration of immigrant communities and
although the native language has continued to be used at home and some
distinctive cultural traditions have been maintained, English is the language of 96 percent of Americans and the elements of American civic culture have rarely been challenged.

During the last generation educational reformers, minority groups, and
women's organizations have striven to expand these traditional responsibilities to recognize the contributions of various groups to American society
and to end race and sex stereotypes. Integrationists commonly view this as
an important element of successful desegregation, in that it educates domi-

80. Justin R. Moore and Craig A. Ratchner, "Spanish? Mexican? Chicano? The
Influence of Spanish Culture on New Mexico," *Integrated Education* (September–
October, 1976), pp. 23–24.

nant social groups about the background of others. Recent research sustains this view. Some supporters of biculturalism, however, advocate modification of the tradition of a single common language in the schools in favor of using the schools to inculcate and maintain cultural and linguistic differences in segregated settings.

In a country that has been unable to resolve its racial problems, it seems unwise for the government to undertake programs that may encourage or deepen linguistic-cultural cleavages. Linguistic politics in countries with deep ethnic divisions have proved to be volatile, emotional, and persistent. There should be serious investigation of the possibility that policies intensifying separate linguistic and ethnic identities may increase the already high levels of Hispanic segregation and generate bitter linguistic politics.[81]

### An Integrationist Alternative

Although there are obvious conflicts between desegregation orders and bilingual education plans, it may be that the goals of each legal requirement can be better achieved in integrated schools offering special educational programs. One reason for this is that the desegregation right has a stronger legal basis. Two attorneys prominent in bilingual litigation observe:

Because of the broad remedial powers exercised by the courts to eliminate unlawful school segregation, desegregation cases continue to serve as convenient vehicles for court-ordered bilingual education programs. Since a court's power to right unlawful school segregation (a constitutional wrong) may well be greater than its power to redress a *Lau* violation (a federal statutory violation), desegregation cases may provide the best hope for achieving comprehensive court-mandated bilingual-education programs.[82]

Civil rights lawyers litigating cases in communities with large Hispanic populations are usually anxious to have the support of Hispanic groups and

81. One study of the relation between language and residential segregation in Montreal suggests that language identification tends to be strongly associated with residential separatism. Stanley Lieberson, "Residence and Language Maintenance in a Multilingual City," *Plural Societies* (Summer 1971), pp. 63–73. For a view of the relation between linguistic issues and political aspirations, see Joshua A. Fishman, *Language and Nationalism* (Rowley, Mass.: Newbury House, 1973), pp. 44–50.

82. Teitelbaum and Hiller, "Bilingual Education," p. 162. The authors were leading attorneys in a number of the major cases of the Puerto Rican Legal Defense and Education Fund. Vilma Martinez of MALDEF also insists that the two remedies can be mutually supportive.

are willing to support their educational proposals. Federal courts, concerned with the complexity of tri-ethnic desegregation, are often eager to minimize tension by adopting such plans.

It is not clear, on the other hand, that a right to bilingual education can be sustained independently in the long run. Many of the cases have relied on expert testimony attributing Hispanic educational problems to the lack of bilingual-bicultural programs and predicting major gains if such programs are implemented. If evaluation studies continue to undercut these conclusions, the Supreme Court's directive in *Lau* to "do something" might give way to court directives to "do something else." Under *Lau* there is no right to bilingual education unless it helps children function better in English classrooms.

If the strategic reasons for an integrationist strategy are important, the educational ones may be even more so. Children are not learning English very well in existing bilingual classrooms that have a monolingual student body. The existing programs too often resemble the old "Mexican rooms" the Hispanic leaders of the last generation fought.

A number of experts in Hispanic education have argued that classes need students of both Spanish and English backgrounds for effective language learning and job preparation. Thomas P. Carter, a pioneer in the field, observed in 1974:

Spanish for Spanish speakers could be used to justify present or future segregation of the group: if it is best to teach such children in Spanish, it could also be argued that it is most efficient to isolate them from those taught in English. "Spanish speaker" suggests Mexican-American to most educators, and all children with Spanish surnames or dark faces could be "encouraged" to learn their "native tongue," regardless of the status of the language in their homes or their ability to use it. Given only two polar choices, ethnic segregation with instruction in Spanish or desegregation without it, this author would choose the latter as most beneficial to the child and society.[83]

One of the most influential bilingual education advocates, Jose Cardenas, says that no such choice need be made. Bilingual training can be done in integrated schools with appropriate curriculum.[84] Research suggests that only in such a setting are good results with Hispanic learning of English likely and that middle class English-speaking children enrolling in such programs could learn Spanish well without its interfering with the rest of

83. Thomas P. Carter, "Mexican-Americans in School: English and Spanish Programs," in Frank Pialorsi, ed., *Teaching the Bilingual* (University of Arizona Press, 1974), p. 216.
84. Jose Cardenas, "Bilingual Education, Segregation, and a Third Alternative," *Inequality in Education* (February 1975).

their school program. If the question of segregation is not faced, says William Milan, a former federal bilingual education official, the result may be to damage the prospects of Hispanic children in the largely English job market.[85] Nor is it likely, unless Anglo children enter the programs, that the "bicultural" program will really represent an interchange of cultures not only permitting Hispanic children to come to terms with the dominant society but also helping white and black children understand the cultural heritage of an important and growing third group in American society.

By some measures Hispanic children are more segregated than blacks and a 1977 report on Hispanic achievement indicates that they face severe educational problems in all sections of the country.[86] So far little is known either about the impact of bilingual education or about the best way to desegregate Hispanic children. Given the enormous internal diversity of the Hispanic population and the different circumstances in which children must function, it is unlikely that there will be a single "best" policy.

Until we know more about the effects of various policies on Hispanic children and more about the values and preferences of their families, common sense suggests that we refrain from pushing policies to their extremes. Evidence available so far suggests that there is not necessarily a conflict between the educational needs of Hispanic children and school integration. But the most effective way of combining the two must still be found.

85. Noel Epstein, "The Bilingual Battle: Should Washington Finance Ethnic Identities?" *Washington Post*, June 5, 1977.

86. The first nationwide study of Hispanic educational gains, covering 1971–75, was issued by the National Assessment of Educational Progress in May 1977. It reported large gaps in achievement scores in all subjects tested and far higher levels of grade retention than experienced by other groups. Conditions were said to be worst in the Northeast, the most segregated area in the country. *Washington Post*, May 21, 1977.

# PART TWO

# Politics and Nonenforcement

# 8

# The President, Congress, and Antibusing Politics

WHEN President Lyndon Johnson signed the Civil Rights Act of 1964, it seemed certain to begin a period of revolutionary change in American race relations, a change then supported by a broad spectrum of political forces and evoking virtually unanimous support from American blacks. The first southern President since before the Civil War signed the bill as supporters—including conservative Republicans—looked on. Soon he chose the bill's floor leader and one of the nation's most eloquent civil rights advocates, Hubert Humphrey, as his running mate. In the fall, against one of the bill's few prominent nonsouthern opponents, Barry Goldwater, the President won a landslide victory that produced the most progressive congressional majority in recent history. All of the six major civil rights organizations had strongly supported enactment of the law and there was a seemingly unanimous black commitment to enforcement. Southern opponents were defeated and demoralized. Seldom has a social movement achieved a more unambiguous triumph.

The act brought about change in southern racial practices. Public accommodations were integrated. More black students went into desegregated schools in the first year of enforcement than had in the previous decade. The 1965 Voting Rights Act enfranchised blacks of the Deep South for the first time in the century. Changes that had seemed all but impossible took place rapidly and peacefully.

The underlying political consensus soon began to erode, however, particularly on the question of school segregation. By the early 1970s white Americans had consolidated against urban school desegregation. Now, after more than a decade of political attacks on busing and annual battles over antibusing legislation, little of consequence has been accomplished. Congress has enacted few significant antibusing amendments and presidential promises of more decisive action against the courts have come to nothing.

Still, the political battles and public statements deserve attention because of their influence on the national discussion of integration. They have left the federal courts more isolated than ever. They have been used to justify the removal of executive branch agencies' power to enforce civil rights laws. Finally, the negative character of the antibusing movement has meant that there has been no serious examination for some time of the ways in which the power of government could be used to produce an integrated society in the cities.

The Goldwater campaign, the emergence of George Wallace as a national figure, and the Nixon campaign strategies injected racial polarization into national politics. Presidential candidates apparently decided that there was more to be gained by dwelling on whites' fear of racial change than by appealing for black votes. The shift of the southern white vote to the GOP in the 1960s seemed to vindicate the strategy. Nixon was elected president with almost no black votes. More and more Republicans in the House and some in the Senate followed a similar strategy. This break with the progressive element of the party's tradition brought to office officials whose effective constituencies were almost entirely white.

When the courts began to order desegregation through busing the prominence in American politics of racial change rapidly became apparent on Capitol Hill. Long-time civil rights supporters suddenly encountered polarized public feeling unprecedented in their careers. A number of congressmen from Michigan and Massachusetts and other trouble spots executed fast, 180-degree changes in voting. Major education bills and huge appropriations measures were often ignored as busing amendments took precedence. Presidents Nixon and Ford threatened to veto entire programs if antibusing provisions were not tough enough.

The House, with its short terms and narrow constituencies, responded to the issue first and consistently approved presidential proposals to restrain the courts. The Senate—where many members are free of immediate election worries, where statewide constituencies encourage responsiveness to both black and white demands, and where, unlike in the House, the rural western states, which have very few minority children, are represented equally—consistently restrained the House and blocked presidential demands.

The story of antibusing legislation is rich in examples of how policy is affected by tactics. Committed civil rights supporters with positions of seniority have used conference committees, control of committee agendas, filibusters, muddled legislative language, and a variety of other strategems to frustrate antibusing majorities. Time after time the tactics the South used to preserve segregation have been used to defend desegregation requirements.

Both presidential and congressional politics reflected the decentralized nature of American society. The Wallace movement and the southern congressional attacks crested in the late 1960s and early 1970s, when the threat of change was imminent and the people were aroused. In 1972 the *Milliken* case in Detroit dominated Michigan politics. But by the time of the 1976 primaries, busing was a fact of life in many parts of the South and the issue was one of secondary importance. In many states it was academic since no cases were pending or there was almost no one to desegregate. Only in Boston was it dominant.

The long battles illustrated a feature of American politics that is too seldom described—the willingness of a surprising number of political leaders to go against strong public opinion on behalf of a principle they believe in or simply in defense of the law. During the most intense local polarization many members of Congress spent their political resources to prevent limitations on the courts. Most northern Democrats in the Senate and many in the House consistently voted against the national consensus. So did a number of Senate Republicans. The men and women who defied public opinion were a minority, but they prevented a collision between Congress and the Supreme Court.

## The Erosion of Support

The initial breakdown of the civil rights consensus can be ascribed to many causes. The changes soon reached beyond issues peculiar to the South. Deciding to act against vicious official racism in another region did not imply support for social transformation at home. Even when people agreed that something was wrong, they were divided on how much the *federal government* should do.

The divisiveness emerged rapidly during the process of enforcing the Civil Rights Act. When the Office of Education required southern school districts to begin token desegregation under "freedom of choice" plans in the fall of 1965, the adjustment was difficult but it was accepted. The next year, when federal civil rights officials realized that freedom of choice was not going to work, the Department of Health, Education, and Welfare escalated its requirements. The focus of enforcement changed from the surface equity of the process to the result—actual annual progress toward genuinely integrated schools. This went beyond what many courts were requiring at the time and was bitterly protested.

At the same time the civil rights movement was breaking up. In 1964 it had been completely integrationist. Within two years, some groups had turned to the issues of black power, cultural nationalism, and community building. Although these groups represented only a small fraction of the black population, they received a great deal of attention. Politically this meant that there was no unified black voice on civil rights issues. For the next several years some widely publicized black leaders attacked the premises of desegregation head on. Those who remained steadfast to the principles of 1954 and 1964 were belittled as traditionalists of declining importance. The movement was in disarray.[1]

The problems were magnified by the urban riots of 1965–68 and by the growing preoccupation of liberals with the Vietnam War. White Americans were shocked and terrified by the mass rioting and looting of blacks. The riots forced the public to focus on the immense racial problems of the cities, but hardly in a way designed to foster support for the changes necessary to produce desegregation.

The mood of Congress changed quickly. Even before a more conservative Congress was elected in 1966, the most liberal Congress in many years had unceremoniously killed a new civil rights bill. The House voted to limit federal school desegregation powers. It was the first of a long series of annual setbacks.

### Congressional Views of Segregation

The first signs of resistance to urban desegregation appeared in the congressional debate on the 1964 Civil Rights Act. Many members believed the South was a special case.

The House adopted amendments to one section of the bill forbidding the Justice Department to file litigation to force the busing of children for the purpose of racial balance.[2] In the Senate the fear of future busing actions was voiced by Senator Robert Byrd of West Virginia (who became the Democratic Senate leader in 1977). Under pressure from Byrd, the bill's

1. During this period Hispanics were only beginning to emerge as a major force. They were never clearly integrationist and many espoused goals of cultural and linguistic separatism.

2. House Committee on the Judiciary, *Civil Rights Act of 1963*, House Report 914, 88:1 (GPO, 1963), pp. 44, 85.

floor manager, Hubert Humphrey, stated his belief that the fund-withholding sanction could not be applied to de facto segregation. He assured opponents that President Johnson would reject "racial balancing" requirements.[3]

The statements about desegregation rested on the then prevailing understanding of constitutional requirements. Humphrey said that de facto segregation had been omitted from the bill because the Supreme Court had recently let stand a lower court decision that the Gary, Indiana, schools had no obligation to abolish segregation.[4] The Supreme Court's refusal to hear the case was widely cited as proof that northern segregation was constitutional.[5]

The Civil Rights Act, however, emerged from Congress with its major enforcement provision intact. In one of the most sweeping and important sentences in federal statutory law, the act stated: "No person in the United States shall on the ground of race, color, or national origin, be excluded from participation in, be denied the benefits of, or be subjected to discrimination under any program or activity receiving federal financial assistance."[6] This language laid the groundwork for broad administrative power to define and enforce standards: as the Court fleshed out constitutional requirements, the responsibilities of the Department of Health, Education, and Welfare would expand.

When HEW began actively enforcing the law in 1965, the initial response was calm. Congressional opponents turned belligerent only when the agency made clear that it was actually aiming at transformation of the southern school systems. Southerners were shocked that HEW was prepared to take the almost unprecedented step of cutting off large amounts of federal grants-in-aid. Many agencies had the power to cut the flow of federal money under certain conditions, but they almost never did. Under President Johnson, HEW frequently did.

When enforcement began, southern members of Congress were still reeling from their first serious defeat on civil rights legislation in Congress in almost ninety years. For some time southern leaders had denounced desegregation orders as undemocratic usurpations by the courts. Now that

---

3. *Congressional Record,* June 4, 1964, pp. 12715–17.
4. Ibid.
5. *Bell* v. *School City of Gary, Indiana,* 324 F.2d 209 (7th Cir. 1963), *cert. denied,* 377 U.S. 924 (1964). The Gary case was repeatedly mentioned in both committee and floor consideration. Although it is improper to infer any judgment on the substance of a case from the Supreme Court's refusal to hear it, the fact that a denial of review left standing a lower court's finding that the de facto segregation was constitutional was often seen as Court support for this proposition.
6. 78 Stat. 241, Title VI, 42 U.S.C. §2000(d).

Congress had ratified the policy of the courts, that rationale was gone. Only after HEW raised its requirements and southern opponents regrouped was there real resistance.[7]

### The Beginning of Northern Opposition

The first political confrontation to undermine congressional support took place outside the South, in Chicago. Neither Congress nor HEW had given much thought to the issue of northern and western segregation. It was clear, however, that both the Constitution and the 1964 Civil Rights Act prohibited intentional segregation in the North. How intent could be proved was unclear.

A 1965 civil rights complaint in Chicago not only alleged that there was a wide variety of segregationist practices but also claimed that the city intended to use the funds it would receive from the new Elementary and Secondary Education Act to reinforce segregation.[8] A confrontation between the city's black community and the local school system led to mass boycotts, hundreds of arrests, and a congressional hearing on the local situation.

Just a week after a small team of HEW staff members began to investigate Chicago, Commissioner of Education Francis Keppel deferred $32 million in new federal aid funds the city had been due to receive. The action came before the HEW staff had gathered any of the evidence necessary to sustain a fund cutoff and it put the administration in direct conflict with the most powerful Democratic political organization in the country. Commissioner Keppel had expected that the Chicago school officials would cooperate quietly to avoid publicizing the fact that their funds were being held up, but his action quickly became known.

The action drew attacks from the Chicago congressional delegation and from Senate GOP Leader Everett Dirksen of Illinois. Mayor Richard J. Daley threatened to end his delegation's support for all federal education legislation. Though HEW quickly retreated, the affair aroused the suspicion and hostility of a number of northern urban congressmen.

In 1966 the most liberal House since the depression voted against the

7. The 1965 school desegregation guidelines developed by the U.S. Office of Education are reprinted under the title "General Statement of Policies," in *Guidelines for School Desegregation,* Hearings before a special subcommittee of the House Judiciary Committee, 89:2 (GPO, 1966), pp. A20–A24.

8. See *Integrated Education* (December 1965–January 1966), pp. 10–35, for text of complaint submitted by Chicago's Coordinating Council of Community Organizations.

HEW school desegregation program. In the same House that had passed the Voting Rights Act, the Elementary and Secondary Education Act (ESEA), Medicare, Model Cities, and many other social reforms, opposition to school desegregation was growing. This was the first sign of what was to become a long-term shift. Each year from 1966 to 1977 the House passed at least one amendment designed to restrain school integration.

HEW had magnified its political problems when it issued new guidelines requiring far more desegregation in the South. Southern congressmen claimed that the tougher requirements were illegal and that HEW was forcing arbitrary changes which disrupted local educational systems.[9] By August 9, 1966, things had changed enough for the House to pass an amendment sponsored by Representative Howard "Bo" Callaway, a very conservative Georgian, which forbade HEW to require "assignment of students to public schools in order to overcome racial imbalance." The amendment was intended to prohibit any desegregation action in the South beyond "free choice" plans, which usually left schools highly segregated, and it appealed to northerners disturbed by the Chicago incident and beginning to worry about busing.[10] An even more sweeping amendment, submitted by North Carolina Congressman Basil Whitener but always called the Whitten amendment because Mississippi Congressman Jamie Whitten has resubmitted it annually, directing HEW to allow the perpetuation of segregation in southern "free choice" systems failed by nine votes.[11]

As the 1966–67 school year approached, opponents in Congress grew increasingly active. Eighteen southern senators had appealed in May to their old comrade, President Johnson, for a relaxation in the policy, but he supported enforcement.[12] Southern members inundated the enforcement staff with requests and letters and denunciations.

September also saw the first attempt by a northern congressman to exploit the backlash. Republican Representative Paul Fino of New York City, formerly one of his party's strong civil rights supporters, attacked a draft policy proposal, prepared for discussion within the administration, calling for a $6 billion program to find new answers to urban school problems. Fino assailed what he saw as a plan to force busing across school district lines into the suburbs, although this was immediately disavowed by the administration. When the high priority Model Cities bill came before the House, its sponsors initiated an amendment, which was approved by voice vote,

9. *Congressional Record*, August 9, 1966, pp. 18703–10.
10. Ibid., pp. 18717, 18721.
11. Ibid., pp. 18701, 18715.
12. Letter from the southern caucus to President Johnson, May 2, 1966.

forbidding administrators to require desegregation as a condition for receiving the funds.[13] This became part of the act.[14]

One of the few positive ideas of the period was quietly sidetracked in a Senate committee. Senator Edward Kennedy had proposed federal aid for northern and western school districts that voluntarily desegregated. This relatively noncontroversial proposal had enjoyed good prospects, but in September the liberal Senate Labor and Public Welfare Committee killed it. Even voluntary action in the North was not popular.

The southerners in the House concentrated their attack at first on obscure enforcement procedures little understood by civil rights supporters. Frontal attacks on desegregation would come later. First, they weakened HEW's power to hold up money for new federal aid programs in school districts where the department believed illegal segregation was taking place. The House passed an amendment to the ESEA by Representative L. H. Fountain of North Carolina forbidding the deferral procedure.[15]

However, this was the first of many occasions when liberal senior members of conference committees protected civil rights agencies. The general practice of relying on committee and subcommittee seniority in selecting conferees meant that the House members of the conference committee were a liberal group headed by Harlem Congressman Adam Clayton Powell, Jr., and that the Senate conferees too were led by strong supporters of civil rights. The 1966 conference committee eviscerated the Fountain amendment. Angry southerners were unable to persuade the House to risk defeat of the entire ESEA bill by attempting to force the Senate to reconsider in the final days of the session.[16]

Civil rights supporters had managed to preserve the basic structure of the 1964 Civil Rights Act in the first skirmishes, but these battles would go on incessantly into the mid-seventies. Supporters were reduced to skillful use of the tools of minorities attempting to frustrate majorities in Congress. The tactics that had prevented congressional passage of civil rights legislation for decades now forestalled its repeal.


### The Threat to Education Legislation

In 1967 Democratic opponents of civil rights enforcement by HEW joined Republicans to attack both the structure of federal aid to education

13. *Congressional Record,* October 14, 1966, pp. 26922, 26927.
14. 80 Stat. 1257.
15. *Congressional Record,* October 6, 1966, pp. 25573, 25578.
16. *Congressional Record,* October 20, 1966, pp. 28207–15.

and civil rights enforcement. The race issue threatened to split northern and southern Democrats. The danger in the House was so grave that HEW tacitly approved some of the less damaging civil rights amendments being drafted in the House and reorganized the enforcement program.

Again the HEW program was protected, but only because its enemies on the House floor were disorganized. Southerners, most Republicans, and some northern Democrats had rallied behind proposals drafted by Representative Edith Green of Oregon requiring that all HEW guidelines be based on particular parts of the Civil Rights Act and that they be applied equally to all fifty states. Southerners believed that the vague words of the statute would make it hard to justify the specific requirements of the guidelines. Since no one was going to launch a serious enforcement effort in the North, they thought, much less would be done in the South in the future.

When the 1967 ESEA amendments reached the House floor, however, Congresswoman Green confused everyone by accepting an amendment that allowed HEW to rely on court decisions to support standards. In the end the amendments were so unclear that HEW could continue its existing program while the program's foes could take credit for votes against it. This was to become a frequent pattern.

One thing showed the direction of the drift. The Fountain amendment limiting the deferral of funds, fought so hard the previous year, was enacted in the 1967 education bill. The administration accepted the weakening of the deferral power as part of a bargain intended to gain southern votes for extending the life of the ESEA.

Southern senators threatened to filibuster against the bill, and Dirksen came within a hair's breadth of amending it to forbid the use of any federal money to bus students, even for voluntary integration. Dirksen's move was defeated only by the opposition of freshman GOP Senator Robert Griffin of Michigan.[17] This was ironic, since Griffin later became a leader of the antibusing drive when Detroit was threatened with desegregation.

To extricate the education bill from the Senate, HEW Secretary John W. Gardner finally offered another compromise. HEW promised to further limit deferral actions, persuading the Senate's southern caucus to end any threat of filibuster.[18]

Again the liberal conference committee threw out the House restrictions. House opponents were once more presented with a take-it-or-leave-it package, brought to the floor on the final hectic day of the 1967 session. HEW retained its powers.

17. *Congressional Record,* December 4, 1967, pp. 34964–80.
18. *New York Times,* December 12, 1967.

The second year of congressional combat had left some marks on HEW's effort to enforce the Civil Rights Act. The most visible and committed spokesman for the effort, Commissioner of Education Harold Howe II, had lost his authority over the program. The enforcement staff was scattered in regional offices. The deferral power and enforcement credibility had been weakened.

### The 1968 Campaign

Although there was still very little city school desegregation in the nation, the fear of change grew after the Supreme Court's 1968 decision in *Green* v. *New Kent County,* which held that school systems segregated by official action must actually integrate, not merely offer blacks "free choice" to transfer for desegregation. In the courts civil rights lawyers were pressing the urban districts.

Both George Wallace and Richard Nixon emphasized desegregation in their campaigns. Wallace roused southern audiences with his passionate attack on HEW bureaucrats. His rapidly rising strength in the polls and his dominance in the Deep South suggested that he might gain enough votes to hold the balance of power in the electoral college.[19]

In his victorious campaign, Nixon attacked busing. He told the southern caucus at the GOP national convention that he believed judges were unqualified to make local school decisions. He promised a more conservative Supreme Court. He endorsed "freedom of choice." He said it was "dangerous" to use the threat of federal aid cutoffs to "force a local community to carry out what a Federal administrator or bureaucrat may think is best for that local community."[20] It was the first overt attack on civil rights enforcement by a successful presidential candidate in recent history.

During the election campaign Congress, through an amendment to a spending bill, came close to ending HEW's authority to desegregate southern schools by outlawing HEW's regulations. As the courts and HEW had begun to insist on the desegregation of southern city schools, southerners had been pointing out that similar segregation was ignored in the North and West. They succeeded in inserting into the 1968 HEW appropriations measure a directive that half of HEW's enforcement staff be used to in-

19. Theodore H. White, *The Making of the President 1968* (Pocket Books, 1970), pp. 429–36.
20. Regional television broadcast from Charlotte, North Carolina, reported in *Washington Post* and *New York Times*, September 13, 1968.

vestigate northern cases.[21] Appropriations bills in future years would frequently be the targets of congressional attacks on civil rights enforcement. This approach had two important tactical advantages: appropriations bills must be passed every year and they go to conservative conference committees.

### Nixon's Racial Politics

After President Nixon's inaugural, enforcement officials in the federal agencies found themselves under pressure from Capitol Hill and the White House to slow down. For the first time since 1954, both elected branches of government opposed the courts, attempting to delay change and hoping eventually to restrict judicial power to order desegregation. Pressure grew, first for a partial repeal of the Civil Rights Act and later for a showdown on the issue between the judiciary and the elected branches of government.

Nixon won election as the first president since Woodrow Wilson committed to slowing the momentum of racial change. After taking office he had to decide what to do about the existing drive to complete desegregation in the rural South and about desegregating urban areas. On both issues he decided to oppose desegregation.

As a result there was less and less disposition in Congress to fight efforts to narrow the Civil Rights Act. Once again Whitten submitted the amendment that would force HEW to accept "free choice" plans as being in full compliance with the Civil Rights Act. The Johnson administration had fought the proposal, but this time the new attorney general, John Mitchell, told a meeting of GOP congressmen that he could see nothing wrong with the amendment. The House promptly passed it. Only Senate resistance and a belated HEW statement of opposition succeeded in defeating the measure.[22]

The Nixon administration politicized the enforcement process, and negotiations between local officials, HEW's civil rights staff, and congressional offices were transferred to Washington. The momentum and credibility of the federal drive for integration were greatly diminished.[23] Only the unanimous October 1969 Supreme Court decision, *Alexander* v. *Holmes*,[24] pre-

---

21. Public Law 90-557 (1968), §410.
22. Interview with William van den Toorn, Office of Civil Rights, May 1, 1974.
23. Interview with OCR Atlanta Regional Director Paul Rilling, July 3, 1969.
24. 396 U.S. 19 (1969).

vented a collapse of the southern desegregation effort. This, the first major decision of the Court under Chief Justice Warren Burger, a Nixon appointee, summarily rejected the administration's insistence on delay and ordered that plans be carried out at once.

The busing issue was growing. In his long-awaited March 1970 statement of school desegregation policy, President Nixon sharpened the White House attack on the courts. He denounced "extreme" court orders, which, he said, "have raised widespread fears that the nation might face a massive disruption of public education: that wholesale compulsory busing may be ordered and the neighborhood school virtually doomed."[25] In conformity with the President's policy, the Justice Department went into court in 1970 to fight a federal district court decision ordering desegregation of the Charlotte, North Carolina, school system, carrying its battle to the Supreme Court.

### The Senate

By early 1970 congressional civil rights supporters appeared to have been routed. A skillful drive, led by Senator John Stennis of Mississippi and supported by the White House, produced the first serious Senate defeat for school integration.

Stennis documented northern segregation in great detail and then challenged northern senators to require all cities to meet the standards that had been set for the South. His amendment to the ESEA of 1965 to apply the law *equally* "without regard to the origin or cause of such segregation" meant that, unless the administration was prepared to move out in front of the federal courts and require desegregation in the North, nothing could be done in the South. Since the President had consistently opposed the desegregation of northern cities, civil rights supporters believed he would use the Stennis amendment to equalize conditions by ending change in Dixie. Senate Democratic leaders and GOP leader Hugh Scott fought the amendment but could not defeat it so long as it enjoyed quiet White House backing.[26]

The Senate vote indicated that the nation's backward movement on desegregation had now reached major proportions. A Gallup poll published shortly after the Senate vote reported that nine people in ten were opposed

25. "Statement about Desegregation of Elementary and Secondary Schools, March 24, 1970," *Public Papers of the Presidents: Richard Nixon, 1970* (GPO, 1971), p. 305.
26. Congressional Quarterly, *Civil Rights Progress Report, 1970*, pp. 39–41.

to busing, even though most of the whites against busing said they were willing to send their children to half-black schools.[27]

Civil rights groups were deeply discouraged. The President was hostile to urban desegregation, his appointments were making the Supreme Court more conservative, the House had been hostile for years, and now the last bastion, the Senate, seemed to have fallen. If the Senate joined the White House and the House of Representatives in resisting, the pressure on the courts would be immense. It was a congressional election year—the year of Spiro Agnew's biting attacks on liberals, of campus polarization on Cambodia, and of GOP efforts to mobilize the "silent majority"—and the administration used the busing issue in a strident campaign to put a new conservative majority on Capitol Hill.

The obituary for school integration turned out to be premature. When the House and Senate went to conference on the Stennis amendment, a strange thing happened. The bill emerged from conference not only without the Stennis provision, but with directions to HEW to formulate separate policies for de facto and de jure segregation and to apply each nationally.[28]

In February 1970 the Senate established the Select Committee on Equal Educational Opportunity, with Walter Mondale as chairman, to explore the complex issues. In its three years of existence, the Mondale committee investigated and attacked the Nixon administration's failure to enforce civil rights laws. It gave school officials and civil rights spokesmen an opportunity to rebut the administration's contention that desegregation was failing in communities across the country. The committee's work helped improve the Emergency School Aid (desegregation aid) legislation. More important, it provided some counterforce to the heavy weather that was pushing the Senate toward an attempt to override the courts.[29]

## Aid for Desegregation

One section of President Nixon's March 1970 school desegregation policy statement was well received by both civil rights supporters and school officials—his call for a large grant program to help desegregating school

27. Gallup poll, April 5, 1970; reprinted in *Congressional Record*, April 8, 1970, p. 10908.

28. 84 Stat. 121.

29. The committee published thirty-six volumes of hearings on the major issues involved in school desegregation, more than a dozen special studies, and a final report, *Toward Equal Educational Opportunity*, 92:2 (GPO, 1972).

systems do the job better. Since the Supreme Court had made further delays in desegregating the rural South impossible, the President proposed to ease the transition with a two-year $1.5 billion emergency program.

The administration soon faced the necessity of translating the President's broadly stated promise, inserted in his desegregation statement at the last moment, into a specific legislative proposal. The resulting bill was built around helping districts that were facing "emergencies" created when the courts ordered sudden massive desegregation. When a local school district was directed to desegregate immediately, its major out-of-pocket expense was often the purchase of new buses. Local administrators, not wanting to disrupt educational plans on short notice, hoped to use federal funds for this purpose.

After HEW had drafted the bill, the President added a new provision prohibiting use of the money for busing. This, in effect, dissociated the administration from busing, and it was strongly opposed by school officials and civil rights groups and provoked new battles in Congress. Congress rapidly approved interim 1970 appropriations of $75 million while committees worked on the legislation for the much larger program.

The pilot program produced serious administrative abuses. White House insistence on rapid action meant that there were no effective civil rights reviews and the money was simply sent out. Jackson, Mississippi, for instance, was granted $1.3 million four days *before* HEW received the city's official application.[30] It was discovered that much of the money had gone to districts continuing to segregate. In some places, the districts receiving the money were systematically firing black teachers and principals and segregating black children in classes in nominally "desegregated" buildings. The General Accounting Office, Congress' investigatory agency, reported that in many of the approved applications there was no pretense that the money would be spent for integration.[31]

The battle over the Emergency School Aid Act stretched into 1971 and 1972. In the end, Congress transformed an amorphous plan for a one-shot grant without strings to southern districts into a program with a more national orientation, strong administrative strings, and some incentives for desegregation. The desegregation requirements were so unambiguous that

30. Earl Browning, Jr., "Emergency School Assistance: Financing the Desegregation Retreat" (unpublished paper, 1971).

31. "The Emergency School Program—An Evaluation," a report prepared by a coalition of civil rights organizations including the NAACP Legal Defense Fund, the American Friends Service Committee, and the Washington Research Project (1970; processed); Report of the General Accounting Office, 1971.

HEW continued enforcing them long after it stopped enforcing the Civil Rights Act. The temporary two-year program was twice extended. On the other hand, President Nixon eventually had his way on the prohibition against using the money for busing. His opposition and that of President Ford to increased appropriations for the program were effective; the effort peaked in 1973 but was severely eroded by inflation during the next four years.

## Politics and Polarization

The politics of antibusing legislation began to change rapidly after the Supreme Court handed down its unanimous and surprisingly tough 1971 decision in the Charlotte case.[32] The busing remedy became available in the North too, once lawyers had proved de jure violations. That fall the issue was suddenly brought home to the white suburbanites of the country when a federal district judge in Michigan ordered the preparation of a desegregation plan for metropolitan Detroit.[33]

The votes on antibusing measures in the House in 1971–72 consolidated Republican sentiment against school desegregation and began to weaken northern Democratic support. In 1972, antibusing forces started out with a large, stable core of House votes and tended to pick up more votes as a growing number of northern Democrats joined their southern counterparts (see table 8-1). Southerners had always said that the politics of the issue would change when the North was forced to desegregate. They were right. Some members of the Michigan, Colorado, Massachusetts, and Delaware congressional delegations suddenly reversed their position. In the House the antibusing fights that had been led by southerners were now taken over by Michigan members.

This produced odd coalitions. Often moderate and liberal members felt they had to vote for amendments sponsored by extremely conservative members whose lead they would follow on no other issue. A principal author of the House antibusing language, for example, was Representative John Ashbrook of Ohio, a leader of the most conservative Republicans. A number of Democrats who had recently enjoyed almost perfect (by the standards of Americans for Democratic Action) voting records found themselves supporting Ashbrook. On the Senate side, antibusing authors included such improbable figures as Senator Jesse Helms of North Carolina,

32. *Swann* v. *Charlotte-Mecklenburg Board of Education*, 402 U.S. 1 (1971).
33. *Bradley* v. *Milliken*, 338 F. Supp. 582 (E.D. Mich. 1971).

Table 8-1. *Changing Factional Alliances on House Antibusing Votes,*
*1968–72*

Percent

| Factional agreement | Whitten amendment[a] | 1972 ESEA amendments[b] | Nixon antibusing bill[c] |
|---|---|---|---|
| Republican– southern Democrat | 65.6 | 89.6 | 86.2 |
| Northern Democrat– southern Democrat | 20.4 | 48.9 | 46.0 |

Source: James Bolner and Robert Shanley, *Busing: The Political and Judicial Process* (Praeger, 1974), pp. 116, 118–19.
a. From 1968 to 1971 there were five roll call votes on the Whitten amendment.
b. In 1972 there were seven roll call votes on the ESEA amendments.
c. In 1972 there were nine votes on the Nixon bill, the most drastic effort to limit judicial power.

whose views made most of the older southern Democrats look liberal by comparison, and Senator Edward Gurney of Florida, who at the time was under indictment in a political scandal.

As the controversy intensified, political leaders faced an unusual situation. Opinion against busing was so strong that many congressmen with largely white constituencies could see no support for the policy the courts were attempting to implement. In middle class communities threatened by court orders, the public protested on an unprecedented scale. There was little organized support for the policy from the black community, and social scientists publicly stated that the policy did no good anyway. Politically, there was little to lose by opposing busing and there was the possibility of gaining an active new constituency.

The congressional mood in the 1971–76 period was reminiscent of that in southern state legislatures in the late 1950s. Although most legislators knew they lacked the authority to repeal Supreme Court decisions, public pressure was so intense that legislators often cast almost unanimous ballots for patently ridiculous positions. In the 1950s the Virginia legislature pronounced the 1954 Supreme Court decision null and void and gave the governor authority to shut down public schools if integration was threatened. On Capitol Hill in the 1970s members of Congress found themselves debating measures to cut off the gasoline for school buses, to permit resegregation of southern schools, and to tell the Supreme Court how to handle its school cases. Many of these measures had been proposed or strongly endorsed by the President and all passed the House. In the 1950s

the southern legislators had attempted to forestall litigation by laws restricting the NAACP; in 1974 Congress restricted legal services lawyers. Though
they could handle most legal problems of the poor, legal services lawyers
could not represent clients who were attempting to end their children's
unconstitutional segregation in a de jure segregated school system.

### The Constitutional Amendment

The most extreme response was a drive to amend the Constitution so that
federal authority to require positive local action to desegregate urban
schools would be ended. The favored vehicle was an amendment reading:
"No public school student shall, because of his race, creed, or color, be
assigned to or required to attend a particular school." This "affirmation of
equal opportunity" would of course proscribe any desegregation plan that
attempted to overcome de jure segregation by reassigning children. It
would prohibit not only busing but also numerous other techniques of
urban school desegregation. With existing urban housing patterns, it would
mean almost nothing could be done.

The amendment drive peaked in early 1972, when President Nixon
publicly stated that he might support a constitutional amendment unless
Congress could end busing by legislation. This statement, however, was
promptly attacked by both Republican and Democratic leaders of the
Senate and even by Vice-President Agnew.[34] Gerald Ford, then House
GOP Minority Leader, and Senator Henry Jackson, a Democrat, strongly
endorsed amendments but theirs was a minority view.[35]

The amendment was introduced by thirty-one members of the House in
early 1972, and supporters organized a discharge petition to force it out
of the Judiciary Committee. After more than one-third of the House had
signed the petition, the committee agreed to hold hearings. Some seventy
members of the House either appeared before the committee or submitted
statements on the amendment. The great majority favored it.[36] But the
committee bottled it up after the President decided to first try legislation
limiting court orders. The amendment process, he told a national television
audience, has "a fatal flaw—it takes too long."[37]

An analysis of the voting records of the more than 150 members who

34. *Washington Post,* February 15, 1972.
35. *New York Times,* February 16 and 17, 1972.
36. *School Busing,* Hearings before Subcommittee No. 5 of the House Committee
on the Judiciary, 92:2 (GPO, 1972), pp. 1877–78, iii–xii.
37. *New York Times,* March 17, 1972.

signed the discharge petition showed that they had consistently been opponents of civil rights measures. From 1968 to 1971, in a series of crucial votes,
they had been against actions to strengthen civil rights enforcement by
more than 7–1. Although opponents of busing frequently said they favored
integration so long as neighborhood schools were naturally integrated, the
amendment's supporters had voted almost 5–1 against the 1968 fair housing law on its key test. Ten out of eleven also opposed strong enforcement
against job discrimination.[38]

If legal authorities are correct in stating that a constitutional amendment
is the only way to reverse judicial decisions requiring student transportation, opponents of busing are up against extraordinarily difficult political
obstacles; among them, that in almost half of the states there are almost no
minority students to bus and in a few states segregation has been virtually
eliminated. Even if an amendment could be extracted from a hostile House
Judiciary Committee, proponents would have to muster two-thirds margins
in both House and Senate and overcome a probable Senate filibuster. They
would then need ratification by three-fourths of the states. This would take
years at best.

In a 1972 national poll a majority of the respondents supported legislation limiting desegregation but fewer than one-third favored a constitutional amendment (see table 8-2). A 1976 poll for *Time*, however, reported
a 51–39 percent majority for an amendment.[39] The House Democratic
caucus in November 1975 voted 2–1 to table an amendment proposal although at the time there were protests and disruption in Boston and
Louisville.[40]

Constitutional amendments can be enacted only when there is a broad
national consensus on an issue. Strong minority opposition can easily block
the drive for two-thirds majorities in both houses. Polls indicate that the
proposed constitutional amendment to permit prayer in schools, for instance, is supported by a much larger (77–17 percent) majority of the
public yet has been blocked in Congress.[41]

Congress is hesitant to tamper with the Constitution or with the tradition
of an independent judiciary. In the busing debates, arguments were often
based on constitutional law and the separation of powers, not on substance.
Many members of Congress are lawyers, as are all members of the Judiciary

38. Analysis of voting records by Orfield, in *School Busing*, Hearings, p. 734.
39. *Time* poll reported in *Integrated Education* (November–December 1976),
p. 24.
40. *Washington Post*, November 20, 1975.
41. *Gallup Opinion Index* (May 1975), p. 22.

Table 8-2. *Public Support for Antibusing Legislation and Constitutional Amendment*

Percent

| | Answer | | |
|---|---|---|---|
| Question | Favor | Oppose | No opinion |
| A law has been introduced in Congress to prohibit busing of children beyond the nearest schools even where the courts have found unlawful segregation. Do you feel it would be right or not right for Congress to pass such a law? | 57 | 29 | 14 |
| Would you favor or oppose a constitutional amendment which would make it lawful to keep schools segregated? | 30 | 53 | 17 |

Source: U.S. Commission on Civil Rights, "Public Knowledge and Busing Opposition" (March 13, 1973; processed), appendix, p. 2, reporting data collected by Opinion Research Corporation in November and December 1972 based on 2,006 interviews.

Committees, which must handle constitutional amendments. This is a substantial barrier to precipitate constitutional change and has surely influenced the politics of the issue. President Nixon never submitted an amendment, nor did President Ford, even after the idea was endorsed in the 1976 GOP platform. Antibusing leaders in the House continued to try to force a vote with a discharge petition in 1977 but failed to obtain enough signatures.

### The Midnight Amendments

Until 1971 the battles in Congress had been primarily over limiting HEW's power to enforce the 1964 Civil Rights Act. But in a late evening House debate on November 4, 1971, the Michigan delegation led the House toward a direct challenge to the authority of the federal courts. The fight was over a complex higher education bill that also carried the Nixon desegregation assistance program.

Without hesitation, the House adopted an amendment introduced by suburban Detroit Congressman William Broomfield which said that future court orders requiring transportation of students to achieve racial balance must not take effect until the school system concerned had had a chance to appeal the case to the Supreme Court. This directly opposed a decision by the Court, which had ruled unanimously in 1969 that desegregation orders must be carried out immediately, even though appeals were pending.[42] Although the amendment was obviously intended to delay the execution of a metropolitan Detroit desegregation plan, it was drafted so broadly that it would have blocked plans even where there were no unsettled legal issues. The amendment was adopted with little discussion, 235–125.

A second amendment devised by Representative John Ashbrook, which would come up time after time in the debates of the next several years, prohibited the use of federal grant money for busing students or teachers for desegregation. The amendment was a break with the tradition of giving local districts discretion in the use of school aid and would constitute a special hardship on some 2,000 districts already under desegregation plans requiring busing. Though it was strongly opposed by many school officials, it passed by a huge margin.

Next the House adopted Congresswoman Edith Green's amendment forbidding federal officials to encourage integration. The amendment stated that federal administrators must not "urge" or "persuade" local authorities to use their own state or local money for busing. Federal officials, sworn to uphold the Constitution, would be forbidden even to suggest that local governments comply with the clear requirements of the Constitution as interpreted by a unanimous Supreme Court. More ominous was the amendment's partial repeal of the 1964 Civil Rights Act. If the Green amendment became law, HEW would lose its power to cut off federal aid to school districts that defied federal court orders requiring busing.[43]

When the House finally passed the higher education bill with all these amendments included, much more attention and energy had been devoted to busing than to all the complex provisions of one of the most significant college aid measures in U.S. history.

### Election Year Showdown

The issue plagued the Senate in 1972, producing a close and ugly fight during the spring primary campaigns and a down-to-the-wire battle, complete with an unusual liberal filibuster, in the session's final days. A district court order for desegregation of the Richmond, Virginia, city and suburban school systems and George Wallace's triumphant victory in his one-issue Florida primary campaign made it impossible for Democrats to ignore the issue.[44] No civil rights question had divided the party so deeply for many

42. *Alexander* v. *Holmes,* 396 U.S. 19.
43. *Congressional Record,* November 4, 1971, pp. 39317–18.
44. *Washington Post,* January 6, 1972; *Congressional Quarterly,* March 18, 1972, p. 585.

years. President Nixon did his best to exploit the opposition's division and to strengthen his antibusing credentials by repeatedly demanding congressional action to stop busing.

During the spring battle the civil rights forces held their tiny majority by offering a "compromise" on the moratorium issue: Majority Leader Mike Mansfield and Minority Leader Hugh Scott jointly sponsored an amendment that would delay only the enforcement of metropolitan orders and only until 1973. While the amendment made little practical difference at the time, it was a significant change of principle. In the Senate, which had usually opposed even attempts to restrain HEW, the moderate leadership now felt it was necessary to endorse a compromise restraining the courts.

Although disheartening to civil rights groups, the Scott-Mansfield amendment was only another tactical retreat. It gave the conservatives rhetorical satisfaction while attempting to protect most of the authority of the judiciary.

Things really heated up at this stage. Before the House and Senate could work out their differences on the higher education bill, Wallace's victory in Florida and a nationally televised antibusing speech by the President two days later intensified the pressure on Congress. The administration demanded action by the conference committee supporting the House position and quickly prepared its own antibusing package, which would come to the floor later in the session.

The executive branch concentrated first on the conference committee, encouraging votes in the House instructing conferees to insist on antibusing language. The House instructed its conferees twice, each time by approximately 2–1.[45] Discouraged civil rights supporters prevented Senate adoption of the wide-ranging House amendments by a single vote.[46]

A compromise was eventually hammered out. The conferees accepted the sweeping language of the House's moratorium amendment in the hope that the courts would find the poorly drafted language either meaningless or unconstitutional. On the other hand, the amendment forbidding the spending of federal aid money for busing was rendered harmless.[47]

The compromise was attacked by liberals and conservatives in both houses, but it held and the higher education bill was enacted.[48] The Presi-

45. *Congressional Record*, March 8, 1972, pp. 7554, 7562; May 11, 1972, pp. 16841–42.

46. *Congressional Record*, March 1, 1972, p. 6276.

47. *Congressional Quarterly*, May 27, 1972, pp. 1242–43.

48. *Congressional Record*, May 24, 1972, p. 18862; *Congressional Quarterly*, June 10, 1972, p. 1371.

dent signed it but called the antibusing language "inadequate, misleading and entirely unsatisfactory" and the most "manifest congressional retreat from an urgent call for responsibility" of his entire administration.[49] The busing fight had completely overshadowed the educational sections of the bill.

The contest was far from over for the year. Unsatisfied, President Nixon pressed hard for the passage of an "Equal Educational Opportunities" bill he had presented in March. It not only attempted to delay court orders but also incorporated deep infringements of judicial autonomy. It prescribed the kind of desegregation plans courts could approve and the priority they must give to various remedies. It said that courts could neither order the transfer of any elementary school student further from his neighborhood than the next closest school nor substantially increase the total busing in a school district. School boards would be authorized to reopen existing court orders that went beyond these standards, permitting the resegregation of many blacks who had been integrated in southern schools.[50]

Civil rights supporters were on the defensive again. The liberals on the House Education and Labor Committee dragged out committee action on the President's plan as long as possible, hoping to delay House action until near the end of the session.

The committee reported an amended version in August, which the House proceeded to make more rigid: the majority voted to prohibit the busing of secondary as well as elementary students beyond the next closest school.[51]

The administration's draft bill had been written to go to the limit of whatever authority Congress might have to restrain the judicial branch. Most constitutional authorities thought it went well beyond. More than 500 law professors signed a letter expressing their belief that the bill was unconstitutional. The administration could produce only one authority, Robert Bork of Yale Law School, to testify that the measure was probably constitutional.[52] Changes made on the House floor, however, had moved the measure so much further toward detailed congressional control of the courts that even some of the administration loyalists balked. Representa-

49. "Statement on Signing the Education Amendments of 1972, June 23, 1972," *Public Papers of the Presidents: Richard Nixon, 1972* (GPO, 1974), pp. 701, 703.
50. Ibid., March 25, 1972, pp. 642–48.
51. *Congressional Record*, August 17, 1972, pp. 2888–2907.
52. His testimony appears in *Equal Educational Opportunities Act of 1972*, Hearings before the Subcommittee on Education of the Senate Committee on Labor and Public Welfare, 92:2 (GPO, 1972), pp. 1312–20. (Bork later became solicitor general in the Nixon administration.)

tive Albert Quie, GOP spokesman on education, for example, found that he could not support them.[53]

The administration bill finally came to the Senate floor in October 1972, about a month before the presidential election. Feeling certain of a Nixon landslide victory over George McGovern, most senators seemed ready to vote for almost any bill. Civil rights supporters decided that their only choice was to filibuster.

The filibuster began on October 6, and liberals proved in three successive votes that they had the strength to prevent cloture. Conservatives, who had used a filibuster earlier in the year to block a bill granting strong enforcement powers to the Equal Employment Opportunities Commission, found their favorite tool being used against them. Longtime enemies of the filibuster system joined in the delaying tactic only to hear their obstructionism denounced in southern accents. The filibuster held in spite of White House lobbying and a strong appeal from President Nixon.[54]

### Turning Off the Gas

Although the President promised to give the matter "highest priority" in 1973, antibusing legislation may well have been one of the many casualties of Watergate. It was not an election year and the Supreme Court removed some of the pressure when it failed to order metropolitan desegregation in Richmond. Congress did not attempt to enact major education legislation during the year. Only at the end of the year, when legislation dealing with the Arab oil embargo was being seriously considered, did busing again become significant. Congress voted against every proposed cutback in the use of gasoline—from recreational aviation to recreational travel—but busing was different.

Congressman John Dingell, a Democrat from the Detroit suburbs, offered an amendment denying gasoline "for the transportation of any public school student to a school farther than the public school closest to his home offering educational courses for the grade level and course of study of the student within the boundaries of the school attendance district wherein the student resides.[55]

Representative Jonathan Bingham of New York protested, saying that the House would "allow oil to be allocated . . . for all kinds of recreational

53. *Congressional Record*, August 17, 1972, p. 28906.
54. "The President's News Conference of October 5, 1972," *Public Papers of the Presidents: Richard Nixon, 1972* (GPO, 1974), p. 338.
55. *Congressional Record*, December 13, 1973, p. 41268.

and nonessential purposes but here is an educational purpose and we say no oil for this purpose." He pointed out that one effect of the amendment would be to prohibit voluntary desegregation efforts. The restriction would not apply to private schools, which would still be allocated gasoline to bus students as far as they wished. Only school systems attempting to enforce federal court orders would be denied.[56] Representative Bella Abzug of New York called it "scandalous demagoguery." In response to her claim that the amendment was "demagogic or racist," Speaker Carl Albert took the extraordinary step of striking her words from the *Congressional Record*.[57] It was the first time in a decade that this had been done.

Representative Charles Wiggins of California, a critic of busing, thought that Dingell had the wrong answer. "To me," he said, "this is much like the Congress denying to the Supreme Court energy and power, because we are unhappy with its decisions."[58]

Representative Dale Milford of Texas claimed that the amendment would win "public acceptance" for conservation. "The fuel saved will help to heat a few more homes. It will help to save a few more jobs and it will make literally millions of people happier."[59] The amendment was not really "anti-minority," said a Florida member, but "pro-American."[60]

Black congressmen denounced the tactic. Ronald Dellums, who came from Berkeley, where busing had stabilized racial patterns in a community for the better part of a decade, told the House of his "feeling of desperation, anguish, and cynicism."[61] Parren Mitchell of Maryland recalled his sadness when a young black student asked, "Why do they hate us so?" "Mr. Chairman," said Baltimore's first black congressman, "that question may well be raised on this floor today, and I do so raise it."[62]

The debate was largely wasted. Everyone knew that any antibusing amendment would pass. This one did, 221–192.[63]

The next day two Democratic congressmen from Texas attempted to modify the ban. Bob Eckhardt of Houston proposed that gas be allocated for transporting students when a local school board wished to do so. He did not want to cut off a program in his district where white families were voluntarily sending their children to a formerly black school. J. J. (Jake)

56. Ibid., p. 41270.
57. Ibid., pp. 41270–71.
58. Ibid., p. 41271.
59. Ibid., pp. 41272–73.
60. Ibid., p. 41275.
61. Ibid.
62. Ibid., p. 41280.
63. Ibid.

Pickle endorsed this approach, fearing chaos in the Austin desegregation plan. Even this modest, southern-sponsored amendment was defeated quickly, 202–185.[64]

The Senate was not yet ready for such arbitrary action. The conference committee removed the Dingell amendment.

The idea of cutting off the gas continued to appeal to the House—it incorporated a similar proviso in a 1975 energy bill, though there was no current gas shortage. It was all reminiscent of Georgia Governor Lester Maddox's suggestion that the answer was to let the air out of the school bus tires. At any rate, the restriction was again quickly removed by the conference committee.

### Throttling Legal Services

Since the beginning of the Nixon administration, the legal services program, one of the most controversial remnants of the War on Poverty, had been threatened. As the climax approached it became entangled with the busing issue.

Neighborhood legal services had been in trouble ever since they stopped merely representing ghetto residents who claimed to have been cheated by local merchants and began to raise difficult test cases challenging basic legal assumptions. Governors in five states had attempted to veto funding for their offices. California's Governor Ronald Reagan was the leading critic, continually feuding with the California Rural Legal Assistance program. Senator George Murphy of California led unsuccessful 1967 and 1969 Senate battles to prohibit all test cases.[65]

An analysis of 2,050 of the program's test cases between 1967 and 1972 showed that less than 1 percent dealt with the field of civil rights. Few of these were school cases. Of the early northern and western school cases, only two in the small Southern California communities of Inglewood and Oxnard were litigated by legal services lawyers.[66] Legal services offices in larger cities, including Hartford, Springfield, Illinois, and Dallas, later initiated litigation. While these efforts consumed only a tiny fraction of the resources of the legal services program, they were an important addition to the meager legal means of private civil rights organizations. They soon pro-

64. *Congressional Record*, December 14, 1973, pp. 41701–03.

65. Earl Johnson, Jr., *Justice and Reform: The Formative Years of the OEO Legal Services Program* (New York: Russell Sage Foundation, 1974), p. 193.

66. *Johnson v. Inglewood Board of Education*, L.A. Super. Ct., No. 973669 (1969); *Soria v. Oxnard School District Board of Trustees*, 328 F. Supp. 155 (S.D. Cal. 1971).

voked congressional anger. It is indicative of the extraordinary pressure of
the race issue that it overshadowed all other legal services work in congressional debate.

Conservatives were particularly critical of the Harvard Center for Law
and Education, one of a series of "backup centers" the legal services program created to do research and help manage important test cases. The
Harvard center worked on many types of educational cases. When Marian
Wright Edelman, a militant black integrationist, became the center's
director in 1972, desegregation action accelerated. In the ensuing years,
the center was involved in the litigation in Boston, Detroit, Indianapolis,
Pittsburgh, and Dayton.[67]

The House had acted to forbid desegregation litigation by legal services
offices in June 1973, even if only private funds were being used. (The only
other categories of proscribed litigation were cases on abortion and the
draft.)[68]

Representative Robert Drinan of Massachusetts, a former law professor,
strongly objected. "Singling out" school cases, he said, might well be unconstitutional.[69] Senator Edward Kennedy said that any attorney "would have
been professionally remiss to have ignored totally any requests for help"
from victims of illegal segregation.[70] But the White House promised to sign
the legal services bill only if the Senate eliminated the backup centers immediately. Under this threat the Senate acceded and the House happily
agreed by a 2–1 majority.[71]

After years of confrontation on legal services, the President got just
what he wanted. In fact, in the busing provisions, he got more than he had
asked for. At a time when neither the Justice Department nor HEW's Office
for Civil Rights was enforcing school desegregation requirements, the
last public resources for enforcing the constitutional requirements had been
closed off. The organizations could finish the cases they had begun, but
nothing new could be initiated. This ban was renewed in 1977.

## Extending the Elementary and Secondary Education Act, 1974

The gasoline and legal services debates were minor sideshows compared
to the long struggle in 1974 over the extension of the basic education pro-

67. *Congressional Record,* January 31, 1974, p. 1675.
68. *Congressional Record,* May 16, 1974, pp. 14995–15014.
69. Ibid., p. 15012.
70. *Congressional Record,* January 31, 1974, p. 1640.
71. *Congressional Record,* July 16, 1974, pp. 23543–48, 23359.

grams in the Elementary and Secondary Education Act. The authorizing legislation was expiring and the President wanted changes. Even without the desegregation issue, Congress would have faced the necessity of rebuilding the old education coalitions by working out accommodations on major regional issues and disputes between the urban, suburban, and rural members over how money should be allocated. Democratic leaders saw the legislation as an opportunity to preserve the main educational programs of the Great Society at least through the 1976 presidential election and perhaps permanently.

The busing issue magnified the obstacles. Although the President's power had been sapped by Watergate, there was no doubt about the popularity of his attack on busing. He maintained the pressure, threatening to torpedo the entire $26 billion measure. Congress, caught up in the impeachment proceedings in the House and an expected trial in the Senate, strove to find a way to keep the school programs operating. The President, on the other hand, needed policies—like busing—that might help him hold his conservative support and prevent a two-thirds vote for removal.

After a year of debate, the House Education and Labor Committee cleared a new bill in February 1974, with only four Michigan members opposing because the committee had voted down antibusing language. This calm mood was not to last.

The real donnybrook came on the floor when Republican Congressman Marvin Esch of Michigan proposed a package of restrictions similar to those adopted by the House in 1972. Once again the opponents of desegregation were led by Michigan members. They insisted on absolute restraints on the courts. Efforts of a group of self-styled moderates to devise some kind of compromise were rejected both by civil rights supporters, who insisted that Congress had no right to restrain the courts, and by opponents of busing.

The "moderate" effort, led by Congressmen John Anderson of Illinois, Richardson Preyer of North Carolina, and Morris Udall of Arizona, failed to win black support. Their "National Equal Educational Opportunities" bill was introduced by Anderson, who said that Congress had been "derelict in its responsibility to take affirmative and constructive action in this sensitive area."[72] The bill called for ten years of federal aid to upgrade ghetto schools and to pay for "free choice" transfers of black students to white schools they wished to attend. It prohibited court orders sending children to "significantly inferior" schools. It said busing must not be ordered until the

72. *Congressional Record*, March 26, 1974, p. 8274.

courts had considered other remedies first.[73] Preyer said the bill was an answer to "the most serious challenge to the political center we have ever had in this country."[74]

The effort got short shrift. Liberal Representative Lloyd Meeds of Washington said that it "comes into conflict with what the Court has already said." Representative Esch dismissed it as "a probusing amendment."[75] The moderates' amendment was overwhelmingly defeated in a voice vote. The House then immediately passed the Esch amendment, 293–117.[76]

House Education and Labor Committee Chairman Carl Perkins and Representative Quie had appealed without success to the members to avoid a busing brawl that would endanger an extremely important education measure. Perkins said, "We are just fooling ourselves" by trying to "reverse Supreme Court decisions." He was sick of the whole issue:

We have had busing amendments introduced in every appropriation bill, we have had busing amendments introduced in all the school bills, and to complicate the greatest school bill that we have in existence by adding an antibusing amendment at this stage of the game, in my judgment, would be doing serious harm . . . because we are going to have a great many problems in working this matter out with the other body.[77]

Quie urged the members not to "complicate the future of a good education bill" with amendments that were probably unconstitutional.[78] South Carolina Representative William Jennings Bryan Dorn said that tacking on antibusing amendments, trying to "set up a special arrangement for the northern metropolitan areas," was "an exercise in futility"; it was an attempt to preserve "the outmoded, outdated, segregated neighborhood school system of the past."[79]

The critics were ignored. The House added the perennial amendment barring the use of federal aid money for busing even when there was an "express written request of appropriate local school officials." It passed easily, 239–168.[80]

As was by now so typical, passage of the basic education bill was anticlimactic, its substance overshadowed by busing.

73. Ibid.
74. Ibid., p. 8276.
75. Ibid., p. 8275.
76. Ibid., pp. 8281–82.
77. Ibid., pp. 8279–80.
78. Ibid.
79. Ibid., pp. 8281–82.
80. *Congressional Record,* March 27, 1974, pp. 8505–06.

## The Senate Decides

The Senate got the bill in May 1974. Busing dominated the debate. The twentieth anniversary of the *Brown* decision found the Senate closely divided on various proposals intended to preserve segregation.

When debate began, the situation was ominous for the civil rights forces. The education legislation had only two months to run. School organizations urged action. Liberals had been able to manage a brief filibuster near the end of the 1972 session, but this year adjournment was months away. The Supreme Court's decision in the Denver case meant that many northern cities were vulnerable to court orders. Desegregation battles were raging in major cities of Massachusetts, Colorado, California, Ohio, and Michigan. President Nixon and the new vice-president, Gerald Ford, attacked congressional inaction.

The Senate Labor and Public Welfare Committee tried to head off further amendments by including language delaying the enforcement of court orders to achieve "racial balance."[81] A more controversial provision forbade federal civil rights officials to bus students to "substantially inferior" schools; this could be read as an affirmation of the "one-way" busing plans criticized by most minority leaders.

In the Senate debate, one side cited polls and argued for majority rule, the other argued for constitutional rights and judicial independence. Many members claimed that a fall 1973 Gallup poll showed 95 percent of the public as opposed to busing. (Actually, the question asked was whether people favored busing over other ways of achieving integrated schools, assuming that alternatives existed.) Most of the opposition to the bill was based squarely on the argument that it was unconstitutional.

Civil rights organizations sought to counter the criticism of busing. A series of reports by the Civil Rights Commission and materials prepared by the Washington Research Project and the Center for Civil Rights at Notre Dame University provided limited ammunition. The united position of the congressional black caucus and the determined leadership of the Senate's only black member, Edward Brooke of Massachusetts, were important in offsetting assertions that blacks opposed busing.[82]

The antibusing crusade was led by Senator Edward Gurney, who tried to get the House Esch amendment enacted. "It is interesting," Gurney said,

81. *Congressional Record,* May 8, 1974, p. 13740.
82. *Congressional Record,* May 14, 1974, pp. 14601–05.

"to note that the farther busing spreads, the closer the vote here in Congress on antibusing measures."[83]

Local problems strongly influenced some members. A case in point was the reaction of the senators from Colorado. Both conservative Peter Dominick, who was up for reelection in 1974, and liberal Floyd Haskell were critical of desegregation in Denver and supported a succession of antibusing moves.[84] Senator Robert Dole of Kansas described controversies in Wichita and Topeka. Wichita had responded to six years of threats of fund cutoffs from HEW with a plan busing 90 percent of the black children and about 1,200 whites, mostly volunteers attracted by special programs in the formerly black schools. In Topeka, the principal site of the original *Brown* case, children were still segregated in seven ghetto schools.[85]

Critics of the antibusing moves emphasized the costs of stirring up futile public hopes that desegregation would be reversed. Senator Claiborne Pell of Rhode Island said the bill would "lay bare wounds which have only recently closed."[86] Senator Harold Hughes of Iowa blamed the President for treating "legislation which goes to the heart of one of the most profound moral imperatives of our history" as "just another amendment."[87] Senator Alan Cranston of California, the state with the most desegregation experience outside the South, blamed the controversy on a deliberate decision by the administration to "stir things up."

I find this situation especially saddening because so many communities across America—including California—have tried so hard to make these desegregation plans, including busing, work in the best interests of their children and in the interest of community cooperation and peace. It is appalling to me to think of disrupting the progress these good-spirited citizens have fought for and won.[88]

The most passionate denunciation of the Gurney proposal came from Senator Edward Brooke. He said the amendment was a direct encouragement for the "small minority" of whites and blacks favoring racial separatism who would "put us back decades" and foster resegregation where integration was working well. Congress, Brooke said, must not return to the separate but equal doctrine of *Plessy* v. *Ferguson*.[89] "I have never seen anything both separate and equal in this Nation."

83. *Congressional Record,* May 15, 1974, p. 14815.
84. Ibid., pp. 14850–51, 14909.
85. Ibid., pp. 14902–03.
86. Ibid., p. 14821.
87. Ibid., p. 14829.
88. Ibid., p. 14924.
89. 163 U.S. 537 (1896).

The hope for an end to racial division lies in our educational system. The opportunities we afford our young people determine the shape of our Nation's future. . . . If we perpetuate separate societies, divided by ignorance and suspicion, we risk an unsteady and uncertain future.[90]

Senator Philip Hart, the only prominent Michigan politician to steadfastly support desegregation through the Detroit panic, reminded members of their oath to support the Constitution, saying, "Some of these amendments . . . are dead wrong in terms of what the Constitution says we may or may not do."[91] Senator Robert Taft, Jr., of Ohio said: "I cannot in good conscience support an approach to this difficult problem that seems to me to be patently unconstitutional."[92]

A few members like Brooke and Hart were ready to risk their seats, if necessary, over a clear stand on the issue. Those who did, like Hart and Edward Kennedy, were able to survive antibusing opponents. Most of the other civil rights supporters, however, were looking for some constitutional way to show that they opposed "unreasonable" busing while they respected the courts. One senator to use this approach was Indiana Democrat Birch Bayh, who was facing a hard reelection battle from a strong GOP candidate, Indianapolis Mayor Richard Lugar, a critic of busing. With Indianapolis threatened by a metropolitan desegregation case, Bayh proposed a convoluted amendment forbidding busing unless courts found that "all alternative remedies are inadequate." It prohibited desegregation plans crossing city-suburban lines unless the lines had been created for discriminatory purposes or had the *effect* of fostering segregation.[93]

The Bayh proposal, which was more rhetoric than substance, infuriated the conservatives. Senator William E. Brock of Tennessee said it "does absolutely nothing to change the situation as it exists." Senator Gurney said it was a "probusing amendment." Bayh replied that Brock was trying to go "back to the old segregation system that we fought a civil war to prohibit."[94]

The Senate debate came to an end with Vice-President Ford waiting to cast the decisive vote against busing if the closely divided chamber deadlocked. By a single vote, the Gurney amendment was tabled, and the Senate promptly adopted the Bayh measure, 56–36. Bayh's proposal drew votes from a bevy of civil rights supporters, including Thomas Eagleton,

90. *Congressional Record,* May 15, 1974, pp. 14858–61, 14853–54.
91. *Congressional Record,* May 16, 1974, p. 15074.
92. *Congressional Record,* May 15, 1974, p. 14913.
93. Ibid., p. 14862.
94. Ibid., pp. 14864–65, 14866–67.

Warren Magnuson, Mike Mansfield, Charles Mathias, Gale McGee, George McGovern, Gaylord Nelson, John Pastore, James Pearson, and Robert Taft, all of whom could now claim a vote against cross-district busing.[95]

The next day the Senate adopted another amendment forbidding the implementation of new desegregation court orders in the middle of a school year. Although this amendment flew in the face of the Supreme Court's unanimous 1969 decision, *Alexander* v. *Holmes,* which required immediate correction of unconstitutional segregation, the impatient members showed little interest in Senator Javits's effort to explain the constitutional principles. The amendment quickly passed, 71–20.[96]

### Another Compromise

As the debate came to an end on May 16, 1974, the balance of power seemed suddenly to switch to the opponents of desegregation. Senator Griffin made a last attempt to revive the House amendments without the controversial provision permitting the reopening of court orders. A liberal-moderate effort to table this proposal failed by a single vote. At this point, with the clear danger of strong Senate action against the courts, Senate Minority Leader Hugh Scott and Majority Leader Mansfield offered a less drastic substitute amendment prepared for such a contingency. The tactic worked. The conservatives failed by three votes to table the Scott-Mansfield amendment.[97] Once again the leaders combined forces to take the edge off antibusing efforts.

The substitute contained Griffin's text but added at various points language stating that its restrictions were "not intended to modify or diminish the authority of the courts of the United States to enforce fully the Fifth and Fourteenth amendments to the United States Constitution."[98] Scott said that the "only question" before the Senate was whether members would state that the Senate "does not intend to violate the Constitution of the United States."[99] Forty-six senators voted against it anyway.[100]

The Scott-Mansfield proposal passed, 47–46, without any serious debate. The complex document was laid on the Senate desks minutes before the vote. Although it appeared to leave the status quo largely untouched, it had a crucial provision that went unnoticed by both the Senate and the sub-

95. Ibid., pp. 14924, 14926.
96. *Congressional Record,* May 16, 1974, pp. 15069–70.
97. Ibid., p. 15078.
98. Ibid., p. 15076.
99. Ibid., p. 15078.
100. Ibid., p. 15079.

sequent conference committee. It forbade not only the courts but also federal "departments or agencies" to order the busing of students beyond the next closest school. The language protected the courts but said nothing specific about HEW's powers. The Senate may have accidentally approved an amendment to the 1964 Civil Rights Act. With Congress contemplating legislative nullification of Supreme Court decisions, an attack on the century's most important civil rights law—a change that a few years earlier would have been considered a terrible defeat for civil rights—now went unnoticed. HEW, of course, did not fight to retain its authority.

Still more severe restrictions remained to be voted on. Senator William Lloyd Scott of Virginia, for instance, proposed altering the constitutional system by denying all federal courts jurisdiction over cases concerning public schools. This proposal was supported by twenty-five senators.[101] (Two years later it got more votes.)

As the Senate finished debate on the education bill, Senate leaders praised the muddled compromise. Hugh Scott called it "sound wisdom," but Senator James Pearson of Kansas pointed out that the Senate had substantially modified existing policy with a series of constraints on the courts, which meant that "busing can be used only as an extreme and last resort and as the only final alternative to the continuation of a segregated and, therefore, unconstitutional school system."[102] Whatever it meant, senators were glad to send it on to the conference committee. The bill passed, 81–5.[103]

Everyone knew that the conference struggle would be long and difficult. During the six weeks that the conference worked House members took the extraordinary step of voting three different times to instruct their conferees against compromise on busing.

All those involved reported that the conference committee negotiations were contentious and sensitive. The busing issue, said Senator Pell, consumed "endless days and hours of debate. The language the Senate brought into the conference was totally unacceptable to the House. . . . Nevertheless, the Senate conferees held to the belief that there were also certain House provisions that were totally unacceptable to them. The final language is a melding of the two."[104]

The conference bill was attacked, said Pell, by both liberal and conservative senators. Senator Javits, for instance, thought the compromise might well be unconstitutional but the best obtainable in the face of House

101. *Congressional Record,* May 20, 1974, p. 15424.
102. Ibid., pp. 15443–44.
103. Ibid., p. 15444.
104. *Congressional Record,* July 23, 1974, pp. 24772–73.

antagonism.[105] He said that the conferees had "sat into the small hours of the morning" until they hit upon an agreement to modify the tradition of continual judicial supervision of desegregation plans by allowing the termination of court orders in certain circumstances.[106]

Later, House Democratic and Republican leaders told a similar story. "We have scraped the bottom of the barrel," said Representative Carl Perkins of Kentucky. "There is no way where we can get anything further. These are all of the antibusing provisions we will get, and we will not get any more this year."[107] Perkins's Republican colleague, Albert Quie, said that the conferees had accepted all the major House provisions, adding only the Senate language that Congress intended to "conform to the requirements of the Constitution."[108]

Just exactly what the conference agreement meant was not clear. Most of the floor debate was on whether the package was tough enough. There was little serious analysis of the compromise.

The fifty-nine sections of the new law incorporated a miscellany of overlapping and contradictory provisions, most of which had not been discussed at all on the floor. A few of the sections actually were advances in civil rights laws. Many others attempted to constrain the process of devising desegregation plans while proclaiming Congress' intention to avoid encroachment on the authority of the judicial branch.

A major new area of discretion for federal judges was provided. Since 1954 desegregation cases had remained open for many years. Judges retained jurisdiction and litigants could file new motions asking that the old orders be tightened. Southerners in cities with rapid outward movement of whites wanted the urban court orders limited to a single decision that would, by legal definition, correct the vestiges of de jure segregation. Then the court could relinquish its jurisdiction, leaving new segregated schools invulnerable to legal attack. In a society where the average family moves every five years and residential segregation is pervasive, such a policy would normally guarantee resegregation of schools. Although judges already had the power to terminate cases, the amendments encouraged the courts to use it.

The provisions of the law most directly in conflict with the courts had become familiar in earlier legislative fights. It said that neighborhood school assignment practices did not violate students' rights unless they were designed to intentionally segregate students. One passage read: "No court,

105. Ibid., p. 24775.
106. *Congressional Record*, July 24, 1974, p. 24891.
107. *Congressional Record*, July 31, 1974, pp. 26103, 26111.
108. Ibid., p. 26110.

department, or agency of the United States shall . . . order the implementation of a plan that would require the transportation of any student to a school other than the school closest or next closest to his place of residence which provides the appropriate grade level and type of education for such student."[109] The Esch language included a list of remedies the courts must consider before ordering busing.

The net effect of the antibusing language on the courts was probably minor. Congress clearly recognized that the restrictions on the courts would not apply when they limited the constitutional rights of minority children. Since the courts generally ordered busing only when there was no other way to achieve desegregation, judicial compliance with the provisions of the act presumably would involve only a recitation of this fact and a declaration of the preeminent requirements of the Constitution. This is just what happened in several cases after the legislation was passed.

The most important changes were the possible political and legal effects of the act on HEW's desegregation enforcement program. Since HEW had not seriously enforced the fund-cutoff provisions of the 1964 Civil Rights Act since mid-1969, little attention had been paid to its role. The department, however, had powers of great importance. It had been found guilty of failing to enforce the 1964 law by a federal court and had been ordered to act promptly against segregation in scores of southern and border state school districts. HEW officials used the existence of a law forbidding it to order systems to carry out busing plans as a defense against compliance with the court order. The really serious constraint on HEW under this policy came when a court order required HEW to enforce the 1964 law in the big cities.

The law could be construed in ways that would eliminate its restrictive effect on HEW. In actual practice, HEW provides guidelines; it never "orders" the implementation of a desegregation plan; it does not have the authority to do so. The department's enforcement policy, when it uses it, is merely to withhold funds from or recommend the initiation of litigation against school systems that refused to comply with constitutional requirements for desegregation.[110]

## Final Passage

The compromise held. The vote came first in the Senate, where many members asked the body to consider the educational issues in the bill for a

---

109. *Congressional Record*, July 23, 1974, pp. 24543–44, text of bill sec. 215(a).
110. See Gary Orfield, *The Reconstruction of Southern Education: The Schools and the 1964 Civil Rights Act* (Wiley, 1969), pp. 47–150.

change. The dominant desire was to get the bill enacted. It rapidly passed, 81–15.[111]

The real battle was expected from antibusing forces in the House. Their leader, Congressman Esch, opposed the entire bill. The language on the supremacy of constitutional requirements, he said, "raises a cloud over the effectiveness of the rest of the Esch amendment." He asked that the bill be sent back to conference. Louisiana Congressman Joe Waggoner, Jr., insisted that "the vote on the conference report is a busing issue vote."[112]

Representative Marjorie Holt, whose district included two large Maryland school systems with busing problems, called the compromise "nearly worthless, because the Federal courts are expressly invited to continue imposing racial quotas requiring mass busing."[113]

The debate, however, was neither as long nor as passionate as the earlier ones. When the final vote came on July 31, 1974, in Nixon's chaotic last days, the House voted to accept the conference committee report, 323–83—almost four to one.[114]

When President Ford suddenly took office he found the education bill on his desk awaiting action. In his first address to Congress he announced that he would sign the bill. "Any reservations I might have about its provisions . . . fade in comparison to the urgent needs of America for quality education."[115] He later added that he was still unsatisfied with the busing provisions.[116]


## Separate, not Equal

Congressional action on the ESEA bill showed that, though Congress and the President were ready to restrain desegregation, they were not disposed to provide additional resources for improving education in ghetto schools. Nixon and Ford had frequently proposed upgrading inner city education as an alternative, but both consistently submitted education budgets proposing yearly cuts in school programs (after allowing for inflation). And the House Education and Labor Committee reported a bill raising school aid for suburbs and southern and rural states, sharply cutting

111. *Congressional Record,* July 24, 1974, p. 24926.
112. *Congressional Record,* July 31, 1974, pp. 26111–12.
113. Ibid., p. 26125.
114. Ibid., p. 26128.
115. *Congressional Quarterly,* August 17, 1974, p. 2211.
116. *Congressional Quarterly,* August 24, 1974, p. 2321.

funds for New York City, Los Angeles, and Chicago, and somewhat reducing funds for many other cities.[117]

The New York delegation, with the support of other urban members, attempted to amend the bill to reverse New York City's loss of almost $50 million under the new distribution formula. They pointed out that it would give Montgomery County, Maryland (one of the wealthiest U.S. counties), 44 percent more money while the District of Columbia would lose 12 percent.[118] The New York proposal was buried in an avalanche of opposition, losing 87–326.[119]

Some suburban members of the House urged still greater redistribution to the suburbs. Michigan Democrats James O'Hara and William Ford, antibusing leaders, proposed a plan that would give $5.6 million more to the two Detroit suburban counties, both among the nation's twenty richest, while taking $4.4 million from nearly bankrupt Detroit, $2.4 million from Baltimore, and some from other central cities. This proposal was too overt. The amendment went down, 103–312.[120]

As passed, the House bill cut funds to forty-one of the country's largest cities at a time of rapid inflation. The biggest losses came in some of the cities with the largest ghettos—New York, Chicago, Los Angeles, Philadelphia, Cleveland, Newark, and Washington.[121]

Nor was the Senate interested in channeling more money into ghetto schools. The Senate committee bill had protected funds for the big cities. On the floor, however, Senator John McClellan of Arkansas moved to substitute the House formula. It was adopted, 56–36.[122]

Futile efforts were made by two Senate moderates, Lowell Weicker, Jr., of Connecticut and Lawton Chiles of Florida, to enact large compensatory education programs for ghetto children. Chiles proposed a $2.5 billion program that would give any neighborhood school with more than 40 percent poor children additional funds equal to at least two-thirds the national annual average total per-pupil costs. Chiles said he thought people were ready to pay to avoid the "tremendous discombobulation" of the busing controversy. His measure did not even come to a vote.[123]

Weicker's "Quality School Aid" bill would have more than doubled federal compensatory aid. He asked senators to commit themselves to raising

117. *Congressional Record*, March 12, 1974, pp. 6339–42.
118. *Congressional Record*, March 26, 1974, p. 8237.
119. Ibid., p. 8243.
120. Ibid., pp. 8246, 8247.
121. *Congressional Record*, May 13, 1974, pp. 14333–34.
122. *Congressional Record*, May 15, 1974, p. 14838.
123. *Congressional Record*, May 20, 1974, pp. 15281, 15282.

taxes sufficiently to cover the costs of eliminating "inferior schools with inferior teachers and opportunities." Weicker did ask for a vote. He lost, 4–83.[124]

Thus in the end Congress responded to the financial problems of big city schools by diverting some of their funds to the suburbs and the South.

Senator Brooke later described the issue well:

We have many debates on the Senate floor about whether we should go forward with integration . . . or whether we should try to make the segregated ghetto and barrio schools more equal. . . . Our decisions about investing money in education show that Congress has rejected both approaches. Each year we are providing less assistance, in dollars of constant value, both for helping the integration process work better and for compensatory education.[125]

Brooke supported his contention with statistics showing that the compensatory education program had one-seventh less money than three years earlier and that the desegregation aid program had shrunk 30 percent (see table 8-3).

### The Holt Amendment

Before the 1974 session ended, there was a final skirmish. Another previously obscure member injected the issue into the debate in a new way. As congressional adjournment neared, Congresswoman Holt tried to eviscerate what remained of the 1964 Civil Rights Act as it applied to education. She offered an amendment that would have prohibited withholding federal aid funds to force school systems to carry out desegregation plans and would have stopped the collection of records and statistics HEW needed to determine the extent of segregation.[126] Her amendment, she said, would end the government's "obsession" with "racial quotas." Without data, enforcement was of course impossible.

Although the provision was narrowly defeated on the Senate floor, the conference committee accepted the Holt language in the final days of the Congress. The *Washington Post* described the situation:

HEW Secretary Caspar Weinberger is among those who have seen this deceptive language for what it is—an attempt to terminate the federal government's pursuit of its duty to enforce the Civil Rights Act of 1964 and related laws. . . .

There has been an almost haphazard, not to say irresponsible, note to the way the legislators in both sides of Congress have let this momentous bit of legislation come so near to passage.[127]

124. Ibid., p. 15424.
125. *Congressional Record* (daily edition), May 27, 1976, p. S8153.
126. *Congressional Record*, October 1, 1974, p. 33364.
127. *Washington Post*, December 4, 1974.

Table 8-3. *Appropriations for Selected Federal Education Programs, Fiscal Years 1965–76*

Thousands of 1965 dollars[a]

| Fiscal year | Title I, ESEA[b] | Emergency School Aid Act[c] | Title IV, Civil Rights Act[d] |
|---|---|---|---|
| 1965 | 0 | 0 | 6,000 |
| 1966 | 1,161,118 | 0 | 6,109 |
| 1967 | 993,666 | 0 | 6,164 |
| 1968 | 1,084,258 | 0 | 7,738 |
| 1969 | 976,355 | 0 | 8,041 |
| 1970 | 1,103,083 | 0 | 9,885 |
| 1971 | 1,175,416 | 58,771 | 12,538 |
| 1972 | 1,196,780 | 56,187 | 10,938 |
| 1973 | 1,298,110 | 178,580 | 15,563 |
| 1974 | 1,143,841 | 157,319 | 14,435 |
| 1975 | 1,129,476 | 129,444 | 16,075 |
| 1976 | 1,081,507 | 122,391 | 15,198 |

Source: Calculations by Congressional Research Service, *Congressional Record* (daily edition), May 27, 1976, p. S8154.

a. The appropriations are stated in constant dollars to show the real purchasing power of the programs from year to year.

b. Title I of the ESEA is designed to aid "target" schools with high concentrations of children from poor families.

c. The Emergency School Aid program is designed to facilitate the transition from segregation to desegregation and to provide aid for schools in central cities that remain segregated.

d. Title IV is a small program of technical assistance and staff training for desegregation.

Once again Majority Leader Mansfield and Minority Leader Scott joined forces at the last minute to head off disaster by persuading the Senate to reject the conference report. Pressing toward adjournment, senators swept aside a conservative filibuster, cut off debate, and voted down the Holt measure.[128]

The House soon followed suit. Once the Senate majority made its position clear, the initiative shifted. House members knew that getting programs funded and adjourning the session now depended on accepting the Senate position. The House agreed in a 224–138 vote.[129]

The victories against the Holt amendment were unexpectedly swift and decisive. The 1974 election was over and there was less pressure for action against busing.[130]

128. *Congressional Record*, December 10, 1974, p. 39114.

129. *Washington Post*, December 15, 17, 1974.

130. The election showed that busing was still an important issue but not one that destroyed political careers. Florida's Governor Reubin Askew won by a landslide in spite of his defense of busing orders. Oklahoma's Senator Henry Bellmon, who was criticized by his opponent for opposing legislation attempting to override the Supreme Court on busing, was reelected. Birch Bayh won reelection over Richard Lugar, who

Desegregation in Delaware, Defeat in Washington

Any hope that the worst was past proved to be illusory in September 1975. After a year of little discussion of the issue, the publicity accompanying desegregation in Boston and metropolitan Louisville revived political debate. The sudden intervention of President Ford, who claimed that the courts were requiring unnecessary busing without looking for better alternatives and thus violating the provisions of the Esch amendment, added to the pressure.

Attitudes crystallized in a sudden Senate reversal, probably the most important move against school integration in the upper chamber at any time. An amendment attempting to end any authority to require busing remaining in HEW was offered by a young progressive senator from Delaware, Joseph Biden. For the first time, such an amendment had the support of northern liberal Democrats, including Majority Leader Mansfield.

Senator Biden's leadership was the direct result of community reaction to a pending lawsuit in Wilmington. After the 1974 battle, when Biden had voted with the civil rights forces, he was denounced by leaders of the influential New Castle County Neighborhood School Association.[131] Publicly challenged to speak about his future votes on the issue, Biden was condemned as "the number one phony in Delaware" by the head of the suburban antibusing organization.[132] Realizing that he could be harassed for the next four years, he agreed to discuss the issue at a public meeting on July 9, 1974, in the suburbs,[133] where he faced a hostile crowd for two hours

---

strongly opposed busing. (*New York Times*, November 6, 1974.) Denver Congresswoman Patricia Schroeder, representing the first northern city ordered by the Court to desegregate, soundly defeated a challenge by a school board member who built much of his campaign around the busing issue (*New York Times*, September 9, 1974).

It was not that busing was popular. A Gallup poll published the day before the election showed the public opposed by a majority of 68 to 32 percent (*Baltimore Sun*, November 4, 1974). On the question of busing across city-suburban lines, an NBC poll taken on election day showed 77 percent opposed (*Washington Star-News*, November 6, 1974). The issue, however, was not decisive. Perhaps, as later surveys would show, people no longer believed that elected officials could do much about the problem. At any rate, it was still possible to support desegregation and survive politically, at least in some parts of the country.

131. *Wilmington Morning News*, June 15, 1974.
132. *Wilmington Evening Journal*, June 28, 1974.
133. Ibid., June 29, 1974.

of questioning. Although he told the audience that his "liberal friends" were criticizing him and promised to support a constitutional amendment that would forestall the court-ordered metropolitan racial-balance for Wilmington, he won little support. He said he still favored busing when it was necessary to correct intentional local gerrymandering for segregationist purposes.[134]

But as the antibusing movement grew in the Wilmington suburbs in 1975, Biden again raised the issue, which he now saw as a "domestic Vietnam." He led the liberal turnabout, received favorable national press attention as a tough-minded realist, and restored his white political base in the state.

Nor was Senator Biden the only one to receive national attention from the media; Minority Whip Robert Byrd came up with a similar amendment of his own. He had been a leading opponent of the 1964 Civil Rights Act, one of the few nonsouthern members of the Democratic party to oppose the legislation. He had then joined the southern filibuster with a long speech about biblical justification for segregation.[135] Now, eleven years later, he won Senate passage of an amendment repealing part of the 1964 law.

After days of parliamentary in-fighting and heated public statements, the Biden and Byrd amendments came up for final votes in late September. Both passed.

The amendments, which required HEW to follow a neighborhood school policy, had little immediate significance, since HEW was not requiring any urban school desegregation anyway except where specifically ordered to act by federal court decision. The votes were symbolically important, however. Senator Humphrey said of the Senate's shift:

The message is that the Senate, the last bastion of civil rights support, has now joined the President and the House in opposing desegregation of towns and cities across the North and West. The message to segregated children is that Congress is ready to destroy the only existing machinery for systematic enforcement of their constitutional rights, even though the machinery has not been used for 6 years and was severely limited by legislation just last year. . . . The symbolic power of congressional action is immense, often more important than the specific legislative action. . . . The action can only encourage supporters of segregation and increase the already immense pressures on the Federal courts.[136]

When the bill went to conference, the conferees struck the confusing Biden amendment but retained the Byrd restrictions, which became law

---

134. *Wilmington Morning News*, July 10, 1974.
135. *Congressional Record*, June 10, 1964, pp. 13207–09.
136. *Congressional Record* (daily edition), September 26, 1975, p. S16905.

in early 1976. The last redoubt of defense for urban school desegregation seemed to be crumbling on Capitol Hill.

## An Election Year Lull

As the 1976 election year approached, another round of battles over busing seemed likely. After a year of relative quiet, President Ford began to speak out against busing in speech after speech.[137] Protests and violence in Boston and Louisville during the fall of 1975—the worst fall since 1972— were widely publicized.

At the National Democratic Issues Conference in November, Democratic presidential candidates confronted three thousand demonstrators from an antibusing group led by labor union activists. The issue fragmented the candidates. Senator Lloyd Bentsen of Texas attacked busing as a "bankrupt social policy," Representative Udall blamed Congress for failing to search for alternatives, and former nominee George McGovern delivered an emotional speech calling racial equality a "transcendent moral issue." "All of us," he said, "should warn any candidate who turns to the tactics of racial division and fear that in conscience we cannot support him even if he is the nominee."[138] A poll showed that the party activists were deeply divided.[139]

If the Democrats were divided, the Republican candidates were strongly united on the popular side of the issue, debating merely which tactics should be used to fight busing. The President attacked the courts just as Boston faced citywide implementation.[140]

The Democratic campaign opened as expected, but it soon took a new direction, in part because of the emergence of an unexpected leading candidate, Jimmy Carter. The busing issue was most prominent in the Massachusetts primary, where Senator Henry Jackson fought George Wallace for the support of voters aroused by Boston's turmoil. Jackson won the primary after running large ads announcing "I am against forced busing" and outlining his plan to limit the remedy. Closer analysis of the Massachusetts results, however, showed, first, that Jackson had not been able to take the votes of strong antibusers away from Wallace, and second, that an anti-

137. *New York Times*, August 20, 1975; *Education Daily*, August 21, 1975; *Washington Post*, September 17, 1975.
138. *Washington Post*, November 23, 1975; *Washington Star*, November 23, 1975.
139. *New York Times*, November 24, 1975, reporting findings of Peter Hart poll.
140. *Boston Globe*, August 27, 1975.

busing stance could cost the party support among its many liberal and minority voters. Udall, the leading liberal contender, argued that politicians should "give the courts some help and not try to undercut them."[141]

The issue was turned against Jackson in Florida by Carter, who saw the primary there as vital to eliminating Wallace as the principal southern candidate. Running in the state with the most extensive busing orders in the country (most of the state had countywide busing on a racial-balance model), Carter claimed that Jackson was exploiting "racist" feelings. "I don't believe that a candidate is going to be successful in this country who concentrates on that kind of emotional issue, which is divisive, which is a negative issue. . . . I don't say he is a racist. . . . But he exploited an issue with racist connotations."[142]

Carter won the primary decisively, making himself the dominant political figure in the South and the leading contender for the nomination. Although busing was not popular in Florida, it was no longer a paramount issue. The key to Carter's victory was winning the votes of three-fourths of the state's blacks while holding moderate whites.[143]

Carter staked out a position on the busing issue early and held to it throughout his campaign. Among other things:

1. He strongly supported integrated education, often calling HEW's enforcement of the 1964 Civil Rights Act the "best thing that ever happened to the South" and pointing out that his daughter Amy attended an integrated school with a black majority.

2. He stated his personal opposition to court-ordered busing and his preference for the arrangement in Atlanta, where the busing issue was dropped in exchange for increased black control of the school bureaucracy.

3. He promised to oppose antibusing amendments to the Constitution and to support the desegregation orders of federal courts.

But after the Florida primary had eliminated Wallace and damaged Jackson's campaign, little was heard of the busing issue during the remainder of the Democratic campaign.

In contrast to the Republican platform, which promised the party would support an antibusing amendment to the Constitution, the Democratic platform strongly endorsed integrated education and reluctantly accepted the necessity for some busing. It was adopted without any floor fight.

Mandatory transportation of students beyond their neighborhoods for the purpose

141. *Washington Post,* March 1, 1976.
142. *New York Times,* March 4, 1976.
143. Robert Reinhold, "Voting Reflects Shifts in Florida," *New York Times,* March 11, 1976, interpreting a statewide poll.

of desegregation remains a judicial tool of last resort. . . . The Democratic Party will be an active ally of those communities which seek to enhance the quality as well as the integration of educational opportunities. We encourage a variety of other measures, including the redrawing of attendance lines, pairing of schools, use of the "magnet school" concept, strong fair housing enforcement, and other techniques for the achievement of racial and economic integration.[144]

President Ford attempted to reactivate the issue during the spring campaign. In May and June he made a series of widely publicized statements about busing and directed the Department of Justice to intervene in litigation to limit busing and to draft legislation for consideration in Congress. The result was the School Desegregation Standards and Assistance bill, which the President sent to Congress with a message saying that some of the courts had "gone too far" and thus "slowed our progress toward the total elimination of segregation."[145]

The bill was designed to block busing unless there was school-by-school proof that segregation was intentional. It required the courts to ignore evidence that school segregation had resulted from de jure housing segregation, stipulated that desegregation orders should terminate after three to five years, and instructed the courts to ignore resegregation that emerged in the meantime.[146] It would have limited desegregation to temporary orders integrating schools near the ghetto or barrio line, concentrating the burden of change on lower-income whites and probably accelerating racial transition in the affected neighborhoods.

The most interesting thing about the bill was the contrast between its fate and that of the Nixon proposal four years earlier. The Nixon bill produced a major fight and was blocked only by a Senate filibuster. The Ford bill was sent to committee and never heard of again in either house.

There were, of course, other skirmishes over busing during the year, but the results showed a gradually changing mood. Except for the final enactment of the Byrd amendment early in 1976, no antibusing amendment was passed by Congress during the election year. A Senate that had been ready to directly attack the courts four years earlier now defeated a number of far more limited antibusing measures by substantial votes.

One of the perennial proposals—by Senator William Scott, to end the

---

144. Democratic platform reprinted in *Congressional Record* (daily edition), July 2, 1976, p. S11580. Republican platform summarized in *Congressional Quarterly*, August 21, 1976, p. 2296.

145. "The President's Message to the Congress Transmitting the Proposed School Desegregation Standards and Assistance Act of 1976," *Weekly Compilation of Presidential Documents*, vol. 12 (June 28, 1976), p. 1080.

146. Ibid., pp. 1081–82.

right of lower federal courts to hear any cases dealing with education—surfaced again. This was tabled by a better than two to one majority. A related proposal, limited to busing, was also quickly defeated.[147]

A more serious proposal, sponsored by Senators Dole and Biden, would have imposed limitations on civil rights litigation by the Department of Justice. The 1964 Civil Rights Act had given the department broad authority to initiate or intervene in civil rights cases, and Justice had been an important participant in many school cases. The Dole-Biden amendment would have prohibited any Justice Department participation in busing cases unless the department intervened against civil rights groups. Dole said that the goal was to bring Justice in line with the policy imposed on HEW by the Byrd amendment. This was tabled by a 55–39 vote.[148]

After the national conventions, busing received no serious discussion in the presidential campaign. The issue was never raised in the televised debates between Ford and Carter, and the few desegregation plans that took effect in September were carried out peacefully.

There were signs of probusing action in Congress. Some southern senators expressed their refusal to support amendments designed to prevent the changes the South had already lived through from reaching the North.[149] Senators Javits and Brooke attacked the premises of the antibusing forces in a series of statements culminating in a January 1977 conference in the Senate Caucus Room, the first major meeting supporting school integration on Capitol Hill in years. Congress enacted a modest civil rights bill, providing fees for lawyers bringing civil rights cases.

One sign of the changing mood was the leadership of Senator John Glenn of Ohio. Representing a state where virtually all of the major cities were involved in the most concentrated campaign of urban school litigation ever launched by the NAACP, Glenn refused to join the antibusing forces. He proposed legislation granting funds to districts for providing better education through the development of "magnet schools" offering special programs to encourage voluntary integration. Glenn's amendment did nothing to restrict the power of the courts; it simply gave local school systems more educational options. The amendment received wide support in the Senate and passed easily.[150]

147. *Congressional Record* (daily edition), April 1, 1976, pp. S4831, S4837.
148. *Congressional Record* (daily edition), June 24, 1976, pp. S10398–403.
149. See remarks by Senators Dale Bumpers of Arkansas and Robert Morgan of North Carolina, ibid., pp. S10403–04.
150. Glenn's speech introducing the amendment appears in *Congressional Record* (daily edition), April 14, 1976, pp. S5733–36; debate and passage in ibid., August 27, 1976, pp. S14773–86.

## A New Administration

The election of President Carter and the transition to a new administration made the future of the school desegregation issue uncertain. The 1977 session of Congress was the first in years without executive branch support of some kind of antibusing legislation. Nor did the administration push desegregation—in fact, the new attorney general, Griffin Bell, and his deputy, Peter Flaherty, were criticized by congressional liberals during their confirmation hearings for a history of opposing urban desegregation. On the other hand, civil rights groups were pleased with appointments in HEW and with the selection of the black attorney who had desegregated much of Florida, Drew Days III, as assistant attorney general for civil rights. In his first year in office, President Carter sent Congress neither negative nor positive proposals; he said nothing about the issue. When HEW made a modest attempt to revive desegregation enforcement, the White House did not intervene, nor did the President say anything when Congress promptly passed an amendment quashing the attempt. Although polls showed continued public opposition, for the moment it seemed possible that the worst was over.

# 9

# Toward Separate
# but Equal at HEW

ONE OF the most important accomplishments of the civil rights movement
in the 1960s was the creation of federal sanctions and administrative
machinery sufficiently powerful to enforce constitutional requirements for
dismantling the dual school structure in the rural South. The 1964 Civil
Rights Act made the Department of Health, Education, and Welfare responsible for either assuring compliance or cutting off federal aid funds,
empowered the Justice Department to intervene in school cases, and provided some money for desegregation assistance. The law multiplied enforcement resources, shifted the burden of initiating cases from private
groups, and made local officials realize that they were eventually going to
have to desegregate.

The results were phenomenal. In 1965, the first year of enforcement, desegregation began in virtually every rural school district in the South, most
of which had been totally segregated.[1] The next year faculty desegregation
and the first moves beyond token desegregation of students began. By 1968
the schools of the rural South were on notice that they must finish desegregation by fall 1969.

The law had less effect on urban segregation, but that was beginning
to change at the end of the Johnson administration. The HEW staff was
investigating several middle-sized cities, and the Justice Department had
filed its first four lawsuits against northern urban school districts.

As the courts began to require urban desegregation, the importance of
enforcing the Civil Rights Act increased. Title VI of the law prohibited
giving federal funds to school districts that failed to comply with the mini-

1. *Southern Education Report*, vol. 1 (January–February 1966), pp. 28–29; Southern Education Reporting Service, *Statistical Summary* (Nashville: SERS, 1967), p. 43.

mum constitutional standards set by the Supreme Court. After the Court's 1971 busing decision this meant that HEW had to cut off federal aid unless southern communities where there was no other way to end unconstitutional segregation bused children. After the Supreme Court's 1973 decision in the *Keyes* case in Denver, HEW had a similar legal obligation in the North.

## The Transformation of an Enforcement Bureaucracy

In his campaign President Nixon had attacked HEW enforcement practices. But because he took office without carrying either house of Congress, where there were bare congressional majorities against openly changing the law, he had to find more subtle ways to change policy.

The HEW Office for Civil Rights at that time employed hundreds of staff members who specialized in school district compliance and supported the movement for racial integration. Civil service laws made it impossible to remove most of the staff. The new administration could assign only a thin layer of political appointees to the top positions.

The evolution of the Office for Civil Rights from then on was one of changing goals and organizational adaptation. The regulations did not change. The regional offices continued to pursue investigations of existing cases. Investigations were written up and papers recommending compliance activities were sent up through channels to Washington. On the surface, everything was the same.

Civil rights compliance, however, is a distinctive type of bureaucratic activity. Initiation of compliance procedures requires the approval of ranking political appointees. A decision actually to withhold federal aid from even the smallest school system with the most blatant civil rights violations must be signed by the secretary of HEW. Without the continuous positive support of appointed officials the process bogs down. Once local officials perceive indecision, resistance multiplies.

During the first year of the Nixon administration both internal handling of particular cases and public downgrading of the fund-cutoff procedure discouraged the processing of further cases. Staff members soon realized that it was useless to pursue desegregation goals.

In the next few years, the Office for Civil Rights passed through several stages of goal transformation from its early focus on integration. The process could be outlined as follows:

1. ambiguity, inconsistency, and inaction;
2. test of alternative enforcement procedures;

3. polarization and assertion of political control;
4. futile efforts by civil rights groups to reassert original goals through the courts;
5. de facto definitions of new missions and response to new constituencies.

By the mid-1970s the Office for Civil Rights had almost totally redefined its basic objective, giving only passing attention to the old goal of eliminating dual school systems. Some of the change was eventually legitimated in the courts and in Congress. Congress acted during the 1970s to add responsibility for ending discrimination against women and the handicapped to the office's goals. The Supreme Court upheld the office's authority to issue regulations against linguistic discrimination. And Congress limited HEW's powers to desegregate schools.

The result was ironic. An agency that had carried out perhaps the most effective drive against racial discrimination in American history grew in size and resources under a hostile administration but had less and less impact on the problem it was designed to solve. By the mid-1970s its principal civil rights goal was to make separate institutions more nearly equal. The vision of the 1954 Supreme Court decision had given way to the doctrine of the 1896 *Plessy* decision. The Carter administration inherited an agency that would have been unrecognizable to its founders.

### The Record under President Johnson

During the Johnson administration, a federal agency for the first time was willing to back up desegregation requirements by turning off the flow of federal money to offenders. Until HEW began enforcement of the school desegregation guidelines there had been few occasions in the entire history of federal aid programs when federal administrators had cut off funds for any reason. President Johnson and the top HEW officials were prepared to enforce the law even at considerable political cost. ( The Democratic loss of five southern states in 1964 and ten of the eleven southern states in 1968 was clearly related to this commitment. )

As President Johnson left office in 1969 a number of the goals of civil rights leaders were in sight.[2] By the fall of 1965 most southern school systems had executed plans more demanding than those earlier won by litigation. The next year, HEW toughened its requirements. As President

2. Potomac Institute, *Americans Are Law Abiding Citizens: A Survey of Community Compliance* (Washington: Potomac Institute, 1969).

Nixon was sworn in, school assignment policies in the rural South were rapidly approaching parity with those in the North.[3]

This was a remarkable change. As in all social revolutions, however, attaining the first goal disclosed the need for further change. While the schools of the rural South could be effectively desegregated by simply sending children to the nearest school, the majority of southern black children lived in cities and would remain segregated under a neighborhood school policy.

HEW had little experience with big cities. It had early adopted a policy of not attempting to regulate school systems already under court order, which included many of the leading cities of the southern and border states.

HEW officials had begun to negotiate plans with officials in small southern cities and sometimes succeeded in winning acceptance of busing plans that went beyond a simple neighborhood school policy. In the late 1960s, they were seriously negotiating with several of the cities in the South still under HEW's jurisdiction, particularly with the capital cities of South and North Carolina, Columbia and Raleigh, and with the nation's largest suburban system, Prince Georges County, Maryland. All three of the negotiations were stalled and the cutoff of funds was a very real possibility in late 1968.

HEW policy virtually ignored the northern cities, many of which showed spectacularly high levels of segregation, after the effort to investigate a major civil rights complaint against the nation's second largest public school system, Chicago, collapsed in 1965.[4] That humiliating backdown delayed any serious exploration of HEW's northern enforcement responsibility and undermined both the morale of the staff and the political leverage of the entire enforcement program. When the northern enforcement effort timidly began again in 1967 and 1968, it was quite different. Instead of being an ad hoc response to a huge city, it emphasized quiet fact-gathering and investigation of manageable medium-sized communities.

HEW officials recognized the problem of severe and rapidly spreading urban segregation, but their response was largely rhetorical. During 1966, for example, HEW Secretary John Gardner announced the creation of a special office to investigate de facto segregation. In a May 1966 speech, Commissioner of Education Harold Howe II called for national action, proposing experiments with education parks enrolling 20,000 students from many neighborhoods throughout a metropolitan area:

We could . . . alter political boundaries to bring the social, economic and intellec-

3. M. Hayes Mizell, "Southern School Desegregation: Reflections on the Consequences of Reform" (unpublished paper, May 1969).

4. See p. 238.

tual strengths of the suburbs to bear on problems of the city schools. Building programs for the future could be planned so that new schools break up, rather than continue, segregation of both the racial and economic sort. The Office of Education will provide Federal planning funds for such efforts right now . . . and, if I have my way, the Office will provide construction funds before long. . . . Altering political boundaries or consolidating the educational facilities of a large city would involve major organizational changes . . . major educational surgery. But I believe that major surgery is required if we are to liberate the children of the slums.[5]

The idea even got as far as a draft bill, the "Equal Educational Opportunity Act of 1967," prepared by an Office of Education task force for the consideration of the secretary. The plan called for $5.7 billion over five years to build new schools that would be integrated and provide financial incentives for suburban cooperation in metropolitan desegregation. The draft bill, however, was leaked to two GOP congressmen and attacked on the House floor.[6] The administration never made a formal proposal, and the next year control of the funds the commissioner of education had hoped to use to encourage voluntary experiments was transferred by Congress to state governments.

In the fall of 1967 HEW began to study northern cities for "patterns of overcrowded classes and less qualified teachers in largely Negro schools, inadequate and inferior equipment, gerrymandering of school attendance zones, and racial discrimination in teaching assignments." The department made it clear, however, that it would not act against segregation "arising solely from fair and reasonable application of neighborhood school attendance zoning to segregated housing patterns."[7]

Southerners in Congress succeeded in 1967 in winning enactment of a requirement that school desegregation be enforced equally across the country. In the 1968 HEW appropriations bill, Congress accepted a southern proposal that half of HEW's desegregation staff be devoted to northern cases. New guidelines were developed to apply to the North.[8]

Investigations in the late 1960s focused on either little-known small districts or moderate-sized cities. Investigators spent a great deal of time, for instance, studying segregation in the suburbs of Ferndale, Michigan, and Penn Hills, Pennsylvania.

Funds were withheld in 1969 from Ferndale, but the case had little intrinsic significance. HEW documented local decisions to build a segregated

5. "The City Is a Teacher," speech of May 13, 1966, reprinted in *Congressional Record*, June 8, 1966, pp. 12656–57.

6. *Congressional Record*, September 15, 1966, pp. 22754–57.

7. *Washington Post*, September 15, 1967.

8. Ibid., July 8, 1967.

black school and to maintain segregated faculties and student bodies within walking distance of each other. This one case, which affected only 800 minority students, consumed nine months of an HEW lawyer's time, much of it spent recording Ferndale's history and writing a lengthy brief.[9]

A more important case was Wichita, Kansas, where HEW developed extensive evidence of segregation. After much debate HEW decided, as the end of the Johnson administration approached, to risk a cutoff. The threat worked just as the law intended. The school district began serious negotiations, eventually devising a citywide desegregation plan. This was to be the only triumph for HEW desegregation policy outside the South during the first decade of the Civil Rights Act's existence.

Although HEW had begun to create the capacity for dealing with northern segregation cases, there was little disposition to act. By September 1968 the department had designated about twenty-five systems of "manageable" size with serious segregation and less than one-third black enrollment for close study. Among them were Pueblo, Colorado; Toledo and Middletown, Ohio; Union Township, New Jersey; McKeesport, Pennsylvania; Pontiac and Saginaw, Michigan; Omaha, Nebraska; Tucson, Arizona; Pasadena, California; and Fort Wayne and Hammond, Indiana. Some staff members believed the department had sufficient information to act, particularly in Pasadena, Omaha, and Tucson. In several communities large teams had already made several visits and accumulated a great deal of data.[10]

But progress was slow. One reason was the uncertain state of the law. The Supreme Court had never heard a northern case. Decisions of lower courts were inconsistent and offered little encouragement except where there was clear evidence of intentional local segregation. Many of HEW's investigations found evidence of faculty segregation and of racial "containment" through variations of neighborhood school plans. The Office for Civil Rights was still searching for a definition of urban discrimination "that a court would buy." With rulings going both ways, the tendency to pull back was strong. The office had been, in the words of one staff member, "very cautious since Chicago."[11]

Forceful action in the North during the Johnson period would have required breaking new legal ground. The department had moved ahead of the courts in 1966 in forcing the rural South to go beyond token desegrega-

9. Interview with Roderick Potter, attorney for HEW, September 23, 1968.

10. Interviews with Joshua Zatman, B. Hunton, and Lillian O'Connor of OCR, September 23, 1968.

11. Interview with Avery Smith of OCR, September 23, 1968.

tion, but the action was taken against a single region and with the backing of a president still near the height of his power. In 1968 a weakened administration trying to cope with riots and urban polarization needed no more problems.

The mood of discouragement was reflected by Johnson's last HEW secretary, Wilbur J. Cohen. In an August 1968 interview, Cohen said that the country was far from ready to face the ordeal of urban desegregation after several years of riots. "I think we have to be realistic," he said. "In a large number of big city areas we have a lot of neighborhoods that are going to be completely black." The real problem, he said, was to upgrade services to stop "fear and riots." "Maybe another generation," he speculated, "will have to deal with integration." The secretary said that he did not believe busing was the answer and thought the public agreed with him. His solution was to increase federal funds for segregated black schools.[12]

Commissioner of Education Howe, who had led the HEW enforcement effort in the South, was also discouraged by the obstacles that remained as the Johnson administration ended. He described the progress to date as minimal, and saw the task as a protracted one. "Some people have a notion that Americans can solve any problem that they've got in short order. . . . Well, you don't change 100 years of history in short order. We have become accustomed to discrimination and it's hard to stop doing it."[13]

The Johnson administration achieved only the bare beginnings of an urban desegregation policy. As the President left office, the Justice Department was prosecuting its first northern desegregation cases, hoping to define the constitutional requirements. HEW was pressing several southern cities for busing plans but was cautious about testing its enforcement powers in the North, waiting for judicial leadership.

## The Nixon Administration Begins

When the Nixon administration took office, the President had to square his campaign promises with the facts that the Civil Rights Act was still on the books and that HEW's Office for Civil Rights was still processing cases. After a period of confusion, the administration stopped significant HEW action against school systems in the rural and urban South as well as in northern cities.

12. *Washington Post,* August 8, 1968; see also *Southern Education Report* (November 1968), p. 17.

13. *Washington Post,* November 10, 1968.

THE RURAL SOUTH. Almost immediately a series of decisions had to be made about withholding funds from small southern school districts that had been found guilty by hearing examiners. The administration faced an uncomfortable choice—it could either drop the cases and openly concede that it would not enforce the civil rights law, or it could enforce the penalties and be accused by the South of violating campaign promises.

Indecision dominated the first six months. HEW Secretary Robert Finch changed direction repeatedly, vacillating between decisions to enforce the law and White House pressure for compromise. The fall 1969 deadline for completing rural desegregation was near.[14]

Days after taking office, Finch granted delays to five recalcitrant districts threatened with fund cutoffs. In one of the systems, Marion County, North Carolina, the acceptance of a desegregation plan opposed by HEW experts was announced by the county Republican leader, who said he had been informed of HEW's reversal by a member of the White House staff.[15] HEW eventually withheld funds from three of the five districts, but federal policy became more and more fuzzy.

From the beginning, the administration tried to find a way to shift the burden back onto the courts. When a few courts responded, however, another kind of indecision arose. A federal court in South Carolina, for instance, directed twenty-one school districts to use HEW's help in developing acceptable desegregation plans. After HEW staff had prepared plans for fall 1969 desegregation, HEW leaders overruled the experts and directed that eighteen of the districts be given another year's delay. As hundreds of communities around the South facing the September deadline watched, word circulated that the administration was considering simply junking the deadline. Jerris Leonard, head of the Justice Department's Civil Rights Division, announced, "It's wrong to set an arbitrary deadline we can't meet."[16]

On July 3, 1969, a new policy was announced by the secretary of HEW and the attorney general. Almost exactly five years after the signing of the 1964 Civil Rights Act, federal officials were to end reliance on fund withholding and rely instead on Justice Department enforcement through lawsuits. Included in the statement's ten pages of confusing language was an open invitation for delay: "A policy requiring all school districts, regard-

14. The best journalistic account of this period appears in the news stories of Peter Milius in the *Washington Post*.

15. *Charlotte Observer*, March 1, 1969.

16. *Washington Post*, June 20, 1969. See also Gary Orfield, "The Politics of Resegregation," *Saturday Review* (September 20, 1969), pp. 58–60, 77–79.

less of the difficulties they face, to complete desegregation by the same terminal date is too rigid to be either workable or equitable."[17]

The statement even outlined some of the possible justifications for delay. For example, it said delays based on "serious shortages of necessary physical facilities, financial or faculty" would be considered. The message was clear to much of the South. Headlines in southern newspapers read SCHOOL DEADLINES SCRAPPED and NIXON KEEPS HIS WORD.[18] The administrative machinery for which the civil rights movement had fought so long had been abolished after all but the last few hundred of the 4,476 school systems of the southern and border states had committed themselves to ending segregation rapidly. Most established educational leaders of the region had conceded the inevitability of desegregation; the reversal of policy rewarded the remaining intransigent minority. Paul Rilling, HEW's Atlanta regional compliance director, argued that without a clear and firm policy "the whole thing goes down the drain."[19] NAACP Executive Director Roy Wilkins said that the government was "breaking the law."[20]

The director of the Office for Civil Rights, Leon Panetta, fought to keep his program alive by ignoring the negative sections of the July 3 statement and emphasizing the other parts. Disagreement in the administration came out in the first press briefing, as reported July 4 by the *New York Times:* "In an hour of questions and answers, Mr. Mitchell's man repeatedly left the impression that the Administration favored giving school districts more time to complete desegregation. But every time this view was expressed, Mr. Finch's men would emphatically declare that their department was for the fastest kind of desegregation enforcement."[21]

The HEW staff announced that it would send letters to all southern school districts stating that the guidelines had not been changed after all. The letter was blocked by the White House.[22]

A month later the government took the unprecedented step of asking the federal courts to delay desegregation in Mississippi. Secretary Finch wrote to the chief judge of the Fifth Circuit Court of Appeals warning that the desegregation plans recently submitted by his own department would produce "chaos, confusion and a catastrophic educational setback."[23] The

17. Departments of Justice and Health, Education, and Welfare, joint press release, July 3, 1969.
18. *Columbia State,* July 6, 1969; *Montgomery Advertiser,* July 4, 1969.
19. Interview with Paul Rilling, July 2, 1969.
20. Leon Panetta and Peter Gall, *Bring Us Together* (Lippincott, 1971), p. 222.
21. Ibid., p. 221.
22. Ibid., pp. 235–37.
23. Ibid., p. 255.

Justice Department filed a motion for delay. Finch then participated with Jerris Leonard in interrogating HEW education experts, with a court stenographer present, until they finally found some willing to testify for the secretary's request for a delay.[24]

Although a stern and unanimous Supreme Court rapidly ruled that the Mississippi school districts would have to desegregate at once,[25] HEW continued to approve desegregation plans that allowed a year's delay and left many black children in segregated schools. Panetta could not even win approval of a draft policy statement against the firing of black teachers and principals, a serious problem in the South.[26]

The strange bureaucratic guerrilla warfare went on for seven months as the Nixon administration was buffeted by a series of civil rights crises, including battles over voting rights and job discrimination and Senate defeat of two highly controversial Supreme Court nominees criticized for their role in school litigation.

In February 1970 Panetta learned through a headline in the Washington *Daily News* that he was being fired. White House Press Secretary Ron Ziegler simply announced that Panetta's still unwritten resignation had been accepted.[27] In an unprecedented step, 1,800 career employees of HEW signed a petition to the secretary asking for an explanation of the department's civil rights policies.[28] Paul Rilling described the effect of the policy changes:

The result of this retreat has been the revival of active, increasingly well-organized segregationist opposition in the South. Many districts are backing away from voluntary or court-ordered desegregation plans. . . . There has been one instance of mob violence against school children. The definitive policy statement of the President, finally issued on March 24, adopted much of the verbiage of the segregationists: we must preserve neighborhood schools; busing is bad; education is more important than integration; desegregation heightens racial tension; many Negroes don't want it, etc.

It was false, Rilling pointed out, to raise the busing issue in the South, where school districts showed declining bus mileage after integration.[29] In any event, the administration's efforts were frustrated because the task

24. Ibid., p. 259–62; this report was confirmed in the author's discussions with James Allen, Jr., then commissioner of education, Gregory Anrig, and other ranking HEW officials.
25. *Alexander* v. *Holmes*, 396 U.S. 19 (1969).
26. Panetta and Gall, *Bring Us Together*, pp. 312–16.
27. Ibid., pp. 350, 355.
28. Peter Gall, "Mores of Protest," in Charles Peters and Taylor Branch, eds., *Blowing the Whistle: Dissent in the Public Interest* (Praeger, 1972), pp. 168–81.
29. Paul M. Rilling, "Desegregation: The South *Is* Different," *New Republic* (May 16, 1970), pp. 17–18.

was largely completed and the Supreme Court intervened. By acting decisively in 1969, the Court was able to slow the momentum of backward movement in the school districts.

THE URBAN SOUTH. After it became clear that trying to delay rural desegregation was futile, the administration concentrated its resistance on emerging requirements for busing in southern cities. The lower federal courts and HEW had been pressing southern cities to accomplish desegregation even if it required moving away from neighborhood school assignment patterns.[30] Many southern cities had schools that had been built for blacks, operated under state segregation laws, and had never enrolled a white; these, they argued, were simply "innocent" neighborhood schools that just happened still to be all-black. The Supreme Court had not yet decided the issue. As Nixon took office, HEW was close to a showdown on urban desegregation plans in Columbia, South Carolina, Raleigh, North Carolina, and other southern city school districts.

In Columbia, a relatively simple pairing plan combining schools on opposite sides of the ghetto line would have largely solved the problem. The school board had tentatively approved the plan, but a local meeting was taken over by angry opponents. Nixon had told Senator Strom Thurmond of South Carolina when they discussed the city's plight at the 1968 GOP Convention that he opposed the HEW requirements.[31] Secretary Finch later refused to enforce the finding of HEW's Reviewing Authority, which required a fund cutoff.

In Raleigh, which HEW reportedly viewed as a test case in eliminating segregation in southern city school systems, fewer than one-seventh of the black students were in integrated schools in 1967.[32] In August 1968 negotiations broke down completely and HEW began fund-cutoff proceedings. In the largest school system affected by HEW enforcement since the Chicago controversy, HEW rejected the simple neighborhood school system and asked for a pairing scheme, redrawing attendance zones to improve integration. The Raleigh schools rejected this, and Raleigh remained segregated until civil rights lawyers gave up on HEW and took the case into federal court. It was finally desegregated in the fall of 1971. The court required much more than HEW had asked.

In Prince Georges County, Maryland, HEW's statistics showed that

30. Particularly important was a major case of the Fifth Circuit Court of Appeals, *United States* v. *Jefferson County Board of Education*, 372 F.2d 836 (5th Cir. 1966); 380 F.2d 385 (5th Cir. 1967).

31. Article from *Columbia State*, reprinted in *Congressional Record*, September 12, 1968, p. 26736. See also Thurmond's description of the situation; *Congressional Record*, July 24, 1968, p. 23058.

32. *Richmond Times-Dispatch*, August 7, 1968.

there had been relatively little desegregation in the huge system in spite of the transition to a "neighborhood school" concept after 1954. HEW's Office for Civil Rights ordered the county to come up with a desegregation plan by December 31, 1968. When local officials asked for help, federal analysts drafted a plan. The problem was the concentration of some 30,000 blacks in twelve square miles of ghetto just across the Washington line. The immediate need was to transfer 1,500 black children to white schools. Under the implicit threat of an end to the $12 million annual federal subsidy, local school officials quietly discussed HEW's proposals from August until the election, when things suddenly came to a head. The day after the Nixon victory, Prince Georges officials made public HEW's plan and their opposition to it.[33] The day after that HEW backed off, announcing that the plan needed "further study."

During the entire Nixon administration, HEW never took enforcement action in spite of the county's clear failure to comply. Eventually local parents sued the school district. They quickly won their case, and desegregation was ordered in the middle of the 1972–73 school year.[34]

The administration sent HEW "experts" to testify in court proceedings that extensive urban desegregation was unsound. In cases of great legal importance involving the largest cities of Virginia and North Carolina, they testified in favor of minimal desegregation plans.

The administration's coolness toward HEW enforcement was shown by Attorney General John Mitchell when he told House GOP leaders that he saw nothing wrong with an amendment permitting resegregation of the rural South through return to "free choice" plans. The House Republicans then joined southerners in writing the idea into an HEW appropriations bill. Only Senate resistance and a long-delayed statement from HEW prevented a sudden collapse of federal standards.[35]

Vice-President Spiro Agnew went to the Southern Governors Conference and put the administration to the right of the southern politicians. Agnew delivered a stinging attack on busing, but the governors straddled the issue in a resolution calling for "quality nondiscriminatory education" with "good judgment in the use of any busing."[36]

33. *Washington Post,* November 7, 1968.

34. *Vaughns* v. *Board of Education of Prince George's County,* 355 F. Supp. 1034 (D. Md. 1972).

35. Interview with William van den Toorn of OCR, May 1, 1974; *New York Times,* October 15, 1969; *Washington Post,* December 18, 1969.

36. *Atlanta Constitution,* September 18, 1969; *New York Times,* September 27, 1969.

When the administration set up an ad hoc committee in October 1969 to review desegregation plans, the busing issue dominated. In the first action, which concerned a Florida school district, both HEW's chief legal officer and Justice's top civil rights official attacked busing because of "all the heat we're getting."[37] As the word filtered down, HEW officials and local school officials began submitting weaker plans. The ad hoc group often watered plans down even at the cost of retaining segregation. The policy, HEW's civil rights director later wrote, was "to shade the plans so that the legal minimum of busing, or pairing black and white schools" would result.[38]

By 1971 it was clear that HEW had given up its mission of bringing the nation's public schools into compliance with constitutional requirements. The ultimate sanction of fund cutoffs had been publicly abandoned and its last administrative proponent fired. The White House openly warned federal officials that they would be fired if they continued to urge busing.[39] The Office for Civil Rights seemed to have become an agency without a mission.

The early 1970s brought continuing pressure to change the agency's direction, from both inside and outside. Civil rights groups went to court to try to force the administration to comply with the law by reactivating their fund-cutoff machinery. Agency leaders, on the other hand, often worked to redirect resources into new and different missions. Congress assigned it additional, unrelated duties. This substitution of goals ultimately permitted the agency to expand and even prosper under an administration strongly opposed to its original purpose.

Much of the justification for the shift in goals was couched in technical and administrative terms. Administration leaders declared, for example, that Justice Department litigation would be more efficient and that HEW had so many other responsibilities it simply lacked the capacity to do the job. Both claims would be tested and rejected in the federal courts.

JUDICIAL INTERVENTION: *Adams* v. *Richardson.* Soon after HEW ceased enforcing the 1964 law, southern efforts slowed down, with a number of school districts rescinding their plans, others refusing to submit new plans, and still others searching for ways out. Civil rights groups sued HEW despite the heavy odds against the likelihood that they could convince the

37. Panetta and Gall, *Bring Us Together,* p. 295; John Egerton, "Title IV of the 1964 Civil Rights Act: A Program in Search of a Policy" (Nashville: Race Relations Information Center, 1970; processed), pp. 14–15.

38. Panetta and Gall, *Bring Us Together,* p. 313.

39. *Congressional Quarterly,* August 28, 1971, p. 1829.

courts that HEW should resume civil rights enforcement. Two legal barriers normally defeated such attempts.

First, a case against an agency cannot even be argued in federal court unless the court decides that those bringing the case have "standing to sue." The Constitution does not authorize the courts to make abstract general policy decisions; they are empowered only to decide genuine "cases or controversies" concerning tangible interests of those bringing suit. In general, courts had refused to hear cases on the administration of federal aid programs, citing a half-century-old doctrine that no individual or group normally has standing to sue. The Supreme Court stated the principle in 1923:

The administration of any statute . . . is essentially a matter of public and not of individual concern. If one taxpayer may champion and litigate such a cause, then every other taxpayer may do the same. . . . The bare suggestion of such a result, with its attendant inconveniences, goes far to sustain the conclusion which we have reached, that a suit of this character cannot be maintained.

Before a court could consider such a case, the plaintiff must show "that he has sustained or is immediately in danger of sustaining some direct injury as the result of its enforcement, and not merely that he suffers in some indefinite way in common with people generally."[40]

This principle was a formidable obstacle. The courts had relaxed it only when there was an assertion of a violation of a basic constitutional right.

Second, even if a court did hear the case, judges were often reluctant to deny reasonable executive discretion to a coequal branch of the federal government. In view of the great number of statutory responsibilities of major agencies and their limited administrative resources, substantial discretion in establishing priorities is a basic part of the executive function. Federal judges usually avoid supervising federal administrators. The courts are ill equipped to make decisions about the motives and political goals of executive branch officials and to devise alternative administrative standards, priorities, and procedures. If an agency can offer a plausible explanation for its actions, the courts rarely intervene.

Nevertheless, when a Washington, D.C., law firm brought suit in cooperation with major civil rights groups, the case ended in victory. In *Adams v. Richardson* Federal District Judge John H. Pratt found HEW guilty of subverting the law and ordered the agency to resume enforcement in certain neglected cases. He found that 113 school districts had backed down on their promises to desegregate after HEW stopped enforcing the law in

40. *Massachusetts* v. *Mellon,* 262 U.S. 447 at 487 (1923).

1969 and that 74 of them were still illegally segregated. HEW had begun administrative enforcement against only 7 defiant districts and the Justice Department had filed suits against only 3.[41]

Judge Pratt was particularly critical of HEW's failure to enforce both the Supreme Court's 1969 *Alexander* v. *Holmes* decision forbidding more delays and its 1971 *Swann* ruling against urban segregation in the southern and border states. He said that HEW had illegally ignored the Court's "presumption against schools that are substantially disproportionate in their racial composition."[42]

HEW had identified 300 school systems that still had imbalanced, predominantly black schools. Judge Pratt found that the agency had arbitrarily dismissed the problem as only minor in 75 systems and then eliminated another 134 systems without any investigation. Finally, HEW had sent letters to the remaining 91 districts requesting compliance with constitutional requirements. Less than half had complied. Even in totally resistant districts no funds were cut off.

The district court ruled that the 1964 Civil Rights Act gave HEW only "limited discretion" and that it must act against school systems after reasonably prolonged negotiations failed. The court concluded that HEW's enforcement machinery had been almost totally abandoned, in violation of the law. Before 1970 HEW had begun about 600 fund-termination proceedings. In the year following the firing of Leon Panetta, not a single case was initiated.[43]

The court's 1973 decision directed the agency to begin action against 127 districts operating in violation of the *Swann* principles. HEW was also directed to begin work promptly on a number of other neglected cases. The judge set deadlines and ordered the agency to report back to his court.[44] Surprised by this unusual decision, HEW took the case to the court of appeals. Although appeals are normally heard by a three-judge panel, this important judicial-executive dispute was argued before all nine judges of the District of Columbia Circuit Court of Appeals. In June 1973 the court unanimously upheld the basic features of Judge Pratt's order, rejecting HEW's contention that the Civil Rights Act was so broadly drafted that courts must allow "agency discretion." The tribunal said that, although courts should not second-guess individual decisions in a generally adequate

41. *Adams* v. *Richardson*, 351 F. Supp. 636 at 638 (D.D.C. 1972).
42. Ibid. at 638.
43. Ibid. at 639–41.
44. *Adams* v. *Richardson*, 356 F. Supp. 92 at 94–98 (D.D.C. 1973).

enforcement program, this case involved a finding that "HEW has consciously and expressly adopted a general policy which is in effect an abdication of its statutory duty."[45]

Pronouncing the lower court's findings "unassailable," the court of appeals decision concluded that "HEW is actively engaged in supplying segregated institutions with federal funds contrary to the expressed purpose of Congress."

It is one thing to say that the Justice Department lacks the resources necessary to locate and prosecute every rights violator; it is quite another to say HEW may affirmatively continue to channel federal funds to defaulting schools. . . . Congress' clear statement of affirmative duty should not be discounted.[46]

The government decided not to appeal this strong and unanimous decision to the Supreme Court. HEW moved quickly to initiate enforcement proceedings. In contrast to the normal Title VI investigation process, which often lasted for years, the site reviews were accelerated, letters charging noncompliance were rapidly sent out, and a number of the cases were settled.[47]

Much of this activity, however, produced little real change. HEW rarely pressed the hard issues. The court had been able to act so forcefully against HEW not because the agency had made the wrong enforcement decisions but because it had done no enforcing at all. The court orders gave HEW officials new options—either they could take the decisions as an order to begin serious enforcement or they could try to answer the procedural failings noted by the court with a procedural response while making as few substantive changes as possible. HEW did the latter.

Six months after the court order, HEW reported on its progress to the district court. Only nine districts had submitted new plans that eliminated segregated schools. No school district had yet lost its federal aid. Seventeen systems were desegregated through private litigation. In most of the cases declared "successfully desegregated," HEW officials stated that either the local district had voluntarily complied or the changes necessary to bring the district to approximate racial balance simply were not practical. Scores of cases were either still pending or had not yet been seriously considered.[48]

Perhaps the most significant effect of the judicial intervention was to

45. *Adams* v. *Richardson*, 480 F.2d 1159 at 1162 (1973).
46. Ibid.
47. U.S. Commission on Civil Rights, *The Federal Civil Rights Enforcement Effort—1974*, vol. 3: *To Ensure Equal Educational Opportunity* (GPO, 1975), pp. 102–09.
48. Joanne Omang, "HEW Says 80 Areas Meet School Integration Rules," *Washington Post*, August 14, 1973.

restore some credibility to the process of enforcing the Civil Rights Act. Compliance machinery unused for four years now began to operate again. While no system had yet lost federal aid, local officials again had to consider that possibility.

The fundamental problem with the *Adams* order, however, was that it did not spell out the standards HEW must apply. Understandably, the court did not want to become involved in details of administration. Without clear standards, HEW proceedings were often without substance.

A year and a half after the decision, HEW recommended desegregation plans leaving many students segregated, claiming that congressional action in the interim had superseded the requirements of the *Adams* order. In mid-1974, when HEW would either have to cut off some funds or risk being found in contempt of court, Congress enacted a complex antibusing amendment, prohibiting executive agencies from ordering the transportation of students farther than the closest or next-closest school.[49] Congress' intent was not completely clear. Although in previous years HEW lawyers had dismissed a number of amendments as meaningless, HEW officials, caught between a court order commanding them to enforce the Civil Rights Act and a White House threat to fire anyone who recommended busing, saw the amendment as a way out of an intractable problem. If one read it as a partial repeal of Title VI, HEW could no longer be required to do anything more than insist on plans requiring busing no farther than the next closest school. The new law, said Martin Gerry, OCR's acting director, would have a "chilling effect" on remedies.

Gerry saw HEW's future role primarily as a fact-finder. Fund-cutoff remedies would not be invoked if districts refused to prepare adequate desegregation plans. The value, he thought, would come from ending the paralysis of HEW on the entire urban issue. For the last three years, "we have been, in effect, sitting around contemplating the stars" on the busing issue. Now investigators would be free to develop cases, even if they could not require much desegregation. Perhaps HEW could provide witnesses and evidence in federal courts if private organizations or the Justice Department sued the school system.[50] HEW would prove constitutional violations, then continue to pay federal subsidies, hoping someone else might enforce the law.

Lloyd Henderson, long-time chief of the education division in the Office for Civil Rights, similarly saw the central need as the development of enforcement standards. Staff members needed to know what policy they were

49. *Congressional Record*, July 23, 1974, p. 24543. See pp. 266–67, above.
50. Interview with Martin Gerry, September 10, 1974.

supposed to enforce. For too long he had worked where investigations could be conducted, cases prepared, papers drawn up to initiate the hearing process, and then nothing happened. Nor would anyone even explain why nothing happened or what would have to be done to make something happen. This situation, understandably, lowered staff morale.

Emerging from a period when a letter asking a California school district to desegregate one illegally segregated school remained unsigned after two years in the HEW secretary's office, Henderson was glad to have authorization to proceed on anything. Having some standard would enable the office to finish up cases that had been hanging fire year after year and to concentrate resources on districts and issues where some progress could be made even under existing policies. Under any policy, he explained, some desegregation at least could be achieved. Some of the small districts being investigated had very few ghetto schools, and these could be desegregated.

From Henderson's perspective, the *Adams* case had accomplished little of lasting value while consuming substantial administrative resources. Although he conceded that the decision was correct and that the civil rights groups "had us nailed" with clear evidence of many cases where HEW "hadn't done anything" about obvious violations, he found the court's requirements ineffective. An order really expected to work, he said, should have included specific policy guidelines. Otherwise it was just a "paper exercise" of sending out letters by certain deadlines, a "waste of time." Most of the plans that did come in, he said, did the absolute minimum, sometimes moving only a few children from one school to another.[51]

Two results of the *Adams* case are noteworthy. First, it produced an independent judgment of HEW's record on civil rights law enforcement. Second, it showed that, against strong administration resistance, extraordinary judicial intervention in the HEW administrative process would be necessary to bring about any real change in desegregation requirements. But no court was anxious to become involved in the details of individual cases or in continuous supervision of administrative decisions. The case revealed both the extent of the problem of intentional nonenforcement and the limited capacity of the judicial branch to repair the damage.

The court order did clearly demonstrate that HEW had the technical capacity to process large numbers of cases far more rapidly than it had. Between the 1973 *Adams* decision and November 1974, a Civil Rights Commission study reported, HEW staff members concluded 141 of the 197 cases affected by the order,[52] though civil rights groups were critical of

    51. Interview with Lloyd Henderson, September 30, 1974.
    52. Commission on Civil Rights, *Federal Civil Rights Enforcement Effort—1974*, vol. 3, p. 362.

the *way* some of these cases had been resolved. The problem was not inadequate resources; it was the politics of the busing issue.

## New Definitions of Discrimination

Although the Office for Civil Rights had virtually ended its activity on behalf of school integration, its officials were busy with a diversity of social change issues. They were trying to document unequal resources in black and Puerto Rican schools in New York City, drafting regulations against sex discrimination in athletics across the country, and developing bilingual-bicultural education requirements. They were investigating patterns of discipline and expulsion in schools and demanding data on sensitive questions of testing and procedures for channeling children into remedial courses. They were devising policies to cut discrimination against the handicapped. Almost the only thing the OCR was not doing was what it had originally spent almost all its time on, desegregating schools.

The Office for Civil Rights flourished as it changed (see table 9-1). Starting out with a small number of people in 1964, it was a sizable institution a decade later. The original small group of employees who had done much to transform southern education, working out of decrepit offices in a World War II temporary frame building on the Mall in Washington, had become a large staff in nicely decorated, carpeted offices in the HEW headquarters building, and there were miniature bureaucracies in ten regional

Table 9-1. *Growth of the Office for Civil Rights, Fiscal Years 1968–77*

| Fiscal year | Staff positions | Appropriations (thousands of dollars) |
|---|---|---|
| 1968 | 333 | . . . |
| 1969 | 326 | . . . |
| 1970 | 401 | 5,418 |
| 1971 | 550 | 8,581 |
| 1972 | 596 | 10,830 |
| 1973 | 707 | 14,768 |
| 1974 | 872 | 18,747 |
| 1975 | 847 | 22,207 |
| 1976 | 904 | 25,339 |
| 1977 | 1,054 | 31,304[a] |

Source: *Department of Labor and Health, Education, and Welfare Appropriations for 1976*, Hearings before a subcommittee of the House Committee on Appropriations (GPO, 1975), pt. 4, pp. 489, 517; *Department of Labor and Health, Education, and Welfare Appropriations for 1977*, Hearings (GPO, 1976), pt. 6, pp. 830–32.

a. Requested. By the end of calendar year 1977 appropriations had not been passed because of the unsettled question of the use of federal funds to subsidize abortions.

offices. By mid-1973, 116 professional staff members were assigned to work on elementary and secondary education alone.[53] Others dealt with higher education, health care, and job discrimination.

The office continued to grow while ignoring its original mission because there were many other legitimate enforcement duties that raised no serious political problems. The legal understanding of the prohibition of discrimination in Title VI had expanded, and Congress was enacting new statutes requiring HEW to end discrimination against women and the handicapped.

The social movement for southern civil rights in the 1950s and 1960s had stimulated not only blacks but also other groups of deprived Americans to organize and demand government action to protect their rights. The nation's second-largest minority group, the Chicanos, became increasingly vocal and assertive, as did other ethnic groups ranging from Puerto Ricans to Indians. Sometimes their demands presented less difficult challenges to government than those of black organizations. As the 1970s began, women's groups were organizing and pressing their pleas for action against sex discrimination with increasing effectiveness. They quickly became the most powerful constituency of the OCR.

There were also new demands from blacks that did not require busing as discrimination continued in nominally integrated schools. Studies of the displacement of black teachers and administrators in the South and of disproportionate punishment and expulsion of black students produced angry demands for further regulation.[54]

Many of these demands were welcomed and even encouraged by HEW, since they gave the agency important tasks free from the treacherous politics of busing. In most cases involving schools, these were issues that could be dealt with in existing schools without the reconstitution of entire systems. In time, goals not mentioned by the drafters of the 1964 law displaced the objective of ending unconstitutional segregation.

### Separate but Equal in the Big Cities

In 1970 HEW civil rights officials found themselves being drawn back into the study of the nation's largest school systems. Beginning with New York, they eventually created a large special program to study Chicago,

53. Ibid., p. 12.
54. For example, John Egerton, "When Desegregation Comes, the Negro Principals Go," *Southern Education Report* (December 1967), p. 3; Children's Defense Fund, *School Suspensions: Are They Helping Children?*" (Cambridge, Mass.: CDF, 1975), pp. 63–78.

Los Angeles, Philadelphia, and Houston (Detroit was omitted because of the pending NAACP lawsuit). This new burst of interest in the largest systems, however, had a peculiar twist—the investigations were not of segregation but of "equal opportunity."

Senator Jacob Javits, a major state political leader of the President's party, asked HEW to investigate discrimination against Puerto Ricans in New York City. The goal was to discover whether education was "equal" in certain respects, particularly whether instruction was offered in a child's own language. HEW officials, led by a team that had worked on Mexican-American cases, believed that linguistic and cultural discrimination was the primary cause of Latinos' educational problems.

The New York City investigation aimed to answer questions such as "whether educational services being provided to children place them in educational and cultural environments which do not meet their linguistic needs, or include the use of curriculum materials which dictate a permanently lower level of educational achievement regardless of academic potential."[55] It depended on establishing a computerized "data base" incorporating a vast amount of information about the school system. Eventually civil rights officials hoped to collect these data in all five districts, covering about a sixth of the nation's black students, almost a fourth of those with Spanish surnames, and more than a fifth of those of Asian background.[56]

The plan was surprising not only for its ambitious goal but also for its conspicuous change of focus. When HEW officials talked about "equal educational opportunities" in 1968 everyone understood it to mean remedying unconstitutional segregation of black children. The 1968 guidelines had included sections on equal services but no hint that this was the main goal. Four years later, the same phrase described the goal of offering separate, specialized instruction, largely in a distinctive language, for various linguistic minorities.

In all the big city reviews the focus was to be on "comparability." There would be minutely detailed checks on the equality of expenditures and facilities. Schools would be examined not only for differences in courses offered, but also for equivalency in such areas as "attendance services, health services, food services, student body activities, recreational activities, civic activities, services and programs linked with mental health programs, drug abuse prevention programs, etc." Investigators would look for

55. Statement of Martin Gerry, *Bilingual Education Act,* Hearings before the General Subcommittee on Education of the House Committee on Education and Labor, 93:2 (GPO, 1974), p. 10.

56. Ibid., pp. 12–13.

"educational environments which . . . are linguistically and culturally disadvantaging." They would inquire into the reasons for assignment practices that produced in-school segregation or grouping, but they would ignore how the schools themselves had become segregated.[57]

In March 1973 the OCR staff outlined their project for New York in a document more than 160 pages long.[58] It called for data collection on a scale that would have been unimaginable before computerization.

For example, the average square feet per student per school in everything from counselors' offices to laboratories were to be calculated, and data collected on expenditures ranging from security services to electric wiring. Investigators were to count all items, from musical instruments to silverware.[59] Elaborate checks would be made of school budgets. The object was to learn if minority schools were missing something tangible that the system supplies to other schools. A basic assumption was that measurably equal education will produce approximately equal results, that separate schools can indeed be equal, particularly if they reflect the linguistic and cultural background of minority students. It was the assumption of *Plessy*, not of *Brown*.

Research does not sustain these assumptions. Central city expenditures are frequently above the statewide averages. It is difficult and sometimes even counterproductive to try to impose rigid financial controls on a school system. The famous Washington, D.C., case, *Hobson v. Hansen*, directed that expenditures per child be almost precisely equal.[60] Carrying out this order has frequently meant the unpredictable shifting of teachers and other resources, making any kind of planning exceedingly difficult, disrupting the organizational structure of individual schools, and requiring small schools that lose students to double up classes, or even grades, and narrow the range of their curricula.

Although the comparability strategy was chosen, in part, to avoid the political problems of busing, it too proved difficult to carry out. New York City school officials were not happy about the prying into all aspects of school operations. Negotiations resulted in more limited federal requests for data. Even after the city school officials agreed, there was protracted defiance from the decentralized community school boards. In mid-1976 HEW sued to force principals to complete the necessary questionnaires.[61]

57. Ibid.
58. HEW, Office for Civil Rights, Office of Special Programs, "An Outline of Issue Areas to Be Reviewed During Initial Phase of the Equal Educational Review" (March 1973; processed).
59. Ibid., pp. 4, 8–10, 17.
60. *Hobson* v. *Hansen*, 327 F. Supp. 844 at 863 (D.D.C. 1971).
61. *New York Times*, June 28, 1976.

The New York study resulted in a report on discrimination in the hiring of faculty and a long report on unequal programs for blacks and Puerto Ricans late in 1976. At a time when the city was firing teachers and already under a court order to institute bilingual education, the effect either report would have was uncertain. The school board did agree in the fall of 1977 to desegregate its teachers.

The first concrete action was against Chicago in 1976. The Office for Civil Rights had informed the Chicago school board in October 1975 that it was violating the 1964 Civil Rights Act by segregating its faculties, by assigning "teachers with significantly lesser levels of professional training and experience" to black and Latino schools, and by failing to provide special bilingual programs for 6,200 non-English-speaking children. After six months of negotiations Chicago refused to make the necessary adjustments. On March 31 HEW deferred all pending Chicago grant applications for new programs and set in motion fund-cutoff proceedings.[62] It then contracted for a special analysis of Chicago school data and prepared an official set of charges against the city. The data showed, among other things, that 214,000 out of 225,000 black students were attending schools in which 91 to 100 percent of the students were from minority groups and that many Latino students faced similar levels of segregation.[63] The department, however, requested no action against the segregation of students.

After another federal court order directed HEW to enforce its own regulations in the North, a fund-cutoff hearing was held in Chicago in 1976. Then a March 1977 ruling by an administrative law judge prompted Chicago to move rapidly to desegregate its faculties and initiate bilingualism. But student segregation remained untouched.

### Action against Linguistic Discrimination

Some of the new HEW goals coincided with those of the White House. At the same time, for example, that President Nixon was leading the drive against busing, his 1972 campaign committee had set out to win a large part of the rapidly growing Latino vote.[64] This political goal was not the

62. Letter from Martin Gerry to Superintendent Joseph P. Hannon, March 31, 1976.
63. HEW, Office for Civil Rights, "Chicago Student and Faculty Composition—Number of Persons by Level, Year, School Composition and Racial/Ethnic Background" (April 9, 1976; processed), p. 12.
64. The strategy emerges with rare clarity because of the unprecedented publication of internal campaign documents as a by-product of the Watergate investigations.

A memorandum from the campaign committee to Attorney General John Mitchell in late 1971, for instance, identified Spanish-speaking Americans as one of the four key voting blocs that should receive special attention from the White House:

reason HEW chose to concentrate its resources on ending discrimination against Spanish-speaking citizens, but its congruence with HEW's emphasis gave the agency freedom to expand its regulatory efforts.

HEW officials were convinced that something must be done about the neglected educational problems of hundreds of thousands of children who could not understand the language their teachers were using. This conviction produced the major policy innovation of the Office for Civil Rights during the Nixon administration. In 1970 HEW announced in its "May 25th Memorandum" that it now interpreted the Civil Rights Act as forbidding practices that discriminated against students without a working command of English. Since HEW normally only prohibited "discrimination" under Title VI after the courts had already found a practice clearly unconstitutional, this was breaking new ground. Not only that, but the department was proposing to regulate classroom practices with extraordinary vigor.

The policy of May 25, which was aimed at more than a thousand school districts and 3.7 million minority children, required a school to take "affirmative steps to rectify the language deficiency in order to open its instructional program to these students." It challenged existing testing, counseling, and assignment practices which put a child in a lower track (a less demanding curriculum for children below grade level) or a mentally retarded class on the basis of a test that often actually measured his proficiency in English rather than his ability.[65]

The policy generated little controversy at first, when it was applied in small Texas districts. The press ignored it.

---

"Spanish-surnamed Americans comprise approximately 5 percent of the total population . . . [this group] is significant because of its concentration in such key states as California, Texas, Illinois, New Jersey and Florida. . . . All Spanish-speaking Americans share certain characteristics—a strong family structure, deep ties to the Church, a generally hard-line position on the social issue—which makes them open to an appeal from us *if* they can be convinced the President has recognized their social and economic problems. This is especially true now that the Democratic Party is under suspicion for favoring politically potent blacks at the expense of the needs of the Spanish-speaking people."

Campaign officials repeatedly mentioned the political value of HEW's role in bilingual education and discussed ways to dramatize it through visits to programs by the President and one of his daughters. White House memorandums frequently referred to meetings with HEW officials and briefings from them. *Presidential Campaign Activities of 1972,* Hearings before the Senate Select Committee on Presidential Campaign Activities, 93:1 (GPO, 1973), pt. 13, pp. 5533–34: "Memorandum for the Attorney General," December 16, 1971.

65. Memorandum from J. Stanley Pottinger (director of the OCR) to School Districts with More Than Five Percent National Origin–Minority Group Children, May 25, 1970.

But the requirements were predicated on sweeping assumptions new in civil rights enforcement—that the schools had an obligation to achieve equal results for each major racial or linguistic minority and that HEW knew what educational practices would best assure this. Enforcement officials could easily show that the test scores of Mexican-American students were lower than those of Anglos, and they assumed that the school system was responsible. A model plan, devised in response to a federal court decision in a Texas case ordering implementation of a comprehensive educational plan for Mexican-American students, called for bilingual-bicultural education throughout the elementary and junior high schools, new programs of early childhood education, special teacher training programs, and new ways of assigning children to special courses.[66]

When HEW began its program, it was satisfied if a district would merely agree to set up an educational program starting Spanish-speaking children in classrooms taught in Spanish and gradually moving to English. After a time, however, HEW demanded not only bilingualism, bilingual staff recruitment, and an end to the use of unfair tests, but also development of a curriculum respecting Hispanic culture and continuing education in *both* languages.

While the educational demands were expanding, the desegregation demands were disappearing. In 1970 HEW had accused fourteen small districts of actions supporting segregation.[67] Policy had changed, however, by the time HEW conducted a review in one of Texas's urban centers, El Paso, where intensive HEW staff work produced a "comprehensive educational plan." After the school district agreed to sign it, it was hailed within HEW as a model solution. It did nothing, however, about the district's severe segregation.[68]

One of HEW's leading educational consultants, Bambi Cardenas, called the 33-page El Paso plan the "best that's been produced." El Paso officials were responsive to specific HEW recommendations. Cardenas recalls that they were willing to do anything so long as they did not have to desegregate.[69]

The HEW team in El Paso was led by Martin Gerry, who saw the effort to develop the city's plan as an aid both in developing a general enforce-

66. *United States* v. *Texas Education Agency,* 342 F. Supp. 24 (E.D. Tex. 1971), *rev'd on other grounds,* 467 F.2d 848 (5th Cir. 1972).

67. Commission on Civil Rights, *Toward Quality Education for Mexican Americans* (GPO, 1974), pp. 57–62, especially p. 61.

68. El Paso Independent School District, "Educational Philosophy of the El Paso Independent School District" (1972; processed), p. 1.

69. Interview with Bambi Cardenas, September 19, 1974.

ment policy and in training staff. Gerry says that the "issue of student assignment was ducked" in spite of his belief that it was important—a decision made "because of the Administration's position." According to Gerry, Stanley Pottinger, director of the OCR at the time, told him that he could not raise the segregation issue.[70]

The El Paso authorities were ready to change the whole definition of the school's role. Not only did the system renounce the goal of assimilating students into the U.S. culture, but it accepted bilingualism, "especially the need to begin instruction in the language native to the child and to help him develop maximum facility in the other dominant language of our bilingual city as early as possible, while continuing the development of his native language."[71] It was, of course, a complete change of perspective for an American school system to describe English as "the other dominant language." The district promised to review its entire curriculum to find "culturally relevant materials."[72]

One consequence of the decision to emphasize Hispanic curricula for Chicano children was to keep the faculties as well as the student bodies largely segregated. In contrast to the previous HEW policy of faculty desegregation, HEW explicitly authorized principals to retain disproportionate numbers of Chicano teachers to further their programs, ignoring the evidence of Chicano teachers' bias against Chicano children.[73] El Paso parents, worried that unconstitutional segregation would continue under this "model" plan, had to undergo five years of litigation before obtaining a limited court order.[74]

### HEW's Response to Lau

When a Supreme Court decision in 1974 upheld HEW's right to prohibit linguistic discrimination under the 1964 Civil Rights Act, the decision greatly increased the agency's power.[75] It also tested HEW's seriousness in pursuing bilingualism.

The administration showed little disposition either to withhold federal funds from recalcitrant districts or to provide the federal aid necessary for any serious large-scale bilingual education effort. Even the separate but

70. Interview with Martin Gerry, September 10, 1974.
71. El Paso Independent School District, "Educational Philosophy," p. 1.
72. Ibid., pp. 1, 8.
73. Ibid., pp. 29–30; Commission on Civil Rights, *Teachers and Students*.
74. *Alvarado* v. *El Paso Independent School Board*, 426 F. Supp. 575 (W.D. Tex. 1976).
75. *Lau* v. *Nichols*, 414 U.S. 563 (1974).

equal policy was weakly enforced. A full bilingual-bicultural program would cost a large amount of money, at least in the early stages. New teachers would have to be hired, others trained or retrained, new texts, teaching materials, and library materials purchased, and new levels of supervisors, consultants, and administrators installed. Money was not available in many districts. Since the requirements came from a federal agency, backed by federal courts, school boards looked to Washington. The Bilingual Education Act of 1968 had established a convenient mechanism for providing the money and Congress had repeatedly demonstrated its eagerness to increase the funds.

In the first Texas case, when the court had directed HEW experts to help devise a bilingual remedy, much of the resulting plan was never carried out. It depended on the receipt of federal money, which the administration failed to provide.[76]

The *Lau* decision raised the same issue but on a scale potentially affecting millions of children. Once again, the financial response was the same. The administration soon made clear its unwillingness to finance anything more than research and small experiments. The new approach, it said, would have to be a state and local financial responsibility[77]—a decision that was also an indirect decision about enforcement. With no federal financial leverage, the possibility of enforcing any kind of detailed standards diminished. Many of the large urban systems and isolated rural districts that were particularly important for Latino children were already in serious financial trouble.

The Supreme Court had said that something must be done. HEW for some time would not say what. This meant that until HEW spelled out standards no one would know what was required.

San Francisco school authorities, operating a system with substantial numbers of Chinese, Japanese, Filipino, Korean, and Spanish-speaking students, asked, "What steps are necessary to comply?"[78] The answering letter was a masterpiece of vacillation. HEW again said that "officials of each school district" were responsible.[79] Even after Congress extended the bilingual education program and appropriated funds for it, HEW refused to spend much of the money.

76. Commission on Civil Rights, *Toward Quality Education for Mexican Americans*, p. 63.

77. Testimony of Frank Carlucci, under secretary of HEW, *Bilingual Education Act*, Hearings, pp. 309–15.

78. Letter from Superintendent Lane E. De Lara to Peter Holmes, February 20, 1974.

79. Letter from Martin Gerry to De Lara, March 26, 1974.

In his first budget after the *Lau* decision, the President called for a cutback in the modest federal bilingual program. After allowing for inflation, the administration proposed to do *less* after the Supreme Court decision than before. Though praising bilingualism as an alternative to desegregation, the President predicted that the maximum possible effort under the new budget would be 284 classroom projects in the entire country and the training of about 1,500 new bilingual teachers.[80]

Eventually, HEW did decide that schools must institute bilingual education programs for large numbers of children, but without federal funds. Policy was shaped in the summer of 1975 by an advisory task force that included many Hispanic intellectuals and resulted in a statement that came to be known as the "*Lau* remedies." Though not issued as an HEW regulation, the detailed standards for diagnosis, testing, and educating children from non-English-speaking backgrounds were used for enforcement. HEW regional officials made hard, specific demands in letters to local school officials, threatening to punish noncompliance by initiating fund-cutoff proceedings.[81]

Under pressure from local school officials and close questioning from the *Washington Post*, Acting OCR Director Martin Gerry conceded that HEW had no evidence to show that its policies would actually improve the education of linguistic minorities. Publication of an HEW clarifying memorandum stating that the "*Lau* remedies" constituted only a "guideline" spelling out one acceptable kind of education response was widely interpreted as backing down.[82] There was a further twist, however. HEW officials said that if local school systems did not wish to provide bilingual programs they must *prove* that whatever they wanted to do would work as well. Since there was no evidence on how well bilingualism worked, it was impossible to compare anything with it. On such grounds, HEW was prepared to cut off federal aid.

Although bilingual programs did expand rapidly, they were highly segregated. The first national evaluation of the federal bilingual programs showed that only about one in ten Anglo students were enrolled in the typical program. It also showed, in direct opposition to HEW's basic educational assumption, that the children enrolled in the programs did worse

80. *The Budget of the United States Government, Fiscal Year 1976—Appendix*, pp. 415–16, 419.

81. Proceedings were actually initiated against Chicago and several other districts.

82. Memorandum from Lloyd Henderson to Directors, Office for Civil Rights, Regions I–X, and Elementary and Secondary Education Branch Chiefs, Regions I–X, "Application of *Lau* Remedies," April 8, 1976.

in reading and English vocabulary than Hispanic children who remained in normal classrooms with no special services.[83] Another study showed that during the first five years of the seventies, when HEW was working actively for the rights of Hispanic children, their segregation increased significantly.[84]

## Sex Discrimination

A little-noticed provision in Title IX of the Education Amendments of 1972 required an end to sex discrimination in schools receiving federal aid. The responsibility was an extremely complex one for which few additional resources were provided. Proposed regulations covered issues ranging from admissions practices to participation on school athletic teams and sex role stereotypes in textbooks.

The Office for Civil Rights now was confronted by an active, informed, and insistent constituency of women's organizations, a constituency with organizational resources and political power far greater than those of minority groups, as evidenced by the way it transformed the usually invisible process of administrative rule-making and then successfully beat down a challenge to the regulations on the floor of Congress. Normally, after preliminary administrative regulations are published in the *Federal Register,* the issuing agency receives a few comments. After the Title IX regulations were published, there were more than 9,000 comments from across the country. The athletic regulations were widely protested by local school officials, and influential House members led an effort to weaken the demands. The mobilized women's organizations, however, quashed the protest.[85]

The Title IX regulations, finally issued in 1975, took up seventeen pages of small print in the Code of Federal Regulations.[86] They required elaborate investigations of compliance, a difficult task for HEW's elementary and secondary education staff, which was not growing at all. The theory was that most future investigations of local school systems would assess both race and sex discrimination. HEW had tried to free itself from the enormous administrative burden of investigating every complaint, but a coalition of

83. American Institutes for Research, "Evaluation of the Impact of ESEA Title VII Spanish/English Bilingual Education Program," AIR 48300 (February 1977; processed). This is a preliminary evaluation, and its conclusions should be treated cautiously.

84. Center for National Policy Review, *Trends in Hispanic Segregation: 1970–1974,* vol. 2 (Washington: CNPR, 1977), p. 7.

85. *New York Times,* June 4, 1975.

86. 45 C.F.R. Pt. 86 (1975).

women's groups, civil rights groups, and Hispanic organizations attacked the draft regulations and eventually won a court order requiring priority investigation of all complaints received by fixed deadlines and regular reports back to the courts.[87] Compliance with this order required a major redirection of HEW's resources away from enforcement activities with potentially greater impact. Even so, noncompliance with even the most basic requirements was widespread. An HEW report in March 1977 showed, for example, that only one-third of the more than twenty thousand schools and colleges receiving federal aid had even submitted the required form promising to end sex discrimination.[88] The job of forcing districts to submit forms and, later, of monitoring actual compliance was enormous.

### Discrimination against the Handicapped

Not even the women's issues, however, had the universal appeal of the OCR's assignment to enforce fair treatment for some 35 million handicapped Americans. Section 504 of the 1973 Rehabilitation Act forbade discrimination against people with mental or physical handicaps in all programs receiving federal aid.

Ending unfair treatment of handicapped children was an attractive goal, involving little early political controversy. At the same time, drafting and enforcing regulations dealing with such a problem seemed certain to be time consuming. Once again, HEW was provided with little additional staff to meet this responsibility.

HEW was so slow in issuing the regulations that lawyers for organizations of handicapped citizens went to court. They won a 1976 court order setting a deadline for the issuance of orders. The Ford administration appealed the court decision and asked Congress for further guidance about the meaning of the 1973 law.[89] Once the writing of regulations began, the heavy costs of compliance soon became evident.

At the beginning of the Carter administration, frustrated organizations began to use the direct action techniques of the early civil rights movement. Demonstrators staged a sit-in at the secretary's office, picketed his home, and occupied HEW's regional office in San Francisco for three weeks. HEW issued the regulations in April 1977, announcing that they would affect one-sixth of the nation's population, or 35 million people, including alcoholics and drug addicts. Among the many required changes would be the elimina-

87. *Brown* v. *Weinberger*, 417 F. Supp. 1215 (D.D.C. 1976).
88. *New York Times*, March 16, 1977.
89. *New York Times*, April 11, 1977.

tion of physical barriers in all facilities of federal grant recipients and the provision of proper public schools for the 5.5 million handicapped school age children.[90]

The multiple compliance responsibilities of HEW were frequently and forcefully cited by HEW officials responding to civil rights critics. The Justice Department asked Judge Pratt to end some of the requirements imposed by the *Adams* decision, arguing that the need to process cases of racial discrimination was interfering with other tasks. The Carter administration later asked Congress to increase the OCR staff to permit simultaneous activity on all fronts.

## Toward Separate and Unequal

During the early 1970s, the Office for Civil Rights developed a new conception of its mission. The change was based both on an adaptation to the political pressures that were making a continued effort for desegregation impossible and on sensitivity to the demands of newly emerging groups demanding equal rights. The new philosophy began to evolve the year after President Nixon ruled out the use of the fund-cutoff mechanism to enforce desegregation. Step by step, case by case, HEW staff members learned that it was futile to pursue the old issues and that something could be accomplished by trying to make separate institutions equal. Cut off from its old constituency, the OCR searched for and found enthusiastic new constituencies with real needs and with intellectuals who had a vision of educational change. In the space of a very few years, an OCR dedicated to the eradication of the doctrine of "separate but equal" in education came to accept separate schools and the goal of making them more nearly equal. The office grew as the original mission shriveled.

### HEW and Northern Segregation

HEW's continuing record of inaction in enforcing desegregation in the nation's urban areas was sharply criticized in two long and detailed reports issued by a private civil rights center and by the U.S. Civil Rights Commission in late 1974 and early 1975.[91] HEW officials, including Secretary Caspar

90. HEW news release, April 28, 1977.
91. Center for National Policy Review, *Justice Delayed and Denied: HEW and Northern School Desegregation* (Washington: CNPR, 1974); Commission on Civil Rights, *The Federal Civil Rights Enforcement Effort—1974*, vol. 3.

Weinberger, said that they lacked resources and that there was no constituency for enforcing the law anyway. Civil rights lawyers reacted by suing HEW again.

The HEW record was documented by the Center for National Policy Review. The center examined hundreds of HEW's files covering most of the northern and western investigations initiated since the Civil Rights Act became law. The report concluded: "In many cases, HEW investigations uncovered violations of the law, but the agency failed to take any effective action. . . . In other cases, HEW failed to conduct any investigation at all."[92]

Lloyd Henderson, long-time director of the OCR's Elementary and Secondary Education Division, said the report "came right out of our files." He blamed the failure to resolve cases primarily on two problems—continual diversion of staff to other tasks and indecision on the busing issue.[93] Martin Gerry described the report as "generally accurate." HEW, he said, was bound to follow the busing policy of the President, and this was the major constraint on enforcement.[94] In the bilingual cases, which were consuming large amounts of staff time, Henderson said, "We've just ignored segregation." Referring to the 1896 Supreme Court's "separate but equal decision," he summed up these investigations: "*Plessy* has been very big."[95]

The fundamental problem in the northern and western investigations was that HEW had developed no administrative standards. The advantage of administrative enforcement as opposed to litigation should come from the capacity of bureaucratic specialists to apply relatively simple standards to large numbers of cases. Without any workable definition of what constituted a violation of the law, the staff gathered vast amounts of data only to be told that whatever they uncovered was not quite enough.

The 1964 Civil Rights Act established one of those complex and time-consuming enforcement procedures that only works when enforcers have succeeded in creating a credible impression that the ultimate remedy will be employed if necessary. The HEW enforcement program had succeeded in making the South believe this by the end of the Johnson administration. The effort was abandoned in 1969.

Even if HEW had accomplished total desegregation in every northern district it investigated in the first decade of Title VI enforcement, the North would still have been highly segregated. HEW reviewed eighty-four northern and western districts, most of which were small. Of the 2.1 million

92. *Justice Delayed and Denied.*
93. Interviews with Lloyd Henderson, February 21, 1975, and September 30, 1974.
94. Interview with Martin Gerry, September 10, 1974.
95. Interview with Henderson, September 30, 1974.

Table 9-2. *Reviews of Northern School Districts Initiated by HEW, 1965–73*

| Year | Number |
|------|--------|
| 1965 | 1 |
| 1966 | 1 |
| 1967 | 2 |
| 1968 | 28 |
| 1969 | 16 |
| 1970 | 15 |
| 1971[a] | 11 |
| 1972 | 9 |
| 1973[b] | 1 |

Source: Center for National Policy Review, *Justice Delayed and Denied: HEW and Northern School Desegregation* (Washington: CNPR, 1974), p. 46.
a. Year of Supreme Court ruling on southern cities.
b. Year of Supreme Court ruling on northern cities.

children enrolled in these districts, almost a tenth were desegregated by private lawsuits before HEW did anything. Another third were in districts where the enforcement task had been turned over to the Justice Department. The remaining districts enrolled 1.2 million students, the large majority of whom were white. Even if HEW succeeded in obtaining plans that desegregated all the minority students, it would influence the educational future of less than one-tenth of the black students in the North and West and less than one-twentieth of the Hispanic children in all public schools.[96]

In contrast, private civil rights groups, whose resources were minuscule compared to HEW's large staff, had filed federal lawsuits affecting more than tw' :e as many black children. Private litigation had desegregated system: enrolling more than 400,000 minority children.[97]

The further the courts went in spelling out legal requirements for urban desegregation, the less interest HEW showed in investigating local violations. The pattern is evident in table 9-2.

The decline in the number of new reviews was accompanied by a shift in their focus. Many of the reviews initiated during the Nixon administration did not even deal with the problem of segregation; most were studies of language and cultural issues and of the equality of facilities.

The net result of the first eight years of HEW's effort in the North and West was movement toward compliance in thirteen local school systems. Most of the systems affected were small. Wichita, Kansas was the largest.[98]

96. Center for National Policy Review, *Justice Delayed and Denied.*
97. Ibid., pp. 40–41.
98. Center for National Policy Review, *Justice Delayed and Denied,* pp. 41, 48.

The HEW cases bogged down in a bureaucratic miasma, with three years or more frequently passing before any decision was reached. HEW lawyers insisted on proof of violations far in excess of that required by most federal courts. In Dayton, Ohio, for instance, investigators found that the great majority of the city's sixty-nine schools were segregated and produced evidence that the city had been intentionally segregated since 1915. The lawyer in charge, however, insisted that a $57,000 computerized analysis of all the schools since 1915 was an "absolute prerequisite" for action. A year and a half later, HEW had still done nothing. The local NAACP finally had to take the case into court on its own.[99] The story was similar in Toledo, Fort Wayne, and elsewhere.

Year after year staff members sent large files of evidence to Washington, only to have the files sit for many months on desks there and eventually be sent back with the explanation that the evidence was now out of date.

### Saved by Congress

On the central issue of busing, HEW was paralyzed after the fall of 1971. The department had initially tried to enforce the Supreme Court's 1971 decision requiring integration of cities with de jure segregation, even drawing up plans requiring considerable busing in Austin and in the Nashville metropolitan school district.[100] After President Nixon intervened and the Justice Department took the extraordinary step of disavowing HEW's plan for Austin, HEW changed. In Evansville, Indiana, for example, years of enforcement had finally persuaded the school board to end segregation of the relatively small number of blacks enrolled in a sizable school system. After the President's statement, however, the school board promptly withdrew its plan. HEW said it would accept a plan requiring no busing. Eventually the school board decided not to submit even that. Convinced that HEW would do nothing, civil rights lawyers sued. The federal judge rapidly ordered desegregation.[101]

When Congress enacted the 1974 amendments to the Elementary and Secondary Education Act, which limited HEW's authority to order busing,

99. Ibid., p. 53.
100. Cynthia Brown, "Nixon Administration Desegregation," and J. Stanley Pottinger, "HEW Enforcement of *Swann*," both in *Inequality in Education* (August 1971), pp. 6–16; Peter Milius, "Nashville Offered Pupil Busing Plan," *Washington Post*, June 2, 1971.
101. Center for National Policy Review, *Justice Delayed and Denied*, pp. 99–101; *Martin* v. *Evansville-Vandenburgh School Corporation*, 347 F. Supp. 816 (S.D. Ind. 1972).

the department welcomed the action. In the past, HEW had often been confronted with confusing congressional restrictions, but had interpreted them narrowly and been sustained by the courts. The various prohibitions on "racial balance" requirements, for instance, were ignored, since HEW said its standards were based on constitutional requirements for desegregation, not on a goal of "racial balance" as an end in itself.

Just two days after President Ford signed the act, the Office for Civil Rights issued a policy memorandum restricting future desegregation plans. It was a display of blinding bureaucratic speed for an agency that commonly takes many months to interpret the intent of Congress in far less complex legislation. Director Holmes wrote: "OCR may not, as part of a desegregation plan, require the transportation of a student to a school other than the school closest or next closest to his or her place of residence which offers the appropriate grade level. This limitation is applicable to elementary as well as secondary school pupils."[102]

HEW now set out to answer charges of inaction by requiring this limited form of desegregation in all the pending cases. In the largest of the districts affected by the *Adams* decision—Baltimore—the department ruled that its standards could be met merely by putting as few as 10 percent white children in a black school just across the ghetto line and transporting enough black children the other way to make the first row of schools inside the white communities 50 to 90 percent black.[103]

This, said OCR Director Holmes, was all that the law permitted, and he would follow a similar policy in devising standards to be applied to the other large cities. In a city like Los Angeles, he said, HEW would not examine segregation unless it found a blatantly discriminatory attendance policy in two adjacent schools. Then those two schools might be required to desegregate. There would be no large-scale desegregation.[104]

The Fresno, California, school district illustrated the implications of the new policy for a smaller system with a simple desegregation problem— three segregated schools. A month after the new legislation was signed, HEW wrote that it would now accept continued segregation at two of the three schools.[105]

HEW emphasized voluntary persuasion even for these modest demands. Secretary Caspar Weinberger said that enforcing the cutoff provisions of

102. Memorandum from Peter Holmes to OCR Director of Elementary and Secondary Education and OCR Regional Directors, August 23, 1974.

103. *Baltimore Sun,* September 5, 1975.

104. Interview with Peter Holmes, February 21, 1975.

105. *Washington Post,* November 11, 1974.

the Civil Rights Act was a "blunderbuss" approach not necessary in a period of "matured" race relations, even though "substantial racial isolation remains, mainly in our large urban centers where feasible and reasonable remedies, short of massive busing, are not readily available."[106]

When Weinberger was replaced in mid-1975 by F. David Mathews, both criticized school desegregation and suggested that perhaps HEW should do still less. In his farewell speech to the San Francisco Commonwealth Club, Weinberger denounced busing as "another example of questionable social engineering."[107]

At his confirmation hearing, Mathews said that busing "is not producing good results" and suggested that something else be tried. He could suggest no alternative. After a strong rebuke from Senator Javits, Mathews promised to "uphold the law of this land as written."[108]

Two months later, however, the new secretary again attacked desegregation policies, saying that fund-withholding punished "innocent third parties." He wanted the whole approach restudied, he told a national television audience.[109]

### Priorities—the First Becomes Last

HEW's intention to downgrade desegregation enforcement was presented in 1974 with great clarity in a series of internal policy and planning decisions that set agency priorities and allocated staff time. This process showed how fundamentally the agency had changed since the Johnson administration. The desegregation effort, which had absorbed most of the OCR staff's efforts in the 1960s, barely survived in the plans for 1975.

During its executive staff conference on March 25–28, 1974, the Office for Civil Rights decided to emphasize in-school problems, not segregation. The conference decided that usually, when a system was reviewed for in-school racial issues, it should also be reviewed for possible sex discrimination, even though this was often "more subtle and difficult to prove."[110] The choice to try to collect "all applicable data" simultaneously, of course, put a heavy additional burden on the investigatory staff.

The conference revealed that HEW's enforcement resources were al-

106. Letter from Secretary Weinberger to Senator Thurmond, September 23, 1974.

107. Text of speech reprinted in *Congressional Record* (daily edition), July 22, 1975, p. S13277.

108. *Washington Post,* July 16, 1975.

109. *New York Times,* July 18, 1975.

110. "Report of Executive Staff Conference, Office for Civil Rights, DHEW, March 25–28" (OCR files), pp. 3–6.

ready heavily mortgaged in various directions. For three years, the OCR would have to spend time on the investigations and reports required by the *Adams* decision. It had promised the RFK Foundation to mount a national attack on "pushout" policies, the disproportionate suspension of minority children in some school systems. Third, reviews under the Emergency School Aid program must be completed. Fourth, the OCR was committed to monitoring "equal education," not segregation, in five of the nation's largest school systems.

After the executive staff policy planning sessions, OCR Director Peter Holmes reached a series of specific priority decisions. He decided that 70 percent of the field work on public schools should go to studying problems within schools.[111] In-school discrimination, the first priority, was to receive 30 percent of staff time, while student discipline, funding equalization, and linguistic-cultural and sex-role discrimination were each allocated 15 percent. The segregation issue was to be given only 10 percent of the division's time.[112] Since school enforcement would get only about one-third of the OCR's resources, this meant that the office was planning to devote about one-thirtieth of its available time to the task of dismantling school segregation.

The central task that had consumed the energies of the Office for Civil Rights at its birth had almost vanished. Even in this minuscule effort the busing policy would mean that in the cities little desegregation would be required. The office was bigger and busier than ever. All that had changed was that somewhere it had lost its purpose.

Holmes said that the OCR could carry out a program to desegregate most major urban systems if it were a priority. It was not.[113] HEW had the capability to do the job but no longer thought it was important. With few exceptions, segregation would be accepted. The OCR would work to make it "more equal."

### Crosscurrents

The major struggles over the future of HEW's enforcement policy had moved to the floor of Congress and to the federal courts. The Senate acted, in the fall of 1975, joining the House in limiting HEW's enforcement power in urban school desegregation cases. The nation's major civil rights groups,

111. The decisions made by Holmes were incorporated in "Annual Enforcement Planning Task, Outline Decision Paper" (March 1974), p. 1.

112. Ibid., pp. 2–4.

113. Interview with Holmes.

on the other hand, continued to press litigation filed on July 3, 1975, asking that HEW be made to enforce the 1964 Civil Rights Act in the North and West.

The two initiatives were confusing and contradictory. After the Byrd amendment became law, HEW adopted a policy of doing nothing about urban segregation; the only actively pursued issue was faculty desegregation. A few months later, however, HEW came under yet another court order. Judge John J. Sirica, who had handled the Watergate case, concluded that HEW had systematically failed to enforce civil rights law in northern and western cities. In a July 20, 1976, decision, he ordered HEW to promptly begin proceedings against some forty-four districts that had been in the enforcement process for years.[114] Even before the final decision, the OCR had begun to review the files and set procedures in motion again, trying to close as many cases as possible.[115]

Like the courts in earlier cases, however, Sirica failed to spell out substantive requirements. The cases that came under the order varied from allegations of discrimination against Indian students in some small Minnesota systems to investigations of faculty segregation and other matters in Chicago and Los Angeles. Most of the districts on the list were small and most of the cases were not built around the student segregation issue.[116] Without further orders or initiative in HEW, it was unlikely that this decision would have much impact on urban desegregation.

In the 1976 election campaign, the Office for Civil Rights, the focus of bitter attacks in earlier campaigns, was not mentioned.


## Postscript: The Carter Administration

The 1976 election transferred control of the executive branch from a party whose national convention had called for a constitutional amendment against busing to one that had reluctantly accepted it as a tool of desegregation. President Carter chose as new secretary of HEW Joseph Califano, the first strong integrationist to occupy the office since John Gardner in the Johnson administration. Califano appointed a group of liberal lawyers committed to enforcing civil rights law to direct the Office for Civil Rights and named long-time civil rights activists to head up HEW's legal office and legislative relations staff. He tried to set the tone with a series of strong statements expressing his commitment to vigorous enforcement.

114. *Brown* v. *Weinberger*, 417 F. Supp. 1215.
115. *New York Times*, August 13, 1975.
116. *Brown* v. *Weinberger*. The list is included in the decision.

During his first week in office Califano announced a review of OCR policies, saying there had been "too much data collection and too little enforcement."[117] The next month he issued a public warning that HEW was prepared to cut off funds from districts that did not comply, promising to "restore the integrity of HEW's civil rights program."[118]

There was little doubt that Califano and the new leadership of HEW were civil rights supporters. The question was, how much could they accomplish? The office was under so many court-imposed deadlines for so many contradictory enforcement tasks that virtually no staff was available for any fresh policy initiative. One of the ironies of the situation was that some of the new enforcement officials were the very civil rights lawyers who had worked so hard to wrap their Nixon and Ford administration predecessors in a straitjacket of judicial decrees. Now they found themselves unable to move, facing a succession of issues that did not reflect administration priorities and were unlikely to accomplish much desegregation. In June 1977 new OCR Director David S. Tatel asked the federal court supervising HEW to consolidate three of the major cases and provide him with time "to develop a rational and balanced enforcement program." Tatel conceded that the office had had a "sorry record of neglect." "I fully understand that in the past the Office for Civil Rights has failed to enforce the civil rights laws in accordance with Congressional mandates, and that lawsuits were necessary to mobilize this department's enforcement energies." But he argued that it was not fair to bind a new administration because of the "mistakes and constraints of the past." Without change, he said, enforcement priorities would be "in large part dictated by present or potential court orders."[119]

The court rejected the request, but eventually an out-of-court agreement was reached. On December 29, 1977, Secretary Califano announced that the various court orders had been consolidated into a new agreement that set firm deadlines for resolving complaints and also gave HEW some discretion in using its staff. The agency promised to hire almost nine hundred more enforcement officials.[120]

Even if the OCR did manage to regain some administrative discretion, it still faced the congressional restrictions of the Byrd amendment. In June 1977 the administration adopted a less narrow view of what the Byrd amendment meant but still did not press for its repeal. Califano and Attor-

117. *Washington Post,* January 27, 1977.

118. Ibid., February 18, 1977.

119. *New York Times,* June 8, 1977, quoting affidavit filed in the federal district court.

120. *Adams* v. *Califano,* C.A. 3095-70 (D.D.C. 1977).

ney General Griffin Bell reversed earlier policy and ruled that HEW need not follow a strict neighborhood school policy. HEW would now withhold funds from school districts that refused to reduce segregation by pairing or clustering schools (techniques that involved combining the attendance areas of two or more schools on opposite sides of the ghetto boundary and assigning all the children from the enlarged zone to attend each of the schools for certain grades). Such redistricting would be required even if it involved some increase in local busing.[121] The new ruling gave HEW enforcers access to a technique that had proved very useful in desegregating small concentrations of minority students, but still left it without a workable policy for the cities with large ghettos and barrios.[122]

Congressional reaction to this modest initiative was almost instantaneous. Within days of the first newspaper stories about the new policy the House of Representatives voted 225–157 to reverse it. The Senate Appropriations Committee promptly voted to put the same restriction in the HEW money bill for fiscal 1978. The White House said nothing.[123] The conference committee retained the limitation and also prohibited the collection of certain kinds of data.[124] Unless there was a change of heart in Congress or a federal court ruling that restrictions on civil rights enforcement were unconstitutional, HEW apparently was excluded from playing any role in urban desegregation. Congress had written into law a requirement that the agency provide local school districts with federal aid even when it had strong evidence that the money would be spent to support discrimination.

Secretary Califano said in early 1978 that there was little HEW could do. Busing, he said, was "in the hands of the federal courts" and would "solve fewer and fewer problems," in part because it was "very difficult" to see what busing could do in central cities where few white students remained.[125] HEW's role would be modest.

The new leaders of HEW wished to redirect a large agency that had passed through years of upheaval and redefinition back toward its original goal. Even with favorable judicial rulings, however, any serious attack on segregation of big city schools would require a major and politically costly commitment from the President, whose policy remained unknown.

121. *Washington Post,* June 8, 1977.
122. Pairing or clustering schools on the outskirts of large, expanding ghettos does not produce lasting integration and may even accelerate the process of neighborhood transition and residential resegregation.
123. *New York Times,* June 17, 1977.
124. *Education USA,* August 1, 1977.
125. *U.S. News and World Report* (January 9, 1978), p. 44.

# 10

# Justice, Politics, and Busing

ONCE the Supreme Court had acted against urban segregation, expanding desegregation requirements in ways that left few cities anywhere in the country in compliance with the law, the Justice Department faced an enormous enforcement task. The Nixon administration's 1969 decision to rely on litigation by the Justice Department rather than enforcement by the Department of Health, Education, and Welfare meant that much would depend on Justice's decisions about the use of its authority.[1]

## The Decision to Rely on Litigation

When the administration announced its policy, civil rights groups were furious. Liberals argued that fifteen years of school litigation proved that case-by-case desegregation through the courts would take a century or two. The Justice Department's Civil Rights Division, with just a few lawyers, was unlikely to have much effect on segregated cities.

Even before the Nixon presidency, civil rights groups had been critical of the department's cautious approach. Its lawyers had ignored urban school desegregation until 1968. Even at the height of the civil rights movement, Justice had often restrained the exercise of HEW's administrative powers. The emphasis was on slow and certain development of the law.

---

1. *Washington Post,* July 4, 1969; *New York Times,* July 4, 1969.

Until 1964 the Justice Department lacked the power to initiate cases. It could only participate by filing "friend of the court" briefs. The 1964 Civil Rights Act, however, empowered Justice's Civil Rights Division to file new cases and to intervene in cases filed by others.

John Doar, then assistant attorney general for civil rights, clung to the theory that the Constitution required only token integration under "freedom of choice" desegregation plans long after HEW began to move toward requiring the abolition of the dual structure of the southern school system.[2]

It was not until late in the Johnson administration, when the President named Ramsey Clark attorney general and appointed Stephen Pollak, an activist, assistant attorney general, that the department's position shifted. It urged the Supreme Court to require systematic dismantlement of the whole segregation system, arguing "effective desegregation is not accomplished so long as there remain all-Negro schools, attended by an overwhelming majority of the Negro children."[3] The department asked the Court to consider not just the abstract equity of offering all students an equal opportunity to choose their schools, but also the real community pressures that restrained desegregation: "Insecurity, fear, founded or unfounded, habit, ignorance, and apathy, all inhibit the Negro child and his parents from the adventurous pursuit of a desegregated education in an unfamiliar school, where he expects to be treated as an unwelcome intruder. And corresponding pressures operate on the white students and their parents to avoid the 'Negro' school."[4]

After the Court sustained Justice's position in 1968,[5] the department concentrated its resources on a major enforcement effort. Across the South, motions were promptly filed to update old desegregation plans. HEW joined the campaign, bringing pressure on the districts desegregating under its guidelines. Desegregation accelerated. This was a model of the way the various elements of the enforcement process could work together.


## The Early Northern Cases

Under Ramsey Clark the Justice Department attacked northern school desegregation. In mid-1968 the department filed its first northern cases. It sued a Chicago suburb (South Holland), a city in Southern California (Pasadena), and the largest city in Indiana (Indianapolis), dealing with an explosive issue in politically important swing states in a presidential election year.

2. Interview with John Doar, June 20, 1967.
3. Memorandum for the United States as Amicus Curiae, *Green* v. *County School Board of New Kent County* (February 1968), p. 2.
4. Ibid., p. 8.
5. *Green* v. *County School Board of New Kent County*, 391 U.S. 430 (1968).

Action came rapidly only in South Holland. The department proved that the system was gerrymandering district attendance lines and choosing school sites to maintain four segregated white schools and two segregated black schools. Department lawyers produced elaborate evidence showing that large numbers of students had been assigned on a discriminatory basis.[6] White resistance was strong; thousands of dollars were collected to finance an appeal. The Illinois state school superintendent supported the local white officials.[7] It all seemed like something that might have happened a decade earlier and five hundred miles south.

Within months Justice won the case and an appeal. In early September, the district desegregated. Although trouble had been predicted, the transfer of 387 black students to the four white schools was peaceful.[8]

Justice became mired in protracted litigation in its other cases. The Pasadena and Indianapolis cases, as originally filed, were not especially complex or difficult, yet litigation was slow. Two years elapsed before an initial order was obtained in Pasadena.

Pasadena in 1968 was a city of 190,000 people with a large ghetto. School construction and assignment policies had increased segregation. HEW investigators who examined the system in 1968 concluded that it had intentionally segregated faculty, provided inferior schools for blacks, and gerrymandered attendance zone lines, but HEW did nothing. Three families sued the system.[9] The Justice Department joined that litigation.

When the suit was filed, the city was aging and its black and Mexican-American communities were growing. White enrollment had dropped by 2,800 students from 1961 to 1968, nine-tenths of the decline having occurred in the last three years. The decline was not due to white flight from integrated schools, but rather to the demographic displacement of the white population, to neighborhood racial transition, and to the fact that the white residents were older and less likely to be in their childbearing years than the minority families. A researcher for a civil rights group estimated that existing trends would produce a black and Chicano majority in 1971.[10]

---

6. Amended Complaint, Motion for Preliminary Injunction, filed May 27, 1968, *United States* v. *School District 151 of Cook County, Illinois*, Civ. No. 68 C 755 (N.D. Ill. 1968).

7. *New York Times*, September 23, 1968; *Chicago Daily News*, January 31, February 25 and 28, 1969.

8. *Chicago Daily News*, September 5, 1968.

9. Roy Reed, "Classic Segregation Crisis: Pasadena," *New York Times*, April 7, 1969.

10. Ibid.

Desegregation was ordered by the federal district court in March 1970. The plan called for busing more than one-third of the 30,600 students, redrawing attendance boundaries, and rearranging grade structures.[11]

The Pasadena decision was a breakthrough for desegregation law, but it did not solve the problem of the city. In the school system the researcher's prophecy was rapidly fulfilled, and whites became a minority. A conservative school board took office determined to undermine the desegregation plan. The district judge had to deal with the problem of noncompliance with little assistance from the Justice Department. The private litigants, supported by the American Civil Liberties Union, had to carry the battle.[12] When the case came before the Supreme Court in 1976, Pasadena officials asked for an end to busing because of the population changes. The Justice Department then defended the plan with a strong brief, but the Court said the lower court had gone too far in requiring continual readjustments to prevent resegregation.[13]

The Pasadena case, however, was simple compared to that in Indianapolis, where the department claimed in 1968 that the local schools were racially labeled by the maintenance of fifty-nine schools with totally segregated faculties and another twenty-six with only one teacher of the opposite race apiece.[14] Since the school district was known to have practiced official segregation until the 1940s, Justice argued that pervasive de jure segregation remained and that the "crucial question" was whether Indianapolis had ever complied with the Supreme Court's 1954 *Brown* decision.

The Indianapolis case involved a great deal of work, particularly since Justice tried to prove intentional segregation at each of the system's 107 schools. It became more complex after the presiding district judge decided that no practical desegregation plan was possible within the boundaries of a two-fifths black school district because of a racial "tipping point," which he said would ensure white flight from the city. The case eventually evolved into a metropolitan desegregation dispute, in which the Justice Department played an ambiguous role and most of the burden fell on private litigants. The Supreme Court vacated the most recent plan early in 1977, sending the case back for still more proceedings. Final resolution of the dispute was not in sight after nine years in court.

11. *Spangler* v. *Pasadena City Board of Education,* 311 F. Supp. 501 (C.D. Cal. 1970).

12. Eventually, when the case was taken by the Supreme Court, the Justice Department filed a brief opposing the school board.

13. *Pasadena City Board of Education* v. *Spangler,* 427 U.S. 424 (1976).

14. Motion for Preliminary Injunction, filed 1968, *United States* v. *Board of School Commissioners of City of Indianapolis.*

## The Limits of Litigation

The few Justice victories were slow and costly and strained the department's small civil rights staff. Assistant Attorney General Pollak began the litigation not because he believed the courts could deal effectively with unconstitutional discrimination in the North, but because a body of case law was needed to establish workable principles for urban school desegregation law. He expected the courts to hold that de facto segregation was actually the product of various forms of state action, but the burden of demonstrating this, even in a few test cases, was "almost beyond the capability of the Civil Rights Division."[15] "This process of litigation," said Attorney General Clark, "is too slow and feeble to achieve the rights we need. . . . I think we are going to have to rely on courts to the maximum extent that they can be effective, but I don't think they can do 10 percent of the job." According to Clark, the Civil Rights Division did not have enough lawyers to handle the task in even one state.[16]

Pollak believed that the early northern and western litigation helped accumulate a body of facts about urban school segregation. Even in the first few cases, he said, "we learned that the distinction between de jure and de facto segregation has little meaning. Once the facts were pursued, the Department found that what had been justified as de facto segregation was in reality caused by governmental action."[17]

The Pasadena and Indianapolis cases had incorporated one of the common problems of urban desegregation—how to devise a remedy that would be realistic in view of the continuing spread of residential segregation and outflow of whites from the city. In Pasadena these changes ultimately limited the effect of the court order. In Indianapolis the district judge made them a central question from the outset. Justice would face the issue directly in later Supreme Court battles over metropolitan plans for Richmond and Detroit.

Justice's first northern cases showed that even an administration strongly committed to desegregating urban schools would face both great cost in managing the cases and difficult questions about the future of the cities that they raised. Decisions in later cases, however, were to be made by an administration in which opposition to busing had become a leading theme.

15. Interview with Stephen Pollak, June 12, 1969.
16. Testimony of Ramsey Clark, *Equal Educational Opportunity*, Hearings before the Senate Select Committee on Equal Educational Opportunity, 91:2 (GPO, 1970), pp. 1613–14.
17. Pollak testimony in ibid., p. 1847.

## External Images and Internal Problems

When it decided to rely only on Justice Department litigation to secure compliance, the Nixon administration assured the public that the department could and would handle the school desegregation task better than HEW had done. To support this assertion, Justice immediately announced eight cases—in Chicago, in southern states, and in Waterbury, Connecticut. The most important of the southern cases was an effort to win a court order in Georgia to make state officials enforce desegregation requirements in local systems. The action in Chicago was the most publicized federal enforcement activity in a northern city for several years.[18]

The blitz of litigation was intended to counter criticism of HEW's retreat, and positive headlines showed that it did have the desired effect. Justice then attempted to consolidate its gains with a press release containing data suggesting that administrative enforcement was less rapid and less effective than case-by-case litigation. Federal statistics and scholarly research show, however, that the administrative process usually works better. A recent analysis comparing levels of desegregation for 1968 and 1970 in districts handled by HEW with those in systems under court order indicates substantially higher levels of segregation in the latter.[19] When administrative enforcement was actively pursued in the South, from 1965 to 1968, desegregation increased several hundred percent.[20]

Advocates of administrative enforcement insist that courts lack the capacity to effectively monitor compliance with their desegregation orders. Available evidence supports this. Not only was the Justice Department able to handle far fewer cases, but it usually achieved less desegregation in the cases it did pursue.

The eight new cases illustrated this lack of achievement. Little came of the two northern cases, and most of the southern cases were against small districts that had already lost federal funds as a result of HEW enforcement and that would automatically regain the money once they came under court order. Only the statewide litigation in Georgia had genuine importance, and even there, controversy arose about the standards for compliance.

The northern actions were simply letters threatening to take action in

18. *New York Times,* July 9, July 10, 1969.
19. Micheal W. Giles, "H.E.W. versus the Federal Courts: A Comparison of School Desegregation Enforcement," *American Politics Quarterly,* vol. 3 (January 1975), pp. 81–90.
20. *Race Relations Reporter,* July 6, 1971.

the future. A lawsuit was eventually filed against Waterbury, but Justice settled out of court for a gradual plan.

The Chicago letter was confined to peripheral issues from the start. It was primarily concerned with the city's pattern of intense faculty segregation, a clear violation of well-established legal requirements. The letter spoke vaguely of further federal investigation: "We expect to continue to examine other practices and policies of the board alleged to be violative of the law." Chicago was given a tough two-week deadline after which a lawsuit would be filed.[21]

The Chicago case never came to trial. After the initial publicity, the department did not even file the necessary papers to open a lawsuit. Seven years later, the faculties were still segregated and the Chicago school system was continuing to receive a large amount of federal aid. HEW was forced by a court order to renew action against faculty segregation in 1976. Student segregation persisted.

Justice also became involved in a desegregation case pending in Houston, asking the court to end freedom of choice in the city. The Houston school board produced a voluntary desegregation plan after local moderates and liberals won control of the board in 1969. The plan was for systematic desegregation of faculty and staff but only partial student integration.[22] Although it moved a great many black students out of black schools, the plan was bitterly protested by Chicanos. In it Chicanos were counted as "whites." Often low-income black students were "desegregated" with low-income Chicano students, many of whom had serious problems with the English language. This pooled the children with the greatest educational needs, exacerbating group tension, and left almost all Anglo children in all-white schools. Eventually the Fifth Circuit Court of Appeals ordered a somewhat more demanding plan, but it left a good deal of segregation and ignored the separate claims of the Mexican-American students.[23] By 1977 the city was still offering only a voluntary magnet school solution.

## The Politicization of Justice

The month after the announcement of the administration's new enforcement policy, the Justice Department's efforts were undermined by a sudden

21. Ibid., July 10, 1969.
22. Ibid., March 1, 1970.
23. *Ross* v. *Eckels*, 317 F. Supp. 512 (S.D. Tex. 1970), 468 F.2d 649 (5th Cir. 1972).

shift in the government's position when the administration tried to delay integration in Mississippi. This induced an unprecedented open protest by Justice lawyers, and eventually led to a humiliating defeat in the Supreme Court.

When HEW prepared plans in August 1969 to desegregate Mississippi's last thirty segregated districts that September, the department informed the district court that "each of the enclosed plans is educationally and administratively sound, both in terms of substance and in terms of timing."[24] Suddenly, without conferring with enforcement officials, Secretary Robert Finch took the extraordinary step of asking the court of appeals to delay desegregation and to ignore the plans his department had just submitted. The new policy had been devised by top HEW and Justice officials.

The turnabout produced an immediate storm. The protest, signed by nine-tenths of the attorneys in the Civil Rights Division, condemned abandonment of "clear legal mandates." The lawyers refused to argue the government's case in court or to defend the policy in other pending cases. In some cases they gave data to the private civil rights lawyers opposing the government's position.[25] In the next few days the attorney general attacked his own staff. The head of the Civil Rights Division, Jerris Leonard, insisted that his lawyers get back in line. A leader of the revolt recounted one confrontation. "On October 1st, Mr. Leonard called me to his office. . . . Our obligation was to represent the Attorney General, he said, and John Mitchell had decided that delay was the appropriate course to follow in Mississippi. . . . 'Around here the Attorney General is the law,' he said. The difference of opinion was irreconcilable, and I was told to resign or be fired."[26] Another Civil Rights Division lawyer, John Nixon, resigned, publicly stating that the entire civil rights enforcement staff was being demoralized: "at the present time, there is no leadership in civil rights enforcement. . . . The whole impetus for civil rights enforcement is coming from the line attorneys attempting to push stuff through rather than from any leadership above."[27]

When the Mississippi case reached the Supreme Court, the solicitor general, who normally represents the government before the Court, accentuated the division in the department by refusing to argue the government's side, forcing an inexperienced assistant attorney general to face a

24. Gary J. Greenberg, "Revolt at Justice," *University of Chicago Magazine* (March–April 1970), p. 24.
25. Ibid., pp. 23, 25–26.
26. Ibid., p. 27.
27. *Washington Post*, October 18, 1969.

panel of angry justices. The NAACP Legal Defense Fund attacked in a bitter full-page newspaper ad: "Our Government for the first time . . . has gone to court and asked that school segregation be allowed to continue."[28] For the first time since 1954, Justice officials were seated in federal courtrooms at tables across the room from civil rights lawyers, working with their former opponents.

After the southern courts acquiesced to the delay, the Supreme Court acted with rare speed in hearing the case and handing down a unanimous decision in October 1969 against the Justice Department's position. "Under explicit holdings of this Court," the Court said, "the obligation of every school district is to terminate dual school systems at once."[29] The decision, announced by the chief justice appointed by Nixon, was a direct rebuke to the President, who had recently denounced advocates of "instant integration" as "extremists," and to the department.[30]

Yet weeks later, in a case potentially affecting many segregated systems in Louisiana, Justice again fought for delay. Once again the Supreme Court promptly rejected the department's plea.[31] Constitutional requirements were clear. Further delays in carrying out desegregation were unconstitutional.

The obvious politicization of the enforcement process had challenged the Court. Ironically, the result was a definite stiffening of desegregation requirements.

Unfortunately for civil rights groups, even such clear standards were not self-enforcing outside the school districts named in the cases before the Supreme Court. Nothing would happen in the many other districts in the South under court order until motions were filed asking the district judges to revise the existing orders to end delays. In the weeks that followed the Supreme Court's October decision, the major private group, the NAACP Legal Defense Fund, filed scores of such motions. The government filed none.

The futility of attempting to delay finally led the administration to change its political calculations again. With the blame placed on the courts, administration leaders decided to finish desegregation in the rural South well before the 1972 election. After George Wallace survived an all-out administration effort to defeat him in the 1970 Alabama gubernatorial campaign, it seemed increasingly unlikely that President Nixon would carry

28. Reg Murphy and Hal Gulliver, *The Southern Strategy* (Scribner's, 1971), p. 58.
29. *Alexander* v. *Holmes*, 396 U.S. 19 (1969).
30. *New York Times*, September 30, 1969; *Alexander* v. *Holmes*, 396 U.S. 19.
31. *Carter* v. *West Feliciana Parish*, 396 U.S. 226 (1970).

much of the Deep South in 1972 anyway. Wallace evidently planned to run as an independent and was expected to repeat his successful 1968 campaign there.

President Nixon explained his policy in a statement issued in March 1970.[32] Conceding that desegregation was inevitable in the rural South, he now drew the line at desegregating urban systems through busing. After the President's statement, Justice officials announced that they would press for prompt compliance in the approximately 200 still segregated districts of the rural South and that they were considering filing statewide desegregation cases in five more southern states.[33] Protests from five southern governors soon led to the abandonment of the latter plan, but the administration did take other actions.

A cabinet-level desegregation committee set up under the chairmanship of Vice-President Agnew worked to persuade systems to comply. The pressure from Washington was sufficiently strong and continuous to have some effect. Within two months, for instance, voluntary desegregation plans were submitted by twenty-three of the thirty-two remaining segregated school systems in Arkansas.[34]

When the new school year began, many of the last resisting systems of the southern black belt had desegregated. For a time, the Justice Department was again playing its traditional role.

### The White House, the Supreme Court, and Busing

The drama of the Mississippi case turned public attention to the rural South at the very time urban integration requirements were emerging. Since the late 1960s federal courts in the South had been evolving a legal theory that required southern cities to move beyond the establishment of neighborhood school systems toward actual integration. This was opposed by President Nixon; both he and HEW Secretary Finch criticized court orders for Charlotte, North Carolina, and Los Angeles. Finch denounced them on national television as "totally unrealistic" moves in the "wrong direction."[35]

32. "Statement about Desegregation of Elementary and Secondary Schools, March 24, 1970," *Public Papers of the Presidents: Richard Nixon, 1970* (GPO, 1971), pp. 311–12.

33. *Washington Post*, March 23 and 30, 1970. Accounts of enforcement actions during this period include Rims Barber, "Swann Song From the Delta," and Cynthia Brown, "Nixon Administration Desegregation," both in *Inequality in Education* (August 1971), pp. 4–5, 11–16.

34. *Washington Post*, May 30, 1970.

35. *Washington Post*, April 19, 1970.

The busing issue came to a head legally and politically when the Justice Department acted on major controversies in the Charlotte and Manatee County, Florida, school districts. In Charlotte the dispute was over a countywide desegregation plan that required extensive busing in one of the South's largest urban centers. In Manatee County, Governor Claude Kirk tried to block a busing plan in a small district. In both cases, Justice lawyers argued against busing.

The Manatee County case was largely political. It was an election year and Kirk was one of the few Republican incumbent governors in Dixie. Polls showed him to be in serious trouble. He had dramatically announced he would personally take over the Manatee County school system and ordered school officials to defy a court-ordered desegregation plan. Kirk justified his resistance by revealing that the Justice Department had decided to intervene on behalf of less busing. Rather than prosecuting the governor for defying the judiciary, the Justice Department provided him with a rationale for his action, arguing before the Fifth Circuit Court of Appeals that the Manatee plan was "so extreme as to constitute an abuse of discretion" and that the district judge had erred in requiring the busing of an additional 2,700 of the system's 17,000 students.[36] "In effect," HEW's civil rights director said later, "what it did was to shake Governor Kirk's hand for standing in the doorway and defying compliance of the order of a public court."[37] When Governor Orval Faubus defied a court order in Little Rock in 1957 and Governor Wallace defied one in 1963, Presidents Eisenhower and Kennedy mobilized the executive branch in support of the courts. The Nixon administration, however, gave implicit support to the other side.

This action supported Kirk's criticism, if not his tactics, which, according to the local superintendent, had produced resistance and indecision in a community that had been prepared to accept integration quietly. The case suggested that there might be a great deal to gain politically in defying federal court orders. The courts, however, quickly rejected the Justice Department's position, and Kirk backed down. His antibusing posturing did not salvage his career. The people of Florida turned him out of office, electing Reubin Askew, a supporter of school integration. Justice lawyers had been used in a futile tactic.

The Charlotte (*Swann*) case was far more important. Federal District Judge James McMillan had concluded that the only way to end unconstitutional segregation was to bus some 13,000 additional students in a plan that would establish an approximately equal ratio of black and white

36. *New York Times*, October 13, 1970; *Washington Post*, October 13–15, 1970.
37. *Washington Post*, April 14, 1970.

students in each school in the consolidated city-county system. The case raised the immediate possibility of similar litigation in cities throughout the seventeen southern and border states and directly threatened the President's policy.

When the case came before the Fourth Circuit Court of Appeals in April 1970, Assistant Attorney General Leonard argued against districtwide integration while his predecessor from the Johnson administration, Stephen Pollak, wrote a brief for the National Education Association supporting the other side. The court of appeals was headed by Chief Judge Clement Haynsworth, Jr., whose 1969 nomination to the Supreme Court had been defeated, in part, by criticism of his unsympathetic handling of school desegregation cases.

The Justice Department's position was determined by the President's policy statement on school desegregation, which maintained that neighborhood schools met all constitutional requirements. The Justice brief argued that Judge McMillan was guilty of "an abuse of discretion" in ordering complete desegregation. It asked the court of appeals to order the preparation of a new desegregation plan emphasizing nonbusing approaches such as pairing and clustering and redrawing attendance zone lines. Justice attorneys argued that there was nothing unconstitutional about the continued operation of all-black schools in the ghettos of this overwhelmingly white school district. The department asked the court to consider "whether, for the purpose of achieving a precise, system-wide racial balance, a plan would require a school board involuntarily to make unreasonable increments in transportation expenditures."[38]

Lawyers for the NAACP Legal Defense Fund argued that in metropolitan Charlotte, containing half a million people, busing clearly was a feasible solution. It should not be turned down because there might be special problems in larger cities: "The exceptional problems of the vast ghettos should not be permitted to paralyze rational inquiry about the extent to which substantial balance may be feasible in a particular community."[39]

The court of appeals supported Justice's position. The majority stated: "Some cities have black ghettos so large that integration of every school is an impractical if not an unattainable goal. If a school board makes every reasonable effort to integrate the pupils under its control, an intractable

38. *Washington Post,* April 9, 1970; Memorandum for the United States, *Swann* v. *Charlotte-Mecklenburg Board of Education,* in the Fourth Circuit Court of Appeals, 1970.
39. *New York Times,* May 29, 1970.

remnant of segregation, we believe, should not void an otherwise exemplary plan." The court held that the busing in the original Charlotte plan was excessive.[40] In October, though the desegregation plan was already in effect, the administration asked the Supreme Court for the restoration of some segregated neighborhood schools, holding out the hope that the problem might someday be solved by unspecified private action to change residential patterns.[41]

Civil rights lawyers responded that eliminating identifiable black schools was an essential part of the South's job of breaking up the dual school structure. At least in the South, they argued, the courts had a continuing responsibility to repair the damage created by a history of inequality under the law.[42]

Everyone waited for the Supreme Court's ruling, probably the most important school decision since 1954.

The Court surprised both the administration and civil rights groups with a strong and unanimous decision. In April 1971 it held that southern cities must use all feasible means, including extensive busing if necessary, to create a nonracial school system. The Constitution required "the greatest possible degree of actual desegregation." There was a constitutional "presumption against schools that are substantially disproportionate in their racial composition."

All things being equal ... it might well be desirable to assign pupils to schools nearest their homes.

But all things are not equal in a system that has been deliberately constructed and maintained to enforce racial segregation. The remedy for such segregation may be administratively awkward, inconvenient and even bizarre in some situations and may impose burdens on some; but all awkwardness and inconvenience cannot be avoided in the interim period when remedial adjustments are being made to eliminate the dual school systems.[43]

The Court gave broad discretion to lower court judges to devise appropriate remedies.

40. Swann v. Charlotte-Mecklenburg Board of Education, 431 F.2d 128 (4th Cir. 1970).

41. The department's brief to the Court described the desegregation plan as one providing "a precise, system-wide racial balance" that probably involved "unreasonable" costs. "Thus," the argument concluded, "we think that the question facing this court is whether, in view of ... the circumstances of the case and the alternatives reasonably available, the court below invoked a remedy so extreme as to constitute an abuse of discretion." Pat Waters, "Charlotte, North Carolina: 'A Little Child Shall Lead Them,'" in Southern Regional Council, The South and Her Children (Atlanta: SRC, March 1971), p. 28.

42. New York Times, October 7, 1970.

43. Swann v. Charlotte-Mecklenburg Board of Education, 402 U.S. 1 (1971).

The decisive action destroyed the legal foundation of the administration's urban school policy. Once again, a Justice Department position had been unanimously rejected. "The Supreme Court," the President said, "has acted and their decision is now the law of the land. It is up to the people to obey that law."[44]

At first it seemed that the Charlotte decision might finally have persuaded the executive branch to finish up southern desegregation, treating the cities as the rural areas had been treated. No political restraints appeared in the first two cases litigated after *Swann*, Austin and Nashville. The Nashville plan called for desegregating all but one of the black schools in the metropolitan area by busing 14,500 additional children. Even the long-dormant HEW enforcement program showed signs of activity.[45] The White House, though continuing to criticize busing and to fight against it in the North, seemed resigned to southern desegregation.

Federal courts moved rapidly in several southern states. Large southern cities found themselves suddenly required to establish a level of busing no large northern city had ever adopted. Protests were loud. Texas Republicans were outraged that the administration (through Justice lawyers) was asking a federal judge to adopt a large busing program in Austin. The protests soon had their effect.

### Total Opposition to Busing

Signs of resistance to the courts emerged in August 1971. HEW Secretary Elliot Richardson told a congressional committee that he had instituted a policy giving very low priority to local requests to use federal desegregation aid for busing costs. The administration, he said, would accept an amendment to the Emergency School Aid Act prohibiting the use of federal money for pupil transportation.[46]

In August President Nixon promised all-out resistance to busing. After George Wallace charged that the agencies were defying administration policy, White House Press Secretary Ronald L. Ziegler, speaking for the President, said that officials "who are not responsive will find themselves involved in other assignments or quite possibly in assignments other than the federal government."[47] The 1970 firing of the director of HEW's Office for Civil Rights, Leon Panetta, for overzealous enforcement made the

44. *New York Times,* April 21, 1971.
45. *Washington Post,* May 20, June 2 and 23, 1971.
46. *Congressional Quarterly,* August 28, 1971, pp. 1829–30.
47. Ibid., p. 1829.

threat credible. Coming just weeks before school was scheduled to open in newly desegregated urban districts across the South, it deepened local confusion and uncertainty.

Once again Justice lawyers faced the humiliation of going into court to oppose a desegregation plan (for Austin) HEW had recently submitted. The new approach rapidly affected other school districts. The department successfully appealed for a delay in the Corpus Christi, Texas, plan. In Columbia, South Carolina, HEW ended years of dispute by accepting a plan that allowed the system to retain a number of segregated schools.[48]

Justice continued to argue for the kind of partial desegregation approach that the Supreme Court had rejected in *Swann*. The department's legal theory now was that only individual schools where the civil rights litigants could prove intentional segregation must be desegregated. In large urban systems with hundreds of schools this required gathering evidence far beyond the capacity of civil rights groups or even of the Justice Department.

## Justice Leadership: The Nixon-Ford Period

While the Justice Department had engaged in only a token enforcement effort, it still had a major role to play in the development of desegregation law. Since the beginning it had participated in every significant school case to come before the Supreme Court. And it had a lesser, though important, role to play in setting the tone of national discussion of desegregation. But the department's record in these roles was ambiguous under Nixon and Ford.

Attorneys General John Mitchell, Richard Kleindienst, Elliot Richardson, William Saxbe, and Edward Levi all actively supported antibusing legislation aimed at limiting the power of the courts to enforce the Supreme Court's urban desegregation requirements. They also said, however, that the department would enforce the law.

In the first Nixon administration, the solicitor general was Erwin Griswold, a former Harvard Law School dean and former member of the Civil Rights Commission. It was Griswold who took the unusual step of refusing to defend the attempt to delay desegregation in Mississippi, leaving the case in the hands of an inexperienced assistant attorney general. He did, however, argue for less desegregation in other cases.

When Griswold retired after the 1972 election, he was replaced by

48. *Washington Post*, August 26, 1971.

Robert Bork. Bork, when a law professor at Yale, had worked with the administration in developing its antibusing legislation and had written the only law review article defending its constitutionality.[49] His selection was a clear sign that the department would take a conservative position on school issues before the Supreme Court.

The day-to-day administration of civil rights litigation rested with the assistant attorney general for civil rights. This position went to a Wisconsin politician, Jerris Leonard, in 1969. Leonard saw himself as a "moderate conservative." After his first enforcement activities were bitterly attacked, he was usually careful to conform to administration policy. He tried to delay Mississippi desegregation, attempting to defend the policy shift before an angry Supreme Court, and helped engineer the end of HEW's use of the fund-cutoff machinery of the 1964 Civil Rights Act.[50]

When Leonard left, the White House replaced him with David L. Norman, a skilled career attorney with a conservative approach to the school issue. Norman had done major work in the early voting-discrimination cases but generally was a believer in small government and "cooperation, not coercion" in enforcement. A long-term opponent of plans requiring extensive busing,[51] he is credited with the major development of the school-by-school approach to litigation.

Norman's successor at the beginning of the second Nixon term was J. Stanley Pottinger, who had brought HEW's Office for Civil Rights into conformity with White House antibusing policies. School cases were assigned a low priority under his leadership at Justice, although he occasionally criticized antibusing tactics within the administration.

The rhetoric of Justice Department officials alternately featured promises to respect court orders, assertions that Congress had ample authority to nullify Supreme Court busing requirements, and proud claims that more civil rights progress was being made than ever before. Justice leaders were repeatedly frustrated. The Court under Chief Justice Warren E. Burger continued to reject administration approaches to school desegregation with monotonous regularity. At the same time, Congress rejected almost all of the administration's efforts to enact legislation restraining the courts.

49. *Congressional Quarterly*, December 16, 1972, p. 3135; March 10, 1973, p. 513.

50. Leon Panetta and Peter Gall, *Bring Us Together* (Lippincott, 1971), pp. 294–99, 306–14; John Carmody, "Jerry Leonard—A Team Man in Justice's Civil Rights," *Potomac Magazine* (March 3, 1970), pp. 7–10, 26–30.

51. Ken W. Clawson, "David Norman: 'Man on the Spot' in the Busing Issue," *Washington Post*, August 16, 1971.

The continuing conflicts between law and politics were evident in comments made by Pottinger in May 1974. He told a conference of journalists that busing had been developed as an "emotional and political issue" by northern politicians who "want to survive" in a national climate of resistance to integration. "Busing is not only right legally, but morally and socially." He appealed for an end to the national preoccupation with it.[52]

The same day, President Nixon again stated his "unequivocal opposition to forced busing." After this statement, the executive director of the President's domestic council talked to Pottinger.[53]

A few days later Pottinger told a reporter that he agreed with the President that "busing as the sole tool to deal with equal education opportunities is an unsatisfactory tool. It hasn't worked in the last 20 years." He said that the civil rights fight for busing was "not a realistic response to the problem." In his own mind, Pottinger said, he was undecided. He saw little support for or prospect of actually accomplishing integration in most big cities outside the South.[54]

Justice officials had to walk a constantly moving, perilously exposed tightrope.

## Election Year and the Antibusing Crusade

The White House pressure on the department increased in 1972 after George Wallace's Florida primary victory demonstrated the power of the busing issue. In a nationally televised speech on March 16 the President asked Congress to enact legislation sharply limiting the desegregation powers of the courts.[55]

When the President sent Congress his 1972 bill, it put Assistant Attorney General Pottinger in a delicate position. After refusing to comment for two weeks, Pottinger strongly endorsed the bill, arguing that it would "greatly aid the forward momentum of equal educational opportunity." The legislation, which attempted to prohibit all significant busing, would produce

52. *Washington Post*, May 23, 1974.
53. "Statement about Proposed Amendments to the Elementary and Secondary Education Act, May 22, 1974," *Public Papers of the Presidents: Richard Nixon, 1974* (GPO, 1975), pp. 449–50. *Washington Post*, May 29, 1974.
54. Ibid.
55. The proposals were outlined in "Special Message to Congress on Equal Educational Opportunities and School Busing, March 17, 1972," *Public Papers of the Presidents: Richard Nixon, 1972* (GPO, 1974), pp. 430–31.

valuable "consensus and clarity," Pottinger said, which would enable the Civil Rights Division to move ahead on other kinds of issues.[56]

The President ordered the Justice Department to actively oppose busing plans.[57] Instead of using the department to argue the conservative position on the unsettled issues of constitutional law, he attempted to use the Civil Rights Division as a weapon against enforcement of the settled law. Justice lawyers hired to defend civil rights were put to work on legislation some experts believed to be unconstitutional.[58]

The political issue mushroomed when the suburbs were threatened. In 1972 two lower court decisions opened up the possibility of busing suburban white students into northern ghetto schools. Federal district judges in Detroit and Richmond concluded that plans limited to the mostly black central cities would be charades and that they must therefore order desegregation across school district boundary lines. "Desegregation" of children through a plan that would merely place each child in a 70 percent black school, the judges held, would neither repair the damage done by segregation nor produce a stable integrated community. Civil rights lawyers and judges elsewhere were reaching the same conclusion.

The Richmond decision, handed down in January 1972, concluded that the Constitution required desegregating entire school systems that were racially identifiable. The judge stated that there was nothing immutable about school district lines and that state school officials had often encouraged mergers to improve school opportunities:

School district lines within a state are matters of political convenience. The claim that the defendant counties have a right to keep their separate systems to be utilized solely by residents of the respective counties has little merit in the face of past discriminatory practices on the part of all of the defendants. . . .

The consolidation of the respective school systems is a first, reasonable and feasible step toward the eradication of the effects of past unlawful discrimination.[59]

A similar decision in Detroit, *Milliken* v. *Bradley,* transformed Michigan politics. Within a week protests began in the Detroit suburbs. The highly segregated working class suburb of Warren responded to a hurried call for a day's boycott by keeping 40 percent of the children at home. Politicians immediately reacted. A previous opponent of antibusing legislation, Sen-

56. *Washington Star,* April 2, 1972.
57. *Washington Post,* August 5, 1971.
58. Five hundred law professors signed a letter to this effect.
59. *Bradley* v. *School Board of the City of Richmond,* 338 F. Supp. 67 at 104–05 (E.D. Va. 1972).

ator Robert Griffin of Michigan, who was up for reelection in 1972, announced his opposition to "forced busing."[60] The *Detroit News* described busing as "the issue which tears mothers' hearts out." Griffin successfully appealed to Attorney General Mitchell for Justice Department intervention against the Detroit decision. Soon he proposed a constitutional amendment against busing.[61] George Wallace swept the Michigan Democratic primary after a campaign emphasizing busing.

While the President was denouncing busing and promising restrictions on the courts the Justice Department could hardly appear in court on behalf of citywide desegregation; instead it attempted to minimize busing and proposed that civil rights groups bear a heavy burden of proof of intentional segregation.

Sometimes the arguments turned out to lack legal foundation. Nashville–Davidson County, Tennessee, for example, was a large metropolitan school district that had already begun to carry out an HEW busing plan. When the case came before the court of appeals, the Justice Department asked the court to send it back to the district court because of the "problems and hardships" caused by the plan.[62] Angrily rejecting this motion, the court went out of its way to administer an unusual public rebuke: "We determine that the representative of the Department of Justice had not had the opportunity to read the District Court record in this case."[63] In its haste to enter the case the last day of the hearing, the department had improperly asked the court to consider issues that had not been raised in the trial. The court ruled that the plan was "the first comprehensive and potentially effective desegregation order ever entered" in the protracted Nashville litigation.[64] Low judicial regard for the department's work also appeared in Detroit, where the court rejected one effort by Justice to intervene.[65] These were rare reprimands for a legal staff with a reputation for excellent and careful work.

The department's unusual posture was reflected in other cases. When a district court in *Adams v. Richardson* found HEW guilty of illegally refusing to enforce the 1964 Civil Rights Act, a Justice attorney appeared before all the judges of the circuit court of appeals. He argued that since the President had *proposed* legislation attempting to limit urban desegregation,

60. *New York Times,* October 3, 1971.
61. *Detroit News,* September 29, 1971.
62. *Kelley* v. *Metro Board of Education of Nashville,* 463 F.2d 732 (6th Cir. 1972).
63. *Washington Star,* May 31, 1972.
64. *Kelley* v. *Metro Board of Education.*
65. *Washington Post,* May 10, 1972.

HEW's inaction was justifiable as it was complying with a policy that the President *wanted* Congress to adopt.[66]

The department was operating under political controls so tight that the head of the Civil Rights Division's education section, Brian Landsberg, found that he could not, in good conscience, sign a number of the briefs submitted in major school desegregation cases.[67] This kind of protest has an immediate effect within an agency and on judges experienced in school litigation. The briefs Landsberg refused to sign included by 1974 many of the department's most important cases—the *Milliken* (Detroit) case, three other major cases that had reached the Supreme Court, and five argued before courts of appeals.[68]

### The Effect on the Staff

The political atmosphere had a dispiriting effect on the staff of the Civil Rights Division. A visible result was the resignation of six attorneys. After President Nixon's televised speech in March, one of them, Arthur Chotin, wrote a letter to the *Washington Post* beginning: "As I sit here watching President Nixon make his statement on school busing I am sickened. Sickened because it is the job of the President to unite and lead the nation to the future, not buckle under the weight of political pressure and retreat to a dark and miserable past."[69]

The administration's proposed 1972 antibusing bill also evoked a general statement of opposition by most of the Civil Rights Division's lawyers as well as more specific protests from a group of Justice's black attorneys.

The general protest was a letter to Congress signed by ninety-five attorneys appealing for defeat of the President's antibusing bill. The measure, it said, "would limit the power of federal courts to remedy, through busing, the unconstitutional segregation of public school children."[70]

The argument was stated more forcefully in a bitter open letter to Congress from ten black Civil Rights Division staff members. The lawyers attacked the administration's yielding to "racist pressure groups and political expedience."

Recent developments . . . tell us in no uncertain terms that there are those so

66. William I. Taylor, "The Justice Department and Race Relations," *Integrated Education* (May–June 1974), p. 8.
67. Memorandum from Brian Landsberg to J. Stanley Pottinger, October 12, 1973.
68. Ibid.
69. *Washington Post,* May 10, 1972.
70. Ibid.

Table 10-1. *Caseload of the Civil Rights Division, Department of Justice, Fiscal Years 1973–78*

| Status | 1973 | 1974 | 1975 | 1976 | 1977[a] | 1978[a] |
|---|---|---|---|---|---|---|
| Pending | 692 | 799 | 898 | 915 | 966 | 998 |
| Filed | 209 | 236 | 163 | 198 | 202 | 220 |
| Closed | 102 | 137 | 146 | 172 | 170 | 172 |
| Pending at end of year | 799 | 898 | 915 | 941 | 998 | 1,046 |

Source: *The Budget of the United States Government,* relevant years; *Departments of State, Justice, and Commerce, the Judiciary, and Related Agencies Appropriations for 1978,* Hearings before a subcommittee of the House Committee on Appropriations, 95:1 (GPO, 1977), p. 315.
a. Estimated.

determined to keep the two societies separate and distinct that such traditionally American concepts as the sanctity of the Constitution, the "separation of powers," as well as "oaths of office" will willingly be sacrificed. Quite clearly they, and their unwitting allies, have no qualms about raping the Fourteenth Amendment, prostituting the courts, and defaming the efforts of those who have worked so hard to promote desegregation, including those who have put their economic and political lives on the line.

What we have been witnessing . . . is . . . a camouflaged effort to resurrect the concept of "separate but equal."[71]

It was a low point for the Civil Rights Division. Some staff members resigned angrily, others quietly. Many risked their jobs with open protests.

During this period the education section of the division lost experienced lawyers and had increasing difficulty in recruiting replacements from the country's strongest law schools. A staff that had been at the center of the legal drive for racial justice was now branded as an enemy of the movement. As a result, the division had to recruit from second-level law schools. Education section chief Landsberg said: "Some of our sources have dried up. I think it's a tragedy personally that pro-civil rights people get so carried away with their anti-Nixon rhetoric that they scare people away."[72]

Recruitment problems were compounded by the low priority the division's director and the deputy attorney general's office gave to filling vacancies. Staff size remained static, about twenty lawyers working on all education cases, as the huge caseload grew (see table 10-1). In early 1974 Landsberg described his staff as "very inexperienced," saying that "half of my lawyers have been here less than a year."[73]

Each year the division was less able to manage its backlog of pending

71. *Congressional Record,* April 26, 1972, pp. 14535–36.
72. Interview with Brian Landsberg, April 4, 1974.
73. Ibid.

cases. Even when the Justice Department later requested more staff, it was primarily to handle new functions such as protecting the rights of the handicapped and prosecuting credit discrimination cases.

### Accommodation by the Civil Rights Division

In spite of the uproar, the division did evolve a legal strategy compatible with the President's goals. The basic issues during this period were how much evidence was needed to prove unconstitutional segregation in urban areas and how extensive the remedies must be once segregation was proved. The Justice Department came down strongly on the conservative side of both issues.

Judgments about the amount of proof required to show that segregation is intentional, and thus unconstitutional, must take into consideration legal philosophy, the appropriate role of the courts in a democratic society, practical problems of litigation, and political pressure. Civil rights groups believed these judgments could be speedily made. The courts should recognize society's pervasive racism by accepting evidence on the racial effects of general urban trends as sufficient to show intentional segregation. Court decisions, official reports, and scholarly evidence had clearly established that some housing had been intentionally segregated through governmental action. In virtually every case where there were the resources to investigate the history of a local school board fully, evidence of a policy supporting segregation had been uncovered. To desegregate merely part of a district, they believed, was not only wrong in principle but also impractical, leading to resegregation as white students left for white schools.

The policymakers remaining in the Civil Rights Division saw things differently. Political considerations could not be dismissed. They were painfully aware that the President had broad authority over his legal representatives, that the administration was quite prepared to end careers over the question, that the attorneys general would not fight the White House position, and that there was no substantial local or national political constituency supporting a vigorous program of litigation. Even minority groups were divided.

As the legal counsel for the President, the Justice Department staff is expected to defend the White House position when there is any legitimate way it can be defended. The lawyer's job is not to judge the case, but to search for a rational argument to defend his client. There were major unsettled areas in school law and it was perfectly legitimate for the President to require his attorneys to adopt the most conservative, reasonable legal arguments.

It was a different matter, however, when the administration opposed Supreme Court requirements. When attorneys believed the Justice position was intended to undermine established constitutional principles, they could refuse to sign briefs or ask for another kind of assignment. But the effect of this was limited since their superiors could simply turn the cases over to more conservative, less experienced lawyers who were prepared to accept policy direction.[74]

The spectacle of Justice Department lawyers protesting to the press, signing letters and petitions, and appealing to Congress for defeat of the administration's legislative proposals was astonishing in a city of quiet bureaucracies. Less dramatic, though important, was the more subtle resistance—narrowing the statements of the President's policy, openly informing the courts that the department did not know the facts of a case on which it purported to offer advice, inserting in briefs evidence supporting the other side's arguments, and favoring a stronger desegregation plan in the oral arguments than had been spelled out in the printed briefs.

In general, however, the department did urge the courts to accept a restrictive legal theory. It relied on a school-by-school approach, requiring proof of intentional discrimination at every school in a system before that system could be desegregated. Education section chief Landsberg said this was justified by the political atmosphere of the time: "We have thought that at a time in our history when the very concept of school desegregation is under serious attack it is especially important to establish a strong factual basis for desegregation relief."[75] The Justice Department had been able to use this apparently cumbersome standard to show that every school in some districts was, in fact, intentionally segregated. In the department's first settled case in the North, South Holland, government lawyers developed evidence on the two segregated schools that "was literally student-by-student, not just school-by-school." The evidence was so strong that the department had stood fast in enforcing the court's busing order. Landsberg

74. The differing concepts were clear in an exchange between a dissident lawyer and Assistant Attorney General Jerris Leonard. Leonard asked the lawyer if he could defend "the administration's Mississippi position in future cases," saying that he must represent the attorney general. The lawyer replied: "My oath of office requires that I support and defend the Constitution of the United States and vigorously enforce the civil rights laws." *Washington Post*, October 18, 1969.

75. Interview with Landsberg, April 4, 1974.

claims that the technique did not prevent effective department litigation in Pasadena, California. It was also used in Indianapolis.[76]

It was possible, in other words, to achieve significant desegregation through the school-by-school approach if one had enormous resources to invest in it. The Justice Department's inability in the average year to win even one northern or western case did not negate the legal logic of the argument.

Lawyers defending the administration's position could cite modern legal philosophy for support. The idea of judicial self-restraint, the belief that the judicial branch should use its powers sparingly, deferring whenever possible to the elected branches of a democratic government, was associated with some of the most important jurists of the century, notably Justice Felix Frankfurter. There was also a troubling philosophic question in contemporary civil rights law about the degree to which the courts should depart from the normal individualism of American law to accord minority groups special treatment to remedy past discrimination against them as a group. Justice Department conservatives could argue that they were merely supporting a policy minimizing departures from tradition.

Civil rights groups, however, called the legalistic approach a sophisticated way to make desegregation impossible. Norman J. Chachkin, then the NAACP Legal Defense Fund's principal expert in school law, wrote:

No one should know better than Justice Department attorneys the difficulties of producing direct proof of individual segregatory acts affecting every individual school within a system. Likewise, no one should appreciate better than Justice Department attorneys that inability to make such a detailed showing should not detract from a finding of pattern and practice which justified across the board relief. . . .

With its . . . long experience, surely the Civil Rights Division was aware that as an educational matter, desegregation plans which were not system-wide were unlikely to be successful. Yet, the government advanced and pressed the idea that the remedy for school segregation should reach only those facilities as to which individual acts of discrimination had been shown.[77]

The *Keyes* case, the first northern school case to reach the Supreme Court, illustrated the anomalies of Justice's efforts to foster desegregation and comply with the policy of the President. The department opposed the effort of the civil rights groups to win a broad decision against de facto segregation. At the same time, its school-by-school analysis showed that the lower federal courts should have ordered the desegregation of a somewhat larger fraction of Denver than they did. The Justice brief also dealt

76. Ibid.
77. Letter from Chachkin to J. Stanley Pottinger, October 4, 1973.

with some of the special problems of Mexican-American students that had not been adequately treated in the initial decision.[78] The department was thus simultaneously asking for more desegregation in the local area and supporting the side of the argument that would still integrate only part of the city and put a heavy burden of proof on the private litigants.

The Supreme Court rejected the school-by-school approach in 1973, holding that once there was convincing evidence of intentional segregation in any significant part of a school district the courts must presume the entire district to be illegally segregated unless there was conclusive evidence to the contrary. The decision recognized that segregation in one part of a city had demographic effects on other parts of the city and that without some diminution in the burden of proof little integration would take place. The record of intentional urban segregation was sufficient to justify shifting the burden of proof.

The Justice Department failed to take steps to see that the *Keyes* decision was carried out, unlike its action after the *Green* decision.[79] After *Green*, Landsberg says, "a great deal of our energy went into enforcing what was a fairly clear mandate of the court to complete desegregation of the rural South."[80] Similarly, after the 1971 *Swann* decision the department had pursued desegregation in the urban South until directly forbidden to by the President.

In the year after the *Keyes* ruling, the department held back, filing two urban cases, against Tulsa and Omaha. Since the Tulsa system had historically been a southern-style dual system, the only new effort to enforce the *Keyes* doctrine was the Omaha case. Omaha in 1972 had only 12,000 black students and 1,000 Chicanos, about half of whom were in predominantly minority schools.[81] In addition, the department had broadened the issues in its pending case against Kansas City, Kansas. This, said Landsberg, was all the litigation Justice's available manpower permitted. Two lawyers had worked full time for a year preparing the Omaha case, for example, before it was filed. The next stage had required another year of work by a lawyer and two research analysts.[82]

The net response of the Justice Department to the Denver decision, then, was to bring an action against the nation's fifty-seventh largest school

78. Brief of the United States as Amicus Curiae, *Keyes* v. *School District No. 1, Denver, Colorado* (1973).

79. *Green* v. *County School Board of New Kent County*, 391 U.S. 430 (1968).

80. Interview with Landsberg, April 4, 1974.

81. HEW, Office for Civil Rights, *Directory of Public Elementary and Secondary Schools in Selected Districts, Fall 1972* (GPO, 1973), p. 802.

82. Interviews with Landsberg, April 4, 1974, and April 22, 1975.

system and to modify one pending against a smaller one. If both were eventually won, desegregation of less than 0.4 percent of the nation's black students could be achieved.[83]

Since in *Keyes* the Court had required proof in a "substantial portion" of a district, the Justice Department's chief school segregation experts maintained that school-by-school analysis was still appropriate. This approach led the department to advocate the retention of some segregated schools in Austin.

The school-by-school method made the process of litigating a case immensely time-consuming. For example, the management of the government's role in the Indianapolis case had "tied up one and one-half lawyer-years [annually] almost ever since it was filed [in 1968]."[84] Though the government was advocating more modest change than private groups in Indianapolis, it was investing far more legal time than any private group could afford.


## New Goals Emerge

As with HEW, during the early 1970s the integrationist goals of the Civil Rights Division were displaced by an increasingly diverse set of reform objectives. The education section was dealing with a wide range of issues, including college segregation, discrimination in hiring faculty and staff, discriminatory assignment of children to classrooms for the mentally retarded, equal treatment of the handicapped, and bilingual-bicultural education for linguistic minorities. In 1972 the section was made responsible for fighting sex discrimination in education. Despite all these added responsibilities the education section had the same size staff in 1974 as in the far simpler days of 1969.

The Justice Department reacted to the rise of new social movements, the changed political climate, and the weakened integrationist drive. Justice lawyers, like private civil rights lawyers, became involved in a complex set of second-generation southern desegregation questions, the demands of the Hispanic movement, and other issues. The new issues were not only intrinsically interesting but free of the ugly politics of busing as well.

"As the issues have gotten tougher," Landsberg conceded, "the solidarity of the civil rights movement has just crumbled. . . . Along with the explosion of school law has come a lessening of the effort that goes into any one

83. Data from HEW, Office for Civil Rights, *Directory . . . 1972,* pp. vii, 472, 802.
84. Interview with Landsberg, April 4, 1974.

thing.... We've been guilty of that within the division.... It has resulted in our cutting back the resources that are available for straight black desegregation cases."[85]

Assistant Attorney General Pottinger said that the *Keyes* and *Milliken* decisions created a framework of legal principles that made substantial desegregation possible, but he had decided that his division would assign low priority to enforcing those principles. The case law probably meant that wherever the necessary resources were invested civil rights litigants could get a citywide desegregation plan,[86] but no cases were filed.

The task of enforcing the urban desegregation principles appeared nowhere in Pottinger's 1975 list of priorities for the division. Traditionally the first priority had been remedying de jure segregation in the South, and that continued to receive a great deal of attention. The second priority was to protect other minority groups against discrimination, particularly linguistic discrimination, by special programs, not integration. The third was desegregating faculties, particularly by hiring minority teachers in largely white systems. The fourth was desegregating state colleges and universities in the southern and border states. But northern urban school desegregation cases were initiated rarely and prosecuted cautiously.

Pottinger believed it inappropriate for the Civil Rights Division to attempt to desegregate northern cities. Northern segregation problems, he felt, were "intractable." An "immense effort" was required, and the nation no longer believed that the effort should be made. There was "no pressure ... on enforcement agencies to bring cases." Nor was Pottinger aware of any significant pressure for housing desegregation.[87]

Attorney General Levi viewed the problem from a similar perspective, often publicly criticizing the Supreme Court's busing decisions. He foresaw a much more limited role for the Civil Rights Division. "Today the Civil Rights Division's effort against race discrimination is a more subtle one. Often it is difficult now to show a history of *de jure* segregation, and more importantly, as the quest for equal opportunity becomes more successful, some of the demands of minority groups might, if met, involve unfair deprivations of others. A difficult balance is required." He praised the broadening of the division's work to "other disadvantaged groups within society," mentioning cases on the rights of the mentally ill, treatment of juvenile offenders, nursing home standards, and child placement procedures. He stressed the general need for caution: "As lawyers we must

85. Ibid.
86. Interview with J. Stanley Pottinger, April 22, 1975.
87. Ibid.

know the limits of the law and the fact that other social institutions are sometimes able to do that which law cannot do."[88] Levi was a legal scholar in the Frankfurter mold and a strong conservative on urban desegregation.

When asked about busing on the CBS "Face the Nation" program in December 1975, Levi equivocated. He said that school systems should not "be run by the courts" but defended some busing as the "last remedy" for proven state-imposed segregation. The Justice Department, he said, would ask the courts to reconsider the citywide plans first devised in the 1971 *Swann* case; the approach needed to be "rethought." In response, NAACP Executive Director Roy Wilkins accused Levi of "capitulation": "We find it shocking and unworthy . . . for . . . you, as Attorney General to participate in shaping this strategy of retreat."[89]

### The Development of Education Law

The issues now occupying the Civil Rights Division reflected not only political constraints, but also the trend in education litigation, which was to deal with more and more matters traditionally outside judicial purview. The political frustration of activists in the late 1960s and early 1970s, a new style of public interest law, and the development of specialized law reform groups financed with public funds or foundation grants to develop legal theories and bring test cases brought a smorgasbord of educational issues into the courts.[90] Capable legal representation was available to raise issues ranging from expulsion procedures to school finance. Once lawyers began to probe into the internal workings of schools, they often found discrimination and procedural irregularities. Once the courts or Congress recognized the new rights, activist groups naturally began to demand stricter and broader government enforcement of them.

Activist lawyers were stimulated by their new leverage to deal with abuses that could be corrected by apparently simple means. Handling the case of a Chicano student who was condemned to a school career in classrooms for the mentally retarded merely because his English was not yet

88. Speech before the American Bar Association, Montreal, August 1975; text in *Congressional Record* ( daily edition), January 19, 1976, p. E44.

89. *New York Times,* December 22, 1975.

90. The rapidly expanding scope of education litigation is discussed in a contemporary casebook by David L. Kirp and Mark G. Yudof, *Educational Policy and the Law: Cases and Materials* (Berkeley, Calif.: McCutchan Publishing, 1974). And statistics showed the explosion in litigation—more education cases were filed in federal courts between 1967 and 1971 than ever before. John C. Hogan, *The Schools, the Courts, and the Public Interest* (Lexington Books, 1974), p. 7.

good enough to complete an IQ test rapidly, a lawyer was exposing a procedure educators could not justify.[91] It was not difficult for a court to devise a reasonable procedure limiting the most blatant of such abuses.

Civil rights activists urged HEW and Justice to give higher priority to building into informal school processes legal notions of regularity and due process. The Children's Defense Fund asked HEW to forbid the assignment of a disproportionate number of minority children to "special education programs" and "racial disproportions in suspensions."[92] Other liberal groups, the RFK Foundation and the Southern Regional Council, appealed for action on the issue of "pushouts," or expulsions, of students in recently desegregated systems.[93]

Not only did procedural cases appear to have a better chance of victory, but they were also much more susceptible to traditional legal analysis than the busing cases, which raise complex questions of demographics, politics, and urban development. Procedural requirements that unbiased general rules be established and a proper hearing held applied traditional legal thinking to new issues.

It may be that aiming litigation at such targets indicates a sound understanding of the capacities of courts. One student of law reform efforts observes: "Courts can . . . be of some use in implementing policies that apply principally to government agencies—particularly those policies relating to procedural matters turning on questions of due process. The deeper that it is necessary to penetrate into society, however, the more undependable courts become."[94]

Ultimately, however, procedural victories may be hollow. Even after due process is provided, more black children may still be expelled from southern schools. Even if the tests are given without language bias, more Hispanic children may be assigned to less challenging course sequences because of the weakness of their educational background and the poverty of their families. Equalizing funds for schools may make no educational dif-

91. Henry J. Casso, "A Descriptive Study of Three Legal Challenges for Placing Mexican-American and Other Linguistically and Culturally Different Children in Educably Mentally Retarded Classes" (Ph.D. dissertation, University of Massachusetts, 1973).

92. Children's Defense Fund, *Children Out of School in America* (Cambridge, Mass.: CDF, 1974), pp. 8–9.

93. Southern Regional Council, *1974 Annual Report* (Atlanta: SRC, 1975), pp. 17–18.

94. Stuart A. Scheingold, *The Politics of Rights: Lawyers, Public Policy, and Political Change* (Yale University Press, 1974), p. 130. A similar view is expressed in Abram Chayes, "The Role of the Judge in Public Law Litigation," *Harvard Law Review* (May 1976), p. 1315.

ference. The early victories may have been relatively easy because they were relatively insignificant. Real change may require substantive educational and administrative judgments from the court, which federal judges are understandably reluctant to make.

Desegregation may eventually prove to be a function far more suitable to effective judicial resolution than most in-school issues. It is easily measurable and the official act of assigning particular students to particular schools is concrete and unambiguous. Although it may be difficult for the courts to determine how well desegregation is carried out over the years, it is certainly possible to order that segregation be ended and to fix the responsibility for ending it.

At least for the present, however, the growth of education law has helped legitimate the dispersion of the resources that were once concentrated on segregation. The impact was freely admitted in the Justice Department. The Civil Rights Division's new responsibilities meant that without large additions to the staff the strategy of urban desegregation through litigation would become steadily less realistic. New staff was not provided.

Its limited resources and demanding standards of proof therefore forced Civil Rights Division leaders to judge that the staff's total capacity for handling urban cases amounted to three or four active cases involving school districts with 40,000 to 100,000 students. Since the division's interest in the South continued, it could handle only two or three active cases in the North and West.

Pottinger and Landsberg saw urban cases as a kind of vast open-ended commitment for years of effort, including the tedious job of educating inexperienced judges in the complexities of desegregation law. Even after a judge had accepted proof of discrimination,[95] they pointed out, the process of developing a remedy often took several more years. But if an administration made urban desegregation a top priority, the existing Justice Department staff could not come close to doing the job across the country. Enforcement would probably require the general application of HEW standards for integration, as it had in the South.

### The Department and the Development of the Law

Though Justice could not enforce school desegregation requirements, it could help develop stronger principles of desegregation law. The department carries great influence in litigation, particularly on controversial cases

95. Interview with Landsberg, April 4, 1974; interview of Deputy Assistant Attorney General Frank Dunbaugh on WRC-TV, August 11, 1974.

raising unsettled legal issues. It was well aware of this. Pottinger saw the Civil Rights Division as a powerful "conservative force for change," chiefly focusing on incremental development of the law. The courts respect the department, he said, and "almost invariably agree" with its positions because they know it will "use the massive resources that it has and its incomparable authority" on behalf of a solid conservative position.[96]

During the Nixon period, the department usually did take a conservative position. When there was direct White House involvement it veered to the right; it edged subtly to the left when the Civil Rights Division was given more freedom of action.

Civil rights critics who accused the department of taking illegitimate positions were often wrong. The positions could frequently be defended by plausible legal reasoning. Actually the critics were reacting to a major change in the Civil Rights Division's definition of its constituency. Since the beginning of the Kennedy administration the division staff had defined the civil rights movement as an important constituency which it never directly opposed, though often doing less than the civil rights groups wished. But now the groups had to deal with a "Civil Rights" Division that took a neutral or hostile position on some of the most important unsettled issues of civil rights law, one that increasingly emphasized its role as the representative of a president the groups saw as their leading enemy. The authority and resources provided by the civil rights statutes were being used to slow or reverse civil rights progress.

Watergate clearly demonstrated that there are cases in which the Justice Department must not act merely as the President's lawyer, but must recognize its primary duty to the law and the Constitution. Many civil rights leaders felt this point had also been reached in the area of civil rights law.

Justice officials proffered various rationales. Some department lawyers argued that the courts ought to move slowly to help people understand the history of segregation.[97] Others spoke of careful legal craftsmanship to gradually extend existing precedents, a strategy appropriate to a precedent-based legal system. Caution was defended as a way to avoid defeats. "The thing that hurts desegregation efforts the most," said Landsberg, "is losing a case" so it became essential to "try to make as strong a case as I can on every incident."[98] A similar view had been taken by John Doar, head of the Civil Rights Division under President Johnson.[99] Hostile local courts, in

96. Interview with Pottinger, April 22, 1975.
97. Interview with Landsberg, April 4, 1974.
98. Ibid.
99. Interview with John Doar, June 20, 1967.

fact, sometimes rejected the most moderate and modest efforts to enforce the law.[100] Some federal district judges either could not understand simple principles of desegregation law or were unwilling to apply them. In Austin in 1971, for example, the district judge refused to order any significant desegregation of the city's schools. In October 1974 the department met the same problem in Omaha, where the judge dismissed the case, ruling that Omaha had a neighborhood plan "honestly and conscientiously framed and administered."[101] Courts of appeals eventually reversed both decisions.

Since district judges had wide discretion and the issues were volatile, these problems could recur. Erroneous decisions could be reversed through appeal, but the process placed a heavy additional burden on the department. To minimize the risk, the department overprepared its cases, often using the legal standards of the district judges most hostile to civil rights as its minimum standard. Existing resources made it impossible for the department to win more than a few cases this way.

Thus the Justice Department cases commonly rested on legal theories that did nothing to advance the state of the law. Intensive investigations permitted judges to decide cases without raising new legal issues. The department was engaged in neither a significant enforcement process nor a major effort to develop the law. It was operating a program of symbolic enforcement and marginal legal development.

The advances in legal theory that did occur were subtle and usually specific to the case at issue. In Indianapolis, for example, the department rejected the broad metropolitan approach favored by the local district judge but did not foreclose the possibility of some desegregation outside the central city school district in the special local circumstances. In his oral argument, the Justice attorney took a marginally stronger position than had the brief.[102]

In most cases, though, any real breakthrough on the principles of urban segregation would have to come through private litigation and the decisions of federal judges, often against Justice opposition.

### Nonenforcement of the 1964 Act

As all these limitations became evident, the old idea that the Justice Department could replace HEW in enforcing the 1964 Civil Rights Act was

100. Leon Friedman, ed., *Southern Justice* (Pantheon, 1965), pp. 260–68.
101. *Race Relations Law Survey*, vol. 3 (1971), p. 94; *New York Times*, October 16, 1974.
102. Interview with Landsberg, April 4, 1974; interview with Craig Pinkus, attorney for the intervening plaintiffs, March 20, 1974.

discarded. The attorney general and the secretary of HEW, in announcing the new strategy in July 1969, had said that the Justice Department would file lawsuits against districts flagrantly violating HEW's desegregation standards. Justice officials had insisted that the alternative procedure would be workable. They were wrong.

A bureaucratic ritual had been devised in which HEW would turn case files over to the Justice Department. This procedure had been followed for several northern cases during the Johnson administration and had led to the filing of the first northern lawsuits in the Nixon presidency. Eventually, however, HEW and Justice developed a procedure limiting the number of cases referred by HEW to the attorney general's office.[103] Unless private litigation against a school system had already begun, the case was not sent to Justice unless the department agreed to accept it. After early 1971 no more northern cases were referred.[104] HEW would not enforce the law and Justice could not, partly because of the way it had complicated the task.

The HEW-Justice relationship was largely meaningless after mid-1971. The Justice Department was initiating no new northern or western cases, and HEW's enforcement machinery had been cranked up for only one district, Boston, where its focus was primarily on language discrimination with a narrower attack on the racial implications of different grade structures in the black and white sections of the city.[105] After the courts ordered HEW to resume enforcement, most of its efforts were limited to tangential issues. Justice's only significant move was to file a lawsuit against Ferndale, Michigan, the small Detroit suburb with one segregated school that had defied HEW and where segregation persisted after funds were cut off in 1972.

Desegregation critics, however, tried to limit the department's role even more. Senator Robert Dole of Kansas attempted to amend Justice's appropriations bill for fiscal 1976 to prohibit the department's participation in litigation to remove children from their neighborhood schools. The amendment, which would have precluded not only litigation requiring busing but also most other segregation remedies, was tabled by a narrow seven votes.[106] The next year it appeared again.

Justice officials claimed their minimal enforcement merely reflected

103. U.S. Commission on Civil Rights, *The Federal Civil Rights Enforcement Effort—1974,* vol. 3: *To Ensure Equal Educational Opportunity* (GPO, 1975), pp. 129–30.

104. Ibid.; interview with Peter Holmes, director of HEW's Office for Civil Rights, February 21, 1975.

105. Interview with Martin Gerry, September 10, 1974.

106. *Congressional Record* (daily edition), September 3, 1975, p. S15160.

public opinion. Pottinger saw support for integration as continuing to decline.

The busing issue, having cracked the coalition, forced a lot of people who would have been for busing in the North to look for other problems to solve. As a result, now we are dealing with a proliferation of issues, not just busing, in an atmosphere where the pressure is essentially off. . . .

It's because that pressure is gone that you find a different kind of atmosphere operating in the executive branch, and in Congress, and I think in the courts.[107]

Pottinger later tried to qualify his remarks, saying that Justice would not "decide whether or not to get into a case on the basis of whether congressional pressure exists." He said, however, that though he no longer faced "committee hearings, criticism speeches, letter-writing, pressure on enforcement officials," Congress was now pressing the opposite way.[108] There was almost no political support for enforcement.


## Justice and the 1976 Campaign

By the time the 1976 campaign began, HEW and the Justice Department had almost completely withdrawn from the enforcement process in the cities and Congress had put restraints on future HEW activity. Attorney General Levi had avoided much of the partisan involvement in the busing question that had characterized several of his precursors in the Nixon administration. Only two northern cities faced new desegregation plans in the fall, and the primaries showed that the issue had little prominence anywhere but in Boston.

This relative calm disappeared in May when there was a policy dispute in the Justice Department. Solicitor General Bork had long been critical of extensive busing and had been watching for an opportunity to bring his views on the proper limits before the Supreme Court. Bork drafted a brief asking the Court to hear the appeals of the Boston plan and summarizing the Justice Department's view on the need to reduce busing. Pottinger argued strongly against such action.[109]

When the pending action became public, civil rights groups and high-ranking black Republicans Senator Edward Brooke of Massachusetts and

---

107. *Washington Star,* October 8, 1975.
108. *Washington Star,* October 20, 1975.
109. *Washington Post,* May 18, 1976.

Transportation Secretary William T. Coleman, Jr., appealed to Attorney General Levi not to deepen division in the nation's most racially polarized city. Roy Wilkins wrote to the attorney general: "Seeking Supreme Court review of a case of a record so marked with defiance, recalcitrance, and violence by school officials and street mobs practically insures continued undermining of the judicial process."[110] Senator Brooke cited the danger of "violence in my city" and argued against "retreat in the face of lawlessness."[111]

Although Attorney General Levi opposed Supreme Court review of the Boston case, he said that the department would recommend limiting busing if the Court took the case. The Court did not. At the same time, President Ford directed Justice to continue searching for an appropriate case. The President said that he had also told Justice officials to quickly develop new antibusing legislation to try to limit court orders.[112]

Both the President and GOP challenger Ronald Reagan emphasized the issue repeatedly near the close of the 1976 Republican primaries. Reagan renewed his call for a constitutional amendment and antibusing legislation. The Republican platform echoed Reagan.[113] President Ford met with the attorney general and other advisers to discuss legislation to limit busing to parts of cities. He told newsmen from Ohio (where the primary was only days away and several cases were pending) that his legislation would restrain the courts. The courts had erred, Mr. Ford said, in "taking over a whole school system, as the courts did in the Boston case and several others."[114]

Critics of Justice's role in the process argued that both the Supreme Court brief and the proposed legislation involved futile challenges to settled constitutional doctrines. The Justice Department had filed suits based on essentially the same arguments when the Court was considering the Charlotte and Denver cases. Each time the department's position was rejected. Black columnist William Raspberry, a frequent critic of busing, now criticized the department's role as intentionally misleading and politically inspired.[115] Finally, when the Austin case was awaiting possible

110. *New York Times*, May 17, 1976.

111. *Washington Star*, May 19, 1976.

112. *Washington Post*, May 30, 1976.

113. GOP Platform, in *Congressional Record* (daily edition), September 2, 1976, p. H9475.

114. *New York Times*, June 3, 1976.

115. William Raspberry, "Mr. Ford's 'Alternatives' to Busing," *Washington Post*, June 4, 1976.

Supreme Court review, the department filed a brief, reiterating its philosophy of school-by-school analysis.[116]

President Ford's new antibusing bill went to Congress with the attorney
general's support on June 24, 1976. It was far too late in the year for any
serious consideration and Congress did not even hold hearings on the
measure. It was, however, submitted in plenty of time to have an effect on
the President's contest with Ronald Reagan for GOP conservative support
at the party's August convention. The bill proposed that court orders be
dissolved after three to five years, permitting extensive resegregation, and
that the Justice Department be allowed to go into federal court on the side
of school districts trying to get out from under existing court orders. It suggested limiting the courts to school-by-school remedies, attempting to accomplish by legislation a Justice Department preference the courts had
rejected.[117] It proposed minimal temporary desegregation, primarily around
the boundaries of ghettoes and barrios. Once again, the Justice Department
had been mobilized to join in an antibusing crusade.

## Transition and the Carter Administration

In his successful pursuit of black support in the primaries and in the fall
election—he received 94 percent of the black vote in November[118]—Jimmy
Carter often promised unprecedented black representation in the cabinet.
It was widely speculated that he might name the first black attorney general. Few agencies had been so disappointing to blacks in recent years as
the Justice Department and few offered such prospects for sudden change
in an administration with little money for new social programs.

No nomination, however, was as bitterly criticized by black leaders as
Carter's choice of Atlanta attorney Griffin Bell as attorney general. Much
of the congressional fight over Bell concerned his record on school desegregation. He had helped design Georgia's 1959 "massive resistance" laws permitting the closing of schools to resist integration. He had helped formulate

116. Brief for Certiorari for the United States, *Texas Education Agency (Austin
Independent School District)* v. *United States,* October term 1976, No. 76-200.

117. *Congressional Record* (daily edition), June 24, 1976, pp. S10471–77. The bill,
S3618, was titled "School Desegregation Standards and Assistance Act of 1976."

118. *Washington Post,* November 11, 1976, estimates of the black vote based on a
national survey.

strategies to limit Atlanta desegregation and had served on a state commission which denounced the 1954 *Brown* decision.[119]

As a member of the Fifth Circuit Court of Appeals, he cast the deciding vote and wrote the 1963 opinion limiting integration in Atlanta.[120] When civil rights lawyers brought the case back to court after the 1971 *Swann* decision, asking that citywide desegregation be ordered, Bell intervened again. Although he was not hearing the case, he helped engineer a negotiated compromise solution, leaving the schools overwhelmingly segregated in exchange for transferring more administrative jobs to blacks.[121] The NAACP denounced this agreement, but the Georgia court denied their efforts to intervene and the compromise stood. Jimmy Carter frequently cited it as a model solution.[122]

Civil rights organizations attacked Bell's civil rights decisions in the Fifth Circuit during his confirmation hearings, and their evidence was persuasive to a number of senators. Senator Charles Mathias of Maryland said Bell's record was certainly not favorable and could be seen as "designed to retard the march of the law toward equality and justice." Another opponent, Senator Donald Riegle of Michigan, commented: "I expected an Attorney General that could unite us as a people. . . . Griffin Bell's nomination is greatly deficient in this respect." Senator William Proxmire saw "nothing in his record to show that he will be the kind of champion of civil rights that the principal law-enforcement official of the Federal Government must become." Senators John Chafee and Jacob Javits agreed.[123] A number of prominent Republicans claimed that Democratic liberals were voting for Bell only because of party ties and that a similar nominee from a Republican president would have been defeated.[124]

Several of his liberal supporters conceded that they were concerned and urged approval only because of promises made during the controversy. Senator Birch Bayh, who led the floor battle, cited Bell's "specific pledges of strong enforcement of civil rights laws."[125] In its editorial, the *Washing-*

119. Details of record recounted in *Congressional Record* (daily edition), January 25, 1977, pp. S1301–06.

120. *Calhoun* v. *Lattimer*, 321 F.2d 302 (5th Cir. 1963).

121. *Congressional Record* (daily edition), January 25, 1977, p. S1301.

122. "What Carter Believes: Interview on the Issues," *U.S. News and World Report* (May 24, 1976), pp. 22–23.

123. *Congressional Record* (daily edition), January 25, 1977, pp. S1296, S1308, S1312, S1321, S1328.

124. See, for example, comments of Senators Robert Dole and Edward Brooke, ibid., pp. S1314, S1337.

125. Ibid., p. S1298.

*ton Post* thought Bell's selection of a black federal judge, Wade McCree, Jr., as solicitor general, was a good sign.[126] Edward Kennedy told the Senate that he had asked numerous questions about civil rights and received specific commitments from Bell that "he would personally insure vigorous enforcement of the Federal civil rights laws and the Constitution."[127] Bell was eventually confirmed 75–21, but it was by far the most controversial nomination to the new cabinet.[128]

Criticism from blacks flared up again when President Carter named Pittsburgh Mayor Peter Flaherty deputy attorney general. When the Pennsylvania Human Rights Commission had ordered desegregation of Pittsburgh schools in 1971, Flaherty had actively fought busing, saying that "this community is against it" and it "cannot be enforced." He told the school board:

The people of this City have made it clear that they want their neighborhood schools preserved. . . . The bond which parents have for their children and the natural concern of parents for the safety and well-being of their children cannot be overcome by any social reform.[129]

The NAACP criticized the appointment before it was formally announced, but White House Press Secretary Jody Powell dismissed the complaint. "The President is aware of those feelings. And, as I understand it, that opposition is based on Flaherty's opposition to busing, a position the President shares and made very clear during the campaign."[130]

The civil rights groups gained little support in the Senate, but Senator Javits did obtain unusual agreements from Flaherty: that he would defer to the assistant attorney general for civil rights on the busing issue and that he would "vigorously enforce the law in all areas, including school desegregation, regardless of his personal views."[131] He was confirmed 87–4.[132]

Contradictory impulses in the administration were evidenced, however, by both the appointment of Judge McCree, a strong school integration supporter, as solicitor general and the naming of Drew Days III, a black lawyer who had managed school cases for the NAACP Legal Defense Fund, as head of the Civil Rights Division. Days had won some of the broadest

126. *Washington Post,* January 25, 1977.
127. *Congressional Record* (daily edition), January 25, 1977, p. S1309.
128. Ibid., p. S1345. A Louis Harris Survey of May 19, 1977, showed that Bell was the least popular member of Carter's new cabinet.
129. Statement to Pittsburgh School Board, May 16, 1972, reprinted in *Congressional Record* (daily edition), April 5, 1977, p. S5538.
130. *New York Times,* March 10, 1977.
131. *Congressional Record* (daily edition), April 5, 1977, p. S5542.
132. Ibid., p. S5543.

metropolitan desegregation orders in the country in Florida. When anti-busing leader Senator Joseph Biden attempted to obtain commitments from the two nominees, he failed, and he opposed their confirmation.[133]

Days compounded the confusion with a series of vague statements that seemed to affirm the previous administration's school-by-school policy. "If there are limited violations shown," he said, "I would hope the courts will not necessarily conclude that a systemwide desegregation plan is neces- sary."[134] His interview with the *Chicago Tribune* carried the headline NEW RIGHTS CHIEF WON'T PUSH BUSING. He described himself as "neutral" on bus- ing. He opposed complete racial balancing of school systems and found the assumption that a good plan must eliminate all predominantly black schools "basically patronizing."[135] At the same time, however, he asked public officials to stop attacking busing and favored a more positive Justice De- partment stance. His sharp differences with his predecessors were most apparent when he was asked, "Do you feel there have been any cases where courts have perhaps gone too far with busing?" He said simply, "No."[136]

The direction the new administration would take remained unclear throughout the first months. No new urban school cases were filed, no positive civil rights legislation was introduced, and the administration did not ask Congress to repeal the various antibusing measures that were ham- stringing executive branch enforcement. On the other hand, there were a move toward more supportive briefs and a brief effort to revive HEW's enforcement program by administrative rulings. The new administration had no strategy for desegregating the nation's cities, but it was prepared to defend and perhaps gradually expand existing legal principles. That in itself was a substantial change.

During its first months, the Carter administration submitted briefs to courts of appeals on two leading metropolitan cases, Wilmington and Indianapolis, and on Austin, and to the Supreme Court on important cases from Dayton and Detroit. Although there was no clear break with the legal principles of the Nixon-Ford Justice Department, they were usually applied in a manner supporting more desegregation. The pattern was clearest in the Supreme Court submissions.

The district court in Dayton had made few findings of de jure segrega- tion because the judge had then believed that little proof was needed to justify a citywide remedy. Now that the Supreme Court had made clear

133. *Congressional Record* (daily edition), March 9, 1977, p. S3819.
134. *New York Times,* March 18, 1977.
135. *Chicago Tribune,* April 11, 1977.
136. Ibid.

that more was necessary, Justice had to choose between recommending limited desegregation and urging the Court to take note of additional evidence that might justify a broad remedy.

The brief was the strongest affirmation of urban desegregation submitted by the Justice Department in years. Endorsing the principles of the *Keyes* decision, the department asked the Court to sustain the existing Dayton order without requiring further proceedings. Though conceding the inadequacies of the lower court conclusions, the Justice brief marshaled evidence from other parts of the trial record to show "pervasive racial discrimination with persistent effects" in Dayton. If the Court was worried about white flight, the brief argued, it would be better to order the development of specially attractive education in desegregated schools than to limit desegregation.[137]

The second important 1977 brief submitted to the Supreme Court supported a significant expansion of judicial power to foster successful desegregation. In Detroit the courts had ordered the state government to help pay for a variety of special education and teacher training programs intended to make the entire process work better. The State of Michigan claimed that the district judge had exceeded his authority. The Justice Department, however, defended the plan, arguing that segregation "often has pervasive effects on the educational process" and justifies educational remedies.[138]

The Supreme Court unanimously upheld educational remedies in Detroit.[139] Although the Dayton case was sent back to the lower courts for further evidence, the unanimous decision did not abandon the doctrines of the *Keyes* case.[140]

The Justice briefs in the courts of appeals were a somewhat mixed bag. In the Austin case, the department offered no comfort to antibusing forces. It argued that, although the court of appeals had previously erred in making a broadside attack on the neighborhood school system, there was ample proof that children in the major Mexican-American barrio had been intentionally segregated and a broad remedy should therefore be imposed.[141]

The briefs for Indianapolis and Wilmington were far more cautious on

137. Brief for the United States as Amicus Curiae, *Dayton Board of Education* v. *Brinkman*, No. 76-539, April 1977.

138. Brief for the United States as Amicus Curiae, *Milliken* v. *Bradley*, No. 76-447, March 1977.

139. *Milliken* v. *Bradley*, 45 U.S.L.W. 4873 (1977).

140. *Dayton Board of Education* v. *Brinkman*, 45 U.S.L.W. 4910 (1977).

141. Brief for the United States, *United States and Overton* v. *Texas Education Agency* (Austin), in the Fifth Circuit Court of Appeals, March 23, 1977.

the issue of metropolitan desegregation. In Indianapolis, Justice said, there was not yet sufficient proof of de jure segregation to justify compulsory busing of children across district lines. It recommended prompt desegregation in the central city, in spite of a judicial finding that this would accelerate white flight, and only voluntary desegregation in the suburbs.[142]

In Wilmington, where the Supreme Court had already sustained the finding that the state had violated the Constitution, the department faced the pressure generated by Senator Biden, who had been national chairman of the Carter campaign. On the other hand, conditions in Wilmington were favorable for a successful metropolitan approach. The total metropolitan area was smaller and had fewer students than a number of single districts that had already desegregated. A plan limited to the central city was unrealistic when the city's school population was only about one-sixth white.

The department's brief claimed that the lower courts had ordered too much desegregation and supported the development of a less stringent plan. Although it called the district court order "in large part appropriate," it also criticized the court's assumption that the predominantly black schools of the central city could not be desegregated without "a substantial injection of whites." The government asked the Court to specifically reject the goal of racial balance and yet provide "a substantial inter-district remedy." In other words, the court was told to cut back its existing order somewhat but not too much.[143]

In 1977 the federal courts handling cases in St. Louis and Cleveland invited Justice to participate, and in each case the department intervened on behalf of a citywide desegregation plan in the predominantly minority central city. The department argued in the Cleveland case that the Supreme Court's ruling in Dayton should not limit the Cleveland plan—a stand that was acclaimed by black leaders. In Kansas City, Kansas, the department appealed a district court plan that called for limited desegregation.[144]

The department's role was changing from that of an opponent of existing school desegregation law to that of a defender of basic rulings; sometimes it advocated less far-reaching plans, other times it called for extensions of the law, at least in relatively noncontroversial fields like the provision of

142. Statement of Position for the United States, *United States and Buckley* v. *Board of School Commissioners of the City of Indianapolis,* in the Seventh Circuit Court of Appeals, March 21, 1977.

143. Brief for the United States as Amicus Curiae, *Evans* v. *Buchanan,* in the Third Circuit Court of Appeals, March 18, 1977.

144. Department of Justice press release, August 10, 1977; *New York Times,* June 23 and August 16, 1977; *Cleveland Press,* August 16, 1977.

funds for educational programs supporting desegregation. It was a major change but not one likely to substantially increase the integration of urban schools.

The briefs were complex and technical and received little public attention outside the communities directly affected. The only Justice initiative that was widely publicized and closely followed in Congress was the effort to revive HEW's enforcement program.

Assistant Attorney General Days concluded that HEW could still require reorganization of nearby schools through pairing or clustering, even if the indirect result was to make some busing necessary. He argued that unless HEW retained some kind of enforcement authority the courts might hold the entire Byrd amendment unconstitutional.[145]

The policy was short-lived. Before HEW had time to begin action under the ruling, both houses of Congress voted to change the law. The House acted within days. There was no word from President Carter on the new antibusing language. In the Senate the battle was much closer—an amendment maintaining the status quo failed by only four votes.[146] It was a stormy initiation for those hoping to involve the executive branch in desegregating the schools.

After eight years in which the Justice Department had often helped lead the opposition to large-scale school desegregation, no one could say quite where it was going. Certainly the mood had changed and attacks on the courts had ended. But school integration was not an administration priority, and no general policy for urban integration had been devised. The issue, it seemed, would be largely left to the courts, with modest assistance from Washington.

145. Memorandum from Days to Attorney General Bell, undated; reprinted in *Congressional Record* (daily edition), June 28, 1977, pp. S10909–10.

146. *Congressional Record* (daily edition), June 28, 1977, pp. S10918–19.

# 11

# The Limits of
# Private Enforcement

THE FAILURE of federal officials during the Nixon and Ford administrations to enforce the legal principles of Supreme Court decisions requiring desegregation in northern and western cities left most of the burden of litigation on private civil rights organizations and individual lawyers. In the cities there was little voluntary local compliance with the law—nothing like that in the border states after the 1954 *Brown* decision. Civil rights groups faced not only a staggering burden of complex and expensive litigation, but also opposition that was frequently led by the nation's chief law enforcement official, the President. In a number of the most important urban school cases, the Justice Department was their opponent. From their standpoint, it was much worse than the neutrality of the 1950s.

Suits were filed by a variety of groups, ad hoc coalitions, and individual lawyers—NAACP chapters, lawyers cooperating with the Legal Defense Fund, local legal services lawyers, lawyers from American Civil Liberties Union chapters, volunteer attorneys serving local groups, the Harvard Center for Law and Education, the Mexican-American Legal Defense and Education Fund, the Center for National Policy Review, and many others. Most of the cases proved time-consuming and expensive. None of the groups had much money, nor was there a coherent national strategy.

## Can Private Enforcement Work?

In the first ten years after the 1954 decision the school desegregation battle in the South tested the capacity of private civil rights lawyers to enforce a bitterly resisted social change. A small group of capable civil rights lawyers working under the leadership of the NAACP Legal Defense and Education Fund filed hundreds of desegregation cases. In case-by-case litigation, they were up against not only well-financed and determined opposition but also ingenious state and local resistance schemes, endless delays, and ineffectual decisions.

The lawyers' effort was prodigious but the results were meager, although eventually they did manage to eliminate the unconstitutional "massive resistance" laws in most states. The desegregation process began in the larger districts. The pace accelerated slightly after the neutral Eisenhower administration was replaced by a supportive Kennedy government, but only about one black child in fifty was in a desegregated school after ten years. When the 1964 Civil Rights Act was passed, most school districts were still completely segregated and judges were still ordering plans calling for token integration of one grade a year to be carried out over a decade or more.[1] Black children continued to be assigned to all-black schools unless their parents defied threats and intimidation to ask for a transfer. Jack Greenberg, director of the Legal Defense Fund, summarized the situation: "Of thousands of school districts, there were but a few hundred cases. No formula could have desegregated these districts until civil rights lawyers became available to press cases there. That was impossible until 1964 when the Civil Rights Act provided additional enforcement personnel through the Departments of Justice and Health, Education, and Welfare."[2]

The difficulties of case-by-case private enforcement led the NAACP and congressional civil rights supporters to seek executive branch enforcement. This was the issue in the most important congressional civil rights struggles of the 1950s. The 1964 Civil Rights Act accomplished this goal.

The enforcement of the 1964 law broke the logjam of resistance. By the end of the Johnson administration most of the rural South was desegregated and executive branch initiative had stimulated much tougher judicial requirements. Even when the Nixon administration ordered the federal agencies to stop active enforcement, the Supreme Court was able to preserve the momentum of change in the rural South by stepping in decisively against retreat.

1. For descriptions of the judicial struggle during this period, see Jack W. Peltason, *Fifty-Eight Lonely Men* (Harcourt, Brace and World, 1961), and Reed Sarratt, *The Ordeal of Desegregation* (Harper and Row, 1966), pp. 209–20.

2. Jack Greenberg, Letter to the Editor, *New York Times Magazine* (November 3, 1968), p. 16.

## The NAACP

A 1962 federal district court decision desegregating the schools of New Rochelle, New York, stimulated interest in northern school cases. Local NAACP chapters, which often led demonstrations and political struggles for school integration, favored lawsuits. Much of the burden fell on the small legal staff of the NAACP. When the activist phase of the civil rights movement began in the early 1960s, segregated schools were the most important target of many of the urban NAACP chapters. The issue was raised in scores of cities and led to important test cases. At the NAACP 1961 national convention the local units were directed to work to "ensure the end of all segregated public education in fact or by law by all means available."

In early 1963 the organization reported action on this issue in "more than sixty-nine cities in fifteen states." Across the country twenty-one lawsuits had been filed against segregated urban schools, eighteen of them by the NAACP. These included important cases in Gary, Indiana, and Kansas City, Kansas.[3]

In the early litigation the hope was for a rapid extension of the principle of *Brown* to northern schools through a finding that all segregation was unconstitutional, regardless of its origin. The *Brown* decision's condemnation of the harm done to black students by segregation encouraged NAACP lawyers to believe that, if they could show similar harm as a result of northern policies, the courts would act. It was a high-risk strategy and it failed. Between 1963 and 1966 the NAACP lost its cases against Gary, Kansas City, and Cincinnati in lower federal courts.

NAACP lawyers believed they had proved intentional segregation by Kansas City in setting attendance boundaries and approving transfer policies that intensified segregation. The court disagreed. In Cincinnati they tried another strategy, introducing proof that the schools were unequal. But expert testimony about unequal programs and facilities and their psycho-

---

3. *Bell* v. *School City of Gary*, 324 F.2d 209 (7th Cir. 1963), *cert. denied*, 377 U.S. 924 (1964). *Downs* v. *Board of Education of Kansas City*, 336 F.2d 988 (10th Cir. 1964), *cert. denied*, 380 U.S. 914 (1965). See also Robert L. Herbst, "The Legal Struggle to Integrate Schools in the North," *Annals*, vol. 407 (May 1973), p. 47; June Shagaloff, "Public School Desegregation in the North and West," NAACP memorandum, January 1963.

logical and educational effect on children was in vain. The judge dismissed the case.[4]

The northern drive stalled. The Supreme Court refused to hear a case from a northern or western city until it finally decided the *Keyes* case in 1973, nineteen years after *Brown*. The lower courts, it appeared, would act only when the NAACP could provide incontrovertible proof of intentional, broad discrimination by school boards. Finding such evidence about the intentions of past school board members was almost impossible. Although they may have been well aware of racial patterns and of the racial implications of their zoning, site selection, transfer policy, and other decisions, they rarely discussed them in public. A clear pattern of decisions that had intensified segregation usually emerged, but they were not the kind of thing explicitly noted in the board's minutes.

### The NAACP Legal Staff

An angry dispute within the NAACP, which ultimately resulted in the dissolution of the legal staff, was touched off by a young NAACP lawyer's article on the Supreme Court in the *New York Times Magazine* of October 13, 1968. The article, "Nine Men in Black Who Think White" by Lewis Steel, infuriated many NAACP leaders and prominent supporters. It stated that the Supreme Court continued to treat blacks as "second-class citizens," delaying enforcement of civil rights. "Never in the history of the Supreme Court," said Steel in describing the school cases, "had the implementation of a constitutional right been so delayed or the creation of it put in such vague terms." He charged the Court with ducking the difficult urban issues of housing segregation and northern school segregation: "the Court refused to review a series of conservative lower court decisions which upheld what school officials described as accidental segregation in Gary, Ind.; Kansas City, Kan.; and Cincinnati. As a result the schools of the North have become segregated faster than Southern schools have been desegregated."[5]

When Steel was fired, the controversy divided normal allies. Lawyers for the American Jewish Congress, for example, charged that Steel had distorted the Warren Court's favorable record. An American Civil Liberties Union official, on the other hand, called Steel's analysis "correct and valuable." Jack Greenberg said, "We have felt that the Court has played a

4. Herbst, "Legal Struggle," p. 51.
5. Lewis M. Steel, "Nine Men in Black Who Think White," *New York Times Magazine*, October 13, 1968, pp. 56, 112, 115.

courageous role in freeing this nation from the shackles of a racist past."[6] Civil rights groups were eager to avoid alienating either the Court, before which they must argue cases, or the contributors who helped finance litigation. Some civil rights activists also believed that Steel was wrong and that the NAACP had failed to develop cases sufficiently for Supreme Court review.

NAACP General Counsel Robert Carter and the other lawyers threatened to resign unless Steel was reinstated. After a long and acrimonious dispute, the NAACP board stood firm. All the lawyers quit.[7]

The fight dissipated the only group in the country experienced in northern school litigation (the NAACP Legal Defense Fund, an independent organization, focused its resources on the South) at a time when the initiation of the Justice Department's northern litigation and the rulings in a number of lower court cases suggested the possibility of greater success. Aside from the work of the NAACP, only one other urban school case—brought by local civil rights activist Julius Hobson in Washington, D.C.—had been completed in the entire country from 1966 to 1969.[8]

## The NAACP Legal Defense Fund

The development of urban desegregation law had to come for a time from cases brought to the Supreme Court by the NAACP Legal Defense Fund, which began as the legal arm of the NAACP but in 1956 became a separate tax-exempt organization with its own leadership. The LDF brought the first major southern city case against Charlotte, North Carolina, which led to the 1971 *Swann* decision for citywide desegregation. Then in 1973, the LDF victory in *Keyes* relaxed the standards for proving de jure segregation outside the South.[9]

The LDF had compiled an excellent record in managing hundreds of southern cases. It was responsible for some important early northern cases, including those in Denver and Las Vegas, and for part of the Detroit case.

6. Letters from Will Maslow, Leo Pfeffer, Martin Garbus, and Jack Greenberg to *New York Times Magazine*, October 27, 1968, pp. 21, 24, and November 3, 1968, p. 16.

7. *New York Times*, October 15, 16, 21, 27, and 29, November 20, 24, and 28, December 10 and 14, 1968.

8. Herbst, "Legal Struggle," p. 52. *Hobson v. Hansen*, 269 F. Supp. 401 (D.D.C. 1967), aff'd sub nom. *Smuck v. Hobson*, 408 F.2d 175 (D.C. Cir. 1969).

9. *Swann v. Charlotte-Mecklenburg Board of Education*, 402 U.S. 1 (1971); *Keyes v. School District No. 1, Denver, Colorado*, 413 U.S. 189 (1973).

It had long been considered one of the best staffed and best run civil rights organizations in the country.

By the end of 1972 the LDF had some 1,200 cases on its docket and approximately twenty-three full-time lawyers. But it handled only a few northern and western school cases, which, although they helped develop legal principles, probably had at best a marginal impact on achieving urban desegregation. It had a substantial national budget, drawing funds from a number of foundations and individuals, but relatively little of the money was available for the direct costs of litigation. Donations have not kept pace with rising costs in the recession and inflation of the 1970s.

In the years after the 1954 decision, the small LDF staff in New York and the cooperating attorneys in the South had one principal mission—southern school desegregation. The load of school cases was heavy as district after district went through the legal mill. The entire staff was involved, and there was no division or indecision about what needed to be done.

The unity of the civil rights movement and its liberal constituency against southern school segregation was shattered when the issue moved north. As the busing controversy erupted in the intellectual community and even some black leaders voiced doubts, there was far less incentive for an organization to make a heavy commitment of its resources to school litigation. Thus the priority of the issue declined as the cost and difficulty of pursuing each case were multiplied by the need to prove intent and to devise a remedy in a complex urban setting. It was easier and more popular to invest resources in cases on job discrimination, housing segregation, voting rights, affirmative action, capital punishment, and other issues that unified the LDF's constituency and staff. As the recession of the 1970s deepened, the job issue became the first priority, and the LDF played an increasingly unimportant role in enforcing urban desegregation.

The initial plan had been for a much larger role. For example, after the 1973 *Keyes* victory strategy sessions were held to work out "criteria for selecting which Northern school districts to pursue in the wake of Denver." The sessions had reportedly concluded: "One clear limitation on litigation targets is size. Cities larger than Denver would overtax the Fund's limited resources."[10] There was a plan, though, to sue as many as thirty-six smaller cities over a period of several years.

Although in *Keyes* the Supreme Court had eased the burden of proving intentional segregation, civil rights litigants still had to gather as much and

10. *Equal Justice* (LDF newsletter), August 1973, p. 1.

as detailed evidence as possible—a demanding task. The LDF was considering further litigation to try to move toward a more explicit "effect-oriented, not intent-oriented rule."[11]

The staff talked about starting litigation promptly in half a dozen cities, with emphasis on places of moderate size whose racial composition permitted "a workable desegregation plan." An experienced local attorney would spend all his time handling the litigation and helping the community organize for integration. But new funds were not found, and the drive never began.[12] Such failure to raise special funds partially explained the LDF's unwillingness to develop cases, but it was also explained by the shift in priorities.

Although the LDF was one of the few legal resources available to apply the Supreme Court's school decisions across the country, its staff conceded that it could do little to enforce *Keyes*, that it had no enforcement strategy, and that its primary role was in developing legal principles. James M. Nabrit III, associate counsel and second-ranking officer of the LDF, saw it as "continuing to be a law-making role rather than an enforcement role," not filing "dozens of cases." The *Keyes* decision, Nabrit said, "nailed down" the tendency of the lower courts to hold school boards responsible for practices resulting in segregation. There were many communities where the necessary proof could be obtained, but somebody else would have to do it. The LDF was "not geared up for major enforcement of northern school desegregation."[13]

The LDF approach, as described by Nabrit, was to have "enough cases so that the natural legal issues arise." The idea was not "to concoct any elaborate theories in advance" but to try to figure out "how to get the job done" in the case. The organization's role in enforcement was limited to trying to enforce the law in the cases it had already filed.[14]

Some LDF officials were not convinced that solutions through litigation were possible. Even a case such as the one in Denver, a relatively small northern city, Nabrit said, was almost unmanageable. The group had been involved in long, frustrating, and often unsuccessful litigation in some of the South's leading cities, including Atlanta, Houston, and Miami, none of which were ever thoroughly desegregated under a citywide plan.[15]

11. Ibid.
12. Ibid.; interview with James Nabrit III (associate counsel of the LDF), February 8, 1974.
13. Interview with Nabrit.
14. Ibid.
15. Ibid.

The limited resources of the LDF were already heavily engaged in managing southern urban desegregation plans. In 1972–73, for instance, it was active in litigation in Richmond, Memphis, Atlanta, Tulsa, Houston, Fort Worth, Norfolk, Oklahoma City, and other southern and border state school systems. In other southern cities it fought the way desegregation plans were being implemented, trying to prevent various forms of segregation in nominally integrated schools.[16]

The LDF did not expand its modest docket of northern school litigation. This tendency was confirmed by the outcome of the *Milliken* case in Detroit, which left the staff pessimistic about the possibility of finding practical plans for big cities. In the four years after *Keyes* the LDF filed no new northern school cases in any city bigger than Springfield, Illinois.[17] After Springfield desegregated in September 1977, it had no new cases pending.

### NAACP Leadership Again

In the early 1970s a new NAACP legal staff responded to renewed demands for school cases from a number of local chapters, usually limiting its role to consultation and paying for outside legal help.

The pace accelerated after the Supreme Court's 1971 *Swann* decision, and the NAACP began to win northern cases. By 1974 it was involved in cases in Michigan, Ohio, and elsewhere. Its general counsel, Nathaniel Jones, was a principal attorney when the Supreme Court heard the *Milliken* case.

The courts, said Jones, had begun to modify their position in 1970 and 1971, showing growing willingness to accept the NAACP argument that "schools do not and would not become segregated without the indispensable help of government action or inaction." A 1970 decision in Benton Harbor, Michigan, was the first breakthrough. In rapid succession came cases in Pontiac and Kalamazoo, in which the federal judges held government officials responsible for the consequences of inaction in the face of spreading segregation. There were also early signs that the courts might order school desegregation based on evidence that housing was intentionally segregated by official policy.[18]

The NAACP concentrated on the Midwest because the Sixth Circuit

16. "LDF Annual Report: NAACP Legal Defense and Educational Fund, Inc., 1972–73 Annual Report on Services to the People of the United States," p. 4; interview with Norman Chachkin of the LDF, February 8, 1974.

17. Telephone interview with Drew Days III at the LDF, April 22, 1976.

18. Nathaniel R. Jones, "Brown—20 Years Later," *Crisis* (May 1974), p. 153.

Court of Appeals was more favorable than other appellate tribunals and because publicized lawsuits in the region generated demands for litigation from other cities. Three of the early suits were filed in the late 1960s after local governments had reversed previous decisions to integrate. In Kalamazoo and Dayton, new local boards rescinded earlier plans. The Michigan legislature blocked the desegregation plan in Detroit.

Pressure to file cases in other communities in the Midwest soon involved the NAACP in five major cases in Ohio (Cincinnati, Cleveland, Columbus, Dayton, and Youngstown). In the final weeks of 1973, the group filed suit in Cleveland, where 56 percent of the 76,000 students were black, more than nine-tenths of them in segregated schools. The racial identity of the schools was reinforced by intense faculty segregation. When the outgoing school board in Cincinnati adopted a plan to desegregate the almost half-black school system, only to have it promptly rescinded by the new board, the NAACP filed suit in May 1974. A week later it sued Youngstown.

The NAACP would have filed many more cases in response to local insistence if it had had the necessary funds. Money was so short, however, said Jones, that he had to tell local chapters that requested help or had already filed cases that they must first raise funds.[19]

### Problems

The lack of money was not the only constraint on pursuing school cases. As part of an organization serving more than 400,000 members, the NAACP lawyers are pulled in many directions. Local chapters demand litigation in fields like employment discrimination, segregation in the armed forces, and police harassment. In late 1974 only one NAACP lawyer was working full time on school litigation; General Counsel Jones devoted a mere fraction of his time to it.[20]

NAACP leaders also had to deal with internal problems. One was the "Atlanta compromise," a deal in which the Atlanta NAACP chapter dropped its desegregation suit when the school board agreed to turn over a number of top administrative posts to blacks. (Both President Carter and Attorney General Bell were involved and have praised it as a model solution.) Although the city's overwhelmingly black enrollment limited the possibility of desegregation within the city limits, the compromise was cited

19. Interview with Nathaniel Jones, November 16, 1974. See also *Crisis*, February 1974, pp. 60–61, and August–September 1974, pp. 243–44.
20. Interview with Jones; comments by lawyers and consultants working on NAACP litigation.

by conservatives as a harbinger of things to come as the commitment to integration declined. The national organization denounced the local action and threw out the leadership of the local chapter.[21]

Other conflicts came from an angry organizational battle over the choice of a leader to replace long-time Executive Director Roy Wilkins, from financial problems so severe that the continued existence of the organization was in doubt, and from labor disputes in the headquarters staff.

There was also some rivalry between the NAACP and the Legal Defense Fund for primary credit for desegregation litigation. Days before the twentieth anniversary of the *Brown* case, for instance, Roy Wilkins issued an angry memorandum charging the media with giving too much credit to the LDF. Wilkins reminded the media that in 1954 the LDF had been just a component of the NAACP and that the NAACP had made the policy choices leading to *Brown*.[22] On a less lofty level, however, attorneys from the two organizations often cooperated on cases. Both groups recognized the primary claim of the NAACP to northern litigation.

## Other Organizations

Although the NAACP and the NAACP Legal Defense Fund sponsor much of the urban school litigation carried on by the private civil rights organizations, the American Civil Liberties Union has become an increasingly important sponsor of school litigation. The ACLU usually concentrates on civil liberties but sometimes takes on major civil rights cases. Its local chapters, which have considerable autonomy, have taken the lead in some areas but done nothing in others. Sometimes the organization shares the burden with other groups.

The ACLU was active in the early 1970s in a number of the first cases in the North and West. Several volunteer attorneys in Denver managed the first phase of the *Keyes* case. In New York and California local chapters took part in the lawsuits overturning state antibusing laws. In New York City the group sought integration of Queens, which still had a white majority.

The strongest impact of the ACLU on school desegregation has been in California. The largest ACLU case was *Crawford* v. *Board of Education of the City of Los Angeles*,[23] filed by volunteer counsel recruited by the

21. Jones, "Brown—20 Years Later," p. 154.
22. "NAACP Strategy Caused 1954 *Brown* Edict," *Crisis*, August–September 1974, p. 239.
23. This case was originally filed in 1963 and in 1977 was still pending in California state courts. The most recent decision is Minute Order, No. C822854, July 5, 1977.

Southern California Civil Liberties Union. In Santa Barbara, the Southern California chapter filed a brief supporting the school board's desire to implement a desegregation plan that conflicts with the antibusing provision in the state constitution. The group also participated in litigation in San Diego and Pasadena.

The New York Civil Liberties Union was active in two cases. The more important was desegregation litigation in Buffalo. In New York City, the organization challenged the city when it rescinded a neighborhood integration plan.

In Prince Georges County, Maryland, the ACLU won orders for desegregation of the sprawling suburban system. In the South, it played a role in litigation in Miami, Atlanta, Austin, and Louisville. The Illinois chapter sued the Waukegan school district. The Delaware chapter took part in the Wilmington metropolitan litigation. The organization led the desegregation movement in Seattle.[24]

ACLU involvement is not always seen as an unmixed blessing by the civil rights groups. While the local chapters can mobilize resources not available to the national civil rights litigators in some cases (drawing on a constituency of skilled white liberal lawyers), they may occasionally run against the grain of whatever fragmentary litigation strategy has been evolving by consensus among the small group of civil rights professionals. Thus, for example, the lawyers from the major groups were unhappy when the Atlanta ACLU chapter pushed forward with a metropolitan desegregation case after the defeat in Detroit. They believed that litigating a case involving a large metropolitan area with sparse resources before a conservative court invited further tightening of the strictures of the Supreme Court's metropolitan decision.

Local ACLU volunteers showed signs of growing interest in the school issue in 1976. At the ACLU's biennial conference spontaneous interest produced an unscheduled workshop which led to resolutions urging increased activity by the national organization, both in fighting antibusing legislation and in filing cases. The national office later began to work on community organization and assisting local groups.[25]

Another group that has played a role in litigation is the Center for National Policy Review at the Catholic University of America School of Law in Washington, D.C., a private, foundation-funded organization developed to monitor civil rights enforcement. Its director, William Taylor, a major theorist of metropolitan litigation, has been particularly active in the

24. *Civil Liberties* (December 1971), p. 11; ACLU Docket, 1974, "School Desegregation," 27,000 series; *Seattle Times*, June 11, 1977.
25. *ACLU* (newsletter of National Capital Area Chapter), July 1976, p. 4.

Richmond, Wilmington, and Buffalo cases. The center also prepared a report on HEW's failure to enforce the 1964 Civil Rights Act in the North, and it has participated in litigation aimed at forcing HEW to enforce the law.[26]

Finally, an important legal resource for representing the rights of the poor has been the 300 local programs supported by the Legal Services Corporation, one of the surviving fragments of President Johnson's War on Poverty. Legal services lawyers took the leadership in some early California cases, in litigation in El Paso and Dallas, and in a number of other cases. The Harvard Center for Law and Education, a "backup center" intended to do research and provide assistance to local offices, became actively involved in the controversial Boston and Detroit cases. Congress outlawed such activity by the legal services offices, however, forcing them to try to find other counsel for minority children in the cases they had already started. If they could not, the corporation ruled, the legal code of ethics obligated the attorneys to continue to represent their clients. Even this shrinking residual role—involving twelve cases—was strongly attacked during congressional consideration of the 1977 legal services bill.[27]

## The Lack of Coordination

A variety of groups active in the same field of litigation at the same time naturally face problems of coordination. Some of the national organizations are really only decentralized confederations of local groups. No one group has the money, the administrative structure, or even the desire to coordinate all the school cases. No one group even maintains a list of all the cases. Some civil rights lawyers are, in fact, ideologically opposed to national coordination, believing that their primary duty is to try to right the injustices affecting their local clients, raising whatever legal issues might help win the case. Another incentive for uncoordinated activity is organizational competition. Organizations receive funds, for example, at least in part because of perceptions of their relative importance and effectiveness. Obviously an organization, or even an individual, leading the way toward a major legal breakthrough is likely to gain both recognition and increased support.

The tendency toward fragmentation is principally restrained by the division of the actual work on many major cases among several members

26. Center for National Policy Review, *Annual Report,* August 1974.
27. *Congressional Record* (daily edition), June 27, 1977, pp. H6547–50.

of the small pool of lawyers who know the issues and work on them regularly. Those most active in federal court litigation tend to remain in contact with each other and exchange information, at least once cases get to the court of appeals level. (This is not necessarily the case for the lawsuits and administrative enforcement actions brought under state law.)

So cases are begun ad hoc, often on local initiative. A suit is filed and tried in a district court or a state court, and the record is shaped, often with little development of the kind of evidence that will be important in the higher courts. When it seems evident that a case may become the basis for an important appellate decision—a lawmaking case—the leading national civil rights lawyers may attempt to establish relations with the local lawyers that will permit them to shape and argue much of the appeal.

This is a delicate and not always soluble problem. In Indianapolis, for example, a metropolitan case with a unique legal setting attracted the interest of national organizations, but local attorneys wanted neither to relinquish the case nor to do much work on it.

The Indianapolis case was first filed by the Justice Department. When the department failed to press the metropolitan issue, the judge granted the request of two local lawyers to intervene on behalf of the black children. At the same time a loosely knit coalition of teachers, the League of Women Voters, other women's group members, clergy, and academics worked on developing a metropolitan plan, "Quality Integrated Education for Marion County."

At this point it became for civil rights lawyers a major test of metropolitan desegregation.[28] But the case went to the court of appeals with little input from any attorney with real experience in school desegregation cases except for Justice Department lawyers, who took an ambiguous position. The local NAACP lawyers reportedly refused to tell their local allies what they were doing. A supporting attorney was told nothing except the date and time of the scheduled hearing.[29] Since the local lawyers would not permit outside preparation of the case, the national experts had no opportunity to develop the record, the briefs, and the proposed remedies in ways likely to produce extensions of important principles of case law.

The local coalition of desegregation supporters eventually submitted an *amicus* brief in the lower court litigation, written by a young volunteer, Craig Pinkus, which heavily influenced the decision. When the time came

28. Interview with Chachkin; interview with David Kirp, former director of the Harvard Center for Law and Education, March 22, 1974.
29. Interview with Craig Pinkus, volunteer attorney for the Marion County coalition, April 20, 1974.

for appeal, Pinkus had to deal with a poor trial record. Ironically, it was possible to draw up a substantial appeal brief only because the threatened suburbs had retained an astounding total of thirty-five lawyers for the trial. Each tried to show the court why his or her suburb should be left alone while others desegregated. In the process of fighting each other they inserted in the trial record voluminous data that later permitted civil rights groups to raise major appeal issues.[30]

The Indianapolis story illustrates some of the weaknesses in the system of case-by-case enforcement that make it extremely difficult to develop a comprehensive national strategy through litigation. The lawyers are not all closely associated with one organization that is paying the costs. Inexperienced lawyers are centrally involved in many of the cases. The litigation tends to "grow" rather than to develop in logical fashion. Accidental factors such as the availability and interest of skilled lawyers can be decisive. Cases often develop in localities where segregation has become so intense and suburbanization so far advanced that there is no good remedy within the city.

Anyone can file a lawsuit by typing up a few simple papers and paying the necessary fees. There is no assurance that a lawsuit reflects any thought-through policy, that those filing it will be able to prosecute it, or that a victory will influence anyone outside the immediate locality. The resulting court order may be shortsighted and self-defeating.

In view of the many obstacles to making and enforcing public policy through private litigation, the accomplishments of the private groups have been considerable. Private litigation by the NAACP Legal Defense Fund won Supreme Court approval of urban desegregation requirements against Justice Department opposition. Litigation has kept the issue alive and has desegregated more urban children than the actions of HEW and Justice combined. Nonetheless, it is expensive, slow, and unpredictable, especially in the lower courts. It is impossible to nationally enforce a controversial policy against active opposition without far greater resources than civil rights groups possess.

Frustrated by their limited gains, the major civil rights organizations worked together on a 1975 lawsuit to make HEW enforce the 1964 Civil Rights Act in the North. The groups had reached the same conclusion their predecessors had about the South in the mid-1950s—the only way there could be more than token change was through executive branch enforcement. This time, however, there were differences. In the mid-1950s it had

30. Interview with Pinkus.

seemed unlikely that Congress would ever pass a law requiring action from HEW and Justice. In the mid-1970s, on the other hand, that law was already on the books but it seemed unlikely that the President would decide to enforce it. Civil rights advocates struggled to obtain an order compelling administrators to enforce the law even as Congress moved to repeal some of its provisions.

Once again, the court decision went against HEW, but the victory was an equivocal one. The district court found HEW guilty of failure to enforce the 1964 law and ordered the agency to promptly begin bringing cases to a close within fixed time limits.[31] Under this directive HEW insisted on faculty desegregation in some cities and pushed bilingual education requirements. It continued, however, to avoid urban plans that required substantial busing; this was reinforced by the passage of restrictive legislation in 1976 and 1977. Thus in spite of an important legal victory, the burden of urban desegregation remained on the private groups.

## Money

Money has consistently been a problem for the private civil rights groups. The NAACP has been especially squeezed.

Though many local school boards view the NAACP as a large and powerful organization, it is a fragile and precarious structure that must patch together funds and promises to keep its existing cases in federal court. It can still threaten to bring new cases, as General Counsel Jones did in Chicago in July 1976,[32] but it simply lacks the money to carry through. Barring a major turn of fortune, the NAACP effort will shrink. Since it is the dominant organization active in the field, this means that the entire movement will slow.[33]

### The Costs of Litigation

Few kinds of legal action approach the complexity and cost of urban school cases. Researching the history of a city's school system may require the examination of hundreds, even thousands, of school board decisions made over many years. Lawyers must try to track down and question pos-

31. *Brown* v. *Weinberger*, 417 F. Supp. 1215 (D.D.C. 1976).
32. *Chicago Daily News*, July 26, 1976.
33. The NAACP calculated that it would cost $750,000 to sue the Chicago school board. No one had even estimated the cost of a metropolitan case.

sible witnesses and locate and analyze voluminous old records, clippings, and other sources. Usually they also gather detailed information on the educational and physical differences between the city's white and minority schools. The analysis must be sufficiently well-grounded to offset the special knowledge and access to records of school officials and their lawyers.

Since district judges are seldom familiar either with the constitutional law of school desegregation or with the racial history of the community on which they must sit in judgment, the task of persuading them to order major changes in local schools requires lengthy trials and much expert testimony. Trials in big cities frequently require copious and expensive records. Merely printing the record of the *Keyes* case cost the NAACP Legal Defense Fund more than $35,000.[34]

In the South, where the schools had been officially segregated by state law until 1954, the history of violation was clear and the remedy often simple. In most of the rural cases desegregation could be achieved simply by ordering the school district to send all black and white students to the closest school. There were almost no cases where Anglo-Latino-black desegregation was necessary.

In the North and West, proving the violation has been an arduous task, heavy even for HEW with its large staff of investigators. HEW officials estimated that it took 10,000 hours of staff time to develop and prosecute the case against the small suburb of Detroit, Ferndale.[35] If a private organization invested similar resources, even charging a modest rate for the legal time, the cost of eliminating discrimination would be prohibitive.

When the NAACP decided in 1950 to launch a broad long-term assault on the "separate but equal" doctrine, it set aside $150,000 for the entire campaign.[36] In those days this was enough to attack the nation's long-established doctrine in race relations law, financing the development of all the cases through the Supreme Court level. But the cost of the first stage of a large city case in the 1970s may exceed the total NAACP budget for all the cases leading to the *Brown* decision, particularly if one considers the value of the time donated by local counsel.

An example of this is *Crawford,* the original Los Angeles trial in the California state court system, which was handled by ACLU volunteers. Filing the case was delayed for years because the Southern California branch of the ACLU had difficulty locating a volunteer able and willing

34. Interview with Nabrit.
35. Interview with Roderick Potter (attorney for HEW), September 23, 1968.
36. Daniel M. Berman, *It Is So Ordered* (Norton, 1966), p. 29.

to do it.[37] Finally a leading Beverly Hills law firm offered its services. The firm was involved from the 1966–67 school year through a 1976 state supreme court decision.

When the case was tried before the municipal court, the firm's senior partner, Bayard Berman, worked in court for more than sixty-eight days and two associates reportedly worked for at least twelve hours a day, seven days a week, throughout the trial.[38] At the firm's normal billing rates, the bill for Mr. Berman's services alone would have been $65,000 or more for the trial. At least $25,000 worth of the firm's attorneys' time was invested in preparing the appeal brief, a document of 446 pages. In addition, the firm absorbed substantial out-of-pocket costs for secretarial services, copying, and other items.

Even so, the firm had to cut corners. Early in the trial, for example, it had no funds to pay for the high-priced copies of the previous day's proceedings, useful in planning courtroom strategy. Eventually the ACLU raised a donation for this.[39] More serious was the inability to bring in national specialists as witnesses or to devise sound desegregation objectives that could be built into a strategy for trying the case. The legal burdens of the case and the finite resources of the law firm precluded careful consideration of such important issues as housing segregation and the demographic patterns of the community. The debate centered around a plan calling for systemwide racial balance simply because the school system insisted that no other approach would work. No serious analysis was made of this proposition. Lawyers were fully occupied proving a history of de jure segregation and rebutting the contentions of the Los Angeles school district.

When the first phase of the case was won, after two lower court decisions and the state supreme court's decision that the district had violated the state and federal Constitutions, it merely set in motion the second phase of the action, the remedy hearing. To handle this, the ACLU had to find another volunteer lawyer, Edward Medvene. Medvene, who had had no experience in this kind of litigation, had to counter the resources of the school system and its lawyers. This stage involved litigation as complex as that of the proof stage. It raised a multitude of educational, administrative, social, and political judgments difficult for the lawyers to deal with. By the time the court devised a plan for the city, the social composition of the city might have changed so much since the beginning of the litigation a decade earlier that only a metropolitan approach would work.[40] Judge Paul Egly ordered the participants to submit a brief on the metropolitan approach in July 1977.[41]

Desegregation litigation handled without large amounts of civil rights group resources or legal services staff time has usually been through the voluntary labors of a law firm or an individual attorney. (If one was not available, the schools remained segregated.) In Minneapolis, for instance, the case was filed by a volunteer, Charles Quaintance, Jr., formerly an attorney with the Justice Department's Civil Rights Division who had handled the government's case in Pasadena before entering private practice.[42] Since the school board wanted to desegregate and did not appeal the first decision, the work was less overwhelming.

In Denver, vital work in developing the case was done by Gordon Greiner, normally an antitrust lawyer. In Boston, the prime mover was the Harvard Center for Law and Education, but a major firm devoted most of its pro bono time to the case, providing a full-time attorney, John Leubsdorf.[43] In Indianapolis, much of the work has been handled by three volunteer attorneys.[44]

### Financial Problems: The NAACP

The civil rights movement has always been in financial trouble, but the 1970s were particularly difficult for the groups most important in bringing cases to enforce the requirements of *Keyes*. During a period when some of the major civil rights organizations of the 1960s ceased to operate and when huge financial judgments against the NAACP were ordered by Mississippi state courts, the NAACP strained to the limit trying to support an expensive program of unpopular litigation.

Although the NAACP has more than 400,000 members, its national

40. Interview with Rintala; telephone conversations with Edward Medvene, April–June 1977.
41. *Los Angeles Times,* July 9, 1977.
42. *Minneapolis Tribune,* August 11, 1971.
43. Interview with John Leubsdorf, August 5, 1974.
44. Interview with Pinkus.
In many places where desegregation might be feasible no case has been filed. In other communities the lawyers who filed a case and received the early publicity never took the case to trial or, if they did, performed badly. David L. Kirp, "Multitudes in the Valley of Indecision: The Desegregation of San Francisco's Public Schools" (unpublished paper, 1975), p. 121, quotes San Francisco attorney Ben James: "Here I am, handling a divorce today, a drunk driving case tomorrow, and in between a major civil rights case."

budget is surprisingly small. Its total income in 1972 was $1.7 million, $300,000 of it from federal grants for day care centers and other programs not related to specific civil rights objectives. Litigation was financed from the additional $2 million the NAACP raised for its Special Contribution Fund, a tax-exempt mechanism used also to support NAACP programs for education, housing, youth activities, training, discrimination in the military, voter registration, and other activities. Most of the organization's non-tax-exempt funds were devoted to supporting the elaborate structure of local branch organizations.[45]

The national organization could control local cases only if it was financing them. Local chapters lacked the resources to support urban cases adequately. The insistence of the local demands and the desire to be responsive in a membership organization led to overextension of litigation commitments and involvement in cases with little potential either for stable desegregation or for developing new legal principles.[46]

The Detroit case, though it raised important issues, was a financial morass for the NAACP, costing several hundred thousand dollars even though it received extensive free legal counsel from the Harvard Center. The organization had still not paid the attorneys involved almost a year after the Supreme Court argument. Delay in paying consultants was even longer. The burden grew after the Supreme Court assessed $20,000 court costs because the NAACP lost the case.[47]

When the NAACP received a special half-million-dollar grant in 1974 from the Ford, Carnegie, and Rockefeller Brothers foundations specifically for its northern school litigation program, the bills from Detroit were still stacked up on Jones's desk in New York. The grant was intended to finance two dozen school cases for two years and to ease the financial burden of the Detroit case.[48] Initially it and other support enabled the NAACP legal programs to continue to operate rather than to expand. Jones used some of the second installment of the foundation money to pay the most pressing old debts.[49]

Even with the grant, Jones said, the group would be fortunate to be able to handle the cases already filed. There was no chance, he believed, of nationally enforcing the *Keyes* decision through private civil rights litigation.

45. *Crisis* (June–July 1972), p. 212.
46. Interview with Jones.
47. Ibid.
48. *Crisis* (October 1974), pp. 285–86.
49. Interview with Jones.

In 1975 there was another in the organization's history of financial crises. About a quarter of a million dollars in debt and under heavy pressure from its creditors, the group could not pay its utility and travel bills.

The NAACP had always found some way out of its previous crises, but its problems were compounded by defeat in a Mississippi court. An August 1976 decision by the Hinds County Chancellery Court ruled that the NAACP was guilty of conspiracy in a 1966 boycott by the local branch against white merchants in Port Gibson, Mississippi. The court awarded the white merchants $1.25 million. Under state law, the NAACP had to post a bond of $1.56 million if it wished to appeal the ruling. The organization already had posted more than a quarter of a million dollars in bond money in the county to appeal an earlier ruling that the organization had libeled a white policeman.

The ruling, said Jones, "threatens to put us out of existence."[50] The NAACP sharply cut back its staff and launched an emergency fund-raising drive, which produced enough loans and donations to cover the bond. Eventually the bond was lowered by a federal court decision.[51] Nonetheless, the case continued to imperil the national organization and to absorb energies and funds. Jones estimated that it would require five years of litigation.[52]

A 1977 NAACP report showed that local chapters had some involvement in about fifty cases. Chapters wishing to file new cases were told to raise their own funds. The difficulty of completing the cases already in court was compounded by the Supreme Court's 1977 decisions laying a heavier burden of proof on civil rights lawyers.

### Financial Problems: The LDF

The LDF is neither a rich nor a large organization. As it works on more and more issues, its accomplishments in any given field necessarily diminish. Its reported income in 1970 for all purposes was $3.15 million; in 1971 it was $3.85 million; and in 1972, $4.16 million. In each year, the organization ran a deficit.

Although the budget sounds substantial, most of the money was not spent on civil rights litigation but on training programs, fund raising, community service work, and special projects. Foundation grants were used

50. *New York Times*, August 12, 1976; "NAACP Statement on the Mississippi Boycott Case," *Crisis* (October 1976), pp. 265–66.
51. *Washington Post*, October 21, 1976.
52. *New York Times*, October 21, 1976.

to establish new activities, not to assist existing programs. In 1971 the budget for litigation was $1.68 million; in 1972, $1.74 million;[53] and in 1975, $2.27 million, of which only $0.6 million was devoted to all school cases in the North and the South.[54]

Only one LDF lawyer, Norman Chachkin, was working full time on school desegregation in 1974. After Chachkin left, his successor, Drew Days III, worked only part of the time on school cases. Other litigation had far higher priority.

## The Role of the Foundations

The major civil rights organizations financing school desegregation litigation receive contributions from many individuals but are largely dependent on the grants of a few of the nation's largest private foundations. The late 1960s and the first half of the 1970s were a poor time for the growth of individual contributions but a period of rapidly rising costs, both through inflation and through the increased complexity of the urban issues in the North and West. This has made the decisions of the large foundations all the more important.

Integrationist organizations have been caught between the traditional conservatism of most foundations and the tendency for liberal foundations to give school integration a low priority and to divide diminishing resources among a constantly growing number of competing organizations and constituencies.

The foundations with a record of interest in race relations have emphasized research and education rather than litigation. While some research grants are useful in the general maintenance of organizations, they can be mixed blessings. They may fragment the time and attention of the top leadership without directly contributing to the organization's original mission.

Grants to the NAACP Legal Defense Fund, for example, helped draw the group into setting up a poverty law program and organizing a sizable division concerned with community relations. Such efforts do not desegregate schools and may create diversionary forces in the organization.

53. Statements of Income and Expenditures, 1970–72, "A Report on the Services to the People of the United States by the Legal Defense Fund, 1970–71," p. 26; "Report on Services to the People of the United States by the NAACP Legal Defense and Education Fund, Inc., 1971–72," p. 18; "LDF Annual Report . . . 1972–73," p. 21.

54. Robert B. McKay, *Nine for Equality under Law: Civil Rights Litigation* (Ford Foundation, 1977), p. 12.

Philanthropic activity often reflects the national mood. The executive director of the Urban League, Vernon Jordan, criticized the foundations for what he described as a "withdrawal" from racial issues in the 1970s. The new mood, he said, "has spread to foundations and foundation executives as surely as it has touched politicians, businessmen and housewives."[55]

Three of the nation's large foundations have provided most of the support for civil rights litigation—Ford, Carnegie, and Rockefeller Brothers. Another small group of foundations such as the Field Foundation have been regular but relatively small contributors.

As the largest, richest, and one of the most imaginative American philanthropies, Ford has for years been of great importance in planting the seeds of intellectual movements and social experiments. Even though it has been the major source of civil rights funds from foundations, however, it has displayed considerable ambivalence toward the goal of urban school integration. A review of Ford grants since 1964 shows that funds were largely limited to research in the early years and that more money was often allocated to ghetto improvement strategies than to desegregation.

Ford grants supported the compensatory education movement in 1964 and 1965. These pilot projects helped shape national policy incorporated into the Elementary and Secondary Education Act of 1965 and Operation Head Start. The foundation's most ambitious urban school policy initiative was the proposal for "community control" of schools in New York City, a commitment that climaxed in 1968 with grants of almost $900,000.[56] The disappointing results and the racial polarization produced by the New York experiment were discussed in chapter 6.

Significant amounts of Ford money began to flow into the operating budgets of civil rights agencies only after the 1967 ghetto uprisings in Detroit and Newark climaxed three years of urban riots. Ford provided grants to the NAACP and the Legal Defense Fund, though the grant to the latter was aimed at reform of the criminal justice system, not desegregation.[57]

In 1968, when Martin Luther King, Jr., was assassinated and there was an unprecedented outbreak of urban riots in many parts of the country,

55. Vernon E. Jordan, "The Foundation and Society," *Foundation News* (September–October 1972), p. 29.

56. This discussion and the following section are based on analysis of successive volumes of *Ford Foundation Annual Report* published between 1964 and 1973. Direct quotations are specifically cited.

57. *Ford Foundation Annual Report, 1967*, p. 2.

concern mounted. More than $300,000 of Ford money went to religious fair housing groups. Kerner Commission research efforts and special public opinion polls received more than three-quarters of a million dollars. There were substantial grants to educate the clergy and the mass media on race issues. Kenneth Clark's Metropolitan Applied Research Corporation, the NAACP, the Urban League, the Southwest Council of La Raza, the Legal Defense Fund, and the Mexican-American Legal Defense and Education Fund (MALDEF, the new litigation organization created by the Ford Foundation), all received large grants.

The year 1969 was the high point in Ford civil rights support; some grants were doubled.

In the early 1970s Ford made substantial grants to the LDF, the NAACP Special Contribution Fund, and MALDEF.[58] Support for litigation began tapering off, however, by 1971. Emphasis was again on groups oriented to ghetto improvement.[59]

Like other liberal foundations, Ford was losing both money and focus in the early 1970s as the stock market deteriorated and social change groups proliferated. It also felt the need to respond to a broader range of minority organizations. Ford created separate legal defense funds for Mexican-Americans, Puerto Ricans, American Indians, and women, and felt obligated to sustain them.[60] In fiscal year 1972, for example, both MALDEF and the Native American Rights Fund received far more money than did the NAACP Legal Defense Fund.[61] Urban Coalition President Carl Holman observed: "The same dollars get shifted from plate to plate. First it's the blacks' turn, then Puerto Ricans, Chicanos, peace groups and ecologists."[62]

Ford reported in August 1976 that it had given $4.4 million to the NAACP during the past decade and announced a new two-year grant of $850,000 to the NAACP Special Contribution Fund to finance future litigation and pay some of the outstanding bills[63]—a contribution vital to the survival of NAACP litigation.

Only a small portion of the funds granted for litigation programs and related efforts went to support school cases and even the total grants were relatively small by Ford standards. They did not rise as inflation and the

---

58. *Ford Foundation Annual Report, 1969*, pp. 32, 116, and *1970*, pp. 16, 18, 20.
59. *Ford Foundation Annual Report, 1971*, pp. 17, 19, 22.
60. McKay, *Nine for Equality under Law*, pp. 17–27.
61. *Ford Foundation Annual Report, 1972*, pp. 18, 21.
62. *New York Times*, November 8, 1974.
63. *Ford Foundation Letter*, August 1, 1976.

increasing complexity of the cases drove costs upward. The following table shows Ford's grants through March 1977 to organizations handling school desegregation litigation:[64]

|                                        | *Millions of dollars* |
|----------------------------------------|:---------------------:|
| NAACP Special Contribution Fund        | 4.35                  |
| MALDEF                                  | 4.29                  |
| NAACP Legal Defense Fund               | 2.39                  |
| Center for National Policy Review      | 1.23                  |

The foundation's declining ability to support its many beneficiaries was a matter for serious concern as the market value of its stock holdings fell sharply and inflation eroded purchasing power. By late 1974 Ford's assets could buy only about one-fourth of the services the foundation could have bought a decade earlier.[65] Even though civil rights litigation was given high priority, it would not receive more dollars.

With few exceptions, other foundations have not been seriously interested in financing civil rights litigation in general or school cases in particular. During the first two years of the 1970s, when reported foundation grants totaled $1.86 billion, only a few foundations provided as much as $25,000 in general expenses for the Legal Defense Fund and even fewer supported the NAACP Special Contribution Fund.[66] One large investment in civil rights—$3.75 million in grants from twenty-one foundations between 1969 and 1973—was for training black lawyers in white, southern law schools. In addition, thirty-eight foundations contributed two-thirds of a million dollars to the related efforts of the Law Students Civil Rights Research Council.[67]

Perhaps the New York City location of most of the major foundations that are actively interested in social problems has affected their view of the school issue. In an enormous school system with more than two-thirds minority enrollment, the obstacles to integration may well seem intractable.

Foundations are understandably reluctant to underwrite the large operating expenditures of a few organizations over a long period. Foundation staff members perceive their job as one of initiation and innovation, not long-term sustenance. Foundations, with their freedom from both govern-

---

64. McKay, *Nine for Equality under Law*, p. 35.

65. *Ford Foundation Annual Report, 1974*, p. 62.

66. Lee Noe, ed., *The Foundation Grants Index, 1970–71* (New York: The Foundation Center, 1972), pp. x–xi.

67. Robert Spearman and Hugh Stevens, *A Step Toward Equal Justice: Programs to Increase Black Lawyers in the South, 1969–1973* (Carnegie Corp., 1974). The contributions are listed on p. 68.

ment and business constraints, are constantly appealed to by leaders of new and seemingly important movements. They are urged by skillful packagers of ideas to make relatively small investments, which, they are assured, promise vast social or intellectual returns. Frequently they know that if they refuse the innovators will have no further recourse.

Without federal enforcement, private support is essential to civil rights groups if they are to secure integration, even in the moderate-size districts most easily desegregated. Support on this scale can only come from the foundations. Only a few, however, have been willing to provide money for litigation, and none have made a large commitment to school litigation per se.

### Court Awards of Legal Fees

One other potential source of funds for litigation deserves consideration. In 1972 Congress enacted legislation empowering the courts to order local school boards found guilty of unconstitutional segregation to pay the fees of the lawyers who sued them.

Volunteer attorneys who have invested years of effort in major cases have been awarded fees. A prominent Arkansas civil rights attorney, John W. Walker, for instance, was awarded $150,000 in legal fees for six and a half years of work in the Oklahoma City litigation.[68] In the Swann case, the court awarded $175,000.[69] In Prince Georges County, the ACLU volunteer received $68,000.[70] After a long delay, the Internal Revenue Service ruled in late 1974 that public interest law firms could accept awards of legal fees so long as they did not exceed "50% of total costs of legal functions" of the organization.[71]

The NAACP filed for the costs of sixteen years of litigation in Memphis in late 1976. The group calculated that the case had required 4,987 hours of legal time and the lawyers asked for an award of $1,017,725. In November 1976 the NAACP won a $350,000 award from the Kalamazoo, Michigan, school board.[72] In Denver $360,000 in fees were awarded.

Provision for the payment of fees has stimulated much of the litigation

68. *Washington Post,* May 16, 1976.

69. 66 F.R.D. 483 ( W.D.N.C. 1975).

70. *Busing of Schoolchildren,* Hearings before the Subcommittee on Constitutional Rights of the Senate Committee on the Judiciary, 93:2 ( GPO, 1974), p. 241.

71. Robert L. Rabin, "Lawyers for Social Change: Perspectives on Public Interest Law," *Stanford Law Review,* vol. 28 ( 1976), p. 260.

72. The cases were *Northcross* v. *Board of Education of Memphis City Schools* and *Oliver* v. *Michigan State Board of Education and School Board of Kalamazoo.*

dealing with fair employment practices under Title VII of the 1964 Civil Rights Act.[73] The chance of collecting large fees in connection with class action against leading firms can sustain law firms otherwise unable to bear the costs or obtain necessary funds from individual victims.

There are drawbacks, however, to relying on fees to finance school litigation. One is the magnitude of the task of proving de jure segregation. Another is the long lead time before any payment can be received. (This is also a problem in Title VII cases. However, a given community can produce many job cases and only one school case.) It is not uncommon for major urban cases to languish in the courts for a decade as the Milwaukee, Indianapolis, and Los Angeles cases did. Volunteer attorneys wishing to devote much of their time to such litigation must have funds to finance the pretrial investigation, to handle a long trial, to prepare and print appeal briefs, and to appear in court to argue the almost inevitable appeal. Expert testimony and assistance in planning are expensive but often crucial to a case. Supreme Court decisions in 1976 and 1977 that demanded more proof and required reargument of many major cases increased the burden.

Even when there is a good chance of winning a case and being awarded a large fee, few firms and fewer individual attorneys can make such a heavy investment or wait so long. This means that cases are often poorly prepared, handled slowly, or not filed at all. After the exhausting job of proving the violation, there may be neither time nor money for the careful preparation of a desegregation plan. If there were some kind of revolving fund to advance lawyers a fraction of the anticipated fees, the mechanism might work better.

## The Limits of Private Enforcement

The limited resources and fragmentation of private civil rights groups and the inherent limitations on case-by-case litigation have made progress slow and hard. Urban desegregation litigation is tediously complex and endlessly protracted. Managing a major northern case usually entails years of work. Delay has often, in fact, been the principal tactic of local officials since they can gain political credit for appeals that are foredoomed but that put off the inevitable.

Enforcement of constitutional principles through private litigation is inherently uneven since suits can be filed against only a small proportion of

73. Rabin, "Lawyers for Social Change," p. 258. Congress provided for payment of such fees in 42 U.S.C. §2000e–5(k) (1970).

communities that are violating constitutional rights. This problem is intensified because civil rights lawyers often feel obligated to litigate cases from communities with particularly desperate problems, even though stable integration within the city boundaries is no longer possible and the case makes no contribution to the development of the law.

Civil rights groups have been unable to mount a coordinated, adequately financed drive for private enforcement of school desegregation law. In the 1950s civil rights lawyers were able to begin desegregation in only a few southern school districts each fall. In the 1970s private litigation wins even fewer urban cases each year. These cases have brought some form of desegregated education for hundreds of thousands of minority children and have established a framework of law that would permit more extensive change under a supportive national administration. Most important, they have kept the issue of integrated education alive through a period of rapidly declining public support for civil rights. These are real accomplishments. The fact remains, however, that private resources are hopelessly inadequate to desegregate the children of the nation's urban areas.

# PART THREE

# Policy Choices

# 12

# Metropolitan Desegregation

THE ISSUE of desegregation across city-suburban boundary lines arose almost as soon as the Supreme Court authorized citywide desegregation plans. Less than a year after the 1971 Charlotte (*Swann*) case, two federal courts had ordered metropolitanwide desegregation plans.[1] The reason was simple—the judges in Richmond and Detroit saw no other way to provide real and lasting desegregation. They concluded that the entire city school system had become identified as an inferior minority institution in the metropolitan community.

The movement for metropolitan remedies received a major setback when the Supreme Court deadlocked on the Richmond case and decided 5–4 in favor of a central-city-only desegregation plan in the Detroit (*Milliken*) litigation. The Detroit case had been exhausting and very expensive, and its loss was discouraging. Almost immediately the steam went out of plans to press for metropolitan solutions in a number of other older cities.

The *Milliken* decision, of course, did lower the national fever over the busing issue. The drive for a constitutional amendment dissipated, politics in Michigan returned to normal, and the threat of a direct congressional confrontation with the courts became less serious. The newspapers announced that the suburbs were safe, meaning that most urban whites were beyond the reach of any court order.

Nothing was permanently resolved, however, by the Supreme Court decision. Cases continued where there were special local circumstances.

1. *Bradley* v. *Milliken,* 345 F. Supp. 914 (E.D. Mich. 1972). *Bradley* v. *School Board of the City of Richmond,* 338 F. Supp. 67 (E.D. Va. 1972); *rev'd,* 462 F.2d 1058 (4th Cir. en banc 1972), *aff'd by an equally divided Court,* 412 U.S. 92 (1973).

Civil rights lawyers and central city school administrators expressed their belief that the issue would inevitably have to be dealt with. Demographers projected population trends showing a seemingly inexorable spread of urban ghettos and barrios, reaching well into the inner suburbs. Two states threatened by desegregation decisions, Wisconsin and Delaware, enacted state laws permitting the transfer of some central city students to the suburbs. In urban education, there was a widespread conviction that the real city was the metropolitan area and the central city was the ghetto.

The task of the Supreme Court, of course, is not to practice amateur sociology; it is to define and apply principles of law. The closely divided *Milliken* Court left the law unsettled. The gap between the four members who joined in the majority opinion and the four who dissented was wide. The fifth member of the majority, Justice Potter Stewart, took an ambiguous position that made it difficult to describe the controlling principles of law clearly.

The Court was divided on several questions:

1. Does the autonomy of local school districts have constitutional status?

2. Can a desegregation plan meet all constitutional requirements by placing all children in predominantly minority schools?

3. Is suburban segregation accidental?

4. Do the courts have an obligation to produce a remedy that can be reasonably expected to last?

5. Are state governments and state education officials responsible for the segregationist practices of local school boards?

6. Is metropolitan desegregation institutionally feasible?

The fragmented opinion meant that there was no set of strong legal arguments, no coherent and plausible legal theory to close the issue. The angry tone of the dissenters indicated that the debate would continue.

One conclusion in the majority opinion in *Milliken* is that infringing on the autonomy of a local school district is permissible only where there is clear evidence that intentional governmental action had produced the segregation between the city and the suburbs. In contrast to its willingness to look at the *effects* of patterns of decisions within individual districts and to assume that discrimination in one part of a city affects the movement of the people in the city, the Court imposed a much higher burden of proof on those who wished to incorporate suburban jurisdictions in desegregation plans. The decision was summarized by the *Harvard Law Review:* "the Court held that federal courts cannot order multidistrict remedies absent proof that school district lines have been drawn in a racially discriminatory manner or that other discriminatory acts of state officials or of one or more school districts have substantially caused interdistrict segregation."[2] It was the judgment of the lower courts that the unconstitutional segregation of Detroit blacks could only be ended by a metropolitan remedy, but Chief Justice Warren Burger argued that the courts should only try to restore conditions to what they would be if the illegal segregation had not happened. Whether the schools were predominantly black or whether they rapidly resegregated was legally irrelevant, in his view. Thus the courts could not order metropolitan desegregation unless civil rights lawyers could prove that blacks would be attending school in the suburbs if they had not been segregated as a result of unconstitutional actions. This put a heavy burden of proof on civil rights organizations. None had the capacity for analyzing the historic development of school and housing patterns in the communities of a large metropolitan area.

The Court's majority held that it was important to maintain the autonomy of local school districts, which must not be infringed unless there were grave violations. It dismissed the argument that state governments were responsible for segregation caused by their instrumentalities and that state school boards exercise considerable control over local districts. It simply stated that metropolitan integration in a complex area like the Detroit region would involve unacceptable judicial intervention in the development and operation of new institutions of school government, new financing arrangements, and other changes. The four dissenters disagreed on each issue.

The *Milliken* decision left dangling the question of the origin of segregation in metropolitan areas. The question was raised in a brief passage in the opinion of Justice Stewart, who cast the decisive fifth vote for the majority and who indicated that his position might change if civil rights lawyers could prove that the residential patterns and trends in the metropolitan area resulted from government action. In a footnote he revealed his view of how segregation spread. The growth of housing and school segregation, he said, was "caused by unknown and perhaps unknowable factors such as immigration, birth rates, economic changes, or cumulative acts of private, racial fears." The one ray of hope Stewart offered civil rights groups was that "other factual situations" might justify crossing suburban lines.

Were it to be shown, for example, that state officials had contributed to the separation of the races by drawing or redrawing school district lines ... by trans-

---

2. "The Supreme Court, 1973 Term," *Harvard Law Review*, vol. 88 (1974), p. 61.

fer of school units between districts . . . or by purposeful, racially discriminatory use of state housing or zoning law, then a decree calling for transfer of pupils across district lines or for restructuring of district lines might well be appropriate.[3]

After the *Milliken* decision lawyers and other experts came to Washington for two post mortem sessions. The U.S. Commission on Civil Rights held hearings on its meaning and implications. Later, lawyers managing affected cases across the country and social scientists who had done relevant research gathered to share impressions and discuss future tactics. Pessimists among them thought that Stewart's comment meant little and that hoping to win cases through better proof of intentional housing discrimination would be futile. Optimists detected openness to change. They hoped to build the law by beginning with cases that would be relatively easy for the courts to handle.

Experts in the two national civil rights organizations most deeply involved in school litigation took the pessimistic view. NAACP General Counsel Nathaniel Jones, who had argued the case before the Court, saw the decision as a political judgment. There was plenty of proof in the record, he argued, to justify the metropolitan remedy if the Court had been willing to move in that direction. The major motive, he thought, was to "stall" the explosive issue.[4] Norman C. Amaker, formerly with the NAACP Legal Defense Fund, viewed the decision similarly. Amaker's analysis of Stewart's position was that civil rights groups must still produce overwhelming proof that the policies increasing housing segregation were "purposeful" and that "the communities created across school district boundaries are a direct result" of the policies.[5] Legal Defense Fund lawyers agreed that there was little chance of any real breakthrough on the legal issues.[6]

The lawyers generally agreed that it would be unwise to bring any more metropolitan desegregation suits resembling the Detroit case. Litigation seeking metropolitan desegregation should include convincing evidence of specific state or local policies or actions that intentionally produced segregated schools or residentially segregated communities.[7]

---

3. *Milliken* v. *Bradley*, 418 U.S. 717 at 755–56 (1974).

4. Testimony of Nathaniel Jones before the U.S. Commission on Civil Rights, November 9, 1974.

5. Testimony of Norman Amaker before the Commission on Civil Rights, November 9, 1974.

6. Testimony of James Nabrit III (associate counsel of the NAACP Legal Defense Fund) before the Commission on Civil Rights, November 9, 1974.

7. See particularly ibid.

## After *Milliken*

When the *Milliken* case was decided, metropolitan lawsuits at different stages were pending in cities from Hartford to Atlanta. After the 1971 and 1972 decisions by district judges favoring metropolitan desegregation in Detroit and Richmond, lawyers had explored the issue in many settings.

The two cases offering the best chance after *Milliken* were Louisville and Wilmington. Lawyers felt that local legal and factual circumstances distinguished them clearly from Detroit. In both cases the federal courts agreed.[8] In other pending cases, such as those in Indianapolis and Atlanta, however, the courts moved more slowly.

### Louisville

The Sixth Circuit Court of Appeals had ordered consideration of a desegregation plan encompassing Louisville and the rest of Jefferson County.[9] The city school board supported consolidation, but the county school board had appealed the decision to the Supreme Court. The day the Supreme Court decided the Detroit case, it also made a procedural decision on the Louisville litigation, returning it to the circuit court "for further consideration in light of *Milliken v. Bradley*."[10]

Louisville was typical of cities well on the way to having a ghetto school system. The population of the metropolitan area in 1970 was almost 900,000, having increased by a healthy 15 percent during the 1960s. In the same period, the central city's white population had fallen by one-seventh and the black population had increased by more than one-fifth. By 1970 the suburbs contained almost two-thirds of the area's whites but only about one-seventh of the blacks. There was growing residential separation.[11]

The Louisville school board had adopted a desegregation plan in 1956

8. *Newburg Area Council v. Board of Education of Jefferson County, Kentucky*, 510 F.2d 1358 (6th Cir. 1974); *Evans v. Buchanan*, 393 F. Supp. 428 (D. Del. 1975).

9. *Newburg Area Council v. Board of Education of Jefferson County*, 510 F.2d 1358. Louisville had its own school district; the rest of the county made up the Jefferson County district.

10. *Board of Education of Jefferson County, Kentucky v. Newburg Area Council, Inc.*, 418 U.S. 918 (1974).

11. U.S. Bureau of the Census, *Statistical Abstract of the United States* (GPO, 1974), pp. 878–79.

that was then widely hailed as a model. The system's attendance areas were redrawn and each student was offered a "free choice" of which school he wished to attend. The result was a peaceful first step toward desegregation. At the time, the schools were almost three-quarters white.[12]

Neither the city nor the county ever underwent thorough desegregation. Between 1956 and 1966 the proportion of segregated schools in Louisville gradually fell from 78 percent to 55 percent. But it began to rise again as transitional neighborhoods became ghettos.

By 1971 almost three-fourths of the city's schools were highly segregated. Segregation was worst in the elementary schools, where children were less integrated than in 1956.[13] The enrollment in the city system was almost half black. Each year the percentage increased, primarily because the white enrollment fell so rapidly.[14]

Since suburbanization had jeopardized the possibility of stable desegregation in the city, the Kentucky Human Rights Commission in 1972 recommended merging the city and suburban schools. The migration from the city had not been "white flight" from desegregation; most of the city's white children were in segregated white schools anyway. But the combination of rapid suburbanization and an expanding ghetto had produced accelerating resegregation. The commission warned that "soon all the gains made in the early years of desegregation will be wiped out," and recommended: "Louisville and Jefferson County school officials should begin planning together now for the complete merger and desegregation program which is inevitable."[15] Housing segregation had grown worse. Louisville had been among the top third of cities in housing integration in 1940 but had declined to the bottom third by 1970. In 1940 about four black families in five would have had to move to achieve a random nonracial distribution of population. In 1970 nine black families in ten would have had to move.[16]

It was useless for Louisville to wait for a change in housing patterns to produce school integration. Demographic trends were moving the city inexorably toward more and more rigid school and housing segregation.

When the issue came back to the court of appeals after *Milliken*, how-

12. Don Shoemaker, ed., *With All Deliberate Speed* (Harper, 1957), p. 83.
13. Kentucky Commission on Human Rights, "Louisville School System Retreats to Segregation" (1972; processed), p. 8.
14. Ibid., p. 10.
15. Ibid., pp. 16, 17.
16. Kentucky Commission on Human Rights, "Louisville Still Among Most Segregated Cities: Information Regarding Louisville from the Council on Municipal Performance Report" (November 7, 1974; processed), pp. 1–4.

ever, the substantive problems of the city were far less important than the distinctive legal situation. The court ruled in December 1974 that metropolitan Louisville could be desegregated not because its problems were more severe than Detroit's but because Kentucky laws and history were different. Though there was no evidence of de jure segregation against the schools in the Detroit suburbs, it found that "the opposite is true" in Louisville. Not only was the Jefferson County system guilty of intentional discrimination, but "school district lines in Kentucky have been ignored in the past for the purpose of aiding and implementing continued segregation."[17]

There were important practical distinctions as well. Whereas the Detroit case involved fifty-three separate school systems, in Louisville there were only two major systems operating in a single county in a state whose education laws made the county the "basic educational unit." The administrative complexities that had troubled the Supreme Court in *Milliken* would not arise in Kentucky "since the merger or consolidation . . . could be effectuated under the express provisions of a Kentucky statute. This statute authorizes the reconsolidation of school districts within a single county even without the consent of the county school board."[18]

Early in 1975 the Supreme Court refused to delay Louisville desegregation by reviewing the decision.[19] Any possibility of avoiding desegregation was lost when the city's school board voted itself out of existence. Under state law, this automatically transferred responsibility to the county system. The desegregation plan was implemented in September 1975. For the first time in the United States, city and suburban children from formerly separate school systems participated in a desegregation plan.

### Wilmington

In an earlier form the Wilmington case had been part of the original 1954 decision by the Supreme Court. Two decades later Wilmington had undergone demographic changes much like those that afflicted Louisville and many other central cities.

Wilmington was a small fifteen-square-mile city in the center of a single county with 386,000 people. There were fewer than 14,000 students in the city schools and more than 73,000 in the suburbs. The racial differences

17. *Newburg Area Council* v. *Board of Education of Jefferson County,* 510 F.2d 1358, *cert. denied,* 421 U.S. 931 (1975).
18. Ibid.
19. 421 U.S. 931.

were intensifying. By 1970, 44 percent of the city's residents were black but in the suburbs less than 5 percent were. Demographic trends indicated that the city would become one large ghetto.

The Wilmington case differed from the Detroit case in at least four respects. First, Delaware had had legal segregation in all districts until 1954. Second, the state legislature had passed in the 1960s a school consolidation law that permitted state school authorities to consolidate any districts in the state except Wilmington and one other. Third, metropolitan Wilmington was a far smaller area than Detroit and its governmental structure was much less complex. Fourth, there was an explicit finding of intentional housing segregation.

A three-judge district court ruled in March 1975 that the *Milliken* case did not bar a metropolitan plan in Wilmington and that the state of Delaware was historically responsible for segregation. It found city and suburbs guilty of de jure segregation, both in the school systems and in housing. For years, for instance, the suburbs had sent many of their black students into black schools in the city for education. The court ruled that "*de jure* segregation in New Castle County was a cooperative venture involving both city and suburbs."[20]

In its decision, the court reached firm conclusions on the housing issue that the Supreme Court had not considered in Detroit. It found that both federal housing policy and specific local policies, especially those affecting public housing, had reinforced racial separation. Even the President, the court pointed out, had recognized the segregationist impact of national housing policy in his message to Congress in 1971: "Until 1949, FHA officially sanctioned and perpetuated community patterns of residential separation based on race by refusing to insure mortgages in neighborhoods not racially homogeneous. The effects of this policy have persisted for many years after its reversal and are still evident in metropolitan areas today."[21]

Public housing authorities in metropolitan Wilmington had concentrated more than 98 percent of the units within the city. "The evident effect was to concentrate poor and minority families in Wilmington."[22]

The court held that the intense segregation of schools in the central city undermined the possibility of stable integration. School enrollment often became heavily black before neighborhoods changed. The Delaware

20. *Evans* v. *Buchanan,* 393 F. Supp. 428 at 437 (D. Del. 1975).
21. Message to Congress from President Nixon, June 29, 1971, quoted by the court in ibid. at 434.
22. *Evans* v. *Buchanan,* 393 F. Supp. 428.

Human Relations Commission's surveys of people leaving for the suburbs showed that, even for families without children in school, the changing racial composition of a school was a sign that the neighborhood was destined to become a ghetto. This meant that the transition from a virtually all-white to a mostly black school enrollment could happen with surprising speed.[23]

The strain on integrated public schools in Wilmington had been increased, the court decided, by Delaware's practice of using public funds—about three-quarters of a million dollars a year—to bus city children to private and parochial schools, even to those in the suburbs. State payments had doubled after the legislature authorized busing across district lines.[24]

The crucial legal circumstance in the Wilmington case, however, concerned the state's 1968 school consolidation act, which authorized the state board of education to consolidate school districts for a year without approval of the voters of the affected districts. The important feature of this law was that it excluded Wilmington, which then contained 44 percent of all the black pupils in the state. This made it harder for the state board to use consolidation for easing segregation than for almost any other educational goal, since it implicitly created "a suspect racial classification." A number of precedents, said the court, "have made clear that educational authorities . . . have an obligation to consider the racial consequences of major educational policy decisions."

The court ruled that the act was unconstitutional.[25] This and other policies meant that the state government was legally compelled to devise a remedy, probably one incorporating metropolitan desegregation.

Desegregating metropolitan Wilmington, the judges concluded, was much simpler than Detroit. "The New Castle County population is less than one-tenth that of the Detroit metropolitan area. . . . The proposed *Milliken* remedy would have involved three counties . . . any remedy here would be confined to New Castle County and, at most, twelve school districts. There were 779,000 students in the Detroit 'desegregation area,' but there are only 87,696 in all of New Castle County." The entire Wilmington metropolitan area presented no more problems of feasibility than those the Supreme Court had faced in 1971 in upholding the desegregation of Charlotte. New Castle County was physically smaller than the North Carolina system and there were about the same number of students.[26]

23. Ibid. at 435–36.
24. Ibid. at 436.
25. Ibid. at 441.
26. *Evans* v. *Buchanan*, 393 F. Supp. 428.

Although the Wilmington case was not of decisive importance, particularly since the ultimate ruling depended on specific local facts and history, it did keep the metropolitan issue open.

Without even hearing arguments, the Supreme Court sustained the finding of constitutional violations by Delaware and upheld the decision of the court of appeals in November 1975.[27] A metropolitan desegregation plan would go into effect in the fall of 1978.[28]

### Atlanta

The issue in Atlanta, the principal metropolitan area of the Deep South, is still in court. Atlanta had a long and disappointing history of litigation for the central city. In 1958, when the Atlanta case began, the school system was 70 percent white; by the 1974–75 school year it was 83 percent black and had never undergone more than token integration.[29]

This racial change and the shifting goals of some black activists produced an embarrassing public battle over the management of the case. By 1970 the local NAACP lawyer, Howard Moore, who was moving toward the "black power" position, was ready to accept continued segregation in exchange for increasing black control of the city schools. Moore's proposal was denounced by the president of the Atlanta branch of the NAACP, Lonnie King, who said that NAACP's opposition to segregation "has not changed one scintilla." At the same time, the Department of Health, Education, and Welfare responded to a court directive by drafting a desegregation plan for the city that included no busing, but relied on "pairing" nearby schools to marginally increase integration.[30]

The city's school board concentrated on the desegregation of faculties and "free choice" enrollment for black students. The district judge supported this opportunity to "desegregate" the city, holding that more integration would drive whites away.[31]

27. *Evans* v. *Buchanan*, 423 U.S. 963 (1975).

28. In 1976 the district court ordered preparation of a plan for September 1977 but delayed its order. *Evans* v. *Buchanan*, 435 F. Supp. 832 (D. Del. 1977). Later in the year the Justice Department urged the Supreme Court to limit the reach of the Wilmington remedy. But the Court ensured the implementation of a metropolitan plan when it refused in October 1977 to review the case.

29. Gene Guerrero, "Atlanta Schools: The Case for Metro Relief," *Civil Liberties* (April 1975), p. 3.

30. *Atlanta Constitution*, January 14, 1970.

31. *Calhoun* v. *Cook*, 332 F. Supp. 804 (N.D. Ga. 1971).

Rapid white suburbanization continued and few white pupils remained. In early 1973 the NAACP's Atlanta branch attracted national attention when it accepted a "compromise," dropping busing but granting over half the administrative leadership jobs in the system to black educators. The angry national NAACP drew on rarely used authority to suspend the entire Atlanta leadership.[32]

The compromise was implemented, and the system became more overwhelmingly black each year. One group of black parents collected thousands of books of trading stamps to purchase a school bus to carry students to integrated schools and asked the American Civil Liberties Union to sue for metropolitan desegregation. The ACLU lawyers faced the obstacles of a hostile federal court, lack of support from the city's school officials, and little money to invest in research and preparation of the case. Although the case offered the ACLU a possibility of leadership in an important area of civil rights law, it also risked creating a destructive precedent.

Overriding the advice of national civil rights groups, the ACLU decided to pursue the case in 1974. The lawyers believed that the history of segregation in Atlanta was so much worse than in Detroit that the Supreme Court might well reverse its position.

ACLU volunteer attorney Margie Hames was sure that she could prove interdistrict violation as well as a long history of intentional housing segregation and of local and state support for sending suburban blacks to city schools and allowing white students to transfer to the suburban systems.[33]

The housing evidence was extensive. The local zoning law had once openly defined black and white residential areas. So had city planning authorities. Through the mid-1950s, Hames said, zoning decisions had clearly been made on the ground of race. Buffer areas of greenery had been built between white and black areas. In some places urban renewal had been used to intensify residential segregation.[34]

The courts had already found suburban Atlanta governments guilty of intensifying "racial concentration" by confining public housing to the central city. In its 1971 decision, the court observed that these actions had helped produce a situation where "it has become virtually impossible to achieve meaningful school desegregation." In the original Atlanta school case in the 1950s, the court held that federal housing programs and local

32. "NAACP Suspends Atlanta Unit: Repudiates School Agreement," *Crisis* (May 1973), pp. 168–69.

33. Statements by Margie Hames at Conference on Metropolitan School Integration, Center for National Policy Review, Washington, November 16, 1974.

34. Ibid.

administrators had "engaged in a broad pattern of affirmative acts to promote racial housing segregation in Atlanta and suburbs."[35]

The case was pursued because of the determination of an extraordinary
volunteer lawyer. Before the Atlanta case, Margie Hames's activities had
brought her before the Supreme Court twice in the successful campaign to
legalize abortion. She prepared for the school case by spending much of her
time for two years reading records in local archives and taking depositions
from scores of public officials.[36]

In 1975 the ACLU claimed leadership on the metropolitan issue. "The
ACLU," said the organization's national newsletter, "has largely inherited
the field of metropolitan desegregation cases, because other civil rights
organizations fear that the Supreme Court will continue to . . . reject metro
relief."[37] The outcome of this case (which went to trial in the fall of 1977)
may influence the future of the metropolitan issue in many American cities.
It reflects both the openness of the judicial process and the inability of national civil rights organizations to manage a coordinated strategy of litigation, even on issues of sovereign importance.

### Hobson's Choice in Detroit

The *Milliken* decision was a major defeat for metropolitan desegregation
plans. It explicitly affirmed the right of black children to integrated education but specifically rejected the finding of the lower federal courts that it
was impossible to successfully desegregate the schools in a system with 70
percent black enrollment. Not only did the Supreme Court hold that
Detroit could be desegregated within the city boundaries, but it ordered the
lower courts to do it quickly.[38]

The relevant standard for desegregation, the Court majority indicated,
was not a national or metropolitan one, but one confined to a single school
system.[39] This standard meant that if a black student in an 80 percent black
system had been segregated in a 95 percent black school, he would receive
his constitutional rights when the system "desegregated" and all children

35. Guerrero, "Atlanta Schools," p. 3.
36. *Civil Liberties* (January 1976), p. 6.
37. *Civil Liberties* (April 1975), p. 3.
38. *Milliken* v. *Bradley*, 418 U.S. 717.
39. Ibid.

attended schools approximately four-fifths black. The Court said that if the remaining whites left, as the lower courts said they would, this raised no legal problem; if the city lost many of its remaining middle class taxpayers, that raised no issue of constitutional dimensions.

Not only did the Supreme Court reject the commonsense meaning of "desegregation," but it employed language carrying a tone of reprimand. It implied that a quixotic quest for a metropolitan solution had delayed real justice, and ordered "prompt formulation of a decree directed to eliminating the segregation found to exist in Detroit city schools, a remedy which has been delayed since 1970."[40]

The Milliken decision forced the NAACP to make an unpleasant choice in Detroit. After arguing forcefully and at great expense for metropolitan desegregation and insisting that central-city-only integration would not work, it was told to take it or do nothing at all. Local black political leaders urged the agency to drop the case. Faced with a rapid decline in local jobs and abandonment of housing since the 1967 riots, the city administration was not eager to increase pressure on the remaining middle class residents. The NAACP, however, publicly rejected the appeal for restraint in a statement calling for "citizens, and particularly public officials," to stop fighting the effort and start working for public support of the plan.[41]

The schools were by now 72 percent black and the number of whites was dropping rapidly. Fewer than a third of the schools were more than half white. The city school board devised a plan to desegregate these schools by busing 35,000 students to 122 elementary schools, but the NAACP called for racial balance at every school. The district judge, however, rejected both plans. Eventually he ordered a modest plan busing 21,800 white students (less than one-tenth) and integrating 38 ghetto schools.[42]

The Detroit desegregation plan brought most of the city's remaining white schools to at least 40 percent black enrollment, but 83,000 black children were still in schools with few, if any, white students. Although they had been found to be unconstitutionally segregated, the court of appeals could find no remedy. When the NAACP asked for approximate racial balance throughout the city, the court rejected the idea of busing children from one set of largely black schools to another set of schools with only a slightly larger white minority. This would "accelerate the trend toward

40. Ibid. at 753.
41. Christian Science Monitor, March 26, 1975.
42. Washington Post, August 21, 1975; Milliken v. Bradley, 540 F.2d 229 (6th Cir. 1976).

rendering all or nearly all Detroit's schools so identifiably black as to represent universal school segregation within the city limits." The court concluded that additional desegregation was essential in Detroit but that it could find no way to accomplish it. The judges were convinced "that genuine constitutional desegregation cannot be accomplished within the school district boundaries of the Detroit School District."[43]

Detroit was not alone in facing this dilemma. There were a number of other cities with large black majorities which were either operating under old court orders or in court. Baltimore and Richmond had overwhelmingly black systems that were supposedly "desegregated." Years earlier, a federal judge had eliminated one of the last remaining pockets of integration in the Washington, D.C., system by ordering that the white children who made up 30 percent of the enrollment of one school be distributed among three schools where they would constitute only 10 percent of each.[44] Cases concerning Cleveland and Philadelphia were in court.

Similar issues arose in litigation in other big cities—for instance, Cleveland and St. Louis. The St. Louis school district, with 73 percent black enrollment, presented serious obstacles to full desegregation. Initially local civil rights lawyers had settled out of court for a plan creating eight "magnet schools" for 4,000 of the district's 88,000 children, but even these limited goals were not met, and the NAACP went to court in an attempt to bring about further desegregation. In May 1977 the Justice Department suggested desegregating the high schools by making the three remaining white schools more than half black and assigning about 30 percent of the white students to three all-black schools. Enrollment in one of the schools involved was 96 percent white; after "desegregation" it would be 71 percent black if all whites assigned to it enrolled.[45] St. Louis Superintendent Robert Wentz, who earlier had said that "long-term solutions are not going to be found in the city itself," called for careful study of metropolitan approaches.[46]

43. *Bradley* v. *Milliken,* 540 F.2d 229. In September 1977 the Detroit schools were 83 percent black; only one-tenth of them had as many as half white children. *Detroit Free Press,* September 7, 1977.

44. *Baltimore Sun,* November 3, 1975; *Hobson* v. *Hansen,* 269 F. Supp. 401 (D.D.C. 1967).

45. *St. Louis Globe-Democrat,* May 25, 1977; *St. Louis Post-Dispatch,* May 25, 1977.
Even before desegregation, St. Louis had a serious problem with students illegally enrolling in suburban districts. Marjorie Mandel, "Students Sneak into Suburban Schools," *St. Louis Post-Dispatch,* May 27, 1977.

46. *St. Louis Globe-Democrat,* February 16, 1977. A 1977 Danforth Foundation study concluded that stable desegregation would require metropolitan plans in cities like St. Louis. *St. Louis Post-Dispatch,* November 8, 1977.

When the Cleveland school board was found guilty of unconstitutional segregation in August 1976, Judge Frank Battisti noted the extreme racial division between school districts in the metropolitan area and found that both housing policies and illegal practices by the state board of education had contributed to the problem. Some 86,000 black children attended schools in Cleveland and other predominantly black school systems in the metropolitan area, but only 6,000 black pupils and more than a quarter of a million white students attended school in the white-majority districts. Observing that one major suburb, East Cleveland, already had schools with 97.4 percent black enrollment, he warned of a possible trend "to wholly separate school districts."[47]

The fundamental social insight of the 1954 *Brown* decision by the Supreme Court was that a system in which minority children were forced to attend segregated schools was "inherently unequal." It was unequal not because there was something wrong with black children but because there were deep social prejudices about the inferiority of black institutions. This meant that the dominant society would not treat the minority schools equally and would assume that the children who attended them were inferior and would devalue their education, both by expecting less during the educational process and by assuming that graduates had had inferior training.

These expectations and fears still persist strongly. In the 1960s, when hundreds of school districts operated "freedom of choice" plans permitting transfer by students to schools of the opposite race, many thousands of blacks but almost no whites transferred even though many of the black schools were closer and offered distinctive educational programs. Some expensive "magnet schools" located in the ghetto whose educational programs are far superior to those offered in all-white schools have found it difficult to attract volunteer transfer students.[48] Gallup polls show that, although acceptance of school integration grew considerably from 1963 to 1973, the resistance of white parents to enrolling their children in predominantly black schools remained high. Only 6 percent of northern

---

47. *Reed* v. *Rhodes,* 422 F. Supp. 708 ( D. Ohio 1976 ).

48. The failure of the Harlem magnet school I.S. 201 to attract white students led to the development of New York City's drive for community control. Recent major efforts in Houston and Cincinnati to use magnet schools as a desegregation strategy have had little success in drawing white students into schools that previously had large majorities of black and Hispanic students. Daniel U. Levine and Connie Campbell, "Developing and Implementing Big-City Magnet School Programs," in Levine and Robert J. Havighurst, eds., *The Future of Big-City Schools: Desegregation Policies and Magnet Alternatives* ( McCutchan Publishing, 1977), pp. 258–59.

parents surveyed said in 1973 that they objected to their children attending
school with a few blacks but 23 percent objected to schools where half the
students were black and 63 percent to schools where more than half were
black.[49]

Desegregation that produces a predominantly black school system is
obviously seen by whites as something quite different from other forms of
desegregation, and has the least chance of acceptance.

## Institutional and Social Class Effects of *Milliken*

The courts are concerned with ending illegal segregation, not with
designing the optimal plan for successful integration. Even if the Supreme
Court were authorized by the Constitution to carry out detailed adjustments, it has no special competence for doing so.

The debate over metropolitanism, however, revolves around a more
serious charge. Critics of the *Milliken* doctrine claim that the Court ignored
social reality so completely that it supported a remedy with no chance at
all of producing desegregated schools for more than a brief period. Limiting
remedies to schools with few white students in cities where long-established
demographic trends guaranteed resegregation meant, in effect, that there
was no remedy, only an intensification of conflict and possibly a speeding up
of the normal process of ghetto and barrio expansion.

Growing minority domination of urban schools is accompanied by a
substantial decline in the socioeconomic and educational background levels
of the white families that continue to use the central city school systems.
At advanced stages of suburbanization in a metropolitan area, a disproportionate number of the white families remaining in the central city are
those without school age children and those whose economic status denies
them access to the suburban housing market. Unfortunately, the white
students left in the city's public schools often represent the population
groups most threatened by ghetto expansion and most hostile to blacks.

When desegregation is limited to central cities, particularly to the older,
decaying ones, it is unlikely to result in minority children's attending
middle class schools with strong education programs. Since 1920, there has
been a steady increase in the segregation of children in the urban North by
social class.[50]

49. *Gallup Opinion Index*, October 1973, p. 14.
50. Robert J. Havighurst, *Education in Metropolitan Areas* (Allyn and Bacon,
1966), p. 59.

Chicago illustrates this stratification. The city and its suburbs were relatively similar in 1940, both relatively close to the national average of the proportion of high- and lower-status jobs. By 1950, however, a gap had appeared, and after the in-migrations of the 1950s, the gap was wide—the percentage of upper-status families was almost twice as high in the suburbs as in the city. The gap broadened steadily in the 1960s and 1970s.

The *Milliken* principles, when applied to old cities, embody a social policy that whites with the least income, status, and power must bear the entire burden of desegregation, while those who can afford upper-income housing in segregated suburbs may be completely insulated. The 1970 census data made it evident that the outward movement of the white middle class during the 1960s had intensified the problem. The statistics showed that limiting desegregation to the central cities in the metropolitan areas of significant size would effectively insulate almost 70 percent of the white families earning more than $10,000.[51] By the mid-1970s, the social class isolation was even greater. In several metropolitan areas, not only was almost all the white middle class gone from the central city schools, but most of the black middle class was attending either a public school outside the central city or a private school.[52]

## Is Metropolitan Segregation Accidental?

Limiting desegregation to central cities introduces all kinds of apparent inequities in the enforcement of civil rights. It means that minority and white students in different states, with different traditions of local government organization, are treated in radically different ways. It means that millions of minority children must forgo desegregation or be desegregated in schools with few whites, schools still perceived as minority schools by most Americans. It means that black leaders must choose between giving up the rights of their children and possibly accelerating the flight of the remaining whites in the old cities. It tends to turn white working class people against protected white middle class suburbanites. It combines, in the desegregated schools of the old cities, groups who often have in common only the weaknesses of their school background, the powerlessness of their

51. Commission on Civil Rights, *Hearings Held in Washington, D.C.* (GPO, 1971), p. 535, special tabulation of U.S. Census Bureau data.
52. This was particularly apparent in Washington, Newark, Cleveland, and St. Louis.

parents, and among older children a tendency toward overt hostility. It offers little chance for educational gain.

This policy is based on the premise that the segregation of the suburbs just happened, that people sorted themselves out along racial lines without any significant public intervention or influence. Therefore, the Supreme Court reasons, there is no justification for infringing on suburban communities' right of self-government.

Outside the southern and border states, where blacks have always lived in the counties that became suburbs and where the boundary lines between city and suburban school districts were established long before there was any substantial minority population in a metropolitan area, it is rarely possible to show extensive racially motivated action to foster segregation either in the creation or in the operation of suburban school systems. Nor is it generally possible to show that the actions of most nonsouthern suburban school systems fostered school segregation. Seldom have they needed to segregate schools because the system of housing separation is so efficient. It is hard to imagine how intentional school segregation could be proved in a school district with only three or four minority families.

In the suburbs the policy of treating each school district as a separate entity puts the entire burden of accomplishing school integration on the communities that have been fairest to minority home buyers and renters and insulates the communities that have the most exclusionary land-use practices and the most segregationist housing markets. Since the suburbs that are fair often have a lower per capita tax base and a high and rapidly growing proportion of minority residents, resources for integrated education are limited. Communities like the St. Louis suburb of University City, the Philadelphia suburb of Willingboro, and the Chicago suburb of Park Forest South are being penalized for their fair housing practices with heavy school desegregation burdens while many other nearby communities remain almost all-white and need do nothing.

The underlying legal question is whether the whole structure of school segregation is the direct result of unconstitutional housing segregation. If suburban neighborhoods were created by unconstitutional state action, can the courts limit remedies to those outside the suburban sanctuaries?

*Housing Policy Evidence*

If the Supreme Court should begin to consider the relation between housing segregation and school segregation, it would find a formidable array of evidence. Lawyers concerned with housing discrimination, the impact of public housing programs, zoning and land use regulation, and a variety of other urban policy issues with clear racial implications have been developing proof for years. Students of urban policy and the history of particular cities have accumulated data potentially important to litigation of the housing question.

The consensus of the court decisions and of the scholarly research is that urban housing patterns have indeed been affected by action by state, local, and federal government officials fostering segregation, although the precise extent of the impact is unclear. Evidence can be produced in many metropolitan areas on several forms of housing discrimination:

1. Racial zoning ordinances (legal until 1917 and often on the law books later).

2. Restrictive covenants (prohibitions on sales to racial and ethnic minorities, required on federally insured developments in the suburbs and enforced by the courts until 1948).

3. Local condemnation of land occupied by minority groups in suburbs or land slated for minority or integrated housing.

4. Exclusion of subsidized housing (through a variety of devices).

5. Discrimination by home finance institutions operating under federal and state charters and supervision and by realtors licensed by the state government.

6. Federal Housing Administration and Veterans Administration mortgage policies supporting segregation.

7. Inadequate police response to protect safety and property when mob action, violence, and intimidation threaten minority homebuyers in white neighborhoods.

8. Use of subsidized housing programs in ways that intensify segregation and destabilize integrated neighborhoods.

The courts have found local housing authorities and federal housing agencies guilty of intentional segregation in several major cases, some of which were discussed in chapter 4. In recent years, federal housing officials, including former Secretary of Housing and Urban Development George Romney, have openly conceded that the federal programs historically followed segregationist policies. In an important 1976 decision, *Hills* v. *Gautreaux*, the Supreme Court authorized the lower courts to direct that some subsidized housing be constructed in the Chicago suburbs to remedy the segregation in local and federal public housing programs.

### —And Remedy

But although the evidence is clear, its effect on the Supreme Court is uncertain. Experts specializing in civil rights law find different meanings in the *Milliken* decision, both for what it implies about the Court's perception of urban realities and for what it suggests about the views of the justices on the proper limits of the judiciary. In 1976 and 1977 the Court significantly increased the burden of proof for civil rights advocates, insisting that the discriminatory motivation of policies, as well as their impact, be proved.

In *Milliken* the Supreme Court set aside the housing question because the court of appeals had not dealt with it. One housing expert analyzed the legal situation:

the threshold problem for plaintiffs is not that of proving that all of the conduct of the state or suburbs is unlawful, but the more basic one of demonstrating to the Court that . . . the bland assumption that residential segregation is the result of neutral, impersonal factors beyond the control of government is totally wrong, and that government at all levels is heavily, and even decisively implicated as a major causal factor.[53]

Accepting Justice Stewart's invitation, civil rights lawyers began to press the housing issue in cases argued after the Detroit case. This was successful in Wilmington. In Indianapolis and Cleveland the federal courts hearing the cases made explicit findings of intentional housing segregation.[54] Judges faced with the practical problems of desegregating urban schools continually turned to the issue of why the nearby suburban systems were almost completely white. The question arose during proceedings in July 1977, for instance, in both New York City and Los Angeles. Federal Judge John F. Dooling commented on pending litigation on high school segregation in Queens: "We're going to have to stop looking at this in terms of political boundaries. To parcel out children along political lines is so silly it's going to fail eventually."[55] In Los Angeles, Superior Court Judge Paul Egly asked all parties to the desegregation suit to submit briefs on the metropolitan issue by September 1977. The school district concluded that a metropolitan approach would be more feasible than one limited to the city.[56]

More and more central city school boards were examining the demographics of their cities and joining the battle for metropolitan solutions. In Detroit and Richmond, the central city school boards joined civil rights groups in suing the suburbs. At first opposed to the idea, the Indianapolis board changed its mind. In Louisville the board precipitated a merger by voting to dissolve the city system. In Kansas City the board filed a suit in

---

53. Martin E. Sloane, "*Milliken* v. *Bradley* and Residential Segregation," paper presented to the U.S. Commission on Civil Rights, November 9, 1975, p. 25.

54. *Reed* v. *Rhodes*, 422 F. Supp. 708; *United States* v. *Board of School Commissioners of City of Indianapolis*, 541 F.2d 1212 (2d Cir. 1976).

55. *New York Times*, July 9, 1977.

56. *Los Angeles Times*, July 9, 1977, and September 22, 1977.

May 1977 attempting to force reassignment of students among eighteen school districts, five of them across the state line in Kansas. The board claimed that "state action sanctioned, and at times required racial segregation in housing, employment, recreation, transportation, and public employment."[57]

The *Milliken* decision, in which the Court did not foreclose the possibility of metropolitan desegregation where there was compelling evidence of housing violations, had left a small chink in the wall around the suburbs. Eventually the Court would be forced by lower court findings on the housing issue to make a decision that would either open a passage through the wall or brick it shut.

## Do Metropolitan Plans Work?

Substantial experience with metropolitan plans has already been gained. In a number of states most or all school districts are organized on a county-wide basis. Many of these states are in the South. As a result, a number of southern districts, as well as Las Vegas, Nevada, have operated under court-ordered metropolitan plans for several years. These include some of the country's largest and most important school districts (see table 12-1).

A recent analysis of the enrollment trends between 1968 and 1973 in all U.S. districts with over 75,000 students found sharp differences in the stability of metropolitan and city-only desegregation plans. All but one—Albuquerque—of the districts that had undergone relatively substantial desegregation during the period with less than average loss of white enrollment were metropolitan systems. All those experiencing greater than average losses were central city systems—in fact, many large central cities that had *not* desegregated lost white students much faster than systems with desegregation plans that had achieved racial balance throughout the metropolitan area.[58]

A confirmation of this pattern came, for example, in the second year of desegregation in Louisville. During the first year desegregation was bitterly controversial in the city, which became the national focal point of the antibusing movement and the site of numerous nationally publicized protests. Enrollment declined substantially during this crisis. In the second year enrollment was almost precisely the number projected. In a number

57. *New York Times*, May 28, 1977.
58. Thomas F. Pettigrew and Robert L. Green, "School Desegregation in Large Cities: A Critique of the Coleman 'White Flight' Thesis," *Harvard Educational Review*, vol. 46 (February 1976), p. 35.

Table 12-1. *Major School Systems under Court-Ordered Metropolitan Desegregation*

| Metropolitan area (county and county seat) | Enrollment (1972–73) | Rank among all continental U.S. districts | Central city systems of comparable size |
|---|---|---|---|
| Dade (Miami) | 241,000 | 6 | Detroit |
| Jefferson (Louisville) | 139,000 | 13[a] | Cleveland |
| Broward (Fort Lauderdale) | 129,000 | 17 | Milwaukee |
| Duval (Jacksonville) | 112,000 | 20 | St. Louis |
| Hillsborough (Tampa) | 105,000 | 22 | Columbus, Ohio |
| Pinellas (Clearwater) | 90,000 | 29 | Indianapolis |
| Orange (Orlando) | 86,000 | 31 | Denver |
| Nashville–Davidson County | 83,000 | 34 | Fort Worth |
| Charlotte-Mecklenburg | 78,000 | 36 | Newark |
| Clark (Las Vegas) | 75,000 | 41 | San Francisco |

Source: National Center for Educational Statistics, *Education Directory, 1973–74*, p. 251.
a. If the city and county systems had been consolidated when the data were collected.

of schools, particularly those where black students were bused into the suburbs, enrollment was significantly higher than projected. The school system found itself in the position of refusing to transfer credits for some white students who had enrolled in unaccredited "segregation academies" the previous year and wished to return to the public system. In the third year (the fall of 1977) school opened peacefully, family efforts to gain permission to return to neighborhood schools declined, and the enrollment pattern became stable.[59]

The only systematic effort to assess the metropolitan plans directly, rather than just analyzing enrollment statistics, was a study of the eight countywide school systems in Florida made by researchers at Florida Atlantic University and supported by the National Science Foundation. The research studied the beliefs and actions of a large sample of parents, permitting the researchers to relate the parents' decisions either to keep their children in public school or to withdraw them to racial attitudes, busing, and other factors.

The study found that whether a child was bused or not made little difference to his or her family's attitude. In the first year of desegregation resistance apparently peaked, then declined. There was more opposition to sending children to schools with over 30 percent black enrollment, but that declined too after the family got used to the school. Most white families calmly complied with the court orders. Of those that protested the decision,

59. *Louisville Times,* August 22, 1977; *Louisville Courier-Journal,* August 31, 1977.

seven in eight ended up sending their children to the desegregated public schools.[60]

Between fall 1971 and fall 1972—when the busing issue was brought to a high pitch in Florida by George Wallace's presidential primary victory and a state referendum on the subject—about one white family in thirty left the public schools. Most of the loss came in the first year of desegregation. The initial loss was higher but still small in schools with more than 30 percent black students. Once families had had experience in schools with higher numbers of black students, the number of transfers fell substantially.

Once the process had begun the findings of our study strongly support a policy of equalizing racial balances throughout a district's schools thus eliminating the problem of upward shifting black ratios. When those ratios can be kept below 30 percent, a school district may experience minimal "white flight." When this is not possible . . . racial balances still should be equalized. Our study has shown that once the initial impact of crossing the threshold has occurred, the rate of rejection falls over successive years. This suggests that as time passes white resistance may be overcome, provided that racial balances remain relatively constant. To this end busing may be used as an intelligent tool in the desegregation process, perhaps with surprisingly good results.[61]

The Florida evidence shows that statewide metropolitan desegregation, with racial balance applied throughout large school districts, need produce neither declines in white support for the public schools nor erosion of enrollment beyond that normally expected. Enrollment trends hold firm after the transition. The statistics usually show remarkable stability compared with those resulting from desegregation plans in large central cities where whites are in the minority. In some cases, at least, metropolitan desegregation clearly works.

### Black Attitudes toward Metropolitan Desegregation

Proposals for shifting authority from central city institutions to the metropolitan level have often been criticized by black leaders as schemes to dilute black political control. And it is true that most of the referenda on

60. The research findings of the Florida Atlantic University study have been reported in the following articles and reports: Everett F. Cataldo, Douglas S. Gatlin, and Micheal Giles, "Determinants of Resegregation: Compliance/Rejection Behavior and Policy Alternatives," reported to National Science Foundation (June 30, 1975; processed); Giles, Cataldo, and Gatlin, "Desegregation and the Private School Alternative," in Gary Orfield, ed., *Symposium on School Desegregation and White Flight* (Washington: Center for National Policy Review, 1975), pp. 21–31; Giles, Cataldo, and Gatlin, "The Impact of Busing on White Flight," *Social Science Quarterly*, vol. 55 (September 1974), pp. 493–501.

61. Everett F. Cataldo, Micheal Giles, Deborah Athos, and Douglas S. Gatlin, "Desegregation and White Flight," *Integrated Education* (January 1975), p. 5.

metropolitan government have not carried in black neighborhoods. In a number of cities, black politicians have urged that first priority be given to consolidating a black political base.[62] A number of prominent blacks, among them Washington, D.C., School Superintendent Vincent Reed, have opposed metropolitan desegregation proposals.[63] Hispanics have voiced similar views.

Although the preference of minority groups may have no legal significance to the courts, it is crucial both for setting the agenda of the civil rights groups that manage litigation and for policymakers considering proposals to aid metropolitan integration.

There are two sources of information on black support for metropolitan solutions. The first is the experimental voluntary metropolitan plans of Boston, Hartford, and Rochester. In each case there have been many volunteers year after year. In each case hundreds of black families have sent their children to the suburbs though it was inconvenient and their children were isolated outsiders in the suburban schools. These voluntary programs could be expanded if the necessary funds and the necessary suburban cooperation were available.[64]

The second source, surveys of black families directly affected by existing metropolitan plans in Louisville, several Florida districts, and Nashville, provides better information. In each case most of the burden of busing falls on black families, since black students are far more likely to be bused than whites under most court-ordered plans. In spite of problems with local plans and difficulties at particular schools, black parents in Florida supported the desegregation plans. About one-fourth of the families opposed them and only one-twelfth actively disapproved of "the way desegregation has been handled around here." Support was strongest when children were sent to a school with more than 70 percent white enrollment and less than ten miles away.[65]

The desegregation process was much stormier for black families in the Louisville area, where there was active and intense white resistance. Blacks also experienced a greater loss of political influence as the schools in the formerly independent city school system (headed by a black superintendent) came to be dominated by the more conservative school administra-

62. Dale Rogers Marshall, Bernard Frieden, and Daniel W. Fessler, "Metropolitan Government: Views of Minorities," in Marshall and others, *Minority Perspectives* (Johns Hopkins Press for Resources for the Future, 1972), pp. 9–30.

63. *Washington Post*, October 14, 1976.

64. Norman Gross, "An Interdistrict Transfer Program," *Integrated Education* (May–June 1975), pp. 135–36.

65. Cataldo, Gatlin, and Giles, "Determinants of Resegregation," pp. 37–42.

tion of surrounding Jefferson County. In spite of these difficulties, a survey conducted by Duke University scholars and the Louis Harris polling organization during the first year of change found a high level of black support for desegregation. On the general policy issue, 90 percent of the black respondents said that it was a good idea for children to attend schools that reflected the racial balance of the metropolitan area. Only 6 percent said it was a bad idea. Black adults tended to believe (incorrectly) that their neighbors were less enthusiastic about desegregation than they were.[66]

When the question was changed from general values to one about support for the area's current busing plan, there was a deeper division. Sixty-one percent of the families surveyed favored the plan; 35 percent opposed it. Of the supporters, half said that busing was the "only way to achieve quality in education," one-sixth cited the need for blacks and whites to learn about each other and improve race relations, and one-tenth mentioned their belief in integration and racial equality. Forty-three percent of all black residents said that the quality of education for black children had improved since busing began; only one-fifth believed it had declined during the transition.[67]

The survey results from metropolitan Nashville were similar. After four years of desegregation 72 percent of blacks said that the schools were "operating on the right track" and 82 percent believed that the teachers were working to improve instruction. Blacks were much more likely than whites to believe that children were being treated fairly in school and that school officials understood and tried to help resolve problems that parents brought to their attention.[68]

66. Willis Hawley and John McConahay, "Attitudes of Louisville and Jefferson County Citizens Toward Busing for Public School Desegregation: Preliminary Results" (Durham, N.C.: Duke University and Louis Harris and Associates, 1976; processed), pp. 4–5.

67. Ibid., pp. 6–19. In Charlotte-Mecklenburg, the system affected by the Supreme Court's 1971 busing decision in *Swann*, the sharp difference between white and black attitudes again appeared. A survey conducted by Message Factors, Inc., reported that 78 percent of whites but only 30 percent of blacks opposed busing children out of their neighborhoods. (Another 42 percent said they were "both for and against some aspects.") Eighty-two percent of blacks said they preferred integrated schools and more than a third gave the higher quality of education as their principal reason for supporting busing their children out. The next most popular reason was that children should "learn to live together." Message Factors, Inc., "Parental Preferences for Pupil Assignment Plan" (Charlotte: Quality Education Committee, 1974; processed), pp. 18–20.

68. Urban Observatory of Metropolitan Nashville, "Community Survey of Public Education in Metropolitan Nashville" (August 1976; processed), pp. 53, 56, 66, 80.

Since no northern city has yet carried out metropolitan desegregation, the reactions of minority parents there cannot be analyzed. It is significant, however, that when the metropolitan area litigation was under way in Detroit, a poll showed that most blacks were willing to bus children across district lines for desegregation. Only 43 percent were satisfied with existing schools and three-fourths thought that equal education was more likely in integrated classrooms. A 1977 survey in Wilmington found that most black parents believed their children's education would be improved after desegregation on a metropolitan level.[69]

Until recently there was a plausible economic basis for black arguments against metropolitanism. Central city school systems often spent more per pupil than the statewide average and more than many inner suburbs. Research showed that the chief effect of policies built around equalizing expenditures would be to upgrade the receipts of the poorer suburban school systems.

Since the late 1960s, however, conditions have changed in very important respects. It is no longer possible to make an argument that the segregation of a central city school district should be accepted in return for minority control of the wealth and power of the district. There is an increasing correlation between segregation and fiscal distress. Even if one wished to do nothing about segregation, it is apparent that merely maintaining present levels of central city school programs will require access to resources outside the city. Central cities must decide not what new programs they will add but what existing programs and personnel they can eliminate. They cannot bring in imaginative new teachers but must often fire the youngest, best-trained staff and cancel parts of the core curriculum. The fragmentation of urban school systems promises both spreading segregation and deepening inequality.

### Regional Inequities

The Supreme Court's *Milliken* decision means that the chance of minority children receiving an integrated education depends not only on the metropolitan area but also on the region of the country in which they happen to live. Old central cities like Boston, where growth was cut off by independent suburbs many decades ago, encounter particularly difficult problems even though they lie in metropolitan areas with few minority resi-

69. *Detroit Free Press* poll taken in 1972, reported in Phyllis Myers, "From Auto City to School Bus City," *City* (Summer 1972), p. 37; Wilmington poll in *Integrated Education* (September–October 1977), p. 29.

dents. (There were only 4 percent black residents in the Boston metropolitan area in 1970.) The advanced state of suburbanization in the East and Midwest, and the traditions of governmental fragmentation, doom these regions to higher levels of segregation indefinitely.[70]

Under the *Milliken* policy there can be substantial and lasting desegregation in a single school district in many of the major urban areas of the South and West, but little in the great industrialized cities of the Midwest and East, which have shown no progress in desegregation during the last decade while great change was taking place in the southern and border states.

Southern school districts are more often countywide. Southern and western cities are apt to spread into regions that would be suburbs elsewhere and to retain annexation powers to keep up with population movements. Southern cities usually have few Hispanics and their black population is older, less concentrated in the child-bearing years. There are more likely to be blacks in southern suburbs, which often absorbed small rural black communities. Finally, some southern cities are still experiencing in-migration of young rural and out-of-state whites.

The differences are increased by the regional concentration of parochial schools, which have long educated large fractions of the white students in the older central cities and far fewer in the cities of the West and South. These large private school systems make one-district desegregation in older cities even less practical.

The consequence of all these regional differences is that much of the South can be desegregated under the one-district principle, but the largest urban centers of the North cannot.

In practice, the *Milliken* approach institutionalizes a new kind of regional legalized segregation. In the past, because federal courts deferred to state law, a black student who had the misfortune to be born in one of the seventeen states of the southern and border regions had a right to attend only a segregated black school. Today, for different reasons, urban black and Hispanic children in the industrial belt from Connecticut to Illinois must often attend a segregated school, even if a history of de jure segregation has been proved, because they happen to live in a region where the school district lines define segregated residential areas. In the 1950s and 1960s, southern opponents of racial change seldom argued in favor of segregation, claiming instead that they were opposed to the idea of federal infringement of "states' rights." In the 1970s in metropolitan areas where

---

70. The differences between Florida's metropolitan districts and the districts of older cities in the North are particularly striking.

there is a history of unconstitutional segregation, opponents defend "local control." In *Brown* and succeeding cases, the courts rejected the southern defense. In the *Milliken* decision the Supreme Court accepted the northern argument.

### Practical Considerations

The two metropolitan cases that reached the Supreme Court revealed no serious practical impediments to a metropolitan solution. Tentative planning during the Richmond litigation showed that the city and its two surrounding suburban counties could be desegregated with little increase in busing. A plan built around creating six administrative subdivisions, equalizing the burden of busing for whites and blacks and producing schools that were all 20 to 40 percent black, would require no new buses and the rides would be no longer than those already usual in the area. The city-suburban boundary lines frequently separated nearby black and white schools. There were numerous city schools with few whites only a few blocks from suburban schools with few blacks.[71]

The Detroit case posed the issue in one of the most complex settings imaginable. Yet desegregation was surprisingly feasible. Justice Thurgood Marshall wrote:

As far as the economics are concerned, a metropolitan remedy would actually be more sensible. . . . Since no inventory of school buses existed, a Detroit-only plan was estimated to require the purchase of 900 buses. . . . The tri-county area, in contrast, [would need] almost two-thirds fewer than a Detroit-only remedy. Other features of an inter-district remedy bespeak its practicality, such as the possibility of pairing up Negro schools near Detroit's boundary with nearby white schools on the other side of the present school district line.[72]

The Court majority did not dispute Marshall's summary of the evidence on feasibility. The issue was held to be irrelevant since the Court found no constitutional violation in the suburbs.

## Metropolitan Remedies and State Governments

One matter that clearly concerned the Supreme Court majority in the *Milliken* case was the fear that metropolitan court orders would draw the

71. Brief for the Petitioners, *Bradley* v. *State Board of Education of the Commonwealth of Virginia*, in the Supreme Court, October term 1972, No. 72-550, pp. 47–48, 69.

72. *Milliken* v. *Bradley*, 418 U.S. 717 (1974).

federal courts into an endless administrative and political quagmire, in which the judiciary would have to function as a "super-legislature," redrawing the structure of educational governance across the country.

In actuality, the job would probably be a considerably smaller technical burden than the implementation of the Court's reapportionment decrees of the 1960s for the following reasons:

1. Many metropolitan areas have no significant minority enrollment.

2. In most smaller metropolitan areas desegregation is possible without crossing district lines.

3. Many of the largest southern metropolitan areas have already carried out metropolitan desegregation plans.

4. Private civil rights groups can handle only a small number of these cases at any given time, producing perhaps two or three plans a year.

5. In contrast to the reapportionment situation, there are both a body of state law dealing with some issues of school district consolidation and large state administrative agencies (departments of education) that can assume major administrative and coordination responsibilities.

Of course, there would be difficult and complex problems. The litigation would be time-consuming and exceedingly complex, particularly if it depended on detailed proof of housing violations in various suburbs. Major changes in school district structure would be needed in the northern industrial cities and in some of the aging cities of the South.

The result need not be huge metropolitan school districts. In both Richmond and Detroit, the plans under consideration called for dividing the metropolitan area into a number of separate, integrated administrative units, each considerably smaller than the old central city system. The Louisville case produced a merger into a single county system that took place almost automatically under state law once the city school board had voted to dissolve the city's separate system. In Wilmington the court made the state responsible for planning. The likelihood is that a somewhat different kind of plan will emerge in each major metropolitan case.

Much of the responsibility for devising and administering solutions eventually will rest on state governments. Local school districts are legally creatures of state governments, and state education authorities have long played a crucial role in school finance and setting curriculum requirements. When district courts decided to order metropolitan school desegregation plans in Detroit and Richmond, they asked the state departments of education to participate in planning solutions.[73] In each case, the state did until a higher court overturned the decision. The Wilmington metropolitan case

73. *Bradley* v. *Milliken,* 345 F. Supp. 914 (E.D. Mich. 1972); *Bradley* v. *School Board of the City of Richmond,* 338 F. Supp. 67.

was directed principally at the state level, and the state government was given substantial initial planning responsibility.

The first major metropolitan solution permitted to stand by the Supreme Court was deeply influenced by state law and state agencies. The Kentucky Commission on Human Rights intervened in a pending Louisville case directed only at the central city, urging a metropolitan order. Later, when the case was being appealed to the Supreme Court and the Louisville school board voted to dissolve the city district, the Kentucky State Board of Education used its authority under state law to order consolidation of the two systems.[74] This action rendered the legal controversy moot.

A weaker but potentially significant element of state support came when the Massachusetts legislature provided funds for voluntary metropolitan desegregation. The Wisconsin legislature enacted a substantial program of assistance for voluntary suburban participation at its 1976 session.[75] The Illinois State Board of Education has proposed a similar program. Delaware passed a law permitting open enrollment transfers across district lines. Many states have laws specifying procedures for district consolidation, designed originally to facilitate joining small rural districts, but potentially applicable to the new situation.

It would be ironic if a school desegregation battle beginning with the assertion of states' rights to preserve segregation were to evolve toward an assertion of state responsibility to end metropolitan segregation. Early experience suggests that the states would not welcome this role, but that they might display considerable ingenuity and flexibility in carrying it out.[76]

The metropolitan issue is one that will not go away because it reflects the social reality of our largest urban centers. Eventually either the Supreme Court or the nation's political leaders will have to choose between segregation and metropolitan change.

74. Martin M. Perley, "The Louisville Story," *Integrated Education* (November–December 1975), pp. 11–14; *Louisville Courier-Journal*, April 22, 1975.

75. Wisconsin State Legislature, Assembly Substitute Amendment 2 to 1975 Assembly Bill 1040, reprinted in *Congressional Record* (daily edition), June 3, 1976, pp. S8501–02.

76. Experience in state governments is discussed by Bert Mogin, "The State Role in School Desegregation" (Stanford Research Institute, 1977; processed).

# 13

# Making Desegregation Work

THERE IS NO simple solution to the problems of school segregation, which flourishes in our aging metropolitan communities. Without positive action, it will intensify. Persistent action and long-range planning on many fronts will be necessary to achieve integration that works and that lasts.

Millions of American children, mostly in the southern and border states, attend desegregated schools, though much remains to be done to make the process work better. For most children and their communities, however, segregation is still the rule.

Although the central preoccupation of this book is with the feasibility and the enforceability of the Supreme Court's urban desegregation require-ments, it has nowhere been the presumption that the courts could resolve the problem, even with greater wisdom and power than they possess. Any major social change requires strong public and political support. This is particularly the case for the complex metropolitan areas.

The courts are often pictured as arbitrary and extremely powerful in-struments of government, but they have seldom been effective in forcing acceptance of policies without public support.[1] Members of the Supreme Court are acutely aware of the Court's limited power and of the real dangers of political reprisals or constitutional amendments from an aroused public. Judges have no special competence to make decisions about education, school administration, and local governmental structure.[2]

1. Theodore L. Becker, ed., *The Impact of Supreme Court Decisions* (New York: Oxford University Press, 1969), p. vi.
2. Interesting perspectives on the judges' own views of their work can be found in articles by federal judges John Minor Wisdom, J. Braxton Carven, Jr., and James B. McMillan, *Law and Contemporary Problems*, vol. 39 (Winter 1975), pp. 135–63. Another interpretation is Donald L. Horowitz, *The Courts and Social Policy* (Brookings Institution, 1977).

Only the leadership of elected officials and administrators can generate a mutually supportive pattern of enforcement actions to create stable desegregation and to build genuine integration. Without this, no lasting solution seems imaginable. The courts can define the issues and stimulate analysis to show that change is feasible and necessary, but left exclusively to them, desegregation will be spotty and often temporary. Only public commitment can mobilize the resources to do the job. If that commitment develops, there are many approaches to integration—interrelated, moving with varying speed and decisiveness, but moving in a common direction. If we do not choose to move in that direction, demographic trends will sweep us backward to more extreme segregation.

Local leaders seem to believe that politics requires not only that they oppose busing but that they fight efforts to make integration work after it becomes inevitable. School officials refuse to prepare sensible local plans for fear someone will think they are "soft on busing." Superintendents who actively lead a drive for integration often lose their jobs. Similarly, federal officials refuse to provide grants for busing costs required by federal court orders. This does not stop busing but does shift the blame. When integration comes, city councils or school boards frequently attempt to demonstrate their firmness by voting down requests for money to aid the transition. An important social change is often carried out in circumstances sure to make it work as poorly as possible, with local officials taking actions that can only hurt their communities. Researchers who question desegregation because it fails to end educational differences rapidly should perhaps devote more attention to the surprising frequency with which positive results are found in the most unlikely circumstances.

The experience of the South shows the limited ability of the federal courts to accomplish social change by themselves. Not until there was congressional support and growing local acceptance did southern desegregation move beyond the token level. Without comparable support, northern desegregation will at best be gradual and at worst unsuccessful.

If desegregation is to work, two distinct policy issues need serious attention from the executive and legislative branches of government. First, should there be a blanket national policy either requiring or prohibiting urban integration? If so, what kind? Second, what can be done to make the desegregation process work well where it has already happened or is inevitable?

These two questions are separate. Even if it is now impossible to win agreement about general policy, surely much wider public approval can be won for the proposition that desegregation plans should be approached in a way that maximizes positive results and limits the possibility of damage to a community and its children. Policies designed to accelerate desegregation require a commitment to act for integration despite strong opposition. Policies designed to make an inevitable transition work, in districts where the courts have made a decision, require a more modest commitment—a belief in the values of good education and better race relations and a willingness to muster public support for a city's schools.

## Public Leaders and Compliance with the Law

School desegregation is probably the only process fulfilling well-defined constitutional rights that is consistently assailed as illegal or illegitimate by many public officials who have sworn to uphold the Constitution. The explosiveness of the transition in some communities is directly related to politicization. In Boston, for example, the issue had dominated city politics for a decade before desegregation began. Political leaders had built careers by promising to stop integration. The people believed it could be stopped.[3] The U.S. Civil Rights Commission criticized Presidents Nixon and Ford for reinforcing opponents of integration by attacking the court orders for Boston.[4]

Leaders usually hold out false hope that the orders can be overturned through appeal, protests, or some kind of federal legislation. A few urge defiance. Rarely do they tell the truth—that desegregation is inevitable once a constitutional violation has been found. Hostile public leadership undermines acceptance of the law and respect for the legitimacy of the judicial process and tends to generate or justify organized drives to subvert the implementation of the order. Such drives never overturn the order, but they can increase racial hostility and multiply the barriers to making desegregated schools work.

The busing issue has brought north a staple of southern politics of the last generation. Cynical political exploitation of racial fears and strategies of racial polarization have become commonplace.

There is no way to stop court-ordered desegregation short of a constitu-

3. Peter Schrag, *Village School Downtown: Boston Schools, Boston Politics* (Beacon Press, 1967).
4. Nixon also openly criticized specific court orders for Charlotte and Los Angeles and frequently attacked the general policy of urban desegregation. Ford criticized the Boston plan shortly before the opening of school in both of the first two years of that controversial desegregation plan and charged the courts with ordering more busing than the Constitution requires.

tional amendment. A plan may be expanded or limited on appeal—but there will be a plan. Even in a special case such as Detroit, where the Supreme Court overturned the effort of a lower court to expand the law, some form of desegregation is eventually imposed.

Whatever they may think about desegregation, public officials must assume responsibility for peaceful compliance with the law. They must support and encourage efforts by school officials and community organizations to manage the transition as smoothly as possible. Once a case has been decided, enforcement becomes a test of the willingness to uphold a system of constitutional justice and a choice about the future of the local schools. Merely by urging respect for law and telling the public that change is inevitable after a court decision, local leaders could lighten the burden on school administrators and improve the local climate.

## Supporting Successful Desegregation

When desegregation is inevitable, the next logical question is whether there are ways to make it work better. The answer, of course, is yes. There are various policy changes that would ease the tension of the transition and increase the chances of a positive outcome. Many are relatively uncontroversial.

### Aid for Initial Costs

Although the recurring yearly cost of operating a desegregation plan is usually only a small fraction of the local school budget, particularly after state reimbursement for transportation, the initial costs can be substantial and arise suddenly. Local school officials almost never budget in advance for new buses or other items necessary to carry out a plan. This means that after the court order they face hard financial choices in an atmosphere of pressure and public confusion.

In the first year the costs of purchasing large fleets of buses, providing parking and maintenance facilities, altering school facilities for different age groups, training teachers, and so forth, drain school finances. Because this fiscal strain comes with the initiation of an unpopular social change, claims that the educational process has been undermined gain credibility. At a time when the school system might profit from supplementary resources, it finds itself unusually pinched.

The school system must thus choose between cutting back other programs and failing to carry out the desegregation plan effectively. To cut down the number of buses that must be purchased, for example, some systems resort to split schedules, which may require the children in a single family to leave for and return from school at very different hours. Without skillful planning and sufficient reserve buses, breakdowns of vehicles can leave busloads of children stranded for long periods, deepening opposition to the plan. Without adequate funds for adapting a building for use by children of a different age group, the transition becomes more abrasive.

Several state and local governments have sued for federal payment of the funds required to carry out the orders imposed by federal courts.[5] Whatever the legal merit of the cases, the idea is sensible, especially at the onset of desegregation. The federal government should provide grants to school districts during the first year of desegregation. Such grants should be separate from the regular Emergency School Aid program, which should be redesigned not as a solution to the one-time cash flow problem, but as a long-term effort to aid education and human relations after desegregation. Too often, this money has been seen as strictly transitional, and has been tendered with a prohibition against spending it for busing. It meets neither the initial need for money to buy buses nor the long-term need for developing new educational programs and continuing teacher training.

While federal grants for initial costs clearly would be the best solution, a less costly method would be the establishment of a revolving fund to provide districts with low-interest loans that would permit them to spread the initial costs over a number of school years. Perhaps the appeal of this method could be increased by including in the loan program systems under court order to correct discrimination in facilities for handicapped children and female students.

State legislatures also should consider giving special financial aid to districts suddenly ordered to desegregate. The Supreme Court in 1977 authorized lower courts to order states to pay for some of the educational programs necessary to make a desegregation plan work,[6] but state legislation, together with the allocation of discretionary funds by state departments of education, would be a more positive step. State leaders should reject counterproductive and unconstitutional measures such as the Kentucky law excluding Louisville from normal student transportation subsidies.[7]

Local businesses and foundations might make special gifts or provide

5. The State of Kentucky and Prince Georges County, Maryland, are among the jurisdictions that have sued for such payments.

6. *Milliken* v. *Bradley* (*Milliken II*), 45 U.S.L.W. 4873 (1977).

7. Federal District Judge James F. Gordon ruled that the state law was unconstitutional. *Louisville Courier-Journal*, September 15, 1976.

services to the schools and to community coalitions organizing for peaceful desegregation. The social and financial costs of community upheaval such as that in Boston make aiding a peaceful transition not only a useful civic contribution but also a practical way for business to protect its investment in a community. When business leaders have mobilized, as they did successfully in Dallas, they have been a powerful constructive force.[8] City universities have a similar stake in the future of the community and a variety of special resources that should be used to aid successful desegregation. In the second phase of the Boston plan, and in several other cities, major efforts have been made to draw leading universities and businesses into the process of designing and managing new specialized educational programs permitted by movement away from standardized neighborhood school curricula.[9]

### Preparation of Better Desegregation Plans

Although almost everyone involved admits that many desegregation orders are poorly designed, little attention has been given to improving them. Often there is virtually no educational planning, although educational changes in the schools may be the crucial factor in making desegregation work well in the long run.[10] Worried by the politics of the issue, educational leaders frequently claim that desegregation is not an educational issue. But it is one of the most important educational issues teachers and administrators ever face. Some relatively simple changes in policy could help improve plans.

Federal funds should go to each school district engaged in desegregation litigation for contingency planning should the district lose its legal battle, as almost all of them eventually do. If planning began when the case was filed, there would be far more time to consider the changes necessary for a

8. Among the cities where foundation grants assisted the work of community coalitions supporting a peaceful transition were Cleveland and Detroit. There were large contributions from businesses in Dallas, Detroit, and Dayton. Elinor Hart, *Desegregation Without Turmoil: The Role of the Multi-Racial Community Coalition in Preparing for a Smooth Transition* (National Conference of Christians and Jews, 1977), p. 7. In Dallas the Chamber of Commerce played a central role.

9. *Morgan* v. *Kerrigan,* 338 F. Supp. 581 (D. Mass., 1975), *aff'd,* 520 F.2d 401 (1st Cir. 1976).

10. Meyer Weinberg, "Desegregation and Quality Education: Quality and Equality in Our Schools," paper written for the Southern Regional Council, March 1976; Neil V. Sullivan and Evelyn S. Stewart, *Now Is the Time: Integration in the Berkeley Schools* (Indiana University Press, 1969). See also Gary Orfield, "How to Make Desegregation Work: The Adaptation of Schools to Their Newly-Integrated Student Bodies," *Law and Contemporary Problems,* vol. 39 (Spring 1975), pp. 314–40.

smooth transition. This would afford an opportunity to learn from other districts about the problems and advantages inherent in the process, so the grant should include travel funds for direct exchange of information. One of the strange facts about desegregation planning is the tendency of each city to face its problems without being aware of solutions developed and lessons learned in similar cities. Since much of the planning would involve educational techniques, the district could make important gains even if it happened to win its case.

Grants should require representation of both minority and white leaders in the planning process. In school systems that refuse to participate in planning busing, the federal money could support the development of a comprehensive educational plan for retraining teachers, restructuring school facilities and grades, creating both curricula and teaching methods that would allow teachers to function successfully with students of varying backgrounds, and starting bilingual programs. When school officials refuse to participate even in educational planning, the money might be awarded directly to a private group or groups representing the Parent-Teacher Association, teachers' organizations, and other education and community groups. Communities with well-designed plans that are the product of substantial local efforts both within and outside the school system begin desegregation with a great advantage.

### Reviving Title IV

Expert help in planning for effective desegregation might be furnished by expanding a small existing program—Title IV of the 1964 Civil Rights Act, which was designed to aid desegregation by providing technical assistance—and removing the political constraints that have rendered it largely ineffective. By 1974 the Title IV program supported twenty-six desegregation assistance centers and staff in forty state departments of education, and had made small grants—averaging about $40,000[11]—to only fifty-two of the nation's school systems. Top priority was given university-based assistance centers, mostly in the South. Much of the effort has been concentrated on counseling and briefly training local school personnel in human relations and the educational changes needed to make desegregation work better. Evaluations of these centers have criticized many for poor performance.[12]

Throughout most of the history of Title IV, most experts employed by the

11. *The Budget of the United States Government, Fiscal Year 1976—Appendix,* p. 419.

12. U.S. Commission on Civil Rights, *Title IV and School Desegregation* (GPO, 1973), pp. 24–40; John Egerton, *Title IV of the 1964 Civil Rights Act: A Program in Search of a Policy* (Nashville: Race Relations Information Center, 1970), pp. 1–2.

program have been able to avoid playing any part in the actual drawing-up of desegregation plans. Typically they wish to appear as "professionals" concerned with education but unentangled in the dispute over court-ordered desegregation. They were, however, briefly drawn into designing plans in 1969 by orders of federal judges who needed help in dealing with large numbers of school districts. The Nixon administration's decision to halt active enforcement by the Department of Health, Education, and Welfare of the 1964 Civil Rights Act placed the burden on the courts, which then ordered HEW to provide technical assistance.[13]

But HEW, not wishing to become involved, decided in 1972 that experts in Title IV centers could no longer respond to requests from judges.[14] As in the case of paying for the costs of busing, the administration wished to emphasize its opposition even if it meant removing a potentially important resource for better plans.

Serious desegregation planning, at any rate, cannot be best carried on by small, vulnerable Title IV staffs in university-based centers in schools of education. Adequate planning for large urban areas requires independent interdisciplinary analysis combining national expertise and understanding of special local conditions. Funds should be provided to establish a private nonprofit desegregation research and analysis group, with a board of directors made up of representatives of national teachers', school board, and administrators' organizations, civil rights groups, and academic researchers. The group should assemble a small staff of skilled researchers to diagnose community demographic trends, develop suggested approaches, and comment on the probable consequences of alternative approaches. As a desegregation case proceeded, this staff would be available to work with local officials, scholars, and community leaders in preparing plans incorporating both physical desegregation and educational change. This would be supplemented by a careful analysis of the effects of local housing policy, job location trends, and so forth, on the continuing feasibility of various approaches to desegregation and by a report on alternative policies that would support the integration process. Such information would be invaluable to all the parties in school litigation as well as to the judge. It would also provide local leaders and citizens with information about their area that is seldom available now. Though responsibility for designing specific plans would remain at the local level, discussion would begin with a broader perspective than it now does.

13. Egerton, *Title IV*, pp. 15–16; see also Leon Panetta and Peter Gall, *Bring Us Together* (Lippincott, 1971), pp. 135–37.
14. Commission on Civil Rights, *Title IV*, p. 38.

Since the quality of an urban desegregation plan may have a powerful effect not only on many thousands of children but on future social relationships within the metropolitan area, the plan should not be designed haphazardly by out-of-town consultants who briefly visit the city or by federal judges attempting to make sense of complex school district maps and administrative subdivisions. The frequent failure of HEW, local school boards, state school authorities, and professional educators to intelligently plan the most substantial move against segregation in this generation has been recklessly irresponsible.

Even though much of the initial planning for desegregation could best be carried out by a staff independent of HEW, there would still be ample work for the existing assistance centers. They could provide the kind of follow-up, training, and communication needed in the transformations that take place over several years in desegregated schools.

The opportunities that come with systemwide desegregation are rarely exploited. When a system reassigns many of its students, teachers, and administrators simultaneously, it in effect creates new schools. In an atmosphere of crisis and uncertainty many of the normal institutional constraints against change in urban school systems are attenuated, at least temporarily. Teachers and administrators are often unusually eager for new ideas to help them cope with the altered situation, and judges are often willing to order into operation any reasonable changes in school organization proposed by local educators as a necessary part of the desegregation plan. The Supreme Court has explicitly recognized their right to do this. Constructive use of this opportunity can produce educational gain in a community.

### Multiyear Educational Aid

Planning assistance is vital but it is not enough. Even with grants or loans to meet the start-up costs of desegregation, administrators may be unable to find sufficient funds to help individual schools meet the educational needs of teachers and students in integrated classrooms. Congress should substantially expand the Emergency School Aid program.

President Nixon's proposal in early 1970 called for a one-time $1.5 billion program to ease the desegregation process in the rural South. After a scandal in the first year of the program, Congress attached controls to it and provided funds for northern as well as southern school districts. The Nixon and Ford administrations opposed extending the program and refused to spend some of the money appropriated.[15] The Ford administration's budget proposals for 1975, for example, slashed spending for the program by 71 percent and eliminated grants to local school systems.[16]

The program spent slightly over $250 million in fiscal year 1974, with most of the grants going to some 570 local school districts. The average district received about $275,000.[17] Though this sum seems substantial, it was too small to have any discernible effect on many school systems, often providing only a few dollars per student. The available resources for the program, always small, declined 31 percent between 1973 and 1976.[18]

Congress kept the program alive but could neither provide appropriations large enough to offset inflation nor devise any new effort to help the big city desegregation process, which began in earnest in 1971. (The first Carter administration budget asked for less than a 1 percent increase for the program.[19]) If large-scale urban desegregation was to take place and there was to be significant support for educational changes after the transition, much more would be required.

The grants commonly supported ad hoc programs unrelated to desegregation. There was no concept of desegregation as a long-term process and no commitment to supporting years of work on educational change. The program would be improved by expanding it to give newly desegregating districts substantially larger grants for the first year and gradually diminishing grants for the next four or five years.

A prerequisite for receiving funds would be the preparation of a comprehensive local educational plan with a fully articulated strategy for turning desegregated schools into genuinely integrated ones. Such a plan might include new educational options in magnet schools (which draw children voluntarily into integrated schools with special programs), helping teachers individualize instruction (allowing each child in a classroom to learn as fast as he can), reviewing social studies curricular materials, language training programs, and training in crisis management and human relations. While HEW should provide technical planning assistance from outside experts, specific educational decisions should be made locally so long as they are consistent with desegregation.

15. For a legislative history of this program, see Gary Orfield, *Congressional Power: Congress and Social Change* (Harcourt Brace Jovanovich, 1975), pp. 173–88.

16. *The Budget of the United States Government, Fiscal Year 1976—Appendix*, p. 419.

17. Ibid.

18. Calculations of appropriations in constant dollars by Congressional Research Service, *Congressional Record* (daily edition), May 27, 1976, p. S8154.

19. Ibid., June 15, 1977, p. H5955.

## Integration and Title I

The most important source of federal aid to public schools is the Elementary and Secondary Education Act. Title I, the largest segment, is aimed at compensatory education for children in low-income communities. To increase the impact of Title I, federal and state officials have aimed the available funds at a relatively small number of "target" schools so the increment will be large enough to make a difference.

The target school concept makes sense in a segregated school system but not in a fully integrated system. Eliminating concentrations of low-income, low-achieving students is a basic goal of a good desegregation plan, yet if the money follows the individual desegregated students to their new schools, it is dispersed. On the other hand, the money may be transferred to the school with the most poor children after desegregation. Since minority students are often distributed roughly equally, this means the money may go from the school with the most minority children to the school with the most poor white children. HEW regulations require continued concentration on target schools and were enforced by litigation in Wichita. Only a few districts have been exempted under a special experimental program.[20] One trouble is that black and Hispanic students who were receiving special reading instruction or other compensatory programs in their segregated school may not get the same service in their new school. Denying help to children poorly prepared by a ghetto or barrio school at the time they face the greater challenge of integrated classrooms is senseless.

Congressional legislation and the regulations of HEW and state departments of education fail to recognize the special educational situation of fully integrated urban school systems. Teachers in desegregated schools often have to deal with educational problems very different from those in either low-income ghetto schools or middle class schools and need different forms of help. The aim should be not solely to design compensatory techniques but also to help teachers find ways to meet the individual needs of a group of children with a wide range of experience and achievement levels and different backgrounds. In a well-designed individualized program in an integrated school, many of the children needing special help may not come from families eligible under Title I.

20. Lawyers' Committee for Civil Rights under Law, *Federal Education Project Newsletter,* March 1976, p. 5; April 1976, p. 6; and May 1976, p. 4. Lawyers' Committee experts believe HEW has the authority to designate an entire desegregated school district a target area.

Federal policy must permit fully desegregated districts much more flexibility in the use of Title I funds so long as their program is designed to improve the quality of education in the desegregated classroom. A plan, to be worked out in cooperation with a districtwide Title I parent advisory committee, the representatives of the minority groups involved in the desegregation litigation, state school officials, HEW, and expert consultants, could try to identify and help students with the greatest academic problems. The federal requirement that the money be used not for normal expenditures but rather for additional educational efforts would remain in effect.

HEW and state officials should devise a broad set of objectives to be included in the plan, such as curriculum revision, special help for children with learning problems suddenly placed in desegregated classrooms, the development of basic skills for all students, provision of specially trained aides to make individual instruction work, and other changes likely to aid effective desegregation. Legislation and regulations are needed to permit combining Title I and Emergency School Aid money for such a plan.

Congress began the reform of the Emergency School Aid program in amendments enacted in September 1976. The legislation authorized a small increase in appropriations and provides a modest new program of assistance for magnet school planning and programs. The House conferees' report on the legislation expresses Congress' concern about the denial of "much needed services" to children transferred from Title I schools but provides no legislative solution.[21] More may be done when the education laws are renewed in 1978.

### Federal and State Bilingual-Bicultural Programs

The development of bilingual-bicultural programs, discussed in chapter 7, raises the important question of whether they should operate in a segregated setting. In practice, most do—only about one-tenth of the children in the typical bilingual class are Anglo. The question is both educational and legal. Can a bilingual program be expected to work in a monolingual school where there is little opportunity or necessity to use the new language with anyone except the teacher? Is it a substitute for integration?

In developing "comprehensive educational plans" to end discrimination against linguistic minorities, HEW officials have accepted segregation. But if bilingual programs are to be used to foster integration and to make desegregation work better, integration should be a necessary component of

21. The relevant portion of the report appears in *Congressional Record* (daily edition), September 27, 1976, p. H11109.

these plans in areas that have historically segregated Latinos in schools and housing. Integrated schools need not mathematically balance small minority groups, dispersing them in so many schools that special language help cannot be provided; there should be sufficient concentrations of minority and Anglo children interested in bilingual programs to support teachers in individual schools.

The federal program receives far more requests for assistance than it can fund. Priority should be given those that would be an integral part of communitywide integration. This would increase the chance that the change will be peacefully accepted.

## Research

One would expect more than two decades of national controversy over school desegregation to have produced an impressive body of research on the integration process. Congress made a beginning in 1964, when an unnoticed item in the Civil Rights Act directed HEW to undertake a national study of the effects of segregation. The result, *Equality of Educational Opportunity*, has influenced the national debate since that time. While it was a remarkable piece of short-term research, it had severe deficiencies that render it increasingly less helpful (see chapter 5).

The study was based on data collected at one time and concentrated on the most easily measurable aspects of school programs. Integration was viewed as a condition, not a process. In other words, the analysis starts by assuming that, if integration influences achievement levels, the effect comes from the mere fact of contact, not from educational processes within the school. It does not measure the cumulative changes in individual teachers, students, and schools over time. Thus it is almost useless as a source of ideas on how to make integration work better: beyond the general though important findings that integration works better when begun in the early grades and that its positive educational effect appears to come from social class rather than racial mixing, it has little to offer.[22]

Astonishingly, the federal government has sponsored little new research on the effects of desegregation since the 1966 study. There have been hundreds of local studies and some significant efforts to assess the Emergency School Aid program, but few longitudinal studies or studies effectively measuring noncognitive impacts.[23] Research offers an opportunity to obtain

22. James Coleman and associates, *Equality of Educational Opportunity* (GPO, 1966).

23. For reviews of existing research, see Nancy St. John, *School Desegregation:*

potentially useful information, ranging all the way from sensitive, detailed interpretations of individual schools to carefully constructed, broadly conceived national research following the process over several years.

Two federal evaluation studies published in 1976 show the potential value of research that moves beyond simple measurements of academic achievement and describes what is happening in schools. The Educational Testing Service's *Conditions and Processes of Effective School Desegregation* and the System Development Corporation's multiyear study of the Emergency School Aid program both found that the way the desegregation process is handled by teachers and principals—school rules, the way teachers discussed race issues in class, and other factors—and the number of years a child spends in integrated classes can make a substantial difference in the long-term effects.[24] Much more research on these issues is needed.

Congress might well follow its 1964 precedent, directing HEW to institute a major program of desegregation research, providing a special appropriation as was recently done for a study of compensatory education. In designing this research, HEW should consult with the Civil Rights Commission, the Department of Justice, leading academic researchers, civil rights organizations, and major associations of educators and parents.

Congress should provide enough funds to carry on the research for at least five years to permit a study or studies of the scale and complexity necessary to sort out the factors that appear to make desegregation work and to formulate policy recommendations for local educators, for Congress, and for federal administrators. Research should be sponsored about effective ways to accomplish integration and bilingual-bicultural programs simultaneously. A sophisticated design for several interrelated longitudinal studies, prepared for the Civil Rights Commission in 1974, estimated that a reasonably comprehensive national six-year study could be carried out for "between $9 million and $15 million."[25]

Such research not only would improve our understanding of the process

---

*Outcomes for Children* (Wiley, 1975); Meyer Weinberg, "The Relationship Between School Desegregation and Academic Achievement: A Review of the Research," *Law and Contemporary Problems,* vol. 39 (Spring 1975); and Nancy St. John, "The Effects of School Desegregation on Children: A Re-Review of Research Evidence," paper presented to the American Academy of Arts and Sciences Study Group on Urban School Desegregation, October 1977.

24. Garlie A. Forehand, Marjorie Ragosta, and Donald A. Rock, "Conditions and Processes of Effective School Desegregation" (Princeton, N.J.: Educational Testing Service, 1976; processed); John E. Coulson and associates, "The Second Year of the Emergency School Aid Act (ESAA) Implementation" (Santa Monica: System Development Corp., 1976; processed).

25. Robert L. Crain and associates, *Design for a National Longitudinal Study of School Desegregation* (Santa Monica: Rand Corp., 1974).

of desegregation, but would doubtless furnish new insights into the nature of the educational process itself. Congress should not expect research of this kind to make value or legal choices for the nation; rather it would illuminate the relative value of different techniques for accomplishing integration.

## The Search for Housing Alternatives

Many opponents of urban school desegregation plans explain that they support instead the "natural" method of producing integrated schools—the building of integrated neighborhoods. Available data show that, without some drastic change, this is a forlorn hope. In the 1970s ghettos and barrios continue to expand, and suburban communities that conducted mid-decade censuses report only small increases in integration[26]—even though polls show that blacks have a strong preference for integrated neighborhoods, that a growing number of whites accept integration, and that the number of black families with the money to buy homes in the suburbs is increasing.[27] It is indisputable, however, that action on the housing front could support school desegregation, lower the cost, and increase the likelihood of stable racial contact.

Congress outlawed housing segregation without providing any credible enforcement machinery. Few cases have been filed. Most of the state and local agencies have small staffs and no real enforcement powers. This is also true of the Department of Housing and Urban Development. The Justice Department has not supported broad judicial action against exclusionary practices of suburban communities.[28] If housing segregation and the continuing spread of ghettos in American metropolitan areas are seen as serious problems, enforcement powers and administrative resources should be increased and penalties made more severe.

At best, however, case-by-case enforcement would have limited con-

26. Thomas F. Pettigrew, "A Sociological View of the Post-Milliken Era," in U.S. Commission on Civil Rights, *Milliken* v. *Bradley: The Implications for Metropolitan Desegregation* (GPO, 1974), p. 66; William Gorham and Nathan Glazer, eds., *The Urban Predicament* (Washington: Urban Institute, 1976), pp. 145–55; panel presentation by Reynolds Farley, January 28, 1977; and analysis of special censuses in 119 Chicago suburbs, *Chicago Tribune*, July 10, 1977. Pettigrew estimates that four to five centuries would be required to desegregate this way.

27. Reynolds Farley, "Residential Segregation and Its Implications for School Integration," *Law and Contemporary Problems*, vol. 39 (Winter 1975), pp. 167–77.

28. The Justice Department had filed only 135 suits to enforce the fair housing requirements in the entire United States by mid-1973. HUD, *Housing in the Seventies* (GPO, 1973), pp. 2–31; Commission on Civil Rights, *The Federal Civil Rights Enforcement Effort—A Reassessment* (GPO, 1973), pp. 98–130.

sequences. The compliance machinery is so cumbersome that discriminators run little risk of being found guilty. If discrimination is proved, usually the only penalty is completion of the sale or rental that should have been made in the first place. By the time the laborious investigation is completed, the victim of discrimination has long since been forced to find housing elsewhere. Although a few victims have won substantial cash damages, the danger that such a sanction will be invoked against any individual realtor is so small it can be discounted. A serious policy against residential segregation should include severe sanctions and perhaps tangible incentives.

The 1968 fair housing law contains language of potentially far greater significance: it stipulates that all federal agencies "shall administer their programs and activities relating to housing and urban development in a manner affirmatively to further the purposes of this title [housing integration] and shall cooperate with the Secretary to further such purposes."[29] The language has been interpreted by some federal courts as a binding directive in the administration of federal programs.[30] At the very least it authorizes rejection of urban development proposals that intensify segregation and gives priority to those that stabilize and expand integration. HUD makes no such assessment. ( Its low-income housing program—cash supplements under Section 8—may well increase segregation.) If housing integration is to diminish school segregation, such information must be gathered and acted on.

An integrationist housing policy would also require that programs to produce subsidized housing in segregated white suburbs be revived.[31] It would be of the greatest importance to see that both this housing and conventional housing were actively and effectively marketed in minority communities. Segregationist practices and expectations are so deeply embedded in the housing market that strong positive action is necessary to abolish them.


### Programs to Stabilize Integrated Neighborhoods

The 1968 fair housing law creates an ample legal basis for a policy giving priority to programs designed to stabilize integration and maintain the attractiveness of integrated neighborhoods to majority and minority

29. Public Law 90-284, §808( d).
30. *Shannon* v. *HUD*, 436 F.2d 809 ( 3d Cir. 1970).
31. Patricia Harris, secretary of HUD in Carter's administration, has indicated that she will pursue this issue.

buyers. An obvious example would be to concentrate housing rehabilitation funds in integrated neighborhoods that are beginning to deteriorate. Such a policy would not only support integration, but also work better than existing rehabilitation policies. Rehabilitation of terminal slum areas has often led to vandalism and rapid deterioration or abandonment of the rehabilitated housing. It almost always condemns the residents of the rehabilitated houses to poor segregated schools. In a relatively strong area just beginning to decline, less money is required for rehabilitation.

Financial incentives in the form of favorable financing and special tax credits or direct payments could be used to begin residential integration in areas of extreme segregation. Such incentives, used for a variety of other objectives related to housing, have accelerated suburbanization, and there is no reason they should not be used to diminish racial separation. (In 1974, for example, a special $2,000 tax credit for the purchase of new homes functioned as a subsidy for moves to the outermost suburbs. And depreciation allowances were designed to stimulate investment in new housing, usually in the suburbs, through higher rates of write-off than were granted investors in older city housing.)

Although a great deal of thought has been given to the need to break open the ring of suburban exclusion of blacks, little serious attention has been paid to the reverse—that housing integration can also be accomplished by whites moving back into ghetto neighborhoods. Such a movement, generated largely by realtors, speculators, and preservation groups, has been taking place on a significant scale in a number of cities even though existing housing policies work directly against it. This is, of course, beneficial to central cities, creating additional standard units of housing at little or no cost to taxpayers and diminishing the extent of urban racial separation. But it is needlessly hampered by financing problems, including "redlining" by mortgage institutions.

Federal policy should aim at equalizing the financial choices, permitting young families to choose central city living without paying heavy penalties. Cities need legislation requiring the Federal Housing Administration and the Veterans Administration to offer low-down-payment, insured mortgages covering both the purchase price and the renovation costs in a single package in basically sound urban neighborhoods. Tax credits or other subsidies for the purchase of homes could include renovated housing, and there should be equal tax treatment for new and newly renovated housing (equally rapid depreciation, for example) to stimulate rehabilitation.

The fear that such restoration might ultimately produce resegregation by driving low-income minority families from the neighborhood could be alleviated. HUD and local officials could channel funds for rehabilitation and for low-income homeownership programs and senior citizen housing programs into such areas, permitting substantial numbers of low-income residents to remain. These residents would then share in the rapidly increasing housing values common in this process.

With reasonable administrative care, these policy changes would require little long-run expenditure by the federal government and would generate additional revenue for city governments. They would provide a rare opportunity to reinforce and consolidate some of the few positive trends now under way in the cities.

Serious civil rights enforcement by the agencies supervising federally chartered or federally insured savings institutions would help. When full investigation disclosed violations, the agency could order prompt corrective action and compensation to proven victims of discrimination. Lending institutions with segregationist policies should be severely disciplined.

### Suburban Integration

Although it might be possible to speed up the return of middle class whites to central cities and the suburbanization of middle class minorities at little cost, if substantial numbers of low- and moderate-income black and Hispanic families are to enter the white suburbs, a major commitment of federal housing resources will be required. Serving low-income families is particularly important for school integration because almost half of America's black children are in families headed by females, which usually have low incomes.

An important study by Anthony Downs calls for creating metropolitan agencies to supervise housing and community development. Downs proposes large-scale suburban development, with requirements that a specific share of each new project be set aside for low-cost and subsidized housing units. He supports the establishment of counseling centers to help minority and low-income families trapped in the dual housing market.[32]

A study by the Commission on Civil Rights also calls for the creation of metropolitan or even state housing and community development agencies to plan housing development throughout metropolitan areas. A metropolitan agency would be empowered to override local zoning and land use requirements and directly sponsor housing construction when the existing producers failed to do so. Applications from area jurisdictions for federal

32. Anthony Downs, *Opening Up the Suburbs: An Urban Strategy for America* (Yale University Press, 1973), pp. 161, 163.

funds for projects with possible effects on housing would have to be approved by the metropolitan agency.[33]

These are some of the changes that would be necessary to create genuinely integrated neighborhoods in many suburban areas. They are hardly easy or "natural" alternatives to busing, would be far more expensive, and have little political support.

Some small steps in this direction have been taken through local voluntary action in a few metropolitan areas, where "fair share" approaches to the development of subsidized housing have been worked out. One pioneer was the Dayton, Ohio, metropolitan area; plans have also been developed in metropolitan Washington, D.C., and other jurisdictions. The trend may be encouraged by the Supreme Court's 1976 decision authorizing lower courts to order some metropolitan public housing desegregation in Chicago.[34] Federal encouragement, leadership, and incentives could lead others to use this approach, particularly if subsidized housing construction programs were reactivated. Existing programs are too small and rental ceilings too low to permit more than token integration in newer suburbs.

### Supporting Integrated Neighborhoods through School Policies

Although at any given time there are many neighborhoods with an integrated residential population, most are communities in transition, not stable integrated areas into which both white and black families continue to move. Shockingly few neighborhoods have achieved stable integration for a number of years. Experts—planners, developers, HUD officials, academics, local housing officials—surveyed in 1970 identified only nineteen in the United States.[35] Many people, of course, lived in temporarily integrated areas.

Two modest congressional initiatives could help stabilize existing integration. The first would be to reward integrated neighborhoods by exempting them from citywide busing plans.[36] The second would be to stabilize existing integrated schools by guaranteeing that their integration will be preserved if the neighborhood begins to resegregate residentially.

33. Commission on Civil Rights, *Equal Opportunity in Suburbia* (GPO, 1974), pp. 69–70.

34. *Hills* v. *Gautreaux*, 425 U.S. 284 (1976).

35. Nina Jaffe Gruen and Claude Gruen, *Low and Moderate Income Housing in the Suburbs* (Praeger, 1972), pp. 119–21.

36. Communities are justifiably outraged by desegregation plans that bus children away from their own, integrated neighborhood. Such an order in Prince Georges County, Maryland, was described by William Raspberry, "Busing without Purpose," *Washington Post,* May 27, 1977.

Whenever a neighborhood school comes reasonably close to districtwide racial distribution, it should be excluded from the desegregation plan. Where there is still significant imbalance but also substantial integration, the level of integration should be improved by bringing additional children into the integrated school while retaining those already enrolled. When declining enrollment forces districts to close schools, the "naturally integrated" schools should remain open.

Since these procedures would support and reinforce the goal of long-term integration, Congress could constitutionally establish this policy under its power to define specific Fourteenth Amendment protections. Courts and school officials could also carry it out on their own initiative. Some orders already exempt integrated communities. In Louisville this has produced substantial movement into some integrated areas. Such a policy would require a procedure that automatically reassigned children to prevent school segregation in once-integrated neighborhoods that resegregated and ended busing in newly integrated residential areas.

Many civil rights experts are so distrustful of Congress because of its record on school desegregation that they would prefer that it merely provide additional resources for the courts. William Taylor of the Center for National Policy Review in Washington, D.C., for example, has suggested that Congress might provide a technical assistance program for school districts that wish to minimize busing by combining school and housing desegregation plans. As the federal courts begin to explore the relation between housing and school violations more closely, such technical assistance might also be useful to judges who wished to consider remedies dealing simultaneously with both dimensions of the problem.

Another useful step would be to establish a national policy that no additional segregated schools will be permitted in any school district. It is to everyone's advantage to stop the expansion of segregation and to stabilize integration in as many community schools as possible. Expanding segregation victimizes both the black homebuyer who wishes to escape ghetto conditions and the remaining white homeowners, who do not wish to send their children to ghetto schools but cannot afford to move to the suburbs. Having no policy for school desegregation is really having a policy of making the people in the transitional area bear the full burden of racial change and ensuring that the process will produce nothing more than ghetto or barrio expansion.

This national policy would mean that integrated schools remained integrated. As blacks and Hispanics continued to move outward, the number of stably integrated schools would slowly increase. Although many cities now lack enough Anglo students to integrate all schools, almost all could maintain integration in the schools undergoing racial change at any given time. The additional white students required would be sent not to former ghetto schools but to already integrated schools, a much easier form of desegregation. Suburbs beginning to receive minority migration would not repeat the process of developing ghetto and barrio schools.

Such a policy normally would work in a single school district for years. Where cross-district desegregation was necessary, the legislation could direct state education departments to formulate the appropriate plans, which would often involve few students. Such an arrangement might be more acceptable to suburban communities if they were convinced that it was the only alternative to segregated suburban systems created by big city ghettos spilling across the city-suburban boundary line. Inner suburban neighborhoods would be prime beneficiaries.

One advantage is that it would integrate whites and upwardly mobile middle class blacks and Hispanics, at least initially, thus avoiding the difficulties of simultaneously adjusting to race and class differences. The job of integrating whites and residents of the "crisis ghetto" would come later.

## Designing Positive National Policy

In more than two decades of executive and legislative activity concerning school desegregation, little has been accomplished. Many pieces of state legislation have been enacted, mostly in the South, but only a few have been effective in making integration work. Only one—the Massachusetts Racial Imbalance Act of 1965—established a legislative requirement for integrated schools, and it was repealed in 1974. Most of the state legislative activity, including all of the "massive resistance" laws of the late 1950s, has attempted to prevent integration. Many of these laws were clearly unconstitutional and were struck down by the federal courts.

Congress' record has been more mixed. The 1964 Civil Rights Act was decisive in ending segregated education in the rural South. Since 1966, however, there has been little positive action, only repeated, ineffectual congressional attempts to restrain the courts and a successful effort to weaken the capacity of HEW to enforce urban desegregation (see chapter 8). Though numerous antibusing bills are introduced, Congress probably has little further power to restrain desegregation by statute, and the issue of a constitutional amendment, for the present, at least, is dead.

If Congress cannot end busing, its options are to devise policies improving the desegregation process or even setting national desegregation requirements congruent with the Constitution. The annual antibusing proposals do not preserve segregation; they only increase local confusion and conflict. There has been little serious discussion of the many ways Congress could exercise its power to address public concern about the desegregation process, to set national minimum standards that would produce some desegregation even without court orders, and, on the most ambitious level, to replace the judicial process by enacting legislation that would remedy all constitutional violations.

Only two proposals for positive national policy had received much discussion in Congress by 1977, and neither had come close to passage in either House. More than a third of the Senate voted for Senator Abraham Ribicoff's 1971 plan to require gradual metropolitan desegregation. And there has been recurring discussion in the House of a plan to establish national, freedom-of-choice metropolitan desegregation, allowing minority students to transfer to suburban systems with federal funds paying the cost. This plan was drafted by Representative Richardson Preyer of North Carolina and supported by a number of influential House figures, including John Anderson of Illinois and Morris Udall of Arizona.[37] The sponsors, knowing they lacked sufficient support, never brought it to a roll call vote on the House floor, although Preyer argued vigorously for it in December 1975 before the House Democratic Caucus, and hearings were held in 1976. In October 1977 Preyer introduced another version.

### Metropolitan Open Enrollment

Although neither plan has any immediate chance of passage, the Preyer proposal is clearly the least controversial. A number of cities have experimented with small voluntary metropolitan integration programs, and Wisconsin and Delaware have state laws encouraging it. These plans and virtually all of the thousands of earlier southern plans based on a freedom-of-choice model have one thing in common—they will affect few minority children and they will send no white children into ghetto schools unless such schools are successfully reconstituted as areawide magnet schools with special educational programs. Under such a plan a suburban community would incur no costs, would enroll only a few highly motivated

37. Speech of March 8, 1972, cited in Richardson Preyer, "Beyond Desegregation— What Ought to Be Done?" *North Carolina Law Review*, vol. 51 (1973), p. 673.

black or Hispanic children, and would be under no compulsion to send white children to the city. Some funding formulas would subsidize the suburban schools.

This proposal is not a national desegregation program and it could not displace the authority of the courts since it would rarely, if ever, eliminate unconstitutional segregation.[38] It nonetheless deserves support. Congressional action for civil rights serves many different functions. Symbolically, enactment of such legislation would be the first step toward moving the issue from the courts to the elected branches of government, a change that could only increase the legitimacy of desegregation requirements. It would produce national experience with an easily manageable form of desegregation and perhaps diminish fears of more basic changes. It would reach many districts that would never be affected by case-by-case litigation, and it would demonstrate that voluntary plans cannot do the job in most communities.

When Congress first acted on the issue of southern voting rights in 1957 and 1960, it fashioned laws that did not work, that achieved only modest changes in a few locations. The legislation and the ensuing judicial enforcement efforts did, however, put the issue of devising a workable national policy on the political agenda. Eventually, when the public mood changed, Congress passed the 1965 Voting Rights Act. Enactment of a version of the Preyer legislation might serve the same function as the 1957 law—it would not restrict the right of anyone to turn to the courts for further desegregation, and it would end the isolation of the judicial system.

While open enrollment is inadequate as an overall desegregation plan, it would be an inexpensive way to begin. It would not incorporate compulsory changes for large numbers of children, but it would make possible the transfer of a few of the most talented and highly motivated minority

38. The Commission on Civil Rights analyzed the failure of freedom-of-choice plans to desegregate the hundreds of southern school systems where they were attempted in the mid-1960s in the following publications: *Survey of School Desegregation in the Southern and Border States, 1965–66* (CCR, 1966) and *Southern School Desegregation, 1966–67* (GPO, 1967). HEW decided in 1966 that such plans were not adequate unless they produced substantial annual increases in desegregation. The Supreme Court held that they were constitutionally deficient except on the rare occasions when they worked rapidly to end segregation, as in the important 1968 decision, *Green* v. *County School Board of New Kent County*, 391 U.S. 430. Some scholars, notably Nathan Glazer, continue to argue that such plans can be constitutionally adequate and effective in urban districts. Several cities, including Milwaukee, are experimenting with combination free-choice and magnet-school plans as the first phase of their desegregation process. These have never been more than partially successful in large cities.

children, children who are specially damaged by the narrow curricula and lack of academic challenge in many inner city schools.

## Phased Metropolitan Desegregation

Senator Ribicoff's 1971 "Urban Education Improvement" bill called for desegregating metropolitan areas in twelve years. Its aim was that each suburban school have a minority student enrollment at least half but not more than double the average minority proportion of the whole metropolitan area. Local authorities could use any technique that worked and proceed gradually. Nowhere, according to Ribicoff, would suburban schools be required to have more than four or five black and Hispanic children in a typical class even at the end of twelve years.[39]

When the measure came to a vote in April 1971, there were only 35 votes for passage, with 51 opposed. The supporters included all of the prominent Senate Democrats then considered active candidates for the 1972 presidential nomination, plus eight southerners who wanted to extend desegregation north.[40] When it came up for a vote again in 1972, Ribicoff noted that increasing racial polarization had lessened support and ended consideration of the issue. "In the face of pressure in the presidential primaries from Governor George Wallace, Senate Hubert Humphrey and Senator Henry Jackson changed their positions and opposed my education proposal when it came to a vote again in the Senate in February 1972, losing 65 to 29."[41]

The Ribicoff proposal was the sole positive effort to set a national policy of desegregating metropolitan areas during the first half of the 1970s, but it contained defects that would have to be corrected to make it an appropriate model for national policy. First, there is no need for a metropolitan approach in the many areas where minority students make up only a small percentage of central city enrollment, nor does it make sense for minority groups that are already highly suburbanized. In an area where black students make up 15 percent of the central city enrollment but only 5 percent of the metropolitan enrollment, say, integration could easily be accomplished in the central city, and a policy of scattering minority students in very small numbers in distant suburban schools is unnecessary and might well be psychologically harmful. Nor is a metropolitan plan necessary for Mexican-American students when they constitute a fifth of central city enrollment and a fifth of suburban enrollment, though there should be some

39. Abraham Ribicoff, *America Can Make It!* (Atheneum, 1972), pp. 42–45.
40. *Congressional Quarterly*, April 23, 1971, p. 932.
41. Ribicoff, *America Can Make It!* pp. 47–48.

exchanges among individual suburbs. Metropolitan plans could be limited to situations where the central city schools contained more than one-fourth minority children and where there was a notable difference in minority enrollment between the central cities and the suburbs. Although there is no educational reason to follow a racial balance model, there is substantial evidence that such an approach would lessen white flight.

Any plan for metropolitan desegregation should also recognize the special needs of non-English-speaking children. Desegregation plans need to be flexible enough to prevent these children from being dispersed so thinly in a school system that it becomes impossible to offer them the special language instruction they may need.

Finally, the Ribicoff plan takes far too much time. Experience with desegregation plans in both the South and the North shows that the strongest resistance usually arises between the time the public first becomes aware that desegregation is a real possibility and the time it becomes a reality, so school systems rarely do much planning until desegregation is imminent. It would be more realistic to allow a year for initial planning, followed by two years to implement and adapt to elementary school desegregation. Only then would junior and senior high schools be desegregated. This would not meet all constitutional requirements until the end, but any dissatisfied minority parent or civil rights group would retain the right to sue for more rapid action. There would probably be few suits, however; litigation normally takes several years and is undertaken only when minority leaders see no other alternative.

The plan would have the advantage of permitting orderly planning, acquisition of buses, and changes in physical facilities. It would begin integration at the age level where it is easiest and has the most positive effect on learning and attitudes. By the time the upper grade integration process was set in motion, school officials would have acquired valuable experience and some of the older children would have attended integrated elementary schools. These years of experience would moderate community attitudes and remove the pressure from the courts.

### Supporting Policies

Should Congress decide to exert its positive power, it not only could establish a framework of national desegregation policy but also might address a number of related matters—among them: minimizing violence; the legal status of nonblack minority groups in desegregation plans; efficient busing and use of schools; cooperation with urban private schools; and community-based school desegregation in cities where white pupils are in the minority.

Existing desegregation plans often embody principles devised with little serious analysis by school officials, plaintiffs, or federal judges. Where mechanistic approaches may be self-defeating, Congress should establish new policies. If the authority is used wisely, it may reduce opposition and increase the stability of the resulting desegregation.

MEETING THE FEAR OF VIOLENCE. One concern that consistently figures in busing disputes is the fear of white and minority parents that their children will be exposed to violence. Even without desegregation, school violence is a growing problem, particularly in the high schools, and there is fragmentary evidence to suggest that it may increase somewhat during the first phase of integration at the secondary level.[42] This may be partly because every fight in a newly integrated school is a visible and frightening incident. Usually little happens in the elementary schools, and after the transition the upper schools return to normal. Clear policies, however, might alleviate the fear.

The fear is vague. Sometimes it is believed that the ghetto neighborhood itself is dangerous and that this danger somehow seeps into the school. In most cases, of course, a bused student has no contact with the neighborhood since he or she goes directly from the bus into the school.

Much of the trouble in high schools occurs early in desegregation and is related to specific problems in the schools that could be minimized by careful planning and providing high school principals and faculties with good technical assistance. Tension arises, for example, over the lack of minority representation on the student government, the cheerleading squad, and other sources of high school prestige. Schools often fail not only to honor Black History Week or special national days of Hispanic students, but also to provide either a social studies program that recognizes the contributions of each group to American society or elective courses for children who wish to study their heritage more intensively. Creative solutions to these and other problems have been worked out by many school administrators and the Community Relations Service.[43] Federal education officials could assemble examples of effective techniques, incorporate them in model

42. Subcommittee to Investigate Juvenile Delinquency of the Senate Committee on the Judiciary, *Our Nation's Schools—A Report Card: "A" in School Violence and Vandalism,* 94:1 (GPO, 1975).

43. Ben Holman, "Dealing with Racial Conflicts in Schools" (Department of Justice, Community Relations Service, February 23, 1975; processed).

staff training programs, disseminate handbooks to local officials, and provide funds for the training required to put the ideas into practice.

In a few cities education in some of the schools may be severely disrupted by either neighborhood gangs or the systematic harassment of bitterly opposed parent and community groups. Most of the violence in the cities with problems has been among adults outside the schools.[44] Philadelphia school authorities claim that in some areas they cannot guarantee that children will be safe from gangs that have achieved a kind of neighborhood sovereignty. Antibusing protestors have engaged in severe long-term harassment of students and teachers in a few Boston schools. In most cities such protests are small and rapidly die away. In the rare cases when they can be sustained indefinitely, they do significantly impair education.

School boards whose schools are threatened by sustained violence and intimidation might close these buildings. Congress, the courts, and HEW should recognize the legitimacy of such actions. This would not end desegregation but it would ensure that all the children from the neighborhood in question would ride the bus rather than walk to their integrated school. It might build pressure for order in neighborhoods facing the loss of their school. Although experience suggests that such closings would rarely be necessary or justified, the existence of such a policy might help calm parents' fears.

Virtually all urban school systems facing desegregation now have excess school capacity because of the rapid drop in the birthrate and suburbanization. Efficient plans for the use of school resources should include the closing of schools operating far below capacity, which is costly.

In determining which schools to close, school boards could use any reasonable nonracial criteria. (Most courts recognize this right.) Obsolescent facilities or buildings without modern fireproofing, for instance, might be selected in some jurisdictions. Where violence and disruption cannot be controlled, this in itself would be a legitimate reason for closing a school—no students or faculty members should be subjected to such conditions, and closing the school, applying a reasonable standard in minority and white neighborhoods alike, would surely raise no constitutional difficulty. Finally, although busing burdens should be equalized, this need not be done in an arbitrary or mechanical fashion that exposes children to danger or inadequate facilities.

Desegregation plans should include strong, specific rules on in-school

44. Report by Assistant Attorney General Ben Holman to Senators Edward Brooke and Jacob Javits, June 10, 1976.

discipline. Federal and state technical assistance could help in developing rules and training school administrators in fair procedures for effective desegregation. It is not discipline that produces minority protests in schools, but rather the belief that discipline is not applied fairly.

WHO IS ILLEGALLY SEGREGATED? Until the Supreme Court's 1973 *Keyes* decision, school segregation was normally thought of as a problem involving only black Americans. The Court then found that Mexican-Americans had an essentially similar constitutional right. When HEW's enrollment reports asked for separate information on blacks, those of Spanish origin, Asians, and Indians, it further broadened the concept of desegregation obligations. Since Hispanic, Oriental, and Indian populations are all growing far faster proportionately than blacks or Anglos, the difficulty of accomplishing integration grows even as the rationale becomes more diffuse.

Not only does the broader definition of segregated minority groups increase the difficulty of integration, but it also extends legal recognition to cleavages that may already be closing. Had the law recognized earlier ethnic groups as permanently separate and permanently entitled to special civil rights protections, it would not make sense today. More than that, in many urban areas there would be no majority group. Most people would be members of one or another legally recognized minority continuing to press its separate claims.

Wise social policy suggests that categorizing people rigidly risks further fragmentation of American urban society. When the division is already present, has been fostered by government action, has deep historical roots, and thus seems irreversible in the foreseeable future, the law should recognize and attempt to remedy the resulting obstacles to equal opportunity. When, on the other hand, the situation is similar to the early phases of immigrant assimilation into American society, the law should attempt to help individuals with special needs rather than a whole group, so as to both automatically lessen governmental intervention as the group's special difficulties diminish and avoid crystallizing lasting social and political divisions.

The problem of black Americans surely resulted from fundamental social cleavages and led to the formulation of the Fourteenth Amendment's protections. The problem of contemporary Italian-speaking children, on the other hand, applies only to some members of a group most of which has been successful in American society. Italian-speaking children should be accorded special educational help not because they are Italian-Americans, but because they are individuals who need assistance in learning English.

The difficult cases involve groups that were clearly the victims of serious discrimination until relatively recently but that now show signs of rapid integration. These include Asians and, in some areas, Hispanics. In many communities Asian-Americans do not face serious residential or school segregation. Despite a history of official discrimination culminating in the removal of Japanese-Americans to detention camps during World War II, Asian-Americans in most cities show remarkable educational and economic success and a swiftly rising level of intermarriage with Anglos. There are, of course, exceptions, such as San Francisco's Chinatown. In most communities, however, the courts might well deny special treatment to Asians without proof that it is necessary and then limit it to those with special educational needs or those who still face local segregation.

The appropriate forum for other decisions on special language and cultural programs in the schools is not the court or HEW but the local school board. When there is no illegal segregation, the political process is better adapted to making the continuing incremental changes to serve evolving group needs and perceptions.

Hispanic groups present the courts with a far more complex challenge. They are far more segregated than Asians and often encounter serious academic problems in school. At the same time, however, Hispanics are suburbanizing more rapidly than blacks, experiencing greater economic mobility, and intermarrying with Anglos at much higher rates. Middle class Hispanics face fewer castelike barriers to integration than blacks do. There is no simple way to characterize the overall status of the complex subgroups of Hispanic people in American society. Perhaps a court should reach a judgment specific to a community or even to major portions of a large city in determining whether or not Hispanic children are a victimized minority. In the many communities where there are high levels of segregation and severe socioeconomic and educational inequalities, the courts should provide remedies.

"Minority groups" that have achieved significant social and economic success, do not encounter severe residential or school segregation, and are generally successful in school should be considered part of the majority for school desegregation purposes. Perhaps the law should move toward defining all residents of stable integrated middle class communities as part of the "majority," whatever their ancestry. If residential and educational integration proceeds, a time may eventually come when blacks in such communities are no longer considered members of a legally defined victimized minority.

The issue is too complex and there is too much variance from region to region to permit one simple national rule. Congress might try, however, to establish some basic policies. For instance, it could require HEW and HUD to make regular reports on segregation trends for nonblack minorities and to explain HEW's own classifications. This is another instance where technical assistance might be useful to the courts.

EFFICIENCY IN DESEGREGATION PLANNING. If Congress wants to minimize the amount and cost of busing, it might require school districts to undertake, while desegregation cases are pending, federally financed research on the most efficient transportation policies and the most efficient use of facilities. In the last-minute planning for carrying out court orders, school districts are seldom able to do such analysis. The research could include a survey of school space throughout a district and recommendations about the closing of excess and obsolete buildings to produce savings that could help finance the cost of the busing plan.

Local officials and federal judges should not be bound by such findings, however. There may be many educational, organizational, and community relations reasons for selecting a more expensive desegregation plan. The findings, however, would be a useful guide for planning. If policymakers are concerned about the financial burden of busing plans, this process would surely provide cost figures that would allay public worry. People would realize that much of the cost of a local plan could arise from educational and community decisions, not simply from the necessity for desegregation.

PRIVATE SCHOOL PARTICIPATION. Most major northern and western cities contain large numbers of white children enrolled in parochial and other private schools, sometimes far more than in public schools. If these schools could play a voluntary role in desegregation, integration would become somewhat more feasible.

The practical and constitutional difficulties of working out public-private school cooperation are so great that the idea should be first explored on a small scale in states with a favorable legal structure. A number of states already permit dual enrollment in private and public schools; for example, in allocating school funds the Illinois School Code stipulates that "pupils regularly enrolled in public school for only part of the school day may be counted on the basis of 1/6 day for each class attended."[45] Cooperative arrangements between nearby private and public schools, with each spe-

45. National Catholic Educational Association, *Catholic Schools in the United States, 1973–74* (Washington: NCEA, 1974), p. 30.

cializing in particular aspects of the curriculum and with dual enrollment for many children, would often draw more white children into the public school and more minority children into the nonreligious part of the private school's program. The additional costs could be reimbursed by the federal government. Enrollment in cooperative programs of even a small fraction of the white children from parochial schools, for instance, would significantly improve the possibility of big city desegregation.[46] In view of the dismal demographic trends of the older central cities and the barriers to metropolitan integration raised by the *Milliken* decision, this is one of the few remaining possibilities for integration in some central cities—in fact, since many middle class black and Hispanic children are already enrolled in private schools, it may be the only way to avoid severe class segregation even in minority communities.

One great barrier to cooperation with parochial schools is constitutional. In recent years the Supreme Court has taken a strict view of the "establishment of religion" clause of the First Amendment, defending the legal wall between church and state. The Court, for example, rejected state efforts to indirectly aid parochial schools in New York by granting tax credits to parents using the schools.[47] Parochial schools do, however, receive some federal aid directed at the nonreligious educational needs of individual children, though not general assistance to the school. Desegregation subsidies would be another form of federal aid, a major incentive for cooperation by financially threatened private schools.

To reach an agreement might well require evidence that the private schools could offer a secular education controlled by laymen and with no religious training for students from the public schools. Even in Catholic schools most of the teaching staff are now laymen and nonclerical school boards control the schools in many cities.

The courts must constantly balance constitutional provisions that, stated in their absolute form, are frequently mutually contradictory. The courts must work out reasonable boundaries. In situations where the rights of minority students have been violated by unconstitutional official action, the post-*Milliken* courts are frequently troubled by the seeming absence of a feasible central city remedy. Faced with a clear constitutional conflict, they might well decide that providing a nonsegregated education outweighed indirect aid to religiously affiliated schools.

46. Chris Ganley, ed., *Catholic Schools in America* (Denver: Curriculum Information Center with National Catholic Educational Association, 1975), p. xiii.
47. *Committee for Public Education* v. *Nyquist*, 413 U.S. 756 (1973).

Two other issues concerning private schools deserve attention. The federal government and private foundations might consider grants to parochial systems for carrying out desegregation plans. As the enrollment of blacks and Hispanics has grown rapidly in Catholic and other private schools, private school segregation has become a significant problem in some cities. Funds and technical assistance might stimulate private action to increase integration.

At the same time there should be more vigorous action against private schools that are intentionally segregated and often built by opponents of public school desegregation. These schools, often called "Christian academies," operate in violation of the Supreme Court's decision against private school segregation and should be denied tax-exempt status by the Treasury Department and any form of direct or indirect federal assistance. State school authorities should vigorously enforce accreditation standards.

CREATING ISLANDS OF INTEGRATION IN GHETTO SCHOOL SYSTEMS. Once a school system has become overwhelmingly minority, desegregation policies premised on a white majority or a relatively even population split are nonsensical. To take an extreme example, a racial-balance plan could "integrate" all the schools in Washington, D.C., by making each 96 percent black. If the primary legal goals are to overcome the effects of prolonged illegal separation of white and black children and to end the racial identifiability of minority schools, neither is accomplished by such plans.

While the obvious solution is metropolitan desegregation, sensible approaches are needed to handle the issue in systems with few Anglo children until the courts, the states, or Congress provide metropolitan answers. The emphasis should be on a flexible approach to achieve the maximum feasible genuine integration, not to disperse symbolic whites in as many schools as possible. The Supreme Court has consistently stated that there is no constitutional requirement for racial balance. Courts and school administrators should be given considerable latitude to assign students in a way intended to maintain racial and ethnic diversity in the school system, stabilize neighborhood integration, and provide a growing number of high-quality integrated public schools that will attract both white and black middle class families. Integration should be required if a school would otherwise be overwhelmingly white because of residential patterns, but it might be limited to about half minority children. Public opinion studies show that most white parents are prepared to accept this level of integration.[48] And educa-

48. See table 4-1, above.

tional research suggests that schools integrated at that level are more likely to provide educational benefits for minority children than schools with a small white minority.

Eleanor Holmes Norton, former chairperson of the New York City Commission on Human Rights, has suggested that in cities with small and declining white minorities, it is only rational to treat white children as the "minority."[49] If whites were treated as both a minority and an essential resource for maintaining racial and class diversity, integration plans could be developed that operate like the affirmative action plans used to begin the integration of blacks in white institutions.

There should be special efforts to retain middle class children in the schools, perhaps by devising multiethnic curricula for schools in neighborhoods with substantial residential integration but segregated schools. Permissive transfer policies might be developed, allowing children from minority and nonminority groups who live in an area where there are no integrated schools to attend schools where most students are from the other group. Minority students could transfer to a nonminority school until it became fully integrated with half minority enrollment, and vice versa. Similarly, major new residential developments, such as "new towns in-town" or large middle income projects, might be allowed to set up new schools so long as they would ultimately serve at least half local minority students. Without new schools it would probably be impossible to win a long-term commitment to the city from middle class families. By any reasonable standard, producing a school that is half white in a ghetto school system should be considered an increase in integration.

If such policies were adopted and were held constitutional by the courts, the incentives for young white families to move back into inner city neighborhoods undergoing housing renovation would increase. Although this movement already has reached substantial proportions in parts of Washington, Philadelphia, New York, and some other cities, the present condition of the schools has been a major constraint. Since most white parents, even strong supporters of integration, are unwilling to enroll their children in ghetto or barrio schools, the reverse movement to the cities has so far been largely limited to those who can afford private schools or those with no school age children.

Reverse migration of more white parents to the central city would create a momentum of expanding integration that might become self-perpetuat-

49. *Integrated Education* ( May–June 1975 ), p. 145.

ing. The number of integrated inner city schools would stop shrinking and begin to grow again.

Policies for stabilizing and expanding islands of integration in central city minority school systems should be transitional since they offer no overall solution and would have little short-term impact on patterns of metropolitan segregation. They would be chiefly a holding action, designed to maintain the best feasible level of genuine integration and avoid further deterioration. In the long run, however, the only way to reverse the underlying trends of racial and class change in the central city is metropolitan desegregation.

## The Choice

The choice before the nation is not whether its urban schools should be desegregated—that issue has been settled by the findings of unconstitutional segregation in most cities, judicial recognition of the right to desegregation, and insistence by civil rights groups on enforcing this right. The choice is whether we will integrate in a peaceful, beneficial, and lasting way. Although there can be many disagreements about particular strategies, it should not be difficult to make the choice once the issue is honestly faced.

Political leaders must choose between accepting a process of spreading segregation, punctuated by isolated and bitterly controversial court orders in a few cities each year, and devising a positive policy for school integration and the eventual creation of integrated communities. The limited reach of the courts and private civil rights groups means that public officials can easily find ways to delay desegregation, to make it harder, and to make it less successful. If they choose to work for integration, on the other hand, positive change can be promoted with targeted aid programs, with the provision of better research and technical assistance, with policies for integrated housing, and with procedures that incorporate major local participation in designing plans.

More important than these is the development of a public policy, formulated in the elected branches of government, positively committing the nation to integration, recognizing the metropolitan dimensions of the problem in aging urban centers, and setting some deadlines for action. A commitment by the nation's political leaders always has more force and legitimacy than a judicial pronouncement. Leadership is necessary to place this problem on the agenda of unfinished business that must be dealt with and constructively resolved.

If the nation chooses segregation—and doing nothing is accepting segregation—it faces a future as divided, angry, and separate peoples. If it chooses integration it will demonstrate that the majority in a free society can act to bring about institutional change remedying the enduring consequences of a history of discrimination, moving the cities beyond an issue that has been dividing the people and distracting attention from education, and beginning to build integrated schools. School desegregation may be merely a first bridge across the racial gulf, but it is the only bridge we can build in our generation. We must build it well.

# Index